Readings in Applied Microeconomics

A central concern of economics is how society allocates its resources. Modern economies rely on two institutions to allocate: markets and governments. But how much of the allocating should be performed by markets and how much by governments? This collection of readings will help students appreciate the power of the market. It supplements theoretical explanations of how markets work with concrete examples, addresses questions about whether markets actually work well and offers evidence that supposed "market failures" are not as serious as claimed.

Featuring readings from Friedrich Hayek, William Baumol, Harold Demsetz, Daniel Fischel and Edward Lazear, Benjamin Klein and Keith B. Leffler, Stanley J. Liebowitz and Stephen E. Margolis, and John R. Lott, Jr., this book covers key topics such as:

- Why markets are efficient allocators
- How markets foster economic growth
- Property rights
- How markets choose standards
- Asymmetric Information
- Whether firms abuse their power
- Non-excludable goods
- Monopolies

The selections should be comprehended by undergraduate students who have had an introductory course in economics. This reader can also be used as a supplement for courses in intermediate microeconomics, industrial organization, business and government, law and economics, and public policy.

Craig M. Newmark is Associate Professor of Economics at North Carolina State University, USA. His research focuses on U.S. antitrust policy and has been published in the *Journal of Political Economy*, *Journal of Law and Economics*, *Review of Economic Statistics*, and other journals. He teaches graduate courses in microeconomics and writing for economists, and an undergraduate course on the moral foundations of capitalism.

Readings in Applied Microeconomics

The power of the market

Edited by

Craig M. Newmark

Routledge
Taylor & Francis Group

LONDON AND NEW YORK

First published 2009
by Routledge
2 Park Square, Milton Park, Abingdon, Oxon, OX14 4RN

Simultaneously published in the USA and Canada
by Routledge
270 Madison Avenue, New York, NY 10016

Routledge is an imprint of the Taylor & Francis Group,
an informa business

Typeset in Perpetua and Bell Gothic by Keyword Group Ltd
Printed and bound in Great Britain by CPI Antony Rowe, Chippenham, Wilts

British Library Cataloguing in Publication Data
A catalogue record for this book is available from the British Library

Library of Congress Cataloging in Publication Data
Readings in applied microeconomics: the power of the market / edited by Craig Newmark.
p. cm.
Includes bibliographical references and index.
1. Microeconomics. I. Newmark, Craig.
HB 172.R328 2009
338.5--dc22
2008046385

ISBN13: 978-0-415-77739-1 (hbk)
ISBN13: 978-0-415-77740-7 (pbk)
ISBN13: 978-0-203-87846-0 (ebk)

INBN10: 0-415-77739-9 (hbk)
INBN10: 0-415-77740-2 (pbk)
INBN10: 0-203-87846-9 (ebk)

To my wife, Betsy, and to my children, Katie and Meredith

Contents

PART EIGHT
Abuse of Firm Power

Notes on Contributors

Richard Alm is Senior Economics Writer at the Federal Reserve Bank of Dallas.

Ronald Bailey is Science Editor at *Reason* magazine.

William J. Baumol is Professor of Economics and Director of the C.V. Starr Center for Applied Economics at New York University and Senior Research Economist and Professor of Economics, Emeritus, Princeton University. He is a past president of the American Economic Association (1981).

Eric W. Bond is the Joe Roby Professor of Economics at Vanderbilt University.

Geoffrey Colvin is Senior Editor-at-Large at *Fortune* magazine.

W. Michael Cox is Senior Vice President and Chief Economist at the Federal Reserve Bank of Dallas.

Harold Demsetz is Professor Emeritus of Economics at the University of California, Los Angeles.

Robert C. Ellickson is the E. Meyer Professor of Property and Urban Law at the Yale Law School.

Daniel R. Fischel is the Lee and Brena Freeman Professor of Law and Business, Emeritus at the University of Chicago Law School.

Fred E. Foldvary is a lecturer in economics at Santa Clara University and a research fellow at the Independent Institute.

F. A. Hayek shared the Nobel Prize in Economics in 1974. He died in 1992.

David Hemenway is Professor of Health Policy at the Harvard School of Public Health and Director of the Harvard Injury Control Research Center and the Harvard Youth Violence Prevention Center.

Steven Horwitz is Charles A. Dana Professor of Economics at St. Lawrence University.

Benjamin Klein is Professor Emeritus of Economics at the University of California, Los Angeles and Director, LECG.

Daniel B. Klein is Professor of Economics at George Mason University.

Charles R. Knoeber is Professor of Economics at North Carolina State University.

Clement G. Krouse is Professor of Economics at the University of California at Santa Barbara.

Edward P. Lazear is the Steele Parker Professor of Human Resources Management and Economics at Stanford University and the Morris Arnold Cox Senior Fellow at the Hoover Institution. He served as the Chairman of the U.S. Council of Economic Advisors from 2006 to 2009.

Keith B. Leffler is Associate Professor of Economics at the University of Washington.

Kenneth Lehn is Samuel A. McCullough Professor of Finance at the Katz Graduate School of Business of the University of Pittsburgh.

S. J. Liebowitz is the Ashbel Smith Professor of Economics at the University of Texas at Dallas.

John R. Lott, Jr. is Senior Research Scientist at the University of Maryland Foundation.

Michael T. Maloney is Professor of Economics at Clemson University.

Stephen E. Margolis is Professor of Economics at North Carolina State University.

Charles Maurice was Professor Emeritus of Economics at Texas A & M University. He died in 1999.

J. Harold Mulherin is Professor of Banking and Finance at the University of Georgia.

Michael C. Munger is Professor of Political Science, Economics, and Public Policy at Duke University. He served as President of the Public Choice Society and as North American editor of *Public Choice*.

Craig M. Newmark is Associate Professor of Economics at North Carolina State University.

David G. Raboy is Chief Economic Consultant at Patton Boggs LLP.

Leonard E. Read was the founder of the Foundation for Economics Education. He died in 1983.

Russell Roberts is Professor of Economics at George Mason University, the J. Fish and Lillian F. Smith Distinguished Scholar at the Mercatus Center, and a research fellow at Stanford University's Hoover Institution.

Michael Satchell is a writer at *U.S. News & World Report*.

Eugene Silberberg is Professor Emeritus of Economics, University of Washington.

Charles W. Smithson is a Partner with Rutner Associates, New York, NY.

Richard L. Stroup is Adjunct Professor of Economics at North Carolina State University and an Adjunct Scholar at the Cato Institute.

Steven N. Wiggins is Professor of Economics at Texas A & M University.

Acknowledgments

The publisher would like to thank the following for their permission to reprint their material:

Blackwell Publishing for permission to reprint Steven N. Wiggins and David G. Raboy, "Price Premia to Name Brands: An Empirical Analysis," *Journal of Industrial Economics,* 44, 4 (December 1996), pp. 377–388.

Elsevier Limited for permission to reprint Micheal T. Maloney and J. Harold Mulherin, "The Complexity of Price Discovery in an Efficient Market: The Stock Market Reaction to the Challenger Crash," *Journal of Corporate Finance,* (2003) 9, pp. 453–419; Craig M. Newmark, "Price and Seller Concentration in Cement: Effective Oligopoly or Misspecified Transportation Cost?" *Economics Letter,* 60, 2 (August 1998), pp. 243–250.

Federal Reserve Bank of Dallas for permission to reprint W. Micheal Cox and Richard Alm, "These Are the Good Old Days," *Federal Reserve Bank of Dallas 1993 Annual Report,* 1993, pp. 3–25.

Hoover Institution Press for permission to reprint Charles Maurice and Charles W. Smithson. "The Timber Crisis" and "America's First Oil Crisis," *The Doomsday Myth: 10,000 Years of Economic Crises* (Stanford, CA: Hoover Institution Press, 1984), pp. 45–59 and 61–71; Russell Roberts. "The Great Outsourcing Scare of 2004," *Hoover Digest,* 2004, 2 (Spring 2004).

Mercatus Center for permission to reprint Steven Horwitz, "Making Hurricane Response More Effective," George Mason University, Mercatus Center, Policy Comment No. 17, March 2008.

Oxford University Press for permission to reprint Robert C. Ellickson, "A Hypothesis of Wealth-Maximizing Norms: Evidence from the Whaling Industry," *Journal of Law, Economics, and Organization,* 5, 1 (Spring 1989), pp. 83–97.

Pearson for permission to reprint Eugene Silberberg, "Shipping the Good Apples Out," *Principles of Microeconomics,* 2nd Ed. (Needham Heights, MA: Pearson Custom Publishing, 1999), pp. 81–84.

Regnery Publishing for permission to reprint John R. Lott, Jr., *Freedomnomics* (Washington, DC: Regnery Publishing, Inc., 2007), pp. 27–30, 35–39, and 86–87.

Southern Economic Association for permission to reprint Clement G. Krouse, "Brand Name as a Barrier to Entry: The ReaLemon Case," *Southern Economic Journal,* 51, 2 (October 1984), pp. 495–502.

Springer for permission to reprint Fred E. Foldvary and Daniel B. Klein, "The Half-Life of Policy Rationales: How New Technology Affects Old Policy Issues," *Knowledge, Technology, & Policy,* 15, 3 (Fall 2002), pp. 82–92.

The American Economic Association for permission to reprint F. A. Hayek, "The Use of Knowledge in Society," *American Economic Review,* 35, 4 (September 1945), pp. 519–30; Harold Demsetz, "Toward a theory of Property Rights," *American Economics Review,* 57, 2 (May 1967), pp. 347–359; Eric W. Bond, "A Direct Test of the 'Lemons' Model: The Market for Used Pickup Trucks," *American Economics Review* 72, 4 (September 1982), pp. 836–840; Charles R. Knoeber. "Golden Parachutes, Shark Reppellents, and Hostile Tender Offers," *American Economics Review,* 76, 1 (March 1986), pp. 155–167; Benjamin Klein, "Transaction Cost Determinants of 'Unfair' Contractual Arrangements," *American Economics Review,* 70, 2 (May 1980), pp. 356–362.

The Freeman for permission to reprint Leonard E. Read, "I, Pencil," *The Freeman,* 46, 5 (May 1996), pp. 274–278; Daniel B. Klein, "Private Highways in America, 1792–1916," *The Freeman,* 44, 2 (February 1994), pp. 75–79.

The Independent Institute for permission to reprint Richard L. Stroup, "Free Riders and Collective Action Revisited," *The Independent Review,* 4, 4 (Spring 2000), pp. 485–500.

The Liberty Fund for permission to reprint Michael C. Munger, "Orange Blossom Special: Externalities and the Coase Theorem," The Liberty Fund, Library of Economics and Liberty, www.econlib.org/library/Columns/y2008/Mungerbees.html.

The National Interest for permission to reprint Ronald Bailey, "The Law of Increasing Returns," *The National Interest,* 59 (Spring 2000), pp. 113–121.

The University of Chicago Press for permission to reprint William J. Baumol, "Entrepreneurship: Productive, Unproductive, and Destructive," *Journal of Political Economy,* 98, 5, part 1 (October 1990), pp. 893–921; S. J. Liebowitz and Stephen E. Margolis, "The Fable of the Keys," *Journal of Law and Economics,* 33, 1 (April 1990), pp. 1–25; Benjamin Klein and Keith B. Leffler, "The Role of Market Forces in Assuring Contractual Performance," *Journal of Political Economy,* 89, 4 (August 1981), pp. 615–641; Harold Demsetz, "Industry Structure, Market Rivalry, and Public Policy," *Journal of Law and Economics,* 16, 1 (April 1973), pp. 1–9; Craig M. Newmark, "Does Horizontal Price Fixing Raise Price? A Look at the Bakers of Washington Case," *Journal of Law and Economics,* 31, 2 (October 1988), pp. 469–484; Daniel R. Fischel and Edward P. Lazear, "Comparable Worth and Discrimination in Labor Markets," *University of Chicago Law Review,* 53, 3 (Summer 1986), pp. 891–918; Harold Demsetz and Kenneth Lehn, "The Structure of Corporate Ownership: Causes and Consequences," *Journal of Political Economy,* 93, 6 (December 1985), pp. 1155–1177.

Time Inc. for permission to reprint Geoffrey Colvin, "We're Worth Our Weight in Pentium Chips," *Fortune*, 141, 6 (March 20, 2000), p. 68.

University Press of American for permission to reprint David Hemenway, 'The Ice Trust," in *Prices and Choices*: *Microeconomic Vignettes* (Cambridge, MA: Ballinger Publishing Company, 1977), pp. 153–169.

U.S. News and World Report for permission to reprint Michael Satchell, "Save the Elephants: Start Shooting Them," *U.S. News & World Report*, 121, 21 (November 25, 1996), pp. 51–53.

Preface

A central concern of economics is how society allocates its resources. Modern economies rely on two institutions to allocate: markets and governments. But how much of the allocating should be performed by markets and how much by governments?

In economics classes students learn—in a rather abstract way—that markets are generally good allocators. They are also taught that in some instances markets do not work well and that in these instances of "market failure," including externalities, non-excludable goods, asymmetric information, and monopoly, allocation by government is better. But even before the instructor discusses market failure, students typically question whether markets work well. Do they work well if companies become large? Won't large companies exploit their "power"? If markets work well, why are people forced to use inferior products such as Windows software? Won't market exploitation of vital natural resources, such as oil, cause us to run out? How can markets work well if information is costly? How can consumers trust what firms tell them?

As I write this in October 2008, concerns about the market system are especially intense. But people have always feared and suspected markets. Markets—and the idea of capitalism—don't inspire loyalty or love like other ideas. Peter Saunders wrote:

> Capitalism lacks romantic appeal. It does not set the pulse racing in the way that opposing ideologies like socialism, fascism, or environmentalism can. It does not stir the blood, for it identifies no dragons to slay. It offers no grand vision for the future, for in an open market system the future is shaped not by the imposition of utopian blueprints, but by billions of individuals pursuing their own preferences.
>
> Peter Saunders, "Why Capitalism is Good for the Soul,"
> *Policy*, 23, 4 (Summer 2007–8, pp. 3–9)

This collection of readings is intended to address that problem. The book will help students appreciate the power of the market. It supplements theoretical explanations of how markets work with concrete examples. It addresses questions about whether markets actually work well. And it offers evidence that supposed "market failures" are not as serious as claimed.

Over one-third of the readings focus on vital aspects of markets that are insufficiently stressed in economics courses. Part one of the book looks at how market prices efficiently aggregate and transmit information while simultaneously also providing individuals with incentives to take good actions, good for both themselves and society. Part two's readings look at how and why markets create wealth. Part three reminds students that property rights are important to the market system.

The other parts of the book present more standard topics but from a perspective that differs from the one undergraduate students usually see. Sections on externalities, non-excludable goods, and asymmetric information demonstrate that these problems are not as serious, or as common, as introductory textbooks imply. The readings in part seven on monopoly and collusion indicate that even if a market has a small number of sellers, monopolistic behavior does not necessarily result. Finally, part eight's readings demonstrate that often-alleged abuses of firm power are powerfully constrained by the market.

Virtually every selection included in this book contains a story or a concrete example of the power of the market. The selections are non-technical, use almost no math, and should be comprehended by college students who have had an introductory course in economics. (It would be helpful if the students have also had introductory statistics up to basic regression analysis. Eight of the articles report regression results. But even if students haven't had statistics, I believe they will readily grasp the main points of those articles.) I have assigned many of these articles in undergraduate courses in microeconomics and industrial organization with success.

Each section begins with an introduction. Review and discussion questions follow each reading. And each section ends with some annotated suggestions for further readings. This reader can be used as a supplement in courses in intermediate microeconomics, industrial organization, business and government, and public policy.

I thank my editors at Routledge, Rob Langham and Emily Senior, for their encouragement and help. I thank my colleagues at North Carolina State University for their support and kindness. And, as always, I thank my wonderful family for everything: my wife, Betsy, and my two daughters, Katie and Meredith.

PART ONE

Information and Incentives

Introduction

The power of the market comes from prices. Prices do two important things simultaneously. First, they aggregate and transmit information—information about consumers' demands and suppliers' costs—cheaply and quickly. And second, they provide everyone incentives to act in ways that benefit not only themselves, but benefit others.

In the classic article, "The Use of Knowledge in Society," Friedrich Hayek explains how important it is that prices transmit information and provide incentives. Hayek notes that solving the fundamental economic problem—coping with scarcity—would be easy for a "central planner" if the planner had perfect information about all the tastes, skills, and technologies in the economy. But the planner doesn't have that all information. He doesn't have it because much valuable information is known only at specific places and times by widely dispersed individuals.

A market economy, on the other hand, obtains that information through the price system. Prices induce people who have valuable information to use it, because using it will make them money. The information is thereby revealed in the market price.

And the market price then induces people to act in desirable ways. If a new source of tin is discovered, demanders will conserve tin and suppliers will produce more. These are the same actions a central planner would want to take, but they happen quickly and automatically through the power of market prices.

The other four readings in Part One provide examples of the power of prices at work. Leonard E. Read notes that a pencil is a simple product. So simple that pencils are extremely common: billions of them are sold each year.[1] But Read's article states a surprising fact about the simple pencil: there isn't a single person on Earth that knows everything about how to manufacture one. The manufacture of a single pencil involves, directly or indirectly, literally thousands of people and dozens of technologies. To manufacture a typical pencil, cedar trees are grown in California, graphite is mined in Sri Lanka, and an oil is extracted from plants in Indonesia. Nobody can possibly know all the details about these processes, and all the others, needed to manufacture a pencil. How, then, does a pencil get made? Answer: it is made largely through the price system. As Hayek observed, the price system means that a single individual needs to know very little. A grower of California cedar trees or a firm mining graphite in Sri Lanka need only compare its costs to a market price. If the prices are high enough compared to costs, these firms will ship their products to other firms, who then repeat the process. The process works without central control, without explicit orders, and with no one person knowing all the details.

The process is so powerful, in fact, that as Charles Maurice and Charles W. Smithson discuss in two excerpts from their book, *The Doomsday Myth*, market prices have so far allowed us to avoid an economic Doomsday. The economic Doomsday that some people fear would come because we are using up our vital natural resources, such as oil. The amount of oil we have is finite. As the world's population and economy grows, we might ask: won't we run out of oil, and when we do, won't the world economy suffer a massive blow, even "Doomsday"?

Maurice and Smithson note that people have had similar fears a number of times before. Two of the similar instances were a concern in the nineteenth century about running out of whale oil, and a worry in the early twentieth century U.S. about running out of timber. But in both cases, Doomsday didn't arrive. It didn't arrive because of the information and incentive effects of market prices. As use of whale oil grew and whales grew scarce, and as use of timber skyrocketed, prices for whale oil and timber rose. Higher prices gave people powerful incentives to change their behavior. Users reduced consumption. Producers tried to produce more efficiently, and more importantly, developed substitutes for the scarce resources. Whale oil was replaced by "rock oil"—petroleum or what we just call oil today—and the timber used by railroads was gradually replaced by steel. As with the production of pencils, these big, beneficial changes were accomplished without central control, relatively quickly, and efficiently.

Quick and efficient actions fostered by the market are emphasized in the article by Steven Horwitz about the aftermath of Hurricane Katrina. After Katrina devastated parts of Louisiana and Mississippi, residents desperately needed relief. Which organization provided especially effective relief? The huge retailer, Wal-Mart. According to Horwitz, Wal-Mart was effective because the market gave it "the right *incentives* to respond well and [it] could tap into *local information* necessary to know what the response should be" emphasis added.

Finally, following the tragic explosion of the U.S. space shuttle Challenger, a blue-ribbon panel of distinguished engineers and scientists determined that the explosion should be blamed on faulty parts manufactured by the firm Morton Thiokol. The panel took more than four months to reach that conclusion. The U.S. stock market, on the other hand, identified Morton Thiokol as the likely culprit, on the day of the crash, *within less than five hours*. The article by Michael T. Maloney and J. Harold Mulherin illustrates how the market is an extremely efficient processor of information.

Note

1 Baron D. (2007) "Don't Write Off the Pencil," *Los Angeles Times*, January 23, A-15.

Chapter 1

F. A. Hayek

THE USE OF KNOWLEDGE IN SOCIETY

I

WHAT IS THE PROBLEM, we wish to solve when we try to construct a rational economic order?

On certain familiar assumptions the answer is simple enough. *If* we possess all the relevant information, *if* we can start out from a given system of preferences and *if* we command complete knowledge of available means, the problem which remains is purely one of logic. That is, the answer to the question of what is the best use of the available means is implicit in our assumptions. The conditions which the solution of this optimum problem must satisfy have been fully worked out and can be stated best in mathematical form: put at their briefest, they are that the marginal rates of substitution between any two commodities or factors must be the same in all their different uses.

This, however, is emphatically *not* the economic problem which society faces. And the economic calculus which we have developed to solve this logical problem, though an important step toward the solution of the economic problem of society, does not yet provide an answer to it. The reason for this is that the "data" from which the economic calculus starts are never for the whole society "given" to a single mind which could work out the implications, and can never be so given.

The peculiar character of the problem of a rational economic order is determined precisely by the fact that the knowledge of the circumstances of which we must make use never exists in concentrated or integrated form, but solely as the dispersed bits of incomplete and frequently contradictory knowledge which all the separate individuals possess. The economic problem of society is thus not merely a problem of how to allocate "given" resources—if "given" is taken to mean given to a single mind which deliberately solves the problem set by these "data." It is rather a problem of how to secure the best use of resources known to any of the members of society, for ends whose relative importance only these individuals know. Or, to put it briefly, it is a problem of the utilization of knowledge not given to anyone in its totality.

This character of the fundamental problem has, I am afraid, been rather obscured than illuminated by many of the recent refinements of economic theory, particularly by many of the uses made of mathematics. Though the problem with which I want primarily to deal in this paper is the problem of a rational economic organization, I shall in its course be led again and again to point to its close connections with certain methodological questions. Many of the points I wish to make are indeed conclusions toward which diverse paths of reasoning have unexpectedly converged. But as I now see these problems, this is no accident. It seems to me that many of the current disputes with regard to both economic theory and economic policy have their common origin in a misconception about the nature of the economic problem of society. This misconception in turn is due to an erroneous transfer to social phenomena of the habits of thought we have developed in dealing with the phenomena of nature.

II

In ordinary language we describe by the word "planning" the complex of interrelated decisions about the allocation of our available resources. All economic activity is in this sense planning; and in any society in which many people collaborate, this planning, whoever does it, will in some measure have to be based on knowledge which, in the first instance, is not given to the planner but to somebody else, which somehow will have to be conveyed to the planner. The various ways in which the knowledge on which people base their plans is communicated to them is the crucial problem for any theory explaining the economic process. And the problem of what is the best way of utilizing knowledge initially dispersed among all the people is at least one of the main problems of economic policy—or of designing an efficient economic system.

The answer to this question is closely connected with that other question which arises here, that of *who* is to do the planning. It is about this question that all the dispute about "economic planning" centers. This is not a dispute about whether planning is to be done or not. It is a dispute as to whether planning is to be done centrally, by one authority for the whole economic system, or is to be divided among many individuals. Planning in the specific sense in which the term is used in contemporary controversy necessarily means central planning—direction of the whole economic system according to one unified plan. Competition, on the other hand, means decentralized planning by many separate persons. The half-way house between the two, about which many people talk but which few like when they see it, is the delegation of planning to organized industries, or, in other words, monopoly.

Which of these systems is likely to be more efficient depends mainly on the question under which of them we can expect that fuller use will be made of the existing knowledge. And this, in turn, depends on whether we are more likely to succeed in putting at the disposal of a single central authority all the knowledge which ought to be used but which is initially dispersed among many different individuals, or in conveying to the individuals such additional knowledge as they need in order to enable them to fit their plans in with those of others.

III

It will at once be evident that on this point the position will be different with respect to different kinds of knowledge; and the answer to our question will therefore largely turn on the relative importance of the different kinds of knowledge; those more likely to be at the disposal of particular individuals and those which we should with greater confidence expect to find in the possession of an authority made up of suitably chosen experts. If it is today so widely assumed that the latter will be in a better position, this is because one kind of knowledge, namely, scientific knowledge, occupies now so prominent a place in public imagination that we tend to forget that it is not the only kind that is relevant. It may be admitted that, so far as scientific knowledge is concerned, a body of suitably chosen experts may be in the best position to command all the best knowledge available—though this is of course merely shifting the difficulty to the problem of selecting the experts. What I wish to point out is that, even assuming that this problem can be readily solved, it is only a small part of the wider problem.

Today it is almost heresy to suggest that scientific knowledge is not the sum of all knowledge. But a little reflection will show that there is beyond question a body of very important but unorganized knowledge which cannot possibly be called scientific in the sense of knowledge of general rules: the knowledge of the particular circumstances of time and place. It is with respect to this that practically every individual has some advantage over all others in that he possesses unique information of which beneficial use might be made, but of which use can be made only if the decisions depending on it are left to him or are made with his active cooperation. We need to remember only how much we have to learn in any occupation after we have completed our theoretical training, how big a part of our working life we spend learning particular jobs, and how valuable an asset in all walks of life is knowledge of people, of local conditions, and special circumstances. To know of and put to use a machine not fully employed, or somebody's skill which could be better utilized, or to be aware of a surplus stock which can be drawn upon during an interruption of supplies, is socially quite as useful as the knowledge of better alternative techniques. And the shipper who earns his living from using otherwise empty or half-filled journeys of tramp-steamers, or the estate agent whose whole knowledge is almost exclusively one of temporary opportunities, or the *arbitrageur* who gains from local differences of commodity prices, are all performing eminently useful functions based on special knowledge of circumstances of the fleeting moment not known to others.

It is a curious fact that this sort of knowledge should today be generally regarded with a kind of contempt, and that anyone who by such knowledge gains an advantage over somebody better equipped with theoretical or technical knowledge is thought to have acted almost disreputably. To gain an advantage from better knowledge of facilities of communication or transport is sometimes regarded as almost dishonest, although it is quite as important that society make use of the best opportunities in this respect as in using the latest scientific discoveries. This prejudice has in a considerable measure affected the attitude toward commerce in general compared with that toward production. Even economists who regard themselves as definitely above the crude materialist fallacies of the past constantly commit the same mistake where activities directed toward the acquisition of such practical knowledge are concerned—apparently because in their scheme of things all such knowledge is supposed to be "given." The common idea now seems to be that all such knowledge should as a matter of course be readily at the command of everybody, and the reproach of irrationality leveled against the existing economic order is frequently based on the fact that it is not so available. This view disregards the fact that the method by which such knowledge can be made as widely available as possible is precisely the problem to which we have to find an answer.

IV

If it is fashionable today to minimize the importance of the knowledge of the particular circumstances of time and place, this is closely connected with the smaller importance which is now attached to change as such. Indeed, there are few points on which the assumptions made (usually only implicitly) by the "planners" differ from those of their opponents as much as with regard to the significance and frequency of changes which will make substantial alterations of production plans necessary. Of course, if detailed economic plans could be laid down for fairly long periods in advance and then closely adhered to, so that no further economic decisions of importance would be required, the task of drawing up a comprehensive plan governing all economic activity would appear much less formidable.

It is, perhaps, worth stressing that economic problems arise always and only in consequence of change. So long as things continue as before, or at least as they were expected to, there arise no new problems requiring a decision, no need to form a new plan. The belief that changes, or at least day-to-day adjustments, have become less important in modern times implies the contention that economic problems also have become less important. This belief in the decreasing importance of change is, for that reason, usually held by the same people who argue that the importance of economic considerations has been driven into the background by the growing importance of technological knowledge.

Is it true that, with the elaborate apparatus of modern production, economic decisions are required only at long intervals, as when a new factory is to be erected or a new process to be introduced? Is it true that, once a plant has been built, the rest is all more or less mechanical, determined by the character of the plant, and leaving little to be changed in adapting to the ever-changing circumstances of the moment?

The fairly widespread belief in the affirmative is not, so far as I can ascertain, borne out by the practical experience of the business man. In a competitive industry at any rate—and such an industry alone can serve as a test—the task of keeping cost from rising requires constant struggle, absorbing a great part of the energy of the manager. How easy it is for an inefficient manager to dissipate the differentials on which profitability rests, and that it is possible, with the same technical facilities, to produce with a great variety of costs, are among the commonplaces of business experience which do not seem to be equally familiar in the study of the economist. The very strength of the desire, constantly voiced by producers and engineers, to be able to proceed untrammeled by considerations of money costs, is eloquent testimony to the extent to which these factors enter into their daily work.

One reason why economists are increasingly apt to forget about the constant small changes which make up the whole economic picture is probably their growing preoccupation with statistical aggregates, which show a very much greater stability than the movements of the detail. The comparative stability of the aggregates cannot, however, be accounted for—as the statisticians seem occasionally to be inclined to do—by the "law of large numbers" or the mutual compensation of random changes. The number of elements with which we have to deal is not large enough for such accidental forces to produce stability. The continuous flow of goods and services is maintained by constant deliberate adjustments, by new dispositions made every day in the light of circumstances not known the day before, by B stepping in at once when A fails to deliver. Even the large and highly mechanized plant keeps going largely because of an environment upon which it can draw for all sorts of unexpected needs; tiles for its roof, stationery for its forms, and all the thousand and one kinds of equipment in which it cannot be self-contained and which the plans for the operation of the plant require to be readily available in the market.

This is, perhaps, also the point where I should briefly mention the fact that the sort of knowledge with which I have been concerned is knowledge of the kind which by its nature cannot enter into statistics and therefore cannot be conveyed to any central authority in statistical form. The statistics which such a central authority would have to use would have to be arrived at precisely by abstracting from minor differences between the things, by lumping together, as resources of one kind, items which differ as regards location, quality, and other particulars, in a way which may be very significant for the specific decision. It follows from this that central planning based on statistical information by its nature cannot take direct account of these circumstances of time and place, and that the central planner will have to find some way or other in which the decisions depending on them can be left to the "man on the spot."

V

If we can agree that the economic problem of society is mainly one of rapid adaptation to changes in the particular circumstances of time and place, it would seem to follow that the ultimate decisions must be left to the people who are familiar with these circumstances, who know directly of the relevant changes and of the resources immediately available to meet them. We cannot expect that this problem will be solved by first communicating all this knowledge to a central board which, after integrating *all* knowledge, issues its orders. We must solve it by some form of decentralization. But this answers only part of our problem. We need decentralization because only thus can we ensure that the knowledge of the particular circumstances of time and place will be promptly used. But the "man on the spot" cannot decide solely on the basis of his limited but intimate knowledge of the facts of his immediate surroundings. There still remains the problem of communicating to him such further information as he needs to fit his decisions into the whole pattern of changes of the larger economic system.

How much knowledge does he need to do so successfully? Which of the events which happen beyond the horizon of his immediate knowledge are of relevance to his immediate decision, and how much of them need he know?

There is hardly anything that happens anywhere in the world that *might* not have an effect on the decision he ought to make. But he need not know of these events as such, nor of *all* their effects. It does not matter for him *why* at the particular moment more screws of one size than of another are wanted, *why* paper bags are more readily available than canvas bags, or *why* skilled labor, or particular machine tools, have for the moment become more difficult to acquire. All that is significant for him is *how much more or less* difficult to procure they have become compared with other things with which he is also concerned, or how much more or less urgently wanted are the alternative things he produces or uses. It is always a question of the relative importance of the particular things with which he is concerned, and the causes which alter their relative importance are of no interest to him beyond the effect on those concrete things of his own environment.

It is in this connection that what I have called the economic calculus proper helps us, at least by analogy, to see how this problem can be solved, and in fact is being solved, by the price system. Even the single controlling mind, in possession of all the data for some small, self-contained economic system, would not—every time some small adjustment in the allocation of resources had to be made—go explicitly through all the relations between ends and means which might possibly be affected. It is indeed the great contribution of the pure logic of choice that it has demonstrated conclusively that even such a single mind could solve this kind of problem only by constructing and constantly using rates of equivalence (or "values," or "marginal rates of substitution"), *i.e.*, by attaching to each kind of scarce resource a numerical index which cannot be derived from any property possessed by that particular thing, but which reflects, or in which is condensed, its significance in view of the whole means end structure. In any small change he will have to consider only these quantitative indices (or "values") in which all the relevant information is concentrated; and by adjusting the quantities one by one, he can appropriately rearrange his dispositions without having to solve the whole puzzle *ab initio*, or without needing at any stage to survey it at once in all its ramifications.

Fundamentally, in a system where the knowledge of the relevant facts is dispersed among many people, prices can act to coordinate the separate actions of different people in the same way as subjective values help the individual to coordinate the parts of his plan. It is worth contemplating for a moment a very simple and commonplace instance of the action of the price system to see what precisely it accomplishes. Assume that somewhere in the world a new opportunity for the use of some raw material, say tin, has arisen, or that one of the sources of supply of tin has been eliminated. It does not matter for our purpose—and it is very significant that it does not matter—which of these two causes has made tin more scarce. All that the users of tin need to know is that some of the tin they used to consume is now more profitably employed elsewhere, and that in consequence they must economize tin. There is no need for the great majority of them even to know where the more urgent need has arisen, or in favor of what other needs they ought to husband the supply. If only some of them know directly of the new demand, and switch resources over to it, and if the people who are aware of the new gap thus created in turn fill it from still other sources, the effect will rapidly spread throughout the whole economic system and influence not only all the uses of tin, but also those of its substitutes and the substitutes of these substitutes, the supply of all the things made of tin, and their substitutes, and so on; and all this without the great majority of those instrumental in bringing about these substitutions knowing anything at all about the original cause of these changes. The whole acts as one market, not because any of its members survey the whole field, but because their limited individual fields of vision sufficiently overlap so that through many intermediaries the relevant information is communicated to all. The mere fact that there is one price for any commodity—or rather that local prices are connected in a manner determined by the cost of transport, etc.— brings about the solution which (it is just conceptually possible) might have been arrived at by one single mind possessing all the information which is in fact dispersed among all the people involved in the process.

VI

We must look at the price system as such a mechanism for communicating information if we want to understand its real function—a function which, of course, it fulfills less perfectly as prices grow more rigid. (Even when quoted prices have become quite rigid, however, the forces which would operate through changes in price still operate to a considerable extent through changes in the other terms of the contract.) The most significant fact about this system is the economy of knowledge with which it operates, or how little the individual participants need to know in order to be able to take the right action. In abbreviated form, by a kind of symbol, only the most essential information is passed on, and passed on only to those concerned. It is more than a metaphor to describe the price system as a kind of machinery for registering change, or a system of telecommunications which enables individual producers to watch merely the movement of a few pointers, as an engineer might watch the hands of a few dials, in order to adjust their activities to changes of which they may never know more than is reflected in the price movement.

Of course, these adjustments are probably never "perfect" in the sense in which the economist conceives of them in his equilibrium analysis. But I fear that our theoretical habits of approaching the problem with the assumption of more or less perfect knowledge on the part of almost everyone has made us somewhat blind to the true function of the price mechanism and led us to apply rather misleading standards in judging its efficiency. The marvel is that in a case like that of a scarcity of one raw material, without an order being issued, without more than perhaps a handful of people knowing the cause, tens of thousands of people whose identity could not be ascertained by months of investigation, are made to use the material or its products more sparingly; *i.e.*, they move in the right direction. This is enough of a marvel even if, in a constantly changing world, not all will hit it off so perfectly that their profit rates will always be maintained at the same constant or "normal" level.

I have deliberately used the word "marvel" to shock the reader out of the complacency with which we often take the working of this mechanism for granted. I am convinced that if it were the result of deliberate human design, and if the people guided by the price changes understood that their decisions have significance far beyond their immediate aim, this mechanism would have been acclaimed as one of the greatest triumphs of the human mind. Its misfortune is the double one that it is not the product of human design and that the people guided by it usually do not know why they are made to do what they do. But those who clamor for "conscious direction"—and who cannot believe that anything which has evolved without design (and even without our understanding it) should solve problems which we should not be able to solve consciously—should remember this: The problem is precisely how to extend the span of our utilization of resources beyond the span of the control of any one mind; and, therefore, how to dispense with the need of conscious control and how to provide inducements which will make the individuals do the desirable things without anyone having to tell them what to do.

The problem which we meet here is by no means peculiar to economics but arises in connection with nearly all truly social phenomena, with language and most of our cultural inheritance, and constitutes really the central theoretical problem of all social science. As Alfred Whitehead has said in another connection, "It is a profoundly erroneous truism, repeated by all copy-books and by eminent people when they are making speeches, that we should cultivate the habit of thinking what we are doing. The precise opposite is the case. Civilization advances by extending the number of important operations which we can perform without thinking about them." This is of profound significance in the social field. We make constant use of formulas, symbols and rules whose meaning we do not understand and through the use of which we avail ourselves of the assistance of knowledge which individually we do not possess. We have developed these practices and institutions by building upon habits and institutions which have proved successful in their own sphere and which have in turn become the foundation of the civilization we have built up.

The price system is just one of those formations which man has learned to use (though he is still very far from having learned to make the best use of it) after he had stumbled upon it without understanding it. Through it not only a division of labor but also a coordinated utilization of resources based on an equally divided knowledge has become possible. The people who like to deride any suggestion that this may be so usually distort the argument by insinuating that it asserts that by some miracle just that sort of system has spontaneously grown up which is best suited to modern civilization. It is the other way round: man has been able to develop that division of labor on which our civilization is based because he happened to stumble upon a method which made it possible. Had he not done so he might still have developed some other, altogether different, type of civilization, something like the "state" of the termite ants, or some other altogether unimaginable type. All that we can say is that nobody has yet succeeded in designing an alternative system in which certain features of the existing one can be preserved which are dear even to those who most violently assail it—such as particularly the extent to which the individual can choose his pursuits and consequently freely use his own knowledge and skill.

VII

It is in many ways fortunate that the dispute about the indispensability of the price system for any rational calculation in a complex society is now no longer conducted entirely between camps holding different political views. The thesis that without the price system we could not preserve a society based on such extensive division of labor as ours was greeted with a howl of derision when it was first advanced by von Mises twenty-five years ago. Today the difficulties which some still find in accepting it are no longer mainly political, and this makes for an atmosphere much more conducive to reasonable discussion. When we find Leon Trotsky arguing that "economic accounting is unthinkable without market relations"; when Professor Oscar Lange promises Professor von Mises a statue in the marble halls of the future Central Planning Board; and when Professor Abba P. Lerner rediscovers Adam Smith and emphasizes that the essential utility of the price system consists in inducing the individual, while seeking his own interest, to do what is in the general interest, the differences can indeed no longer be ascribed to political prejudice. The remaining dissent seems clearly to be due to purely intellectual, and more particularly methodological, differences.

A recent statement by Professor Joseph Schumpeter in his *Capitalism, Socialism, and Democracy* provides a clear illustration of one of the methodological differences which I have in mind. Its author is preeminent among those economists who approach economic phenomena in the light of a certain branch of positivism. To him these phenomena accordingly appear as objectively given quantities of commodities imping-ing directly upon each other, almost, it would seem, without any intervention of human minds. Only against this background can I account for the following (to me startling) pronouncement. Professor Schumpeter argues that the possibility of a rational calculation in the absence of markets for the factors of production follows for the theo-rist "from the elementary proposition that consumers in evaluating ('demanding') consumers' goods *ipso facto* also evaluate the means of production which enter into the production of these goods."[1]

Taken literally, this statement is simply untrue. The consumers do nothing of the kind. What Professor Schumpeter's *"ipso facto"* presumably means is that the valuation of the factors of production is implied in, or follows necessarily from, the valuation of consumers' goods. But this, too, is not correct. Implication is a logical relationship which can be meaningfully asserted only of propositions simultaneously present to one and the same mind. It is evident, however, that the values of the factors of produc-tion do not depend solely on the valuation of the consumers' goods but also on the conditions of supply of the various factors of production. Only to a mind to which all these facts were simultaneously known would the answer necessarily follow from the facts given to it. The practical problem, however, arises precisely because these facts are never so given to a single mind, and because, in consequence, it is necessary that in the solution of the problem knowledge should be used that is dispersed among many people.

The problem is thus in no way solved if we can show that all the facts, *if* they were known to a single mind (as we hypothetically assume them to be given to the observing economist), would uniquely determine the solution; instead we must show how a solution is produced by the interactions of people each of whom possesses only partial knowledge. To assume all the knowledge to be given to a single mind in the same manner in which we assume it to be given to us as the explaining economists is to assume the problem away and to disregard everything that is important and significant in the real world.

That an economist of Professor Schumpeter's standing should thus have fallen into a trap which the ambiguity of the term "datum" sets to the unwary can hardly be explained as a simple error. It suggests rather than there is something fundamentally wrong with an approach which habitually disregards an essential part of the phenomena with which we have to deal: the unavoidable imperfection of man's knowledge and the consequent need for a process by which knowledge is constantly communicated and acquired. Any approach, such as that of much of mathematical economics with its simultaneous equations, which in effect starts from the assumption that people's *knowledge* corresponds with the objective *facts* of the situation, systematically leaves out what is our main task to explain. I am far from denying that in our system equilibrium analysis has a useful function to perform. But when it comes to the point where it misleads some of our leading thinkers into believing that the situation which it describes has direct relevance to the solution of practical problems, it is time that we remember that it does not deal with the social process at all and that it is no more than a useful preliminary to the study of the main problem.

Note

1   J. Schumpeter, *Capitalism, Socialism, and Democracy* (New York, Harper, 1942), p. 175. Professor Schumpeter is, I believe, also the original author of the myth that Pareto and Barone have "solved" the problem of socialist calculation. What they, and many others, did was merely to state the conditions which a rational allocation of resources would have to satisfy, and to point out that these were essentially the same as the conditions of equilibrium of a competitive market. This is something altogether different from showing how the allocation of resources satisfying these conditions can be found in practice. Pareto himself (from whom Barone has taken practically everything he has to say), far from claiming to have solved the practical problem, in fact explicitly denies that it can be solved without the help of the market. See his *Manuel d'économie pure* (2nd ed., 1927), pp. 233–34. The relevant passage is quoted in an English translation at the beginning of my article on "Socialist Calculation: The Competitive 'Solution,'" in *Economico*, New Series, Vol. VIII, No. 26 (May, 1940), p. 125.

Review and Discussion Questions

1   What is an example mentioned in the article of information that is specific to time and place?
2   Discuss what happens, according to Hayek, when a new use of tin is discovered.
3   How does the price system help "dispense with the need of conscious control"?
4   Hayek wrote:

> What is the problem we wish to solve when we try to construct a rational economic order? On certain familiar assumptions the answer is simple enough. *If* we possess all the relevant information, *if* we can start out from a given system of preferences and *if* we command complete knowledge of available means, the problem which remains is purely one of logic ... This, however, is emphatically not the economic problem which society faces ... The reason for this is that the "data" from which the economic calculus starts are never for the whole society "given" to a single mind which could work out the implications, and can never be so given.

Explain what Hayek means. (Why can the data "never be so given"?) How does Hayek's argument relate to a fundamental idea of economics?

Chapter 2

Leonard E. Read

I, PENCIL

I AM A LEAD PENCIL—the ordinary wooden pencil familiar to all boys and girls and adults who can read and write.[1]

Writing is both my vocation and my avocation; that's all I do.

You may wonder why I should write a genealogy. Well, to begin with, my story is interesting. And, next, I am a mystery—more so than a tree or a sunset or even a flash of lightning. But, sadly, I am taken for granted by those who use me, as if I were a mere incident and without background. This supercilious attitude relegates me to the level of the commonplace. This is a species of the grievous error in which mankind cannot too long persist without peril. For, the wise G. K. Chesterton observed, "We are perishing for want of wonder, not for want of wonders."

I, Pencil, simple though I appear to be, merit your wonder and awe, a claim I shall attempt to prove. In fact, if you can understand me—no, that's too much to ask of anyone—if you can become aware of the miraculousness which I symbolize, you can help save the freedom mankind is so unhappily losing. I have a profound lesson to teach. And I can teach this lesson better than can an automobile or an airplane or a mechanical dishwasher because—well, because I am seemingly so simple.

Simple? Yet, not a single person on the face of this earth knows how to make me. This sounds fantastic, doesn't it? Especially when it is realized that there are about one and one-half billion of my kind produced in the U.S.A. each year.

Pick me up and look me over. What do you see? Not much meets the eye—there's some wood, lacquer, the printed labeling, graphite lead, a bit of metal, and an eraser.

Innumerable antecedents

Just as you cannot trace your family tree back very far, so is it impossible for me to name and explain all my antecedents. But I would like to suggest enough of them to impress upon you the richness and complexity of my background.

My family tree begins with what in fact is a tree, a cedar of straight grain that grows in Northern California and Oregon. Now contemplate all the saws and trucks and rope and the countless other gear used in harvesting and carting the cedar logs to the railroad siding. Think of all the persons and the numberless skills that went into their fabrication: the mining of ore, the making of steel and its refinement into saws, axes, motors; the growing of hemp and bringing it through all the stages to heavy and strong rope; the logging camps with their beds and mess halls, the cookery and the raising of all the foods. Why, untold thousands of persons had a hand in every cup of coffee the loggers drink!

The logs are shipped to a mill in San Leandro, California. Can you imagine the individuals who make flat cars and rails and railroad engines and who construct and install the communication systems incidental thereto? These legions are among my antecedents.

Consider the millwork in San Leandro. The cedar logs are cut into small, pencil-length slats less than one-fourth of an inch in thickness. These are kiln dried and then tinted for the same reason women put rouge on their faces. People prefer that I look pretty, not a pallid white. The slats are waxed and kiln dried again. How many skills went into the making of the tint and the kilns, into supplying the heat, the light and power, the belts, motors, and all the other things a mill requires? Sweepers in the mill among my ancestors? Yes, and included are the men who poured the concrete for the dam of a Pacific Gas & Electric Company hydroplant which supplies the mill's power!

Don't overlook the ancestors present and distant who have a hand in transporting sixty carloads of slats across the nation.

Once in the pencil factory—$4,000,000 in machinery and building, all capital accumulated by thrifty and saving parents of mine—each slat is given eight grooves by a complex machine, after which another machine lays leads in every other slat, applies glue, and places another slat atop—a lead sandwich, so to speak. Seven brothers and I are mechanically carved from this "wood-clinched" sandwich.

My "lead" itself—it contains no lead at all—is complex. The graphite is mined in Ceylon. Consider these miners and those who make their many tools and the makers of the paper sacks in which the graphite is shipped and those who make the string that ties the sacks and those who put them aboard ships and those who make the ships. Even the lighthouse keepers along the way assisted in my birth—and the harbor pilots.

The graphite is mixed with clay from Mississippi in which ammonium hydroxide is used in the refining process. Then wetting agents are added such as sulfonated tallow—animal fats chemically reacted with sulfuric acid. After passing through numerous machines, the mixture finally appears as endless extrusions—as from a sausage grinder—cut to size, dried, and baked for several hours at 1,850 degrees Fahrenheit. To increase their strength and smoothness the leads are then treated with a hot mixture which includes candelilla wax from Mexico, paraffin wax, and hydrogenated natural fats.

My cedar receives six coats of lacquer. Do you know all the ingredients of lacquer? Who would think that the growers of castor beans and the refiners of castor oil are a part of it? They are. Why, even the processes by which the lacquer is made a beautiful yellow involves the skills of more persons than one can enumerate!

Observe the labeling. That's a film formed by applying heat to carbon black mixed with resins. How do you make resins and what, pray, is carbon black?

My bit of metal—the ferrule—is brass. Think of all the persons who mine zinc and copper and those who have the skills to make shiny sheet brass from these products of nature. Those black rings on my ferrule are black nickel. What is black nickel and how is it applied? The complete story of why the center of my ferrule has no black nickel on it would take pages to explain.

Then there's my crowning glory, inelegantly referred to in the trade as "the plug," the part man uses to erase the errors he makes with me. An ingredient called "factice" is what does the erasing. It is a rubber-like product made by reacting rape-seed oil from the Dutch East Indies with sulfur chloride. Rubber, contrary to the common notion, is only for binding purposes. Then, too, there are numerous vulcanizing and accelerating agents. The pumice comes from Italy; and the pigment which gives "the plug" its color is cadmium sulfide.

No one knows

Does anyone wish to challenge my earlier assertion that no single person on the face of this earth knows how to make me?

Actually, millions of human beings have had a hand in my creation, no one of whom even knows more than a very few of the others. Now, you may say that I go too far in relating the picker of a coffee berry in far off Brazil and food growers elsewhere to my creation; that this is an extreme position. I shall stand by my claim. There isn't a single person in all these millions, including the president of the pencil company, who contributes more than a tiny, infinitesimal bit of know-how. From the standpoint of know-how the only difference between the miner of graphite in Ceylon and the logger in Oregon is in the *type* of know-how. Neither the miner nor the logger can be dispensed with, any more than can the chemist at the factory or the worker in the oil field—paraffin being a by-product of petroleum.

Here is an astounding fact: *Neither* the worker in the oil field nor the chemist nor the digger of graphite or clay nor any who mans or makes the ships or trains or trucks nor the one who runs the machine that does the knurling on my bit of metal nor the president of the company performs his singular task because he wants me. Each one wants me less, perhaps, than does a child in the first grade. Indeed, there are some among this vast multitude who never saw a pencil nor would they know how to use one. Their motivation is other than me. Perhaps it is something like this: Each of these millions sees that he can thus exchange his tiny know-how for the goods and services he needs or wants. I may or may not be among these items.

No master mind

There is a fact still more astounding: The absence of a master mind, of anyone dictating or forcibly directing these countless actions which bring me into being. No trace of such a person can be found. Instead, we find the Invisible Hand at work. This is the mystery to which I earlier referred.

It has been said that "only God can make a tree." Why do we agree with this? Isn't it because we realize that we ourselves could not make one? Indeed, can we even describe a tree? We cannot, except in superficial terms. We can say, for instance, that a certain molecular configuration manifests itself as a tree. But what mind is there among men that could even record, let alone direct, the constant changes in molecules that transpire in the life span of a tree? Such a feat is utterly unthinkable!

I, Pencil, am a complex combination of miracles: a tree, zinc, copper, graphite, and so on. But to these miracles which manifest themselves in Nature an even more extraordinary miracle has been added: the configuration of creative human energies—millions of tiny know-hows configurating naturally and spontaneously in response to human necessity and desire and in the absence of any human master-minding! Since only God can make a tree, I insist that only God could make me. Man can no more direct these millions of know-hows to bring me into being than he can put molecules together to create a tree.

The above is what I meant when writing, "If you can become aware of the miraculousness which I symbolize, you can help save the freedom mankind is so unhappily losing." For, if one is aware that these know-hows will naturally, yes, automatically, arrange themselves into creative and productive patterns in response to human necessity and demand—that is, in the absence of governmental or any other coercive master-minding—then one will possess an absolutely essential ingredient for freedom: a faith in free people. Freedom is impossible without this faith.

Once government has had a monopoly of a creative activity such, for instance, as the delivery of the mails, most individuals will believe that the mails could not be efficiently delivered by men acting freely. And here is the reason: Each one acknowledges that he himself doesn't know how to do all the things incident to mail delivery. He also recognizes that no other individual could do it. These assumptions are correct. No individual possesses enough know-how to perform a nation's mail delivery any more than any individual possesses enough know-how to make a pencil. Now, in the absence of faith in free people—in the unawareness that millions of tiny know-hows would naturally and miraculously form and cooperate to satisfy this necessity—the individual cannot help but reach the erroneous conclusion that mail can be delivered only by governmental "master-minding."

Testimony galore

If I, Pencil, were the only item that could offer testimony on what men and women can accomplish when free to try, then those with little faith would have a fair case. However, there is testimony galore; it's all about us and on every hand. Mail delivery is exceedingly simple when compared, for instance, to the making of an automobile or a calculating machine or a grain combine or a milling machine or to tens of thousands of other things. Delivery? Why, in this area where men have been left free to try, they deliver the human voice around the world in less than one second; they deliver an event visually and in motion to any person's home when it is happening; they deliver 150 passengers from Seattle to Baltimore in less than four hours; they deliver gas from Texas to one's range or furnace in New York at unbelievably low rates and without subsidy; they deliver each four pounds of oil from the Persian Gulf to our

Eastern Seaboard—halfway around the world—for less money than the government charges for delivering a one-ounce letter across the street!

The lesson I have to teach is this: *Leave all creative energies uninhibited*. Merely organize society to act in harmony with this lesson. Let society's legal apparatus remove all obstacles the best it can. Permit these creative know-hows freely to flow. Have faith that free men and women will respond to the Invisible Hand. This faith will be confirmed. I, Pencil, seemingly simple though I am, offer the miracle of my creation as testimony that this is a practical faith, as practical as the sun, the rain, a cedar tree, the good earth.

Note

1 My official name is "Mongol 482." My many ingredients are assembled, fabricated, and finished by Eberhard Faber Pencil Company.

Review and Discussion Questions

1 Read writes, "*Leave all creative energies uninhibited. . . .* Have faith that free men and women will respond to the Invisible Hand. This faith will be confirmed." What does he mean?
2 Read's article is several decades old. Are pencils made in approximately the same way today? Do you think it's still true that "not a single person on the face of this earth knows how to make" one?

Chapter 3

Charles Maurice and Charles W. Smithson

THE TIMBER CRISIS

W E NOW GO BACK TO THE TURN OF THE CENTURY to examine another resource crisis in America.[1]

And it was a bona fide crisis. America was running out of its most important, most necessary, and (purportedly) most nonsubstitutable natural resource.

At the turn of the century, America was experiencing the greatest period of economic growth in its history—indeed, this was probably the greatest period of growth in the history of the world. But America was running out of one of the two primary ingredients for sustaining this growth—wood. (The other essential input was iron.) As reported by the doom merchants of the period, the reason was easy to see: we were cutting down forests much faster than they could be replaced.

According to the doom merchants, the railroads, the driving force behind the industrialization, were doomed. After all, the railroads accounted for 20–25 percent of annual timber consumption. Most of this wood was used to replace crossties; 15–20 percent of the crossties had to be replaced every year. You simply couldn't run a railroad without wood.

And, for most uses, there was apparently no substitute for wood. It appeared there were only two choices: (1) follow the lead of the U.S. Forest Service, an important division of the Department of Agriculture, and force reforestation of the continent or (2) conserve wood by slowing down or ending the growth of the nation. Those were the only apparent choices. Only a fool couldn't see that these were the only solutions. Somebody had to do something and fast.

A few headlines from the *New York Times* during the first decade of the twentieth century give a picture of how we viewed the situation (see overleaf).

The headlines, reminiscent of those in the 1970s, convey the feeling at the time. And the feeling was utter gloom. Really, banning Christmas trees to save wood! Was nothing sacred? We can't recall such a draconian measure having been suggested even during the height of the oil crisis, although President Carter did refuse to light the White House Christmas tree in 1979. We all have to sacrifice during a crisis.

Dec. 31, 1900	"THE END OF LUMBER SUPPLY"
Jan. 6, 1905	"TIMBER FAMINE NEAR, SAYS ROOSEVELT [AND] NATIONAL FOREST SERVICE"
Aug. 31, 1908	"NEW PLAN TO SAVE NATIONAL FOREST. SENATOR SMOOT TO RECOMMEND THAT THEY BE TURNED OVER TO STATES, CITIES, AND COUNTIES. REFORESTRY THE OBJECT"
Oct. 31, 1908	"HICKORY DISAPPEARING, SUPPLY OF WOOD NEARS END—MUCH WASTED AND THERE'S NO SUBSTITUTE"
Dec. 7, 1908	"BANISH CHRISTMAS TREES, DR. MACARTHUR SAYS THIS HEATHENISH PRACTICE DENUDES FORESTS"
Dec. 16, 1908	"URGES LAWS TO SAVE TREES, FOREST WILL BE WIPED OUT IN TEN YEARS AT PRESENT RATE, WHIPPLE SAYS"

The U.S. Forest Service was still forecasting a resource disaster even as late as the early 1920s, when the crisis had been resolved. Sherry Olson, in *The Depletion Myth* (pp. 141–42), quotes a Forest, Service publication of 1923:

> Directly or indirectly, every commodity of life will cost more because of the depleted supply of forest products. Every American will pay an unnecessarily large part of his income for shelter, and food, and clothing and fuel, transportation and amusements, necessities and luxuries alike, because wood will be no longer plentiful and near at hand.
>
> This economic punishment will increase in severity as time goes on. There is only one way by which its pressure can be relieved and removed, and that is by growing enough timber for the national needs.

Change "wood" to "oil" and the last sentence to "… that is by becoming self-sufficient in oil." A report of the Department of Energy in 1979? A speech by the energy czar in 1975? Remember? We really did have an energy czar in 1975.

But there was clearly a problem in 1900. Public officials, the media, the president, and the informed public were justifiably worried about it. If people continued to consume timber at the same rate and if the growth rate of timber did not increase significantly, our forests would be quickly depleted. We would be a second rate economic power. We would become practically a "banana republic" except we couldn't grow bananas very well in our climate.

Well, where do we stand today? When was the last time you worried about running out of wood? Out of lumber? Possibly you experienced a timber crisis when you were caught short while building a dog house on Saturday afternoon and the lumber yards were closed. Certainly lumber prices rise and fall in response to building booms and busts. But Americans now worry about other kinds of conservation issues—energy, water, pollution, soil exhaustion—rather than timber.

Why aren't people lining up at the Smithsonian to look at America's last living tree? What happened to the timber crisis? What caused it? More significantly, what ended it? How did such a serious national problem with such dire consequences become practically inconsequential? Let's face it. It was a serious problem; but it did end—and in a relatively short period of time. Let's see what happened.

Evolution of a crisis, 1865–1896

After the Civil War, America began the greatest economic expansion in history. In less than thirty years, the railroads spanned a continent. Prairie crossroads became towns, towns became cities, and cities became metropolises. The so-called robber barons were investing and building industrial empires at an unprecedented rate.

The economic expansion required labor; and labor came, by the millions in the form of the "poor and huddled masses" from Europe and Asia. Rapid growth also required iron, steel, coal, and oil—all in increasing amounts. Pittsburgh made iron and steel from the seemingly unlimited ore deposits of Minnesota. Men discovered coal seams in the northern Appalachian Mountains that would last 500 years at prevailing rates of depletion. When the Pennsylvania oil fields petered out, seemingly infinite deposits were found in Texas. A single well, Spindletop, outside of Beaumont, Texas, pumped more oil in its first year of operation than had been previously pumped from the earth. Everything was apparently unlimited. That is, almost everything.

If the nation was built with iron, it was also built with wood. If the nation moved on iron rails, it also moved on wood ties. And Pittsburgh couldn't forge timber. Neither could Cleveland, Chicago, or New York.

Timber had to be grown; and that took time, a long time. Much more time than late nineteenth-century use would allow. We were using up our forests faster than they could grow. Why?

One problem, of course, was the depletion of eastern forests to make room for farms prior to the Civil War. For a long time, the prevailing method of extracting timber was clear cutting. This technique also led to forest fires, further depleting the forests. Furthermore, such cutting was not conducive to reforestation. Indeed, the railroads had switched from wood to coal for fuel by the end of the Civil War, partially as a result of this problem.

Wood, however, was a major ingredient in the expansion following that war. It had many advantages as a building material. In most areas, it was a low cost material; since wood was light relative to its size, it was inexpensive to ship. Unskilled labor, using relatively simple equipment at the building site, could handle the material quite easily. Most significantly, however, it was abundant.

During the years following the Civil War, American woodworking machinery became the most advanced in the world. American power saws were the fastest anywhere. American mills could handle more timber in less time, by far, than any other mills anywhere in the world.

But it is important to note that no other country adopted the American technology. Although they were extremely fast, American saws turned a very large proportion of the lumber into sawdust. European saws were much slower and required far more labor but returned considerably less sawdust. Nathan Rosenberg, an expert on technological change in America, quotes an observer familiar with American and British woodworking in the 1870s as remarking that "lumber manufacture, from the log to the finished state, is, in America, characterized by a waste that can truly be called criminal." The oil guzzlers of the 1970s were the wood guzzlers of the 1870s.

But were the methods used by Americans in the 1870s really "criminal" or even wasteful? Certainly, the methods used in America would indeed have been wasteful in England or France at that time. In Western Europe at the end of the nineteenth century, timber was very scarce and very expensive. On the other hand, labor was relatively cheap. Europeans conserved wood and expended labor.

In America, timber was abundant and therefore cheap. Conversely, because of the relatively small population and the opportunities available in the frontier, labor was very expensive. So American business expended wood and conserved labor as it built a nation. Whenever possible, Americans substituted the abundant wood for the scarce labor. And they continued to do so, until wood became expensive.

Businesses weren't the only guilty parties. Consumers "wasted" wood also. Fireplaces were designed for very large logs, which saved labor time in cutting but burned up a lot of wood relative to the heat provided. More efficient stoves, like those used in Europe, were more expensive and required more labor to prepare the logs. So, as you would expect, the use of these stoves was not widespread in the United States until wood prices rose considerably.

Builders in America used wood for purposes not dreamed of in Europe, where metal or stone would have been used. Houses were constructed using labor-saving, wood-guzzling technology. As the frontier moved west, town after town sprung up. And they were built entirely of wood. The buildings weren't built to last, but they went up fast, and it didn't take much labor to get them built.

But don't call these methods inefficient. They were very efficient. Businesses and consumers were smart. They were niggardly with the expensive factors of production—labor and time. To conserve these expensive resources, they were profligate with the abundant, cheap, and easily used natural resource—timber. And as industrial growth increased, the rate of depletion of wood increased also.

But the real wood users, the major depleters during this period, were the railroads. From the 1870s to 1900, the railroads consumed as much as one-fourth of the annual timber production in the United States. The railroads being built across the prairies were much more wood intensive than the older eastern railroads. Everything except the rails, spikes, car wheels, and locomotives was made of wood.

The reason was simple. These railroads were built through areas that were rather sparsely populated. To survive, they had to begin to yield a return on the investment quickly. So what would the owners do? Clearly, they were induced to build rapidly, lightly, and cheaply. There would be time enough to rebuild substantially when population and traffic increased. Also, both labor and capital were more scarce on the prairie and hence more expensive than in the East. These expensive resources had to be carefully conserved.

Wood was the answer. It was light, easily worked, and, until the 1890s, cheap. Moreover, it could be replaced and repaired more easily. So the prairie railroads began to use wood in great volume. In addition to using wood for crossties, the railroads used wood for bridges, tunnels, fences, culverts, and telegraph poles. Round timbers were frequently used in bridge construction to save sawing, a technique that used a lot of wood but saved time and labor.

The pattern was established. The nation was experiencing the most rapid growth in its history. And the railroads, one of the most wood-intensive sectors of the economy, were the major industry.

In all areas, but especially in the westward expansion, labor was relatively expensive. So was capital. These had to be conserved. The answer was to build with wood, and they did.

But by 1880, only a fool would have suggested that timber could continue to be used at this rate for very long without a gigantic increase in timber production. If this prevailing trend continued, the nation would run out of wood. No wood, no growth, no more prosperity.

The problem was that no good substitute was available. And because it rotted, wood was almost impossible to recycle. In short, a timber famine was inevitable, and economic collapse (or stagnation) would surely follow. Or so the doom merchants of the time told us.

The railroad experiment, 1880–1896

Since the railroads were the largest consumers of wood in the country, they were among the first to begin preparations for the time when timber prices would start climbing. Three types of response were thought to be possible: (1) substituting alternative materials for the wood currently used, either different types of wood or steel and concrete; (2) improving design to conserve wood; or (3) using chemical preservation to extend the life of wood.

There were several areas of wood use where one or more of these possibilities might be applied. Since crossties were the major source of wood consumption, this was a possible area for study. The railroads also used an extremely large amount of timber for bridges, piling, car construction, telegraph poles, fences, tunnels, wharves, buildings, and platforms. The most promising area for study by the railroads, when they became convinced that wood would become increasingly scarce, was increasing the efficiency of wood use.

Prior to 1896, the railroads made great progress in acquiring knowledge about the properties of wood and wood substitutes. This knowledge made it possible to substitute less scarce grades of wood and in some instances steel and concrete for the scarcer woods in some uses. Research on track stress allowed some conservation of crossties. It was found that a significant economy in wood use could be achieved in two ways: (1) proper species selection for the appropriate use and (2) correct wood seasoning to develop wood strength. For example, proper air seasoning was shown to reduce wood decay and lengthen the useful life of the wood. So by 1896, the railroads could economize on wood use through seasoning, species selection, and alternative design. But except in some regions in which timber was extremely scarce, there was little incentive to actually implement wood conservation techniques—and considerable incentive not to—until the price of wood rose much higher.

Bridge design was an important area that could yield great savings in wood consumption. The railroad bridges constructed after the Civil War used designs developed for construction during that war. As you can imagine, these designs were developed for rapid construction with little attention paid to wood conservation. Such methods were ideal for the prairie railroads. They sacrificed materials to gain speed in construction and save labor. To test a new bridge design, the designer would just build the bridge, load a car with iron, and pull it back and forth over the bridge, increasing its load until the bridge collapsed. The breaking weight per linear foot was recorded. Consequently, since the weakest part of the bridge collapsed, bridges were over-designed or overstressed, with a resulting over-usage of wood. When wood was cheap, a lot of it was used.

Advances in metallurgy showed that steel or iron bridges were, in many places, more cost effective than those made of wood. As many hastily built wooden bridges reached the end of their lives and as the price of wood rose, more and more were being replaced by metal bridges. The first general substitution of metal bridges for wood took place in the 1890s in regions where wood had always been expensive— particularly the Middle West. This replacement began even before the general increase in the price of timber. But while the price of timber was not rising, the price of iron was falling during this period. So the price of wood relative to iron rose, and some substitution was economical.

One use where substitution occurred was the construction of culverts. Between 1888 and 1895, 500 wood culverts a year were replaced. Four-fifths of the replacements were built with iron; the remainder were made from used bridge timber.

Prior to 1900, the railroads made a great deal of progress in developing designs that used less timber in wooden trestles. The type of testing we described, in which individual segments were not designed and tested independently, led to much more wood being used in a trestle than was necessary. So as knowledge of bridge construction advanced, the railroads were able to save considerably on the amount of timber used.

Another innovation that allowed the railroads to save on timber use was wood preservation. As you would expect, the technology of preserving wood from rot was much more advanced in Europe, where wood was extremely scarce, than in America, where it was much more abundant. The first American railroads that experimented to any great extent with preservation of crossties were located in the old settlement areas around Boston, New York, and Philadelphia and on the prairies. In both areas, timber, as you might expect, was more expensive than in other areas of the country. Prior to 1880, several different methods of preservation were tried, with little success. But in 1881, three prairie railroads, the Sante Fe, Union Pacific, and Rock Island (all located in areas characterized by high timber prices), developed a process for preserving crossties. However, at that time the high cost of preservation relative to the cost of timber made tie preservation uneconomical in most areas.

To illustrate why it was not economical to preserve timber, let us provide a typical example from that period. In 1883, the Burlington railroad considered treating hemlock ties with zinc oxide so they could be used in place of the more expensive oak ties. Hemlock ties cost 24 cents each. The treatment added another 24 cents and additional costs were between 6 and 12 cents, depending on the location. The total cost of a treated hemlock tie was between 54 and 60 cents, a figure that did not differ substantially from the cost of an oak tie. Since the expected life was the same—about eight years—for either type of tie, preservation was not adopted.

An important advance in 1885 came in a report of a special committee of the American Society of Civil Engineers. This report concluded that many sources of timber supply were being rapidly depleted. It predicted generally increasing timber prices and growing difficulty in obtaining wood. The report made available the more advanced European processes for wood preservation, especially creosoting.

So although conditions were changing, in all but a few regions where timber was especially expensive it was not economical to practice preservation. Sherry Olson (p. 67), quoting a report of the American Society of Civil Engineers, notes:

> So long as wood was cheap, the cost of efficient preparation, including interest on plant and price of antiseptics, was so great in proportion to the ruling timber prices … timber preparation did not pay. It was cheaper to let it rot in the good old way.

Preservation would not be economical until timber prices rose. Predictions about future wood prices forced the railroads to think about preservation and other types of wood conservation. But in most areas of the United States, economic conditions simply did not justify its practice. Not yet at least.

In 1896, conditions changed—wood prices began to rise rapidly. The earlier research undertaken by the railroads would begin to pay dividends.

The railroads adapt, 1896–1914

In 1896, timber prices began to rise. As the price of wood rose between 1896 and 1907 (the price of crosstie stumpage increased 500–800 percent during this period), the relative price of substitutes, such as concrete and steel, fell. The railroads now began to adapt; slowly at first, rapidly later on. If the possibility of timber famine induced research in conservation methods, rising prices caused the new developments to be used.

At first the railroads, at the urging of the U.S. Forest Service, considered reforestation of the country as a remedy. Some railroads even went so far as to invest in forests. But they soon realized that this was not the answer. The production of wood took longer than they and the Forest Service had at first believed, and the projects proved uneconomical, even with the higher prices of timber. Almost all the railroads abandoned their forestation projects.

The railroads became increasingly disillusioned with the recommendations of the Forest Service. During this period, they found that the real remedy lay in more efficient and more limited use of timber. Reduced consumption replaced increased production as the solution. Substitution was the answer. Olson (p. 97) quotes an executive of the Pennsylvania Railroad, who explained in 1910:

> So far, much less emphasis has been placed on the equally important question of reducing the consumption of forest products. It is very well to make an area produce two sticks of timber where before there was but one; still, it is just as good lumber

economy to double the life of the first stick, and there is the added advantage of an immense saving to the consumer.

So more and more the railroads turned to wood preservation and more efficient uses of timber. Many of the innovations were truly ingenious. Many new, more plentiful species of timber were found to be suitable for crossties after preservation was done. Research showed that ties made of hardwood, such as untreated white oak, could be saved for steep grades, sharp turns, and heavy traffic areas where the ties wore out before they rotted. Treated softer woods could be used in less demanding places. New, more efficient methods of sawing ties were found. These methods reduced the amount of wood used in a given tie. Furthermore, sawing instead of hewing the ties allowed wood that was previously scrap or chips to be used for boards and flooring. All sizes of trees could then be used for ties, whereas hewing of ties required the trees to be eleven to fifteen inches in diameter.

During this transition period, seasoning and preservation of much of the wood destined both for ties and for other uses became quite widespread. Again, these processes permitted considerable saving in timber. But in addition to rotting out, crossties wore out because of mechanical stress. From 1900 to 1914, many innovations were introduced to reduce the stress on ties. For example, tie plates and new types of fastening were designed to protect ties from wear. Different types of fastening and plates were added to protect the wood fibers. More scientific track design also was used to conserve wood.

From 1900 to 1914, the railroads paid a great deal of attention to substitution of other materials for wood. Iron, steel, and concrete were substituted in many uses. For example, there was a rapid shift from all-wood to all-metal cars between 1900 and 1914. As we noted earlier, there was a substitution away from wood in bridge construction. When wood was used in bridge repair and construction, it was treated wood.

We could go on and enumerate the different methods the railroads used to adapt to higher wood prices, but there would be little point in doing so. The major point is, as Sherry Olson notes (p. 7), that the response of the railroads to the timber crisis "demonstrates that the industrial consumer has substantial power to bring about greater efficiency in the use of resources and to confound predictions that look only at his past habits and fail to take into account his powers of choice and change." In other words, consumers are not at the mercy of suppliers.

The role of the U.S. Forest Service, 1898–1920

What was the role of the government during the crisis? Let's look at what the Forest Service was doing at the time. Until 1898, the U.S. Forest Service, established to protect and increase the nation's forests, was little more than a research organization. It carried out research both in wood conservation and in efficient forestry methods. But the budget was very small and little was accomplished.

In 1898, Gifford Pinchot, later to be known as the great conservationist, became chief of the Forest Service. Two statements from the service after Pinchot became chief illustrate its position: "We have never been so near to the exhaustion of our lumber supply," and "the forest of the private owners will have to be set in order if the overwhelming calamity of a timber famine is to be kept from the nation" (Olson, p. 72). With a couple of word changes, the two statements could have come from the Department of Energy in 1979, couldn't they? Let's look at what the Forest Service wanted to do.

To understand what the service recommended, we must first understand the basic theory their plans were based on. The main point was that depletion of the forests was causing wood prices to rise. Starting in 1896, timber prices, especially the prices of replacement railroad ties, began to increase. These rising prices pointed to a decreasing supply of timber.

Since the Forest Service and many people interested in the problem assumed that the quantity of wood (per capita) demanded by the economy was fixed, regardless of price, the price of wood depended upon conditions of supply. Now, admittedly, a decrease in the supply of something will increase its price. But the Forest Service had a different interpretation. And it was a simple theory. Wrong, but simple.

According to the Forest Service, as timber was exhausted in one area, customers had to buy timber from another, more remote area, and therefore had to pay a higher price. The price remained at the new level until that region was depleted and a new timber region brought in, at an even higher price. People used the same amount of wood, regardless of price. If the Forest Service didn't do something, the nation would be denuded, except for the trees in museums.

Based on this line of reasoning, the only salvation was to fill the gap between the amount of wood demanded and the amount supplied. Clearly, the only solution for the Forest Service—an agency staffed primarily by foresters—was increased planting and growing. Silviculture would reforest the nation and save it from its own greed and waste. And a massive reforestation it would have to be, since the nation was using annually 40 cubic feet of timber per capita, while the growth of the forests produced only 13 cubic feet per capita annually.

So you can see that the gapsmanship approach is not just a phenomenon of the past decade. It has a long, though not particularly distinguished, history. If a resource is being used up only two things can be done: find (or grow) more of the stuff or force people to use less. Either way, the gap must be closed.

Although some of the Forest Service's resources were used for product research, most of its efforts went into forestry and, after 1905, to administering the national forests. By 1912, only 4–5 percent of the total budget was devoted to forest products, down from 12 percent in 1904. The primary interest of the Forest Service was how to grow more trees.

For a time, the Forest Service even interested the railroads in forestry as a solution to the problem. Many of the railroads promoted and even practiced forestry. After all, the experts were saying that more efficient forestry was the solution, and the railroads believed the experts. Wouldn't you have believed? But the experts were wrong, as the railroads soon discovered.

During the crucial period between 1900 and 1915, the Forest Service gave the railroads some more poor advice, in addition to encouraging them to promote and practice forestry. For example, foresters encouraged the railroads to use half round ties and short, eight-foot ties, in order to conserve wood. The railroads learned that such ties actually used more wood. The heavier, longer rectangular ties were more economical and gave longer service. Also, the Forest Service urged tie makers to use trees with larger diameters than was customary, in order to save the smaller trees for other, higher valued use. That, of course, meant that the service was recommending smaller ties made from larger trees, an economic contradiction that the railroads didn't buy.

The Forest Service also recommended planting faster-growing species of trees. This recommendation was followed, but it was an economic failure. All in all, the advice given by the service was not very effective. According to Olson (pp. 96–97):

> The silviculturists continued through World War I to predict rising prices for wood, critical shortages, and a painful "wood famine." They continued to agitate for large investments in plantations and forest holdings as profitable and patriotic ventures … [The railroads] were advised to adopt practices in line with an idealized concept of "good forestry," instead of forest practices that would actually promote railroad economies.

The crisis is over

So that's our story. By 1922, the problem was virtually solved. With the exception of a brief problem in housing, the shortages disappeared. Wood prices rose sharply between 1915 and 1920, then continued to rise gradually relative to the prices of alternative materials. But there was no alarm. Not many predicted a timber famine or forest exhaustion.

The Forest Service continued to emphasize silviculture and management of the national forests. The railroads, which were the biggest timber users, became the greatest economizers. Railroad consumption fell from 20–25 percent of the timber cut in 1909 to 3 or 4 percent (excluding pulpwood) in the 1960s.

Other users followed the lead of the railroads in wood conservation. High timber prices encouraged a shift from wood to other building materials in the construction industries. Wood preservation, begun by the railroads, extended the life of wood in other uses, such as fence posts, telephone poles, and buildings.

To appreciate the shift in emphasis, consider the fact that in 1911 the Forest Service investigated the "hickory problem." The annual hickory cut was depleting 3 percent of the U.S. supply (which was the world supply) each year. There was no satisfactory substitute, and hickory trees would soon disappear. Many uses of hickory should be discouraged.

Forty years later the Forest Service formed the Hickory Group to again attack the hickory problem. However, this time the problem was different. Because of the low demand for hickory, hickory trees were taking over the eastern hardwood forests—up to 30 percent of the timber. The Hickory Group was formed to encourage consumer demand for hickory. So much for depletion.

Was there a crisis? Certainly. Unquestionably, timber use could not have continued at the same rate without total depletion, and fairly quickly. There was a problem, and something did have to be done. However, the U.S. Forest Service was of little use. The primary consumers of wood, led by the railroads, adapted their levels of consumption through technological change.

They substituted other materials for wood when the relative price of timber rose. Under the same incentive, they were able to extend the effective life of the wood they did use and to use wood more efficiently.

So market forces overcame this crisis. No one had to force consumers to economize and substitute. Instead it was a case of the users of wood wanting to make a profit and responding to scarcity and price change. The famine was over. As a matter of fact, it never really came.

Note

1 Much of this chapter is based on the work of Sherry H. Olson in *The Depletion Myth*. To the reader interested in more detailed information about America's timber crisis, we recommend this excellent book.

AMERICA'S FIRST OIL CRISIS

DURING THE PAST DECADE, we have heard much about alternative energy sources and synfuels. However, few people remember that petroleum is itself an "alternative energy source." Petroleum—or, as it was called, "rock oil"—was the alternative energy source of the nineteenth century.

Prior to the Civil War, America lubricated its machinery and fueled its lamps with oil from whales. Sperm oil, obtained from the sperm whale, was the best illuminant available at the time. But oil from other types of whales, because it was considerably cheaper than sperm oil, was widely used also. At the time, these oils were practically "essential" to an industrializing economy.

Nonetheless, during and after the Civil War, the whaling industry experienced a rapid decline. Table 3.1 shows some illustrative figures for oil production and the size of the American whaling fleet that should demonstrate the decline in this previously important industry.

What led to such a dramatic decline? Why did such an important industry become so insignificant? Many writers have argued that the discovery of petroleum led to the demise of the whaling industry. For example, in *The Whalers* (p. 150), A. B. C. Whipple asserted that:

It is a safe assumption that in 1859 very few, if any, whalemen had heard the name Edwin L. Drake. And there was no reason why they should have, for Drake was an obscure entrepreneur. But over the next decades every whaleman would come to know, and curse, Drake's name. For on August 27 of 1859, his Seneca Oil Company succeeded in extracting petroleum from the earth by drilling 69 feest down into the soil near Titusville, Pennsylvania. In so doing he put an end to Yankee whaling industry just as surely as if he had drilled a hole in the hold of every whaleship.

The same theme was expressed by F. D. Ommanney (p. 92) in *Lost Leviathan*:

> But in 1859 the greatest and most lasting blow was struck at the whaling fleet. This was the discovery of petroleum and the production of oil from mineral sources which competed with sperm oil and, in the end, drove it off the market as a fuel and illuminant.

Unquestionably, petroleum did replace the previously necessary sperm and whale oil as the primary illuminant and lubricant during the decade after the Civil War. But many who have written about the rise of the petroleum industry tell a different story from that told by the chroniclers of the demise of whaling. For example, in the centennial issue of *World Oil* (p. 135), we find the following:

> Oil had been known since the beginning of history. The pitch used to caulk Noah's Ark undoubtedly was petroleum. Many other simple uses are recorded in the early pages of history and down through the centuries. Early American settlers found Indians skimming oil from seeps and using it for both internal and external medicine. A few enterprising American business pioneers were selling "Rock Oil" as medicine by the middle of the 19th Century. Their sources of supply were seepages or salt brine wells in which they were "unfortunate" enough to find oil.
>
> However, no one gave any serious study to the commercial possibilities of oil until the simultaneous beginnings of the Age of Light and the Machine Age *created the world's first and most serious oil shortage.* [Emphasis added.]

Table 3.1 The American whaling industry, 1856–1876

Whale industry production		
Year	Sperm oil production (barrels)	Whale oil production (barrels)
1856	80,941	197,890
1861	68,932	133,717
1866	36,663	74,302
1876	39,811	33,010
The whaling fleet		
Year	Number of whaling vessels	Tonnage
1856	635	199,141
1861	514	158,745
1866	263	68,536
1876	169	38,883

Walter S. Tower, *A History of the American Whale Fishery*, pp. 121, 126.

Keep in mind that the preceding quotation was published in 1959, fourteen years before our own serious oil shortage. However, the important assertion made in this article was that the rise of the petroleum industry was itself the result of a shortage of whale oil—America's first oil crisis.

Which was it? Did the rise of the petroleum industry sink the whaling industry? Or, was the advent of the oil industry the result of a shortage in whale oil? Was there a whale oil crisis? Let's look at some historical evidence.

The early whaling industry

The first whaling in North America was done by Indians on the East and West coasts, long before Europeans arrived. The search for whales probably began with the killing of stranded whales, for which the Indians kept watch. After killing the whale, they used the oil for heat and illumination, the meat for food, and the bones for building.

After Europeans settled New England, they also kept watch for and killed stranded whales. Not long after the settlement of New England, American whalers began to go to sea and hunt whales, probably because relative to the expanding population, fewer and fewer whales were becoming stranded in coastal bays.

New Englanders became familiar with the new (to them) and superior sperm whale when one of their species became stranded close to shore. All parties involved—Indians, settlers, and the Crown—claimed the whale. The next sperm whale captured was struck and killed in 1712 by a boat hunting other types of whales in the Atlantic. As people became familiar with the superiority of sperm oil as an illuminant and as certain other types of whale were becoming scarce, whalers increasingly searched for sperm whales. A new industry was born.

As boats ventured farther and farther out into the ocean, they consequently were built larger and larger. The whaleboats progressed from rowboats with a single sail to ships up to 50 tons and 40 feet long with multiple sails. Early in the eighteenth century, whale ships could be fitted for voyages up to seven weeks long.

The demand for whale products in England and the colonies increased rapidly during the first half of the eighteenth century. Consequently, the price of sperm oil rose substantially during the century until the beginning of the Revolutionary War. In 1731, the price of sperm oil was 7 pounds sterling per ton. In 1768, the price had risen to 17 pounds sterling per ton; at the beginning of the war, the price was over 40 pounds sterling. Since the index of consumer prices remained relatively stable in this period, the increase was large in both nominal and real terms.

As we would expect, the increase in price led to a substantial increase in the number of whaling vessels. By the start of the war, 60 ships were sailing from New Bedford alone, making that city the capital of the North American whaling industry, with Nantucket close second.

Since whaling ships could not leave port during the Revolutionary War because of the high probability of being sunk by British ships, the New England whaling industry lay dormant from 1776 to 1784. But when the whaling fleet was rebuilt, the whalers found that the whale population had increased during the period of no hunting. By 1788, the New England fleet reached the same size as before the war. And by this time, whalers were venturing around Cape Horn into the Pacific Ocean.

The increased hunting had the obvious consequence. Whales were becoming increasingly scarce in the Atlantic. Further contributing to the problems of the whaling industry, Great Britain, in an effort to build its own whaling industry, imposed a tariff of eighteen pounds sterling per barrel on imported oil. (The U.S. auto industry didn't invent this tactic. It has been around for centuries.) So this tariff effectively eliminated British markets. France, however, had in the meantime become a good market, and the demand in the United States was increasing. As we would expect, ships became larger and larger, and whalers were now able to undertake voyages of up to three years.

At the beginning of the nineteenth century, the U.S. whale oil industry was hit with three blows. First, the French Revolution closed the French market. Then, in 1807, because of privateers, the Embargo Act prohibited whalers from leaving port. Finally, during the war of 1812, the British fleet practically destroyed the American whaling fleet.

But after the war of 1812, the whaling fleet began once more to increase rapidly. The number of ships (though not tonnage) peaked in 1846 when 729 American whaling ships were afloat. At the time, the price of sperm oil was 88 cents a barrel, and the price of whale oil was 33 cents a barrel, still relatively cheap. But cheap oil couldn't continue. High volume whaling was rapidly depleting the raw material—the whales. The more whales killed, the fewer there were to reproduce. The birthrate declined dramatically, as you would expect. Spurred on by the declining whale population, the whaling ships sailed farther and farther from New England. Whaling became more and more efficient. But no matter how efficient the whalers were, the whales wouldn't cooperate by reproducing at a more rapid rate. Regardless of the efficiency of the whaling fleet, the whales just weren't there in the numbers they had been in the past.

By the 1840s, American whalers covered the sea. The Pacific was heavily hunted. During the 1830s and 1840s, there were at times more than a hundred ships off the coast of Japan alone. And, of course, the heavy hunting clearly decreased the supply of whales even further. Once again, America was using up an important natural resource. And as in the case for all natural resources, when the supply of whales decreased, the price of whale oil began to increase.

How high can oil prices go?

By 1850, the price of sperm oil had risen to $1.20 a barrel, and that of whale oil to 49 cents, increases of 36 and 48 percent, respectively, over a four-year period. (The increases in real terms were essentially the same since the price index remained practically unchanged over this period.) By 1856, the price of sperm oil had risen to $1.62, an increase of 84 percent over the ten-year period; the price of whale oil went to 80 cents, an increase of 143 percent over the same period. While the prices of sperm and other whale oil fell somewhat from 1856 until the beginning of the Civil War, the price in real terms fell only about 5 percent, since the price index declined over this period. In any case, in 1860 the price of oil was substantially above what it had been 20 years before.

As you would expect, induced by the rising price of oil, even more ships went to sea to hunt the whales. Total ship tonnage employed in whaling increased from

171,484 tons (543 ships) in 1850 to a peak of 208,299 tons in 1854. Tonnage remained above 200,000 tons as late as 1858, the year before the discovery of petroleum.

But increased hunting did not mean increased oil production for the whaling fleet. Although the price of oil remained relatively high and the whaling fleet remained large, whales grew increasingly scarce and more difficult to find. Just before the Civil War, there seemed to be no solution in sight. How could a country fight a war without lubricants? Whale and sperm oil was "essential" and we were about to run out of it.

The beginning of the age of petroleum

Of course, there was a solution in sight. As a matter of fact, the solution was just around the corner. As we know now, the solution was crude petroleum. And we know also that petroleum quickly became not only superior to whale oil as a lubricant and illuminant but also cheaper.

As noted earlier, petroleum had been known since the dawn of time. People knew it could be used for caulking, and its medicinal properties were widely known early in the nineteenth century. And as we will show, by the late 1850s people knew how to use petroleum as an illuminant and lubricant. The problem was, people didn't know how to get it out of the ground in any significant quantities.

In the early part of the 1800s, no one really experimented with petroleum as an illuminant or lubricant, because whale and sperm oil was so cheap. There was no need for a substitute oil when cheap whale oil was readily available. But when the machine age began, the demand for lighting increased and whales became scarcer. Consequently, the price of whale oil rose, and people began to search for a suitable substitute. Crude petroleum was seen by some persons to have possibilities as a solution to the whale oil crisis as early as 1853.

By 1859, A. C. Ferris was actively working with petroleum as an illuminant in New York. He was able to make fuel from oil and he greatly improved the kerosene lamp. But he had trouble finding a supply. He was importing oil from as far away as Canada, California, and even the East Indies. This oil, as did all other oil, came from seepages and from wells that were dug rather than drilled. Ferris himself tried unsuccessfully to dig for oil in the brine area of western Pennsylvania. But don't feel too sorry for him; he later became one of the pioneers in the new petroleum industry.

Even earlier, in 1853, George H. Bissell, a journalist and teacher, had become interested in what was then called "rock oil" when he became convinced that this oil would make an excellent illuminant. So convinced was he, that he purchased land on Oil Creek in Pennsylvania, an area known for its frequent oil seepage. Bissell and some other men joined together in the Pennsylvania Oil Company and were soon selling oil from seepages on their property at $1.50 a gallon. In 1855, the company hired a famous scientist, Benjamin Silliman, to analyze the properties of oil. Silliman reported that oil would make an excellent illuminant and would also be a good lubricant.

Bissell and some of his partners planned to drill for oil in 1857 using methods that others used to drill for water and salt brine. But since some of the stockholders in the Pennsylvania Oil Company objected strenuously to the venture, Bissell had to reorganize the company as the Seneca Oil Company. The company was continually plagued by disturbances over financing. It then hired Edwin L. Drake, a retired railroad conductor who was totally unfamiliar with the technology of drilling wells, to drill a well on Bissell's property near Titusville, Pennsylvania. Fortunately, Drake hired William Smith, an experienced well driller, to carry out the actual drilling. The crew consisted of Smith's two young sons. On August 27, 1859, late on a Sunday afternoon, this group struck oil, made history, and changed the world.

Even before Bissell and Silliman began exploring the properties of oil, Samuel Kier of Tarentum, Pennsylvania, then the center of a large salt well region, became interested in petroleum. In 1844, the salt brine wells in the area began to produce a nuisance in the form of sludge, which had to be drained off onto the ground or into a canal. When the sludge caught fire one day, people recognized that this oil would burn. By 1846, many people were burning the oil in their lamps even though it was smokey and smelled bad. It did, however, give off a good light and the price was right—the stuff was free for the taking.

Kier, who was selling petroleum, or rock oil, as a medicine, sent a sample to a chemist in Philadelphia, who reported that the oil would make a good illuminant and designed a still that might prove suitable for refining. Acting on these plans, Kier in 1854 built the first oil refinery in America in Pittsburgh, Pennsylvania. The refined oil was sold as a lighting oil. But the oil still stank when it was burned even though it did illuminate well. It also stank when being refined—so badly that the neighbors forced Pittsburgh's city officials to run both Kier and his refinery out of the city. Kier rebuilt the refinery out of the city and sold a considerable amount of lamp oil. He actually refined much of the oil from Drake's first well after 1859. Although he never could eliminate the bad odor, he did improve it. It was left to Silliman to develop the refining process further.

By 1859, there were 53 other refineries operating in the United States, but these refineries were designed to produce coal oil. The refining process, developed by Dr. James Young in Scotland, produced illuminants and lubricants from shale, peat, and coal. While some of these coal oil refineries went out of business after the Pennsylvania oil field came in, many were transformed into petroleum refineries.

After Drake's well came in, many others began drilling in the area. Thousands of people were attracted to the region almost immediately. Very quickly, well after well came in. Less than one year after Drake's well hit, oil was selling for $10 a barrel. At the end of 1861, it was selling for 10 cents a barrel. By late 1860, there were 15 refineries in the area; three years later there were 61. The world's first oil glut occurred. The price was so low that people all over the country were introduced to oil as a cheap, efficient, and reliable illuminant and lubricant.

The demands of a rapidly expanding manufacturing industry increased the demand for oil. Production leaped from a rate of 1,200 barrels a day in 1860 to more than 5,000 a day in 1861. On November 14, 1861, landowners in the Pennsylvania oil field met to organize and take measures to raise the price of oil. All business was to pass through a central authority. At the next meeting, the Oil Creek Association was formed to regulate production; and in January, 1862, the organization set the price of oil at $4 a barrel, up $3.90 from 1861. The first OPEC had emerged. At first, they sold little oil. But by the end of 1862, because of the increased demand, the market price actually became $4 a barrel. The price steadily increased thereafter. It remained high, though, not because of the loosely formed cartel, which soon broke up, but because demand kept increasing as people became more familiar with the properties of oil. By the end of the Civil War, petroleum was the sixth most important export of the United States, ranking behind only gold, corn, tobacco, wheat, and flour. Certainly oil had become an important commodity, and it was destined to become more and more important over time.

What was happening in the whaling industry as the petroleum industry was expanding? During the Civil War, the American whaling fleet was virtually destroyed. Confederate warships, the *Shenandoah* and the *Alabama*, sank a huge number of whalers both in the Atlantic and the Pacific. The remainder stayed in port to avoid being sunk. Many of the older whaling ships were loaded with stones and sunk by the U.S. Navy in Charleston harbor as part of the blockade of Southern ports during the war.

There was a brief revival in whaling after the war when the price of whale oil went to $2.50 a gallon. The number of whaling ships recovered to 253, but the number of whales was simply too small; whales were just too hard to find. Whaling as a major industry was dead by the 1870s. It died, just as the production of "whale-sized" automobiles died as a major industry a hundred years later, because of a resource crisis. But if whaling had peaked in tonnage and number of ships years before the first oil well came in, could the decline of whaling as a major industry be blamed on the discovery of petroleum?

Reconciliation

Returning to the question we posed at the beginning of the chapter, what can we conclude about the beginning of the age of petroleum? Did the discovery of petroleum destroy whaling or did petroleum arise as a result of an oil (whale oil) crisis? Certainly, we can agree that the increased scarcity of whales drove up the price of the primary illuminant and lubricant in the United States and Europe, causing, one might say, the world's first oil crisis. However, we must also agree that, after the discovery that previously known drilling techniques would work for oil and after the development of refining, whaling as a major industry was doomed.

But what can we conclude about the hypothesis that the increased scarcity of whales was an important, possibly the most important, cause of the rise of petroleum as a major industry? Well, we know that man had known about oil for centuries. People knew that oil burned and gave light many years before 1859. We also know that men were working on lamps to burn oil prior to that year. It was a relatively simple step to adapt existing lamps to facilitate the burning of refined petroleum, once the problem of odor was solved. Also, the methods used in coal oil refineries were easily adaptable to petroleum refining. The technology was already available in 1859, as evidenced by the rapid building of refineries in the Titusville area almost immediately after oil was struck.

Finally, the drilling techniques were well known. The drilling methods used for brine water were easily adaptable to petroleum. Bissell, who decided to drill for oil rather than dig for it, had absolutely no experience in drilling, but he must have known something about the process. As noted in *The American Petroleum Industry* (p. 81):

> As a driller, Drake was a rank amateur. At a time when it usually took only six to
> eight months to bore 1,000 feet or more through solid rock in the great salt fields

along the Kanawha River, it took him two years to drill 69½ feet. When Drake finally reached his peak rate of 3 feet a day in August, 1859, he was boring at only about one-half the Kanawha rate of a decade earlier.

Nonetheless, Drake demonstrated that oil could be extracted from the ground at a substantial rate, just as Kier had earlier demonstrated that it could be refined in large quantities. But we must wonder: what if sperm whales had multiplied so prodigiously that whale oil remained at around 25 to 30 cents a gallon? Would people have been experimenting with petroleum refineries? With petroleum lamps? With methods to extract petroleum from the ground?

It's somewhat doubtful. And it would have been inefficient and wasteful to have done so. If whale oil had been 30 cents per gallon, few resources would have been expended to obtain petroleum. Whatever their contribution to mankind, the pioneers of the oil industry, Bissell, Kier, Ferris, Drake, Silliman, and their associates, were primarily, if not solely, interested in profits. Everything we read about the early days of the Pennsylvania (later the Seneca) Oil Company leads us to believe that the stockholders were mainly interested in turning a buck or two. They were continually arguing over money. There is strong reason to believe that if Drake had not struck oil when he did, or soon thereafter, the project would have been discontinued. Some of the stockholders did not even want to send him the last expense installment of $500. When the well hit, the company was really financially strapped. These men were profit seekers, not saints.

This is not to say that if the men of Seneca had abandoned the project others would not have struck oil soon. They would have. As evidenced by the onslaught of successful wells in the Titusville area after Drake struck oil, the technique was too simple to be delayed for very long. Certainly if Kier had not developed the first refinery, someone else would have. But the pioneers, as well as those who would have succeeded them had they quit or failed, were, or would have been, motivated by potential profits.

But would there have been these potential profits from innovation had whales remained plentiful and the price of whale oil low? Or what would potential profits from petroleum have been had whales become more plentiful and whale oil fallen in price? It doesn't appear likely that there would have been as great an incentive to drill for oil and experiment with refineries.

Certainly the petroleum pioneers were well aware of what was happening to the price of whale oil. From *Pennsylvania Petroleum* (p. 232), we quote William H. Abbott, who built the first refinery in the Titusville area. In a news story published in 1888 he wrote:

> The first person to experiment with petroleum, and make a success at refining it, was Samuel M. Kier, of Pittsburgh. He procured his supply from the ... wells at Tarentum. When refined he called it carbon oil. I purchased from him, paying $1.25 a gallon by the barrel. This was far superior to the oil made at that time in Canfield, Ohio, from the fine channel coal; or to whale oil which cost from $1.75 to $2.25 a gallon. It was a fortunate circumstance that on the decline of the whale-fisheries, and particularly, after the destruction of our whaling fleet by the rebels, during the last year of the war, there should be at hand so cheap and abundant a substitute; thereby preventing the public generally from suffering any inconvenience from the loss of whale oil.

Clearly, the introduction of petroleum was not simply a fortunate circumstance. The whale oil crisis and the potentially greater crisis were certainly ended by the emergence of petroleum. Certainly there is evidence that the pioneers of petroleum were strongly motivated by profits, and the high prices of whale oil pointed to potentially high profits in petroleum. No one sent them to the oil fields of Pennsylvania to benefit humanity or to alleviate suffering. They went to benefit themselves and in doing so benefited mankind.

On that note, we find it interesting to see what Ida M. Tarbell wrote in the introduction to *The Birth of the Oil Industry* (p. xxxix) in 1938:

> It is certain, however, the development could never have gone on at anything like the speed that it did except under the American system of free opportunity. Men did not wait to ask if they might go into the Oil Region: they went. They did not ask how to put down a well: they quickly took the processes which other men had developed for other purposes and adapted them to their purpose. Each man made his contribution.
>
> Taken as a whole, a truer exhibit of what must be expected of men working without other regulation than that they voluntarily give themselves is not to be found in our industrial history.

Review and Discussion Questions

1 Why was timber wasted in the 1870s?
2 What actions did the railroads take when timber prices began to rise?
3 What was the later problem with the hickory trees?
4 Why weren't the commercial possibilities of rock oil—petroleum—explored until the 1800s?
5 In 1977, President Jimmy Carter stated that the world might use up all the proven reserves of oil by "the end of the next decade." How are "proven reserves" estimated? Why was President Carter wrong?
6 Currently, some people believe that oil production will inevitably decline (look up references to "peak oil"). Should we worry about this?

Chapter 4

Steven Horwitz

MAKING HURRICANE RESPONSE MORE EFFECTIVE: LESSONS FROM THE PRIVATE SECTOR AND THE COAST GUARD DURING KATRINA

Introduction

MANY PEOPLE BELIEVE that the government, particularly the federal government, should finance and direct both the response to and recovery from natural disasters. Such centralized political solutions have, after all, been the standard practice in recent U.S. history. This belief often rests on the assumption that the private sector's profit motive would thwart the charitable impulses generally regarded as essential for effective relief. However, the private sector's involvement in the response to Hurricane Katrina along the Gulf Coast has provided strong reasons to be skeptical of this argument.

The dramatic failures of the Federal Emergency Management Agency (FEMA) during Hurricane Katrina have been well-publicized and thoroughly dissected by the political process.[1] Both critics and supporters of vigorous government responses to natural disasters have noted those failures and offered analyses of the reasons behind them.[2] These discussions and analyses have led to some fairly minor changes in FEMA's structure and operations for future crises.[3] Despite FEMA's massive failures, the debate to this point has been focused largely on improving the government's response to future disasters and catastrophes. Policy makers and the public alike continue to assume that government must be responsible for nearly all disaster recovery activities.

However, the reality of the response to Katrina demonstrates that the private sector is far more effective than the conventional wisdom suggests.[4] Media accounts during the relief and recovery process and reports from local residents and private-sector actors make it clear that the private sector was extraordinarily successful in providing help to damaged communities across the Gulf, especially in New Orleans. While the major media and political actors rightly focused on the failures of FEMA, the major government agency responsible for disaster relief, the successes of the private sector[5] and of one particular government agency, the U.S. Coast Guard, have been much less publicized. Their effective responses deserve greater consideration as we seek to improve disaster relief and recovery policies. During the Katrina relief efforts, the more successful organizations were those that had the right incentives to respond well and could tap into the local information necessary to know what that response should be. The private sector had the right incentives and, along with the Coast Guard, was able to access the local knowledge necessary to provide the relief that was needed. FEMA lacked both of these advantages.

Post-Katrina, profit-seeking firms beat most of the government to the scene and provided more effectively the supplies needed for the immediate survival of a population cut off from life's most basic necessities. Though numerous private-sector firms played important roles in the relief operations, Wal-Mart stood out. The nearly unanimous agreement by local officials that Wal-Mart's response was crucial in preventing the crisis from being even worse than it was suggests that an analysis of that success is in order.

The other major success story of Katrina was that of the Coast Guard, which rescued more than 24,000 people in the two weeks following the storm. Why were big-box stores like Wal-Mart and one particular government agency able to respond so effectively when other organizations were not? In this Policy Comment, I argue that, contrary to the conventional wisdom, the incentives facing private-sector organizations actually lead them to outperform public agencies in many disaster relief tasks. Furthermore, where a government response is deemed necessary, agencies with more decentralized structures will perform better because they are able to tap into local knowledge and conditions.

Disaster researchers have argued that the most effective responses to disasters involve a combination of "discipline" and "agility."[6] Responders need the discipline of an organizational structure that keeps them focused on solving the problems at hand. At the same time, they also need to be agile in the face of the unexpected in order to respond promptly to the ever-changing conditions characteristic of most disaster recovery efforts. Private-sector firms operate in an institutional environment of profit and loss, which provides an external discipline that ensures they stay focused on their specific purposes. Additionally, decentralized and local organizations have the ability to know the communities they serve very well, thus making them agile in ways that more centralized organizations are not.

These organizational and institutional factors can help explain why simply reorganizing responsibility among government agencies or enhancing the expertise of leadership will not be enough to significantly improve the performance of government disaster relief agencies. Because the problems government agencies face when trying to provide disaster relief are inherent in the agencies' structures, disaster-planning processes and official public policy should include a larger role for the private sector and should limit government's role to being as unobtrusive as possible. Additionally, where government action remains appropriate, policy makers should aim to decentralize governmental responses.

This Policy Comment offers policy makers four specific recommendations for improving responses to natural disasters:

1. Give the private sector as much freedom as possible to provide resources for relief and recovery efforts and ensure that its role is officially recognized as part of disaster protocols.
2. Decentralize government relief to local governments and non-governmental organizations and provide that relief in the form of cash or broadly defined vouchers.
3. Move the Coast Guard and FEMA out of the Department of Homeland Security (DHS).
4. Reform "Good Samaritan" laws so that private-sector actors are clearly protected when they make good faith efforts to help.

Section 1 of this Policy Comment explores the successful responses to Hurricane Katrina by the private sector and the Coast Guard. Section 2 develops a framework for understanding those successes, focusing on the benefits offered by the institutional environment of the private sector and the agility of decentralized organizations. Finally, Section 3 addresses the more detailed recommendations for improving policy.

1 The private sector and the Coast Guard during Hurricane Katrina

In exploring exactly which relief efforts were most successful, it becomes clear that the private sector's efforts were generally much more effective than the government's. Wal-Mart arrived in the New Orleans area long before FEMA and had the supplies that the community needed. Both President Aaron Broussard and Sheriff Harry Lee of Jefferson Parish in suburban New Orleans lauded Wal-Mart's work. In an appearance on *Meet the Press*, Broussard noted that Wal-Mart had delivered three trailers of water only to be turned back by FEMA and quoted Lee in saying, "if [the] American government would have responded like Wal-Mart has responded, we wouldn't be in this crisis."[7] Philip Capitano, mayor of the New Orleans suburb of Kenner, reported, "the only lifeline in Kenner was the Wal-Mart stores. We didn't have looting on a mass scale because Wal-Mart showed up with food and water so our people could survive." Similar reports of Wal-Mart's prompt and effective involvement came from community leaders across the Gulf Coast.[8] Other private-sector firms, especially other so-called "big-box" stores such as Home Depot and Lowe's, also provided much-needed supplies, many of which were free, in the immediate aftermath of the storm. However, because Wal-Mart's response was the largest and most publicized, this Policy Comment will focus on Wal-Mart.[9]

Hurricane Katrina made landfall in southeast Louisiana and southwest Mississippi on August 29, 2005. Between August 29 and September 16, Wal-Mart shipped almost 2,500 truckloads of merchandise to the affected areas and had drivers and trucks in place to ship relief supplies to community members and organizations wishing to help.[10] Home Depot provided more than 800 truckloads worth of supplies to the hard-hit areas and also used buses to transport 1,000 employees from other areas into the region.[11] Wal-Mart also provided a large amount of free merchandise, including prescription drugs, to those in the worst-hit areas of the Gulf Coast. For example, several truckloads of free items went to evacuees in Houston at the Astrodome and the Brown Convention Center. Most importantly, Wal-Mart and Home Depot were able to get this assistance to the disaster areas almost immediately after the storm had passed, in comparison to the days—in some cases weeks—that residents waited for government agencies to provide relief.

Private-sector planning for the storm began days ahead of landfall. On the Friday prior to the Monday landfall, Home Depot activated the "war room" at its Atlanta headquarters, negotiating with various vendors to get needed supplies staged to move into the hurricane zone.[12] Wal-Mart's response began slightly earlier. As part of its regular operations, the company maintains an emergency command center run by Jason Jackson, Wal-Mart's Director of Business Continuity. The center is normally staffed by six to ten employees who respond to incidents at individual stores. When large-scale events threaten "the staff is joined by senior representatives from each of the company's functional areas." When an even more widespread catastrophe like a major hurricane is imminent, the office might include as many as 60 employees. Jackson notes that the easily expandable structure "drives the ability to be agile and flexible."[13] Wal-Mart also uses its own hurricane tracking software and contracts with private forecasters for the latest information on storms. By Wednesday, August 24, the command center had gone into planning mode in anticipation of Katrina's landfall. Two days later, when Katrina struck Florida, the complement of personnel in the command center was over 50.[14]

Having responded to smaller-scale hurricane damage in the past, and with a substantial number of stores along the Gulf Coast and in Florida, Wal-Mart has a protocol for dealing with such events. One key part of the process is passing information down from the senior management level to regional, district, and store managers. The idea, Jackson reports, is to get a response that is "uniform across the company."[15] Once the emergency command center saw that the storm had crossed over Florida and into the Gulf, it applied those protocols to the impending landfall. Emergency supplies—such as generators, dry ice, and bottled water—were moved from warehouses "to designated staging areas so that company stores would be able to open quickly."[16] Those staging areas were set up just outside the likely worst-hit areas to facilitate a quick response with minimal danger of damage. A distribution center in Brookhaven, Mississippi had 45 trucks in place before Katrina's landfall.[17]

As the storm passed, district and store managers relayed information about store conditions back up the chain of command to the emergency operations center. As the storm knocked out the company's computerized inventory-management system and much of the local phone infrastructure, Wal-Mart relied mostly on satellite cell phones that its own loss prevention teams brought in as early as Tuesday. Those teams in New Orleans were supplemented by the regional vice-president, Ronny Hayes, and Deb Hoover, the regional manager for Wal-Mart's One-Hour Photo group.[18] Having all of its key players in the operations room allowed Wal-Mart to field the information coming from Hayes, Hoover, and others on the scene and quickly make adjustments to the supplies it had staged. The presence of two senior managers in New Orleans also helped to coordinate the relief process. For example, when it became clear that a number of stores had suffered damage and that areas were facing severe flooding, Jackson had his replenishment staff order more mops, bleach, and similar products into the affected areas. Trucks were rolling into New Orleans on the day after the storm.

Aside from numerous reports of Wal-Mart providing supplies to hard-hit areas several days ahead of FEMA, additional evidence of the effectiveness of the private sector's response was the speed at which it re-opened stores closed by the storm. A closer look at Wal-Mart shows that, at the peak of the storm, 126 stores and two distribution centers were closed. Of these closed stores, "more than half ended up losing power, some were flooded, and 89 … reported damage."[19] By 10 days after landfall, a mere 15 stores remained closed, those that had suffered flooding or severe structural damage.

Another element of Wal-Mart's successful response was the great degree of discretion that the company gave to district and store managers. Store managers have sufficient authority to make decisions based on local information and immediate needs. As the storm approached, CEO Lee Scott provided a guiding edict to his senior staff and told them to pass it down to regional, district, and store managers: "A lot of you are going to have to make decisions above your level. Make the best decision that you can with the information that's available to you at the time, and, above all, do the right thing."[20] In several cases, store managers allowed either emergency personnel or local residents to take store supplies as needed. They did not feel the need to get pre-approval from supervisors to do so. In Kenner, Louisiana an employee used a forklift to knock open a warehouse door to get water for a local retirement home. In Marrero, Louisiana employees allowed local police officers to use the store as a headquarters and a sleeping place as many had lost their homes.

In Waveland, Mississippi assistant manager Jessica Lewis, who was unable to reach her superiors to get permission, decided to run a bulldozer through her store to collect basics that were not water-damaged, which she then piled in the parking lot and gave away to residents. She also broke into the store's locked pharmacy to supply critical drugs to a local hospital. Jackson said of both of her actions, "What Jessica did is a good example of autonomy."[21] Given the variety of areas in which Wal-Mart operates, it makes sense to allow local managers significant discretion in their day-to-day operations. That sense of empowerment is particularly useful when unusual local conditions require agility and improvisation.

The value of this decentralization of decision-making authority was also clear in the effective response of the U.S. Coast Guard. According to its own reports, the

---

The importance of local knowledge

Economists have increasingly recognized the importance of local knowledge over the last few decades. In his 1945 essay, F. A. Hayek was the first economist to emphasize that the "knowledge of time and place" is central to understanding how market economies coordinate behavior.[1] In that essay, he emphasizes that the knowledge that matters for making good economic and political decisions is the bits and pieces of knowledge possessed by individual people "on the spot," not large-scale theoretical or statistical information. The people closest to the situation at hand make the best decisions with the information they have from that local context. Distant managers or government officials do not possess the same depth of knowledge or familiarity with nuances.

Hayek's insight has been developed and applied in a variety of ways. One extension, for example, is that a good deal of the knowledge relevant to human action is tacit, or inarticulate, and thus cannot easily be put into words or numbers, if at all. When we make choices in the market, we make this tacit knowledge available to others through the effects that our choices have on prices and profits. Often, we cannot describe explicitly why we make the choices we do, both as consumers and producers, but as long as the market registers our choices, it transmits our knowledge to others.

Producers often develop tacit knowledge from operating in particular market contexts for long periods of time. By getting to know their customers and the local area, they hone their abilites to judge situations and know what others want. Again, they may not be able to articulate what it is they know, but it is knowledge nonetheless. Developing this tacit and contextual knowledge requires detailed and repeated contact with those who are being served.

Organizations can have their own kinds of tacit and local knowledge by developing routines and processes that are crystallizations of the learning they have done in their markets. Such routines, which emerge from the highly competitive learning process of the market, are far more likely to reflect the actual needs of the public than the more sporadic local interaction characteristic of the political process.

1 F. A. Hayek, "The Use of Knowledge in Society," reprinted in *Individualism and Economic Order* (Chicago: University of Chicago Press, 1948).

Coast Guard mobilized a total of almost 5,300 personnel, 62 aircraft, 30 cutters, and 111 small boats, which included a third of its entire air fleet, to perform rescue operations in the immediate aftermath. By September 11, 2005, it "had rescued more than 24,000 people and assisted with the joint-agency evacuation of an additional 9,400 patients and medical personnel from hospitals in the Gulf coast region."[22] The Coast Guard was also part of multi-agency teams dealing with environmental recovery and ensuring access to key shipping ports and waterways. Coast Guard search-and-rescue operations commenced immediately after the weather became calm enough and involved air crews that were "pre-staged" in several adjoining states. This included personnel and equipment from the area the storm was to affect that were moved into a "ring" around the Gulf.

Local residents and media reports lauded the Coast Guard's role in the immediate aftermath of the storm. Sheriff Jack Stephens of St. Bernard Parish, just east of New Orleans, reported, "The Coast Guard was the only federal agency to provide any significant assistance for a full week after the storm."[23] One of the key roles the Coast Guard played was partnering with local fishermen who had both boats and knowledge of the area. The decentralized structure of the Coast Guard gave rescuers who were "on the spot" the freedom to act on their local information and engage in these sorts of partnerships. A large number of people owe their lives to the thousands of Coast Guard rescues and the resources that private-sector firms such as Wal-Mart made available.

2 What explains the success of the private sector and the Coast Guard?

To understand the success of firms like Wal-Mart and the strong performance of the Coast Guard compared with that of other government agencies, we need to explore the factors that promote organizational responsiveness to the needs of the people such organizations serve. In order for organizations to be agile and disciplined, they require both the right knowledge and the right incentives. Whether organizations are able to acquire such knowledge and have the appropriate incentives depends on the institutional environments in which they operate and the way in which the organizations are structured. In general, the environment of market competition is superior to that of the political process in providing both the knowledge necessary to respond to people's needs and the profit incentive to act on that knowledge in ways that create value. Within the political process, agencies face different incentives, as they do not operate by profit and loss. Instead, government agencies are more often concerned with pleasing other political actors and finding ways to expand their budgets and power. This often makes them less sensitive to the direct needs of the people who rely on them to get specific tasks accomplished.[24]

In addition, the absence of a competitive market for their product means that, in general, government agencies face knowledge problems in determining what their output should be and how best to produce it. However, government agencies with a more decentralized structure that puts them in more direct contact with the people they serve may be able to overcome these knowledge problems. Larger, more centralized government agencies will lack the incentives of firms in competitive markets as well as the knowledge provided by true market prices, but more decentralized ones may do better along the latter dimension.

I can illustrate this perspective with respect to disaster relief organizations using the schema in Table 4.1.

As one moves clockwise from the top left quadrant, one sees improvements in performance as the incentives to serve people strengthen and greater decentralization enables better access to the knowledge needed to turn those incentives into action. In the case of Katrina, this helps explain FEMA's abysmal performance: its more centralized structure and its operation outside the discipline of profit and loss

Table 4.1 Categorizing disaster relief organizations

	Centralized (decisions made with insufficient local knowledge)	Decentralized (agile, flexible, access to local knowledge)
Public (incentives of political process for power and larger budgets)	FEMA	Coast Guard
Private (disciplined by profits or civil society competition for funds)		Private sector (e.g., Wal-Mart, Home Depot)

denied it access to local knowledge and removed beneficial incentives. Wal-Mart's effectiveness results from market competition (which provides the right kinds of incentives) and an organizational structure that gives sufficient discretion to local actors who have the requisite knowledge. Non-profit organizations often perform well because of the incentive created by their need to compete for voluntary donations. If they have a sufficiently decentralized organizational structure, they can approach the high level of performance of the private sector. Between FEMA and Wal-Mart is the Coast Guard, an organization that is public, but decentralized. The Coast Guard performed better than FEMA, but perhaps not as strongly as private-sector firms like Wal-Mart.

In analyzing the comparative performance of two government agencies such as the Coast Guard and FEMA, one must consider the missions of each, as well as the ability to define benchmark goals for success. The Coast Guard's mission is more precise than FEMA's, which makes it somewhat easier for the Coast Guard to focus resources and get the job done. Even so, this distinction alone cannot account for the depth and breadth of FEMA's failures. Similarly, without information provided by profit and loss, one has no clear and consistent way to measure the success of government agencies with different goals. For example, could, or should, the Coast Guard have saved more lives than it did? At some level, one simply cannot know when one is dealing with government agencies. What one can do is judge by the results that one sees and the perceptions of those affected by the agency's actions, both of which suggest a much stronger performance by the Coast Guard than FEMA, even given the caveats discussed.

As policy makers look to reform disaster relief policy, it is important that they do not focus on issues such as the quality of leadership to such an extent that they ignore these questions of how institutional environment and organizational structure affect performance. The fact that Wal-Mart and the other big-box stores replicated their excellent Katrina performance during the flooding in the Pacific Northwest in December of 2007 is evidence for the structural nature of their advantages.[25] Below, I look at the differing incentives facing public and private organizations; then I turn to the ways in which decentralization creates better access to relevant knowledge.

2.A Profits, politics, and long-term planning

One major advantage that private-sector firms and organizations have in providing effective disaster relief is that their survival is based on pleasing their customers or donors. Wal-Mart and Home Depot have strong incentives to get relief resources to disaster-stricken areas and to re-open their stores as quickly as possible, as doing both are ways of ensuring their continued profitability. Even providing donated goods to the stricken areas, as both firms did, has long-term financial incentives; the goodwill this gesture creates will likely provide future returns in the form of customer loyalty.

What is crucial is that these incentives—self-interest and public benefit—work hand-in-hand: a private firm's concern with its own reputation and profitability leads it to help rebuild the community. Carl Liebert, a vice president with Home Depot, points out that it does not necessarily profit directly from hurricanes, as any increase in sales is counteracted by the costs it incurs in moving personnel and inventory to the storm areas, as well as the cost of the goods it donates. However, the company does profit in the long run from increased customer loyalty: "If we can be there when a customer needs us most, we can win that customer for life."[26] Jason Jackson observes that even though Wal-Mart may lose money short-term by providing disaster relief, it "will have a community to go back to in the end."[27] Long-term interests also work against the possibility of so-called "price gouging." As another Home Depot executive put it, "I can't think of a quicker way to lose customers than price gouging."[28] Since 2004,

---

Institutional incentives and socially beneficial self-interested actions

Often, people judge the desirability of a certain action or policy proposal by the intentions of those behind it. For example, we create agencies like FEMA with the intention that they will "manage" emergencies. When such agencies fail to perform as expected, our first instinct is to assume that they had incompetent managers and/or insufficient resources. However, it might be the case that the incentives faced within the agencies' institutional frameworks were such that even with the best of intentions, incredible managers, and abundant resources, the agencies would be unable to get the job done.

Much recent study in the field of public choice economics, especially the work of James Buchanan and his colleagues, has focused on the empirical question of whether or not political actors can do what we think they *ought* to do.[1] This approach emphasizes that, regardless of the set of institutions under which they operate, we should assume that human beings are broadly self-interested and possess incomplete knowledge. Policies and institutions should be created with structures that assume not that humans are angels but that we seek our own advantage. The most effective social institutions are those structured such that they minimize the harm from self-interested behavior.

Policies and institutions that ignore the question of what incentives they create for self-interested actors are likely to fall. This is a frequent problem within the political process where agencies are given broad powers to act yet managers find it difficult to acquire the knowledge necessary to do so effectively. Political actors then will tend to please their various constituencies, such as elected officials, interest groups who have supported them, or their bosses higher in the civil service, in ways that advance their own power and prestige rather than their organization's mission. The failures of government agencies during Katrina bear out this theory

By contrast, good institutions are ones in which actors have the knowledge necessary to act and the incentives to behave in ways that serve the needs of others. As economists since Adam Smith have understood, good institutions channel our self-interest to the benefit of others and minimize the harm we can do in the process. The effectiveness of the private sector in Katrina shows how market institutions provide precisely the incentives that harmonize self-interest and public benefit.

---

1 See, for example, James M. Buchanan and Gordon Tullock, *The Calculus of Consent* (Ann Arbor: University of Michigan Press, 1962).

Wal-Mart has had a corporate policy of instituting region-wide price freezes when hurricanes approach so as to avoid any accusations of price gouging. In disaster situations, the ability of private-sector firms to think of the long-term creates a powerful incentive to do the right thing.

By contrast, the self-interest of public agencies is not as harmonized with the interests of the citizenry. First, public agencies do not have the profit and loss incentive to engage in actions that add value. Private-sector firms profit (or see donations rise) when they provide people the things they want. The feedback process facing government agencies is far more roundabout, involving citizens recognizing the good work done and voting for officials who promise to continue to support the agency in question. Even then, much can happen between the promise and the allocation of funds. In addition, it is not only those who directly interact with the agency who get to cast a vote; many voters may know nothing about the good or bad work the agency has done. In general, the feedback mechanism for government agencies is much weaker, slower, and more indirect than that for private firms.

Moreover, public agencies find it much more difficult to adopt the longer-term perspective that private organizations can. These problems are not matters of myopic leadership, but are instead endemic in the institutional structure of politics, as the planning horizon of the political process is often as short as the two-year cycle of House elections and certainly no longer than the four-year cycle of the presidency. Public officials cannot act as if their organization will be an "ongoing concern" in the same way those in the private sector can. Public officials are always under the threat of new leadership, new priorities, reorganization, reassignment, or outright abolition, which makes it difficult for them to engage in long-term planning.

This shorter time horizon also explains why organizations like FEMA have less powerful incentives to promote disaster mitigation and end up just attempting to clean up afterward. Disaster researcher Dennis Mileti notes that "the costs of mitigation are immediate while the benefits are uncertain, may not occur during the tenure of the elected officials, and are not visible (like roads or a new library)."[29] In general, political leaders will be biased in favor of projects that produce immediate, visible, and concentrated benefits and whose costs are longer-term, more subtle, and more dispersed. This enables leaders to reap the political benefits of the project while passing the cost on to others and spreading it out in ways that make it in no one's interest to object to the project. Most disaster mitigation activities have just the opposite characteristics: their benefits are long-term, subtle, and dispersed, making them work against the incentives facing elected officials. The private sector is able to capture the longer-term benefits of effective "mitigation" through preparedness, as it loses when its stores are destroyed or closed for longer than necessary but can profit from readiness that gets resources moved quickly. That is the reason firms like Wal-Mart and Home Depot have invested so much in disaster preparedness and are able to respond not just to their own needs but also to the community's as quickly as they did after Katrina.

2.B Risk and agility

The organizations most successful in responding to Katrina were those willing and able to take risks and be agile in the face of uncertain conditions. Reasonable risk-taking, like other positive responses to disasters, is likely to be more common in institutional contexts where incentives reward such behavior. Private-sector organizations are thus more likely to perform well, which was evident in the response to Katrina.

Disaster researchers have accused FEMA and other government relief agencies of being overly conservative and "rule-bound" in the face of a disaster that required not just discipline, but agility. Russell Sobel and Peter Leeson argue that one reason government agencies are unwilling to take risks is that they have an incentive to avoid errors of *commission* and therefore are more likely to make errors of *omission*.[30] Errors of commission refer to actions taken that end up being mistakes, while errors of omission occur when actions are not taken that should have been. For example, if the police are overly aggressive in pursuing a suspect and raid the house of an innocent person, they are making an error of commission. If they simply allow potential suspects to go free by not pursuing them, they are making an error of omission. The claim is that government agencies are likely to take more cautious and conservative strategies than less cautious ones, even if the net benefit of the less cautious one is greater.

The reason for the public sector's greater willingness to tolerate errors of omission is that overt, visible errors tend to be punished more strongly than less visible ones. To take Sobel's and Leeson's example, if FEMA sends personnel in early and exposes them to the dangers of the storm, any negative consequences will be highly visible and will expose FEMA to more negative feedback, even if such a strategy is likely to save more lives. FEMA is better off playing it safe and accepting the likely lesser blame for simply waiting. As Sobel and Leeson put it, "Victims lost before FEMA enters because it delays action are less obviously linked to FEMA's lack of action."[31]

Alternately, suppose FEMA had moved stocks of food into place very early, perhaps even before the storm, only to see them spoil or go unused if the storm missed the area or as a result of FEMA's incompetence. The visible waste would be harder to explain than the less visible consequences of waiting to react. The incentives facing government agencies are such that errors of omission make it easier for them to argue that they did not have sufficient resources to mobilize to action in the face of a crisis or that "external factors" prevented them from doing the job well. In contrast, errors of commission are more obviously failures of execution rather than a lack of resources or external complications. FEMA therefore not only has much weaker incentives to get its tasks right, but actually has some incentive to avoid being proactive in novel situations. This was very clear in Katrina as Wal-Mart executives reported that FEMA and DHS rejected or ignored numerous overtures to find ways to cooperate and were overly bound to tedious accounting practices that made purchases of supplies from Wal-Mart needlessly cumbersome.[32]

The reluctance of public sector agencies to have large stocks of relief goods sitting on hand for distribution during a disaster is a good example of avoiding a problematic error of commission, as idle workers or supplies that are spoiled, outdated, or just plain sitting there would be much more visible than the error of omission of not acquiring and distributing resources in a timely fashion. For private-sector firms, their daily operations in the market lead them to have precisely the kinds of resources needed for disaster relief, and thus they have the flexibility to respond to either a disaster situation or an ordinary day of sales.

Another example of public agencies fearing errors of commission was FEMA preventing a number of volunteer doctors from working on injured people because the medical personnel were not officially registered with FEMA and the agency feared legal liability.[33] FEMA's position was complicated by medical personnel from other states being occasionally uncertain about whether they should offer help because they did not know whether they were covered by Louisiana's and Mississippi's Good Samaritan laws. Such laws generally protect volunteers who offer good-faith medical assistance in a crisis. However, the laws differ from state to state and are generally designed not for large-scale situations like natural disasters, but rather for isolated incidents, such as car accidents. These laws also generally do not protect providers who are paid for their work. Because the legal institutions were insufficiently clear about the actors' potential liability in this case, both public and private actors feared errors of commission.[34]

Unlike the public sector, private-sector firms, when operating under clear legal rules, are no more likely to avoid the risk of errors of commission than they are errors of omission. Both types of errors result in losses for the firm—either absolute losses in the case of errors of commission or lost profit opportunities in the case of errors of omission. What this suggests is that private-sector firms are more likely to be proactive and take reasonable risks in dealing with a disaster. Changes in management strategy or organizational culture within FEMA or other government agencies are unlikely to help this structural problem in any significant way.

2.C Decentralization and organizational culture

From the perspective of generating the incentive structures that promote good disaster preparedness and relief, private solutions outperform public ones. However, having the right incentives is only half the story. Organizations must have the knowledge needed to respond correctly. Here is where the ability to get access to localized knowledge through a decentralized organizational structure matters.

Operating in the marketplace demands that firms selling physical goods or personal services locate where the demand for their outputs are. In Wal-Mart's case, this means opening stores where the population will support a store and having those stores fully stocked for that area's demands. Its stores generally track the population distribution of the United States.[35] As a result of this decentralization of resources inherent in the market, the national big-box firms generally have supplies and human capital near where disasters occur.

Private-sector firms often work hard to create the conditions for employees to exercise discretion within the firm, sometimes called "intrapreneurship." Corporate leaders recognize that in complex organizations, those at the top cannot always know everything that is necessary to direct operations. Their challenge is to find ways to make use of the knowledge of "shop-floor" employees through the very structure of the organization so that knowledge need not be communicated in explicit terms to managers but can be shared through the actions employees take.[36]

One way that firms help ensure that employees use their local knowledge effectively is by creating a consistent and powerful corporate culture. For example, Wal-Mart devotes an entire section of its website to issues of corporate culture, including everything from its "Three Basic Beliefs" to Sam Walton's "Ten Rules for Building Business" to the "Wal-Mart Cheer."[37] Wal-Mart's "Saturday Morning Meetings," which take place at corporate headquarters in Bentonville, Arkansas, provide a forum for explaining and debating core issues facing the firm as well as celebrating the successes of employees. All of these elements of corporate culture are designed to instill a corporate philosophy in every employee. The philosophy provides a common vision and a set of rules to be followed, helping to ensure that when employees far from the top are given discretion, they are more likely to use it wisely. Such decentralization of responsibility can work when the corporate culture is strong and shared. Even here, however, the importance of the "rules of the game" cannot be ignored: both private firms and public agencies with strong organizational cultures will perform notably better when they operate in an environment that provides the incentives, independence, and information to put that culture to good use.

As we have seen, during Wal-Mart's response to Katrina, on-scene associates and managers were allowed discretion to deal with problems as they saw fit, and improvisation was fairly common as store and district managers faced unexpected situations and had to respond creatively. These improvisational responses were the result of the long-term organizational learning that develops in the context of market competition. Individual store managers have developed local and often intuitive knowledge of their own stores and communities that is integral to effective crisis response. It is by virtue of their being located in those communities, constantly facing market pressures to deliver what the community wants, that they are able to know what to do in a crisis presenting unforeseeable challenges.

Similarly, the Coast Guard instills in its members a powerful organizational culture and gives them much latitude for independent decision making. The core of this culture can be found in *America's Maritime Guardian: US. Coast Guard Publication 1*.[38] Published in 2002, the Coast Guard labeled it "Publication 1" in order to emphasize its role as the foundational document that "synthesizes" what the Coast Guard is, what it does, and how it does things. This document lays out organizational culture by offering a mission, a history, and an entire chapter devoted to "principles of Coast Guard operations." Two of those principles were of specific importance to their work during the Katrina disaster. The first is "the principle of on-scene initiative." As the authors describe it:

> [T]he concept of allowing the person on scene to take the initiative—guided by a firm understanding of the desired tactical objectives and national interest at stake— remains central to the Coast Guard's view of its command relationships.[39]

They further develop this principle by recognizing that to take such initiative requires trust from above and a "unity of effort."

In granting on-scene initiative, Coast Guard leadership allows subordinates to alter the particular plan for their specific operation based on their local knowledge, but this must be done without violating the overarching and generally unchanged "commander's intent". The Coast Guard sees communication, especially informal discussions among captains and commanders, as central to preparing individual crews to act independently. This communication enables them to grasp the commanders' intent with a minimum of formal orders. The sort of decentralized teamwork that the Coast Guard expects "works through the common understanding of how individual incidents or situations are normally handled."[40] This organizational culture and empowerment of local actors were key aspects of their effective response after Katrina, which parallels Wal-Mart's in many interesting ways.

Media reports also emphasized these points. The then-Vice Admiral of the Coast Guard (who was put in charge of the federal response to Katrina after FEMA's multiple failures) pointed to that autonomy as a reason it was able to move personnel and equipment into place so much faster than other agencies were. The importance of decentralization of authority was echoed by a former Coast Guard Commandant who told *Time*, "We give extraordinary life-and-death responsibilities to 2nd class petty officers."[41] Even a Coast Guard reservist with only two years of experience has higher-ranking officers reporting to her if she is piloting a boat.

The flatter organizational structure and the nature of the daily tasks of the Coast Guard suggest that it can access local knowledge more effectively than other related government agencies. The Coast Guard is organized by geographic region, with Atlantic and Pacific divisions. Each division is composed of districts, which are composed of units, which in turn consist of sector offices in specific coastal cities. From the Coast Guard Commandant down to the sector office (e.g., a field office in Mobile, Alabama) are four organizational levels. In the Navy, by contrast, there are five steps from the Secretary of the Navy just to the Director of Navy Staff, who is still located in Washington.[42] In addition, the average time at a station for a member of the Coast Guard is thirty-five to thirty-six months, which gives him or her time to get to know the local community.[43] There is no way to know with certainty the nature of an organizational culture, but based on the Coast Guard's own description of its work and its organizational structure, it is reasonable to conclude that organizational factors matter for its strong performance during Katrina.

In addition to its organizational structure and culture, the Coast Guard's involvement with coastal issues on a daily basis means that officers at specific stations interact with local residents much more frequently than do other branches of the military or officials from FEMA. FEMA has fewer individuals stationed in potential disaster areas on a regular basis, and the work in which they are engaged is far less likely to involve contact with members of the general public upon whom FEMA might call in a disaster. By contrast, because of their regular contact with the local residents, local Coast Guard officers knew who had boats and where to find them during Katrina. Put differently, the Coast Guard's other activities, such as search and rescue operations, dealing with drug and immigration issues, and work with the marine environment may be more complementary to its ability to respond effectively to natural disasters than are the day-to-day activities of FEMA.[44]

The ability to respond to novel situations based on local knowledge is crucial to developing the agility needed for effective disaster response. Decentralized organizational structures, along with personnel in the field having a reasonably wide range of discretion, characterized the firms and agencies that responded well to Katrina. Developing the organizational mission and trust to facilitate that decentralization and discretion is the challenge. It is particularly difficult to develop this sort of culture in government agencies where structure and mission are often changed at the whim of the short-run electoral cycle. The Coast Guard's long-standing independence has given it a favorable institutional environment for developing the right sort of culture. Whether its recent move into the much larger and more politicized Department of Homeland Security will undermine that culture and hamper its future effectiveness is a matter of concern.

All of the explanations for why the private sector out-performed the public sector and why the Coast Guard did comparatively well come back to the institutional environment in which the organizations operate. Private firms face the incentives of profit and loss and are able to access the relevant local knowledge because they operate in a market context that provides those incentives and makes that knowledge available to them. The intentions of corporate managers are far less important than the fact that the institutional environment rewards or punishes certain types of behavior, and even the most skilled organizational leader will be ineffective without access to the knowledge and feedback the market generates. In thinking about reforming disaster-relief policy, one must always keep in mind that changing captains will not help if the problem is with the structure of the ship.

3 Implications for disaster-relief policy

The broad lesson to be learned from the private sector's positive role during Katrina is that disaster response should provide as much scope as possible for private-sector contributions and, where government responses are deemed necessary, policy makers should take steps to make the agencies involved as independent and decentralized as possible. Additionally, it is worth noting that hiring agency administrators with more expertise in disaster management is *not* one of the lessons to be drawn. It is not clear that such professional expertise can address the fundamental structural problems FEMA and other government relief agencies face. Redesigning protocols and rules will be of little help if the real problems are the incentives facing public agencies, although expertise might help on the margin in decentralizing some elements of the organization. The argument for decentralization is that the relevant knowledge is that of time and place rather than more global or technical expertise. This is a point that disaster research and policy recommendations have not taken seriously enough in their calls for reform. The following recommendations for policy flow out of the successes and failures in the responses to Katrina and generally follow the framework laid out in Table 4.1, which suggests a move from the upper-left area to the lower-right area of the table.

3.A Ensure that private-sector responses are a recognized part of disaster protocols

Like the Hippocratic Oath, the first recommendation is that government policy makers "do no harm" by making sure that they do not interfere with the private sector's attempts to provide relief within the parameters of non-disaster related laws and regulations. Allowing the private sector to do what it does best in the same ways that it does during non-crisis times is the most important principle for policy makers to follow. Because governments at various levels will have oversight roles to play in any disaster response, it is critical that they recognize the legitimate role of private firms when developing response protocols.

One concern that many have about giving the private sector explicit permission to be central to disaster relief is that its desire for profits would conflict with its willingness and ability to help. Corporations, indeed, are not charities, but as the analysis above shows, engaging in disaster relief is in these companies' long-term self-interest, as it both helps the communities they depend on for their business and creates goodwill amongst their customers. As the Home Depot executive noted, the last thing firms that are in a community for the long haul want to do is alienate their actual and potential customers by either idly standing by or dramatically raising prices during a natural disaster.[45] The incentives of the private sector are very much aligned with its ability to provide disaster relief in the way we saw during Katrina.

The challenge for the public sector is that lacking the incentive of profit and its alignment with getting the job done, the temptation will always be for government agencies to want to be overly involved so that they can continue to justify their current budgets. Although agencies wish to avoid errors of commission, they want to remain involved to justify their existence. Thus, agencies often move in after the fact in the most conservative ways possible. However, the bottom line in any disaster situation is getting the needed resources to those lacking them. As the glowing terms in which Gulf Coast residents speak of the work done by Wal-Mart demonstrate, people do not care whether assistance comes from FEMA or Wal-Mart; they just want someone to get the job done. If the lesson of Katrina is that the private sector is better at marshalling resources and delivering them quickly, then disaster-relief policy should remove the barriers that hinder the private sector from getting the job done.

Various levels of government can take two specific actions that would facilitate the private sector's involvement in disaster response. First, governments should include local firms in the communications protocols that would be implemented during disasters (such as who is to be notified about disaster declarations, who has the authority to make particular decisions, etc.). Second, governments should make publicly available a list of the firms included in such protocols so that all levels of government are aware that these firms will be part of the disaster response. One of the problems during Katrina was that local, state, or federal authorities rebuffed some attempts by private firms and agencies, such as the Red Cross, to provide supplies to stranded Gulf residents, turning back resources headed to New Orleans, keeping first responders away, and sending a group of firefighters who came to help to two days of sexual harassment seminars.[46] Calls from Wal-Mart's Deb Hoover to New Orleans Mayor Ray Nagin's office and the Homeland Security outpost in Baton Rouge were either not returned or returned several days later. She said that government officials "didn't know who we were, and we didn't know who they were. We didn't know who was in charge."[47] If private-sector firms that want to be part of the relief process are in the communications loop from the start and various levels of government know that they are officially part of the process, state actors will be less likely to prevent them from providing the needed relief. Relief efforts need not take the form of public private partnerships; rather, policy makers must ensure that public sector actors know that private firms are authorized to be part of the response and relief effort.

3.B Increase decentralization of government relief

Because no natural disaster is identical to any other, particularly in the case of catastrophic events such as Katrina, each will have unique elements that require local knowledge and the ability to respond quickly to novelty. Additionally, because such disasters always involve the intersection of the forces of nature and a variety of social and cultural processes, disaster response and recovery organizations have to be especially attuned to the complexities and subtleties of local norms, cultures, and demographics. Strategies that work for hurricane relief along Florida's Gold Coast may not work in the Ninth Ward of New Orleans or in the agricultural communities of the Carolinas. Effective response requires the ability to tap into local knowledge and to give the affected citizens themselves maximum control over how they engage in the process of relief and recovery. Where government agencies are needed, they should attempt to act in the most decentralized, flexible ways possible.

FEMA was criticized for being insufficiently responsive to the particular needs of Gulf Coast residents, especially those in the New Orleans area who are characterized by a unique mix of races and cultures with a long, complex history. FEMA is large, highly centralized, and driven by fairly inflexible rules and hierarchies, all of which made it ill-prepared for the complexities of Katrina recovery. Local organizations were better situated to provide assistance, given their knowledge of the geography and culture of the area. It is likely that future relief efforts will be more effective if FEMA dollars are transferred to local governments or non-governmental organizations rather than being allocated directly by FEMA officials at the state or federal level.[48] Local governments and nonprofits are more likely to have the relevant on-the-spot knowledge, but often lack resources in a crisis. Where the private sector is unable to do the job, tax dollars should flow directly to the most local level possible, and the government should give such organizations maximum discretion in using them.

In addition, finding ways to decentralize FEMA's organizational structure by empowering employees at more local levels would improve its responsiveness to some degree. The Coast Guard remains the model to be followed. Policy makers should seriously explore decentralizing FEMA; however, the agency's lack of a clear mission, the fact that it has been reorganized (given different missions) and moved within the bureaucracy multiple times in its history, and its current location within the Department of Homeland Security are factors likely to limit the effectiveness of this effort.

Another way in which relief can be effectively decentralized is by using cash or broadly defined vouchers rather than in-kind transfers as the preferred form of assistance. Vouchers are cash that the recipient can only spend on specific things, similar to a gift certificate from a specific retailer, while in-kind transfers are specific goods or services that government agencies supply directly to the recipient, like the trailers that FEMA provided for many Gulf Coast residents. The economic case for cash instead of in-kind transfers is fairly straightforward: people who wish to acquire the item that would have been provided as an in-kind transfer can do so using the cash, while those who do not can acquire the other things they might wish to have. Vouchers, while still offering fewer options than cash and therefore providing less reliable information about what people really need, are a step up from in-kind transfers in that they at least allow citizens to find the supplier of the product they prefer, which leads to greater competition and higher-quality supplies of the product. Both cash and vouchers empower citizens to make their own choices based on their own knowledge of the trade-offs they face rather than assuming that federal or state officials know better. Rather than receive a FEMA trailer, for example, some Katrina survivors might have preferred a housing voucher that would help them obtain housing in an area outside New Orleans. Others might have preferred cash to tide them over while they stayed with friends or relatives and looked for a new job in a new area. From the recipient's end, at worst, cash or a voucher leaves them no worse off than an in-kind transfer and offers the opportunity for choices that in-kind transfers do not. Cash or vouchers are also easier and cheaper to administer than in-kind transfers, reducing the overall cost of disaster relief. It is much cheaper to simply cut and mail checks than it is to contract for trailers and pay for their delivery and setup.

Replacing in-kind transfers completely with cash or vouchers would eliminate much of the excessive rule-following and red tape that has characterized the disaster recovery process and would allow local residents to deal more directly with the private sector. This enables both residents and firms to coordinate based on their own knowledge and resources, rather than being restricted by tedious rules made hundreds or thousands of miles away by people who are less aware of the particulars of the affected communities.

3.C Move the Coast Guard and FEMA out of the Department of Homeland Security

The Coast Guard has a history of more than 200 years of a fairly specific, observable mission, particularly during Katrina where it was charged with "saving lives." These characteristics have enabled it to develop a powerful organizational culture, which in turn allows it to give great latitude to low-ranking members (as noted earlier). The Coast Guard has also had a great deal of political independence. It is this decentralization and independence that served it so well during Katrina. Even in the absence of market signals and the profit incentive, it is possible for organizations with strong cultures, well-defined missions, and observable outputs to perform well. However, these sorts of organizations are much more the exception than the rule in government for the reasons articulated previously.

The exceptional nature of the Coast Guard's performance is all the more reason to protect the conditions that produced it. The Coast Guard was moved under the Department of Homeland Security in the aftermath of Katrina, ostensibly as a way to motivate the other disaster-relief agencies in the DHS. However, the result may be that the influence flows in the opposite direction. The DHS remains politically controversial, with its mission subject to constant flux by both geopolitical events and the preferences of the president or a Congressional majority. One of the problems plaguing FEMA over the years has been constant changes in its mission and structure as those in power have changed. Moving the Coast Guard into DHS has exposed it to the same sorts of dangers. If it is the case that the Coast Guard's strong performance was a function of its organizational culture of decentralization and discretion that grew, in part, from its independence, then moving it back out of DHS and re-establishing it as an independent agency within the Department of Defense or elsewhere would be one way to ensure that its work during Katrina is repeated in other natural disasters.

FEMA was moved under DHS in the aftermath of 9/11 with the belief that it would be part of any comprehensive response to a terror-related disaster scenario. Unfortunately, that move has had three problematic consequences. First, it continues to hamper FEMA's ability to engage in long-term planning and organizational learning by moving it within a bureaucracy, changing its mission, and exposing it to the rapidly changing and highly politicized environment of anti-terrorism policies. Second, adding the various layers of complexity and potential competing missions that come with the DHS makes it more difficult for FEMA to do its traditional work with natural disasters. This was clearly a problem during Katrina. In prior years, when FEMA was more independent (though not as much so as the Coast Guard), it seemed to perform somewhat better. Third, to the extent that FEMA diverts DHS resources to natural disasters that FEMA could address as a more independent agency, the current organizational structure weakens the department's ability to engage in the rest of its mission.[49] Moving both the U.S. Coast Guard and FEMA out of the DHS would better serve disaster response.

3.D Clarify Good Samaritan laws

One implication of increasing the private sector's role in disaster preparedness and response is that states and localities may have to take a closer look at their Good Samaritan laws. Although these laws differ from state to state, they generally shield from any civil liability those who attempt to aid others in good faith at the scene of an emergency but are unsuccessful (assuming they were not "willfully or wantonly negligent" or the like).[50] Whether commercial actors are protected by these laws is currently unclear in many states. For example, Texas law explicitly excludes the shielding of "a person who was at the scene of the emergency because he or a person he represents as an agent was soliciting business or seeking to perform a service for remuneration." Although such a law may at first appear to clearly exclude private companies from protection under Good Samaritan laws, the ambiguity lies in whether employees of private-sector firms who are engaged in disaster relief in an official capacity are considered agents performing a service for remuneration.

If there is not a quid pro quo (such as employees being directly paid for specific acts), or if, for example, Wal-Mart employees are clearly just distributing donated goods, it seems that they would be shielded from civil action if they were to somehow cause injury or death. However, some private-sector leaders are concerned that there is still room for legal action when the law is not sufficiently clear. Several states have begun both to redraft their Good Samaritan laws to take disaster response into account and to incorporate that redrafting into their larger disaster response revisions. In fact, the American Public Health Association has developed model legislation,[51] which accounts for lessons learned from Katrina and other recent disasters and explicitly extends Good Samaritan protection to commercial and non-profit organizations. All 50 states and the federal government should look at this legislation as a model for reform. The ambiguity of what actions the existing laws would and would not protect caused needless and wasteful uncertainty, delays, and work-arounds during the Katrina response, particularly by medical personnel. These problems need to be addressed, especially as more localities include the private sector in other forms of disaster response.

Conclusion

The goal of disaster preparedness and response is to save lives and relieve suffering. It should not matter who does this and how, as long as it gets done in the quickest and most effective way possible. The private sector, especially big-box firms such as

Wal-Mart and Home Depot, demonstrated during Katrina what they also demonstrate every day in the market: they are very effective at logistics and supply chain management because they have strong incentives to provide the goods and services that people want. As those affected by Katrina directly acknowledged, sometimes grudgingly, the big-box stores were much better at this task than were the official government agencies. Those agencies face a very different set of institutional incentives within the political process, incentives that lead them to be less able to work in the genuine public interest, less willing to take appropriate risks, and more concerned with their own power and budgets, all of which explain their failures during Katrina. The first principle of disaster relief should be to allow private-sector firms as much of a role as possible in the response and government agencies should do all they can to get out of their way.

The one government agency that did perform admirably was the U.S. Coast Guard. Its decentralized organizational culture and relative political independence enabled the Coast Guard to grant a large degree of discretion to on-the-spot actors who could take advantage of their access to local knowledge. These same benefits of decentralization explain the success of private-sector firms, in that decentralization enables better use of local and contextual knowledge. To the extent that the private sector cannot accomplish disaster relief operations, policy makers should strive to structure government efforts in ways that take maximum advantage of local knowledge by providing relief in the form of cash or broadly defined vouchers, decentralizing federal agencies, and making as much use of local government and non-governmental organizations as possible. When future natural disasters occur, policy makers should remember that, as the relief efforts after Hurricane Katrina demonstrate, increased private-sector involvement and more locally oriented government efforts are critical to saving lives and easing suffering quickly and effectively.

Notes

1 See U.S. Senate, *Hurricane Katrina: A Nation Still Unprepared* (Washington, DC: U.S. Government Printing Office, 2006), http://hsgac.senate.gov/_files/Katrina/FullReport. pdf; U.S. House of Representatives, *A Failure of Initiative* (Washington, DC: U.S. Government Printing Office, 2006), http://www.gpoaccess.gov/katrinareport/mainreport.pdf.

2 Russell Sobel and Peter Leeson, *Flirting with Disaster: The Inherent Problems with FEMA*, Policy Analysis No. 573 (Washington, DC: Cato Institute, 2006); Raymond Burby, "Hurricane Katrina and the Paradoxes of Government Disaster Policy: Bringing About Wise Governmental Decisions for Hazardous Areas," *Annals of the American Academy of Political and Social Sciences* 604 (2006): 171–91.

3 Most of these are part of the Post-Katrina Emergency Management Reform Act, which was part of the 2007 Department of Homeland Security Appropriations Act.

4 At least one academic study has recognized this point. See the analysis of political failure and brief discussion of private-sector successes in William F. Shughart II, "Katrinanomics: The Politics and Economics of Disaster Relief," *Public Choice* 127 (April 2006): 31–53.

5 For the purposes of this study, I will use "private sector" to refer both to profit-making firms and non-profits, such as the Red Cross.

6 John Harrald, "Agility and Discipline: Critical Success Factors for Disaster Response." *Annals of the American Academy of Political and Social Sciences* 604 (2006): 256–72.

7 Aaron Broussard, interview by Tim Russert, *Meet the Press*, MSNBC, September 4, 2005, transcript available online at http://www.msnbc.com/id/9179790.

8 Devin Leonard, "The Only Lifeline was the Wal-Mart," *Fortune*, October 3, 2005, 7.

9 An expensive and detailed summary of Wal-Mart's involvement in the Katrina relief effort can be found in Susan Rosegrant, *Wal-Mart's Response to Hurricane Katrina: Striving for a Public Private Partnership*, The Kennedy School of Government Case Program C16-07-1876.0 (Cambridge, MA: Kennedy School of Government Case Studies in Public Policy & Management, 2007), https://articleworks.cadmus.com/doc/800164.

10 Wal-Mart Facts.com, "Wal-Mart's Hurricane Relief Efforts," http://www.walmartfacts.com/FactSheets/8302006_Katrina_Relief.pdf.

11 Patti Bond, "Home Depot: As Experience Grows, Big Orange Refines Script for Storm Response," *Atlanta Journal-Constitution*, September 4, 2005, 1C.

12 Andrew Ward, "Home Depot Prepares for Katrina," *Financial Times*, August 29, 2005, 18.

13 Ben Worthen, "How Wal-Mart Beat the Feds to New Orleans," *CIO Magazine*, November 1, 2005, http://www.cio.com/article/13532/How_Wal_Mart_Beat_Feds_to_New_Orleans. See also Kennedy School of Government Case Program C16-07-1876.0.

14 Ann Zimmerman and Valerie Bauerleia, "At Wal-Mart, Emergency Plan Has Big Payoff," *Wall Street Journal*, September 12, 2005, B1.

15 Kennedy School of Government Case Program C16-07-1876.0, 3.

16 Zimmerman and Bauerlein, B1.

17 Michael Barbaro and Justin Gillis, "Wal-Mart at Forefront of Hurricane Relief," *Washington Post*, September 6, 2005, D01.

18 Kennedy School of Government Case Program C16-07-1876.0, 7.

19 Zimmerman and Bauerlein, B1.

20 Kennedy School of Government Case Program C16-07-1876.0, 5.

21 Ibid., 9–10.

22 U.S. Coast Guard, "Coast Guard Response to Hurricane Katrina," http://www.uscg.mil/hq/g-cp/comrel/factfile/Factcards/Hurricane_Katrina.htm.

23 Amanda Ripley, "How the Coast Guard Gets it Right," *Time*, October 23, 2005. See also Stephen Barr, "Coast Guard's Response to Katrina a Silver Lining in the Storm," *Washington Post*, September 6, 2005, B02.

24 On the market's superiority at providing both the knowledge and incentives for efficient resource use and greater value creation, see the essays in F. A. Hayek, *Individualism and Economic Order* (Chicago: University of Chicago Press, 1948).

25 Laura Gunderson, "Retailers to the Rescue," *The Oregonian*, December 9, 2007, http://www.oregonlive.com/oregonian/stories/index.ssf?/base/business/1197095130228920.xml&coll=7.

26 Ward, 18.

27 Kennedy School of Government Case Program C16-07-1876.0, 5.

28 Terri Langford, "Disaster Plan Teams State and Retailers," *Houston Chronicle*, July 15, 2007, http://www.chron.com/disp/story.mpl/hurricane/4967735.html.

29 Dennis S. Mileti, *Disasters by Design* (Washington, DC Joseph Henry Press, 1999), 160.

30 Sobel and Leeson, 6–7.

31 Ibid., 7.

32 Kennedy School of Government Case Program C16-07-1876.0, 15–16.

33 Katrinacoverage.com, "USCG, FEMA Ordered Doctor to Stop Saving Victim's Life," September 17, 2005. http://katrinacoverage.com/2005/09/17/uscg-fema-ordered-doctor-to-stop-saving-victims-life.html.

34 The Texas Medical Association notes the lack of coverage for those who are paid. Erin Prather, "Volunteers Protected," *Texas Medicine* 102, No. 12 (2006), http://www.texmed. org/Template.aspx?id=5555. According to Gene Matthews and Milissa Markiewicz at the North Carolina Institute for Public Health, "Most state Good Samaritan laws leave significant gaps of liability exposure for both business and non-profit entities that assist in preparing for and responding to an emergency posed by a natural disaster, emerging infection, or terrorist event. This gap can lead to hesitation or lack of coordination on the part of business and non-profit entities providing help during an emergency situation," Gene Matthews and Milissa Markiewicz, "Good Samaritan Liability Preparedness Initiative," *Public Health Preparedness* (July 2007), http://www.astho.org/newsletter/ newsletters/9/display. php?u=Jmk9OSZwPTMyNiZzPTI1NDE%3D.

35 See Michael J. Hicks, *The Local Economic Impact of Wal-Mart* (Youngstown, NY: Cambria Press, 2007), 46–53.

36 See Frederic Sautet, *An Entrepreneurial Theory of the Firm* (New York: Routledge, 2000).

37 Wal-Mart Stores.com, "Wal-Mart Culture," http://www. walmartstores.com/ GlobalWMStoresWeb/navigate.do?catg=251.

38 U.S. Coast Guard, *America's Maritime Guardian: U.S. Coast Guard Publication 1* (2002), http://www.uscg.mil/top/about/doc/uscg_pub1_complete.pdf.

39 Ibid., 52.

40 Ibid., 53.

41 Ripley, 3.

42 See the organizational charts at http://www.uscg.mil/top/about/organization.asp and http://www.navy.mil/navydata/organization/org-cno.asp.

43 U.S. Government Accountability Office, *Coast Guard Station Readiness Improving, but Resource Challenges and Management Concerns Remain* GAO-05-161 (Washington, DC: 2005). 25, http://www.gao.gov/new.items/d05161.pdf.

44 The Coast Guard's budget is pretty evenly divided among its major tasks, with none taking more than 21.3 percent in FY 2007 and the top five items all between 9.9 percent and 21.3 percent. None of its tasks appears to siphon away resources from any of the others.

45 In my extensive reading of the media coverage of Katrina, I could find no reports of charges of price gouging against the big-box stores or other major retailers along the Gulf Coast.

46 A compendium of FEMA's blocking of relief, with links to the media stories, can be found at http://www.rense.com/general67/femwont.him.

47 Kennedy School of Government Case Program C16-07-1876.0, 12.

48 In the particular case of New Orleans during Katrina, the relatively high level of corruption in local government suggests that non-governmental organizations would have been the better choice. Generally, however, any move toward local solutions would be desirable.

49 FEMA's response to the California wildfires in the fall of 2007 was better than its response to Katrina, perhaps because although the fires themselves threatened a large area, the property damage was of a smaller scale and did not involve infrastructure to anywhere near the extent that Katrina did. The fires threatened or destroyed only about 10 percent as many homes as Katrina did. Several interesting comparisons can be found in a *New Orleans Times-Picayune* analysis, available at http://blog.nola.com/times-picayune/2007/ 10/california_fires_cant_be_compa.html. FEMA may have learned a little from Katrina; however, FEMA was heavily criticized during its wildfire relief efforts, and had to fire several managers who were involved in staging a "news conference" where FEMA staffers posed as reporters and made it appear as though FEMA was doing great work. This suggests that what FEMA learned from the aftermath of Hurricanes Katrina and Rita was

limited. The aftermath of that public relations disaster required a response from DHS leadership that, presumably, distracted them from their core mission.

50 A set of links to state Good Samaritan laws can be found at http://www.cprinstructor. com/legal.htm.

51 See the "Good Samaritan Legislative Initiative," part of the North Carolina Institute for Public Health's "Public/Private Legal Preparedness initiative," http://nciph.sph.unc. edu/law/apha.pdf.

Review and Discussion Questions

1 What actions did Wal-Mart take after Hurricane Katrina made landfall?
2 According to Horwitz, why did Wal-Mart take those actions? Why didn't FEMA take them?
3 In some places, there are laws that prohibit sellers from charging prices that are "too high" following disasters. (In the U.S. such laws are often said to prevent "price gouging.") How do you think "too high" should be defined? What do you think the effects of such laws are?

Chapter 5

Michael T. Maloney and
J. Harold Mulherin

THE COMPLEXITY OF PRICE DISCOVERY IN AN EFFICIENT MARKET: THE STOCK MARKET REACTION TO THE CHALLENGER CRASH[1]

1 Introduction

IN THIS PAPER, we apply event study techniques to the crash of the space shuttle Challenger. We choose this case because of its unique information attributes. The Challenger crash was a highly visible event whose underlying cause was not publicly revealed until much later. We use this event to highlight the relation between complex information about business activities and the process of price discovery in markets.

In the terminology of the corporate finance and market microstructure literatures, the event we study had both public and private information components.[2] French and Roll (1986, p. 9) note that the dichotomy between public and private information is somewhat artificial and that "most information falls in the continuum between [the two]." More recent theory by Dow and Gorton (1993) argues that this continuum is not linear. They model price discovery in an environment where information is multidimensional and where the resulting price dynamics are complex. The Challenger crash offers an excellent case study of the multifaceted information structures envisioned by these researchers.

Methodologically, the event has appealing features. It was an exogenous occurrence. There was no leakage that induced run-up or run-down in the pre-event period. Hence, the analysis is free of the concerns of endogeneity raised in the conditional event study literature (Eckbo et al., 1990; Prabhala, 1997). We can also exactly time the occurrence of the event. As studied by Brown and Warner (1985) and reemphasized by Fama (1991) and MacKinlay (1997), the precision in timing the event frees the analysis from the sensitivity of a particular technique or asset pricing benchmark. Further avoidance of the bad model problem (Fama, 1998) comes from the internal control sample enabled by the firms proved not to be at fault in the crash. Indeed, we can gauge the speed of the stock market reaction to the crash not only by the time that the guilty firm was discovered, but also by the time in which the innocents were released.

Our basic analysis provides a test of market efficiency. How quickly and accurately did the stock market process the implications of the space shuttle crash? As an extension, we also attempt to exactly discern how the price discovery unfolded on the day of the crash. Who provided the information that was imbedded in market prices? How valuable was the information?

We also examine issues related to the process of price discovery and tie these to avenues for future research: What is the source of trading volume? What are the inter-firm implications of public announcements? Does a trading halt in one firm shift price discovery to firms that are close substitutes? Does the nature of the information spillover vary with news-related versus order-imbalance halts? Finally, we draw on our example to address policy issues facing securities markets: How obvious is the detection of insider trading around visible corporate events? What is meant by fairness in information disclosure?

We develop the paper as follows: Section 2 reports the evidence on the stock market reaction to the crash. Section 3 considers the nature of the price discovery process. Section 4 provides generalizations of the analysis to issues in corporate finance and market microstructure. Section 5 offers concluding comments.

2 The market reaction to the disaster

2.1 Chronology of the crash

The Challenger explosion occurred at 11:39 a.m. eastern standard time on January 28, 1986. (See Appendix A for a list of the news stories and pertinent dates during the Challenger episode.) The announcement of the crash came across the Dow Jones News Wire at 11:47 a.m. In additional stories crossing the Wire in the next hour, Rockwell International, the maker of the shuttle and its main engines, and Lockheed, the manager of shuttle ground support, issued "no-comment" reactions to the crash. Press coverage that day also identified Martin Marietta as the manufacturer of the shuttle's external fuel tank and Morton Thiokol as the maker of the shuttle's solid fuel booster rocket.

The crash caught nearly everyone by surprise. The headlines the following day in the *New York Times* asked "How Could It Happen" and stated that there were "No Ideas Yet to the Cause." Because of the unprecedented nature of the event, the *Financial Times* on January 30th predicted that "it will be months rather than weeks before NASA has any-real answers to the question—What went wrong with the Challenger?"

To find answers to this question. President Reagan appointed a blue-ribbon panel headed by former Secretary of State William Rogers. After several months of testimony and deliberation, the commission concluded that the cause of the crash was the lack of resiliency at low temperatures in the seals of the shuttle's booster rockets supplied by Morton Thiokol.[3] In its June 1986 report, the Rogers Commission also found fault with the chain of command at the booster's manufacturer, Morton Thiokol, as well as within NASA itself.[4]

   Of the four main manufacturing firms involved in the shuttle project, the commission laid blame on only one of them. After more than 4 months of study by engineering experts and renowned scientists, Morton Thiokol was definitively adjudged to be the culprit.

2.2 The stock market on the day of the crash

Table 5.1 reports the stock returns and trading volume of the four shuttle firms on the day of the explosion. Data are taken from the S&P Daily Stock Price Record. As reported in Panel A, Morton Thiokol's stock return stands out from the other three firms. Morton Thiokol's 1-day return was −11.86%, more than 6 standard deviations greater than the firm's average daily stock return in the 3 months prior to the crash. By contrast, the stock returns of Lockheed, Martin Marietta, and Rockwell, while all negative, were less than 2 standard deviations different than the average return for the firms in the 3 months preceding the crash.[5]

   As shown in Panel B of Table 5.1, Morton Thiokol also experienced an unprecedented amount of trading volume on the day of the crash. The 1.74 million shares traded in Morton Thiokol on January 28th were substantially greater than the average of 100,000 shares per day in the 3 months preceding the event. The other three firms also had above-average trading volume on the day of the crash, although not on the order of Morton Thiokol.

2.3 The speed of the market reaction

The daily data on stock returns and trading volume indicate that the Challenger explosion was a major event and that by the end of trading on the day of the event, the

Table 5.1 Daily stock market behavior around the Challenger crash

Variable	Morton Thiokol	Lockheed	Martin Marietta	Rockwell International
Panel A. Daily stock returns				
January 28	−11.86%	−2.14%	−3.25%	−2.48%
3-Month average	0.21%	0.07%	0.14%	0.06%
3-Month standard deviation	1.86%	1.36%	1.79%	1.79%
Z statistic	6.49	1.63	1.89	1.42
Panel B. Daily trading volume				
January 28	1739.9	667.5	446.2	563.2
3-Month average	100.5	347.9	199.9	221.2
3-Month standard deviation	59.5	159.4	136.5	117.1
Z statistic	27.57	2.00	1.80	2.92

This table compares the stock returns and trading volume of the four major space-shuttle firms on January 28, 1986, the day of the Challenger crash, to averages of the same variables in the 3 months (October 28, 1985 to January 27, 1986) prior to the crash. Trading volume is in thousands of shares. Z statistics test the null that the observation on January 28 equals the average from the prior 3 months. Data are taken from the S&P Daily Stock Price Record.

Table 5.2 Intraday stock market behavior around the Challenger crash

Time	Morton Thiokol	Lockheed	Martin Marietta	Rockwell International
Panel A. Stock price movements				
11:30 a.m.	US$37.25	US$47.25	US$35.38	US$34.75
Noon	Halt	US$44.50	US$34.25	US$32.75
12:36 p.m.	US$35.00	US$45.00	US$32.50	US$34.13
1:00 p.m.	US$34.38	US$45.00	US$33.00	US$33.25
Panel B. Stock returns				
11:30–Noon	Halt	−5.82%	−3.18%	−5.76%
Noon–12:36	−6.04%	1.12%	−5.11%	4.20%
12:36–1:00	−1.79%	0.00%	1.54%	−2.56%

This table reports the price movements and stock returns of the four major space-shuttle firms in the period immediately surrounding the 11:39 a.m. crash of the space shuttle Challenger on January 28, 1986. There is no reported price for Morton Thiokol at noon because of an NYSE trading halt in that stock from 11:52 a.m. to 12:44 p.m. The first post-crash trade in Morton Thiokol occurred at 12:36 p.m. on NASDAQ. Data are taken from the price sheets of Francis Emory Fitch.

stock market had seemingly attributed culpability for the crash to Morton Thiokol,[6] but most interesting is the speed and manner in which the market distinguished Morton Thiokol from the other three firms. In the period immediately following the explosion, Morton Thiokol experienced a sell-induced trading halt while the other shuttle firms bore significant price declines.[7]

To analyze intraday price movements, we used data from Francis Emory Fitch. As reported in Table 5.2 by 12 noon, within 21 min of the crash and 13 min of the News Wire account, Lockheed had fallen 5.05%, Martin Marietta had declined 2.83%, and Rockwell was down 6.12%. Martin Marietta continued to slide for the next few minutes, finally reaching a low of 8.51% off from its pre-crash price.

At resumption of trading in Morton Thiokol at 12:36 p.m., it was down 6% from its pre-crash price.[8] As reported in Figure 5.1, which benchmarks intraday prices to the price at the open on January 28th, Morton Thiokol continued to decline throughout the remainder of trading. By contrast, the other three firms rebounded from their initial price declines.

The price movements on the day of the crash were sustained over time. Figure 5.2 plots the movements of the four shuttle firms in the two months following the crash. All prices are relative to their level on January 27, 1986 and the Dow Jones Industrial index provides a market benchmark. As shown in the figure, the decline of Morton Thiokol on January 28th is maintained in the subsequent months while the other three firms track or outperform the market.

In a most important way, traders reacted differently between Morton Thiokol and the other shuttle firms. The fact that market liquidity was available to maintain a market in Lockheed, Martin Marietta, and Rockwell while the market for Morton Thiokol dried up suggests that the stock market discerned the guilty party within minutes of the announcement of the crash.

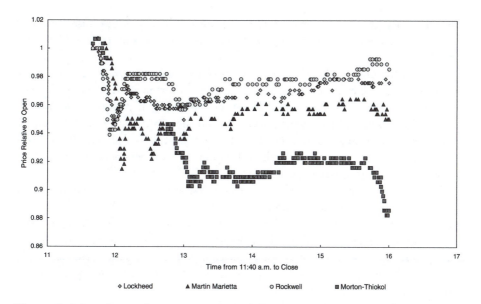

Figure 5.1 Intraday stock price movements following the challenger disaster

2.4 The accuracy of the market forecast

It is clear from the data that all shuttle firms experienced price volatility on the day of the crash. The data also suggest that the trading related to this volatility singled out Morton Thiokol. We build on these two points by addressing the following two queries: What explains the initial price volatility of Rockwell, Martin Marietta, and Lockheed?

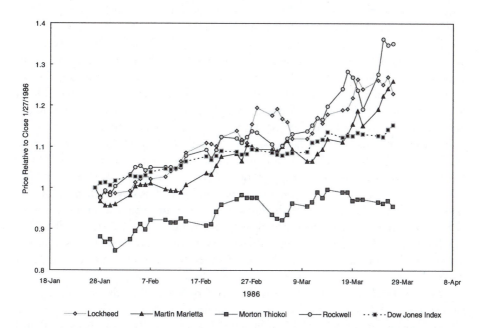

Figure 5.2 Three-month stock price movements following the challenger disaster

Were the stock price movements of all four firms on the day of the crash consistent with an indictment by the market against Morton Thiokol and a no-fault ruling for the other firms?

The crash event clearly had several potential implications. One is that the entire shuttle program might be severely delayed or possibly terminated, which would have hurt all four firms. However, on the day of the crash, President Reagan promised a continued commitment to space exploration, and the shuttle program did maintain operations albeit with a 2-year delay. The other implication is that being judged, the party at fault in the disaster was likely to have serious consequences over and above any delays that the program experienced.

The initial decline of Lockheed, Martin Marietta, and Rockwell may have been attributable to concerns about the continuation of the shuttle program or uncertainty to their culpability in the disaster. At all events, while these firms suffered initial declines of substantial magnitude, their prices rebounded. Morton Thiokol, on the other hand, was not as lucky in either its market valuation or its subsequent expenses. The firm's 1-day price decline was 12%, a loss in equity value of US$200 million.

The stock price decline for Morton Thiokol was substantially larger than the stock price declines for the other firms and hence was not likely based only on an expected delay in the shuttle program. While true that Morton Thiokol had more sales tied up in the shuttle project than the other companies, the difference was not large enough to explain the difference in the stock price movements. The percent of sales coming from NASA for each firm was 8.53% for Lockheed, 10.95% for Martin Marietta, 11.86% for Rockwell, and 18.23% for Morton Thiokol.[9] If the stock price declines for all four firms were only attributable to expected revenue declines because of a slowdown in the NASA shuttle program, Morton Thiokol's price should have dropped only on the order of 4.5%, i.e., about twice the stock price decline of the other firms rather than the 12% that it suffered on the day.

Interestingly, the US$200 million equity decline for Morton Thiokol seems in hindsight to have been a reasonable prediction of lost cash flows that came as a result of the judgment of culpability in the crash by the Rogers Commission. Morton Thiokol suffered substantial costs as an outcome of the shuttle accident. These included legal settlements with the families of the astronauts amounting to US$7 million and a direct forfeiture to NASA of US$10 million in retainers. Additionally, to mitigate future accidents, Morton Thiokol performed repair work of US$409 million at no profit, implying US$40 million in foregone profits (assuming a profit rate of 10%). Most importantly, the firm dropped out of the bidding for a US$1.5 billion NASA contract for the next generation of solid fuel booster rockets, implying US$150 million in lost profits. While this is an undiscounted value, it is representative of the reputational value placed in jeopardy as a result of the disaster.[10] All told, a rough estimate of the losses directly attributable to the shuttle accident is approximately equal to the US$200 million loss in Morton Thiokol equity value on the day of the crash.

Morton Thiokol's stock price reaction was larger than the other companies and by our accounting most of the loss seems to be linked to the expectation of winning future government contracts. All four firms were at risk in this regard because all had wide berths at the government trough. Value Line (1985) reports that while 40% of

Morton Thiokol's sales were to government, Lockheed had 83% of its sales tied to government contracts. Moody's (1985) says that 80% of sales for Martin Marietta were to government. Neither Moody's nor Value Line gives a precise estimate of the percent of sales to government for Rockwell. However, Value Line points out that Rockwell's future opportunities all hinged on winning new government contracts in defense and aerospace one of which was construction of the space station for NASA. All told, culpability in the shuttle disaster would probably have been more devastating in a reputational sense to Lockheed, Martin Marietta, and Rockwell than it was to Morton Thiokol. We think that it is arguable that uncertainty on this margin by some investors may be the explanation for the volatility observed in the stock prices of these firms immediately following the crash.

3 The price formation process

3.1 Where did the information come from?

For most observers, the cause of the crash—the problem with Morton Thiokol's booster rockets—was made public on February 11, 1986, when Nobel-winning physicist Richard Feynman demonstrated that the material forming the shuttle O-rings loses resilience under cold temperatures.[11] However, both NASA and Morton Thiokol had been aware of this problem for at least a year. Testimony indicated that in July 1985, a NASA analyst warned of problems in the seals of the shuttle booster rockets on prior flights, especially those launches done in cold temperatures. Related testimony indicated that NASA had expressed concerns about the seals as early as 1982, and 3 months prior to the crash, Morton Thiokol itself had made a broad call for assistance in solving its O-ring problem to a meeting of experts at the Society of Automotive Engineering. Moreover, on the morning of the launch, Morton Thiokol engineers in Salt Lake recommended that the launch be postponed because of concern over the O-rings given the weather at the launch site.

Although the problem of the O-rings was known to some, it was not public information in the normal sense. A search of the various financial media such as the Wall Street Transcript, the Value Line Investment Survey, and other sources for evidence that analysts were aware of the O-ring problems reveals no obvious concern about Morton Thiokol either before or after the crash. A story from the Wall Street Transcript on January 27, 1986, the day before crash, indicated that Kidder Peabody analysts were quite bullish on Morton Thiokol. Following the crash, a Prudential Bache analyst quoted in the February 17, 1986, Wall Street Transcript considered the decline in Morton Thiokol's price to represent an overreaction by the market. A similar sentiment was conveyed by the analysts of several other securities brokerages following the crash: Donaldson, Lufkin and Jenrette on February 6, 1986, Piper, Jaffray on March 6, 1986, and Bear, Stearns on May 30, 1986. Similarly, the analysts in the April 11, 1986, Value Line Investment Survey considered the shuttle accident to represent "only a moderate setback" for Morton Thiokol. In general, if securities analysts knew about the potential for disaster or even the extent of it for Morton Thiokol, this information was passed to clients via confidential recommendations that were never made public.

3.2 Who brought the information to the market?

The existence of prior knowledge of the O-ring problem suggests that investors who were aware of this private information facilitated the price discovery process on the day of the explosion. It is natural to imagine that insiders at Morton Thiokol were the first to act on the news of the disaster.

We searched the Invest/Net Insider Trading Monitor available from Dialog Information Services for evidence of insider trading by Morton Thiokol people on the day of the crash. The data show no evidence of trading by insiders on January 28, 1986. The sale closest to the event was a disposition of 5000 shares on February 24, 1986, by a divisional officer of the firm. For the 1 year following the crash, the largest insider sale was by the company chairman on August 7, 1986. Both of these sales occurred well after the news of the crash was incorporated into stock prices.

This does not necessarily mean that Morton Thiokol insiders were not responsible for bringing the private information to the market. The information concerning the O-rings was apparently possessed by low-level managers and engineers, people who are not required by law to report their trades. Moreover, higher-up managers might have engaged in trades without reporting them or Morton Thiokol insiders may have bought shares in the other shuttle firms in an attempt to capitalize on their knowledge.

There were 52,500 shares of Morton Thiokol traded on the NYSE from the time of the crash up to the time trading was suspended. Another 200,000 shares traded in the call auction at the resumption of trading on the NYSE. Approximately the same number of shares traded in the other companies over this time period.

Table 5.3 shows the pattern of trading in Morton Thiokol in the minutes following the crash before trading was halted. Five thousand shares were traded at 11:42 a.m.

Table 5.3 Trading in Morton Thiokol immediately following the crash

Time	Trade size	Price
11:40	700	37.375
11:42	5000	37.500
11:45	5000	37.500
11:48	3200 (a)(b)	37.250
11:49	2000	37.375
11:49	16,200 (a)	37.125
11:51	10,000 (a)	37.000
11:52	100	37.000
11:52	1000	37.000
11:52	10,000	37.000
Trading halted		

This table shows trades in Morton Thiokol shares from the time of the crash up to the time trading was suspended (11:39 to 11:52). These are trades occurring on the NYSE. Down-tick trades that are most likely to have been initiated by sell orders are denoted by (a). News of the disaster crossed the Broad Tape on the floor of the exchange at 11:47; the trade immediately following is denoted by (b).

on an up-tick. The fact that this trade occurred on an up-tick suggests that it was not initiated by a sell order and hence was probably not motivated by news of the disaster. At 11:48 a.m., there was a trade of 3200 shares on a down-tick of 1/4th. This was just following the time that the story flashed across the Broad Tape headline service on the floor of the exchange. Both the size of the price change and the coincidence of the news flash suggest that this trade could have been informationally motivated. Although it was followed by up-tick trade, two down-tick trades of 16,200 and 10,000 shares moved price by 3/8ths to US$37. These were followed by trades in the next minute totaling 11,100 shares after which the specialist closed the market. The last three trades occasioned no price change and were likely filled out of the specialist's order book.

Selling shares in Morton Thiokol prior to the trading halt had some value. Sales of Morton Thiokol shares over the 13-min window following the crash prior to the trading halt were US$1.95 million. When the market in Morton Thiokol reopened on the NYSE at 12:44 p.m., the value of these shares was US$1.84 million. Hence, if we attribute the sale of all of these shares to private information about the cause of the crash, US$113,575 in equity losses were avoided by exercise of this knowledge.[12] The 200,000 shares that were exchanged upon resumption of trading were unable to avoid the US$2 price decline, or US$400,000 loss in value.

3.3 How was the information disseminated?

While we cannot attribute the price discovery process to particular informed traders, clearly some segment of the market quickly reacted to the news of the disaster. There was a trading halt in the market for Morton Thiokol shares but not in the market for shares of the other companies. This was true although the share prices in the other companies fluctuated by as much as or more than Morton Thiokol fell when its trading resumed. Liquidity was available to keep these markets operating.

This liquidity may have come from investors possessing private information about the cause of the crash and attempting to profit from this knowledge. However, another possibility is that the private information came to the market, maybe in the form of the early trades in Morton Thiokol—maybe from other sources, where it was quickly digested by floor traders and specialists who then acted on it by providing liquidity for trading in the three innocent companies.[13]

To investigate the first possibility, we estimated how much money might have been made by exercising private information by buying shares in the innocent companies. To estimate the potential value of the private knowledge that Lockheed, Martin Marietta, and Rockwell were not at fault in the crash, we simulate a trading strategy in which an investor purchases shares in these three shuttle firms between the time of the crash through the lowest price reached for each firm on the day of the crash. Table 5.4 notes the prices at which the three firms traded immediately following the crash. Rockwell quickly reached its minimum for the day; the period of decline was 10 min and covered 18 trades. The total position that investors took in the security in this period was US$1.69 million. Lockheed's price decline spanned 14 min and 21 trades in which investors took a cumulative position of US$1.7 million. Martin Marietta's price decline also lasted for 14 min, involved 25 trades, and entailed a US$1.1 million investment.

We next estimate the profits made by unwinding the accumulated positions at the end of trading on the day of the crash.[14] As shown in Table 5.4, the US$1.69 million position in Rockwell was worth US$1.71 million at the end of the day, a return of 1.4%, The position in Lockheed returned 0.41%. Trading in Martin Marietta was actually a losing / proposition, resulting in a −0.62% return. The total profit on buying the three innocent shuttle firms on their way down and then unwinding this position at the end of the day was US$23,625 or 0.53%. As a comparison, the Dow Jones Industrial Index was up 1.13% for the day.

Deferring sales of the accumulated positions until the end of the day following the crash would have led to larger gains for investments in Rockwell and Lockheed, but even more negative returns for Martin Marietta. Buying Rockwell on the way down and selling it the next day yielded a profit of US$58,475 for a return of 3.5%. The same strategy for Lockheed earned 1%, but Martin Marietta lost 2.6%. The total profit across all three firms was US$47,887 or slightly more than 1%. Again by comparison, the Dow Jones Industrial Index was up 1.3% over the 2-day period. As reported at the bottom of Table 5.4 holding the firms for a period of 1 month following the crash would have garnered more sizable gains, but would have exposed investors to market risks that were independent of the private information about the cause of the crash.

Table 5.4 Capitalizing on the knowledge of who was not responsible

Firm	Lockheed	Martin Marietta	Rockwell
Stock price prior to crash	US$47.000	US$35.250	US$34.750
Lowest price	US$44.625	US$32.250	US$32.625
Percent change	−5.05%	−8.51%	−6.12%
Time period of decline	11:45–11:58 a.m.	11:53 a.m.– 12:06 p.m.	11:46–11:55 a.m.
Number of trades	21	25	18
Average size of trades	1767	1292	2616
Largest trade	9000	5000	15,000
Price at time of largest trade	US$46.250	US$35.000	US$34.500
Cumulative volume	37.100	32.300	49.900
Cumulative position	US$1,697,825	US$1,098,575	US$1,688,025
Unwind value on January 28	US$1,704,738	US$1,091,763	US$1,711,550
Percent return	0.41%	−0.62%	1.39%
Unwind value the next day	US$1,715,875	US$1,069,938	US$1,746,500
Percent return	1.06%	−2.61%	3.46%
Unwind value after 1 month	US$2,072,963	US$1,292,000	US$1,889,963
Percent return	22.10%	17.61%	11.96%

This table analyzes trading in the firms who were ultimately judged not to have been responsible for the Challenger disaster. While trading in the at-fault firm, Morton Thiokol, halted as a result of an order imbalance at 11:52 a.m., trading in the not-at-fault firms continued. Each of their prices declined in the same percent as that of Morton Thiokol and over a relatively short time span. This table shows the cumulative position that an informed investor might have taken in each security during the downward price movement. The table also shows the relative gains from unwinding these positions.

3.4 What was the evolution of prices?

The evidence shown in Table 5.4 does not make a compelling case that liquidity in the innocent firms came from outside the market. There does not seem to have been much money to be made by buying shares in the innocent firms. If we assume, then, that the liquidity in the innocent firms was provided by the market makers, it is reasonable to consider how these traders might have reacted.

To this end, we examine the details of the trading in these stocks on the NYSE during the trading halt in Morton Thiokol. The period of interest is from 11:39 a.m. to 12:44 p.m. This is the time of the crash up to the time that trading in Morton Thiokol shares resumed on the NYSE. Table 5.5 gives some details about trades in the other three stocks over this window. There were 120 trades of Rockwell stock totaling 290,400 shares. Lockheed had 101 trades for a total of 233,800 shares. Martin Marietta had 176,000 shares change hands in 85 transactions.

Most trades occurred without changing price although the price of all three stocks did move substantially over the period. The trading was orderly. Of the trades on which price moved, only once did price move by as much as three ticks (37.5¢) and 70% of the trades on which price moved, the price changed by only 1/8th of a dollar. Thus, the overwhelming majority of trades that moved price only moved price by one tick.

3.4.1 The characteristics of trade sizes and price movement

Tables 5.6 and 5.7 put this into perspective by looking at trade sizes and price movements during the entire day. Our analysis here is similar to Barclay and Warner (1993). Table 5.6 shows the distribution of the average number of shares traded at each of the different price changes observed in each stock. For each company, the largest number of trades occurred at zero price change, and while the average trade size is not the

Table 5.5 Trades in other firms during Morton Thiokol trading halt

Stock	Lockheed	Martin Marietta	Rockwell
Total volume	233,800	176,000	290,400
Number of trades	101	85	120
Distribution of trades by price change			
−3/8ths	1		
−1/4th	3	16	6
−1/8th	27	11	16
No change	54	39	78
+1/8th	11	11	18
+1/4th	5	8	2

This table examines trades in the three firms not responsible for the crash. The period examined covers the time of the crash up to the resumption of trading in Morton Thiokol on the NYSE (11:39 a.m. to 12:44 p.m.).

Table 5.6 Price changes and trade sizes

Firm	Absolute price change	Average trade size	Number of trades
Lockheed	no change	2011	160
	1/8th	2302	92
	1/4th	4660	10
	3/8ths	1471	7
	1/2	5000	1[a]
	1	1225	4[b]
Martin Marietta	no change	1894	103
	1/8th	1399	71
	1/4th	3397	37
Rockwell	no change	1789	154
	1/8th	1592	90
	1/4th	4307	14
Morton Thiokol	no change	3278	141
	1/8th	2066	125
	1/4th	5421	29
	3/8ths	600	1
	2	200,000	1[c]

This table shows the average trade size and the number of trades in each of the securities through-out the entire day at each absolute change in price.

[a] Short sale at 1:27 p.m.

[b] Sequence of short sales followed by a bounce-back trades all at 3:03 p.m. Trades sizes in order: 2000, 100, 2500, 300. Short sales depressed price.

[c] Call auction that resumed trading after halt.

largest, more total volume was recorded for each company at no change in price than at any other price movement. The second most common event was for a trade to move the stock price by one tick. Indeed, the relative paucity of price changes in excess of one tick is striking. Except for Martin Marietta, the volume recorded at one-tick price changes was second to zero price change. There were no trades at price changes larger than two ticks for Martin Marietta and Rockwell, and only 14 trades at price changes of three or more ticks across all firms including the US$2 price adjustment occurring at the call auction resumption of trading in Morton Thiokol.[15]

Table 5.6 suggests a loose relation between trade size and price change. Even so, the emphasis is probably best placed on the word "loose." Table 5.7 shows the trade size and price change for the 10 biggest trades in all four companies. Less than 20% of the 10 largest trades in each stock moved price more than one tick. Except for the reopening of Morton Thiokol, none of these trades occasioned a price change of more than two ticks. And, the most common event for these largest trades was no change in price. It is interesting to note that 185,400 shares in Morton Thiokol traded at no price change to close the day. This amounted to nearly the same volume as traded at the reopening after the trading halt in this security.

Table 5.7 Ten largest trades for each firm

Firm	Trade volume	Price change	Price	Time
Lockheed	27,900	no change	47.000	10:22 a.m.
	25,000	−1/8th	47.000	10:44 a.m.
	11,900	no change	47.000	10:54 a.m.
	24,000	1/8th	47.000	11:16 a.m.
	16,000[a]	1/4th	44.750	11:59 a.m.
	20,000	no change	45.250	12:23 p.m.
	10,200	−1/8th	45.250	12:31 p.m.
	28,300	−1/8th	45.000	12:43 p.m.
	15,000[b]	−1/4th	45.000	1:02 p.m.
	10,000	no change	45.375	1:42 p.m.
Martin Marietta	15,000	no change	35.000	11:07 a.m.
	11,400	no change	35.000	11:07 a.m.
	10,000	no change	35.000	11:07 a.m.
	25,000	−1/4th	35.000	11:13 a.m.
	25,000	no change	35.250	11:18 a.m.
	50,000	1/4th	35.500	11:44 a.m.
	14,700	1/8th	33.250	12:39 p.m.
	10,000	1/8th	33.250	1:04 p.m.
	20,000	no change	33.500	1:27 p.m.
	15,700	no change	33.500	1:44 p.m.
Rockwell	15,000	no change	34.500	11:47 a.m.
	10,000	1/8th	32.750	11:56 a.m.
	16,000	no change	32.750	12:00 p.m.
	30,000	1/4th	33.250	12:03 p.m.
	11,000	no change	33.375	12:05 p.m.
	12,000	1/8th	34.125	12:11 p.m.
	10,000	no change	34.125	12:27 p.m.
	10,000	1/8th	33.500	1:06 p.m.
	20,000	no change	33.875	1:56 p.m.
	12,200	no change	34.250	3:37 p.m.
Morton Thiokol	16,200	−1/4th	37.125	11:49 a.m.
	200,000[c]	−2	35.000	12:44 p.m.
	50,000	−1/8th	35.000	12:51 p.m.
	50,000	−1/8th	33.750	1:52 p.m.
	50,000	−1/8th	34.000	2:23 p.m.
	14,000	no change	34.250	2:34 p.m.
	13,000	−1/8th	34.125	3:03 p.m.
	19,000	1/8th	34.000	3:48 p.m.
	100,000	no change	33.000	4:00 p.m.
	85,400	no change	33.000	4:00 p.m.

This table shows the 10 largest trades for each firm, the price, the time of day at which they occurred, and the price change that they occasioned. Except for the resumption of trading in Morton Thiokol, none of the biggest trades were associated with price changes in excess of two ticks.

[a] Short sale.

[b] Time corrected to reflect true sequence of trade.

[c] Shares traded in call auction when trading resumed after halt.

3.4.2 Market liquidity during the halt

Tables 5.6 and 5.7 do give us a way of judging the liquidity that was provided in the three innocent firms from the time of the crash through the trading halt in Morton Thiokol. Although, overall, there is only a loose relation between trade size and price changes, we see that a disproportionately large share of the biggest price changes in the three innocent firms occurred during this period. More than half of the trades associated with price changes in excess of one tick took place during this window.

While we do not have records that tell us which trades were engaged by the specialists in each stock, it is enlightening to examine trades from the perspective of the specialist. For sake of discussion, we assume that the trades that move price are trades that require the market maker to provide liquidity. If price increases, the market needs liquidity on the sell side. That is, if price increases, it increases because buying relative to selling pressure has increased since the last trade. In order to clear the market, liquidity providers must come in on the selling side. On the other hand, if price decreases, there is increased selling pressure and market liquidity is required on the buying side.

Simply enough, we define "liquidity trades" as buys when price decreases and sells when price increases, and given these definitions, we look at the amount of liquidity that the market in these three stocks required over this period. We could choose different definitions. For instance, we could examine only those trades where price changed by two ticks, or where price changed in the same direction twice, or the like. However, the picture is substantively the same.

Table 5.8 shows that there were 42 liquidity trades in Rockwell and 46 in both Lockheed and Martin Marietta. As we might imagine, liquidity trades accounted for a larger percentage of shares than nonliquidity trades. That is, while the majority of trades occurred with no change in price, the majority of shares were exchanged in trades that did change price.

In Rockwell, the largest liquidity-providing buy was a purchase of shares for US$198,000; the largest liquidity providing sell was US$997,500. The largest liquidity buy overall was in Lockheed shares. It was a purchase of US$1,273,500. This trade took place only moments before trading resumed in Morton Thiokol, was for 28,300 shares, and occurred on a down-tick of 1/8th. The largest liquidity sale was for US$1,775,000 in Martin Marietta. It took place at 11:44 a.m., was for 50,000 shares, and occurred on an up-tick of 1/4th.

To get a sense of how much liquidity the market required over this period, we can follow the path of liquidity trades in terms of the net gains and losses to the liquidity providers and the magnitude of their inventory adjustments in shares of the three stocks. In Rockwell, liquidity providers ended the period with a net decrease in shares. Liquidity trades amounted to a net reduction in shares of Rockwell valued at US$2,060,400. This ending inventory is valued at the price of the last trade during the period (whether or not it was a liquidity trade). The maximum inventory reduction over the period was slightly-larger than this. At one point during this window, liquidity traders had gained inventory of US$776,475.

Similarly, liquidity trades in Martin Marietta left market makers with US$1,722,350 less inventory at the end than at the start. On the other hand, liquidity traders in Lockheed were forced to accumulate inventory. Inventory in this stock increased over the period by US$2,835,000.

Table 5.8 Market liquidity during Morton Thiokol trading halt

Liquidity providing trades	Stock		
	Lockheed	Martin Marietta	Rockwell
Number	46	46	42
Volume	119,300	121,600	134,400
Largest buy	US$1,273,500	US$166,250	US$198,000
Largest sell	US$224,375	US$1,775,000	US$997,500
Maximum value of inventory	US$2,835,000	n/a	US$776,475
Maximum inventory deficit	US$(9425)	US$(1,775,000)	US$(2,085,038)
Sum of trades	US$(2,839,813)	US$1,822,925	US$2,027,063
Value of inventory	US$2,820,313	US$(1,722,350)	US$(2,060,400)
Net gain/loss	US$(19,500)	US$100,575	US$(33,338)

This table examines trades in the three firms not responsible for the crash. The period examined covers the time of the crash up to the resumption of trading in Morton Thiokol on the NYSE (11:39 a.m. to 12:44 p.m.). Liquidity Providing Trades are defined as buys when price changes are negative and sells when price changes are positive. In calculating Sum of Trades, buys are negative cash flow and sells are positive. Value of Inventory is based on price at last trade in each stock before Morton Thiokol reopened.

We can see how liquidity traders fared on these transactions by summing the buys and sells and netting the value of the inventory change. In Rockwell, there was more liquidity selling than buying. The sum of the trades, negative cash flow for buys and positive for sells, was US$2,027,063. Given the accumulated inventory deficit of −US$2,080,400, liquidity trades cost the market makers −US$33,338. By the same calculations, liquidity trades in Lockheed also resulted in a loss; in this stock, the loss was −US$19,500. On the other hand, liquidity trades in Martin Marietta resulted in a profit of US$100,575.

Thus, over all three stocks, liquidity providers made a profit of US$47,737. There were a total number of 700,200 shares exchanged in 134 trades with a value of US$11.8 million and requiring capital of US$6.7 million.[16] The profit per trade is not huge: about US$350 per trade. The profit per share traded was 6.8. Both of these are roughly equivalent to the commission on a full commission trade. While the return on the liquidity provided is fairly large if it is considered on an annualized basis, the standard deviation of the profit across the three companies is also large. The simple standard deviation is US$73,646, so the ratio of the total profit to this measure of risk is very similar to average return and risk for the market.

4 Generalizations

4.1 Market efficiency and the source of price movements

The textbook definition of market efficiency gauges the extent to which stock prices quickly and accurately respond to new information. Our case provides broad support for market efficiency. Within an hour, the market seems to have placed the blame for the crash on Morton Thiokol, the party ultimately judged by authorities to have been at fault. The firm's 1-day decline of 12% was quick, permanent, and reasonably corresponds to the subsequent losses in terms of legal liability, repair costs, and lost future business. By contrast, the other firms involved in the shuttle program suffered only temporary stock price setbacks that recovered for the most part by the end of trading on the day of the crash. Similar to research by Mitchell and Maloney (1989) on airline crashes, the stock market seems adept at detecting fault.

Of course, some might interpret the evidence on the innocent firms as noise trading, at least on an ex post basis. The three innocent shuttle firms experienced a great deal of trading volume in the hour following the crash, and this volume was accompanied by a substantial decline in the firms' stock prices. Subsequent trading led to a rebound in the prices of the three firms such that the firms had insignificant stock returns for the day. To some extent, therefore, the market initially overreacted to the Challenger crash.

But viewing the stock price behavior of the three other shuttle firms as a market overreaction seems misguided. Although some uninformed investors chose to sell immediately following the crash, their loss was a gain to the investors who provided liquidity based on their private information. Hence, the case is more consistent with a Grossman and Stiglitz (1980) world rather than an environment of systematic mispricing. Indeed, our case best fits the model of Dow and Gorton (1993, p. 646) in which there is "a rich pattern of price responses, while remaining consistent with rationality."

In seeking explanations for market inefficiencies, Shleifer and Vishny (1997) suggest that there can be persistent deviations from fundamentals because of the costs and risks of arbitrage. Our case finds that the market quickly discovers prices even when the gains from arbitrage are not large. The investors who took positions in the three innocent shuttle firms did not garner large absolute or risk-adjusted gains that day.

The price discovery related to the Challenger crash provides a novel twist on the inquiry accentuated by French and Roll (1986) as to whether stock price movements emanate from public or private information. Clearly, the crash of the Challenger was a public event. And consistent with the French–Roll classification, much of the price movement of Morton Thiokol occurred with no trading volume.

Yet the reason that Morton Thiokol had no trading volume in the period immediately following the crash was because of an NYSE trading halt in the firm's common stock. But while trading in Morton Thiokol was halted, the remaining shuttle firms continued to trade and to provide price discovery. Indeed, an important piece of information to all market participants was which of the shuttle firms had trading halts and which were able to maintain trading.

Hence, the information on Morton Thiokol's O-rings that underpinned the stock market reaction is probably best viewed as private information. Indeed, there is no evidence that the knowledge of the O-ring problem had affected market prices before the day of the disaster. We examine trading in Morton Thiokol on days of prior shuttle launches and found that there had been no abnormal volume or stock price movements. Similarly, there was no abnormal short interest in Morton Thiokol on the days of previous launches, nor were there any short sales of Morton Thiokol on the day of the explosion prior to launch time. Indeed, Morton Thiokol's stock price was marginally up from its open during the period just before the launch.

As noted by French and Roll (1986. p. 9), the simple dichotomy between public and private information is somewhat artificial. The Challenger case reemphasizes that the information processed by the market is not simply some linear combination of private and public components. Instead, the information structure dealt with by market participants is often complex and, as modeled by Dow and Gorton (1993), can produce complicated price patterns in which the relation between information arrival and price discovery is not always direct.

4.2 Implications for corporate finance

The results from the Challenger case have a variety of implications for event study research. We discuss the importance of the sequential, multidimensional nature of information, the sources of trading volume, and the interfirm transfer of information.

4.2.1 The sequential, multidimensional nature of information

Although a rather unique event, the information structure in the Challenger case bears resemblance to the standard sequence in a corporate event. There was internal corporate consideration of information, public revelation of raw data, and finally resolution of the event. Consider the following comparison between the Challenger case and a generic corporate restructuring event:

Information event	Challenger case	Corporate restructuring event
Internal consideration	Internal Morton Thiokol memo on O-ring problem Entreaties at engineering conference to help solve the O-ring problem Call for postponement on morning of launch	Board directs management to consider restructuring alternatives Merger partners considered Merger partner chosen
Public revelation	Challenger crash	Firm publicly announces hiring of investment bank
Event resolution	Rogers Commission concludes fault was in O-rings	Firm announces a formal merger agreement

The similarity indicated by the timeline is that some internal members of a firm and possibly members of the financial community often have private information not known by the representative market participant. But the information is probabilistic and merely one piece of a multidimensional puzzle regarding firm value. Hence, in both the Challenger case and the corporate restructuring event, there is not simply a single piece of information that gestates from private genesis to public maturity. In the Challenger case, it was internally known that cold temperature could compromise the sealing of O-rings, but this was not necessarily a problem given historic weather conditions in Florida. For corporate restructuring, the initial charge of a corporate board has a variety of possible outcomes that even the board itself may not be aware of at the time it assigns the task to management.

This comparison is pertinent to the implementation of event studies. As noted by Fama (1991, p. 1601), the strength of the event study methodology in distilling information lies in the ability to pinpoint the analysis to precise dates. The Challenger example, however, illustrates that even when the event can be precisely dated, the distillation process is often complex. Our results suggest the need for more research along the lines of Lee et al. (1993) that details the microstructure process around earnings announcements.

The comparison between the Challenger crash and corporate restructuring events also has important policy implications. For corporate events such as mergers, the price discovery that occurs prior to the formal public announcement is often offered as de facto insider trading (Keown and Pinkerton, 1981). Jarrell and Poulsen (1989) counter that there are often public rumors prior to formal announcement dates. The Challenger example further illustrates that price discovery does not always obtain from easily identifiable insiders. Instead, the basic competition created by organized financial markets induces analysts, broadly defined, to decipher the implications of a sequence of events. As studied by Dann et al. (1977), some of these "analysts" include transactors on the floor of stock exchanges.

4.2.2 The source of trading volume

The Challenger case also provides implications on the interpretation of trading volume surrounding corporate events. As surveyed by Karpoff (1987), volume is often used to infer the information content of corporate events. Of course, given the definition of French and Roll (1986, p. 9) that "public information affects prices before anyone can trade on it," the use of volume to infer information around reported corporate events is not clear-cut. The Challenger case further indicates the complexity of the volume–information relation. The crash was clearly an information event for Morton Thiokol and that firm had noticeably abnormal volume. But the event also held information for the innocent firms; yet the daily volume in those firms was not as striking relative to recent trading history.

The complexity of the interpretation of trading volume shown in the Challenger case generalizes to corporate restructuring. For example, a number of papers study trading volume surrounding corporate takeover announcements. An often-reported result is that abnormal volume only occurs *after* the public announcement of the takeover (Sanders and Zdanowicz, 1992; Meulbroek and Hart, 1997). Hence, both the Challenger case and the takeover research confirm that there is no simple dichotomy between the effects of public and private information on stock prices.

The complexity of the volume information relation has implications for insider trading policy. The standard measure of damages in insider trading applies to the traders who were hurt by dealing with better-informed traders. But if the above-average trading occurs after the public recognition of the event, does this dampen the apparent harm of insider trading? As Cornell and Sirri (1992, p. 1053) note, "the process by which the market infers information from insider trading is complicated." Perhaps the more important issue is the potential takeovers that are impeded by pre-announcement run-up (Meulbroek, 1992; Meulbroek and Hart, 1997).

4.2.3 The interfirm transfer of information

The Challenger case indicates a rich interfirm information process. In determining the fault of the explosion, the stock market engaged in price discovery not only in the guilty firm but also drew inferences about the firms not at fault.

The active interfirm information process provides support for novel implementation of event studies in corporate finance. For example, research such as Hulburt et al. (2002) contrasts information and agency theories by studying the stock price movement of rivals on the date that a given firm announces corporate restructuring. But the Challenger case also illustrates that, given the active nature of the interfirm information process, researchers must take care to discern the date on which the proposed restructuring first reaches the market and to account for the sequential nature of restructuring information.

One specific event for the future study of interfirm information transfer is a trading halt. A number of papers have studied the informational implications of firms subject to trading halts in securities markets (Lee et al., 1994; Corwin and Lipson, 2000; Christie et al., 2002). A natural extension of this work would be to analyze the price discovery in related firms during the trading halt. A leading cause of trading halts is takeover announcements.[17] In such cases, one could follow Song and Walkling (2000) to define "related firms" as other potential targets from the same industry. A further aspect of such analysis would be to contrast the information spillover that emanates from news-induced trading halts versus order imbalance halts. For a more general treatment of interfirm information spillover during trading halts, one could study close substitutes along the lines of Wurgler and Zhuravskaya (2000).

4.3 Implications for market structure

The Challenger case also provides some implications on various aspects of securities market structure. One straightforward implication is definitional: a firm-specific trading halt is not the same as a market-wide circuit breaker. As illustrated by the Challenger case, the trading halt of Morton Thiokol did not stop the price discovery on the floor of the NYSE.

This simple illustration is quite pertinent to ongoing academic research on market liquidity. For example, Corwin and Lipson (2000, p. 1800) note differences between their results for firm-specific trading halts and the results of Goldstein and Kavajecz (2000) for a market-wide circuit breaker. Future theory and empirical research can add to the conceptual and operational distinctions between firm-specific and market-wide cessations in trading.

Our case also provides some relevant food for thought for a query posed by Professor Stigler some years ago. In what was arguably the first paper on market microstructure, Stigler (1964, p. 133) inquired, "Should floor traders' orders be delayed in execution to achieve parity with outsiders?" In his customary prescience, Stigler anticipated the current era in which the SEC aims towards fairness in information disclosure. When the question is directed at the Challenger event, there was clear parity in knowledge that the disaster had occurred, but it is also clear that there was differential information about the cause. However, regulating parity in information about the cause would have been a difficult matter to operationalize, which may be what Stigler was suggesting in his usual, enigmatic way.

5 Conclusion

The natural reaction to a major event is to ask, What happened? On the NYSE in January 1986, the initial reaction to the Challenger crash was heightened trading in the stock of the four firms most closely linked to the disaster. Out of this trading arose the inference that a single firm was responsible, a conclusion that was substantiated by a presidential commission several months later. But while the commission members were noted scientists and industry experts, the identity of those bringing the information to the market on the day of the crash is much less clear.

These results echo the bipolar aspects of the analysis of securities markets that have been noted recently by O'Hara (1999). The Challenger case is consistent with her statement (p. 84) that "Microstructure models can be viewed as learning models in which market makers watch some particular market data and draw inferences about the underlying true value of an asset." At the same time, the case also reflects O'Hara's observation (p. 83) of "... the perplexing situation that while markets appear to work in practice, we are not sure how they work in theory."

Our analysis of the Challenger case is also pertinent to the information theory of Hayek (1945). He notes (p. 521) that "there is beyond question a body of very important but *unorganized* knowledge ... the knowledge of the particular circumstances of time and place" (emphasis added). What the Challenger episode adds to Hayek's insights is that securities markets are a vehicle for amalgamating unorganized knowledge.

To outside observers, stock exchanges are a scene of "moil and tumult."[18] Yet, evolutionary models such as Alchian (1950) argue that the market as a whole creates knowledge out of the chaos of individual trades. Such knowledge creation lies at the heart of the hypothesis of semistrong market efficiency that is maintained in corporate finance.

Appendix A. News stories and pertinent dates

January 28, 1986

   11:39 a.m.: Shuttle explodes
   11:47 a.m.: *Dow Jones News Wire*: "Space Shuttle Explodes"
   12:17 p.m.: *Dow Jones News Wire*: "Lockheed Has No Immediate Comment"
   12:52 p.m.: *Dow Jones News Wire*: "Rockwell Intl Has No Comment"

January 29, 1986

   New York Times: "How Could It Happen? Fuel Tank Leak Feared"

      Martin Marietta, maker of external fuel tank, has no comment

   Chicago Sun Times: "Morton Big Loser in Dip of Shuttle-Tied Stocks"

      Speculation that the explosion was related to the solid-fuel booster rockets

January 30, 1986

   New York Times: "Inquiry Agenda: Many Questions but No Answers"

      Did a malfunction of the solid fuel rocket booster damage the external fuel tank?

January 31, 1986

   Dow Jones News Wire: "Experts Study Chance that Booster Led to Shuttle Explosion

February 2, 1986

New York Times: "The Shuttle Inquiry"

Faulty seals, flawed casings and poorly packed fuel are among the flaws that could explain a rupture in a solid-fuel booster rocket.

February 3, 1986

Dow Jones News Wire: "Reagan Names Board to Investigate Shuttle Explosion"
New York Times: "Morton Thiokol is Facing the Closest Scrutiny"
Wall Street Journal: "NASA Appears to Be Narrowing Cause of Shuttle Explosion to Booster Rocket"

February 6, 1986

Wall Street Journal: "Frigid Weather at Launch Site Stirs Questions"

February 7, 1986

New York Times: "NASA Was Worried by Cold's Effects"

Rogers Commission told of concern over temperature and booster seals.

February 10, 1986

New York Times: "Panel Asks NASA for its Reports on Booster Risks"

February 11, 1986

Rogers Commission press conference

Nobel-winning physicist Richard Feynman demonstrated that the material forming the shuttle O-rings loses resilience under cold temperatures.

February 13, 1986

New York Times: "Inexperience of Author Led NASA to Discount Warning"

Memo by NASA analyst Richard Cook on July 24, 1985, had noted problem with seals.

February 18, 1986

Wall Street Journal: "Morton Thiokol Trims Work Force at Booster Plant"

February 19, 1986

New York Times: "Rocket Engineer Describes Arguing Against Launching"

Thiokol engineer had warned NASA about temperature and seals.

February 23, 1986

New York Times: "Effects of Cold Emerge as Focus of Shuttle panel"

February 25, 1986

New York Times: "Shuttle Crash: Where Clues Have Led So Far"

NASA concerns with seals dated at least to 1982.

March 4, 1986

Financial World: "The Race for Profits in Space"

Notes that Lockheed, Martin Marietta, Morton Thiokol and Rockwell were all top NASA contractors and all received more than 10% of their revenues from the space agency.

March 24, 1986

Wall Street Journal: "NASA Searches for Reason Seal Failed on Shuttle Booster"

March 31, 1986

Fortune: "Challenger's O-Rings"

In October 1985, Thiokol had made appeal for solution to O-ring problem at annual meeting of Society of Automotive Engineers.

April 30, 1986

New York Times: "Virtual Certainty of failure Shown for Shuttle Seal"

June 6, 1986

Wall Street Journal: "NASA Is Urged to Seek a Second Source for Rockets"

250 members of Congress urge a second supplier for booster rockets.

June 9, 1986

Rogers Commission Report

Report to the President by the Presidential Commission on the Space Shuttle Challenger Accident: Cites faulty seals as cause.
"The consensus of the Commission and participating investigative agencies is that the loss of the Space Shuttle Challenger was caused by a failure in the joint between the two lower segments of the right Solid Rocket Motor. The specific failure was the destruction of the seals that are intended to prevent hot gases from leaking through the joint during the pro-pellant burn of the rocket motor. The evidence assembled by the Commission indicates that no other element of the Space Shuttle system contributed to this failure" (p. 40).
"A careful analysis of the flight history of O-ring performance would have revealed the correlation of O-ring damage and low temperature" (p. 148).

October 30, 1986

Wall Street Journal: "Morton Aide Who Opposed Challenger Launch to Quit"

Roger Boisjoly had been reassigned since testifying to Rogers Commission.

March 2, 1987

Aviation Week and Space Technology: "Morton Thiokol Will Forfeit US$10 Million in Lieu of Contract Penalty"

September 19, 1987

Chemical and Engineering News: "Space Shuttle Passes Final Tests, Is Readied for Return to Space"

March 14, 1988

> *Business Week*: "Morton Thiokol: Reflections on the Shuttle Disaster"

> Company to perform US$409 million worth of redesign work for NASA at no profit.

June 13, 1988

> *Aviation Week and Space Technology*: "Thiokol Drops out of the Bidding for Advanced Shuttle Rocket"

June 20, 1988

> *Time*: "Aerospace: Countdown to a Thiokol Exit"

August 19, 1988

> *Chemical and Engineering News*: "U.S. Space Shuttle: Last Big Tests Clear Return to Space"

February 28, 1989

> *Wall Street Journal*: "Morton Thiokol Is to Spin Off Chemical Line"

> The company broke itself into Morton International, producing salt, specialty chemicals and auto airbags, and Thiokol, an aerospace-only firm.

Notes

1 This paper is an outgrowth of "Efficient Markets: The Space Shuttle Challenger Story," by Erik Larsen, Master's Thesis, Clemson University, July 1992, which reported the stock market reaction to the crash based on daily and monthly returns. We have received helpful comments by a number of individuals and we particularly acknowledge Bobby McCormick, Clark Nardineilli, and Skip Sauer, as well as the referee and editor.

2 Empirical research in corporate finance generally maintains semi-strong form market efficiency and derives valuation implications from identifiable corporate events (MacKinlay, 1997). By contrast, market microstructure considers the roots of the price discovery process and dissects the incorporation of information into market prices (O'Hara, 1999). Using the terminology of French and Roll (1986) and Fama (1970, 1991), corporate finance emphasizes public information while market microstructure focuses on private information.

3 See Report of the Presidential Commission on the Space Shuttle Challenger Accident (1986) called the Rogers Commission Report. See also Lewis (1988).

4 Indeed, subsequent lawsuits raised the possibility that Morton Thiokol and NASA conspired to impede the dissemination of information about the crash. Although such charges were later dismissed, the apparent information failure associated with the Challenger accident is cited by business-school behaviorists as a classic case of organizational miscommunication. See, e.g., Elliot et al. (1993), Lighthall (1991), Maier (1992), and Schwartz (1987).

5 Two other papers report evidence on the daily stock returns of shuttle contractors around the crash. See Chegrin and Herget (1987) and Blose et al. (1996).

6 While we argue that the market ferreted out the pertinent facts of the case, this summary indictment of Morton Thiokol was not universally perceived at the time. While many conjectures as to the cause were offered in the press, only one newspaper, the Chicago *Sun Times*, reported the disparate reactions of the stock prices of the affected firms on the day of the crash.

7 The NYSE defines a trading halt in the following way: "When unusual market conditions arise, such as extreme imbalances of buyers or sellers or significant corporate news, NYSE floor officials consider whether [to implement] a delay or halt in trading." This quote comes from www.nyse.com/content/articles/NT0002412E.html-11k-1999-10-18.

8 Trading resumed on the NYSE at 12:44 p.m. The trade at 12:36 p.m. was on the NASDAQ for 50,000 shares.

9 See Blose et al. (1996).

10 Soon after bowing out of the NASA bidding, the company broke itself into Morton International, producing salt, specialty chemicals and auto airbags, and Thiokol, an aerospace-only firm (announced February 28, 1989).

11 See Feynman and Leighton (1988) for a description of the way the Rogers Commission came to its ultimate conclusion.

12 If we exclude the up-tick trades, then US$83,825 in avoided losses would be attributed to this information.

13 Floor traders and specialists may have pieced together private information from many sources. Possibly they learned the source of the early sell orders in Morton Thiokol. Possibly they made telephone inquiries to rocket scientists. Possibly they learned of insider purchases in the three innocent firms. The data show no purchases by the insiders at Lockheed and Rockwell. Data for Martin Marietta indicate that the company president acquired 30,000 shares on the day of the crash, although this was done via the exercise of options rather than an actual purchase in the market. The timing of this trade during the day is unknown.

14 From the accumulated positions acquired by buying each firm from the time of the crash through their lowest point, we matched trades at the end of the day. For instance, the strategy of buying Rockwell on the way-down accumulated 49,900 shares. We matched these to the trading prices of the last 49,900 shares traded at the end of the day.

15 There were four curious trades in Lockheed at 3:03 p.m. A short sale of 1000 shares is reported to have dropped price US$1, following by a sale of 100 shares that bounced price back up by US$1. This was immediately repeated by a short sale of 1000 again dropping price by US$1. Price again bounced back on a trade of 300 shares. Generally speaking, specialists are not allowed to change price this dramatically. Most likely, these trades were recorded out of sequence and not corrected.

16 We call required capital the sum of the absolute values of the maximum inventory positions in each stock. One could discount this using standard margin requirements.

17 See, e.g., Table 1 in Christie et al. (2002). For a set of 10 takeovers within his broader sample, Asquith (1983) notes that takeover targets experiencing trading halts had different leakage patterns in the pre-announcement period.

18 From O'Rourke (1998, p. 38). Later in the article, he notes some method in the madness.

References

Alchian, A.A., 1950. Uncertainty, evolution and economic theory. Journal of Political Economy 58, 211–221.

Asquith, P., 1983. Merger bids, uncertainty, and stockholder returns. Journal of Financial Economics 11, 51–83.

Barclay, M.J., Warner, J.B., 1993. Stealth trading and volatility: which trades move prices? Journal of Financial Economics 34, 281–305.

Blose, L.E., Bornkamp, R., Brier, M., Brown, K., Frederick, J., 1996. Catastrophic events, contagion, and stock market efficiency: the space shuttle challenger. Review of Financial Economics 5, 117–129.

Brown, S.J., Warner, J.B., 1985. Using daily stock returns: the case of event studies. Journal of Financial Economics 14, 3–31.

Chegrin, A.C., Herget, M., 1987. The space shuttle challenger tragedy and aerospace industry stock prices. Business Forum 12, 25–27.

Christie, W.G., Corwin, S.A., Harris, J.H., 2002. Nasdaq trading halts: the impact of market mechanisms on prices, trading activity, and execution costs. Journal of Finance 57, 1443–1478.

Cornell, B., Sirri, E.R., 1992. The reaction of investors and stock prices to insider trading. Journal of Finance 47, 1031–1059.

Corwin, S.A., Lipson, M.L., 2000. Order flow and liquidity around NYSE trading halts. Journal of Finance 55, 1771–1801.

Dann, L.Y., Mayers, D., Raab Jr., R.J., 1977. Trading rules, large blocks and the speed of price adjustment. Journal of Financial Economics 4, 3–22.

Dow, J., Gorton, G., 1993. Trading, communication and the response of asset prices to news. Economic Journal 103, 639–646.

Eckbo, B.E., Maksimovic, V., Williams, J., 1990. Consistent estimation of cross-sectional models in event studies. Review of Financial Studies 3, 343–365.

Elliot, N., Katz, E., Lynch, R., 1993. The challenger tragedy: a case study in organizational communication and professional ethics. Business and Professional Ethics Journal 12, 91–108.

Fama, E.F., 1970. Efficient capital markets: a review of theory and empirical work. Journal of Finance 25, 383–417.

Fama, E.F., 1991. Efficient capital markets: II. Journal of Finance 46, 1575–1617.

Fama, E.F., 1998. Market efficiency, long-term returns, and behavioral finance. Journal of Financial Economics 49, 283–306.

Feynman, R.P., Leighton, R., 1988. What Do You Care What Other People Think?: Further Adventures of a Curious Character. W.W. Norton & Company, New York.

French, K.R., Roll, R., 1986. Stock return variances: the arrival of information and the reaction of traders. Journal of Financial Economics 17, 5–26.

Goldstein, M.A., Kavajecz, K.A., 2000. Liquidity Provision During Circuit Breakers and Extreme Market Movements. Working paper. New York Stock Exchange, New York.

Grossman, S.J., Stiglitz, J.E., 1980. On the impossibility of informationally efficient markets. American Economic Review 70, 393–408.

Hayek, F.A., 1945. The use of knowledge in society. American Economic Review 35, 519–530.

Hulburt, H.M., Miles, J.A., Woolridge, J.R., 2002. Value creation from equity carve-outs. Financial Management 31, 83–100.

Jarrell, G.A., Poulsen, A.B., 1989. Stock trading before the announcement of tender offers: insider trading or market anticipation? Journal of Law, Economics, & Organization 5, 225–248.

Karpoff, J.M., 1987. The relation between price changes and trading volume: a survey. Journal of Financial and Quantitative Analysis 22, 109–126.

Keown, A.J., Pinkerton, J.M., 1981. Merger announcements and insider trading activity: an empirical investigation. Journal of Finance 36, 855–869.

Lee, C.M.C., Mucklow. B., Ready, M.J., 1993. Spreads, depths, and the impact of earnings information: an intraday analysis. Review of Financial Studies 6, 345–374.

Lee, C.M.C., Ready, M.J., Seguin, P.J., 1994. Volume, volatility, and New York stock exchange trading halts. Journal of Finance 49, 183–214.

Lewis, R.S., 1988. Challenger: The Final Voyage. Columbia Univ. Press, New York.

Lighthall, F.F., 1991. Launching the space shuttle challenger: disciplinary deficiencies in the analysis of engineering data. IEEE Transactions on Engineering Management 38, 63–74.

MacKinlay, A.C., 1997. Event studies in economics and finance. Journal of Economic Literature 35, 13–39.

Maier, M., 1992. A Major Malfunction: The Story Behind the Space Shuttle Challenger Disaster, Research Case. SUNY, Binghamton.

Meulbroek, L., 1992. An empirical analysis of illegal insider trading. Journal of Finance 47, 1661–1699.

Meulbroek. L.K., Hart, C., 1997. The effect of illegal insider trading on takeover premia. European Finance Review 1, 51–80.

Mitchell, M.L., Maloney, M.T., 1989. Crisis in the cockpit? The role of market forces in promoting air travel safety. Journal of Law and Economics 32, 329–355.

O'Hara, M., 1999. Making market microstructure matter. Financial Management 28, 83–90.

O'Rourke, P.J., 1998. In the belly of the beast. Rolling Stone 780 (38–46), 66–67.

Prabhala, N.R., 1997. Conditional methods in event studies and an equilibrium justification for standard event-study procedures. Review of Financial Studies 10, 1–38.

Report of the Presidential Commission on the Space Shuttle Challenger Accident, 1986. USGPO. Washington, DC.

Sanders, R.W., Zdanowicz, J.S., 1992. Target firm abnormal returns and trading volume around the initiation of change in control transactions. Journal of Financial and Quantitative Analysis 27, 109–129.

Schwartz, H.S., 1987. On the psychodynamics of organizational disaster: the case of the space shuttle challenger. Columbia Journal of World Business 22, 59–67.

Shleifer. A., Vishny, R.W., 1997. The limits of arbitrage. Journal of Finance 52, 35–55.

Song, M.H., Walkling, R.A., 2000. Abnormal returns to rivals of acquisition targets: a test of the acquisition probability hypothesis. Journal of Financial Economics 55, 143–171.

Stigler, G.J., 1964. Public regulation of the securities markets. Journal of Business 37, 117–142.

Wurgler, J., Zhuravskaya, V.E., 2000. Does Arbitrage Flatten Demand Curves for Stocks? Working paper. Yale School of Management, New Haven, CT.

Review and Discussion Questions

1 Maloney and Mulherin write, "by the end of the trading day of the event, the stock market had seemingly attributed culpability for the crash to Morton Thiokol." Explain.

2 The value of Morton Thiokol's stock fell about $200 million the day of the crash. What else does the article state $200 million equaled?

3 How, according to Maloney and Mulherin, did the market know that Morton Thiokol was to blame?

4 Can you think of any other explanation for why Morton Thiokol's stock plunged but the stocks of the other shuttle contractors fell significantly less?

5 In the conclusion the authors state that the Challenger case is "pertinent to the information theory of Hayek." Why?

Suggestions for Further Reading

Ault, R. W., Ekelund, R. B., Jr., and Tollison, R. D. (1987) "The Pope and the Price of Meat: A Public Choice Perspective," *Kyklos*, 40: 399–413.

In 1966, Pope Paul VI changed a rule in the Roman Catholic Church that specified Catholics should not eat meat on most Fridays. The rule was centuries old. Why did it change in 1966? The authors explain the change as the response of the Church to incentives, specifically incentives created by prices. In the areas of the world in which the Church's membership was expanding most rapidly, fish was expensive and meat was cheap.

Gross, D. (2003) "The Disaster Market: Can Wall Street Figure Out the Cause of a Space Shuttle Crash Faster Than NASA's Experts?", htttp://slate.msn.com/id/2086811.

Another space shuttle, the Columbia, was destroyed seventeen years after the Challenger disaster studied by Maloney and Mulherin. Gross claims that, unlike the case of the Challenger, for the Columbia disaster the stock market failed to assess blame accurately.

Hahn, R. W. and Tetlock, P. C. (2005), "Using Information Markets to Improve Public Decision Making," *Harvard Journal of Law & Public Policy*, 29: 213–289.

Because markets are so efficient at compiling information, managers and other people have started using "prediction markets" to forecast uncertain values. Hahn and Tetlock briefly review the evidence on how accurate forecasts are, and they argue that such markets could be quite useful for public policy, particularly in evaluating costs and benefits of proposed policies.

Malkiel, M. G. (1989) "Is the Stock Market Efficient?" *Science*, 243 (New Series): 1313–1318.

In this classic article, Burton Malkiel reviews the evidence that the stock market is "efficient." He finds that the evidence supports efficiency, that the stock market quickly incorporates all available information. "Information contained in past prices is included in current market prices, and any publicly available fundamental information is rapidly assimilated into market prices. Prices adjust so well to reflect all important information that a randomly selected and passively managed portfolio of stocks performs as well or better than those selected by the experts" (p. 1317).

Roll, R. (1984) "Orange Juice and Weather," *American Economic Review*, 74: 861–880.

Roll shows that prices determined in a market, the orange juice futures market, can forecast Florida weather better than the U.S. Weather Service can.

PART TWO

Creating Value

Introduction

One of the biggest questions in economics is why some countries are so wealthy while others are so poor. William J. Baumol, in "Entrepreneurship: Productive, Unproductive, and Destructive," focuses on the role of incentives. Some societies provide incentives for individuals to start businesses and to create wealth; other societies provide incentives for individuals to pursue different goals. For example, ancient Roman society offered status and prestige to individuals who extracted income by taxation and military conquest. Medieval China rewarded scholars and government bureaucrats. In contrast, by the Industrial Revolution, Western European societies rewarded business activity and entrepreneurship, activities that created jobs and raised national incomes. Baumol concludes that markets, underpinned by secure property rights and governmental/institutional/social "rules of the game" that reward entrepreneurial effort, create great amounts of wealth. And the degree to which different societies have encouraged markets and business activity helps explain the differences in their economic success.

Some will wonder, however, whether economic growth won't inevitably end as we run out of nonrenewable resources. The readings by Ronald Bailey and Geoffrey Colvin give the reason why not: economic growth is not driven by how much "stuff" the economy produces, it is driven by the stuff's *value*. As illustrated by the high value-to-weight ratio of semiconductor chips—for a chip in 2000, nearly $43,000 per pound— today's economy produces items that embody tremendous intelligence but that use very little raw material. (Compared to 1900 the weight of our total output is about the same, while the value of output per person is about five times higher.) Further, good ideas, commercialized via markets, help us substitute away from scarce natural resources: copper wire is replaced by e-mail and fiber optic cable; the amount of land used to grow food is sharply reduced because of productivity improvements; and clean, abundant natural gas is substituted for wood. Bailey and Colvin conclude human creativity—ideas—plus the power of markets are vital to creating wealth. As long as ideas don't run out, economic growth can continue indefinitely.

Creativity also means that we will probably never run of jobs. While international trade can destroy jobs, Russell Roberts points out that trade, in combination with markets, tends to create an equal or greater number of jobs. It can be quite difficult to predict where the new jobs will come from, but Roberts states that they will indeed arise: "Imagine being told a decade ago that some people would make their living writing software for iTunes at Apple. What's iTunes? Oh, it's a place where people download music into their iPods. What is downloading music?"

W. Michael Cox and Richard Alm make an important point about the usual measure of economic activity, GNP. While GNP is useful, it was never intended to be a complete measure of how well we are living. GNP does not include the value of leisure time; it imperfectly reflects the better quality of products and improvements in product selection; and it doesn't encompass improvements in health, safety, and longevity. Cox and Alm go beyond the usual presentation of dry per capita income and GNP statistics: they discuss how much bigger houses are, how many more families have multiple cars, and how many more have boats, cable TV, and golf club memberships. The GNP (now GDP) measure should be supplemented by other measures if we want a more accurate picture of our standard of living.

Chapter 6

William J. Baumol

ENTREPRENEURSHIP: PRODUCTIVE, UNPRODUCTIVE, AND DESTRUCTIVE[1]

It is often assumed that an economy of private enterprise has an automatic bias towards innovation, but this is not so. It has a bias only towards profit.

(Hobsbawm 1969, p. 40)

WHEN CONJECTURES ARE OFFERED to explain historic slowdowns or great reaps in economic growth, there is the group of usual suspects that is regularly rounded up—prominent among them, the entrepreneur. Where growth has slowed, it is implied that a decline in entrepreneurship was partly to blame (perhaps because the culture's "need for achievement" has atrophied). At another time and place, it is said, the flowering of entrepreneurship accounts for unprecedented expansion.

This paper proposes a rather different set of hypotheses, holding that entrepreneurs are always with us and always play *some* substantial role. But there are a variety of roles among which the entrepreneur's efforts can be reallocated, and some of those roles do not follow the constructive and innovative script that is conventionally attributed to that person. Indeed, at times the entrepreneur may even lead a parasitical existence that is actually damaging to the economy. How the entrepreneur acts at a given time and place depends heavily on the rules of the game—the reward structure in the economy—that happen to prevail. Thus the central hypothesis here is that it is the set of rules and not the supply of entrepreneurs *or the nature of their objectives* that undergoes significant changes from one period to another and helps to dictate the ultimate effect on the economy via the *allocation* of entrepreneurial resources. Changes in the rules and other attendant circumstances can, of course, modify the composition of the class of entrepreneurs and can also alter its size. Without denying this or claiming that it has no significance, in this paper I shall seek to focus attention on the allocation of the changing class of entrepreneurs rather than its magnitude and makeup. (For an excellent analysis of the basic hypothesis, independently derived, see Murphy, Shleifer, and Vishny [1990].)

The basic proposition, if sustained by the evidence, has an important implication for growth policy. The notion that our productivity problems reside in "the spirit of entrepreneurship" that waxes and wanes for unexplained reasons is a counsel of despair, for it gives no guidance on how to reawaken that spirit once it has lagged. If that is the task assigned to policymakers, they are destitute: they have no means of knowing how to carry it out. But if what is required is the adjustment of rules of the game to induce a more felicitous allocation of entrepreneurial resources, then the policymaker's task is less formidable, and it is certainly not hopeless. The prevailing rules that affect the allocation of entrepreneurial activity can be observed, described, and, with luck, modified and improved, as will be illustrated here.

Here, extensive historical illustrations will be cited to impart plausibility to the contentions that have just been described. Then a short discussion of some current issues involving the allocation of entrepreneurship between productive and unproductive activities will be offered. Finally, I shall consider very briefly the means that can be used to change the rules of the game, and to do so in a manner that stimulates the productive contribution of the entrepreneur.

On the historical character of the evidence

Given the inescapable problems for empirical as well as theoretical study of entrepreneurship, what sort of evidence can one hope to provide? Since the rules of the game usually change very slowly, a case study approach to investigation of my hypotheses drives me unavoidably to examples spanning considerable periods of history and encompassing widely different cultures and geographic locations. Here I shall proceed on the basis of historical illustrations encompassing all the main economic periods and places (ancient Rome, medieval China, Dark Age Europe, the Later Middle Ages, etc.) that the economic historians almost universally single out for the light they shed on the process of innovation and its diffusion. These will be used to show that the relative rewards to different types of entrepreneurial activity have in fact varied dramatically from one time and place to another and that this seems to have had profound effects on patterns of entrepreneurial behavior. Finally, evidence will be offered *suggesting* that such reallocations can have a considerable influence on the prosperity and growth of an economy, though other variables undoubtedly also play substantial roles.

None of this can, of course, be considered conclusive. Yet, it is surely a standard tenet of scientific method that tentative confirmation of a hypothesis is provided by observation of phenomena that the hypothesis helps to explain and that could not easily be accounted for if that hypothesis were invalid. It is on this sort of reasoning that I hope to rest my case. Historians have long been puzzled, for example, by the failure of the society of ancient Rome to disseminate and put into widespread practical use some of the sophisticated technological developments that we know to have been in its possession, while in the "High Middle Ages," a period in which progress and change were hardly popular notions, inventions that languished in Rome seem to have spread like wildfire. It will be argued that the hypothesis about the allocability of entrepreneurial effort between productive and unproductive activity helps considerably to account for this phenomenon, though it certainly will *not* be claimed that this is all there was to the matter.

Before I get to the substance of the discussion, it is important to emphasize that nothing that follows in this article makes any pretense of constituting a contribution to economic history. Certainly it is not intended here to try to explain any particular historical event. Moreover, the analysis relies entirely on secondary sources, and all the historical developments described are well known to historians, as the citations will indicate. Whatever the contribution that may be offered by the following pages, then, it is confined to enhanced understanding and extension of the (nonmathematical) theory of entrepreneurship in general, and not to an improved analysis of the historical events that are cited.

The Schumpeterian model extended: allocation of entrepreneurship

The analysis of this paper rests on what seems to be the one theoretical model that effectively encompasses the role of the entrepreneur and that really "works," in the sense that it constitutes the basis for a number of substantive inferences.[2] This is, of course, the well-known Schumpeterian analysis, whose main shortcoming, for our purposes, is the paucity of insights on policy that emerge from it. It will be suggested here that only a minor extension of that model to encompass the *allocation* of entrepreneurship is required to enhance its power substantially in this direction.

Schumpeter tells us that innovations (he calls them "the carrying out of new combinations") take various forms besides mere improvements in technology:

> This concept covers the following five cases: (1) the introduction of a new good—that is one with which consumers are not yet familiar—or of a new quality of a good. (2) The introduction of a new method of production, that is one not yet tested by experience in the branch of manufacture concerned, which need by no means be founded upon a discovery scientifically new, and can also exist in a new way of handling a commodity commercially. (3) The opening of a new market, that is a market into which the particular branch of manufacture of the country in question has not previously entered, whether or not this market has existed before. (4) The conquest of a new source of supply of raw materials or half-manufactured goods, again irrespective of whether this source already exists or whether it has first to be created. (5) The carrying out of the new organization of any industry, like the creation of a monopoly position (for example through trustification) or the breaking up of a monopoly position.
>
> ((1912) 1934, p. 60)

The obvious fact that entrepreneurs undertake such a variety of tasks all at once suggests that theory can usefully undertake to consider what determines the *allocation* of entrepreneurial inputs among those tasks. Just as the literature traditionally studies the allocation of other inputs, for example, capital resources, among the various industries that compete for them, it seems natural to ask what influences the flow of entrepreneurial talent among the various activities in Schumpeter's list.

Presumably the reason no such line of inquiry was pursued by Schumpeter or his successors is that any analysis of the allocation of entrepreneurial resources among the five items in the preceding list (with the exception of the last—the creation or destruction of a monopoly) does not promise to yield any profound conclusions. There is no obvious reason to make much of a shift of entrepreneurial activity away from, say, improvement in the production process and toward the introduction of new products. The general implications, if any, for the public welfare, for productivity growth, and for other related matters are hardly obvious.

To derive more substantive results from an analysis of the allocation of entrepreneurial resources, it is necessary to expand Schumpeter's list, whose main deficiency seems to be that it does not go far enough. For example, it does not explicitly encompass innovative acts of technology transfer that take advantage of opportunities to introduce already-available technology (usually with some modification to adapt it to local conditions) to geographic locales whose suitability for the purpose had previously gone unrecognized or at least unused.

Most important for the discussion here, Schumpeter's list of entrepreneurial activities can usefully be expanded to include such items as innovations in rent-seeking procedures, for example, discovery of a previously unused legal gambit that is effective in diverting rents to those who are first in exploiting it. It may seem strange at first blush to propose inclusion of activities of such questionable value to society (I shall call them acts of "unproductive entrepreneurship") in the list of Schumpeterian innovations (though the creation of a monopoly, which Schumpeter does include as an innovation, is surely as questionable), but, as will soon be seen, this is a crucial step for the analysis that follows. If entrepreneurs are defined, simply, to be persons who are ingenious and creative in finding ways that add to their own wealth, power, and prestige, then it is to be expected that not all of them will be overly concerned with whether an activity that achieves these goals adds much or little to the social product or, for that matter, even whether it is an actual impediment to production (this notion goes back, at least, to Veblen [1904]). Suppose that it turns out, in addition, that at any time and place the magnitude of the benefit the economy derives from its entrepreneurial talents depends *substantially*, among other variables, on the allocation of this resource between productive and unproductive entrepreneurial activities of the sorts just described. Then the reasons for including acts of the latter type in the list of entrepreneurial activities become clear.

Here no exhaustive analysis of the process of allocation of entrepreneurial activity among the set of available options will be attempted. Rather, it will be argued only that at least *one* of the prime determinants of entrepreneurial behavior at any particular time and place is the prevailing rules of the game that govern the payoff of one entrepreneurial activity relative to another. If the rules are such as to impede the earning of much wealth via activity A, or are such as to impose social disgrace on those who engage in it, then, other things being equal, entrepreneurs' efforts will tend to be channeled to other activities, call them B. But if B contributes less to production or welfare than A, the consequences for society may be considerable.[3]

As a last preliminary note, it should be emphasized that the set of active entrepreneurs may be subject to change. Thus if the rules of the game begin to favor B over A, it may not be just the same individuals who switch their activities from entrepreneurship of type A to that of type B. Rather, some persons with talents suited for A may simply drop out of the picture, and individuals with abilities adapted to B may for the first time become entrepreneurs. Thus the allocation of entrepreneurs among activities is perhaps best described in the way Joan Robinson (following Shove's suggestion) analyzed the allocation of heterogeneous land resources (1933, chap. 8): as the solution of a jigsaw puzzle in which the pieces are each fitted into the places selected for them by the concatenation of pertinent circumstances.

Entrepreneurship, productive and unproductive: the rules do change

Let us now turn to the central hypothesis of this paper: that the exercise of entrepreneurship can sometimes be unproductive or even destructive, and that whether it takes one of these directions or one that is more benign depends heavily on the structure of payoffs in the economy—the rules of the game. The rather dramatic illustrations provided by world history seem to confirm quite emphatically the following proposition.

PROPOSITION 1. The rules of the game that determine the relative payoffs to different entrepreneurial activities *do* change dramatically from one time and place to another.

These examples also suggest strongly (but hardly "prove") the following proposition.

PROPOSITION 2. Entrepreneurial behavior changes direction from one economy to another in a manner that corresponds to the variations in the rules of the game.

Ancient Rome

The avenues open to those Romans who sought power, prestige, and wealth are instructive. First, it may be noted that they had no reservations about the desirability of wealth or about its pursuit (e.g., Finley 1985, pp. 53–57). *As long as it did not involve participation in industry or commerce*, there was nothing degrading about the wealth acquisition process. Persons of honorable status had three primary and acceptable sources of income: landholding (not infrequently as absentee landlords), "usury," and what may be described as "political payments":

> The opportunity for "political moneymaking" can hardly be over-estimated. Money poured in from booty, indemnities, provincial taxes, loans and miscellaneous extractions in quantities without precedent in Graeco-Roman history, and at an accelerating rate. The public treasury benefited, but probably more remained in private hands, among the nobles in the first instance; then, in appropriately decreasing proportions, among the *equites*, the soldiers and even the plebs of the city of Rome. ... Nevertheless, the whole phenomenon is misunderstood when it is classified under the headings of "corruption" and "malpractice", as historians still persist in doing. Cicero was an

honest governor of Cilicia in 51 and 50 B.C., so that at the end of his term he had earned only the legitimate profits of office. They amounted to 2,200,000 sesterces, more than treble the figure of 600,000 he himself once mentioned (*Stoic Paradoxes* 49) to illustrate an annual income that could permit a life of luxury. We are faced with something structural in the society.

(Finley 1985, p. 55)

Who, then, operated commerce and industry? According to Veyne (1961), it was an occupation heavily undertaken by freedmen—former slaves who, incidentally, bore a social stigma for life. Indeed, according to this writer, slavery may have represented the one avenue for advancement for someone from the lower classes. A clever (and handsome) member of the lower orders might deliberately arrange to be sold into slavery to a wealthy and powerful master.[4] Then, with luck, skill, and drive, he would grow close to his owner, perhaps managing his financial affairs (and sometimes engaging in some homosexual activity with him). The master then gained cachet, after a suitable period, by granting freedom to the slave, setting him up with a fortune of his own. The freedmen, apparently not atypically, invested their financial stakes in commerce, hoping to multiply them sufficiently to enable them to retire in style to the countryside, thereafter investing primarily in land and loans in imitation of the upper classes.

Finally, regarding the Romans' attitude to the promotion of technology and productivity, Finley makes much of the "clear, almost total, divorce between science and practice" (1965, p. 32). He goes on to cite Vitruvius's monumental work on architecture and technology, in whose 10 books he finds only a single and trivial reference to means of saving effort and increasing productivity. Finley then reports the following story:

There is a story, repeated by a number of Roman writers, that a man—characteristically unnamed—invented unbreakable glass and demonstrated it to Tiberius in anticipation of a great reward. The emperor asked the inventor whether anyone shared his secret and was assured that there was no one else; whereupon his head was promptly removed, lest, said Tiberius, gold be reduced to the value of mud. I have no opinion about the truth of this story, and it is only a story. But is it not interesting that neither the elder Pliny nor Petronius nor the historian Dio Cassius was troubled by the point that the inventor turned to the emperor for a reward, instead of turning to an investor for capital with which to put his invention into production?[5] ... We must remind ourselves time and again that the European experience since the late Middle Ages in technology, in the economy, and in the value systems that accompanied them, was unique in human history until the recent export trend commenced. Technical progress, economic growth, productivity, even efficiency have not been significant goals since the beginning of time. So long as an acceptable life-style could be maintained, however that was defined, other values held the stage.

(1985, p. 147)

The bottom line, for our purposes, is that the Roman reward system, although it offered wealth to those who engaged in commerce and industry, offset this gain through the attendant loss in prestige. Economic effort "was neither the way to wealth nor its purpose. Cato's gods showed him a number of ways to get more; but they were all political and parasitical, the ways of conquest and booty and usury; labour was not one of them, not even the labour of the entrepreneur" (Finley 1965, p. 39).

Medieval China

In China, as in many kingdoms of Europe before the guarantees of the Magna Carta and the revival of towns and their acquisition of privileges, the monarch commonly claimed possession of all property in his territories. As a result, particularly in China, when the sovereign was in financial straits, confiscation of the property of wealthy subjects was entirely in order. It has been claimed that this led those who had resources to avoid investing them in any sort of visible capital stocks, and that this, in turn, was a substantial impediment to economic expansion (see Balazs 1964, p. 53; Landes 1969, pp. 46–47; Rosenberg and Birdzell 1986, pp. 119–20; Jones 1987, chap. 5).

In addition, imperial China reserved its most substantial rewards in wealth and prestige for those who climbed the ladder of imperial examinations, which were heavily devoted to subjects such as Confucian philosophy and calligraphy. Successful candidates were often awarded high rank in the bureaucracy, high social standing denied to anyone engaged in commerce or industry, even to those who gained great wealth in the process (and who often used their resources to prepare their descendants to contend via the examinations for a position in the scholar bureaucracy). In other words, the rules of the game seem to have been heavily biased against the acquisition of wealth *and position* through Schumpeterian behavior. The avenue to success lay elsewhere.

Because of the difficulty of the examinations, the mandarins (scholar-officials) rarely succeeded in keeping such positions in their own families for more than two or three generations (see Marsh 1961, p. 159; Ho 1962, chap. 4 and appendix). The scholar families devoted enormous effort and considerable resources to preparing their children through years of laborious study for the imperial examinations, which, during the Sung dynasty, were held every 3 years, and only several hundred persons in all of China succeeded in passing them each time (E. A. Kracke, Jr. in Liu and Golas [1969, p. 14]). Yet, regularly, some persons not from mandarin families also attained success through this avenue (see, e.g., Marsh [1961] and Ho [1962] for evidence on social mobility in imperial China).

Wealth was in prospect for those who passed the examination and who were subsequently appointed to government positions. But the sources of their earnings had something in common with those of the Romans:

> Corruption, which is widespread in all impoverished and backward countries (or, more exactly, throughout the pre-industrial world), was endemic in a country where the servants of the state often had nothing to live on but their very meager salaries. The required attitude of obedience to superiors made it impossible for officials to demand higher salaries, and in the absence of any control over their activities from below it was inevitable that they should purloin from society what the state failed to provide. According to the usual pattern, a Chinese official entered upon his duties only after spending long years in study and passing many examinations; he

then established relations with protectors, incurred debts to get himself appointed, and then proceeded to extract the amount he had spent on preparing himself for his career from the people he administered—and extracted both principal and interest. The degree of his rapacity would be dictated not only by the length of time he had had to wait for his appointment and the number of relations he had to support and of kin to satisfy or repay, but also by the precariousness of his position.

(Balazs 1964, p. 10)

Enterprise, on the other hand, was not only frowned on, but may have been subjected to impediments deliberately imposed by the officials, at least after the fourteenth century A.D.; and some historians claim that it was true much earlier. Balazs tells us of

the state's tendency to clamp down immediately on any form of private enterprise (and this in the long run kills not only initiative but even the slightest attempts at innovation), or, if it did not succeed in putting a stop to it in time, to take over and nationalize it. Did it not frequently happen during the course of Chinese history that the scholar-officials, although hostile to all inventions, nevertheless gathered in the fruits of other people's ingenuity? I need mention only three examples of inventions that met this fate: paper, invented by a eunuch; printing, used by the Buddhists as a medium for religious propaganda; and the bill of exchange, an expedient of private businessmen.

(p. 18)

As a result of recurrent intervention by the state to curtail the liberty and take over any accumulated advantages the merchant class had managed to gain for itself, "the merchant's ambition turned to becoming a scholar-official and investing his profits in land" (p. 32).

The Earlier Middle Ages

Before the rise of the cities and before monarchs were able to subdue the bellicose activities of the nobility, wealth and power were pursued primarily through military activity. Since land and castles were the medieval forms of wealth most highly valued and most avidly sought after, it seems reasonable to interpret the warring of the barons in good part as the pursuit of an economic objective. For example, during the reign of William the Conqueror (see, e.g., Douglas 1964), there were frequent attempts by the barons in Normandy and neighboring portions of France to take over each other's lands and castles. A prime incentive for William's supporters in his conquest of England was their obvious aspiration for lands.[6] More than that, violent means also served to provide more liquid forms of income (captured treasure), which the nobility used to support both private consumption and investment in military plant and equipment, where such items could not easily be produced on their own lands and therefore had to be purchased from others. In England, with its institution of primogeniture (the exclusive right of the eldest son to inherit his father's estate), younger sons who chose not to enter the clergy often had no socially acceptable choice other than warfare as a means to make their fortunes, and in some cases they succeeded spectacularly. Thus note the case of William Marshal, fourth son of a minor noble, who rose through his military accomplishments to be one of the most powerful and trusted officials under Henry II and Richard I, and became one of the wealthiest men in England (see Painter 1933).

Of course, the medieval nobles were not purely economic men. Many of the turbulent barons undoubtedly enjoyed fighting for its own sake, and success in combat was an important avenue to prestige in their society. But no modern capitalist is a purely economic man either. What I am saying here is that warfare, which was of course pursued for a variety of reasons, was *also* undertaken as a primary source of economic gain. This is clearly all the more true of the mercenary armies that were the scourge of fourteenth-century France and Italy.

Such violent economic activity, moreover, inspired frequent and profound innovation. The introduction of the stirrup was a requisite for effective cavalry tactics. Castle building evolved from wooden to stone structures and from rectangular to round towers (which could not be made to collapse by undermining their corners). Armor and weaponry became much more sophisticated with the introduction of the crossbow, the longbow, and, ultimately, artillery based on gunpowder. Military tactics and strategy also grew in sophistication. These innovations can be interpreted as contributions of military entrepreneurs undertaken at least partly in pursuit of private economic gains.

This type of entrepreneurial undertaking obviously differs vastly from the introduction of a cost-saving industrial process or a valuable new consumer product. An individual who pursues wealth through the forcible appropriation of the possessions of others surely does not add to the national product. Its net effect may be not merely a transfer but a net reduction in social income and wealth.[7]

The Later Middle Ages

By the end of the eleventh century the rules of the game had changed from those of the Dark Ages. The revival of the towns was well under way. They had acquired a number of privileges, among them protection from arbitrary taxation and confiscation and the creation of a labor force by granting freedom to runaway serfs after a relatively brief residence (a year and a day) in the towns. The free-enterprise turbulence of the barons had at least been impeded by the church's pacification efforts: the peace and the (later) truce of God in France, Spain, and elsewhere; similar changes were taking place in England (see, e.g., Cowdrey [1970]; but Jones [1987, p. 94] suggests that some free-enterprise military activity by the barons continued in England through the reigns of the earlier Tudors in the sixteenth century). All this subsequently "gave way to more developed efforts to enforce peace by the more organized governments of the twelfth century" (Brooke 1964, p. 350; also p. 127). A number of activities that were neither agricultural nor military began to yield handsome returns. For example, the small group of architect-engineers who were in charge of the building of cathedrals, palaces, bridges, and fortresses could live in great luxury in the service of their kings.

But, apparently, a far more common source of earnings was the water-driven mills that were strikingly common in France and southern England by the eleventh century, a technological innovation about which more will be said presently. An incentive for such technical advances may have been the monopoly they conferred on their owners rather than any resulting improvement in efficiency. Such monopoly rights were alike sought and enforced by private parties (Bloch 1935, pp. 554–57; Brooke 1964, p. 84) and by religious organizations (see over).

The economic role of the monks in this is somewhat puzzling—the least clear-cut part of our story.[8] The Cistercian abbeys are generally assigned a critical role in the promotion of such technological advances. In some cases they simply took over mills that had been constructed by others (Berman 1986, p. 89). But the Cistercians improved them, built many others, and vastly expanded their use; at least some writers (e.g., Gimpel 1976, pp. 3–6) seem to suggest that the Cistercians were the spearhead of technological advance.

Historians tell us that they have no ready explanation for the entrepreneurial propensities of this monastic order. (See, e.g., Brooke [1964, p. 69] and also a personal communication to me from Constance Berman. Ovitt [1987, esp. pp. 142–47] suggests that this may all have been part of the twelfth-century monastic drive to reduce or eliminate manual labor in order to maximize the time available for the less onerous religious labors—a conclusion with which Bloch [1935, p. 553] concurs.) But the evidence suggests strongly that avid entrepreneurs they were. They accumulated vast tracts of land; the sizes of their domesticated animal flocks were enormous by the standards of the time; their investment rates were remarkable; they sought to exercise monopoly power, being known, after the erection of a water mill, to seek legal intervention to prevent nearby residents from continuing to use their animal-powered facilities (Gimpel 1976, pp. 15–16); they were fierce in their rivalrous behavior and drive for expansion, in the process not sparing other religious bodies—not even other Cistercian houses. There is a "record of pastoral expansionism and monopolies over access established by the wealthiest Cistercian houses ... at the expense of smaller abbeys and convents ... effectively pushing out all other religious houses as competitors" (Berman 1986, p. 112).

As with early capitalists, the asceticism of the monks, by keeping down the proportion of the monastery's output that was consumed, helped to provide the resources for levels of investment extraordinary for the period (pp. 40, 83). The rules of the game appear to have offered substantial economic rewards to exercise of Cistercian entrepreneurship. The order obtained relatively few large gifts, but instead frequently received support from the laity and from the church establishment in the form of exemptions from road and river tolls and from payment of the tithe. This obviously increased the *marginal* yield of investment, innovation, and expenditure of effort, and the evidence suggests the diligence of the order in pursuing the resulting opportunities. Their mills, their extensive lands, and their large flocks are reported to have brought scale economies and extraordinary financial returns (chap. 4). Puritanical, at least in earlier years, in their self-proclaimed adherence to simplicity in personal lifestyle while engaged in dedicated pursuit of wealth, they may perhaps represent an early manifestation of elements of "the Protestant ethic." But whatever their motive, the reported Cistercian record of promotion of technological progress is in diametric contrast to that of the Roman empire.

Fourteenth century

The fourteenth century brought with it a considerable increase in military activity, notably the Hundred Years' War between France and England. Payoffs, surely, must have tilted to favor more than before inventions designed for military purposes. Cannons appeared as siege devices and armor was made heavier. More imaginative war devices were proposed: a wind mill-propelled war wagon, a multibarreled machine gun, and a diving suit to permit underwater attacks on ships. A pervasive business enterprise of this unhappy century of war was the company of mercenary troops—the *condottiere*—who roamed Europe, supported the side that could offer the most attractive terms, and in lulls between fighting, when unemployment threatened, wandered about thinking up military enterprises of their own, at the expense of the general public (Gimpel 1976, chap. 9; see also McNeill 1969, pp. 33–39). Clearly, the rules of the game—the system of entrepreneurial rewards—had changed, to the disadvantage of productive entrepreneurship.

Early rent seeking

Unproductive entrepreneurship can also take less violent forms, usually involving various types of rent seeking, the type of (possibly) unproductive entrepreneurship that seems most relevant today. Enterprising use of the legal system for rent-seeking purposes has a long history. There are, for example, records of the use of litigation in the twelfth century in which the proprietor of a water-driven mill sought and won a prohibition of use in the vicinity of mills driven by animal or human power (Gimpel 1976, pp. 25–26). In another case, the operators of two dams, one upstream of the other, sued one another repeatedly at least from the second half of the thirteenth century until the beginning of the fifteenth, when the downstream dam finally succeeded in driving the other out of business as the latter ran out of money to pay the court fees (pp. 17–20).

In the upper strata of society, rent seeking also gradually replaced military activity as a prime source of wealth and power. This transition can perhaps be ascribed to the triumph of the monarchies and the consequent imposition of law and order. Rent-seeking entrepreneurship then took a variety of forms, notably the quest for grants of land and patents of monopoly from the monarch. Such activities can, of course, sometimes prove to contribute to production, as when the recipient of land given by the monarch uses it more efficiently than the previous owner did. But there seems to have been nothing in the structure of the land-granting process that ensured even a tendency toward transfer to more productive proprietors, nor was the individual who sought such grants likely to use as an argument in favor of his suit the claim that he was likely to be the more productive user (in terms of, say, the expected net value of its agricultural output).

Military forms of entrepreneurship may have experienced a renaissance in England in the seventeenth century with the revolt against Charles I. How that may have changed the structure of rewards to entrepreneurial activity is suggested by Hobsbawm (1969), who claims that at the end of the seventeenth century the most affluent merchants earned perhaps three times as much as the richest "master manufacturers."[9] But, he reports, the wealthiest noble families probably had incomes more than 10 times as large as those of the rich merchants. The point in this is that those noble families, according to Hobsbawm, were no holdovers from an ancient feudal aristocracy; they were, rather, the heirs of the Roundheads (the supporters of the parliamentary, or puritan, party) in the then-recent Civil War (pp. 30–32). On this view, once again, military activity would seem to have become the entrepreneur's most promising recourse.

But other historians take a rather different view of the matter. Studies reported in Thirsk (1954) indicate that ultimately there was little redistribution of property as the result of the Civil War and the restoration. Rather it is noted that in this period the "patrician élites depended for their political power and economic prosperity on royal charters and monopolies rather than on talent and entrepreneurial initiative" (Stone 1985, p. 45). In this interpretation of the matter, it was rent seeking, not military activity, that remained the prime source of wealth under the restoration.

By the time the eighteenth-century industrial revolution ("the" industrial revolution) arrived, matters had changed once again. According to Ashton (1948, pp. 9–10), grants of monopoly were in good part "swept away" by the Monopolies Act of 1624, and, we are told by Adam Smith (1776), by the end of the eighteenth century they were rarer in England than in any other country. Though industrial activity continued to be considered somewhat degrading in places in which industry flourished, notably in England during the industrial revolution there was probably a difference in degree. Thus Lefebvre (1947, p. 14) reports that "at its upper level the [French] nobility ... were envious of the English lords who enriched themselves in bourgeois ways," while in France "the noble 'derogated' or fell into the common mass if [like Mirabeau] he followed a business or profession" (p. 11). (See, however, Schama [1989], who tells us that "even a cursory examination of the eighteenth-century French economy ... reveals the nobility deeply involved in finance, business and industry—certainly as much as their British counterparts. ... In 1765 a royal edict officially removed the last formal obstacles to their participation in trade and industry" [p. 118].) In England, primogeniture, by forcing younger sons of noble families to resort to commerce and industry, apparently was imparting respectability to these activities to a degree that, while rather limited, may have rarely been paralleled before.

The central point of all the preceding discussion seems clear—perhaps, in retrospect, self-evident. If entrepreneurship is the imaginative pursuit of position, with limited concern about the means used to achieve the purpose, then we can expect changes in the structure of rewards to modify the nature of the entrepreneur's activities, sometimes drastically. The rules of the game can then be a critical influence helping to determine whether entrepreneurship will be allocated predominantly to activities that are productive or unproductive and even destructive.

Does the allocation between productive and unproductive entrepreneurship matter much?

We come now to the third proposition of this article.

Proposition 3. The allocation of entrepreneurship between productive and unproductive activities, though by no means the only pertinent influence, can have a profound effect on the innovativeness of the economy and the degree of dissemination of its technological discoveries.

It is hard to believe that a system of payoffs that moves entrepreneurship in unproductive directions is not a substantial impediment to industrial innovation and growth in productivity. Still, history permits no test of this proposition through a set of anything resembling controlled experiments, since other influences *did*, undoubtedly, also play important roles, as the proposition recognizes. One can only note what appears to be a remarkable correlation between the degree to which an economy rewarded productive entrepreneurship and the vigor shown in that economy's innovation record.

Historians tell us of several industrial "near revolutions" that occurred before *the* industrial revolution of the eighteenth century that are highly suggestive for our purposes (Braudel [1986, 3:542–56]; for a more skeptical view, see Coleman [1956]). We are told that two of the incipient revolutions never went anywhere, while two of them were rather successful in their fashion. I shall report conclusions of some leading historians on these episodes, but it should be recognized by the reader that many of the views summarized here have been disputed in the historical literature, at least to some degree.

Rome and Hellenistic Egypt

My earlier discussion cited ancient Rome and its empire as a case in which the rules did not favor productive entrepreneurship. Let us compare this with, the evidence on the vigor of innovative activity in that society. The museum at Alexandria was the center of technological innovation in the Roman empire. By the first century B.C., that city knew of virtually every form of machine gearing that is used today, including a working steam engine. But these seem to have been used only to make what amounted to elaborate toys. The steam engine was used only to open and close the doors of a temple.

The Romans also had the water mill. This may well have been the most critical pre-eighteenth-century industrial invention because (outside the use of sails in transportation by water) it provided the first significant source of power other than human and animal labor: "it was able to produce an amount of concentrated energy beyond any other resource of antiquity" (Forbes 1955, 2:90). As steam did in more recent centuries, it offered the prospect of providing the basis for a leap in productivity in the Roman economy, as apparently it actually did during the eleventh, twelfth, and thirteenth centuries in Europe. Yet Finley (1965, pp. 35–36), citing White (1962), reports that "though it was invented in the first century B.C., is was not until the third century A.D. that we find evidence of much use, and not until the fifth and sixth of general use. It is also a fact that we have no evidence at all of its application to other industries [i.e., other than grinding of grain] until the very end of the fourth century, and then no more than one solitary and possibly suspect reference … to a marble-slicing machine near Trier."

Unfortunately, evidence of Roman technical stagnation is only spotty, and, further, some historians suggest that the historical reports give inadequate weight to the Roman preoccupation with agricultural improvement relative to improvement in commerce or manufacture. Still, the following quotation seems to summarize the weight of opinion: "Historians have long been puzzled as to why the landlords of the Middle Ages proved so much more enterprising than the landlords of the Roman Empire, although the latter, by and large, were much better educated, had much better opportunities for making technical and scientific discoveries if they had wished to do so" (Brooke 1964, p. 88). It seems at least plausible that some part of the explanation is to be found in the ancient world's rules of the game, which encouraged the pursuit of wealth but severely discouraged its pursuit through the exercise of productive entrepreneurship.[10]

Medieval China

The spate of inventions that occurred in ancient China (before it was conquered by the barbarian Yuan dynasty in 1280) constituted one of the earliest potential revolutions in industry. Among the many Chinese technological contributions, one can list paper, (perhaps) the compass, waterwheels, sophisticated water clocks, and, of course, gunpowder. Yet despite the apparent prosperity of the Sung period (960–1270) (see, e.g., Liu and Golas 1969), at least some historians suggest that none of this spate of inventions led to a flowering of *industry*[11] as distinguished from commerce and some degree of general prosperity. And in China too, as we have seen, the rules did not favor productive entrepreneurship. Balazs (1964, p. 53) concludes that

> what was chiefly lacking in China for the further development of capitalism was not mechanical skill or scientific aptitude, nor a sufficient accumulation of wealth, but scope for individual enterprise. There was no individual freedom and no security for private enterprise, no legal foundation for rights other than those of the state, no alternative investment other than landed property, no guarantee against being penalized by arbitrary exactions from officials or against intervention by the state. But perhaps the supreme inhibiting factor was the overwhelming prestige of the state bureaucracy, which maimed from the start any attempt of the bourgeoisie to be different, to become aware of themselves as a class and fight for an autonomous position in society. Free enterprise, ready and proud to take risks, is therefore quite exceptional and abnormal in Chinese economic history.

Slow growth in the "Dark Ages"

An era noted for its slow growth occurred between the death of Charlemagne (814) and the end of the tenth century. Even this period was not without its economic advances, which developed slowly, including the beginnings of the agricultural improvements that attended the introduction of the horseshoe, harness, and stirrup, the heavy plow, and the substitution of horsepower for oxen, which may have played a role in enabling peasants to move to more populous villages further from their fields (see White 1962, p. 39 ff.). But, still, it was probably a period of significantly slower growth than the industrial revolution of the eleventh–thirteenth centuries (Gimpel 1976), about which more will be said presently. We have already seen that this was a period in which military violence was a prime outlet for entrepreneurial activity. While this can hardly pretend to be *the* explanation of the relative stagnation of the era, it is hard to believe that it was totally unimportant.

The "High Middle Ages"

A good deal has already been said about the successful industrial revolution (and the accompanying commercial revolution sparked by inventions such as double-entry bookkeeping and bills of exchange [de Roover 1953]) of the late Middle Ages, whose two-century duration makes it as long-lived as our own (see Carus-Wilson 1941; White 1962; Gimpel 1976).

Perhaps the hallmark of this industrial revolution was that remarkable source of productive power, the water mills, that covered the countryside in the south of England and crowded the banks of the Seine in Paris (see, e.g., Gimpel 1976, pp. 3–6; Berman 1986, pp. 81–89). The mills were not only simple grain-grinding devices but accomplished an astonishing variety of tasks and involved an impressive variety of mechanical devices and sophisticated gear arrangements. They crushed olives, ground mash for beer production, crushed cloth for papermaking, sawed lumber, hammered metal and woolens (as part of the "fulling" process—the cleansing, scouring, and pressing of woven woolen goods to make them stronger and to bring the threads closer together), milled coins, polished armor, and operated the bellows of blast furnaces. Their mechanisms entailed many forms of ingenuity. Gears were used to translate the vertical circular motion of the efficient form of the waterwheel into the horizontal circular motion of the millstone. The cam (a piece attached, say, to the axle of the waterwheel, protruding from the axle at right angles to its axis of rotation) served to lift a hammer and to drop it repeatedly and automatically (it was apparently known in antiquity, but may not have been used with waterwheels). A crank handle extending from the end of the axle transformed the circular motion of the wheel into the back and forth (reciprocating) motion required for sawing or the operation of bellows. The most sophisticated product of all this mechanical skill and knowledge was the mechanical clock, which appeared toward the end of the thirteenth century. As White (1962, p. 129) sums up the matter, "the four centuries following Leonardo, that is, until electrical energy demanded a supplementary set of devices, were less technologically engaged in discovering basic principles than in elaborating and refining those established during the four centuries before Leonardo."[12]

In a period in which agriculture probably occupied some 90 percent of the population, the expansion of industry in the twelfth and thirteenth centuries could not by itself have created a major upheaval in living standards.[13] Moreover, it has been deduced from what little we know of European gross domestic product per capita at the beginning of the eighteenth century that its average growth in the preceding six or seven centuries must have been very modest, since if the poverty of that later time had represented substantial growth from eleventh-century living standards, much of the earlier population would surely have been condemned to starvation.

Still, the industrial activity of the twelfth and thirteenth centuries was very substantial. By the beginning of the fourteenth century, according to Gimpel (1976), 68 mills were in operation on less than one mile of the banks of the Seine in Paris, and these were supplemented by floating mills anchored to the Grand Pont. The activity in metallurgy was also considerable—sufficient to denude much of Europe of its forests and to produce a rise in the price of wood that forced recourse to coal (Nef [1934]; other historians assert that this did not occur to any substantial degree until the fifteenth or sixteenth century, with some question even about those dates; see, e.g., Coleman [1975, pp. 42–43]). In sum, the industrial revolution of the twelfth and thirteenth centuries was a surprisingly robust affair, and it is surely plausible that improved rewards to industrial activity had something to do with its vigor.

The fourteenth-century retreat

The end of all this period of buoyant activity in the fourteenth century (see the classic revisionist piece by Lopez [1969] as well as Gimpel [1976, chap. 9]) has a variety of explanations, many of them having no connection with entrepreneurship. For one thing, it has been deduced by study of the glaciers that average temperatures dropped, possibly reducing the yield of crops (though recent studies indicate that the historical relation between climatic changes and crop yields is at best ambiguous) and creating other hardships. The plague returned and decimated much of the population. In addition to these disasters of nature, there were at least two pertinent developments of human origin. First, the church clamped down on new ideas and other manifestations of freedom. Roger Bacon himself was put under constraint.[14] The period during which new ways of thinking brought rewards and status was apparently ended. Second, the fourteenth century included the first half of the devastating Hundred Years' War. It is implausible that the associated renewal of rewards to military enterprise played no part in the economic slowdown.

Remark on "our" industrial revolution

It need hardly be added, in conclusion, that *the* industrial revolution that began in the eighteenth century and continues today has brought to the industrialist and the businessperson generally a degree of wealth and a respect probably unprecedented in human history. The fact that this period yielded an explosion of output at least equally unprecedented is undoubtedly attributable to a myriad of causes that can probably never be discovered fully and whose roles can never be disentangled. Yet the continued association of output growth with high financial and respectability rewards to productive entrepreneurship is surely suggestive, even if it can hardly be taken to be conclusive evidence for proposition 3, which asserts that the allocation of entrepreneurship *does* really matter for the vigor and innovativeness of an economy.

On unproductive avenues for today's entrepreneur: a delicate balance

Today, unproductive entrepreneurship takes many forms. Rent seeking, often via activities such as litigation and takeovers, and tax evasion and avoidance efforts seem now to constitute the prime threat to productive entrepreneurship. The spectacular fortunes amassed by the "arbitrageurs" revealed by the scandals of the mid-1980s were *sometimes*, surely, the reward of unproductive, occasionally illegal but entrepreneurial acts. Corporate executives devote much of their time and energy to legal suit and countersuit, and litigation is used to blunt or prevent excessive vigor in competition by rivals. Huge awards by the courts, sometimes amounting to billions of dollars, can bring prosperity to the victor and threaten the loser with insolvency. When this happens, it must become tempting for the entrepreneur to select his closest advisers from the lawyers rather than the engineers. It induces the entrepreneur to spend literally hundreds of millions of dollars for a single legal battle. It tempts that entrepreneur to be the first to sue others before those others can sue him. (For an illuminating quantification of some of the social costs of one widely publicized legal battle between two firms, see Summers and Cutler [1988].)

Similarly, taxes can serve to redirect entrepreneurial effort. As Lindbeck (1987, p. 15) has observed, "the problem with high-tax societies is not that it is impossible to become rich there, but that it is difficult to do so by way of productive effort in the ordinary production system." He cites as examples of the resulting reallocation of entrepreneurship "'smart' speculative financial transactions without much (if any) contribution to the productive capacity of the economy" (p. 15) as well as "illegal 'business areas' such as drug dealing" (p. 25).

In citing such activities, I do not mean to imply either that rent-seeking activity has been expanding in recent decades or that takeover bids or private antitrust suits are always or even preponderantly unproductive. Rather, I am only suggesting where current rent-seeking activities are likely to be found, that is, where policy designers should look if they intend to divert entrepreneurial talents into more productive channels.

The main point here is to note that threats of takeovers are sometimes used as a means to extract "greenmail" and that recourse to the courts as a means to seek to preserve rents through legally imposed impediments to competition does indeed occur, and to suggest that it is no rare phenomenon. This does, then, become an attraction for entrepreneurial talent whose efforts are thereby channeled into unproductive directions. Yet, to the extent that takeovers discipline inefficient managements and that antitrust intervention sometimes is legitimate and sometimes contributes to productivity, it would seem that it will not be easy to change the rules in a way that discourages allocation of entrepreneurial effort into such activities, without at the same time undermining the legitimate role of these institutions. Some promising proposals have been offered, but this is not a suitable place for their systematic examination. However, a few examples will be reported in the following section.

Changes in the rules and changes in entrepreneurial goals

A central point in this discussion is the contention that if reallocation of entrepreneurial effort is adopted as an objective of society, it is far more easily achieved through changes in the rules that determine relative rewards than via modification of the goals of the entrepreneurs and prospective entrepreneurs themselves. I have even gone so far as to use the same terms to characterize those goals in the very different eras and cultures referred to in the discussion. But it would be ridiculous to imply that the attitudes of a wealth-seeking senator in Rome, a Sung dynasty mandarin, and an American industrialist of the late nineteenth century were all virtually identical. Still, the evidence suggests that they had more in common than might have been expected by the casual observer. However, even if it were to transpire that they really diverged very substantially, that would be of little use to the designer of policy who does not have centuries at his or her disposal and who is notoriously ineffective in engendering profound changes in cultural influences or in the structure of preferences. It is for this reason that I have chosen to take entrepreneurial goals as given and to emphasize modification in the structure of the rewards to different activities as the more promising line of investigation.

This suggests that it is necessary to consider the process by which those rules are modified in practice, but I believe that answers to even this more restricted question are largely beyond the powers of the historians, the sociologists, and the anthropologists into whose domains it falls. One need only review the disputatious literature on the influences that led to the revival of trade toward the end of the early Middle Ages to see how far we still are from anything resembling firm answers. Exogenous influences such as foreign invasions or unexpected climatic changes can clearly play a part, as can developments within the economy. But the more interesting observation for our purposes is the fact that it is easy to think of measures that *can* change these rules quickly and profoundly.[15]

For example, the restrictions on royal grants of monopolies imposed by Parliament in the Statute of Monopolies are said to have reduced substantially the opportunities for rent seeking in seventeenth- and eighteenth-century England and may have moved reluctant entrepreneurs to redirect their efforts toward agricultural improvement and industry. Even if it did not succeed to any substantial extent in reallocation of the efforts of an unchanged body of entrepreneurs from one of those types of activity to the other, if it increased failure rates among the rent seekers while not impeding others who happened to prefer productive pursuits, the result might have been the same. Similarly, tax rules can be used to rechannel entrepreneurial effort. It has, for instance, been proposed that takeover activity would be reoriented substantially in directions that contribute to productivity rather than impeding it by a "revenue-neutral" modification in capital gains taxes that increases rates sharply on assets held for short periods and decreases them considerably for assets held, say, for 2 years or more. A change in the rules that requires a plaintiff firm in a private antitrust suit to bear both parties' legal costs if the defendants are found not to be guilty (as is done in other countries) promises to reduce the frequency with which such lawsuits are used in an attempt to hamper effective competition.

As has already been said, this is hardly the place for an extensive discussion of the design of rational policy in the arena under consideration. The objective of the preceding brief discussion, rather, has been to suggest that there are identifiable means by which the rules of the game can be changed effectively and to illustrate these means concretely, though hardly attempting to offer any generalizations about their character. Certainly, the few illustrations that have just been offered should serve to confirm that there exist (in principle) testable means that promise to induce entrepreneurs to shift their attentions in productive directions, *without any major change in their ultimate goals.* The testability of such hypotheses indicates that the discussion is no tissue of tautologies, and the absence of references to the allocability of entrepreneurship turned up in extensive search of the literature on the entrepreneur suggests that it was not entirely self-evident.

Concluding comment

There is obviously a good deal more to be said about the subject; however, enough material has been presented to indicate that a minor expansion of Schumpeter's theoretical model to encompass the determinants of the *allocation* of entrepreneurship among its competing uses can enrich the model considerably and that the hypotheses that have been associated with the model's extension here are not without substance, even if none of the material approaches anything that constitutes a formal test of a hypothesis, much less a rigorous "proof." It is also easy to confirm that each of the hypotheses that have been discussed clearly yields some policy implications.

Thus clear guidance for policy is provided by the main hypothesis (propositions 1–3) that the rules of the game that specify the relative payoffs to different entrepreneurial activities play a key role in determining whether entrepreneurship will be allocated in productive or unproductive directions and that this can significantly affect the vigor of the economy's productivity growth. After all, the prevailing laws and legal procedures of an economy are prime determinants of the profitability of activities such as rent seeking via the litigative process. Steps such as deregulation of the airlines or more rational antitrust rules can do a good deal here.

A last example can, perhaps, nail down the point. The fact that Japan has far fewer lawyers relative to population and far fewer lawsuits on economic issues is often cited as a distinct advantage to the Japanese economy, since it reduces at least in part the quantity of resources devoted to rent seeking. The difference is often ascribed to national character that is said to have a cultural aversion to litigiousness. This may all be very true. But closer inspection reveals that there are also other influences. While in the United States legal institutions such as trebled damages provide a rich incentive for one firm to sue another on the claim that the latter violated the antitrust laws, in Japan the arrangements are very different. In that country any firm undertaking to sue another on antitrust grounds must first apply for permission from the Japan Fair Trade Commission. But such permission is rarely given, and, once denied, there is no legal avenue for appeal.

The overall moral, then, is that we do not have to wait patiently for slow cultural change in order to find measures to redirect the flow of entrepreneurial activity toward more productive goals. As in the illustration of the Japanese just cited, it may be possible to change the rules in ways that help to offset undesired institutional influences or that supplement other influences that are taken to work in beneficial directions.

Notes

1 I am very grateful for the generous support of the research underlying this paper from the Division of Information Science and Technology of the National Science Foundation, the Price Institute for Entrepreneurial Studies, the Center for Entrepreneurial Studies of the Graduate School of Business Administration, New York University, and the C. V. Starr Center for Applied Economics. I am also very much indebted to Vacharee Devakula for her assistance in the research. I owe much to Joel Mokyr, Stefano Fenoaltea, Lawrence Stone, Constance Berman, and Claudia Goldin for help with the substance of the paper and to William Jordan and Theodore Rabb for guidance on references.

2 There has, however, recently been an outburst of illuminating writings on the theory of the innovation process, analyzing it in such terms as *races* for patents in which the winner takes everything, with no consolation prize for a close second, or treating the process, alternatively, as a "waiting game," in which the patient second entrant may outperform and even survive the first one in the innovative arena, who incurs the bulk of the risk. For an overview of these discussions as well as some substantial added insights, see Dasgupta (1988).

3 There is a substantial literature, following the work of Jacob Schmookler, providing strong empirical evidence for the proposition that even the allocation of inventive effort, i.e., the directions pursued by inventive activities, is itself heavily influenced by relative payoff prospects. However, it is now agreed that some of these authors go too far when they appear to imply that almost nothing but the demand for the product of invention influences to any great extent which inventions will occur. For a good summary and references, see Abramovitz (1989, p. 33).

4 Stefano Fenoaltea comments that he knows no documented cases in which this occurred and that it was undoubtedly more common to seek advancement through adoption into an upper-class family.

5 To be fair to Finley, note that he concludes that it is *not* really interesting. North and Thomas (1973, p. 3) make a similar point about Harrison's invention of the ship's chronometer in the eighteenth century (as an instrument indispensable for the determination of longitude). They point out that the incentive for this invention was a large governmental prize rather than the prospect of commercial profit, presumably because of the absence of effective patent protection.

6 The conquest has at least two noteworthy entrepreneurial sides. First, it involved an innovation, the use of the stirrup by the Normans at Hastings that enabled William's warriors to use the same spear to impale a series of victims with the force of the horse's charge, rather than just tossing the spear at the enemy, much as an infantryman could. Second, the invasion was an impressive act of organization, with William having to convince his untrustworthy allies that they had more to gain by joining him in England than by staying behind to profit from his absence by trying to grab away his lands as they had tried to do many times before.

7 In saying all this, I must not be interpreted as taking the conventional view that warfare is an unmitigated source of impoverishment of any economy that unquestionably never contributes to its prosperity. Careful recent studies have indicated that matters are more complicated (see, e.g., Milward 1970; Olson 1982). Certainly the unprecedented prosperity enjoyed afterward by the countries on the losing side of the Second World War suggests that warfare need not always preclude economic expansion, and it is easy to provide earlier examples. The three great economic leaders of the Western world preceding the United States—Italy in the thirteenth–sixteenth centuries, the Dutch Republic in the seventeenth and eighteenth, and Great Britain in the eighteenth and nineteenth— each attained the height of their prosperity after periods of enormously costly and sometimes destructive warfare. Nevertheless, the wealth gained by a medieval baron from the adoption of a novel bellicose technique can hardly have contributed to economic growth in the way that resulted from adoption of a new steelmaking process in the nineteenth century or the introduction of a product such as the motor vehicle in the twentieth.

8 Bloch (1935) notes that the monasteries had both the capital and the large number of consumers of flour necessary to make the mills profitable. In addition, they were less likely than lay communities to undergo military siege, which, Bloch notes, was (besides drought and freezing of the waterways) one of the main impediments to adoption of the water mill, since blocking of the waterway that drove the mill could threaten the besieged population with starvation (pp. 550–53).

9 The evidence indicates that the wealth of affluent families in Great Britain continues to be derived preponderantly from commerce rather than from industry. This contrasts with the record for the United States, where the reverse appears to be true (see Rubinstein 1980, pp. 22–23, 59–60).

10 It has been suggested by historians (see, e.g., Bloch 1935, p. 547) that an abundance of slaves played a key role in Roman failure to use the water mill widely. However, this must imply that the Romans were not efficient wealth seekers. As the cliometric literature has made clear, the

cost of maintaining a slave is not low and certainly is not zero, and slaves are apt not to be efficient and dedicated workers. Thus if it had been efficient to replace human or animal power by the inanimate power of the waterways, failure to do so would have cut into the wealth of the slaveholder, in effect saddling him with the feeding of unproductive persons or keeping the slaves who turned the mills from other, more lucrative, occupations. Perhaps Roman landowners *were* fairly unsophisticated in the management of their estates, as Finley (1985, pp. 108–16) suggests, and, if so, there may be some substance to the hypothesis that slavery goes far to account for the failure of water mills to spread in the Roman economy.

11 Also as in Rome, none of this was associated with the emergence of a systematic body of science involving coherent theoretical structure and the systematic testing of hypotheses on the basis of experiment or empirical observation. Here, too, the thirteenth-century work of Bishop Grosseteste, William of Henley, and Roger Bacon was an early step toward that unique historical phenomenon—the emergence of a systematic body of science in the West in, say, the sixteenth century (see Needham 1956).

12 As was already noted, science and scientific method also began to make an appearance with contributions such as those of Bishop Grosseteste and Roger Bacon. Walter of Henley championed controlled experiments and observation over recourse to the opinions of ancient authorities and made a clear distinction between economic and engineering efficiency in discussing the advisability of substituting horses for oxen. Bacon displayed remarkable foresight when he wrote, circa 1260, that "machines may be made by which the largest ships, with only one man steering them, will be moved faster than if they were filled with rowers; wagons may be built which will move with incredible speed and without the aid of beasts; flying machines can be constructed in which a man ... may beat the air with wings like a bird ... machines will make it possible to go to the bottom of seas and rivers" (as quoted in White [1962, p. 134]).

13 But then, much the same was true of the first half century of "our" industrial revolution, which, until the coming of the railways, was centered on the production of cotton that perhaps constituted only some 7–8 percent of national output (Hobsbawm 1969, p. 68). Initially, the eighteenth-century industrial revolution was a very minor affair, at least in terms of investment levels and contributions to output and to growth in productivity (perhaps 0.3 percent per year) (see Landes 1969, pp. 64–65; Feinstein 1978, pp. 40–41; Williamson 1984).

14 The restraints imposed by the church had another curious effect: they apparently made bathing unfashionable for centuries. Before then, bathhouses had been popular as centers for social and, perhaps, sexual activity; but by requiring separation of the sexes and otherwise limiting the pleasures of cleanliness, the church undermined the inducements for such sanitary activities (see Gimpel 1976, pp. 87–92).

15 Of course, that still leaves open the critical metaquestion, How does one go about changing the society's value system so that it will *want* to change the rules? But that is not the issue with which I am grappling here, since I see no basis on which the economist can argue that society *ought* to change its values. Rather, I am positing a society whose values lead it to favor productivity growth and am examining which instruments promise to be most effective in helping it to pursue this goal.

References

Abramovitz, Moses. *Thinking about Growth, and Other Essays of Economic Growth and Welfare.* New York: Cambridge Univ. Press, 1989.

Ashton, Thomas S. *The Industrial Revolution, 1760–1830.* London: Oxford Univ. Press, 1948.

Balazs, Etienne. *Chinese Civilization and Bureaucracy:Variations on a Theme*. New Haven, Conn.: Yale Univ. Press, 1964.

Berman, Constance H. "Medieval Agriculture, the Southern French Countryside, and the Early Cistercians: A Study of Forty-three Monasteries." *Trans. American Philosophical Soc.* 76, pt. 5 (1986).

Bloch, Marc. "Avènement et conquêtes du moulin a eau." *Annales d'Histoire Économique et Sociale* 7 (November 1935): 538–63.

Braudel, Fernand. *Civilization and Capitalism, 15th–18th Century*.Vols. 2, 3. New York: Harper and Row, 1986.

Brooke, Christopher N. L. *Europe in the Central Middle Ages, 962–1154*. London: Longman, 1964.

Carus-Wilson, Eleanora M. "An Industrial Revolution of the Thirteenth Century." *Econ. Hist. Rev*. 11, no. 1 (1941): 39–60.

Coleman, Donald C. "Industrial Growth and Industrial Revolutions." *Economica* 23 (February 1956): 1–22.

———. *Industry in Tudor and Stuart England*. London: Macmillan (for Econ. Hist. Soc), 1975.

Cowdrey, H. E. J. "The Peace and the Truce of God in the Eleventh Century." *Past and Present*, no. 46 (February 1970), pp. 42–67.

Dasgupta, Partha. "Patents, Priority and Imitation or, the Economics of Races and Waiting Games." *Econ. J*. 98 (March 1988): 66–80.

de Roover, Raymond. "The Commercial Revolution of the 13th Century." In *Enterprise and Secular Change: Readings in Economic History*, edited by Frederic C. Lane and Jelle C. Riemersma. London: Allen and Unwin, 1953.

Douglas, David C. *William the Conqueror: The Norman Impact upon England*. Berkeley: Univ. California Press, 1964.

Feinstein, C. H. "Capital Formation in Great Britain." In *The Cambridge Economic History of Europe*, vol. 8, pt. 1, edited by Peter Mathias and M. M. Postan. Cambridge: Cambridge Univ. Press, 1978.

Finley, Moses I. "Technical Innovation and Economic Progress in the Ancient World." *Econ. Hist. Rev*. 18 (August 1965): 29–45.

———. *The Ancient Economy*. 2d ed. London: Hogarth, 1985.

Forbes, Robert J. *Studies in Ancient Technology*. Leiden: Brill, 1955.

Gimpel, Jean. *The Medieval Machine: The Industrial Revolution of the Middle Ages*. New York: Holt, Reinhart and Winston, 1976.

Ho, Ping-Ti. *The Ladder of Success in Imperial China, 1368–1911*. New York: Columbia Univ. Press, 1962.

Hobsbawm, Eric J. *Industry and Empire from 1750 to the Present Day*. Harmondsworth: Penguin, 1969.

Jones, Eric L. *The European Miracle: Environments, Economies, and Geopolitics in the History of Europe and Asia*. Cambridge: Cambridge Univ. Press, 1987.

Landes, David S. *The Unbound Prometheus: Technological Change and Industrial Development in Western Europe from 1750 to the Present*. New York: Cambridge Univ. Press, 1969.

Lefebvre, Georges. *The Coming of the French Revolution, 1789*. Princeton, N.J.: Princeton Univ. Press, 1947.

Lindbeck, Assar. "The Advanced Welfare State." Manuscript. Stockholm: Univ. Stockholm, 1987.

Liu, James T. C., and Golas, Peter J., eds. *Change in Sung China: Innovation or Renovation?* Lexington, Mass.: Heath, 1969.

Lopez, Robert S. "Hard Times and Investment in Culture." In *The Renaissance: A Symposium*. New York: Oxford Univ. Press (for Metropolitan Museum of Art), 1969.

McNeill, William H. *History of Western Civilization*. Rev. ed. Chicago: Univ. Chicago Press, 1969.

Marsh, Robert M. *The Mandarins: The Circulation of Elites in China, 1600–1900*. Glencoe, Ill.: Free Press, 1961.

Milward, Alan S. *The Economic Effects of the Two World Wars on Britain*. London: Macmillan (for Econ. Hist. Soc.), 1970.

Murphy, Kevin M., Shleifer, Andrei, and Vishny, Robert. "The Allocation of Talent: Implications for Growth." Manuscript. Chicago: Univ. Chicago, 1990.

Needham, Joseph. "Mathematics and Science in China and the West." *Science and Society* 20 (Fall 1956): 320–43.

Nef, John U. "The Progress of Technology and the Growth of Large-scale Industry in Great Britain, 1540–1640." *Econ. Hist. Rev.* 5 (October 1934): 3–24.

North, Douglass C, and Thomas, Robert Paul. *The Rise of the Western World: A New Economic History*. Cambridge: Cambridge Univ. Press, 1973.

Olson, Mancur. *The Rise and Decline of Nations: Economic Growth, Stagflation, and Social Rigidities*. New Haven, Conn.: Yale Univ. Press, 1982.

Ovitt, George, Jr. *The Restoration of Perfection: Labor and Technology in Medieval Culture*. New Brunswick, N.J.: Rutgers Univ. Press, 1987.

Painter, Sidney. *William Marshal: Knight-Errant, Baron, and Regent of England*. Baltimore: Johns Hopkins Press, 1933.

Robinson, Joan. *The Economics of Imperfect Competition*. London: Macmillan, 1933.

Rosenberg, Nathan, and Birdzell, L. E., Jr. *How the West Grew Rich: The Economic Transformation of the Industrial World*. New York: Basic Books, 1986.

Rubinstein, W. D., ed. *Wealth and the Wealthy in the Modern World*. London: Croom Helm, 1980.

Schama, Simon. *Citizens: A Chronicle of the French Revolution*. New York: Knopf, 1989.

Schumpeter, Joseph A. *The Theory of Economic Development*. Leipzig: Duncker and Humblot, 1912. English ed. Cambridge, Mass.: Harvard Univ. Press, 1934.

Smith, Adam. *An Inquiry into the Nature and Causes of the Wealth of Nations*. 1776. Reprint. New York: Random House (Modern Library), 1937.

Stone, Lawrence. "The Bourgeois Revolution of Seventeenth-century England Revisited." *Past and Present*, no. 109 (November 1985), pp. 44–54.

Summers, Lawrence, and Cutler, David. "Texaco and Pennzoil Both Lost Big." *New York Times* (February 14, 1988).

Thirsk, Joan. "The Restoration Land Settlement." *J. Modern Hist.* 26 (December 1954): 315–28.

Veblen, Thorstein. *The Theory of Business Enterprise*. New York: Scribner, 1904.

Veyne, Paul. "Vie de trimalcion." *Annales: Économies, Societés, Civilisations* 16 (March/April 1961): 213–47.

White, Lynn T., Jr. *Medieval Technology and Social Change*. Oxford: Clarendon, 1962.

Williamson, Jeffrey G. "Why Was British Growth So Slow during the Industrial Revolution?" *J. Econ. Hist.* 44 (September 1984): 687–712.

Review and Discussion Questions

1 What, in Baumol's terminology, is an "entrepreneur"?
2 How does Baumol account for differences in economic growth across countries and over time?
3 How does his explanation relate to an idea emphasized in this book?
4 What was a key difference among ancient Rome, medieval China, and middle-ages Europe?

5 What policies does Baumol recommend to increase economic growth?
6 A possible way to judge how well economies are performing is to consider how people are "voting with their feet"; that is, how many people are moving to a country, and how many are moving out of a country. Research these immigration and emigration flows. Which countries would you conclude are doing relatively well? Do other factors need to be considered? What does academic research conclude?

Chapter 7

Ronald Bailey

THE LAW OF INCREASING RETURNS

"SUSTAINABLE DEVELOPMENT," WAS DEFINED by the 1987 U.N. report *Our Common Future* as development that "meets the needs of the present without compromising the ability of future generations to meet their own needs." This notion superficially echoes philosopher John Locke's proviso in his *Second Treatise on Government* that every person may remove resources from the state of nature by mixing his labor with them and making them his property as long as "there is enough, and as good left in common for others."

I will show that developed capitalist economies are precisely those economies that "meet the needs of the present without compromising the ability of future generations to meet their own needs." As history has amply shown, technological progress makes possible the economic growth that allows future generations to meet their own needs. There is only one proven way to improve the lot of hundreds of millions of poor people, and that is democratic capitalism. It is in rich democratic capitalist countries that the air and water are becoming cleaner, forests are expanding, food is abundant, education is universal, and women's rights respected. Whatever slows down economic growth also slows down environmental improvement.

At the heart of the debate over sustainable development lay concerns over human population growth and consumption. Two hundred years after Thomas Robert Malthus published *An Essay on the Principle of Population*, demographers, ecologists, economists, biologists and policymakers still debate his theory of population. Leading foundations spend scores of millions of dollars on population programs, while the United Nations holds international conferences on the topic and even has a specialized agency, the United Nations Population Fund, devoted to the issue. Every year, hundreds of weighty studies and books pour from the universities and think tanks discussing what is to be done.

Malthus advanced two propositions that he regarded as completely self-evident. First, that "food is necessary for the existence of man", and second, that "the passion between the sexes is necessary and will remain nearly in its present state." Based on these propositions, Malthus famously concluded that "the power of population is indefinitely greater than the power in the earth to produce subsistence for man. Population, when unchecked, increases in a geometrical ratio. Subsistence increases only in an arithmetical ratio. A slight acquaintance with numbers will show the immensity of the first power in comparison with the second."

Malthus illustrated his hypothesis using two sets of numbers: "the human species would increase in the ratio of—1, 2, 4, 8, 16, 32, 64, 128, 256, 512, &c. and subsistence as—1, 2, 3, 4, 5, 6, 7, 8, 9, 10, &c." He further asserted that "population does invariably increase where there are the means of subsistence." Malthus' dismal summary of the situation in which humanity finds itself is that some portion of mankind must forever be starving to death; and, further, efforts to aid the starving will only lead to more misery, as those initially spared from famine bear too many children to feed with existing food supplies.

In his first edition of the *Essay*, Malthus argued that there were two "checks" on population, "preventive" and "positive." Preventive checks, those that prevent births, include abortion, infanticide and prostitution; positive checks include war, pestilence and famine. In later editions, he added a third check that he called "moral restraint", which includes voluntary celibacy, late marriage and the like. Moral restraint is basically just a milder version of the earlier preventive check. If all else fails to keep human numbers under control, Malthus chillingly concludes,

> Famine seems to be the last, the most dreadful resource of nature. The power of population is so superior to the power in the earth to produce subsistence for man, that premature death must in some shape or other visit the human race. The vices of mankind are active and able ministers of depopulation. They are the precursors in the great army of destruction, and often finish the dreadful work themselves. But should they fail in this war of extermination, sickly seasons, epidemics, pestilence, and plague, advance in terrific array, and sweep off their thousands and ten thousands. Should success be still incomplete, gigantic inevitable famine stalks in the rear, and with one mighty blow, levels the population with the food of the world.

Malthus' principle of population has proved to be one of the most influential and contested theories in history. It provided a crucial insight for Charles Darwin as he was developing his theory of natural selection. In his autobiography, Darwin wrote that in October 1838,

> I happened to read for amusement Malthus on Population, and being well prepared to appreciate the struggle for existence which everywhere goes on, from long-continued observation of the habits of animals and plants, it at once struck me that under these circumstances favourable variations would tend to be preserved, and unfavourable ones would be destroyed. The result of this would be the formation of a new species. Here, then, I had at last got a theory by which to work.

Naturalists, biologists and ecologists have since applied Malthusian theory not only to animals and plants, but to humans as well. Undeniably, his principle of population has an appealing simplicity, and has proved a fruitful hypothesis for ecology and population biology. It undergirds such biological concepts as carrying capacity, which is a measure of the population that a given ecosystem can support. The Kaibab Plateau deer, for example, is a famous case of an animal population outstripping its food supply. In the 1920s, the deer population expanded dramatically. In the absence of predators, a forage shortage ensued, which in turn led to a dramatic reduction of the deer population.

If the concept of carrying capacity can explain fluctuations in animal populations, some intellectuals have reasoned in the second half of the twentieth century, it should apply equally well to human populations. As Stanford University entomologist Paul Ehrlich has explained: "To ecologists who study animals, food and population often seem like sides of the same coin. If too many animals are devouring it, the food supply declines; too little food, the supply of animals declines. ... Homo sapiens is no exception to that rule, and at the moment it seems likely that food will be our limiting resource."

In the late 1960s, Ehrlich was one of many biologists and agronomists who began to issue dire warnings about human "overpopulation", the most famous of which appeared in his book, *The Population Bomb* (1968). "The battle to feed all of humanity is over", Ehrlich wrote. "In the 1970s, the world will undergo famines—hundreds of millions of people are going to starve to death in spite of any crash programs embarked on now." Later, in an article for the first Earth Day in 1970, Ehrlich outlined a horrific scenario in which 65 million Americans and 4 billion other people would die of starvation in a "Great Die-Off" between 1980 and 1989. And in 1990 Ehrlich and his wife Anne published *The Population Explosion*, where they once again asserted that, "One thing seems safe to predict: starvation and epidemic disease will raise the death rates over most of the planet." In these gloomy forecasts, Ehrlich was far from alone. In 1967, William and Paul Paddock asserted in their book, *Famine 1975!*, that, "The famines which are now approaching ... are for a surety, inevitable. ... In fifteen years the famines will be catastrophic." Today, the Worldwatch Institute, a Washington, DC environmentalist advocacy group chaired by Lester Brown, still has a solid Malthusian focus.

Food is not the only resource said to be in short supply. In 1972 the Club of Rome, a group of politicians, businessmen and senior international bureaucrats, famously commissioned *The Limits to Growth* report, which concluded: "If the present growth trends in world population, industrialization, pollution, food production, and resource depletion continue unchanged, the limits to growth on this planet will be reached sometime in the next one hundred years. The probable result will be a rather sudden and uncontrollable decline in both population and industrial capacity."

This is Malthus writ large: not only will humanity run out of food, but it will also run out of non-renewable resources like minerals and fossil fuels. ...

The Primacy of ideas

For decades, economists essentially used a two-factor model in which economic growth was accounted for by adding more labor and more capital to create more goods.

The problem with this model is that over time growth must halt when the marginal value of the goods produced equals the cost of the labor and capital used to produce them. This neoclassical model of economic growth was elaborated in the 1950s by Nobelist Robert Solow and his colleagues, and was later incorporated into *The Limits to Growth* computer model. Relying on it, MIT researchers predicted eventual collapse as the inevitable result of continued economic and population growth.

In the last two decades, economic forecasters, following the lead of economist Paul Romer, have made a conceptual breakthrough that has enabled them to describe more rigorously and accurately—and differently—how economic growth occurs and how, with the proper social institutions, it can continue for the foreseeable future. Romer explains this approach, which has come to be known as the New Growth Theory:

> New growth theorists now start by dividing the world into two fundamentally different types of productive inputs that can be called "ideas" and "things". Ideas are nonrival goods that could be stored in a bit string. Things are rival goods with mass (or energy). With ideas and things, one can explain how economic growth works. Nonrival ideas can be used to rearrange things, for example, when one follows a recipe and transforms noxious olives into tasty and healthful olive oil. Economic growth arises from the discovery of new recipes and the transformation of things from low to high value configurations.

Decoding the clunky economic terminology, "rival" goods are simply things that cannot be used by two or more persons at once, e.g., cars, drill presses, computers, even human bodies and brains. "Nonrival" goods can be used by any number of people simultaneously, e.g., recipes for bread, blueprints for houses, techniques for growing corn, formulas for pharmaceuticals, scientific principles like the law of gravity, and computer programs.

To understand the potency of ideas, consider that a few decades ago silicon was used primarily to make glass. Today it is a crucial component in microchips and optical fibers. Again, until fairly recently petroleum was known mainly as a nuisance for people engaged in drilling water wells; its use as a cheap lighting replacement for increasingly scarce whale oil only began in the 1890s, and soon after came the internal combustion engine.

We make ourselves better off, then, not by increasing the amount of resources on planet earth—that is, of course, fixed—but by rearranging resources we already have available so that they provide us with more of what we want. This process of improvement has been going on ever since the first members of our species walked the earth. We have moved from heavy earthenware pots to ultrathin plastics and lightweight aluminum cans. To cook our food we have shifted from wood-intensive campfires to clean, efficient natural gas. By using constantly improving recipes, humanity has avoided the Malthusian trap while at the same time making the world safer and more comfortable for an ever larger portion of the world's population.

In fact, increasing, rather than diminishing, returns characterize many economic activities. For example, it may cost $150 million to develop the first vial of a new vaccine to prevent Lyme disease. Yet every vial after that is essentially free. The same is true for computer programs: it may cost Microsoft $500 million for the first copy of

Windows 98, but each subsequent copy is merely the cost of the disk on which it is stored. Or in the case of telecommunications, laying a fiber optic network may cost billions of dollars, but once operational it can transmit millions of messages at virtually no added cost. And the low costs of each of these inventions make it possible for the people who buy them to be even more productive in their own activities—by avoiding illness, expediting word processing, and drastically increasing the tempo of information exchanges.

What modern Malthusians who fret about the depletion of resources miss is that it is not oil that people want; they want to cool and heat their homes. It is not copper telephone lines that people want; they want to communicate quickly and easily with friends, family and businesses. They do not want paper; they want a convenient and cheap way to store written information. In short, what is important is not the physical resource but the function to be performed; and for that, ideas are the crucial input. Robert Kates notes that technological discoveries have "transformed the meaning of resources and increased the carrying capacity of the Earth"; economist Gale Johnson concludes that history has clearly confirmed that "no exhaustible resource is essential or irreplaceable"; and economist Dwight Lee asserts that "the relevant resource base is defined by knowledge, rather than by physical deposits of existing resources."

With regard to using physical resources, no less an environmental advocate than Al Gore noted in 1999 in an address to the American Association for the Advancement of Science's annual convention that "throughout our economy, skills, intelligence, and creativity are replacing mass and money—which is why, in the past 50 years, the value of our economy has tripled, while the physical weight of our economy as a whole has barely increased at all." In other words, we got richer not just by using more stuff but by using it more intelligently.

Romer sums it up this way: "Every generation has perceived the limits to growth that finite resources and undesirable side effects would pose if no new recipes or ideas were discovered. And every generation has underestimated the potential for finding new recipes and ideas. We consistently fail to grasp how many ideas remain to be discovered. The difficulty is the same one we have with compounding. Possibilities do not add up. They multiply."

This, it should be noted, is the mirror image of Malthus' argument about exponential growth. Here, however, ideas grow much faster than population.

In fact there are two commons. Ideological environmentalists concentrate solely on the environmental commons and ignore another commons that addresses and solves problems that arise in the environmental commons. Let's call it the knowledge commons. We all draw from the knowledge commons, which consists of the growing pool of institutional, scientific, and technological concepts, and the wealth and capital they create. It is true that the earth is finite, but it is also true that human creativity is not. Our ancestors, by creating the knowledge commons, have in most relevant respects honored Locke's proviso because they have left us much more than they took.

By using a number of simple calculations, Romer illustrates the point that the number of possible discoveries and inventions is incomprehensibly vast. Take, for example, the chemical combinations one can derive from the periodic table of elements. There are about 100 different elements and if one serially combined any four, one would get about 94 million combinations. Romer further assumes that these elements could be combined in differing proportions ranging from 1 to 10. This yields 3,500 proportions times 94 million combinations and provides 330 billion different recipes in total. At the rate of 1,000 recipes per day, it would take scientists nearly a million years to evaluate them all. What is more, this vastly underestimates the actual number of combinations available, since one could combine more than four elements, in different proportions, at different temperatures and pressures—and so on and on.

Again, consider the number of computer programs that could be installed on a single computer hard disk drive. Romer calculates that the number of distinct software programs that can be put on a one-gigabyte hard disk is roughly one followed by 2.7 billion zeros. By comparison, the total number of seconds that have elapsed since the beginning of the universe is only about 1 followed by 17 zeros, and the total number of atoms in the universe is equal to about 1 followed by 100 zeros.

In short, then, people possess a nearly infinite capacity to rearrange physical objects by creating new recipes for their use. Yet some committed Malthusians object that Romer and others who hold that economic growth is potentially limitless not only violate the law of diminishing returns but transgress an even more fundamental physical law: the second law of thermodynamics. According to the second law, in a closed system disorder tends to increase. Think of a droplet of ink as a highly ordered pigment that is diluted when it is dropped into a ten-gallon aquarium. When the pigment's molecules spread evenly throughout the water, disorder is at a maximum—that is, it becomes virtually impossible to reconstitute the droplet. The idea, then, is that the maintenance of order in one part of the system (heating a house) requires an increase of disorder elsewhere (burning oil).

In fact, the solution to the puzzle of life and of a growing economy is that the earth is not a closed system—the energy that drives it comes principally from the sun. It is true that the sun's energy is being dissipated. But it will not burn out for another four to five billion years. Hence, the recipes that humans could devise for obtaining and using energy are for all practical purposes limitless. Until medieval times, people inefficiently heated and cooked with open fires in their homes. Then someone in Europe invented the chimney, which dramatically increased the efficiency of heating and cooking. In the eighteenth century, Benjamin Franklin invented the cast iron stove, which again boosted efficiency—and so on, to today's modern electric heat pumps and gas furnaces. And new ideas and designs continue to be developed all the time, among them passive solar homes, solar cells, fuel cells and nuclear power plants. It seems safe to conclude that so long as the sun shines, the second law of thermodynamics is not terribly relevant.

Indeed, trying to forecast today the energy mix for the next hundred years, especially given the current rate of technological innovation, is as fruitless as someone in 1900 trying to predict our current energy requirements. A person in 1900 would surely not have anticipated scores of millions of automobiles and trucks, thousands of jet planes, and millions of refrigerators. Because of this, the wisest course is for humanity to support institutions and incentive systems that will encourage future scientists, inventors and entrepreneurs to discover, finance and build the technologies that will supply human needs and protect the natural world in the coming century.

Reframing the problems

Insights from New Growth Theory reframe many environmental problems and suggest some surprising solutions. For example, one of the global environmental problems most commonly attributed to population and economic growth is the loss of tropical forests. But is growth really to blame? According to the Consultative Group on International Agricultural Research, the chief factor that drives deforestation in developing countries is not commercial logging but "poor farmers who have no other option to feeding their families other than slashing and burning a patch of forest. ... Slash-and-burn agriculture results in the loss or degradation of some 25 million acres of land per year."

By contrast, the United States today farms less than half of the land that it did in the 1920s but produces far more food now than it did then. The key, of course, is technology. In fact, available farming technology from developed countries could prevent, and in many cases reverse, the loss of tropical forests and other wildlife habitat around the globe. Unfortunately, institutional barriers, the absence of secure property rights, corrupt governments and a lack of education prevent its widespread diffusion and, hence, environmental restoration.

Another environmental problem frequently attributed to population growth is pollution. In 1972 *The Limits to Growth* computer model projected that pollution would skyrocket as population increased: "Virtually every pollutant that has been measured as a function of time appears to be increasing exponentially." But once again, the new Malthusians had things exactly backward. Since 1972, America's population has risen 26 percent and its economy has more than doubled. Western Europe and Japan have experienced similar rates of growth. Yet, instead of increasing as predicted, the Environmental Protection Agency (EPA) reports that since 1976, when national measuring began, ambient air pollutants are way down. The levels of ozone in the air have dropped 31 percent, sulfur dioxides are down 72 percent, nitrogen dioxide was cut by 42 percent, carbon dioxide plunged 76 percent, and particulates (smoke and dust) fell by 31 percent. Air quality in the 10 largest metropolitan areas (four of the five most improved are in California) has improved an average of 53 percent since 1980. Also water use per capita in the United States has been going down for two decades

In fact, a growing body of literature suggests that in most cases there are thresholds of wealth at which the amount of a pollutant begins to decline. Department of Interior analyst Indur Goklany calls these thresholds the "environmental transition." What this means is that when people rise above mere subsistence, they begin demanding amenities such as clean air and water. The first environmental transition is clean drinking water. Goklany has found that the level of fecal coliform bacteria in rivers, which is a good measure of water pollution, peaks when average per capita incomes reach $1,400 per year. The next transition occurs when particulates like smoke and soot peak at $3,200. And again, levels of sulfur dioxide peak at about $3,700. There even appears to be a threshold for forest expansion at about $15,000 per capita annual income.

Jesse Ausubel, director of the Program for the Human Environment at Rockefeller University notes that "forest regrowth appears part of modernity." He points out that U.N. Food and Agriculture Organization studies "of forest biomass for the decade of the 1990s in the boreal and temperate region in more than 50 countries show the forests expanding in every one of them." As global cropland and grazing area shrink, forests will continue to expand. Ausubel estimates that humanity will need to use 20 percent or less of the world's 3 billion hectares of forest to sustainably supply all of our wood needs in the 21st century.

Assuming that man-made global warming is a real problem, there are plenty of ways to handle it. One is to deploy technologies we already have to mitigate its effects on humanity: heating, air conditioning, seawalls, irrigation of farmland, crop switching, and so forth. We could also choose to sequester extra carbon dioxide by pumping it back into the ground whence it came, fertilizing the tropic ocean deserts so that they bloom with phytoplankton that absorbs it from the air, or planting more trees.

In any case, Ausubel doesn't think that carbon dioxide is a long-term problem because the world's energy system has been inexorably decarbonizing for the past two centuries. His research traces humanity's steady progress from wood to coal to oil to natural gas and, eventually, to hydrogen. At each stage, consumers, without being commanded to do so by regulators, have chosen fuels containing more hydrogen over fuels containing more carbon.

Ausubel sees that trend continuing until carbon-based fuels are eliminated by the end of the century. He expects that carbon dioxide concentrations, now about 360 parts per million (ppm), will peak at 450 ppm. That is 100 ppm less than the U.N.'s sometimes stated goal of "stabilizing" carbon dioxide at 550 ppm, and it would happen without draconian increases in energy prices or the creation of global bureaucracies aimed at regulating the atmosphere.

Not surprisingly, committed Malthusians reject such findings. Paul Ehrlich, for instance, stubbornly insists that, "Most people do not recognize that, at least in rich nations, economic growth is the disease, not the cure". To counteract the "disease" of economic growth, Maurice King recommends that people in the "privileged North" should engage in "the deliberate quest of poverty" to curb their "luxurious resource consumption."

The favored target of such critiques is the United States, whose citizens are supposedly consuming more than their fair share of the world's goods and causing more than their fair share of its ills. The average American, however, is not only a consumer but a producer of both goods and ideas. Americans and Europeans get more done with relatively less because of their higher levels of education, greater access to productive tools, superior infrastructure, democratic governments and free markets. As a consequence, output per hour of labor in the United States today is ten times what it was a hundred years ago. Thus, the average Westerner creates far more resources, especially knowledge and technology, than she or he consumes. Thus, too, both Western economies and environments are improving simultaneously.

All that said, if the right social institutions are lacking—democratic governance, secure private property, free markets—it is possible for a nation to fall into the Malthusian trap of rising poverty and increasing environmental degradation. The economies of many countries in Africa are declining, not because of high population growth rates or lack of resources, but because they have failed to implement the basic policies for encouraging economic growth: namely, widespread education, secure property rights and democratic governance.

Democratic governance and open markets have in fact proved indispensable for the prevention of famine in modern times. Nobel Prize-winning economist Amartya Sen notes that "in the terrible history of famines in the world, there is hardly any case in which a famine has occurred in a country that is independent and democratic, with an uncensored press." Why is this? Because, says Sen, "So long as famines are relatively costless for the government, with no threat to its survival or credibility, effective actions to prevent famines do not have the urgency to make them inescapable imperatives for the government." Along with Romer and other theorists, Sen also argues that general economic growth, not just growth in food output, is crucial to ending the threat of famine in Africa. He calls "for measures to encourage and enhance technical change, skill formation and productivity—both in agriculture and in other fields."

In article in the June 11, 2002 issue of the *Proceedings of the National Academy of Sciences* Ausubel concludes, "An annual 2-3% progress in consumption and technology over many decades and sectors provides a benchmark for sustainability." In other words, economic growth and technological progress are sustainable in the long run and make it less and less likely that humanity will overshoot any limits the biosphere may have.

We cannot deplete the supply of ideas, designs and recipes. They are immaterial and limitless, and therefore not bound in any meaningful sense by the second law of thermodynamics. Surely no one believes that humanity has already devised all of the methods to conserve, locate and exploit new sources of energy, or that the flow of ideas to improve houses, transportation, communications, medicine and farming has suddenly dried up. Though far too many of our fellow human beings are caught in local versions of the Malthusian trap, we must not mistake the situation of that segment as representing the future of all of humanity and the earth itself; it is, instead, a dwindling remnant of an unhappy past. Misery is not the inevitable lot of humanity, nor is the ruin of the natural world a foregone conclusion.

Review and Discussion Questions

1 Bailey writes, "Whatever slows down economic growth also slows down environmental improvement." Why?
2 What, according to the article, is the key resource?
3 Why do many production technologies now have declining average costs?
4 Bailey asserts that we've gotten rich not by finding more resources but by doing what with resources?
5 Bailey argues that the West creates more resources than it consumes. Why? Do you agree or disagree?
6 Bailey concludes that famine is almost never an issue of resources, that it almost always has political causes. Research recent instances of famine. Is Bailey right?

Chapter 8

Russell Roberts

THE GREAT OUTSOURCING SCARE OF 2004

PEOPLE ARE WORRIED that Indians are going to take away all of America's good jobs. The "outsourcing" of call-center and software coding jobs to India has been a tough pill to swallow for an educated workforce. The alarmists, from presidential candidates to think tank economists, see a dim future for America if nothing is done to arrest the flow of jobs from West to East.

The level of fear reminds me of an earlier time. In the early 1990s, Japan was thought to be the great threat to the American economy. Japan was strategically pursuing a policy of stealing America's jobs. America was being hollowed out. Back then, Amazon was a river and Spam was a food, sort of, anyway. The focus was mainly on manufacturing jobs, which back in the early 1990s were more numerous than they are today.

I remember a Frontline documentary from those days. It's a wonderful world we live in. A few hits on Google and I was able to find the Frontline web site and a description of the documentary: Losing the War with Japan Frontline looks at the challenge Japanese-style capitalism poses to the U.S. market. The program examines three industries—automobile, video games, and flat panel displays used in computers.

Robert Krulwich introduces the hour-long documentary and anchors a closing half-hour roundtable discussion. The show ended with a parade of returning veterans from the first Iraq war that had recently ended successfully. The voiceover was something like, "We won that war, but can we win the economic war?" The implication of the war imagery was that economic competition was a zero-sum game—the economic pie was a fixed size and every slice that went to Japan was a slice taken from our plate.

Economics takes a different view—trade is mutually beneficial. Both parties benefit and the pie gets bigger. But there was a second part to that documentary that I haven't thought about for a decade. It comes back to me now in the alarm over outsourcing.

The documentary paid a lot of attention to Nintendo. Nintendo was accused of the nefarious strategy of keeping all the best jobs, the creative jobs designing new games, in Japan. The lousy jobs were relegated to America. And as an example of those lousy jobs the Americans were given, we were shown American kids answering the phones, giving advice to gamers who had questions about how the games worked. A call center!

So in 1991, the world was going to hell in a handbasket because we'd be stuck with the call center jobs. In 2004, the world is going to hell in a handbasket because we're losing the call center jobs. Hard to understand how both of those arguments can be right. At the heart of these fears is a theory about how nations prosper—the key is to get the good jobs. Ross Perot had a simple way of expressing it. He said it's better to make computer chips than potato chips.

In this mistaken theory of how jobs affect our standard of living, wages depend on the title on your business card. If somehow the foreigners corner the computer chip market, we're left peeling potatoes for minimum wage, if we're lucky. The problem with this theory is that, if a nation's skill level is low, making computer chips makes you poorer, not richer. It's like me at 5′ 6″ deciding to be a basketball player because basketball players have high salaries. Or Haiti trying to jump-start its economy by creating a domestic pharmaceutical industry sector because pharmaceuticals are very profitable.

Ironically, perhaps, the potato chip business in America is rather high tech. Perot's slogan makes you think of a bunch of folks with potato peelers standing over vats of hot oil. In fact, a potato chip factory (like virtually everything else in a high-wage economy) uses a high ratio of capital to labor. Basically a truck dumps a bunch of potatoes into one end of a highly customized and sophisticated piece of machinery run by a computer. Bags of potato chips come out the other end. Designing and building that machine, along with the software that makes it tick, are not exactly what Perot had in mind. Our wages don't depend on our job titles but on our skills and the amount of capital we have to augment those skills. Opening our economy to trade in goods and services allows us to use our skills and capital as productively as possible.

There are two ways to get things in life. The first is to make them for yourself. The second is to let someone else make it for you and trade for it. When others can make something more cheaply than you can make it for yourself, it makes sense to outsource it. You specialize in what you do most productively and swap for the rest of your desires. That specialization creates wealth. If Indians have low wages and can write computer code more cheaply than Americans, it makes sense to import that code. It's no different from importing inexpensive televisions from abroad and saving our resources for other things we can do more effectively.

It's no different from finding a new production technology that lets you produce at lower cost. It's about getting more from less. That's the true road to wealth. Make the pie bigger by getting more from less. That's the story of the last 100 years of economic progress in America. We've found ways to get more from less. Imagine a world where Indian tech workers were really cheap. Cheaper than cheap. Free.

Suppose India decides to give us free software and run those call centers just out of kindness. Would it ever make sense to refuse the free software in order to preserve high-wage jobs in the software industry? Oh no, not the free software, must be a trick.

Refusing inexpensive software is no wiser. It makes us poorer as a nation, not richer. Imagine reacting that way to high-quality Japanese cars. Imagine refusing to allow Japanese imports into the United States in order to preserve the size and wages of the auto industry. With less competition, the quality of American cars would fall. But the real loss would be all the resources we'd have to devote to cars—all the people and capital and technology and managerial talent—when there would be a less expensive alternative. Savings those resources is what allows us to create the new jobs that come from lower-cost automobiles. In 1900, 40 percent of the workforce was in agriculture.

Technology, figuring out ways to get more from less, allows us to produce more food today with only 2 percent of the workforce. That transition was hard on a lot of farmers, but their children and grandchildren live in a better world because of those changes. The lower costs meant higher profits at first for those farmers who stayed in business, but competition among farmers forced them to share the gains with the rest of us. The result is that food is dramatically cheaper than it was. That means more resources are available to make the myriad of products that we have now in addition to having the food.

The same transition will take place with today's computer programmers who lose their jobs to Indians. There will be personal challenges as workers look to find new jobs. Some new jobs will be created because businesses will have access to less-expensive software. Other opportunities will come along because cheaper software means more resources will be available elsewhere to create new companies and new products. The skeptic wants to know now what the new jobs will be. What if there aren't any?

OK, says the skeptic, I accepted the argument for trade when we outsourced the assembly line jobs or the textile jobs. Those were the bad jobs. But the computer jobs? Those are the jobs we wanted to keep! Those were the good jobs. We went from a manufacturing economy to a service economy to an information economy. There's nothing left! We're going to have to go back to the "bad" jobs, flipping hamburgers and doing each other's laundry. What sector will come along if we've used up all the information jobs? I don't know, but I'm sure it will be something that uses creativity and knowledge. This uncertainty frightens people.

If we can't think of what the next generation of jobs will be, how can we be confident that something will, indeed, come along? Think about that farmer back in 1900. Imagine telling him that in 100 years, farm jobs will only be 2 percent of the workforce. Two percent! What jobs could possibly come along to replace the farming jobs? Well, you explain, there will be jobs at Federal Express and Motorola and Intel and Microsoft and even General Motors. The farmer won't even be able to even imagine the products that those companies will make. Imagine being told a decade ago that some people would make their living writing software for iTunes at Apple. What's iTunes? Oh, it's a place where people download music into their iPods. What is downloading music?

Just think how much the world has changed in only 10 years, all the jobs we couldn't have imagined that are now here. Back in the early 1990s, when people were up in arms about Japan, we ignored the alarmists. We mostly kept to our naive policy of letting people buy freely from around the world. It turned out fine. The alarmists were wrong.

Japan didn't steal our jobs or ruin our country. Employment in the United States grew steadily, as did wages, helped in part by imports from Japan and the rest of the world. Japan, in the meanwhile, has stagnated. My guess is that today's alarmists will turn out to be wrong as well. There's another interesting parallel to the early 1990s. Then and now, the critics of open markets claimed a new paradigm. In the early 1990s, the new paradigm was the unique partnership in Japan between industry and government that supposedly threatened our standard of living.

Today it's the loss of software jobs, the alleged last frontier of employment. But the real reason those arguments have popular and political traction is that both today and in the early 1990s, we're coming out of recessions with sluggish employment growth. When the economy warms up and the jobs come, the worries about outsourcing will fade into the background.

A final thought. Can you imagine how strange our worries about outsourcing must sound to India? Hearing us complain about their low-wage competition is like listening to the Yankees complain that the Red Sox signed Pokey Reese to a contract. You don't know who Pokey Reese is? That's the point. It's the Red Sox who have it rough. But baseball is a zero-sum game—when the Yankees win, the Red Sox have to lose. Unlike sports, international trade makes both sides better off. Outsourcing lets Americans get less-expensive software and the Indians get better wages and the chance to buy more American goods. It's a good deal for both of us.

Review and Discussion Questions

1 What does Roberts conclude by comparing the Nintendo call center jobs of the early 1990s to the call center jobs the U.S. later outsourced to India?
2 Is it better to make computer chips or potato chips? Why or why not?
3 In most of the developed countries the number of farmers today is a tiny fraction of the number there were a century ago. But the number of people in those countries today is greater. How do those countries manage to feed their people?
4 Will we ever run out of jobs?
5 Some countries, because of geography or because of other reasons, don't trade much. How does their economic growth compare with countries that trade more?
6 Try to imagine jobs that don't exist today but that might ten years from now.

Chapter 9

Geoffrey Colvin

WE'RE WORTH OUR WEIGHT IN PENTIUM CHIPS

W E'RE PRODUCING LESS STUFF than we used to, but it's worth a lot more. How did that happen? You can thank the power of the mind.
Have you noticed people getting by with less stuff than they used to? Acting less materialistic? Invoking that stern Yankee adage, "Use it up, wear it out, make it do, or do without"?

Me neither. But believe it or not—and it's hard to believe in this bull-market Babylon—we are, strictly speaking, less materialistic than we used to be. And I can prove it.

Recall Alan Greenspan's arresting statement that America's total economic output weighs about the same now as it did 50 or 100 years ago. His point was that this represents a steadily increasing stimulus to international trade, as shipping costs become a shrinking proportion of the value being shipped. But there's another implication that's at least as important.

The U.S. population in 1900 was 76 million, vs. 275 million today. In the past century our annual economic output per person, in constant dollars, has more than quintupled (to about $33,000). Now, it would be unsurprising to find that in becoming five times richer we were each, on average, turning out five times more physical stuff. It would be remarkable to learn that we had somehow contrived to become five times richer without any increase in per capita creation of physical things. But Greenspan's statistic is far more stunning: By holding the weight of our total output about steady, we have become five times richer while producing 72% less material stuff per person than we did a century ago.

How can this be? The answer goes beyond the economy's long shift from goods to services. Crank the numbers, and you find that even as manufactured goods account for a shrinking proportion of the total economy, their value has risen steadily.

The explanation is that in the Infotech Age, manufactured goods increasingly are congealed brainpower. As Table 9.1 shows, any alchemist still seeking the philosophers' stone should call off the search: Intel turns something baser than base metal—sand (which becomes silicon)—into something far more valuable than gold, Pentium III chips.

Of course, in a general way this is what successful manufacturers have always done: apply intellect in various forms to raw materials to create profitable products. What's new and striking, and what my somewhat fanciful table suggests, is how far the process has gone—how much value some companies are able to extract from ever less physical material. As a rule, those that do it best are the most valuable companies. For example, looking at the car and steel prices in the table, it isn't surprising to learn that DaimlerChrysler (maker of the Mercedes-Benz) is worth more than General Motors (the Chevrolet's maker) or that either one is worth far more than America's ten largest steel producers combined.

Note that the magic ingredient, brainpower, can work in many ways. Sometimes it takes the form of ultrahigh technology, as in the Pentium chip. Sometimes it's brand power, as in the Hermes scarf. Most often it's both, as in the Mercedes-Benz.

The large point to remember about the declining role of physical stuff in the value of manufactured products is that it's good news. As Greenspan pointed out, it fuels trade, which makes all trading partners more prosperous. It may also let firms

Table 9.1 Brainpower weighs in

Product	Price	Weight in pounds	Price per pound
Pentium III 800MHz microprocessor	$851.00	0.01984	$42,893.00
Viagra (tablet)	$8.00	0.00068	$11,766.00
Gold (ounce)	$301.70	0.0625	$4,827.20
Hermes scarf	$275.00	0.14	$1,964.29
Palm V	$449.00	0.26	$1,726.92
Saving Private Ryan on DVD	$34.99	0.04	$874.75
Cigarettes (20)	$4.00	0.04	$100.00
Who Moved My Cheese? by Spencer Johnson	$19.99	0.49	$40.80
Mercedes-Benz E-class four-door sedan	$78,445.00	4,134.00	$18.98
The Competitive Advantage of Nations by Michael Porter	$40.00	2.99	$13.38
Chevrolet Cavalier four-door sedan	$17,770.00	2,630.00	$6.76
Hot-rolled steel (ton)	$370.00	2,000.00	$0.19

respond more quickly to changing markets; just think what business would be like if every warehouse had to be five times bigger than it is. And by processing fewer physical resources per capita, we each put less pressure on the environment.

It's hard to believe while watching your neighbors build bigger houses, buy more cars, and unload more excess junk on eBay. But believe it: As an economy, we're getting richer and thinner. And it feels great.

Review and Discussion Questions

1 Why is the stuff we produce, even though smaller in quantity, worth more now than ever before?
2 The figures in Colvin's table are now several years old. Do his conclusions hold using more recent numbers?

Chapter 10

W. Michael Cox and Richard Alm

THESE ARE THE GOOD OLD DAYS: A REPORT OF U.S. LIVING STANDARDS[1]

R IP VAN WINKLE WAKES to a bright spring day in 1994 and, rubbing his eyes, quickly realizes the world around him has changed. He discovers almost 25 years have flown by since the start of his big sleep. Among his last memories before dozing off in 1970: watching George C. Scott portray *Patton* at a movie theater, seeing *Rowan & Martin's Laugh-In* on television and listening to the Beatles' *Let It Be*. President Richard Nixon had ordered U.S. troops into Cambodia to attack Viet Cong bases. New York's once-hapless Mets had become the "Miracle Mets," starting the 1970 season as World Series champions.

Events since 1970 seem world-shaking. The Soviet Union has fallen apart. The global village has grown together. Yet what amazes Rip the most is the tremendous economic progress the United States has made in just a quarter of a century.

Americans in the 1990s routinely withdraw money from automatic teller machines all over the world. We communicate on cellular phones, cook meals in minutes using microwave ovens, watch movies at home on videocassette players, listen to concert hall-quality music on compact discs and flash instant messages from one computer to another on a global grid called Internet. Americans figure checking-account balances on pocket calculators, use camcorders to film our children playing soccer, fight ulcers and depression with new wonder drugs, flick many things on and off by remote control. We have more cars, more household appliances, more vacation homes, more entertainment options and more free time than Americans two decades ago (see Table 10.1).

The contrast between American life then and now is astounding. Rip surveys the changes and concludes Americans never had it so good. He is puzzled, though, that so few people share his sense of wonderment. People seem glum about the U.S. economy of the 1990s and look back to the time Rip went to sleep—the late 1960s

Table 10.1 The world through Rip's eyes

	1970	1990
Average size of a new home (square feet)	1,500	2,080
New homes with central air conditioning	34%	76%
People using computers	<100,000	75.9 million
Households with color TV	33.9%	96.1%
Households with cable TV	4 million	55 million
Households with VCRs	0	67 million
Households with two or more vehicles	29.3%	54%
Median household net worth (real)	$24,217	$48,887
Housing units lacking complete plumbing	6.9%	1.1%
Homes lacking a telephone	13%	5.2%
Households owning a microwave oven	<1%	78.8%
Heart transplant procedures	<10	2.125*
Average work week	37.1 hours	34.5 hours
Average daily time working in the home	3.9 hours	3.5 hours
Work time to buy gas for 100-mile trip	49 minutes	31 minutes*
Annual paid vacation and holidays	15.5 days	22.5 days
Number of people retired from work	13.3 million	25.3 million
Women in the work force	31.5%	56.6%
Recreational boats owned	8.8 million	16 million
Manufacturers' shipments of RVs	30,300	226,500
Adult softball teams	29,000	188,000
Recreational golfers	11.2 million	27.8 million
Attendance at symphonies and orchestras	12.7 million	43.6 million
Americans finishing high school	51.9%	77.7%
Americans finishing four years of college	13.5%	24.4%
Employee benefits as a share of payroll	29.3%	40.2% **
Life expectancy at birth (years)	70.8	75.4
Death rate by natural causes (per 100,000)	714.3	520.2

* Figures are for 1991.
** Figure is for 1992.
Eisner (1989), Federal Reserve Bulletin (1992 and 1984), National Safety Council (1992), *Statistical Abstract of the United States*, U.S. Department of Commerce (*Current Population Reports* and *Survey of Current Business*). U.S. Department of Energy, U.S. Department of Health and Human Services, U.S. Department of Justice, U.S. Department of Labor (Bulletins 2434, 2422 and 2370: *Employment and Earnings*; and *Monthly Labor Review*—March and July 1992 and 1977).

and early 1970s—as the apex of American prosperity. People reflect on that time as "the good old days" from which the U.S. standard of living has ebbed.

Americans of the 1990s point Rip to many signs of lost vitality in the U.S. economy. Growth is slowing to a crawl. Productivity is stagnating. Paychecks are getting smaller and, for many workers, less certain. Other countries are gaining on us, even as more American families earn two incomes (see "Catching Up" at the end of this essay). Worst of all, perhaps, some Americans worry that their country, for the first time in its history, will fail to provide today's children with living standards as high as their parents'. As if economic deterioration weren't enough, discouraging reports on crime, education, homelessness and other social ills plague the country in the 1990s.

The usual barometers of economic activity show cause for alarm. Inflation-adjusted manufacturing wages rose by 2 percent a year from 1950 to 1973, but they *fell* an average of 1.3 percent a year from 1973 to 1990. Inflation-adjusted median family income gained 3 percent a year from 1950 to 1973, but the annual increase ebbed to 0.1 percent in the past two decades. Productivity, a yardstick of the output from each hour of work, grew at an annual rate of 2.2 percent from 1870 to 1973, then slowed to 1 percent. The broadest measure of the economy's well-being—gross national product, or GNP—sends perhaps the most troubling signal of all. Even with the Great Depression of the 1930s, GNP expanded by an average of nearly 3.5 percent a year from 1870 to 1973 (see Figure 10.1). To the dismay of many Americans, the growth rate slipped to an annual average of less than 2.5 percent in the past two decades.

The two versions of reality could hardly be more at odds. One says the country continues to reap the ever-larger bounty promised by free enterprise; the other, that the increase in Americans' standard of living has slowed markedly in recent years. A loss of dynamism—if real—would challenge Americans' view of who we are. The notion of a falling living standard affronts the American dream, one of the ideals that hold the nation together. It challenges the ingenuity of those in power, confronting them with the task of getting America moving again. Most broadly, it threatens Americans' faith in the free enterprise system at the very moment of its historic triumph over communism.

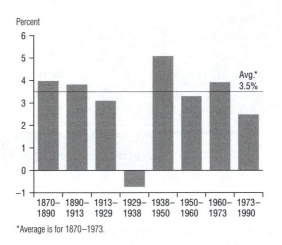

Figure 10.1 Growth of U.S. gross national product, 1870–1990

Balke and Gordon (1989) and U.S. Department of Commerce (*Current Population Reports, Historical Statistics of the United States* and *Survey of Current Business*).

GNP is not standard of living

As Rip learned, there are both bleak and bright views of America's economic progress. To unravel the conflict between them, we must understand how society's standard of living is measured. As a gauge of well-being, economists and policymakers usually rely on GNP, a simple sum of the market value of goods and services our nation churns out in a year. Every measure of how the economy is faring in some way derives from this aggregate. *Growth* is the percentage change in GNP, usually adjusted for inflation by a price index. *Productivity* divides the inflation-adjusted, or real, GNP by the total number of hours worked. *Per capita income* apportions an equal share of real GNP to each person.

At best, GNP offers only a crude measure of Americans' well-being. The meter for GNP is dollars and cents or, through the magic of a price index, real goods and services. The meter for standard of living is happiness, an elusive concept. Even without consulting a philosopher, it's clear they aren't the same. GNP is not standard of living.

By design, GNP counts only a fraction of what human beings might want in a better life (see Figure 10.2). GNP figures ignore the contribution to people's lives of anything. Good or bad, that's not explicitly bought and sold on the open market. For the most part, this is a practical matter: statisticians report what's measurable.

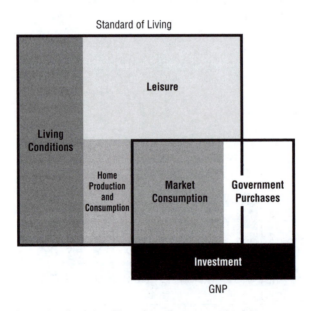

Figure 10.2 What GNP doesn't tell us about living standards

GNP is not standard of living. The two concepts are related, but standard of living has a much broader meaning. GNP does not reflect many factors that affect living standards. Among these are leisure, the value of goods families produce for personal use and conditions of life, such as health and safety, crime, pollution and longevity. GNP in turn, includes some elements that do not affect today's living standards, such as investment spending.

Markets give objective, easily calculated monetary values to shoes, televisions, haircuts, trips to Hawaii—a whole panoply of goods and services.

By far, the largest omission in measured GNP is leisure—time for recreation, family, friends, entertainment, hobbies or just taking it easy. By the choices we make about work hours as incomes rise, Americans show we value leisure highly. Yet because time off from work isn't traded in the marketplace, a trend toward greater leisure in recent decades counts for nothing in the GNP measure of standard of living.

The GNP numbers also ignore the value of services produced and consumed in the home—cooking meals, doing laundry, mowing the lawn, washing the car and dozens more chores. Over time, many household tasks have been shifted toward the market, allowing families even more leisure. As families pay for household chores, GNP data reflect these transactions but can distort comparisons of GNP from one generation to the next.

Time also brings new and improved products that enhance our lives in ways unavailable to previous generations at any price. Each innovation—air conditioners that use less energy, cars that handle more safely, cable television companies that deliver new programs into the home, foods with lower cholesterol and fat—raises the value of these goods and services and lifts consumers' standards of living. Yet various studies suggest that the GNP statistics don't adequately account for improvements, over time, in product quality.

Nor does GNP track a host of other important, nonmarket components of a higher quality of life—longevity, health and safety, working conditions, the environment. These aspects of daily life vary greatly from place to place, from one person's experience to the next, but there's evidence that they've improved decade by decade for most Americans.

It's no easy task to translate much of what's not measured by GNP into dollars and cents. There are inherent difficulties in valuing leisure, home production, product quality, living conditions and whatever else might go into the true standard of living. Yet moving beyond narrow GNP to a broader notion of Americans well-being will help provide a more accurate—and, to many, surprising—view of how well the nation is doing. There's no denying the country would be better off with a faster pace of economic expansion (See "Secrets of Growth" at the end of this essay.) The supposedly lackluster 2.5 percent GNP growth of recent decades, though, doesn't capture all the gains in living standards. The omissions and lapses suggest that GNP, as it comes out of the government's statistical mills, may understate the true income of Americans, perhaps by a large margin.

Time for symphonies and softball

Time is the ultimate scarce resource. Each day contains 24 hours. Each week consists of seven days. In a fast-paced, modern society, once work and chores are done, there almost always seems to be a shortage of time for what we enjoy. Many workers complain about haggard, sleep-deprived lifestyles. Yet, as hard as it may be for many Americans to believe, surveys show the country has never had as much leisure. What's more, evidence from spending patterns and elsewhere suggests that today's Americans are using their time off to squeeze more recreational activities into their lives.

Over the past four generations, the time an average U.S. employee devotes to on-the-job work decreased by nearly one-half (see Table 10.2). Looking at just the most recent two decades, when concerns about American living standards became more pronounced, work hours declined an additional 9.3 percent, the equivalent of 23 days a year.

Table 10.2 Work time

Since 1870, Americans' hours on the job have been cut almost in half. Even since 1970 we've shortened the workweek and gained extra vacation days and holidays.

Year	Work-week (hours)	Work-day (hours)	Work-week (days)	Annual hours Paid for	Vacation (days)	Holidays (days)	Other absence (days)	Annual hours worked
1870	61	10.2	6	3,181	0	3	8	3,069
1890	58.4	9.7	6	3,045	0	3	8	2,938
1913	53.3	8.9	6	2,779	5	3.5	8	2,632
1929	48.1	8	6	2,508	5.5	4	8	2,368
1938	44	8	5.5	2,294	6	4.5	8	2,146
1950	39.8	8	5	2,075	6.5	6	9	1,903
1960	38.6	7.7	5	2,013	7	7	9	1,836
1973	36.9	7.4	5	1,924	8	7.5	9	1,743
1990	34.5	7.3	4.7	1,799	10.5	12	10	1,562

Atack and Bareman (1992), Eisner (1989), Greis (1984), Maddison (1991 and 1964), U.S. Department of Commerce (*Survey of Current Business*) and U.S. Department of Labor (*Bulletin 2370 and Monthly Labor Review*—March and July 1992, 1989, 1977).

Table 10.3 Less work, more leisure

Today's workers may feel pressed for time, but, as a nation, we start to work later in life and work fewer hours than earlier generations. In 1870, Americans could expect to spend 39 percent of their waking hours at leisure. Now, the time we spend in childhood, vacations, evenings, holidays and retirement adds up to 70 percent of our waking hours.

Activity	1870	1950	1973	1990
Age starting work (avg.)	13	17.6	18.5	19.1
Life expectancy (years)	43.5	67.2	70.6	75.0
Retirement age (avg.)	death	68.5	64.0	63.6
Years on job	30.5	49.6	45.5	44.5
Retirement (years)	0	0	6.6	11.4
Annual hours worked	3,069	1.903	1,743	1,562
Annual hours home work	1,825	1,544	1.391	1,278
Lifetime hours				
Working at job	93.604	94,389	79,307	69,509
Working at home	61,594	81,474	67,151	59,800
Waking leisure	99.016	216,854	266,129	308,368

U.S. Department of Commerce (*Historical Statistics of the United States*). U.S. Department of Health and Human Services (*Vital Statistics of the United States*); see also sources for Table 10.2.

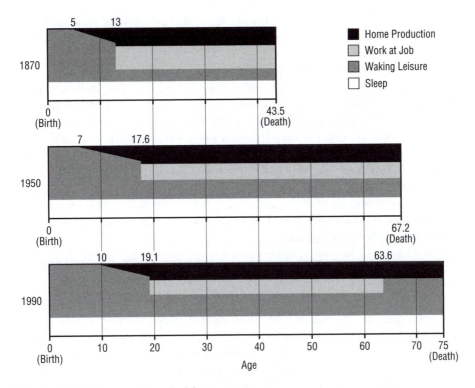

Figure 10.3 Three profiles of a lifetime

U.S. Department of Commerce (*Historical Statistics of the United States*). U.S. Department of Health and Human Services (*Vital Statistics of the United States*); see also sources for Table 10.2.

Daily work hours aren't the end of what's happening to leisure. Americans are starting work later in life and, perhaps even more significant, they are enjoying longer periods of retirement (see Table 10.3). In the two decades after 1970, the age at which an average worker entered the labor force pushed forward by seven months. A typical retirement grew by more than four years. In addition, the average daily time devoted to household chores fell consistently—from 4 hours, 12 minutes in 1950, to 3 hours, 48 minutes in 1973, to an estimated 3 hours, 30 minutes in 1990. Over a year, 18 minutes a day aren't trifling: they add up to more than four extra days off.

Interestingly, the value of work at home might not be declining along with the time spent doing chores. Microwave ovens, no-iron fabrics, self-cleaning ovens, frost-free refrigerators and dozens of other conveniences make household work lighter and faster. In effect, technology is boosting household efficiency by enabling us to accomplish more with the same or less effort.

Today, the typical employee spends less than a third of all waking hours working, either at home or on the job (see Figure 10.3). When totaled, the results are mind-boggling: workers, on average, have added nearly *five years* of waking leisure to their lifetimes since 1973. A look back 120 years shows that an extended childhood, with more years of schooling, and a period of leisure after years of work are strictly modern expectations.

When jobs and work at home are combined, virtually all segments of society worked less in 1990 than they did two decades before. The gain in leisure was a minuscule few minutes a week for employed men. Thanks largely to labor-saving appliances and other helping hands, women who didn't work outside the home reaped 10 extra hours of leisure. Employed women saw a six-hour decline in total work. A trend toward more women taking jobs creates one caveat. Women who used to stay at home and now hold jobs may have increased their work—by about 13 hours a week. Inflexibility in the labor market typically requires them to put in a full week, and household chores await at the end of each day. Nevertheless, women with jobs spend less time on housework than their counterparts did 20 years ago, and they are compensated with higher incomes.

But does having more free time translate into higher living standards? Statistics from the government and trade groups indicate Americans are spending more time and more money on recreation. From 1970 to 1991, the number of Americans who play golf regularly doubled to 11 percent of the population. Even after adjusting for population growth, the number of adult softball teams jumped sixfold in two decades. In 1970, a quarter of Americans bowled; now, a third do. Ownership rates rose 50 percent for recreational boats and more than doubled for vacation homes. Pleasure trips per capita rose from 1.5 a year in 1980 to 1.8 in 1991. Average attendance at baseball games rose from 16.100 in 1973 to 31,377 in 1992. Football, hockey, basketball, golf and car racing are drawing bigger crowds—in person and on television. Cultural activities haven't been short-changed. Per capita attendance at symphonies and operas doubled from 1970 to 1991. We're reading more books; annual sales rose from 6.6 per person in 1974 to 8.1 in 1991.

Money going to leisure activities has risen rapidly, too. From 1970 to 1990, spending rose from $1.2 billion to 54.1 billion for recreational vehicles, $2.7 billion to $7.6 billion for pleasure boats and $17 billion to $44 billion for sporting goods. Total recreational spending, adjusted for inflation, jumped from $91.3 billion in 1970 to $257.3 billion in 1990, an average annual gain of 9.1 percent that well outstrips population growth of 1 percent a year. In 20 years, the money consumers allocated to recreation increased from 5 percent of total spending to nearly 8 percent.

The fact that Americans cram their off-work hours with all these recreational activities suggests we're wealthier—financially better off to make use of the time off we've gained. Work hours and family budgets reveal what GNP numbers don't: an explosion of leisure is improving the American lifestyle.

The lost art of canning vegetables

One way critics put clown the U.S. economy is to say, "We're becoming a nation of hamburger flippers." Truth is, however, somebody always flipped hamburgers, or at least did the equivalent in preparing daily meals, usually in the home. In fact, running a household requires a daunting list of chores—cooking, cleaning, gardening, child care, shopping, banking, ferrying family members to ballet lessons and soccer practice.

As Americans grow richer, many chores once done by family members are moving out of home production and into the market or like gardening and canning, becoming hobbies rather than necessities. More so today than in the past, it's more efficient for workers to spend time earning money doing what they do best on the job, then pay others to perform at least some household tasks. In modern economies, market alternatives to home production are readily available. To the extent they can afford it, households hire professionals to cook, clean, paint, design landscapes, figure taxes and much more. (see Table 10.4.)

Americans, for example, are finding ways to ease the burden of cooking at home. In 1993, restaurants received 43 percent of the country's spending on food, a big gain from the 33 percent of 1972. Eating out, once an occasional luxury, has become a way of life. Even when we eat at home, we often rely more on market goods—heat-and-serve products, microwave meals and carry-out items. Usually, these shortcuts raise the cost of feeding a family, but as consumers become wealthier, they often opt to pay extra for ease and convenience. Entrepreneurs haven't missed the trend away from home production: nearly all businesses whose services replace home production have shown strong gains in employment and sales in recent years.

There's a paradox in the GNP method of accounting. If a person were to marry his or her doctor (gardener, plumber, hair dresser, tax accountant and so forth) and no longer pay for these services, measured economic activity would decline by the amount of the professional fee. The family's true standard of living, however, would remain unchanged. This distortion reveals that GNP understates living standards by the value of what's produced and consumed in the home. Estimates suggest home production, if properly accounted for, would have boosted America's 1992 GNP by about a third, or *$2 trillion*.

Failure to properly account for households' nonmarket production probably wouldn't skew growth rates if the proportion of home and market consumption remained stable over time. The data show, however, that home production fell steadily from 45 percent of GNP at the end of World War II to 33 percent in 1973. It then leveled off. What was the impact on measured growth? The transfer of household chores to the market added 1.3 percentage points to measured annual GNP growth prior to 1973, implying an underlying growth rate for the period of just 2.2 percent. Adjustments after 1973 are insignificant. Merely recognizing the contribution of household production could bring growth rates of the past two decades into line with those experienced in the 1950s and 1960s.

Not just more, but better, too

In judging whether Americans are better off, what should matter most are goods and services that bring enjoyment, provide convenience or reduce discomfort. In other words, the focus ought to be on consumption—the bulk, but not all, of GNP. Artifacts of everyday life provide proof of rising consumption during the past quarter century. The average number of televisions in a household rose from 1.4 in 1970 to 2.1 in 1990. Among those 15 years and older, passenger vehicles per 100,000 people increased from 61,400 in 1970 to 73,000 in 1991. Americans are enjoying more

Table 10.4 Out of home and into the market

As U.S. living standards have risen, and especially as more women have entered the work force, chores once done by family members have become services provided by the marketplace.

Home activity	Business or industry
Yard work	
Mow the lawn	Lawn mowing
Prune trees	Tree service
Trim bushes	Yard maintenance
Weed and fertilize	Lawn and garden care
Install sprinklers	Yard service
Clothing	
Wash and dry clothes	Maid dry cleaning
Iron, starch and fold clothes	Laundry-dry cleaning
Sew, knit and tailor garments	Clothing makes, tailors
Food	
Grow fruit and vegetables	Farming
Raise livestock	Ranging
Preserve fruits and vegetables	Canning, packaging
Slaughter and cure meat	Butchery
Cook and serve meals	Restaurant catering
Clean the dishes	Restaurant
Household maintenance	
Clean house	Maids
Wash windows	Window cleaning
Shampoo rugs	Carpet and rug cleaners
Clean drapes	Drapery cleaners
Make minor repairs	Plumber, electrician
Repair appliances	Appliance repair
Paint the house	House painting
Make or restore furniture	Furniture, upholsterers
Build homes or additions	Home building, construction
Design the home	Architects
Decorate the home	Interior decorators
Exterminate pests	Pest control, exterminator
Family finances	
Fill out tax forms	Accountants, tax preparers
Establish a financial plan	Financial planners
Manage investments	Brokerages
Prepare will, legal documents	Lawyers
Personal care	
Cut and set hair	Barber, beauty salon
Groom (manicures, facials)	Beauty shops
Educate children	Schools, colleges
Babysit	Child care centers
Administer health or medical needs	Doctors, hospital
Care for the elderly	Nursing home
Exercise (jogging, calisthenics)	Health and illness centers
Automobiles	
Maintain vehicles (change oil)	Auto service station
Wash and vacuum vehicles	Car wash
Repair vehicles	Auto repair
Miscellaneous	
Make gifts	Gift and craft shops
Care for pets	Kennel, veterinarian
Cut and split wood	Firewood, central heating
Repair mowers, bikes	Machine shops

luxuries, too. The average amount spent on jewelry and watches, after adjusting for higher prices, more than doubled from 1970 to 1991.

Many Americans live in bigger and better houses. From 1970 to 1992, an average new home increased in size by the equivalent of two 15-foot by 20-foot rooms. New houses are much more likely to have central air conditioning and garages. What about stories that fewer U.S. residents can afford the essential piece of the American dream—a home of their own? The data don't support it. The rate of home ownership has held steady at around 65 percent of the population since 1970, and there's over-whelming evidence that today's houses are stocked with more appliances and gadgets than ever.

Microwave ovens, color televisions, videocassette recorders, answering machines, food processors, camcorders and exercise equipment are all now standard in many American homes. Three-quarters of U.S. homes had a clothes washer in 1990, up from less than two-thirds in 1970. At the same time, ownership of dryers jumped from 45 percent of households to almost 70 percent. About 45 percent of homes had dishwashers, up from 26 percent two decades ago. Between 1970 and 1990, the typical U.S. household gained 4.5 times more audio and video products, more than twice as much gear for sports and hobbies, 50 percent more in kitchen appliances and 30 percent more in furniture. In short, most Americans consume far more than previous generations.

Of course, we could be paying for our consumption by depleting our savings. The evidence, however, says it isn't so. Although Americans may not set aside as much as people in many other countries, the average American still has managed to gain net worth. The stock of real wealth per capita rose by 2 percent a year from 1970 to 1990. The nation has had the best of two worlds: consuming more in the present and setting aside more for the future—not a bad standard for "better off."

The news gets even better As consumers. Americans can now possess products that didn't even exist for past generations (see Table 10.5). Twenty years ago, only a lucky few could show movies at home. Today, two of every three U.S. households own videocassette recorders. When Elvis was king of rock 'n' roll, many of his records succumbed to warps and scratches. Today's compact discs give us concert hall-quality sound. A decade ago, most motorists had to search out a pay telephone to make a call. Today, cellular technology has put a phone in millions of cars. Companies served 11 million subscribers in 1992, up from a mere 92,000 in 1984. The past 20 years also brought many important medical breakthroughs—new drugs, new treatments and new diagnostic tools—to enhance and prolong our lives.

We hardly notice many innovations that improve service. Fiber-optic cables greatly expand the capacity of telephone lines. Lasers on cash registers help speed us through check-out lines by scanning bar codes. Airbags await to cushion us from the impact of traffic accidents. Microprocessors guide pilots and air-traffic controllers. Doppler radar makes weather forecasts more reliable. These and a host of other products, many embedded with tiny silicon brains of their own, make our lives safer, easier, more convenient or just plain more fun.

Few facets of life are untouched by the arrival of new and better products, and GNP's measurement of consumption can easily fall short of properly accounting for improvements in quality. The traditional measures of standard of living—real per capita income, for example—use an index to compensate for rising prices.

Table 10.5 New and improved

From gadgets to wonder drugs, the list of products available to Americans gets longer by the day.

A sampling of new or greatly improved products since 1970

Microwave oven	Videocassette recorder
Camcorder	Laser printers
Voice mail	Cordless phone
Cellular phone	Personal computer
Ultrasound	Answering machine
Home security systems	Small-screen TVs
Synthesizers	CDs and CD players
Pagers	Remote controls
Quartz/digital watches	Sound systems
Fax machines	Digital/LED displays
Coffee makers	Video games
Electronic date books	Food processors
Electric knives	Aspartame
In-line rollerskates	Interactive toys
Miniature radios	Cable TV
Exercise equipment	Airbags
All-terrain vehicles	

Medical advances since 1970

Cosmetics (Retin-A)	Monoclonal antibodies
Organ transplants	In vitro fertilization
Artificial pancreas	Soft contact lenses
	Cornea transplants
Painkillers (acetaminophen, ibuprofen)	Decongestants
Cosmetic surgery (facelifts, implants, liposuction)	Anti-allergenics
	Home pregnancy tests
Biosynthesized drugs (recombinant DNA techniques)	Anti-depressants
	Anti-ulcer drugs
CAT-scan	
Radial kerotonomy	

Statisticians can calculate exactly what Americans pay for cars, clothing, computers and clocks and occasionally try to adjust for better quality, but even their best efforts aren't likely to keep pace with the dizzying blitz of new products and features in a dynamic global economy.

Price indexes, too, are apt to understate gains in product longevity, new features or better performance. The price of a tire, for example, rose from $13 in the mid-1930s to about $70 in early 1994, entering into a price index for tires as an increase of about 1.5 percent a year. However, today's steel-belted radials last more than 10 times longer than the old four-ply cotton tires. Based on cost per 1,000 miles, tires now actually sell for less than half what they did 50 years ago. Even more astounding, an average worker in the 1930s worked almost four hours to buy those 1,000 miles. Today, the cost is less than five minutes. The benefits don't stop there: drivers in safer cars are better off because they have fewer accidents, reducing the amount of time and money spent on repairs. Safer highways may lower GNP, but they raise the standard of living.

Quirks of this sort permeate the price indexes. Modern fabrics last longer and require less care, adding to the value of clothing and linens. Frost-free refrigerators make the messy chore of defrosting a fading memory. In just the past decade, computers and the software to run them improved in speed, memory and ease of use by leaps and bounds. The rapidly rising cost of health care is a major national issue, but at least part of the increase in hospital fees and drug prices is the result of better quality. Car lovers may wax nostalgic about the Corvettes and Mustangs of yesteryear, but today's cars go farther on a gallon of gas. What's more, they've been improved with antilock brakes, fuel injectors, turbochargers, cruise control and sound systems that outperform even the home stereos of 1970. Today's cars, with as many as 25 tiny microprocessors aboard, require less maintenance, too.

Price indexes are also slow to incorporate the myriad of new products coming into common use. Pocket calculators entered the U.S. consumer price index in 1978—only after the prices for these smaller, more powerful models fell by 98 percent from those of the electromechanical desktop devices they replaced. Statisticians missed 99 percent of the price decrease in penicillin. The list could go on: quality improvements are widespread in an age of advanced technology, with new products coming to the market just about every week.

Any failure to properly account for better quality makes price indexes exaggerate increases in the cost of living. Economists frequently debate the extent of upward bias in inflation, but some studies suggest the bias might be significant—from a low of a third of a percentage point a year to as much as 2 percentage points over the past two decades. When price indexes overcompensate for inflation, they make GNP growth seem smaller than it actually is.

Price-index problems have always existed. New products have been introduced and improvements in quality have taken place in previous eras, but there's reason to believe they are greater now, during rapidly expanding technology and trade. Companies face intensifying competition and shrinking product cycles: the latest breakthroughs and updated models seem to be coming faster and faster. Record players reigned for decades before cassette tapes. The time between cassettes and compact discs was much shorter. Now, digital audio tape and recordable CDs are arriving. New models of computer chips once came out every few years. Now, it's nearly an annual event. Accelerated technical progress makes it harder for the statisticians to accurately measure GNP and harder for GNP to serve as a proxy for living standards.

Some other rays of light

More leisure and higher consumption aren't the only ways people's lives have improved. Especially as societies become richer, citizens tend to put greater importance on nonmaterial factors that affect living standards: better health, safety,

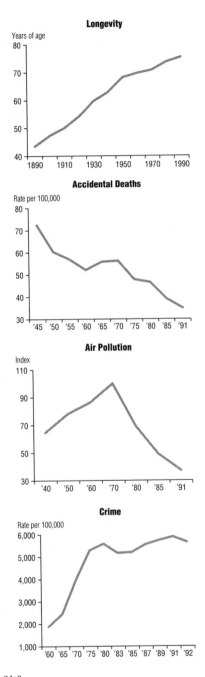

Figure 10.4 Quality of life

While GNP is measured in dollars and cents, many factors affect living standards. Trends toward longer life spans, fewer accidents and decreasing air pollution suggest that U.S. living standards have continued to improve in recent years. New data even show progress in fighting crime.

U.S. Department of Commerce (*Current Population Reports*), National Safety Council, *Statistical Abstract of the United States*, U.S. Department of justice.

more pleasant working conditions, a cleaner environment. All of us could add other considerations we value. "The good life" becomes harder to measure when we move beyond the dollars and cents accounting of GNP data. Even so, there is evidence to counter fears that U.S. living standards are getting worse (see Figure 10.4).

Longevity may be the most important measure of well-being in a modern society. The data show that an average American's life expectancy at birth has increased each decade during the past century. As might be expected, the biggest gains came in the first half of the 20th century, but the upward trend continues. In the past decade, the life span rose by more than one year and eight months.

What's more, the population generally sees itself as healthier. Surveys by the U.S. Department of Health and Human Services show a steady drop in the proportion of Americans who rate their health as "fair or poor," from 12.2 percent in 1975 to 9.3 percent in 1991. Infant mortality rates fell from 20 deaths per 1,000 live births in 1970 to less than nine in 1991. The death rate from natural causes fell by 27 percent from 1970 to 1990, with the most progress coming in diseases of the heart. Cancer death rates are up slightly, but modern medical science provides treatments that prolong life. The portion of the adult population with high cholesterol fell sharply over the past two decades. What once was fatal can in many cases now be treated. Heart, liver and lung transplants, almost unheard of in the early 1970s, are common today.

The country isn't just healthier; it's also safer in some respects. Accidental deaths have declined in every category, especially since 1970. Homes are safer. The workplace is safer. In 1991, 88,000 Americans died in accidents, the lowest figure since 1924. Highway deaths totaled 43,500 in 1991, the lowest they've been since 1962. Even more encouraging, the death rate per 100 million miles traveled on the nation's roads fell from three in 1975 to 1.8 in 1990. At the higher rate, an additional 25,000 people would have died in 1990. The incidence of death from crashes of scheduled airliners has decreased to just a fraction of what it was 20 years ago.

When it comes to time at work, improvement in the quality of life continues, at least for most Americans. The trend toward service employment has rescued many Americans from the daily grind of the manufacturing assembly line. And in manufacturing, modern robots assist worker effort, meaning less wear and tear on the human body. Observers also find greater workplace flexibility in the form of breaks, exercising and socializing. Properly understood, this time isn't shirking. It goes for rest, birthday parties, fitness classes and awards ceremonies that employers support as tools to improve morale and efficiency.

What's more, trends point toward greater flexibility of scheduling to reduce stress involved in meeting family responsibilities. The number of people with flexible job hours rose from 9.1 million in 1985 to 12.1 million in 1991. New technologies—modems, e-mail, fax machines, digital networks—create opportunities for unheard of freedom from the confines of yesterday's 8-to-5 straitjacket. The ranks of white-collar telecommuters, for example, swelled to 6.6 million in 1992, saving at least some employees the bumper-to-bumper grind of an old-style commute. Imagine the possibilities: a lucky worker can type a report into a laptop computer while sitting in a beach chair in Maui, then send it to the office in Dallas via cellular circuits. With improving battery technology, there's no need for even an extension cord.

Safety at work has gotten better, too. Accidental deaths at work have declined consistently since at least 1945. Injuries on the job haven't declined in recent years, but they are well below the levels of previous decades. If the hot, unsavory sweat shop symbolized the workplace of a bygone era, today's standard might be the air-conditioned office and, at an increasing number of firms, employee cafeterias, day-care centers, break rooms and exercise facilities.

Some data show that wages fell over the past 20 years. Yet those statistical series ignore the rapid growth of fringe benefits: with high tax rates, workers often prefer to take their higher pay in the form of additional health care, contributions to retirement funds or employee assistance programs. Figures on total compensation, which include extras employers pay for, don't show a decline. Some workers are finding their benefits packages becoming leaner, but many others are getting new perks. Overall, nonpay compensation as a percentage of payroll is up a third since 1970. Compared with a generation ago, more employers are offering eye care, dental plans, paid maternity leave and stock-purchase plans. Today's most progressive companies are starting to offer day care and paternity leave. It's impossible to prove whether workplace abuses are declining. Even so, workers today have greater redress for unfair dismissal, sexual harassment and other problems.

Americans are also making progress in improving the environment. Levels of such major pollutants as particulate matter, sulfur oxides, volatile organic compounds, carbon monoxide and lead were their highest in 1970 or before. Levels of nitrogen oxides peaked in 1980. Overall, air quality is better now than at any time since data collection in 1940. Water quality has improved since the 1960s, when authorities banned fishing in Lake Erie and fires erupted on the polluted Cuyahoga River near Cleveland. The U.S. Geological Survey, examining trends since 1980, found that fecal coliform bacteria and phosphorous have decreased substantially in many parts of the country. Other traditional indicators of water quality—dissolved oxygen, dissolved solids, nitrate and suspended sediments—have shown little change.

Despite such gains, we live in a complex world, and it would be surprising if by every measure the country's life were getting better. The general gains in health are clouded by the AIDS epidemic. Air and water may be getting cleaner, but they still aren't pristine. Environmentalists warn of global warming, deforestation, hazardous waste dumping and endangered species. Working conditions may have become more pleasant for most Americans, but some workers displaced by downsizing may have new jobs that aren't as good as the ones they lost, or they may have no job at all. Even among the 120 million employed in the United States, reports of widespread layoffs cause anxiety about job security.

We are even more anxious about the increasing incidence of crime and violence. In polls taken in early 1994, crime ranked first among Americans' worries. The data indicate why. Crime worsened in the 1970s and remains high. But even here there's some encouraging news. Figures for the first half of 1993 show that crime rates are ebbing—by 3 percent in violent offenses. Clearly, Americans' well-being will improve if the country can sustain a trend toward less crime.

Diseases, pollution, unemployment and crime are but a few of the threats to our living standards, but we should not let them overshadow two decades of progress.

A last look at standards of living

Rising living standards may be the ultimate test of an economic system. The very notion of economic progress depends in large measure on the potential for most people to become increasingly better off. Successful economies make their citizens richer and happier. Failing ones leave them poorer.

Americans may question whether we're becoming better off. By historical standards, the past two decades' 2.5 percent growth in GNP just doesn't measure up. But GNP does not tell the whole story. A more careful look at leisure, home production, new products, quality improvements and noneconomic indicators casts doubt on claims that the U.S. economy's rate of progress peaked a generation ago. If nothing else, this broader view proves the concept of standard of living cannot be captured by one or two numbers. By broadening our view, we find evidence that Americans are still building a better life. When all's said and done, the gains in recent years probably aren't too different from what they were a generation ago, when capitalism's capacity for progress was hardly questioned.

Why, then, do so many people seem to feel the country has lost its momentum? The question defies an easy answer. Part of the reason may be that many people aren't aware of the quiet improvement in so many areas of their lives—from more leisure to bigger houses and better health. They are, on the other hand, tuned into ills around them on a daily basis—AIDs, global warming and crime, to cite just three examples. And rightly so: these are problems that need attention.

Furthermore, there's a normal human tendency to romanticize the past. Looking back at the high-growth years from 1960 to 1973, for example, the nostalgic may gloss over many unsettling events. The country wrestled with the real possibility of nuclear annihilation, an unpopular war in Vietnam, racial strife that erupted in rioting, assassinations, political scandal and high rates of poverty. Many later problems—inflation in the 1970s, toxic waste dumps that needed cleaning up in the 1980s—trace their origins back to those "good old days."

History books can tell us about how Americans once lived. For the grandparents or great-grandparents of today's workers, life really was a struggle. Hours of work stretched from dawn to well after dusk. Workplaces were often dimly lit, dirty and dangerous. Houses were hot in the summer, cold in the winter. At home, the daily chores were unending and backbreaking. Death came early. The social critics of the time attributed much of the harshness of everyday life to the failings of capitalism.

Looking backward over a century or more, though it's obvious that the free enterprise system works—and works well, so long as private profit incentives are unfettered by government taxes, regulation, debt, policy instability or other burdens. Herein lies the secret to growth. If we let the system work, then every successive generation ought to be able to claim that "these are the good old days." Few Americans would fail to recognize that living standards have improved by leaps and bounds over the long sweep of time. Our Rip Van Winkle, his eyes not blinded by nostalgia or negativism, sees quite clearly that it's still true today. His fresh perspective affirms the promise of even higher living standards in the future—as long as we allow the free enterprise system to work.

Catching up

In the past two decades, Americans worried not only about the country's ability to keep pace with its own past performance but also about a failure to grow as fast as many other countries.

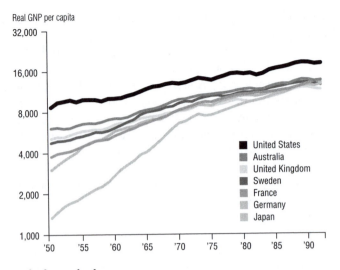

Figure 10.5 A high standard

For decades the United Sates was the unchallenged leader in per capita GNP growth. Since the 1950s, GNP in other countries has risen faster than, but failed to match, the U.S. level.

Maddison (1991).

The numbers are fairly familiar. From 1973 to 1990, per capita GNP in the United States grew by an average 1.5 percent a year (see Figure 10.5). By contrast, average annual economic gains were 3.1 percent for Japan and 2 percent for Germany. While the United States seemed to crawl forward, such developing countries as Korea, Taiwan, Thailand and, most recently, China managed to get their economies moving briskly. About GNP growth, Americans often ask, why are other nations doing so much better?

The answer lies in a notion called *convergence*. Envision an explorer wielding a machete to cut a path through a dense jungle. He goes slowly, hacking his way forward, destination not really known. Those who come behind him have a much easier time of it. They see the path. They know where they're going. They can move faster, gaining ground on the trailblazer.

That's just about what happens with economies. Using the sharp saber of free enterprise, the most advanced nations open the pathway for others by developing markets, technology, business systems and infrastructure—in effect, creating a successful model. Less developed countries can quickly adopt what works and exploit existing markets, and it shows up in faster rates of growth. In short, catching up takes less effort. Some nations don't emulate successful examples. Those that do tend to converge with the leaders in economic performance.

Without question, other nations are catching up to the United States. Per capita output in Japan rose from 50 percent of the U.S. average in 1970 to 72 percent in 1992. Germany moved up from 63 percent to 70 percent. Even so, the United States still hasn't lost its lead—and it's not likely to do so.

As other countries move closer to the U.S. level of development, their growth rates slow and converge toward the U.S. performance. Take Japan, for example. Its average annual growth rate outdid that of the United States by 6.9 percentage points in the 1960s, by 2.3 percentage points in the 1970s and by 1.7 percentage points in the 1980s. At the end of the latest decade, some predicted Japan would overtake the United States as the world's biggest economy. In the 1990s, however, both countries are likely to grow at about the same rate. Unless Japan experiences a renewed spurt of growth, it will not catch the United States.

To some Americans, faster growth abroad is a threat. Nothing could be further from the truth. The United States doesn't benefit when other countries stumble economically. Quite to the contrary, strong growth abroad provides opportunities for U.S. exports and business deals. All countries will move faster if they travel together.

Secrets of growth

Even if Americans' living standards aren't slipping, the U.S. economy can do better. Boosting the rate of GNP growth would make Americans even better off and help solve some of the country's problems—unemployment, poverty and budget deficits, to name just a few.

The U.S. economy has expanded by an average of 2.5 percent a year since 1973. Present and future generations of Americans would end up with much higher living standards if the economy could jump back to the 3.5 percent standard set in the century before 1973. The mathematics of it are straightforward but the results eye-opening: at the end of an average lifetime, the economy would be twice as large with the addition of just one percentage point a year to growth.

Inquiry into what makes economies grow dates back at least as far as Adam Smith's *Wealth of Nations*, published in 1776. In the past decade, with growth slowing in many parts of the world, the question has experienced a revival of interest, becoming one of economists' hottest research topics. The latest thinking recognizes that growth doesn't just happen. Instead, it arises out of the economic environment itself. The key is a stable framework of rights, freedoms and incentives that will spur individuals to work, businesses to produce and entrepreneurs to innovate (see Figure 10.6).

In a free enterprise system, growth is a natural and continuous process, but it must be nurtured by the correct policies. The following are the basic secrets of growth.

Establish and preserve property rights. Private ownership of the means of production allows individuals to reap the rewards from economic activity, thus encouraging efficient use of resources to satisfy consumer wants. People produce more when working in their own self-interest: altruism is a weak motive when compared with the incentive for profit and personal material gain.

Create market-friendly institutions. Markets won't function properly without an appropriate legal code. Contracts need to be enforced. Property rights need to be upheld. Monopoly needs to be controlled. Institutions should facilitate economic activity and complement innovation.

Maintain stable government policies. Households and businesses can pursue their economic interests only if government honors all promises—implicit and explicit.

Frequent changes in tax laws or other government policies create uncertainty and instability that can make a mockery of long-range planning.

Avoid protecting existing jobs, industries or businesses. The natural forces of creative destruction continuously regenerate the economy, but protection from failure prevents new, better or cheaper products from replacing older ones. By rejecting a paternalistic role for government, decision-making and responsibility stay in citizens' hands, where they can be best used to make the hard choices that new opportunities bring.

Keep taxes low and simple. People will work harder and invest more when they can keep a larger share of what they earn. Taxes that don't discourage work or investment— such as user fees or levies on consumption—are less harmful to the economy. Loopholes and special favors divert resources to less efficient uses.

Abstain from excessive regulation. Licenses, permits, fees and other burdens of operating businesses provide the same disincentives as taxes. Efforts to deregulate and privatize will pay off by increasing the rewards of going into business and hiring new-employees.

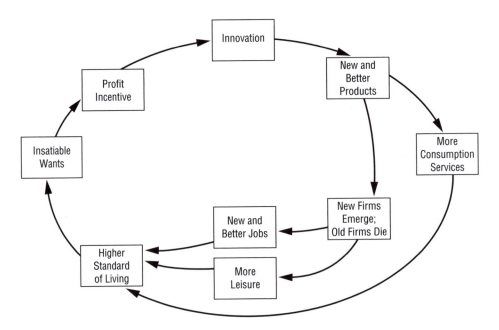

Figure 10.6 Endogenous growth: capitalism's perpetual motion machine

Insatiable consumer wants, combined with the pursuit of self-interest, provide an endless fuel for economic growth. This diagram illustrates now the process works. Consumers will always want more than they have. The profit incentive, when allowed to operate, will continually power a quest for new ways to meet the needs of consumers. Innovation leads to the introduction of new and better produces, which enhances consumption. New firms emerge to produce these products. In the process, they take business from old companies. The rising enterprises hire people for new and better jobs. Living standards rise. Even so, consumers still aren't satisfied and want more. 'Round and 'round it goes. The system slows if something—bad policies, for example—creates an impediment. The secrets of growth make it go faster.

Invest in infrastructure. Government spending on transportation facilities and other investment-type projects can enhance the efficiency of the private sector and facilitate commerce.

Maintain stable prices. Gyrations in the general price level wreak havoc on decision-making by businesses, households and governments. Steady, sensible control of the supply of money is the key to maintaining the currency's purchasing power. Low inflation will facilitate the efficient exchange of goods and services.

Nurture business credit, particularly for entrepreneurs. Keeping government debt low will conserve credit for use by private business. It's tempting to try to legislate away credit risk with government guarantees, but such programs distort the allocation of investment funds and supplant the natural discipline of failure in the marketplace.

Focus unemployment outlays on retraining. The bulk of unemployment funds should be used to prepare displaced workers for new jobs and provide incentives to work. Only a minimum payment should go for passive unemployment.

Make education a priority. A better educated work force is more productive, and it speeds the introduction of new technology. Tax laws ought to treat education as a depreciable capital good, equal to, if not more important than, physical capital. Allowing choice in schools will foster competition and improve quality.

Promote free trade. Tariffs, quotas and other trade barriers decrease competition and deny an economy the full advantage of the production efficiencies offered throughout the world. Free trade makes all nations wealthier.

Note

1 The essay is based on research conducted by W. Michael Cox, vice president and economic advisor. Federal Reserve Bank of Dallas.

Selected bibliography

Atack, Jeremy, and Fred Bateman. "How Long Was the Average Workday in 1880?" *Journal of Economic History*, March 1992.

Balke, Nathan, and Robert J. Gordon. "Prewar Gross National Product." *Journal of Political Economy*, February 1989.

Desmond, Kevin, *A Timetable of Inventions and Discoveries* (New York: M. Evans and Co., 1986).

Eisner. Robert. *The Total Incomes Systems of Accounts* (Chicago: University of Chicago Press, 1989).

Federal Reserve Bulletin, January 1992 and December 1984.

Gordon, Robert J., *The Measurement of Durable Goods Prices* (Chicago: University of Chicago Press. 1990).

Greis, Theresa Diss. *The Decline of Annual Hours Worked in the United States Since 1947*, Manpower and Human Resources Studies, no. 10, The Wharton School (Philadelphia: University of Philadelphia. 1984).

Lund, Robert L., "Truth About the American Productive System," in collaboration with Earl Reeves in *Truth About the New Deal* (New York: Longmans, Green and Co., 1936).

Maddison, Angus, *Dynamic Forces in Capitalist Development* (New York: Oxford University Press, 1991) and *Economic Growth in the West* (New York: The Twentieth Century Fund, 1964).

National Safety Council, *Accident Facts*, 1992.

Statistical Abstract of the United States, various issues.

U.S. Department of Commerce, Bureau of the Census. *Current Population Reports*, series P–65; *Computer Use in the United Stales: 1989*, series P–23, no. 171; and *Historical Statistics of the United States: Colonial Times to 1970*.

U.S. Department of Commerce, Bureau of Economic Analysis, *Survey of Current Business*, January 1992.

U.S. Department of Energy, Office of Energy Markets and End Use, U.S. Residential Energy Consumption Survey, *Housing Characteristics*, annual, 1990 and various issues.

U.S. Department of Health and Human Services, Public Health Services, National center for Health Statistics, *Vital Statistics of the United States*, 1984 and annual; and *Health United States 1992 and Healthy People 2000 Review*, August 1993.

U.S. Department of Justice, Federal Bureau of Investigation. *Uniform Crime Reports for the United States, 1975*, Table 1, Index of Crime, United States, 1990–75; and *Uniform Crime Reports for the United States, 1993*, Table 1, Index of Crime, United States, 1973–1992.

U.S. Department of Labor, Bureau of Labor Statistics, Bulletin 2434, *Employment Cost Index and Levels, 1975–93* (September 1993 and earlier years): Bulletin 2422, *Employee Benefits in Medium and Small Establishments, 1991* (May 1993): Bulletin 2370, *Employment, Hours, and Earnings, United States, 1909–90. Volume 1* (March 1991); *Employment and Earnings*, monthly (Table A–4: "Employment Status of the Civilian Noninstitutional Population by Age, Sex, and Race," 1993 and earlier years); *Monthly Labor Review*, "Trends in Retirement Age by Sex. 1950–2005" (July 1992), "Time-off Benefits in Small Establishments" (March 1992), "Variations in Holidays, Vacations, and Area Pay Levels" (February 1989) and "Absence from Work—Measuring the Hours Lost" (October 1977).

Review and Discussion Questions

1 What indications do Cox and Alm provide that life improved in America from 1970 to 1990?
2 What do Cox and Alm think are important omissions from GNP (GDP)? How do they try to measure the omitted factors? What measures for those factors would you use?
3 What important factors relating to the quality of life do you think GDP omits?
4 Cox and Alm find that people's leisure time, at least in the U.S., has been increasing. But many Americans seem to feel busier than ever. Can the findings of Cox and Alm be reconciled with Americans' feelings?
5 Cox and Alm present data for the U.S. Do you think their findings would hold if other developed economies were examined?

Suggestions for Further Reading

Acemoglu, D. K. (2009) "Fundamental Determinants of Differences in Economic Performance," Chapter 4 in *Introduction to Modern Economic Growth* (Princeton: Princeton University Press).

Daron Acemoglu is one of the leading scholars in the world today on the subject of economic growth. In this chapter from his textbook on economic growth, he summarizes the important research he and his colleagues have done. He concludes, like Baumol, that incentives are extremely important. Some countries provide legal and economic incentives for individuals to create businesses and jobs; in other societies those incentives are weaker, and the result is lower economic growth and less wealth. In addition to statistical evidence in favor of this hypothesis, Acemoglu looks briefly at two "natural experiments": the much different economic results in South Korea vs. North Korea, as well as West Germany vs. East Germany.

Burnham, J. B. (2003) "Why Ireland Boomed," *The Independent Review*, 7: 537–556.

A discussion of why Ireland's economy started to grow much more rapidly in the mid-1980s. Burnham concludes that openness to trade and to foreign investment played an important role, as did more market-friendly government policy.

Cox, W. M. and Alm, R. (2008) "How Are We Doing?" *The American*, 2, www.american.com/archive/2008/july-august-magazine-contents/how-are-we-doing.

Cox and Alm update some of their indicators of consumptions—leisure, and health and safety—to the period 2005–2007.

De Haan, J., Lundström, S., and Sturm, J.-E. (2006) "Market-Oriented Institutions and Policies and Economic Growth: A Critical Survey," *Journal of Economic Surveys*, 20: 157–191.

A survey of recent research about the relation between markets and economic growth. It concludes that economies that are more "market-oriented"—that allow businesses more economic freedom to pursue profit and that have more competition, more trade, and more secure property rights—have higher rates of economic growth.

Gwartney, J. D., Holcombe, R. D., and Lawson, R. A. (2004) "Economic Freedom, Institutional Quality, and Cross-Country Differences in Income and Growth," *Cato Journal*, 24: 205–233.

The authors examine whether differences in institutions help explain differences across countries in income levels and economic growth. The differences in institutions they examine are the degree to which institutions support "secure property rights and freedom of exchange"—that is, the degree to which a country's legal and political institutions support markets. They find that markets matter a lot, that differences in institutions are an important cause of differences among countries in economic growth. Institutions affect both the rate of investment and the productivity of resource use.

PART THREE

Property Rights

Introduction

For markets to work at all, let alone for markets to exert great power, people must be able to buy and sell property. They must have property rights. Property rights are "an instrument of society."[1] They define the ways in which society allows individuals to possess, use, and transfer property. Property may be physical items, like houses and cars, or less tangible items, like an individual's labor or his ideas.

Harold Demsetz, in "Toward a Theory of Property Rights," explains how property rights give individuals powerful incentives to use resources efficiently. In economics jargon, they foster the "internalization of external costs and benefits." ("Internalization" is discussed further in Part Four.) For example, a firm that pollutes the air could impose costs on people. But if the individuals who are harmed have property rights in clean air, the firm will soon take account of those costs, and the firm, one way or another, will reduce the amount of pollution it creates. Demsetz also advances a hypothesis about why property rights emerge and how they change: they emerge, and they change, when the marginal benefit of internalizing external costs and benefits exceeds the marginal cost of establishing, defining, and, importantly, enforcing property rights. Demsetz illustrates this process with an account of how the development of commercial fur trade led North Americans by the early eighteenth century to develop private property rights in land.

In "A Hypothesis of Wealth-Maximizing Norms: Evidence from the Whaling Industry," Robert C. Ellickson provides another detailed example of how property rights emerge and change as the marginal benefits of the rights and the marginal cost of defining and enforcing them change. The property rights that emerge promote efficient resource use, and thus, greater wealth.

Michael Satchell applies the idea that property rights promote the efficient use of resources to argue that, perhaps surprisingly to many people, private property rights can actually help endangered wildlife, specifically African elephants. This is because when African villagers have secure property rights in the elephants—when the elephants are owned—the villagers directly benefit if the elephants are conserved rather than eliminated. Satchell concludes that property rights and the market seem to have improved the elephants' welfare.

Note

1 Demsetz, H. 1989 "Toward a Theory of Property Rights," *American Economic Review*, 57: 347–359.

Chapter 11

Harold Demsetz

TOWARD A THEORY OF PROPERTY RIGHTS

W HEN A TRANSACTION IS CONCLUDED in the marketplace, two bundles of property rights are exchanged. A bundle of rights often attaches to a physical commodity or service, but it is the value of the rights that determines the value of what is exchanged. Questions addressed to the emergence and mix of the components of the bundle of rights are prior to those commonly asked by economists. Economists usually take the bundle of property rights as a datum and ask for an explanation of the forces determining the price and the number of units of a good to which these rights attach.

In this paper, I seek to fashion some of the elements of an economic theory of property rights. The paper is organized into three parts. The first part discusses briefly the concept and role of property rights in social systems. The second part offers some guidance for investigating the emergence of property rights. The third part sets forth some principles relevant to the coalescing of property rights into particular bundles and to the determination of the ownership structure that will be associated with these bundles.

The concept and role of property rights

In the world of Robinson Crusoe property rights play no role. Property rights are an instrument of society and derive their significance from the fact that they help a man form those expectations which he can reasonably hold in his dealings with others. These expectations find expression in the laws, customs, and mores of a society. An owner of property rights possesses the consent of fellowmen to allow him to act in particular ways. An owner expects the community to prevent others from interfering with his actions, provided that these actions are not prohibited in the specifications of his rights.

It is important to note that property rights convey the right to benefit or harm oneself or others. Harming a competitor by producing superior products may be permitted, while shooting him may not. A man may be permitted to benefit himself by shooting an intruder but be prohibited from selling below a price floor. It is clear, then, that property rights specify how persons may be benefited and harmed, and, therefore, who must pay whom to modify the actions taken by persons. The recognition of this leads easily to the close relationship between property rights and externalities.

Externality is an ambiguous concept. For the purposes of this paper, the concept includes external costs, external benefits, and pecuniary as well as nonpecuniary externalities. No harmful or beneficial effect is external to the world. Some person or persons always suffer or enjoy these effects. What converts a harmful or beneficial effect into an externality is that the cost of bringing the effect to bear on the decisions of one or more of the interacting persons is too high to make it worthwhile, and this is what the term shall mean here. "Internalizing" such effects refers to a process, usually a change in property rights, that enables these effects to bear (in greater degree) on all interacting persons.

A primary function of property rights is that of guiding incentives to achieve a greater internalization of externalities. Every cost and benefit associated with social interdependencies is a potential externality. One condition is necessary to make costs and benefits externalities. The cost of a transaction in the rights between the parties (internalization) must exceed the gains from internalization. In general, transacting cost can be large relative to gains because of "natural" difficulties in trading or they can be large because of legal reasons. In a lawful society the prohibition of voluntary negotiations makes the cost of transacting infinite. Some costs and benefits are not taken into account by users of resources whenever externalities exist, but allowing transactions increases the degree to which internalization takes place. For example, it might be thought that a firm which uses slave labor will not recognize all the costs of its activities, since it can have its slave labor by paying subsistence wages only. This will not be true if negotiations are permitted, for the slaves can offer to the firm a payment for their freedom based on the expected return to them of being free men. The cost of slavery can thus be internalized in the calculations of the firm. The transition from serf to free man in feudal Europe is an example of this process.

Perhaps one of the most significant cases of externalities is the extensive use of the military draft. The taxpayer benefits by not paying the full cost of staffing the armed services. The costs which he escapes are the additional sums that would be needed to acquire men voluntarily for the services or those sums that would be offered as payment by draftees to taxpayers in order to be exempted. With either voluntary recruitment, the "buy-him-in" system, or with a "let-him-buy-his-way-out" system, the full cost of recruitment would be brought to bear on taxpayers. It has always seemed incredible to me that so many economists can recognize an externality when they see smoke but not when they see the draft. The familiar smoke example is one in which negotiation costs may be too high (because of the large number of interacting parties) to make it worthwhile to internalize all the effects of smoke. The draft is an externality caused by forbidding negotiation.

The role of property rights in the internalization of externalities can be made clear within the context of the above examples. A law which establishes the right of a person to his freedom would necessitate a payment on the part of a firm or of the taxpayer sufficient to cover the cost of using that person's labor if his services are to be obtained. The costs of labor thus become internalized in the firm's or taxpayer's decisions. Alternatively, a law which gives the firm or the taxpayer clear title to slave labor would necessitate that the slaveowners take into account the sums that slaves are willing to pay for their freedom. These costs thus become internalized in decisions although wealth is distributed differently in the two cases. All that is needed for internalization in either case is ownership which includes the right of sale. It is the prohibition of a property right adjustment, the prohibition of the establishment of an ownership title that can thenceforth be exchanged, that precludes the internalization of external costs and benefits.

There are two striking implications of this process that are true in a world of zero transaction costs. The output mix that results when the exchange of property rights is allowed is efficient and the mix is independent of who is assigned ownership (except that different wealth distributions may result in different demands).[1] For example, the efficient mix of civilians and military will result from transferable ownership no matter whether taxpayers must hire military volunteers or whether draftees must pay taxpayers to be excused from service. For taxpayers will hire only those military (under the "buy-him-in" property right system) who would not pay to be exempted (under the "let-him-buy-his-way-out" system). The highest bidder under the "let-him-buy-his-way-out" property right system would be precisely the last to volunteer under a "buy-him-in" system.[2]

We will refer back to some of these points later. But for now, enough groundwork has been laid to facilitate the discussion of the next two parts of this paper.

The emergence of property rights

If the main allocative function of property rights is the internalization of beneficial and harmful effects, then the emergence of property rights can be understood best by their association with the emergence of new or different beneficial and harmful effects.

Changes in knowledge result in changes in production functions, market values, and aspirations. New techniques, new ways of doing the same things, and doing new things—all invoke harmful and beneficial effects to which society has not been accustomed. It is my thesis in this part of the paper that the emergence of new property rights takes place in response to the desires of the interacting persons for adjustment to new benefit-cost possibilities.

The thesis can be restated in a slightly different fashion: property rights develop to internalize externalities when the gains of internalization become larger than the cost of internalization. Increased internalization, in the main, results from changes in economic values, changes which stem from the development of new technology and the opening of new markets, changes to which old property rights are poorly attuned. A proper interpretation of this assertion requires that account be taken of a community's preferences for private ownership. Some communities will have less well-developed private ownership systems and more highly developed state ownership systems. But, given a community's tastes in this regard, the emergence of new private or state-owned property rights will be in response to changes in technology and relative prices.

I do not mean to assert or to deny that the adjustments in property rights which take place need be the result of a conscious endeavor to cope with new externality problems. These adjustments have arisen in Western societies largely as a result of grad-ual changes in social mores and in common law precedents. At each step of this adjust-ment process, it is unlikely that externalities per se were consciously related to the issue being resolved. These legal and moral experiments may be hit-and-miss procedures to some extent but in a society that weights the achievement of efficiency heavily, their viability in the long run will depend on how well they modify behavior to accommodate to the externalities associated with important changes in technology or market values.

A rigorous test of this assertion will require extensive and detailed empirical work. A broad range of examples can be cited that are consistent with it: the develop-ment of air rights, renters' rights, rules for liability in automobile accidents, etc. In this part of the discussion, I shall present one group of such examples in some detail. They deal with the development of private property rights in land among American Indians. These examples are broad ranging and come fairly close to what can be called convincing evidence in the field of anthropology.

The question of private ownership of land among aboriginals has held a fascina-tion for anthropologists. It has been one of the intellectual battlegrounds in the attempt to assess the "true nature" of man unconstrained by the "artificialities" of civilization. In the process of carrying on this debate, information has been uncovered that bears directly on the thesis with which we are now concerned. What appears to be accepted as a classic treatment and a high point of this debate is Eleanor Leacock's memoir on *The Montagnes "Hunting Territory" and the Fur Trade*.[3] Leacock's research fol-lowed that of Frank G. Speck[4] who had discovered that the Indians of the Labrador Peninsula had a long-established tradition of property in land. This finding was at odds with what was known about the Indians of the American Southwest and it prompted Leacock's study of the Montagnes who inhabited large regions around Quebec.

Leacock clearly established the fact that a close relationship existed, both histori-cally and geographically, between the development of private rights in land and the development of the commercial fur trade. The factual basis of this correlation has gone unchallenged. However, to my knowledge, no theory relating privacy of land to the fur trade has yet been articulated. The factual material uncovered by Speck and Leacock fits the thesis of this paper well, and in doing so, it reveals clearly the role played by property right adjustments in taking account of what economists have often cited as an example of an externality—the overhunting of game.

Because of the lack of control over hunting by others, it is in no person's interest to invest in increasing or maintaing the stock of game. Overly intensive hunting takes place. Thus a successful hunt is viewed as imposing external costs on subsequent hunters—costs that are not taken into account fully in the determination of the extent of hunting and of animal husbandry.

Before the fur trade became established, hunting was carried on primarily for purposes of food and the relatively few furs that were required for the hunter's family. The externality was clearly present. Hunting could be practiced freely and was car-ried on without assessing its impact on other hunters. But these external effects were of such small significance that it did not pay for anyone to take them into account. There did not exist anything resembling private ownership in land. And in the *Jesuit Relations*, particulairly Le Jeune's record of the winter he spent with the Montagnes in 1633–34 and in the brief account given by Father Druilletes in 1647–48, Leacock finds no evidence of private land holdings. Both accounts indicate a socioeconomic organization in which private rights to land are not well developed.

We may safely surmise that the advent of the fur trade had two immediate consequences. First, the value of furs to the Indians was increased considerably. Second, and as a result, the scale of hunting activity rose sharply. Both consequences must have increased considerably the importance of the externalities associated with free hunting. The property right system began to change, and it changed specifically in the direction required to take account of the economic effects made important by the fur trade. The geographical or distributional evidence collected by Leacock indicates an unmistakable correlation between early centers of fur trade and the oldest and most complete development of the private hunting territory.

> By the beginning of the eighteenth century, we begin to have clear evidence that territorial hunting and trapping arrangements by individual families were developing in the area around Quebec. ... The earliest references to such arrangements in this region indicates a purely temporary allotment of hunting territories. They [Algonkians and Iroquois] divide themselves into several bands in order to hunt more efficiently. It was their custom ... to appropriate pieces of land about two leagues square for each group to hunt exclusively. Ownership of beaver houses, however, had already become established, and when discovered, they were marked. A starving Indian could kill and eat another's beaver if he left the fur and the tail.[5]

The next step toward the hunting territory was probably a seasonal allotment system. An anonymous account written in 1723 states that the "principle of the Indians is to mark off the hunting ground selected by them by blazing the trees with their crests so that they may never encroach on each other. ... By the middle of the century these allotted territories were relatively stabilized."[6]

The principle that associates property right changes with the emergence of new and reevaluation of old harmful and beneficial effects suggests in this instance that the fur trade made it economic to encourage the husbanding of fur-bearing animals. Husbanding requires the ability to prevent poaching and this, in turn, suggests that socioeconomic changes in property in hunting land will take place. The chain of reasoning is consistent with the evidence cited above. Is it inconsistent with the absence of similar rights in property among the southwestern Indians?

Two factors suggest that the thesis is consistent with the absence of similar rights among the Indians of the southwestern plains. The first of these is that there were no plains animals of commercial importance comparable to the fur-bearing animals of the forest, at least not until cattle arrived with Europeans. The second factor is that animals of the plains are primarily grazing species whose habit is to wander over wide tracts of land. The value of establishing boundaries to private hunting territories is thus reduced by the relatively high cost of preventing the animals from moving to adjacent parcels. Hence both the value and cost of establishing private hunting lands in the Southwest are such that we would expect little development along these lines. The externality was just not worth taking into account.

The lands of the Labrador Peninsula shelter forest animals whose habits are considerably different from those of the plains. Forest animals confine their territories to relatively small areas, so that the cost of internalizing the effects of husbanding these animals is considerably reduced. This reduced cost, together with the higher commercial value of fur-bearing forest animals, made it productive to establish private hunting lands. Frank G. Speck finds that family proprietorship among the Indians of the Peninsula included retaliation against trespass. Animal resources were husbanded. Sometimes conservation practices were carried on extensively. Family hunting territories were divided into quarters. Each year the family hunted in a different quarter in rotation, leaving a tract in the center as a sort of bank, not to be hunted over unless forced to do so by a shortage in the regular tract.

To conclude our excursion into the phenomenon of private rights in land among the American Indians, we note one further piece of corroborating evidence. Among the Indians of the Northwest, highly developed private family rights to hunting lands had also emerged—rights which went so far as to include inheritance. Here again we find that forest animals predominate and that the West Coast was frequently visited by sailing schooners whose primary purpose was trading in furs.[7]

The coalescence and ownership of property rights

I have argued that property rights arise when it becomes economic for those affected by externalities to internalize benefits and costs. But I have not yet examined the forces which will govern the particular form of right ownership. Several idealized forms of ownership must be distinguished at the outset. These are communal ownership, private ownership, and state ownership.

By communal ownership, I shall mean a right which can be exercised by all members of the community. Frequently the rights to till and to hunt the land have been communally owned. The right to walk a city sidewalk is communally owned. Communal ownership means that the community denies to the state or to individual citizens the right to interfere with any person's exercise of communally-owned rights. Private ownership implies that the community recognizes the right of the owner to exclude others from exercising the owner's private rights. State ownership implies that the state may exclude anyone from the use of a right as long as the state follows accepted political procedures for determining who may not use state-owned property. I shall not examine in detail the alternative of state ownership. The object of the analysis which follows is to discern some broad principles governing the development of property rights in communities oriented to private property.

It will be best to begin by considering a particularly useful example that focuses our attention on the problem of land ownership. Suppose that land is communally owned. Every person has the right to hunt, till, or mine the land. This form of ownership fails to concentrate the cost associated with any person's exercise of his communal right on that person. If a person seeks to maximize the value of his communal rights, he will tend to overhunt and overwork the land because some of the costs of his doing so are borne by others. The stock of game and the richness of the soil will be diminished too quickly. It is conceivable that those who own these rights, i.e., every member of the community, can agree to curtail the rate at which they work the lands if negotiating and policing costs are zero. Each can agree to abridge his rights.

It is obvious that the costs of reaching such an agreement will not be zero. What is not obvious is just how large these costs may be.

Negotiating costs will be large because it is difficult for many persons to reach a mutually satisfactory agreement, especially when each hold-out has the right to work the land as fast as he pleases. But, even if an agreement among all can be reached, we must yet take account of the costs of policing the agreement, and these may be large, also. After such an agreement is reached, no one will privately own the right to work the land; all can work the land but at an agreed upon shorter workweek. Negotiating costs are increased even further because it is not possible under this system to bring the full expected benefits and expected costs of future generations to bear on current users.

If a single person owns land, he will attempt to maximize its present value by taking into account alternative future time streams of benefits and costs and selecting that one which he believes will maximize the present value of his privately-owned land rights. We all know that this means that he will attempt to take into account the supply and demand conditions that he thinks will exist after his death. It is very difficult to see how the existing communal owners can reach an agreement that takes account of these costs.

In effect, an owner of a private right to use land acts as a broker whose wealth depends on how well he takes into account the competing claims of the present and the future. But with communal rights there is no broker, and the claims of the present generation will be given an uneconomically large weight in determining the intensity with which the land is worked. Future generations might desire to pay present generations enough to change the present intensity of land usage. But they have no living agent to place their claims on the market. Under a communal property system, should a living person pay others to reduce the rate at which they work the land, he would not gain anything of value for his efforts. Communal property means that future generations must speak for themselves. No one has yet estimated the costs of carrying on such a conversation.

The land ownership example confronts us immediately with a great disadvantage of communal property. The effects of a person's activities on his neighbors and on subsequent generations will not be taken into account fully. Communal property results in great externalities. The full costs of the activities of an owner of a communal property right are not borne directly by him, nor can they be called to his attention easily by the willingness of others to pay him an appropriate sum. Communal property rules out a "pay-to-use-the-property" system and high negotiation and policing costs make ineffective a "pay-him-not-to-use-the-property" system.

The state, the courts, or the leaders of the community could attempt to internalize the external costs resulting from communal property by allowing private parcels owned by small groups of person with similar interests. The logical groups in terms of similar interests, are, of course, the family and the individual. Continuing with our use of the land ownership example, let us initially distribute private titles to land randomly among existing individuals and, further, let the extent of land included in each title be randomly determined.

The resulting private ownership of land will internalize many of the external costs associated with communal ownership, for now an owner, by virtue of his power to exclude others, can generally count on realizing the rewards associated with husbanding the game and increasing the fertility of his land. This concentration of benefits and costs on owners creates incentives to utilize resources more efficiently.

But we have yet to contend with externalities. Under the communal property system the maximization of the value of communal property rights will take place without regard to many costs, because the owner of a communal right cannot exclude others from enjoying the fruits of his efforts and because negotiation costs are too high for all to agree jointly on optimal behavior. The development of private rights permits the owner to economize on the use of those resources from which he has the right to exclude others. Much internalization is accomplished in this way. But the owner of private rights to one parcel does not himself own the rights to the parcel of another private sector. Since he cannot exclude others from their private rights to land, he has no direct incentive (in the absence of negotiations) to economize in the use of his land in a way that takes into account the effects he produces on the land rights of others. If he constructs a dam on his land, he has no direct incentive to take into account the lower water levels produced on his neighbor's land.

This is exactly the same kind of externality that we encountered with communal property rights, but it is present to a lesser degree. Whereas no one had an incentive to store water on any land under the communal system, private owners now can take into account directly those benefits and costs to their land that accompany water storage. But the effects on the land of others will not be taken into account directly.

The partial concentration of benefits and costs that accompany private ownership is only part of the advantage this system offers. The other part, and perhaps the most important, has escaped our notice. The cost of negotiating over the remaining externalities will be reduced greatly. Communal property rights allow anyone to use the land. Under this system it becomes necessary for all to reach an agreement on land use. But the externalities that accompany private ownership of property do not affect all owners, and, generally speaking, it will be necessary for only a few to reach an agreement that takes these effects into account. The cost of negotiating an internalization of these effects is thereby reduced considerably. The point is important enough to elucidate.

Suppose an owner of a communal land right, in the process of plowing a parcel of land, observes a second communal owner constructing a dam on adjacent land. The farmer prefers to have the stream as it is, and so he asks the engineer to stop his construction. The engineer says, "Pay me to stop." The farmer replies, "I will be happy to pay you, but what can you guarantee in return?" The engineer answers, "I can guarantee you that I will not continue constructing the dam, but I cannot guarantee that another engineer will not take up the task because this is communal property; I have no right to exclude him." What would be a simple negotiation between two persons under a private property arrangement turns out to be a rather complex negotiation between the farmer and everyone else. This is the basic explanation, I believe, for the preponderance of single rather than multiple owners of property. Indeed, an increase in the number of owners is an increase in the communality of property and leads, generally, to an increase in the cost of internalizing.

The reduction in negotiating cost that accompanies the private right to exclude others allows most externalities to be internalized at rather low cost. Those that are not are associated with activities that generate external effects impinging upon many people. The soot from smoke affects many homeowners, none of whom is willing to pay enough to the factory to get its owner to reduce smoke output. All homeowners together might be willing to pay enough, but the cost of their getting together may be enough to discourage effective market bargaining. The negotiating problem is compounded even more if the smoke comes not from a single smoke stack but from an industrial district. In such cases, it may be too costly to internalize effects through the marketplace.

Returning to our land ownership paradigm, we recall that land was distributed in randomly sized parcels to randomly selected owners. These owners now negotiate among themselves to internalize any remaining externalities. Two market options are open to the negotiators. The first is simply to try to reach a contractual agreement among owners that directly deals with the external effects at issue. The second option is for some owners to buy out others, thus changing the parcel size owned. Which option is selected will depend on which is cheaper. We have here a standard economic problem of optimal scale. If there exist constant returns to scale in the ownership of different sized parcels, it will be largely a matter of indifference between outright purchase and contractual agreement if only a single, easy-to-police, contractual agreement will internalize the externality. But, if there are several externalities, so that several such contracts will need to be negotiated, or if the contractual agreements should be difficult to police, then outright purchase will be the preferred course of action.

The greater are diseconomies of scale to land ownership the more will contractual arrangement be used by the interacting neighbors to settle these differences. Negotiating and policing costs will be compared to costs that depend on the scale of ownership, and parcels of land will tend to be owned in sizes which minimize the sum of these costs.[8]

The interplay of scale economies, negotiating cost, externalities, and the modification of property rights can be seen in the most notable "exception" to the assertion that ownership tends to be an individual affair: the publicly-held corporation. I assume that significant economies of scale in the operation of large corporations is a fact and, also, that large requirements for equity capital can be satisfied more cheaply by acquiring the capital from many purchasers of equity shares. While economies of scale in operating these enterprises exist, economies of scale in the provision of capital do not. Hence, it becomes desirable for many "owners" to form a joint-stock company.

But if all owners participate in each decision that needs to be made by such a company, the scale economies of operating the company will be overcome quickly by high negotiating cost. Hence a delegation of authority for most decisions takes place and, for most of these, a small management group becomes the *de facto* owners. Effective ownership, i.e., effective control of property, is thus legally concentrated in management's hands. This is the first legal modification, and it takes place in recognition of the high negotiating costs that would otherwise obtain.

The structure of ownership, however, creates some externality difficulties under the law of partnership. If the corporation should fail, partnership law commits each shareholder to meet the debts of the corporation up to the limits of his financial ability. Thus, managerial *de facto* ownership can have considerable external effects on shareholders. Should property rights remain unmodified, this externality would make it exceedingly difficult for entrepreneurs to acquire equity capital from wealthy individuals. (Although these individuals have recourse to reimbursements from other shareholders, litigation costs will be high.) A second legal modification, limited liability, has taken place to reduce the effect of this externality.[9] *De facto* management owner-ship and limited liability combine to minimize the overall cost of operating large enterprises. Shareholders are essentially lenders of equity capital and not owners, although they do participate in such infrequent decisions as those involving mergers. What shareholders really own are their shares and not the corporation. Ownership in the sense of control again becomes a largely individual affair. The shareholders own their shares, and the president of the corporation and possibly a few other top execu-tives control the corporation.

To further ease the impact of management decisions on shareholders, that is, to minimize the impact of externalities under this ownership form, a further legal modi-fication of rights is required. Unlike partnership law, a shareholder may sell his interest without first obtaining the permission of fellow shareholders or without dissolving the corporation. It thus becomes easy for him to get out if his preferences and those of the management are no longer in harmony. This "escape hatch" is extremely important and has given rise to the organized trading of securities. The increase in harmony between managers and shareholders brought about by exchange and by competing managerial groups helps to minimize the external effects associated with the corporate ownership structure. Finally, limited liability considerably reduces the cost of exchanging shares by making it unnecessary for a purchaser of shares to examine in great detail the liabil-ities of the corporation and the assets of other shareholders; these liabilities can adversely affect a purchaser only up to the extent of the price per share.

The dual tendencies for ownership to rest with individuals and for the extent of an individual's ownership to accord with the minimization of all costs is clear in the land ownership paradigm. The applicability of this paradigm has been extended to the corporation. But it may not be clear yet how widely applicable this paradigm is. Consider the problems of copyright and patents. If a new idea is freely appropriable by all, if there exist communal rights to new ideas, incentives for developing such ideas will be lacking. The benefits derivable from these ideas will not be concentrated on their originators. If we extend some degree of private rights to the originators, these ideas will come forth at a more rapid pace. But the existence of the private rights does not mean that their effects on the property of others will be directly taken into account. A new idea makes an old one obsolete and another old one more valu-able. These effects will not be directly taken into account, but they can be called to the attention of the originator of the new idea through market negotiations. All problems of externalities are closely analogous to those which arise in the land ownership example. The relevant variables are identical.

What I have suggested in this paper is an approach to problems in property rights. But it is more than that. It is also a different way of viewing traditional problems. An elaboration of this approach will, I hope, illuminate a great number of social-economic problems.

Notes

1 These implications are derived by R. H. Coase, "The Problem of Social Cost," *J. of Law and Econ.*, Oct., 1960, pp. 1–44.

2 If the demand for civilian life is unaffected by wealth redistribution, the assertion made is correct as it stands. However, when a change is made from a "buy-him-in" system to a "let-him-buy-his-way-out" system, the resulting redistribution of wealth away from draftees may significantly affect their demand for civilian life; the validity of the assertion then requires a compensating wealth change. A compensating wealth change will not be required in the ordinary case of profit maximizing firms. Consider the farmer-rancher example mentioned by Coase. Society may give the farmer the right to grow corn unmolested by cattle or it may give the rancher the right to allow his cattle to stray. Contrary to the Coase example, let us suppose that if the farmer is given the right, he just breaks even; i.e., with the right to be compensated for corn damage, the farmer's land is marginal. If the right is transferred to the rancher, the farmer, not enjoying any economic rent, will not have the wherewithal to pay the rancher to reduce the number of head of cattle raised. In this case, however, it will be profitable for the rancher to buy the farm, thus merging cattle raising with farming. His self-interest will then lead him to take account of the effect of cattle on corn.

3 Eleanor Leacock, *American Anthropologist* (American Anthropological Assoc.), Vol. 56, No. 5, Part 2, Memoir No. 78.

4 Cf., Frank G. Speck, "The Basis of American Indian Ownership of Land," *Old Penn Weekly Rev.* (Univ. of Pennsylvania), Jan. 16, 1915, pp. 491–95.

5 Eleanor Leacock, *op. cit.*, p. 15.

6 Eleanor Leacock, *op. cit.*, p. 15.

7 The thesis is consistent with the development of other types of private rights. Among wandering primitive peoples the cost of policing property is relatively low for highly portable objects. The owning family can protect such objects while carrying on its daily activities. If these objects are also very useful, property rights should appear frequently, so as to internalize the benefits and costs of their use. It is generally true among most primitive communities that weapons and household utensils, such as pottery, are regarded as private property. Both types of articles are portable and both require an investment of time to produce. Among agriculturally-oriented peoples, because of the relative fixity of their location, portability has a smaller role to play in the determination of property. The distinction is most clearly seen by comparing property in land among the most primitive of these societies, where crop rotation and simple fertilization techniques are unknown, or where land fertility is extremely poor, with property in land among primitive peoples who are more knowledgeable in these matters or who possess very superior land. Once a crop is grown by the more primitive agricultural societies, it is necessary for them to abandon the land for several years to restore productivity. Property rights in land among such people would require policing cost for several years during which no sizable output is obtained. Since to provide for sustenance these people must move to new land, a property right to be of value to them must be associated with a portable object. Among these people it is common to find property rights to the crops, which, after harvest, are portable, but not to the land. The more advanced agriculturally based primitive societies are able to remain with particular land for longer periods, and here we generally observe property rights to the land as well as to the crops.

8 Compare this with the similar rationale given by R. H. Coase to explain the firm in "The Nature of the Firm," *Economico*, New Series, 1937, pp. 386–405.

9 Henry G. Manne discusses this point in a forthcoming book about the American corporate system.

Review and Discussion Questions

1 What are "property rights"?
2 What is a major function of property rights?
3 What causes property rights to emerge? To change?
4 Does Demsetz show that changes in economic variables *cause* changes in property rights or does he merely show that the changes are *correlated*? Explain.
5 How do private property rights differ in their effects from communal property rights? Give the reason why Demsetz states private ownership dominates communal ownership.
6 Copyrights and patents provide inventors of new ideas with some property rights in their ideas. Do you think granting those property rights is a good public policy? What are their advantages and disadvantages? For software, is "open source" development better than property rights?

Chapter 12

ROBERT C. ELLICKSON

A HYPOTHESIS OF WEALTH-MAXIMIZING NORMS: EVIDENCE FROM THE WHALING INDUSTRY[1]

THIS ESSAY ANALYZES the rules that high-seas whalers used during the heyday of their industry to resolve disputes over the ownership of harvested whales. The evidence presented sheds light on two important theoretical issues of property rights.

The first issue is the source or sources of property rights. According to what Williamson calls the "legal-centralist" view (1983:520), the state is the exclusive creator of property rights. Many scholars, including Thomas Hobbes (1909:97–98), Garrett Hardin, and Guido Calabresi (1972:1090–91), have at times succumbed to legal-centralist thinking. An opposing view holds that property rights may emerge from sources other than the state—in particular, from the workings of nonhierarchical social forces. The whaling evidence refutes legal-centralism and strongly supports the proposition that property rights may arise anarchically out of social custom.[2]

The second theoretical issue is whether one can predict the content of informal property rights (norms) that informal social forces generate. This essay advances the hypothesis that when people are situated in a close-knit group, they will tend to develop for the ordinary run of problems norms that are wealth-maximizing. A group is "close-knit" when its members are entwined in continuing relationships that provide each with power and information sufficient to exercise informal social control.[3] A norm is "wealth-maximizing" when it operates to minimize the members' objective sum of (1) transaction costs, and (2) deadweight losses arising from failures to exploit potential gains from trade. This theory of the content of norms is proffered as the most parsimonious explanation of variations among whaling rules.

1 The problem of contested whales

Especially during the period from 1750 to 1870, whales were an extraordinarily valuable source of oil, bone, and other products.[4] Whalers therefore had powerful incentives to develop rules for peaceably resolving rival claims to the ownership of a whale. In *Moby-Dick*, Melville explained why these norms were needed:

> It frequently happens that when several ships are cruising in company, a whale may be struck by one vessel, then escape, and be finally killed and captured by another vessel. ... [Or] after a weary and perilous chase and capture of a whale, the body may get loose from the ship by reason of a violent storm; and drifting far away to leeward, be retaken by a second whaler, who, in a calm, snugly tows it alongside, without risk of life or line. Thus the most vexatious and violent disputes would often arise between the fishermen, were there not some written, universal, undisputed law applicable to all cases. ...
> The American fishermen have been their own legislators and lawyers in this matter.
>
> (1851:504–05)

Melville's last sentence might prompt the inference that whalers had some sort of formal trade association that established rules governing the ownership of contested whales. There is no evidence, however, that this was so. Anglo-American whaling norms seem to have emerged spontaneously, not from decrees handed down by-either organizational or governmental authorities.[5] In fact, whalers' norms not only did not mimic law; they *created* law. In the dozen reported Anglo-American cases in which ownership of a whale carcass was contested, judges invariably held proven whalers' usages to be reasonable and deferred to those rules.[6]

2 The whaling industry

At first blush it might be thought that whalers would be too dispersed to constitute the membership of a close-knit social group. During the industry's peak in the nineteenth century, for example, whaling ships from ports in several nations were hunting their prey in remote seas of every ocean. In fact, however, the entire international whaling community was a tight one, primarily because whaling ships commonly encountered one another at sea, and because whalers' home and layover ports were few, intimate, and socially interlinked. The scant evidence available suggests that whalers' norms of capture were internationally binding.[7]

The Greenland fishery was the first important international whaling ground. The Dutch were the leaders there during the period around 1700, but later encountered increasing competition from French, British, and American whaling vessels. After 1800, ships from the two English-speaking nations became dominant both in Greenland and elsewhere. By the mid-1800s the United States, a fledgling international power, had emerged as the preeminent whaling nation.[8]

American whalers were concentrated in a handful of small ports in southern New England. Nantucket, the dominant North American whaling port in the eighteenth century, was home to over half the New England whaling fleet in 1774 (Stackpole, 1953:53–54). New Bedford, which during the 1820s finally supplanted Nantucket as the leading American whaling center, in 1857 berthed half the whaling ships in the United States (Hohman, 1928:9). Life within these specialized ports centered on the whaling trade. Because of its remote island location and strong Quaker influence, Nantucket was particularly close-knit. "There is no finer example in history of communal enterprise than the Nantucket Whale Fishery. The inhabitants were uniquely situated for united effort. ... Through intermarriage they were generally related to one another, and in fact were more like a large family than a civic community. ... The people were so law-abiding that there was little or no government in evidence on the Island" (Ashley, 1938:31). Many Nantucketers shifted to New Bedford when it emerged as the leading whaling center. There whaling also became a "neighborhood affair."[9]

The captains who commanded the whaling ships occupied pivotal positions in the development and enforcement of whaling norms. Two captains based in the same small whaling port were unquestionably members of a close-knit group and would be vulnerable, for example, to gossip about misconduct at sea. The captains' social circles tended, moreover, to extend well beyond their home ports. Migrants from Nantucket, the world's wellspring of whaling talent, became influential not only in other New England ports but also in foreign whaling nations. By 1812, for example, 149 Nantucketers had commanded British whaling ships.[10]

Even whalers sailing from distant ports tended to socialize at sea. Herman Melville, who in *Moby-Dick* portrays eight meetings between the *Pequod* and other whaling vessels, devotes a chapter to the gam (1851: chap. 53). The gam was a friendly meeting between the officers of two whaling ships that had encountered each other at sea. Typically, the two captains would meet for several hours or more on one ship, and the two chief mates on the other. One reason for the gam was to obtain whaling intelligence. ("Have ye seen the White Whale?") In addition, whaling ships might be on the high seas for three or more years at a stretch. More than most seamen, whalers were eager to pass on letters to or from home[11] and to trade to replenish supplies.[12] Although the gam was hardly a mandatory ritual among whalers, only they, and no other seamen, engaged in the practice.[13]

Whalers also congregated in specialized layover ports. When the Pacific fisheries developed, for instance, the Maui port of Lahaina emerged as a whalers' hangout in the Hawaiian Islands.

3 The calculus of wealth maximization

Wealth-maximizing norms are those that minimize the sum of transaction costs and deadweight losses that the members of a group objectively incur. By hypothesis, whalers would implicitly follow this calculus when developing norms to resolve the ownership of contested whales. As a first cut, this calculus would call for a whaling ship's fraction of ownership to equal its fractional contribution to a capture. For example, a ship that had objectively contributed one-half the total value of work would be entitled to a one-half share. In the absence of this rule, opportunistic ships might decline to contribute cost-justified but underrewarded work, leading to deadweight losses.[14]

This first cut is too simple, however, because utilitarian whalers would be concerned with the transaction costs associated with their rules. They would tend to prefer, for example, bright-line rules that would eliminate arguments to fuzzy rules that would prolong disputes. Finding a cost-minimizing solution to whaling disputes is vexing because there is no ready measure of the relative value of separate contributions to a joint harvest. Any fine-tuning of incentives aimed at reducing deadweight losses is therefore certain to increase transaction costs.

4 Hypothetical whaling norms

In no fishery did whalers adopt as norms any of a variety of rules that are transparently poor candidates for minimizing the sum of deadweight losses and transaction costs. An easily administered rule would be one that made the possession of a whale carcass normatively decisive. According to this rule, if ship *A* had a wounded or dead whale on a line, ship *B* would be entitled to attach a stronger line and pull the whale away. A possession-decides rule of this sort would threaten severe deadweight losses, however, because it would encourage a ship to sit back like a vulture and freeload on others' efforts in the early stages of a hunt. Whalers never used this norm.

Equally perverse would be a rule that a whale should belong entirely to the ship whose crew had killed it. Besides risking ambiguities about the cause of a whale's demise, this rule would create inadequate incentives for whalers both to inflict non-mortal wounds and to harvest dead whales that had been lost or abandoned by the ships that had slain them.

To reward early participation in a hunt, whalers might have developed a norm that the first ship to lower a boat to pursue a whale had an exclusive right to capture so long as it remained in fresh pursuit. This particular rule would create numerous other difficulties, however. Besides being ambiguous in some contexts, it would create strong incentives for the premature launch of boats and might work to bestow an exclusive opportunity to capture on a party less able than others to exploit that opportunity.[15]

Somewhat more responsive to incentive issues would be a rule that a whale belonged to a ship whose crew had first obtained a "reasonable prospect" of capturing it and thereafter remained in fresh pursuit.[16] This rule would reward good performance during the early stages of a hunt and would also free up lost or abandoned whales to later takers. A reasonable-prospect standard, however, is by far the most ambiguous of those yet mentioned, invites transaction costs, and, like the other rules so far discussed, was not employed by whalers.

5 Actual whaling norms

Whalers developed an array of norms more utilitarian than any of these hypothetical ones. Evidence of the details of whaling usages is fragmentary. The best sources are the court reports in which evidence of usages was admitted, especially when the contesting whalers agreed on die usage and disputed only its application.[17] Seamen's journals, literary works such as *Moby-Dick*, and historical accounts provide additional glimpses of the rules in use.

Whaling norms were not tidy, certainly less tidy than Melville asserted in *Moby-Dick* (1851; chap. 89). Whalers developed three basic norms, each of which was adapted to its particular context. As will be evident, each of the three norms was sensitive to the need to avoid deadweight losses because each not only rewarded the ship that had sunk the first harpoon, but also enabled others to harvest dead or wounded whales that had seemingly been abandoned by their prior assailants. All three norms were also sensitive to the problem of transaction costs. In particular, norms that bestowed an exclusive temporary right to capture on a whaling ship tended to be shaped so as to provide relatively clear starting and ending points for the time period of that entitlement.

5.1 Fast-fish, loose-fish

Prior to 1800, the British whalers operating in the Greenland fishery established the usage that a claimant owned a whale, dead or alive, so long as the whale was fastened by line or otherwise to the claimant's boat or ship.[18] This fast-fish rule was well suited to this fishery. The prey hunted off Greenland was the right whale.[19] Right whales, compared to the sperm whales that later became American whalers' preferred prey, are both slow swimmers and mild antagonists.[20] The British hunted them from heavy and sturdy whaling boats. Upon nearing one, a harpooner would throw a harpoon with line attached; the trailing end of the line was tied to the boat.[21] So long as the harpoon held fast to the whale and remained connected by the line to the boat, the fast-fish norm entitled the harpooning boat to an exclusive claim of ownership as against subsequent harpooners. If the whale happened to break free, either dead or alive, it was then regarded as a loose-fish and was again up for grabs. Although whalers might occasionally dispute whether a whale had indeed been fast,[22] the fast-fish rule usually provided sharp beginning and ending points for a whaler's exclusive entitlement to capture and thus promised to limit the transaction costs involved in dispute resolution.

The fast-fish rule created incentives well adapted to the Britishers' situation in Greenland. Because right whales are relatively slow and docile, a whale on a line was not likely to capsize the harpooning boat, break the line, or sound to such a depth that the boats men had to relinquish the line. Thus the fast-fish rule was in practice likely to reward the first harpooner, who had performed the hardest part of the hunt, as opposed to free riders waiting in the wings. Not uncommonly, however, a right whale sinks shortly after death, an event that requires the boatsmen to cut their lines.[23] After a few days a sunken whale bloats and resurfaces. At that point the fast-fish rule entitled a subsequent finder to seize the carcass as a loose-fish, a utilitarian result because the ship that had killed the whale might then be far distant. In sum, the fast-fish rule was a bright-line rule that created incentives for both first pursuers of live whales and final takers of lost dead whales.

5.2 Iron-holds-the-whale

Especially in fisheries where the more vigorous sperm whales predominated, whalers tended to shift away from the fast-fish rule. The evidence on whalers' usage is too fragmentary to allow any confident assertion about when and where this occurred. The fast-fish rule's main alternative—the rule that iron-holds-the-whale—also provided incentives to perform the hardest part of the hunt. Stated in its broadest form, this norm conferred an exclusive right to capture upon the whaler who had first affixed a harpoon or other whaling craft to the body of the whale. The iron-holds-the-whale rule differed from the fast-fish rule in that the iron did not have to be connected by a line or otherwise to the claimant. The normmakers had to create a termination point for the exclusive right to capture, however, because it would be foolish for a Moby-Dick to belong to an Ahab who had sunk an ineffectual harpoon days or years before. Whalers therefore allowed an iron to hold a whale for only so long as the claimant remained in fresh pursuit of the iron-bearing animal. In some contexts, the iron-affixing claimant also had to assert the claim before a subsequent taker had begun to "cut in" (strip the blubber from) the carcass.[24]

American whalers tended to adopt the iron-holds-the-whale rule wherever it was a utilitarian response to how and what they hunted.[25] Following Native American practices, some early New England seamen employed devices called drogues to catch whales. A drogue was a float, perhaps two feet square, to which the trailing end of a harpoon line was attached. The drogue was thrown overboard from a whaling boat after the harpoon had been cast into the whale. This device served both to tire the animal and also to mark its location, thus setting up the final kill.[26] Because a whale towing a drogue was not connected to the harpooning boat, the fast-fish rule provided no protection to the crew that had attached the drogue. By contrast, the iron-holds-the-whale rule, coupled with a fresh-pursuit requirement, created incentives suitable for drogue fishing.[27]

This rule had particular advantages to whalers hunting sperm whales. Because sperm whales swim faster, dive deeper, and fight more viciously than right whales do, they were more suitable targets for drogue-fishing. New Englanders eventually did learn how to hunt sperm whales with harpoons attached by lines to boats (Ashley, 1938:65–66, 92–93). The vigor of the sperm whale compared to the right whale, however, increased the chance that a line would not hold or would have to be cut to save the boat. A "fastness" requirement would thus materially reduce the incentives of competing boatsmen to make the first strike. The iron-holds-the-whale rule, in contrast, was a relatively bright-line way of rewarding whoever won the race to accomplish the major feat of sinking the first harpoon into a sperm whale. It also rewarded only the persistent and skillful because it conferred its benefits only so long as fresh pursuit was being maintained.

Most important, unlike right whales, sperm whales are social animals that tend to swim in schools (Ashley, 1938:75; Melville: chap. 88). To maximize the total catch, when whalers discovered a school their norms had to encourage boatsmen to kill or mortally wound as many animals as quickly as possible, without pausing to secure the stricken whales to the mother ship.[28] Fettering whales with drogues was an adaptive technology in these situations. The haste that the schooling of whales prompted among hunters also encouraged the related usage that a waif holds a whale. A waif is a pole with a small flag atop. Planting a waif into a dead whale came to signify that the whaler who had planted the waif claimed the whale, was nearby, and intended soon to return. When those conditions were met, the usages of American whalers in the Pacific allowed a waif to hold a whale.[29]

Because a ship might lose track of a whale it had harpooned or waifed, whaling norms could not allow a whaling iron to hold a whale forever. When a mere harpoon (or lance) had been attached, and thus it was not certain that the harpooning party had ever fully controlled the whale, the harpooning party had to be in fresh pursuit and also had to assert the claim before a subsequent taker had begun to cut in.[30] On the other hand, when a waif, anchor, or other evidence of certain prior control had been planted, the planting party had to be given a reasonable period of time to retake the whale and hence might prevail even after the subsequent taker had completed cutting in.[31]

Because the iron-holds-the-whale usage required determinations of the freshness of pursuit and sometimes of the reasonableness of the elapsed time period, it was inherently more ambiguous than the fast-fish norm was. By hypothesis, this is why the whalers who pursued right whales off Greenland preferred the fast-fish rule. The rule that iron-holds-the-whale, however, provided better-tailored incentives in situations where drogues were the best whaling technology and where whales tended to swim in schools. In these contexts, according to the theory, whalers switched to iron-holds-the-whale because they saw that its potential for reducing deadweight losses outweighed its transaction-cost disadvantages.

5.3 Split ownership

In a few contexts whaling usages called for the value of the carcass to be split between the first harpooner and the ultimate seizer.[32] According to an English decision, in the fishery around the Galápagos Islands a whaler who had fettered a sperm whale with a drogue shared the carcass fifty-fifty with the ultimate taker.[33] The court offered no explanation for why a different norm had emerged in this context, although it seemed aware that sperm whales were often found in large schools in that fishery. The utilitarian division of labor in harvesting a school of whales is different than for a single whale. The first whaling ship to come upon a large school should fetter as many animals as possible with drogues and relegate to later-arriving ships the task of capturing and killing the encumbered animals.[34] The Galápagos norm enabled this division of labor. It also showed sensitivity to transaction costs because it adopted the simplest focal point for a split: fifty-fifty.

Better documented is the New England coastal tradition of splitting a beached or floating dead whale between its killer and the person who finally found it. The best known of the American judicial decisions on whales, *Ghen v. Rich*,[35] involved a dispute over the ownership of a dead finback whale beached in eastern Cape Cod. Because finback whales are exceptionally fast swimmers, whalers of the late nineteenth century slew them from afar with bomb-lances. A finback whale killed in this way immediately sank to the bottom and typically washed up on shore some days later. The plaintiff in *Ghen* had killed a finback whale with a bomb-lance. When the whale later washed up on the beach, a stranger found it and sold it to the defendant tryworks. The trial judge held a hearing that convinced him that there existed a usage on the far reaches of Cape Cod that entitled the bomb-lancer to have the carcass of the dead animal, provided in the usual case that the lancer pay a small amount (a "reasonable salvage") to the stranger who had found the carcass on the beach. As was typical in whaling litigation, the court deferred to this usage and held the tryworks liable for damages: "Unless it is sustained, this branch of industry must necessarily cease, for no person would engage in it if the fruits of his labor could be appropriated by any chance finder. ... That the rule works well in practice is shown by the extent of the industry which has grown up under it, and the general acquiescence of a whole community interested to dispute it."

The norm enforced in *Ghen* divided ownership of a beached finback whale roughly according to the opportunity costs of the labor that the whaler and finder had expended. It thus ingeniously enabled distant and unsupervised specialized laborers with complementary skills to coordinate with one another by implicit social contract. The remote location and small population of eastern Cape Cod fostered close-knit social conditions that the theory supposes were conducive to the evolution of utilitarian norms. Under those intimate circumstances, offshore whalers were apparently able to use their general community ties to obtain informal control over beachcombers who were not connected to the whaling industry.[36]

The choice between entitling an ultimate seizer to a preestablished fraction of the whale, such as the half awarded in the Galápagos, or to a "reasonable reward," as on Cape Cod, is a typical rule/standard conundrum. "Reasonableness" standards allow consideration of the exact relative contributions of the claimants. Compared to rules, however, standards are more likely to provoke disputes about proper application. For low-level norms, the hypothesis of wealth-maximizing norms supposes that normmakers, seeing that rules best reduce transaction costs and that standards best reduce deadweight losses, make a utilitarian stab at picking the cost-minimizing alternative.[37]

6 Concluding remarks

The example of the high-seas whalers illustrates, contrary to the legal-centralist view, that informal social networks are capable of creating rules that establish property rights. Whalers had little use for law or litigation.[38] The five reported American cases resolving the ownership of whales at sea all arose out of the Sea of Okhotsk. With the exception of an 1872 decision,[39] in which the year of the whale's capture is not indicated, all involved whales caught during the period 1852 to 1862. The lack of litigation over whale ownership prior to that time is remarkable for two reasons. First, it suggests that for more than a century American whalers had been able to resolve their disputes without any reassurance from American courts. Second, whalers succeeded in doing this during a time period in which all British decisions on whale ownership supported norms other than the iron-holds-the-whale rule that the Americans were increasingly adopting.[40]

Because informal norms are in many contexts an important source of rules, analysts should be interested in their content. This essay has offered and defended the hypothesis that members of a close-knit group define their low-level property rights so as to maximize their joint objective wealth. A hypothesis of this sort is most persuasively supported through successful ex ante predictions, not ex post explanations such as those just provided.

An analyst equipped with the hypothesis of wealth-maximizing norms might be unable to predict the precise whaling norms that would develop in a particular fishery. Information about costs and benefits is inevitably fuzzy, both to the normmakers themselves and to analysts. An analyst, however, could confidently identify a large set of norms that would *not* be observed, such as, in the whaling case, "possession decides," "the first boat in the water," or "a reasonable prospect of capture." The content of the three basic norms the whaling community developed tends to support the hypothesis because all three were consistently sensitive to both production incentives and trans-actions costs and varied in utilitarian fashion with conditions prevailing in different fisheries.

Any post hoc explanation risks being too pat, and this one is no exception. A critic might question the analysis on a number of grounds. First, the discussion suggests that whalers might have been wise to use the first-iron rule for sperm whales, and the fast-fish rule for right whales. They did not, and instead varied their rules according to the location of the fishery, not according to species. Perhaps whal-ers anticipated that species-specific rules would engender more administrative com-plications than their fishery-specific rules did. It is relevant that there are dozens of whale species other than sperm and right whales. In light of that fact, it may have been simplest to apply to all species of whales in a fishery the rule of capture best suited to the most commercially valuable species found there. In addition, a cruising whaling ship had to have its boats and harpoons at the ready (Chatterton, 1926:140). Richard Craswell has suggested to me that this necessity of prearming may have lim-ited the whalers' ability to vary their capture techniques according to the species encountered.

Second, a critic could assert that the whalers' norms described were too short-sighted to be wealth-maximizing. By abetting cooperation among small clusters of competing hunters, the norms aggravated the risk of overwhaling. The nineteenth-century whalers in fact depleted their fisheries so rapidly that they were impelled to seek whales in ever more remote seas. Had they developed norms that set quotas on catches, or that protected young or female whales, they might have been able to keep whaling stocks at levels that would support sustainable yields.

The arguments that respond to this second criticism point up some shortcomings of the informal system of social control, as compared to other methods of human coordination. Establishment of an accurate quota system for whale fishing requires both a sophisticated scientific understanding of whale breeding and an international system for monitoring worldwide catches. For a technically difficult and administra-tively complicated task such as this, a hierarchical organization, such as a formal trade association or a legal system, would likely outperform the diffuse social forces that make norms. Whalers who recognized the risk of overfishing thus could rationally ignore that risk when making norms on the ground that normmakers could make no cost-justified contribution to its solution.

Whalers might rationally have risked overwhaling for another reason. Even if overwhaling was not wealth-maximizing from a global perspective, the rapid deple-tion of whaling stocks may well have been in the interests of the club of whalers centered in southern New England. From their parochial perspective, grabbing as many of the world's whales as quickly as possible was a plausibly wealth-maximizing strategy. These New Englanders might have feared entry into whaling by mariners based in the southern United States, Japan, or other ports that could prove to be beyond their control. Given this risk of hostile entry, even if the New Englanders could have created norms to stem their own depletion of world whaling stocks, they might have concluded that a quick kill was more to their advantage. The whaling saga is thus a reminder that norms that enrich one group's members may impoverish, to a greater extent, those outside the group.

Notes

1 This is part of a larger project to be published by Harvard University Press as a book tentatively entitled *Order without Law*. The book will more fully develop the hypothesis and present a wider range of evidence relevant to it.

   I thank Debbie Sivas for exceptional research assistance, and, for their constructive suggestions, Richard Craswell, Geoffrey Miller, Richard Posner, Roberta Romano, and participants in faculty workshops at the Stanford Business School and the Harvard, Yale, and University of Chicago Law Schools.

2 For more evidence to this effect, and also a taxonomy of alternative systems of social control, see Ellickson (1987). Perhaps the classic description of the emergence of informal property rights in a relatively anarchic environment is Umbeck (1977), a study of mining claims during the early years of the California gold rush.

3 Close-knittedness enables a member to monitor others and to use informal means of self-help against deviants. In my forthcoming book I will investigate more fully the linkage between this social condition and the emergence of wealth-maximizing norms. For some glimpses of social control among the close-knit, see Acheson (1988), a description of the customs of Maine lobstermen, and Ellickson (1966), an account of how close-knit rural residents in California informally discipline ranchers who carelessly manage cattle. The present article contains one scrap of evidence that the loss of close-knittedness makes informal cooperation more difficult: American whalers increasingly turned to litigation when their industry began to decline, a trend that would make them see their relationships as less enduring. See n. 40

4 Mid- to late-nineteenth-century judicial opinions recorded the value of single whales (of unreported species) caught in the Sea of Okhotsk, located north of Japan, at over $2,000: *Swift v. Gifford*, 23 Fed. Cas. 558 (D. Mass. 1872) (No. 13,696), $3,000; *Taber v. Jenny*, 23 Fed. Cas. 605 (D. Mass. 1856) (No. 13,720), $2,350. In the latter part of the nineteenth century, mean family income in the United States was on the order of $600 to $800 per year. See Bureau of the Census, 1 *Historical Statistics of the United States: Colonial Times to 1970*, at 322 (1975).

5 Melville (1851:505) asserted that the only formal whaling code was one legislatively decreed in Holland in 1695. The code's contents evoked no description from Melville and also drew no mention in the subsequent Anglo-American case reports.

6 See, for example, *Addison & Sons v. Row*, 3 Paton 339 (1794); *Swift v. Gifford*, 23 Fed. Cas. 558 (D. Mass. 1872) (No. 13,696); see generally Holmes (1881:212). But compare *Taber v. Jenny*, 23 Fed. Cas. 605 (D. Mass. 1856) (No. 13,720) (holding for plaintiff on the basis of general common law regarding abandoned property, despite defendant's [doubtful] assertion that the usage was otherwise).

7 A dictum in *Fennings v. Lord Grenville*, 1 Taunt. 241, 127 Eng. Rep. 825, 828 (Ct, Comm. Pleas 1808), asserts that the fast-fish "usage in Greenland is regarded as binding on persons of all nations." The loneliness of the high seas prompted whalers of different backgrounds to interact with one another. Melville, in chapter 81, provides a fictional account of a mid-Pacific meeting in which the *Jungfrau* of Bremen hailed the *Pequod* of Nantucket in order to obtain needed lamp oil. An actual high-seas trade between a British and a New England ship is described in n. 12

8 See Ashley (1938:23–29); Hohman (1928:5–6, 20–22). The U.S. industry peaked in about 1846, when its whaling fleet consisted of over 700 vessels. At that same time the combined whaling fleets of all other nations totaled 230 ships (Stackpole, 1953:473).

9 Ashley (1938:99). Byers (1987) provides a comprehensive history of early Nantucket.

The hypothesis offered here takes social conditions as exogenous. A more ambitious theory might attempt to attribute the close-knittedness of the whalers' home ports to their recognition that a tight land-based social structure would abet cooperation at sea.

10 Ashley (1938:26). See generally Stackpole (1953:133–44, 390).

11 Melville (1851:341); Hohman (1928:87).

12 See, for example, Chatterton (1926:111) quoting the 1836 journal of Samuel Joy, a New England whaling captain: "I got an anchor from an English ship for 40 lbs tobacco and a steering oar."

13 "So then, we see that of all ships separately sailing the sea, the whalers have most reason to be sociable—and they are so" (Melville, 1851:342). See also Ashley (1938:103–04); Hohman (1928:16); Morison (1921:325).

14 The present discussion assumes that wealth-maximizing whalers would ignore the risk that their actions might excessively deplete the stocks of whales. This assumption will be examined in section 6.

15 According to Bockstoce (1986:61), whalers in the western Arctic had informally agreed to defer to the first boat in the water, but tended to ignore this agreement when whales were scarce. Bockstoce's authority for this proposition is thin. He apparently relies on Williams (1964:368), an old man's remembrance of a whaling voyage taken at age fifteen. The incident that prompted Williams's mention of this purported practice was one in which the ships that chose to defer to another's lowered boats were "too far off to take any interest in the affair." More probative would have been an incident in which a ship nearer to a whale had deferred to a prior lowering by a more distant ship.

16 In his dissent in the staple Property casebook decision, *Pierson v. Post*, 3 Cai. R. 175, 2 Am. Dec. 264 (Sup. Ct. N.Y. 1805), Judge Livingston argued that a fox hunter with a "reasonable prospect of taking" his prey should prevail over the actual taker.

17 See *Hogarth v. Jackson*, 1 Moody & M. 58 (1827) (parties agreed that the fast-fish rule prevailed in the Greenland fishery); *Swift v. Gifford*, 23 Fed. Cas. 558 (D. Mass. 1872) (No. 13,696) (parties stipulated that New England whalers honored the first-iron rule).

18 *Addison & Sons v. Row.* 3 Paton 339 (1794); *Hogarth v. Jackson*, 1 Moody & M. 58 (1827). Melville (1851: chap. 89) identified the fast-fish, loose-fish distinction as the governing principle among American whalers. He also noted at several points, however, that an American whaler who had merely placed a waif on a dead whale owned it so long as he evinced an intent and ability to return (1851:500, 505). The evident tension between these two rules drew no comment from Melville.

19 The ambiguous term *right whale* is used here to refer to a family of closely related species of baleen whales. The two most commonly hunted species were the Biscayan right whale and the Greenland right whale (or bowhead).

20 Ashley (1938:65); Hohman (1928:180); Jackson (1978:3–11). Some whaling crews, "though intelligent and courageous enough in offering battle to the Greenland or Right whale, would perhaps—either from professional inexperience, or incompetency, or timidity, decline a contest with the Sperm whale" (Melville, 1851:279). Melville's fictional and ferocious Moby-Dick was, needless to say, a sperm whale.

21 See Ashley (1938:93).

22 See *Hogarth v. Jackson*, 1 Moody & M. 58 (1827) (whale merely entangled in a line is fast).

23 Hohman (1928:165n). Melville (1851:468) asserted that twenty slain right whales sink for every sperm whale that does.

24 Although the phrase "fresh pursuit" does not appear in whaling lore, it nicely expresses the notion that the crew of the first ship to affix a harpoon had rights only so long as it both intended to take the whale and had a good chance of accomplishing that feat.

25 "The parties filed a written stipulation that witnesses of competent experience would testify, that, during the whole time of memory of the eldest masters of whaling ships, the usage had been uniform in the whole fishery of Nantucket and New Bedford that a whale belonged to the vessel whose iron first remained in it, provided claim was made before cutting in" (*Swift* v. *Gifford*, 23 Fed. Cas. 558, 558 (D. Mass. 1872) [No. 13,696]). The *Swift* opinion also cited *Bourne* v. *Ashley*, 3 Fed. Cas. 1002 (D. Mass. 1863) (No. 1698), to the effect that the usage of the first iron had been proven to exist as far back as 1800. *Swift* held that this usage was a reasonable one and was applicable to a dispute over a whale caught in the Sea of Okhotsk, located east of Siberia and north of Japan.

It is highly doubtful, however, that the usage of the first iron was as universal among New Englanders as the parties had stipulated in *Swift*. The *Swift* opinion itself mentioned British cases that described other usages in effect among the international community of whalers in the Greenland and mid-Pacific fisheries. See also Melville (1851:505) for the irreconcilable assertion that the fast-fish rule was the overriding one among American whalers.

26 See Ashley (1938:89–93); Melville (1651:495). The barrels used to slow the great white shark in the film *Jaws* are modern equivalents of drogues.

27 In *Aberdeen Arctic Co.* v. *Sutter*. 4 Macq. 355, 3 Eng. Ruling Cas. 93 (1862), the defendant had seized in the Greenland fishery a whale that the plaintiff's Eskimo employees had previously fettered with a drogue. The court held for the defendant, finding that no exception to the fast-fish usage, well established for the Greenland fishery, had been proven.

28 In two instances in the Galápagos fishery single ships came upon schools of sperm whales and singlehandedly killed ten or more in one day (Stackpole, 1953:401).

29 In two cases arising in the Sea of Okhotsk, the defendants had slaughtered whales that the plaintiffs had waifed and anchored on the previous day. The plaintiffs prevailed in both. See *Bartlett* v. *Budd*, 2 Fed. Cas. 966 (D. Mass. 1868) (No. 1,075) (plaintiff, who proved the usage that a waif holds a whale, was independently entitled to recover as a matter of property law); *Taber* v. *Jenny*, 23 Fed. Cas. 605 (D. Mass. 1856) (No. 13,720) (plaintiff, who had a high probability of retaking the whale, should prevail as a matter of property law over defendant, who should have known from the appearance of the whale that it had been killed within the previous twelve hours).

30 See *Heppingstone* v. *Mammen*, 2 Hawaii 707, 712 (1863); *Swift* v. *Gifford*. 23 Fed. Cas. 558, 558–59 (D. Mass. 1872) (No. 13,696). Hohman (1928:166) asserted, without citing authority, that a subsequent taker of a sperm whale bearing whaling craft also had to give the owner of the craft a reasonable length of time to retake the whale.

Cutting-in was a laborious process that involved all hands for as long as a day or more. It could not be begun until after the crew had chained the whale to the ship and rigged up special slaughtering equipment. See Melville (1851: chaps. 66–67); Hohman (1928:167). Hohman (1928:166) has alleged that if the first vessel to have attached a harpoon or lance were to come upon a subsequent taker that had justifiably begun to cut in, the first vessel remained entitled to any blubber still in the water.

31 See *Bartlett* v. *Budd*, 2 Fed. Cas. 966 (D. Mass. 1868) (No. 1,075) (defendant had cut in on the day after the plaintiff's crew had killed, anchored, and waifed the whale); see also Hohman (1928:166): "Thus a carcass containing the 'waif' of a vessel believed to be in the general vicinity was never disturbed by another whaler."

32 A fact-specific example of this solution is *Heppingstone* v. *Mammen*, 2 Hawaii 707 (1863), where the court split a whale fifty-fifty between the owner of the first iron and the ultimate taker. The crew of the *Oregon* had badly wounded the whale but was on the brink of losing it when it was caught and killed by the crew of the *Richmond*. The *Richmond* then

surrendered the carcass to the *Oregon*, whose captain refused the *Richmond's* request for a half share. In light of the uncertainty that the *Oregon* would have retaken the whale, the court rendered the Solomonic solution that the *Richmond's* captain had proposed.

33 *Fennings* v. *Lord Grenville*, 1 Taunt. 241, 127 Eng. Rep. 825 (Ct. Comm. Pleas 1808).

34 In *Fennings* the plaintiff had in fact left the drogued whale in order to pursue another.

35 8 Fed. 159 (D. Mass. 1881).

36 Two centuries before *Ghen* New Englanders had enacted ordinances to solve an analogous problem. The seventeenth-century hunters of right whales in the near-shore Gulf Stream were better at killing them than at controlling their carcasses. In 1688 the Plymouth colony had rules that called for whalers to place identifying marks on their lances and that specified how many shillings a finder who towed a dead whale ashore was to receive from the lancer. See Dow (1925:9–10). Long Island laws of the same period called for the killer and the finder of a dead whale at sea to split it equally and also entitled the finder of a whale carcass on a beach to receive a reward (*id*. at 15).

37 The seminal works on choices between *legal* rules and standards are Ehrlich and Posner (1974) and Kennedy (1976:1687–88). See also Diver (1983).

38 Maine lobstermen continue this New England maritime tradition. Informal "harbor gangs" use self-help, not law, to police lobstering territories. See Acheson (1988:73–77).

39 *Swift v. Gifford*, 23 Fed. Cas. 558 (D. Mass. 1872) (No. 13,696).

40 Why litigation burst forth from incidents in the Sea of Okhotsk in the 1850s is unclear. One possibility is suggested by the fact that most of the whales found in that vicinity were bowheads, a relatively passive species (Bockstoce, 1986:28–29). For these baleen whales it may have been utilitarian for whalers to revert from the first-iron rule to the fast-fish rule. American whalers, accustomed to hunting sperm whales in the Pacific, may have had trouble making this switch.

A more straightforward explanation is that the New England whaling community was becoming less close-knit when this spate of litigation occurred. The American whaling industry had begun to decline during the 1850s and was then decimated during the Civil War when several of these cases were being litigated (Hohman, 1928:290–92, 302). The deviant whalers involved in the litigated cases, seeing themselves nearing their last periods of play, may have decided to defect. In two of the five reported cases arising out of the Sea of Okhotsk (*Swift* and *Bourne*), both litigants even operated out of the same port, New Bedford. When the whalers' informal system of social control began to unravel, apparently even its core was vulnerable.

References

Acheson, James M. 1988. *The Lobster Gangs of Maine*. Hanover, N.H.: University Press of New England.

Ashley, Clifford W. 1938. *The Yankee Whaler*. Boston: Houghton Mifflin.

Bockstoce, John R. 1986. *Whales, Ice, and Men: The History of Whaling in the Western Arctic*. Seattle: University of Washington Press.

Byers, Edward. 1987. *The Nation of Nantucket: Society and Politics in an Early American Commercial Center, 1660–1820*. Boston: Northeastern University Press.

Calabresi, Guido, and A. Douglas Melamed. 1972. "Property Rules, Liability Rules, and Inalienability: One View of the Cathedral." 85 *Harvard Law Review* 1089.

Chatterton, Edward Keble. 1926. *Whalers and Whaling*. Philadelphia: J. B. Lippincott.

Diver, Colin S. 1983. "The Optimal Precision of Administrative Rules." 93 *Yale Law Journal* 65.

Dow, George Francis. 1925. *Whale Ships and Whaling*. Salem, Mass.: Marine Research Society.

Ehrlich, Isaac, and Richard A. Posner. 1974. "An Economic Analysis of Legal Rulemaking." 3 *Journal of Legal Studies* 257.

Ellickson, Robert C. 1986. "Of Coase and Cattle: Dispute Resolution among Neighbors in Shasta County." 38 *Stanford Law Review* 623.

———. 1987. "A Critique of Economic and Sociological Theories of Social Control." 16 *Journal of Legal Studies* 67.

Hardin, Garrett. 1968. "The Tragedy of the Commons." 162 *Science* 1243.

Hobbes, Thomas. 1909. *Leviathan*. Oxford: Clarendon Press.

Hohman, Elmo Paul. 1928. *The American Whaleman: A Study of Life and Labor in the Whaling Industry*. New York: Longmans, Green.

Holmes, Oliver Wendell, Jr. 1881. *The Common Law*. Boston: Little, Brown.

Jackson, Gordon. 1978. *The British Whaling Trade*. London: A. & C. Black.

Kennedy, Duncan. 1976. "Form and Substance in Private Law Adjudication." 89 *Harvard Law Review* 1685.

Melville, Herman. 1851. *Moby-Dick*. Middlesex, England: Penguin Books, 1972.

Morison, Samuel Eliot. 1921. *The Maritime History of Massachusetts 1783–1860*. Boston: Houghton Mifflin.

Stackpole, Edouard A. 1953. *The Sea Hunters: The New England Whalemen during Two Centuries, 1635–1835*. Philadelphia: J. B. Lippincott.

Umbeck, John. 1977. "A Theory of Contract Choice and the California Gold Rush." 20 *Journal of Law and Economics* 421.

Williams, William Fish. 1964. "The Voyage of the *Florence*, 1873–1874." In H. Williams, ed., *One Whaling Family*. Boston: Houghton Mifflin.

Williamson, Oliver E. 1983. "Credible Commitments: Using Hostages to Support Exchange." 73 *American Economic Review* 519.

Review and Discussion Questions

1 Do property rights have to be expressed in formal laws or can they be expressed in other ways?

2 What purpose, according to Ellickson, did the whalers' norms serve?

3 Why was the "fast-fish, loose-fish" norm adopted?

4 Why, in some fisheries, was the "fast-fish, loose-fish" norm replaced by the "iron-holds-the-whale" norm?

5 Why didn't the whalers use a quota system?

6 Research the property rights systems used for other marine animals that humans hunt. Can you explain the differences among systems using an approach similar to Ellickson's?

Chapter 13

Michael Satchell

SAVE THE ELEPHANTS: START SHOOTING THEM

ANIMAL LOVERS hail the ivory ban. Many African nations hate it—and say it hurts wildlife

The elephants from Gonarezhou National Park forded the Save River soon after sunup and bore down on the village of Mahenya. The alarm was sounded, but frenzied shouts and the banging of pots and pans failed, as usual, to scare them away. It took the jumbos only minutes to devour a field of ripening maize that Phineas Uketi had coaxed from the thin, desiccated soil of this remote, arid corner of southeastern Zimbabwe. "Not long ago, lions came in the night and killed 14 goats," says the grizzled subsistence farmer, more resigned to than angered by his loss. "Three women were hurt by lion and buffalo; one man was killed by an elephant. Maybe I am not so unlucky."

Just four years ago, marauding wildlife would have spurred Uketi and his fellow villagers to kill the animals with poison and spears. Today, the people in Mahenya and in scores of other Zimbabwean villages tolerate the crop losses, the property damage and the danger, for one reason. They—not the central government—now own the animals in their district. They profit from them. And so they protect them.

There is a growing belief among conservationists that if Africa's big-game animals are to survive—not just inside national parks but outside, where most of them live—people who share the land must benefit. In programs like Zimbabwe's CAMPFIRE, a widely copied model for other African nations, villagers are allowed, under strict controls, to sell permits to big-game trophy hunters and to cull animals for hides, horns and meat.

Sustainable-harvest programs could soon include a return to the ivory trade—the most controversial and most profitable aspect of consumptive wildlife commerce. At least 11 southern African nations including South Africa, Zimbabwe, Malawi, Namibia, Botswana and Tanzania either want to resume—or would support—limited trade in ivory if certain conditions can be met. These include strict measures to prevent poaching and ironclad safeguards to block black-market ivory from entering the legal pipeline.

Prime Minister Ryutaro Hashimoto of Japan, a major ivory-consumer nation, said in October he would "positively consider" supporting a renewed tusk trade. Last week, officials from most of Africa's 35 elephant-range nations meeting in Senegal found that poaching, illegal trade and human conflicts were increasing and agreed "to reconsider the elephant as a renewable natural resource."

Enemy no. 1

African antipathy toward elephants is rooted in the animals' destructive behavior. As the continent's growing human populations gobble up more wildlife habitat, expanding elephant herds compete with cattle farmers for forage and water, raid crop fields and granaries, destroy orchards and forests, damage water lines and dams, wreck buildings and terrorize rural villages.

"Elephants are the darlings of the Western world, but they are enemy No. 1 in Kenya," says David Western, head of the Kenya Wildlife Service. He tacitly supports a return to the ivory trade with strict controls. "The African farmer's enmity toward elephants is as visceral as Western mawkishness is passionate," he says. In the past six years, he points out, close to 400 Kenyans have been killed by wildlife, mostly by elephants but also by lions, buffaloes, hippos, crocodiles and baboons.

Burgeoning elephant herds in southern and eastern Africa are damaging not only wildlife preserves like Kenya's Amboseli National Park but entire countries. Consider Botswana, a nation roughly the size of Texas. "We have 80,000 in our tiny country," says Ketumile Masire, Botswana's president, adding wryly: "That's elephants, not chickens. Many are starving and in some areas destroying their own habitat. We fear they will do irreparable harm to the ecosystem. We would like to reduce our herds and market the ivory."

Fund-raising tool

Legal export sales of elephant tusks were outlawed in 1989 by the member countries of CITES, the United Nations Convention on International Trade in Endangered Species. The ban was a response to rampant poaching—fostered by lax protection and corruption—that had wiped out roughly half of Africa's 1.3 million elephants in the previous decade.

The CITES prohibition was orchestrated by Western nations and their powerful animal-protection groups. They declared the African elephant's very survival to be at stake—ignoring the fact that 600,000 animals is hardly an endangered population. And it didn't hurt that images of dead elephants became an effective membership and fund-raising tool for the animal groups. In the welter of righteous enthusiasm for the ban, they and Western governments promised tens of millions of dollars to African nations to make up for their lost legal ivory revenues. Only a fraction of that money ever materialized.

The ban worked and the slaughter has been drastically reduced, though it has hardly ended. Some 200 elephant carcasses, tusks removed, were found in September in the Congo, reflecting the continued demand for ivory. Southern African nations that protected their elephant populations during the heavy-poaching era and now are overrun by the pachyderms want the ban lifted altogether or modified to allow limited ivory exports from countries with large herds.

The highly charged issue will dominate the agenda next June when the 133 member nations of CITES meet for their biennial conference. The meeting will be held, coincidentally, in Zimbabwe, one of Africa's strongest advocates for resumed ivory trading. With about 70,000 elephants—more than twice the carrying capacity in a country the size of California—and with 45 tons of ivory locked in a government warehouse, Zimbabwe badly wants to find a market for its trove of white gold.

Estimates of stockpiled ivory across the continent range from 500 to 600 tons, perhaps more. For nations mired in poverty, that represents a vast, untapped source of revenue that could underwrite rural development, habitat acquisition and wildlife protection. It also could be siphoned off into the pockets of corrupt bureaucrats. Thus one idea being floated by the World Wildlife Fund is a debt-for-ivory swap in which Western governments would write off a portion of a nation's indebtedness in return for destruction of its stockpiled tusks.

Western animal-protection groups are preparing to mount massive opposition to renewed ivory trading. The Humane Society of the United States, which has launched a $2.5 million elephant contraception experiment in South Africa's Kruger National Park, says that culling and hunting are unnecessary. Believes the society's John Grandy: "Birth control is a humane alternative for African nations who make money from devastating their wildlife, a way for them to embrace compassion."

Ecoimperialism

This sentiment infuriates Africans eager to use their wildlife like any other natural resource, be it timber, copper or diamonds. "Why should our people beg and starve while we are sitting on a stack of ivory worth tens of millions of dollars?" asks Graham Child, an internationally known wildlife scientist in Zimbabwe. Says Botswanan President Masire: "It is environmental imperialism. Let us manage our own resources without interference from the West."

The same ecoimperialism charge is leveled against the United States by Botswana, Zimbabwe, Malawi and Namibia in a related controversy. Together with the 35,000-member Safari Club International, the world's largest big-game-hunting organization, the four southern African nations have petitioned the United States to amend its Endangered Species Act. The law forbids American hunters to bring home trophies of animals the ESA deems threatened or endangered—even though CITES allows limited hunting of some of these species in specific countries.

Big-game hunters typically spend between $20,000 and $60,000 for a safari. Denying them trophy import permits, they argue, is a restraint of trade that costs African nations millions of dollars a year. In South Africa's Pilanesburg National Park not long ago, for example, three very rare black rhinoceros bulls, past breeding age, were approaching the end. SCI members offered up to $250,000 each to shoot them and bring home the trophies. The law, not common sense, prevailed, and the rhinos ended up as hyena food. Likewise, hundreds of cheetahs are killed each year across southern Africa as livestock pests; SCI lobbyist and former Montana congressman Ron Marlenee says the U.S. species protection act actually hampers efforts to provide incentives to rural Africans to halt poaching, to stop converting prime wildlife habitat to livestock pasture and to quit killing the sleek cats that prey on their animals. "If cheetahs killed as pests were instead worth $5,000 apiece to local people, they'd feed their cattle and hogs to them," Marlenee argues.

Some prominent conservationists, like elephant researcher Cynthia Moss, argue that Africa's big game should be protected for its intrinsic worth. Others insist that wildlife must pay its way if it is to survive outside zoos and safari parks. "The protectionist mentality is irrelevant today," believes Hector Magome, manager of planning and development for the South Africa Parks Board. "Wildlife must be used to reduce poverty; otherwise we will lose the parks." The government, he notes, is under tremendous pressure from land-poor South Africans to carve up New Jersey-size Kruger National Park for farms and homesteads. Wildlife officials in southern Africa calculate that managing wildlife on marginal lands can produce twice as much revenue as cattle ranching.

Programs like Zimbabwe's CAMPFIRE, which began in earnest about eight years ago, are a promising start. CAMPFIRE generates $2.5 million a year, 90 percent of that from sport hunting. The money is shared by about 600,000 people living on communal lands.

CAMPFIRE is dependent on a 10-year, $27 million U.S. Agency for International Development grant for administration, training and infrastructure that began in 1990. Though emulated in other countries, the program has recently been tainted by charges of poor management and corruption in some areas of Zimbabwe. Sustainable-use proponents consider it a model for community development despite the blemishes. Opponents say CAMPFIRE is nothing more than U.S. tax dollars subsidizing wealthy trophy hunters.

For Phineas Uketi and his fellow villagers, such controversy is an abstraction. They point out that last year, the 681 households in Mahenya each received a cash payout of 240 Zimbabwean dollars. That's about $25, a significant sum in a subsistence economy in which $100 to $150 is the average annual household income. Revenues from the program, which began in Mahenya in 1992, also have purchased the village two grinding mills and a water line and have built a small school.

CAMPFIRE has brought the villagers of Mahenya full circle. Davison Msimbini says his people once hated nearby Gonarezhou Park because they were forced off the land 30 years ago to create the preserve and were forbidden to hunt the animals that had sustained them for centuries. "Now we use the skills and knowledge of our elders to conserve wildlife as they once did," he says. "Once again, animals are part of our livelihood."

Review and Discussion Questions

1 Why in the past did the villagers kill the elephants?
2 Why did that practice change after the villagers obtained property rights to the elephants?
3 Why aren't cattle in danger of extinction?
4 Are there other endangered animals for which property rights have helped or might help?

Suggestions for Further Reading

Anderson, G. M. and Tollison, R. D. (1985) "Life in the Gulag: A Property Rights Perspective," *Cato Journal*, 5: 295–304.

 The authors use a property rights perspective to argue that the forced-labor system in the Soviet Union (the "Gulag") was less efficient and crueler than slavery in the American South.

Anderson, T. L. and Hill, P. J. (1975) "The Evolution of Property Rights: A Study of the American West," *Journal of Law and Economics*, 18: 163–179.

 How property rights to land, livestock, and water changed in the American West as the marginal benefits and marginal costs of the rights changed.

Benson, B. L. (1989) "The Spontaneous Evolution of Commercial Law," *Southern Economics Journal*, 55: 644–661.

 Benson explains how, in the Middle Ages, traders operating across the many local governments in Europe developed and enforced their own commercial law (*lex mercatoria*). The law was enforced independently from government. Markets are so powerful they can even sustain their own laws!

De Alessi, L. (1983) "Property Rights, Transaction Costs, and X-Inefficiency: An Essay in Economic Theory," *American Economic Review*, 73: 64–81.

 De Alessi shows that a major criticism of neoclassical economic theory, that firms don't actually maximize profits, is at best incomplete and at worst simply wrong. This is because the criticism fails to include the effects of property rights.

De Alessi, M. (2004) "An Ivory-Tower Take on the Ivory Trade," *Economic Journal Watch*, 1: 47–54.

 More on how property rights can help protect and sustain endangered animals like the African elephant.

Jimerson, J. B. (1996) "Good Times and Good Games: How Pickup Basketball Players Use Wealth-Maximizing Norms," *Journal of Contemporary Ethnography*, 25: 353–371.

 An interesting, modern application of Ellickson's "welfare-maximizing norms": the norms developed by pickup basketball players. Jimerson finds that the basketball players' norms "help them play in the best games possible as long as possible" (p. 353).

Lueck, D. (2002) "The Extermination and Conservation of the American Bison," *Journal of Law and Economics*, 31: S609–S652.

 Lueck's detailed history of the American bison ("buffalo") shows that their near-extinction and later (modest) revival is consistent with Demsetz's theory of property rights.

Roll, R. and Talbott, J. R. (2003) "Political Freedom, Economic Liberty, and Prosperity," *Journal of Democracy*, 14: 75–89.

 Statistical analysis by Roll and Talbott concludes that strong property rights are a key determinant of economic growth. "It appears that the critical ingredient of a successful development policy is a fair and just system that invites profitable economic exchange among participants, with no risk of expropriation or repudiation" (p. 76).

Smith, F. L., Jr. (1995) "Markets and the Environment: A Critical Appraisal," *Contemporary Economic Policy*, 13: 62–73.

 Smith argues that property rights and privatization would work better than political means to protect and improve the environment. Why? Consistent with the readings in Part one of this book, Smith contends that information and incentives are better provided by markets.

PART FOUR

Externalities and Coordination Problems

Introduction

Markets are often said to fail because of "externalities." An example of an externality is water pollution: a firm can dump waste into the water, harming parties downstream. But critics argue that unless the polluter is forced to recognize this cost by a government tax on pollution or by laws regulating pollution, the firm will simply continue to pollute, costing the victims and unnecessarily lowering the value of the economy's output.

However, since an important paper by Ronald Coase (1960),[1] economists have understood that the market can at least sometimes solve externality problems by itself. As long as property rights are defined and enforced, and the cost of negotiations between the parties is relatively low, we expect the parties to reach an economically efficient outcome. In the case of water pollution, depending on how property rights are assigned, either the parties downstream will pay the polluting firm to lessen its pollution, or the polluter will pay the downstream parties for the right to continue polluting. The externality is "internalized."

The article by Michael C. Munger describes a situation that was long thought to be an externality requiring government intervention. Fruit and legume growers want to locate near beekeepers because bees pollinate the fruits and legumes. Beekeepers want to locate near the fruits and legumes because some of them provide food for the bees. The fruit and legume growers create a positive externality for the beekeepers, and the beekeepers, in turn, create a positive externality for the fruit and legume growers. How can the market possibly provide efficient amounts of fruit, legumes, and bees? It turns out the growers and the beekeepers solve the problem well by negotiating contracts for the services.

Note that what constitutes an externality is not fixed forever. Technological improvements make it easier for the economy to internalize externalities. Fred E. Foldvary and Daniel B. Klein discuss several ways technology reduces the cost of internalizing, and they present a number of examples. The power of the market is thus enhanced by technology.

An important related criticism of markets is that they can get stuck on bad standards: my choice of standard influences you, your choice of standard influences me, and we could end up with a standard that makes us both worse off. For example, why are the keys of a typewriter arranged in the standard, Qwerty layout? (The keys in the third row from the bottom, on the left side, are Q-W-E-R-T-Y, hence Qwerty.) Many people have heard that early typewriter manufacturers chose Qwerty to slow typists down. They wanted typists to slow down because slower typing reduced the problem of keys jamming, a problem which was irritating and messy. But now that virtually all of us type with computers and there are no keys to jam, why do we still type with the slower Qwerty arrangement?

The answer, critics say, is that the market fails to coordinate a switch to a better standard. You might want to use another arrangement of keys that lets you type faster, but you don't switch because no manufacturer is selling a different arrangement; manufacturers might want to sell a different arrangement, but they don't because they don't think anyone will retrain to use them. The market thus gets stuck on a poor choice. If this problem just involved keyboards, it would be of small import, but critics allege it happens too frequently. We used VHS videotapes instead of allegedly superior Beta tapes; we use PCs running Windows instead of using allegedly far better Macs or Unix machines.

The reading from S. J. Liebowitz and Stephen E. Margolis refutes this criticism theoretically and empirically. Theoretically, any such coordination failure would present a tremendous profit opportunity to someone who could get people to move to the better standard. Given that there are at least a few people interested in making a profit, such coordination problems should be rare. And detailed examination of the history of the QWERTY keyboard indicates that it wasn't—and isn't—a bad choice. (Similarly, VHS videotapes and Windows machines weren't bad choices, either, as discussed by Margolis and Liebowitz in their 2001 book.)[2]

Notes

1 Coase, R. (1960), "The Problem of Social Cost," *Journal of Law and Economics*, 3: 1–44.
2 Liebowitz, S. J. and Margolis, S. E. (2001), *Winners, Losers & Microsoft: Competition and Antitrust in High Technology, Revised Edition*, Oakland: The Independent Institute.

Chapter 14

Michael C. Munger

ORANGE BLOSSOM SPECIAL: EXTERNALITIES AND THE COASE THEOREM

I GREW UP ON A VALENCIA FARM, in orange country south of Orlando. Twice a year, December and June, air was perfumed with orange blossoms, advertising their sweet nectar. Bees filled the air, harvesting that nectar. But the bees looked as if they were wearing thick yellow gaucho pants, carrying pollen from flower to flower.

An old guy with skin like leather, whom we knew as "Bee Man," would bring his hives in, and arrange them in a row. I found that if I looked sad he'd give me a piece of comb, dripping honey (and bee droppings, to be honest) to gnaw on. The bees produced enough honey that Bee Man could pay us in honey and still make money.

Thinking back on it, I was in the middle of one of the most interesting and complex economic situations around. But the sun-warmed, honey-soaked wax comb tasted so good that I missed what some economists call "externalities," bees fertilizing fruit and flowers giving bees nectar for honey.

Externalities

If I do something that affects you, positively or negatively, without your consent or without my own ability to withhold a benefit unless you pay, then that is an *externality*.

Economist A.C. Pigou expressed the problem as a divergence between supply price (what a buyer pays) and the "marginal supply price" (the total amount something costs). Price paid might be less than true cost (a negative externality) or more than true cost (a positive externality). A commonly alleged example is a lighthouse, a *positive* externality. As Henry Sidgwick put it, nearly 150 years ago, "it may easily happen that the benefits of a well-placed lighthouse must be largely enjoyed by ships on which no toll could be conveniently placed."

This conclusion seems perverse, and it is. Folks who would benefit from increased production of a positive externality will try to come up with a solution. As another economist, Ronald Coase, pointed out, Pigou was ignoring an important fact: in real markets, externality problems are often solved privately, which means that the externality disappears. In fact, Coase did a little digging, and found something interesting: in 1820, in England (home of Sidgwick!), more than three quarters of all lighthouses were built and operated privately.

Coase gives a general analysis of externalities in his landmark 1960 paper, "The Problem of Social Cost." He makes three fundamental points. First, externalities are reciprocal. Second, externalities persist only if transactions costs are high. Finally, if transactions costs are low, market processes will lead to the same efficient outcomes, irrespective of the assignment of property rights.

Let's see what a Coasian analysis would tell us about the externality I was interested in. Let's think about bees.

A Coasian analysis: Cheung's "Fable of the Bees"

> Suppose that in a given region there is a certain amount of apple-growing and a certain amount of bee-keeping and that the bees feed on the apple-blossom. If the apple-farmers apply 10% more labour, land and capital to apple-farming they will increase the output of apples by 10%; but they will also provide more food for the bees. On the other hand, the bee-keepers will not increase the output of honey by 10% by increasing the amount of land, labour and capital applied to bee-keeping by 10% unless at the same time the apple-farmers also increase their output and so the food of the bees by 10%. Thus there are constant returns to scale for both industries taken together: if the amount of labour and of capital employed both in apple-farming and bee-keeping are doubled, the output of both apples and honey will be doubled. But if the amount of labour and capital are doubled in bee-keeping alone, the output of honey will be less than doubled; whereas, if the amounts of labour and capital in apple-farming are doubled, the output of apples will be doubled and, in addition, some contribution will be made to the output of honey.
>
> We call this a case of an unpaid factor, because the situation is due simply and solely to the fact that the apple-farmer cannot charge the bee-keeper for the bees' food, which the former produces for the latter. If social-accounting institutions were such that this charge could be made, then every factor would, as in other competitive situations, earn the value of its marginal social net product. But as it is, the apple-farmer provides to the beekeeper some of his factors free of charge. The apple-farmer is paid less than the value of his marginal social net product, and the bee-keeper receives more than the value of his marginal social net product.
>
> (Meade, "External Economies and Diseconomies in a Competitive Situation,"
> pp. 56–7)

In 1952, an economist named J.E. Meade published a paper in the *Economic Journal*. Meade thought that he had discovered a truly new phenomenon, an externality relation so intricate that markets could not handle it. As you can see in the extract above, Meade thought the result would always be inefficiency, because the orchard grower cannot capture all the benefits created by beekeeping. Consequently, he argued, some kind of subsidy or government provision is required.

But Meade was wrong. The first reason is that, unlike oranges, apple blossoms don't produce enough nectar to make "apple blossom honey" viable. Yes, you can buy something called apple blossom honey. It is made mostly from wildflowers that grow in the orchards. But "apple blossom honey" sounds way better than "weed flower honey."

Further, all externalities are reciprocal. Economically, the bee and the flower are as interconnected as the chicken and the egg. And the gains to solving the problem are significant. Meade's claim about the "failure" of markets to capture the externality would have been news to apple growers, as later work by economist Steven Cheung demonstrates.

Remember, the general problem is supposed to be that positive externalities cause underproduction. And Meade argues that the specific problem of beekeeping is a perfect positive externality. Bees kept in one orchard, unless it is very large, will cross boundaries into the neighboring orchard. So pollination is "external" to the decision of any one landowner. And that means that there will be too few bees. Bring in the Federal Bee-reau of Apiation! We need subsidies, and we need them now.

Cheung ignored the economists, and looked at the economics. He found that apple growers had solved the problem. Bees fly far in their search for nectar, sometimes a mile, maybe three miles. Apple orchards can be big (the average size is a little over 50 acres), but bees might easily cross the property line and pollinate trees in the next orchard. So, suppose I have a moderate-sized orchard in the middle of several other orchards. Suppose further that I expect the growers around me to invest in bees. I can free ride, after all! Much, perhaps most, of my orchard will be pollinated by roving bees from the surrounding growers.

But if some economist with a blackboard can figure this out then surely the apple growers can, too. There are real gains to solving this problem, which is local and involves only small numbers of orchardists. Stephen Cheung describes a powerful implicit contract, the "custom of the orchard," that gets farmers out of Meade's predicament:

> [I]f a number of similar orchards are located close to one another, one who hires bees to pollinate his own orchard will in some degree benefit his neighbors. Of course, the strategic placing of the hives will reduce the spillover of bees. But in the absence of any social constraint on behavior, each farmer will tend to take advantage of what spillover does occur and to employ fewer hives himself. Of course, contractual arrangements could be made among all farmers in an area to determine collectively the number of hives to be employed by each, but no such effort is observed.
>
> Acknowledging the complication, beekeepers and farmers are quick to point out that a social rule, or *custom of the orchards*, takes the place of explicit contracting: during the pollination period the owner of an orchard either keeps bees himself or hires as many hives per area as are employed in neighboring orchards of the same type. One failing to comply would be rated as a "bad neighbor," it is said, and

could expect a number of inconveniences imposed on him by other orchard owners. This customary matching of hive densities involves the exchange of gifts of the same kind, which apparently entails lower transaction costs than would be incurred under explicit contracting, where farmers would have to negotiate and make money payments to one another for the bee spillover.

(Cheung, "The Fable of the Bees," p. 30. Emphasis added)

"The custom of the orchard" is an understanding that a certain number of hives are required to pollinate some fixed area, on average. It is true that some bees from farm A will end up on neighboring farm B, and vice versa, in what look like random search patterns. But if both farmers purchase the correct *average* number of hives, and the bees randomly search for pollen and nectar, then the externality is entirely internalized. My bees pollinate some of your trees, and yours some of mine, but the average and marginal allocations of resources are fully optimal! If there is money to be made, and transactions costs are not too high, people will figure out something on their own.

Orange blossom special

Still, what is the market price of bee services? How can markets solve that problem? Cheung (p. 19) proposes a simple answer: since the possible externality is reciprocal, pollination might be worth more, or honey production might be worth more. So, the exchange will be some combination of money and honey, and it is not clear to an outsider who will pay whom. But the actual parties to the exchange can solve the problem among themselves.

Remember that in Washington, apple blossoms produce relatively little nectar. The result is that the beekeepers in Washington are producing more value in pollination than they are taking out in honey. So, apple orchardists pay beekeepers, over and above whatever honey the beekeepers produce, and keep. But the apple orchardists pay less for bee services than if no honey were produced at all.

Orange blossoms, by contrast, are an enormous source of valuable honey. *And, the direction of payment is reversed: In Florida, until recently, beekeepers pay the grove owner.* (The "until recently" caveat is necessary because bee populations have shrunk in the last few years, in many parts of the country, including Florida, so that now grove owners pay beekeepers.)[1]

Thus, at its simplest level, we can see that a remarkably complex theoretical problem is solved in a simple and straightforward way by the price mechanism. Beekeepers will make offers, and so will farmers. Both parties to such transactions benefit. Who pays whom, and how? An outsider might have trouble guessing. The prices will signal the relative scarcities of the inputs (including the bees!), and the demand for the farm products. In apple orchards, the farmers pay the beekeepers. In orange orchards, the beekeepers pay the farmers.

And no one had to tell them what to do to make honey. Sweet.

Note

1 For a related podcast, see Munger on "Subsidies and Externalities" on EconTalk.

Further reading

James Buchanan and W. C. Stubblebine, "Externality," *Economica*, 1962, 29, 371–84.
Steven N.S. Cheung, "The Fable of the Bees: An Economic Investigation," *Journal of Law and Economics*, 1973, 16, 11–33.
Ronald C. Coase, "The Problem of Social Cost," *Journal of Law and Economics*, 1960, 3, 1–44.
J.E. Meade, "External Economies and Diseconomies in a Competitive Situation," *Economic Journal*, 1952, 62, 51–69.
A.C. Pigou, *The Economics of Welfare* (1920), 2001. Piscataway, NJ: Transaction Publishers.
Henry Sidgwick, *The Principles of Political Economy*, 1883. New York: MacMillan and Company.

Review and Discussion Questions

1 What is an "externality"?
2 What three fundamental points about externalities did Ronald Coase make?
3 Economists claim that externalities are reciprocal. What does that mean?
4 Why does raising bees near orchards seem to be an externality?
5 Munger states, "If there is money to be made, and transactions costs are not too high, people will figure out something on their own." Explain what he means. Will transactions costs always be "not too high"?
6 What is a key difference between Washington State apple growing and Florida orange growing? How does the difference illustrate the power of the market to solve externalities?

Chapter 15

Fred E. Foldvary and Daniel B. Klein

THE HALF-LIFE OF POLICY RATIONALES: HOW NEW TECHNOLOGY AFFECTS OLD POLICY ISSUES

T HE JUSTIFICATIONS FOR MANY PUBLIC POLICIES are dissolving as technology advances. New detection and metering technologies are being developed for highways, parking, marine farming, and auto emissions, making property-rights solutions viable. Information becomes more accessible and user-friendly, suggesting that quality and safety are better handled by the private sector, undercutting consumer-protection rationales. As for public utilities, new means of producing and delivering electricity, water, postal, and telephone services dissolve the old natural-monopoly rationales for control and governmental provision.

Most market-failure arguments boil down to claims about market mechanisms being blocked by transaction costs. But technology has trimmed transaction costs and made the old rationales for government intervention increasingly obsolete.

Besides trimming transaction costs, technological advancement accelerates economic change and multiplies the connections between activities. It brings fundamental upsets to even our best understandings of current arrangements and their shortcomings. Thus, by making the economic system ever more complex, it makes the notion that regulators can meaningfully know and beneficially manipulate the system ever less credible.

Technology sets what may be called an intellectual half-life on policies and their justifications.

Introduction

Writers have occasionally noted that a policy's appropriateness depends on the current state of alternative technologies, and that technological changes make old policies obsolete and new policies worthwhile (Hayek 1979: 47; Rosen 1992: 68).

Most market failure arguments boil down to claims about invisible hand mechanisms being obstructed by some kind of transaction costs. If technology trims transaction and production costs—by making it easy to charge users, define and enforce property rights, exit and utilize substitutes, gather information, gain assurance of quality and safety, enter and compete in markets—the invisible hand works better. We argue that *technological advancement tends to enhance the case for free enterprise policy*. It reduces the strength of market failure arguments and the case for intervention.

Our conclusion is bolstered by a second, Smith–Hayek, line of argument. Technology heightens the complexity of the economic system. The more complex a system, the less knowable it is, and the less likely government interventions are to benefit society.

Technological advancement might not enhance the case for free enterprise in every area of policy, but it does in many.

Technology works to resolve market imperfections

Theories of market failure and governmental remedies are not absolute doctrine but depend on the institutional and technological context. The invisible hand—the nexus of voluntary social mechanisms—may fail, in a significant sense, if transaction costs obstruct gainful exchange. But better technology reduces such costs. Applications of market failure theory may be found to have a technological "half-life," after which their validity dissolves.

Some would challenge the general claim, arguing that, just as technology enhances the knowledge and capabilities of private entrepreneurs, so it enhances that of public-spirited regulators and officials. Government becomes more effective because of technology. No doubt there is much to the challenge. Government agencies too can run highways as toll roads. Or, consider a common argument against regulation: that it introduces noncompliance problems and requires costly enforcement. Insofar as technology facilitates government monitoring and enforcement, the case for government regulation gains strength.

However, if both free enterprise and the government are technically capable of, say, producing tomatoes, the sheer incentive argument recommends free enterprise. Good government itself is a public goods problem (Tullock 1971); government often fails to do the good that it is technically capable of. The free enterprise system, on the other hand, generally creates for its participants incentives to pursue what is good for society. Hence, the incentive advantage recommends free enterprise, given technical and institutional workability.

Technology enables metering, excluding, and charging

New technology is making it increasingly possible to define and enforce property rights, and to charge for the use of property. The following are examples of this expanding capability.

Highways and parking

It has traditionally been argued that charging for highway use or parking space would entail significant transaction costs, such as delays and inconvenience for motorists, the handling and securing of bulky cash, and costly or unsightly toll booths or parking meters. Yet these difficulties have been lessened considerably. On highways with electronic tolling, the charge is automatically recorded as the car rolls by, with no need to line up and stop. Highway users can now pay highway tolls as easily as they pay a monthly phone bill, weakening the case for operating highways as "freeways" and strengthening the case for privatization.

Street parking is another service that entrepreneurs can charge for. Modern parking meters no longer require coins for fixed periods of time, but can electronically vary the charge and dispense with time restrictions. New in-vehicle meters with LCD displays operate like pre-paid phone cards; anyone with curb space to rent could do so without even erecting parking meters. One could imagine turning on-street parking space over to private entrepreneurs or adjoining land owners, to rent by the minute using high-tech meters.

Lighthouses

The lighthouse has long served as an example of a public good that cannot be supplied by purely voluntary means. Ronald Coase (1974) explored the history of lighthouse provision in Britain and showed that private entrepreneurs built, owned, and operated lighthouses, and made profits. Payments from ships for lighthouses were mandated at nearby ports, however, so, as David Van Zandt (1993) has explained, the arrangement depended in such cases, after all, on a form of taxation. Whatever the lessons of the historical experience, technology has dissolved any argument for government financing of lighthouse services. By virtue of radar, sonar, satellite-based electronic guidance, and the feasibility of scrambled or encrypted signals, the lighthouse is becoming largely antiquated as a navigational aid. Thus, technology has turned the canonical public good into a museum piece.

Marine resources

The foundation for the invisible hand is private property rights. New technologies are enhancing the ability to define, secure, trade, and enforce private property in marine resources. Just as ranchers and cattlemen in the American West secured and built up their property with such innovations as branding and barbed wire, today entrepreneurs can do likewise in oceans with the technologies of livestock herding, "fingerprinting," tagging, sonar, satellite tracking, habitat creation, fencing, gating, and guarding. Technology has strengthened the intellectual case for aquatic farming and ranching.

Air pollution

Common law traditionally treated air pollution as a nuisance, and that spirit concords with a policy of pollution charges, made feasible by technology. For emissions from cars, the sensor technology developed by Donald Stedman measures pollution levels in the exhaust. When coupled with automatic license plate readers, the technology enables officials to send gross-polluting motorists a pollution bill. A direct polluter-pays approach is much more efficient than command-and-control methods such as smog check programs, alternative-fuel requirements, electric vehicles, and mandates on automakers. Although remote sensing is a program for regional governments to undertake, it is nonetheless a property-rights approach to the problem: It protects the public airshed from violation and leaves nonviolators undisturbed in the use of their own property. It is like protecting public buildings from graffiti by setting up video surveillance, rather than by placing restrictions on who can buy spray-paint and permanent markers at the local hardware stores.

Technology facilitates quality and safety assurance

Many "consumer protection" interventions suppose that quality and safety assurance cannot be adequately provided by voluntary practices and the tort system. Consumers suffer from "imperfect" or "asymmetric" information, which makes for transaction costs in marketplace decisions. The cost of overcoming ignorance is high or even insurmountable, and, in consequence, consumers are vulnerable in a free market to false representations of quality and safety. Services that are hired infrequently or are especially hard to understand need to be restricted according to government approvals and permissions. This line of thinking justifies the Consumer Product Safety Commission, the Food and Drug Administration, the Securities and Exchange Commission, the National Highway Traffic Safety Administration, the Occupational Safety and Health Administration, and local and state occupational licensing, business licensing, and housing codes.

As consumers demand assurance, however, voluntary market processes find ways of supplying it. Service providers assure quality and safety by building and conveying a good reputation. They obtain certifications and seals of approval, seek affiliations with trusted sources, and develop a brand name. Consumers, for their part, also look to rating or recommending agents to ascertain reputations. All these methods and media depend on the generating, collecting, interpreting, formatting, storing, retrieving, and transmitting of information about service providers.

Medical services and products

Information technologies are enhancing quality assurance in medical care. Computer technology coupled with practice review and monitoring have given hospitals, clinics, health organizations, and insurers new means of evaluating practitioner performance. These institutions function as certifiers. Furthermore, because of the Internet and other media, consumers themselves are more able to gain pointed expertise, by learning of available therapies, tapping knowledge of fellow patients, and checking the credentials and affiliations of practitioners. The Internet provides consumers with both technical knowledge and assurances. Also, rating organizations can develop a good reputation for conveying accurate assessments of sellers and manufacturers.

Using the Net, consumers may look merely for the "thumb's up" (or seal of approval), read detailed reviews, or click to another vendor who provides better assurance.

Money and banking

Electronic commerce can be extended to the private issuing of money, revitalizing the case to get rid of banking regulations. Critics of free-market banking suggest that the system would be marred by bank runs and panics, hyperinflation, embezzling, and counterfeiting. These are lapses of quality. Can banks meaningfully assure quality? Would a free banking system prevent such problems? Managing solvency and providing assurances of solvency are especially viable today. Up-to-the-moment financial statements and assessments can be generated and made widely available. Contractual arrangements giving banks options to delay redemption or withdrawal could be more easily posted, managed, and conveyed to worried depositors. Inflation and counterfeiting can be discouraged by rapid feedback mechanisms, such as adverse clearing. In an information age, reputation stays more current and counts for more.

Regulators claim that individuals suffer from an insurmountable ignorance about their own needs and the true quality of available options. Restrictions imposed in the name of quality and safety hamstring many important areas of business and everyday life. Yet in every instance new technology is making claims of information asymmetries and consumer vulnerability less and less credible and proving that the demand for assurance elicits supply.

Technology dissolves natural monopoly arguments

The so-called public utilities—water, sanitation, electricity, natural gas, telephone, and cable television—have long featured an interconnected network or grid, by which water, gas, or electrons are distributed from central sources to users throughout the community. The construction and operation of the distribution system involve large up-front costs that are irreversible. Adding users to the system entails low marginal cost, and distributing product entails low current cost. Thus, in this standard portrayal, a single distribution system continues to enjoy economies of scale as it adds volume over time. The cost structure, therefore, will, in a free market, give rise to a single provider—a natural monopoly. The single provider may then charge high prices, produce low quantity and quality, and make excessive profits. Would-be competitors do not enter and bid down prices because, once they would have sunk investments into a competing system, the incumbent firm will lower its price and possibly bring losses to both firms. Hence no one would be foolhardy enough to challenge the monopolist. Upon this reasoning, regulators and interventionists have argued that government ought to supervise such utilities and control their prices.

Whatever the historical validity of the natural monopoly argument, it is clear that in many service areas technology has brought alternatives that belie the traditional assumptions about costs and integration requirements. Furthermore, rapid change itself complicates the problem of regulators and planners.

Electricity

The current electricity crisis in California is not the result of "deregulation" but, on the contrary, the restructuring of the industry that left in place restrictions on production, control, and pricing. Modern technology favors true deregulation of electricity. Increasingly viable is small-scale generation, powered by diesel, natural gas, or other fuels. On-site generators provide users—office buildings, factories, housing developments, or even single homes—with the option of creating their own self-contained loop. The costs of creating anew competing loops have also fallen by virtue of computer-controlled drilling and line laying, allowing workers to snake under streets and buildings without above-ground disturbance. Such developments dissolve the assumptions of high fixed and sunk costs. Entry and competition in the market would, in a free market, be very viable. Furthermore, technology has greatly advanced the possibility of combining electricity generation with steam power, heat, and air conditioning, and of combining electricity distribution with telecommunications, vastly complicating the job of any regulator who presumes to know how to improve upon the invisible hand.

Water and sanitation

Technology has also made more viable the on-site recycling of water. Homes, developments, businesses, and so on could, if permitted, often choose not to hook up to the centralized utility pipes. The substitute for transporting massive amounts of water via the grid, both to and from users (the latter to deal with waste water), is to develop on-site systems. Such systems would inventory raw water, treat water according to a quality hierarchy for local uses, and then recover raw water from the waste for inventory and reuse. On-site water and waste treatment involves refinement, disposal, and replenishment. So-called gray water could be treated and used for landscaping, cooling, fire fighting, and sanitation. The small amount of water for sensitive human uses, such as bathing, cooking, and drinking, would be distilled to a purity and a safety that the current one-quality-fits-all water systems could not hope to match. The "black water" from toilets and kitchen-disposal units would be treated and disposed of via sewage, vacuum truck, or other method. Depending on recovery rates, the system would need replenishment from rainwater catchments, trucked water, or other sources. Combining on-site utilities may yield economies of scope (the heat from an electricity generator could warm and distill water, for example).

Postal services

Postal service has long been a government monopoly in the United States and most countries, and one could well argue that there was never a good economic reason for this. Modern technology makes a free-market position stronger than ever, since postal communication now competes with alternatives such as faxes, email, and the Internet. Such alternatives make price-gouging fears especially far-fetched. Express mail is already provided by private competitors, and the Internet provides for electronic bill paying and the transmission of documents with electronic signatures. The removal of monopoly protection for the USPS would enable a consolidated contracting of the distribution of goods to rural areas, enabling a company to deliver newspapers, packages, and mail in one delivery.

Telecommunications

Telephone line and television cable networks have been regarded as natural monopolies because laying down multiple grids would duplicate great and uneconomical fixed costs. Long ago, J. Maurice Clark (1923:321) concluded, however, that telephone companies showed no economies of scale, "but rather the opposite." The monopolization of telephony in the United States resulted chiefly from government policy that restricted competition and mandated regulated telephone rates (Thierer 1994). Technology has further weakened any claim of natural monopoly. Fiber optic line and drilling technology make competing lines more viable than ever. Wireless telephones and satellite television transmissions provide expanding dimensions of competition. Technology is blurring the lines of telephony, cable television, and Internet service. Change is rapid, and the hazard of regulatory fossilization is greater than usual.

The complexity/unknowability argument

While admitting some symmetry in the effects of technology, we believe that there is an important asymmetry that goes against government. Any form of government intervention or enterprise depends for its justification on an understanding of what the private enterprise economy would otherwise be lacking or failing to achieve. Justification for occupational licensing depends on consumers being unable, in a regime without licensing, to obtain quality and safety assurance. Utility regulation depends on theories of natural monopoly. Government activism is predicated on a belief that regulators or planners can *know the economy well enough* to restrict, manipulate, or supplement it beneficially.

Yet, after Adam Smith and Friedrich Hayek, the classic argument against government intervention is, aside from incentive problems, that the economy is too complex to know, and therefore too complex to direct or manipulate in a beneficial manner. Like the spontaneous patterns of roller skating in a roller rink, the more complex the system, the more mischievous is the notion of centralized control. In a complex system such as that of 200 skaters in a roller rink, we ought to rely on decentralized decision making. After all, even if the rink is without bound the increased complexity does not pose a comparable problem for the individual skater. He does not interpret the whole: he utilizes pointed knowledge in pursuing opportunities of his particular time and place.

Technology enhances government's ability to gather, collate and convey information, to monitor actions, identify transgressions, and enforce compliance. Technologies expand the informational capability of government. But technology accelerates economic change and multiplies the connections between activities. It integrates dimensions, connects multitudinous variables, and, moment-by-moment, alters constraints and opportunities. To know market arrangements—either those current or those that would exist under alternative policy—such fundamentals would have to remain unchanged for the time being. Yet technology makes the whole economy—that which is to be known—far more complex. It brings fundamental upsets, now and again, to even our best understandings of current arrangements and their shortcomings. After all, society includes the thoughts and potentialities of private individuals and organizations, each of whom has likewise enjoyed vastly expanded informational capabilities.

In his recent book *The Lexus and the Olive Tree*, Thomas Friedman relates comments from a friend that illustrates the contest between informational capability and complexity. He quotes Leon Cooperman, former director of research for Goldman, Sachs:

> When I joined Goldman Sachs in 1967 ... I was the head of research and I hired analysts. In those days, a typical analyst covered seventy-five companies ... I was recently talking to one of the analysts I had hired back then and he told me he was terribly overworked now because he had to cover twelve companies. I just laughed. Only twelve companies? But you have to look into those twelve companies so much more deeply now in order to get some edge that it takes up all of his time.
>
> (Cooperman quoted in Friedman 1999: 101–102)

One might imagine that, because of today's high speed data access, computation, and so on, the analyst would have enhanced informational capabilities, enabling him to cover *more*, rather than fewer, companies. But his informational capabilities do not keep up with the complexity of the world to be analyzed.

In 1879, Cliffe Leslie, an Irish economist and keen expositor of Adam Smith, wrote: "[T]he movement of the economic world has been one from simplicity to complexity, from uniformity to diversity, from unbroken custom to change, and, therefore, from the known to the unknown."[1] In later years Friedrich Hayek took the point further: the economic world has moved not merely to the unknown, but to the *unknowable*. The effect of technology is asymmetric in the epistemic situations in which it leaves, respectively, private actors versus social planners (such as those at the FDA or the Anti-Trust Division). *Technology's heightening of society's complexity outstrips its heightening of the social planner's informational capabilities.*[2] Hayek, like Smith, drew a lesson for policy: Except in the most clear-cut cases of systemic harm like air pollution, the supposition that government officials can figure out how to improve upon the results of decentralized (i.e., voluntary) decision making becomes more and more outlandish. In his Nobel lecture, Hayek (1974) called that supposition the *pretense* of knowledge. As intellectuals who ponder the complex workings of the social world, we really know little aside from one hardy fact: If those who participate in an activity do so voluntarily, each is probably bettering his or her own condition. The more complex the system, the more skeptical we ought to be about claims to knowledge that go beyond and against that hardy fact.

There are, then, two ways in which technological advancement enhances the case for free enterprise: (1) It reduces the costs that had obstructed (actually or supposedly) invisible hand mechanisms, and (2) it makes the economic system ever more complex, and makes the notion that interventionists can meaningfully know and beneficially manipulate the system ever less credible.

Policy areas in which the conclusion may be doubtful

Some cases seem to go against the general tendency. Technology might make it especially difficult to secure and appropriate the value of one's intellectual products, such as basic scientific research, patents, software, music, and writings, because current technology vastly facilitates the replication of "knock-offs" and sharing without authorization. The situation might call for stepped-up government enforcement of patents and copyrights (whether one considers that government intervention or property rights enforcement), or more interventionist measures such as subsidization of knowledge and cultural products—akin to European television subsidies financed by taxes on television ownership (a policy that DeLong and Froomkin 2000 sometimes seem to favor). However, unauthorized replication might, too, have a short technological half-life, as new technologies develop methods to foil unauthorized replication.

It may be argued that technology favors expanded government control of pollution because it enhances the effectiveness of detection, measurement, impact assessment, and enforcement. However, common law traditionally treated air pollution as a nuisance, and direct polluter-pays policies keep to that spirit. If government uses new technologies to define and enforce property rights in water, airs, or animal resources, that might be seen as defensive Nightwatchman functions compatible with the principles of free enterprise.

National security is another area where technology might suggest a larger role for government. Capabilities to create advance quickly, but, alas, not as quickly as capabilities to destroy. New destructive capabilities in arms, biotechnology, and, eventually, nanotechnology might recommend vigorous national security measures. Again, depending on the measures, we might not deem them "government intervention" but rather Nightwatchman functions.

Improved technology, as previously mentioned, might improve regulators' knowledge of particular sets of activities, and recommend more interventions such as anti-trust restrictions. Decades ago, Kenneth Arrow wrote: "Indeed, with the development of mathematical programming and high-speed computers, the centralized alternative no longer appears preposterous. After all, it would appear that one could mimic the workings of a decentralized system by an appropriately chosen centralized algorithm" (Arrow 1974: 5). Even though few today advocate "the centralized alternative," many still feel that by virtue of information technology government can actively manage or guide significant portions of the economy. Again, however, the growth of the complexity of the whole ought to humble even our latest technologies of knowing and intervening. Even at the level of piecemeal intervention such as anti-trust policy, justification relies on a pretense of knowing that such interventions are likely to improve in the whole upon what the un-intervened system would produce.

Finally, it might be argued that technology will make government more transparent and hence more accountable. We may put more trust in government because any abuse or outrage will be more readily exposed and investigated (Brin 1998). This optimistic factor surely has some validity; there has been a profusion of web sites supplying information about candidates, their positions, the voting records, their contributors, and so on. One may argue that technology will facilitate public discourse, public understanding, and participation in direct democracy. Perhaps government can be made more accountable and reliable through "electronic town meetings," in which each citizen may delegate their voting rights to proxies (as in shareholders' meetings). If government were thereby improved, the case for activism would be strengthened.

Our conclusion, therefore, makes no claim to entirety or universality. We do not say that technology favors the case for free enterprise in all areas of policy. We submit a hypothesis that says "tends to," "mostly," "usually," "in general"...

Concluding remarks

The appropriateness of alternate policies depends on the state of technology. As technology advances, the intellectual case for specific policies changes. Thus, technology imposes on policies and their justifications what may be called an expected intellectual half-life. The faster technology advances, the shorter will be the half-life policy rationales.

This paper suggests, more specifically, that technological advancement usually favors the effectiveness of free enterprise over government intervention. If that is the case, interventionists especially need to concern themselves with the intellectual half-life of their positions, lest they promote policies appropriate yesterday but no longer appropriate today or tomorrow.

Just as policy depends on the state of technology, so technology depends on policy. The technological advancements help solve social problems. In doing so, they bring affected parties some kind of profit. Technological advancement is itself a member of the invisible hand, the invisible hand's tending of its current shortcomings. Voluntary social mechanisms and technological advancement enjoy a complex dialectic of mutual improvement.

Notes

1 Cliffe Leslie (1879): 224. He writes also: "And just in proportion ... as industry and commerce are developed, does the social economy become complex, diversified, changeful, uncertain, unpredictable, and hard to know, even in its existing phase" (p. 223).
2 See Roger Koppl (2000), who writes, "the level of complexity is likely to outstrip our analytical engine" (p. 105).

References

Arrow, Kenneth. 1974. "Limited Knowledge and Economic Analysis." *American Economic Review* 64: 1–10.
Brin, David. 1998. *The Transparent Society: Will Technology Force Us to Choose Between Privacy and Freedom?* Reading, MA: Addison-Wesley.

Clark, J. Maurice. 1923. *Studies in the Economics of Overhead Costs*. Chicago: University of Chicago Press.

Coase, Ronald H. 1974. "The Lighthouse in Economics," *Journal of Law and Economics* 17, October: 357–376. Reprinted in Cowen 1988.

DeLong, J. Bradford and A. Michael Froomkin. 2000. "Speculative Microeconomics for Tomorrow's Economy." On DeLong's webpage: http://econ161.berkeley.edu/

Friedman, Thomas L. 1999. *The Lexus and the Olive Tree*. New York: Farrar. Straus and Giroux.

Hayek, Friedrich A. 1979. *Law, Legislation and Liberty: Volume 3, The Political Order of a Free People*. Chicago: University of Chicago Press.

Hayek, Friedrich A. [1974]. "The Pretense of Knowledge" (Nobel lecture). In Hayek's *New Studies in Philosophy, Politics, Economics and the History of Ideas*. Chicago: University of Chicago Press, 1978.

Koppl, Roger. 2000. "Policy Implications of Complexity: An Austrian Perspective," in *The Complexity Vision and the Teaching of Economics*, ed. D. Colander: 97–117. Northampton. MA: Edward Elgar.

Leslie, T.E. Cliffe. 1879. "The Known and the Unknown in the Economic World" (originally published in *Fortnightly Review*, June 1). Reprinted in *Essays in Political Economy*. London: Longmans, Green, & Co., 1888: 221–242.

Rosen, Harvey S. 1992. *Public Finance*. Third edition. Homewood. IL: Irwin.

Thierer, Adam D. 1994. "Unnatural Monopoly: Critical Moments in the Development of the Bell System Monopoly," *Cato Journal* 14, no. 2: 267–285.

Tullock, Gordon. 1971. "Public Decisions as Public Goods," *Journal of Political Economy* 79, no. 4: 913–918.

Van Zandt, David E. 1993. "The Lessons of the Lighthouse: 'Government' or 'Private' Provision of Goods." *Journal of Legal Studies* 22, January: 47–72.

Review and Discussion Questions

1 How does improved technology make it easier to define and enforce property rights? Give an example.

2 How does improved technology make it easier for firms to assure consumers of product quality and safety? Give an example.

3 Can you think of an external cost or benefit that is more likely to be internalized because of the Internet? Explain.

Chapter 16

S. J. LIEBOWITZ and STEPHEN E. MARGOLIS

THE FABLE OF THE KEYS[1]

Introduction

THE TERM "STANDARD" can refer to any social convention (standards of conduct, legal standards), but it most often refers to conventions that require exact uniformity (standards of measurement, computer-operating systems). Current efforts to control the development of high-resolution television, multitasking computer-operating systems, and videotaping formats have heightened interest in standards.

The economic literature on standards has focused recently on the possibility of market failure with respect to the choice of a standard. In its strongest form, the argument is essentially this: an established standard can persist over a challenger, even where all users prefer a world dominated by the challenger, if users are unable to coordinate their choices. For example, each of us might prefer to have Beta-format videocassette recorders as long as prerecorded Beta tapes continue to be produced, but individually we do not buy Beta machines because we don't think enough others will buy Beta machines to sustain the prerecorded tape supply. I don't buy a Beta format machine because I think that you won't; you don't buy one because you think that I won't. In the end, we both turn out to be correct, but we are both worse off than we might have been. This, of course, is a catch-22 that we might suppose to be common in the economy. There will be no cars until there are gas stations; there will be no gas stations until there are cars. Without some way out of this conundrum, joyriding can never become a favorite activity of teenagers[2]

The logic of these economic traps and conundrums is impeccable as far as it goes, but we would do well to consider that these traps are sometimes escaped in the market. Obviously, gas stations and automobiles do exist, so participants in the market must use some technique to unravel such conundrums. If this catch-22 is to warrant our attention as an empirical issue, at a minimum we would hope to see at least one real-world example of it. In the economics literature on standards,[3] the popular real-world example of this market failure is the standard Qwerty typewriter keyboard[4] and its competition with the rival Dvorak keyboard.[5] This example is noted frequently in newspaper and magazine reports, seems to be generally accepted as true, and was brought to economists' attention by the papers of Paul David.[6] According to the popular story, the keyboard invented by August Dvorak, a professor of education at the University of Washington, is vastly superior to the Qwerty keyboard developed by Christopher Sholes that is now in common use. We are to believe that, although the Dvorak keyboard is vastly superior to Qwerty, virtually no one trains on Dvorak because there are too few Dvorak machines, and there are virtually no Dvorak machines because there are too few Dvorak typists.

This article examines the history, economics, and ergonomics of the typewriter keyboard. We show that David's version of the history of the market's rejection of Dvorak does not report the true history, and we present evidence that the continued use of Qwerty is efficient given the current understanding of keyboard design. We conclude that the example of the Dvorak keyboard is what beehives and lighthouses were for earlier market-failure fables. It is an example of market failure that will not withstand rigorous examination of the historical record.[7]

Some economics of standards

Some standards change over time without being impaired as social conventions. Languages, for example, evolve over time, adding words and practices that are useful and winnowing features that have lost their purpose. Other standards are inherently inflexible. Given current technologies, it won't do, for example, for broadcast frequencies to drift the way that orchestral tuning has. A taste for a slightly larger centimeter really can't be accommodated by a sequence of independent decisions the way that increased use of contractions in academic writing can. Obviously, if standards can evolve at low cost, they would be expected to evolve into the forms that are most efficient (in the eyes of those adopting the standards). Conversely, an inappropriate standard is most likely to have some permanence where evolution is costly.

In a recent article on standards, Joseph Farrell and Garth Saloner[8] present a formal exploration of the difficulties associated with changing from one standard to another. They construct hypothetical circumstances that might lead to market failure with respect to standards. To refer to the condition in which a superior standard is not adopted, they coin the phrase "excess inertia." Excess inertia is a type of externality: each nonadopter of the new standard imposes costs on every other potential user of the new standard. In the case of excess inertia, the new standard can be clearly superior to the old standard, and the sum of the private costs of switching to the new standard can be less than the sum of the private benefits, and yet the switch does not occur. This is to be differentiated from the far more common invention of new standards superior to the old, but for which the costs of switching are too high to make the switch practicable. Users of the old standard may regret their choice of that standard, but their continued use of the old standard is not inefficient; would it not be foolish to lay all regrets at the doorstep of externalities?

Farrell's and Saloner's construct is useful because it shows the theoretical possibility of a market failure and also demonstrates the role of information. There is no possibility of excess inertia in their model if all participants can communicate perfectly. In this regard, standards are not unlike other externalities in that costs of transacting are essential. Thus, standards can be understood within the framework that Coase offered decades ago.[9]

By their nature, this model and others like it must ignore many factors in the markets they explore. Adherence to an inferior standard in the presence of a superior one represents a loss of some sort; such a loss implies a profit opportunity for someone who can figure out a means of internalizing the externality and appropriating some of the value made available from changing to the superior standard. Furthermore, institutional factors such as head starts from being first on the market, patent and copyright law, brand names, tie-in sales, discounts, and so on, can also lead to appropriation possibilities (read "profit opportunities") for entrepreneurs, and with these opportunities we expect to see activity set in motion to internalize the externalities. The greater the gap in performance between two standards, the greater are these profit opportunities, and the more likely that a move to the efficient standard will take place. As a result, a clear example of excess inertia is apt to be very hard to find. Observable instances in which a dramatically inferior standard prevails are likely to be short-lived, imposed by authority, or fictional.

The creator of a standard is a natural candidate to internalize the externality.[10] If a standard can be "owned," the advantage of the standard can be appropriated, at least in part, by the owner. Dvorak, for example, patented his keyboard. An owner with the prospect of appropriating substantial benefits from a new standard would have an incentive to share some of the costs of switching to a new standard. This incentive gives rise to a variety of internalizing tactics. Manufacturers of new products sometimes offer substantial discounts to early adopters, offer guarantees of satisfaction, or make products available on a rental basis. Sometimes manufacturers offer rebates to buyers who turn in equipment based on old standards, thus discriminating in price between those who have already made investments in a standard and those who have not. Internalizing tactics can be very simple: some public utilities once supplied light bulbs, and some UHF television stations still offer free UHF indoor antennas. In many industries, firms provide subsidized or free training to assure an adequate supply of operators. Typewriter manufacturers were an important source of trained typists for at least the first fifty years of that technology.[11]

Another internalizing tactic is convertibility. Suppliers of new-generation computers occasionally offer a service to convert files to new formats. Cable-television companies have offered hardware and services to adapt old televisions to new antenna systems for an interim period. Of interest in the present context, for a time before and after the Second World War, typewriter manufacturers offered to convert Qwerty typewriters to Dvorak for a very small fee.[12]

All of these tactics tend to unravel the apparent trap of an inefficient standard, but there are additional conditions that can contribute to the ascendancy of the efficient standard. An important one is the growth of the activity that uses the standard. If a market is growing rapidly, the number of users who have made commitments to any standard is small relative to the number of future users. Sales of audiocassette players were barely hindered by their incompatibility with the reel-to-reel or eight-track players that preceded them. Sales of sixteen-bit computers were scarcely hampered by their incompatibility with the disks or operating systems of eight-bit computers.

Another factor that must be addressed is the initial competition among rival standards. If standards are chosen largely through the influence of those who are able to internalize the value of standards, we would expect, in Darwinian fashion, the prevailing standard to be the fittest economic competitor. Previous keyboard histories have acknowledged the presence of rivals, but they seem to view competition as a process leading to results indistguishable from pure chance.

Consideration of the many complicating factors present in the market suggests that market failure in standards is not as compelling as many of the abstract models seem to suggest. Theoretical abstraction presents candidates for what might be important, but only emprical verification can determine if these abstract models have anything to do with reality.

The case for the superiority of the Dvorak keyboard

Paul David[13] introduces economists to the conventional story of the development and persistence of the current standard keyboard, known as the Universal, or Qwerty, keyboard. The key features of that story are as follows. The operative patent for the typewriter was awarded in 1868 to Christopher Latham Sholes, who continued to develop the machine for several years. Among the problems that Sholes and his associates addressed was the jamming of the type bars when certain combinations of keys were struck in very close succession. As a partial solution to this problem, Sholes arranged his keyboard so that the keys most likely to be struck in close succession were approaching the type point from opposite sides of the machine. Since Qwerty was designed to accomplish this now obsolete mechanical requirement, maximizing speed was not an explicit objective. Some authors even claim that the keyboard is actually configured to minimize speed since decreasing speed would have been one way to avoid the jamming of the typewriter. At the time, however, a two-finger hunt-and-peck method was contemplated, so the keyboard speed envisioned was quite different from touch-typing speeds.

The rights to the Sholes patent were sold to E. Remington & Sons in early 1873. The Remingtons added further mechanical improvements and began commercial production in late 1873.

A watershed event in the received version of the Qwerty story is a typing contest held in Cincinnati on July 25, 1888. Frank McGurrin, a court stenographer from Salt Lake City, who was apparently the first to memorize the keyboard and use touch-typing, won a decisive victory over Louis Taub. Taub used the hunt-and-peck method on a Caligraph, a machine that used seventy-two keys to provide upper- and lower-case letters. According to popular history, the event established once and for all that the Remington typewriter, with its Qwerty keyboard, was technically superior. More important, the contest created an interest in touch-typing, an interest directed at the Qwerty arrangement. Reportedly, no one else at that time had skills that could even approach McGurrin's, so there was no possibility of countering the claim that the Remington keyboard arrangement was efficient. McGurrin participated in typing contests and demonstrations throughout the country and became something of a celebrity. His choice of the Remington keyboard, which may well have been arbitrary, contributed to the establishment of the standard. So it was, according to the popular telling, that a keyboard designed to solve a short-lived mechanical problem became the standard used daily by millions of typists.[14]

In 1936, August Dvorak patented the Dvorak Simplified Keyboard (DSK), claiming that it dramatically reduced the finger movement necessary for typing by balancing the load between hands and loading the stronger fingers more heavily. Its inventors claimed advantages of greater speed, reduced fatigue, and easier learning. These claims have been accepted by most commentators, including David, who refers, without citation, to experiments done by the U.S. Navy that "had shown that the increased efficiency obtained with the DSK would amortize the cost of retraining a group of typists within ten days of their subsequent full-time employment."[15] In spite of its claimed advantages, the Dvorak keyboard has never found much acceptance.

This story is the basis of the claim that the current use of the Qwerty keyboard is a market failure. The claim continues that a beginning typist will not choose to train in Dvorak because Dvorak machines are likely to be difficult to find, and offices will not equip with Dvorak machines because there is no available pool of typists.

This is an ideal example. The number of dimensions of performance are few, and in these dimensions the Dvorak keyboard appears overwhelmingly superior. These very attributes, however, imply that the forces to adopt this superior standard should also be very strong. It is the failure of these forces to prevail that warrants our critical examination.

The myth of Dvorak

Farrell and Saloner mention the typewriter keyboard as a clear example of market failure.[16] So, too, does the textbook by Tirole.[17] Both works cite David's article as the authority on this subject. Yet there are many aspects of the Qwerty-versus-Dvorak fable that do not survive scrutiny. First, the claim that Dvorak is a better keyboard is supported only by evidence that is both scant and suspect. Second, studies in the ergonomics literature find no significant advantage for Dvorak that can be deemed scientifically reliable. Third, the competition among producers of typewriters, out of which the standard emerged, was far more vigorous than is commonly reported. Fourth, there were far more typing contests than just the single Cincinnati contest. These contests provided ample opportunity to demonstrate the superiority of alternative keyboard arrangements. That Qwerty survived significant challenges early in the history of typewriting demonstrates that it is at least among the reasonably fit, even if not the fittest that can be imagined.

Gaps in the evidence for Dvorak

Like most of the historians of the typewriter,[18] David seems to assume that Dvorak is decisively superior to Qwerty. He never questions this assertion, and he consistently refers to the Qwerty standard as inferior. His most tantalizing evidence is his undocumented account of the U.S. Navy experiments. After recounting the claims of the Navy study, he adds "If as Apple advertising copy says, DSK 'lets you type 20 to 40% faster' why did this superior design meet essentially the same resistance as the previous seven improvements on the Qwerty typewriter keyboard?"[19]

Why indeed? The survival of Qwerty is surprising to economists only in the presence of a demonstrably superior rival. David uses Qwerty's survival to demonstrate the nature of path dependency, the importance of history for economists, and the inevitable oversimplification of reality imposed by theory. Several theorists use his historical evidence to claim empirical relevance for their versions of market failure. But on what foundation does all this depend? All we get from David is an undocumented assertion and some advertising copy.

The view that Dvorak is superior is widely held. This view can be traced to a few key sources. A book published by Dvorak and several coauthors in 1936 included some of Dvorak's own scientific inquiry.[20] Dvorak and his coauthors compared the typing speed achieved in four different and completely separate experiments, conducted by various researchers for various purposes.[21] One of these experiments examined the typing speed on the Dvorak keyboard, and three examined typing speed on the Qwerty keyboard. The authors claimed that these studies established that students learn Dvorak faster than they learn Qwerty. A serious criticism of their methodology is that the various studies that they compared used students of different ages and abilities (for example, students learning Dvorak in grades 7 and 8 at the University of Chicago Lab School were compared with students in conventional high schools), in different school systems taking different tests, and in classes that met for different periods of time. Still more serious is that they did not stipulate whether their choice of studies was a random sample or the full population of available studies. So their study really establishes only that it is possible to find studies in which students learning to type on Qwerty keyboards appear to have progressed less rapidly in terms of calendar time than Dvorak's students did on his keyboard. Even in this Dvorak study, however, the evidence is mixed as to whether students, as they progress, retain an advantage when using the Dvorak keyboard since the differences seem to diminish as typing speed increases.

In general, it is desirable to have independent evaluation, and here the objectivity of Dvorak and his coauthors seems particularly open to question. Their book is more in the vein of an inspirational tract than a scientific work. Consider the following (taken from their chapter about relative keyboard performances):

> The bare recital to you of a few simple facts should suffice to indict the available spatial pattern that is so complacently entitled the "universal" [Qwerty] keyboard. Since when was the "universe" lopsided? The facts will not be stressed, since you may finally surmount most of the ensuing handicaps of this [Qwerty] keyboard.
>
> Just enough facts will be paraded to lend you double assurance that for many of the errors that you will inevitably make and for much of the discouraging delay you will experience in longed-for speed gains, you are not to blame. If you grow indignant over the beginner's role of "innocent victim," remember that a little emotion heightens determination.[22]
>
> Analysis of the present keyboard is so destructive that an improved arrangement is a modern imperative. Isn't it obvious that faster, more accurate, less fatiguing typing can be attained in much less learning time provided a simplified keyboard is taught?[23]

The Navy study, which seems to have been the basis for some of the more extravagant claims of Dvorak advocates, is also flawed. Arthur Foulke, Sholes's biographer, and a believer in the superiority of the Dvorak keyboard, points out several discrepancies in the reports coming out of the Navy studies. He cites an Associated Press report of October 7, 1943, to the effect that a new typewriter keyboard allowed typists to "zip along at 180 words per minute" but then adds "However, the Navy Department, in a letter to the author October 14, 1943 by Lieutenant Commander W. Marvin McCarthy said that it had no record of and did not conduct such a speed test, and denied having made an official announcement to that effect."[24] Foulke also reports a *Business Week* story of October 16, 1943, that reports a speed of 108, not 180, words per minute.

We were able to obtain, with difficulty, a copy of the 1944 Navy report.[25] The report does not state who conducted the study. It consists of two parts, the first based on an experiment conducted in July 1944 and the second based on an experiment conducted in October of that year. The report's foreword states that two prior experiments had been conducted but that "the first two groups were not truly fair tests." We are not told the results of the early tests.

The first of the reported experiments consisted of the retraining of fourteen Navy typists on newly overhauled Dvorak keyboards for two hours a day. We are not told how the subjects were chosen, but it does not appear to be based on a random process. At least twelve of these individuals had previously been Qwerty typists, with an average speed of thirty-two words per minute, although the Navy defined competence as fifty words per minute. The typists had IQs that averaged 98 and dexterity skills with an average percentile of 65. The study reports that it took fifty-two hours for typists to catch up to their old speed. After completing an average of eighty-three hours on the new keyboard, typing speed had increased to an average of fifty-six net words per minute compared to their original thirty-two words per minute, a 75 percent increase.

The second experiment consisted of the retraining of eighteen typists on the Qwerty keyboard. It is not clear how these typists were picked or even if members of this group were aware that they were part of an experiment. We are not told whether this training was performed in the same manner as the first experiment (the Navy retrained people from time to time and this may just have been one of these groups). The participants' IQs and dexterity skills are not reported. It is difficult to have any sense whether this group is a reasonable control for the first group. The initial typing scores for this group averaged twenty-nine words per minute, but these scores were not measured identically to those from the first experiment. The report states that because three typists had net scores of zero words per minute initially, the beginning and ending speeds were calculated as the average of the first four typing tests and the average of the last four typing tests. In contrast, the initial experiment using Dvorak simply used the first and last test scores. This truncation of the reported values reduced the measured increase in typing speed on the Qwerty keyboard by a substantial margin.[26]

The measured increase in net typing speed for Qwerty retraining was from twenty-nine to thirty-seven words per minute (28 percent) after an average of 158 hours of training, considerably less than the increase that occurred with the Dvorak keyboard.

The Navy study concludes that training in Dvorak is much more effective than retraining in Qwerty. But the experimental design leaves too many questions for this to be an acceptable finding. Do these results hold for typists with normal typing skills or only for those far below average? Were the results for the first group just a regression to the mean for a group of underperforminig typists? How much did the Navy studies underestimate the value of increased Qwerty retraining due to the inconsistent measurement? Were the two groups given similar training? Were the Qwerty typewriters overhauled, as were the Dvorak typewriters? There are many possible biases in this study. All, suspiciously, seem to be in favor of the Dvorak design.

The authors of the Navy study do seem to have their minds made up concerning the superiority of Dvorak. In discussing the background of the Dvorak keyboard and prior to introducing the results of the study, the report claims: "Indisputably, it is obvious that the Simplified Keyboard is easier to master than the Standard Keyboard."[27] Later they refer to Qwerty as an "ox" and Dvorak as a "jeep" and add: "no amount of goading the oxen can materially change the end result."[28]

There are other problems of credibility with these Navy studies having to do with potential conflicts of interest. Foulke[29] identifies Dvorak as Lieutenant Commander August Dvorak, the Navy's top expert in the analysis of time and motion studies during World War II. Earle Strong, a professor at Pennsylvania State University and a one-time chairman of the Office Machine Section of the Amercian Standards Association, reports that the 1944 Navy experiment and some Treasury department experiments performed in 1946 were conducted by Dr. Dvorak.[30] We also know that Dvorak had a financial stake in this keyboard. He owned the patent on the keyboard and had received at least $130,000 from the Carnegie Commission for Education for the studies performed while he was at the University of Washington.[31]

But there is more to this story than the weakness of the evidence reported by the Navy, or Dvorak, or his followers. A 1956 General Services Administration study by Earle Strong, which was influential in its time, provides the most compelling evidence against the Dvorak keyboard.[32] This study is ignored in David's history for economists and is similarly ignored in other histories directed at general audiences. Strong conducted a carefully controlled experiment designed to examine the costs and benefits of switching to Dvorak. He concluded that retraining typists on Dvorak had no advantages over retraining on Qwerty.

In the first phase of Strong's experiment, ten government typists were retrained on the Dvorak keyboard. It took well over twenty-five days of four-hour-a-day training for these typists to catch up to their old Qwerty speed. (Compare this to the claim David makes about the Navy study's results that the full retraining costs were recovered in ten days.) When the typists had finally caught up to their old speed, Strong began the second phase of the experiment. The newly trained Dvorak typists continued training, and a group of ten Qwerty typists began a parallel program to improve their skills. In this second phase, the Dvorak typists progressed less quickly with further Dvorak training than did Qwerty typists training on Qwerty keyboards. Thus Strong concluded that Dvorak training would never be able to amortize its costs. He recommended that the government provide further training in the Qwerty keyboard, for Qwerty typists. The information provided by this study was largely responsible for putting Dvorak to rest as a serious alternative to Qwerty for those firms and government agencies responsible for choosing typewriters.[33]

Strong's study does leave some questions unanswered. Because it uses experienced typists, it cannot tell us whether beginning Dvorak typists could be trained more quickly than beginning Qwerty typists. Further, although one implication of Strong's study is that the ultimate speed achieved would be greater for Qwerty typists than for Dvorak typists (since the Qwerty group was increasing the gap over the Dvorak group in the second phase of the experiment), we cannot be sure that an experiment with beginning typists would provide the same results.[34]

Nevertheless, Strong's study must be taken seriously. It attempts to control the quality of the two groups of typists and the instruction they receive. It directly addresses the claims that came out of the Navy studies, which consider the costs and benefits of retraining. It directly parallels the decision that a real firm or a real government agency might face: is it worthwhile to retrain its present typists? The alleged market failure of the Qwerty keyboard as represented by Farrell's and Saloner's excess inertia is that all firms would change to a new standard if only they could each be assured that the others would change. If we accept Strong's findings, it is not a failure to communicate that keeps firms from retraining its typists or keeps typists from incurring their own retraining costs. If Strong's study is correct, it is efficient for current typists not to switch to Dvorak.

Current proponents of Dvorak have a different view when they assess why the keyboard has not been more successful. Hisao Yamada, an advocate of Dvorak who is attempting to influence Japanese keyboard development, gives a wide-ranging interpretation to the Dvorak keyboard's failure. He blames the Depression, bad business decisions by Dvorak, World War II, and the Strong report. He goes on to say,

> There were always those who questioned the claims made by DSK followers. Their reasons are also manifold. Some suspected the superiority of the instructions by DSK advocates to be responsible, because they were all holders of advanced degree(s); such a credential of instructors is also apt to cause the Hawthorne effect. Others maintain that all training experiments, except the GSA one as noted, were conducted by the DSK followers, and that the statistical control of experiments [was] not well exercised. This may be a valid point. It does not take too long to realize, however, that it is a major financial undertaking to organize such an experiment to the satisfaction of statisticians. ... The fact that those critics were also reluctant to come forth in support of such experiment[s] ... may indicate that the true reason of their criticism lies elsewhere.[35]

This is one nasty disagreement.[36]

Nevertheless, Yamada as much as admits that experimental findings reported by Dvorak and his supporters cannot be assigned much credibility and that the most compelling claims cited by Yamada for DSK's superiority come from Dvorak's own work. Much of the other evidence Yamada uses to support his views of DSK's superiority actually can be used to make a case against Dvorak. Yamada refers to a 1952 Australian post office study that showed no advantages for DSK when it was first conducted. It was only after adjustments were made in the test procedure (to remove "psychological impediments" to superior performance) that DSK did better.[37] He cites a 1973 study based on six typists at Western Electric, where, after 104 hours of training on DSK, typists were 2.6 percent faster than they had been on Qwerty.[38] Similarly, Yamada reports that, in a 1978 study at Oregon State University, after 100 hours of training, typists were up to 97.6 percent of their old Qwerty speed.[39] Both of these retraining times are similar to those reported by Strong and not to those in the Navy study. Yamada, however, thinks the studies themselves support Dvorak.[40] But unlike the Strong study, neither of these studies included parallel retraining on Qwerty keyboards. As the Strong study points out, even experienced Qwerty typists increase their speed on Qwerty if they are given additional training. Even if that problem is ignored, the possible advantages of Dvorak are all much weaker than those reported from the Navy study.

Evidence from the ergonomics literature

The most recent studies of the relative merits of keyboards are found in the ergonomics literature. These studies provide evidence that the advantages of the Dvorak are either small or nonexistent. For example, A. Miller and J. C. Thomas conclude that "the fact remains, however, that no alternative has shown a realistically significant advantage over the Qwerty for general purpose typing."[41] In two studies based on analysis of hand-and-finger motions, R. F. Nickells, Jr., finds that Dvorak is 6.2 percent faster than Qwerty,[42] and R. Kinkhead finds only a 2.3 percent advantage for Dvorak.[43] Simulation studies by Donald Norman and David Rumelhart find similar results:

> In our studies ... we examined novices typing on several different arrangements of alphabetically organized keyboards, the Sholes [Qwerty] keyboard, and a randomly organized keyboard (to control against prior knowledge of Sholes). There were essentially no differences among the alphabetic and random keyboards. Novices type slightly faster on the Sholes keyboard, probably reflecting prior experience with it. We studied expert typists by using our simulation model. Here, we looked at the Sholes and Dvorak layouts, as well as several alphabetically arranged keyboards. The simulation showed that the alphabetically organized keyboards were between 2% and 9% slower than the Sholes keyboard, and the Dvorak keyboard was only about 5% faster than the Sholes. These figures correspond well to other experimental studies that compared the Dvorak and Sholes keyboards and to the computations of Card, Moran, and Newell ... for comparing these keyboards. ... For the expert typist, the layout of keys makes surprisingly little difference. There seems no reason to choose Sholes, Dvorak, or alphabetically organized keyboards over one another on the basis of typing speed. It is possible to make a bad keyboard layout, however, and two of the arrangements that we studied can be ruled out.[44]

These ergonomic studies are particularly interesting because the claimed advantage of the Dvorak keyboard has been based historically on the claimed ergonomic advantages in reduced finger movement. Norman and Rummelhart's discussion offers clues to why Dvorak does not provide as much of an advantage as its proponents have claimed. They argue,

> For optimal typing speed, keyboards should be designed so that:
> A. The loads on the right and left hands are equalized.

B. The load on the home (middle) row is maximized.

C. The frequency of alternating hand sequences is maximized and the frequency of same-finger typing is minimized.

The Dvorak keyboard does a good job on these variables, especially A and B; 67% of the typing is done on the home row and the left-right hand balance is 47–53%. Although the Sholes (Qwerty) keyboard fails at conditions A and B (most typing is done on the top row and the balance between the two hands is 57% and 43%), the policy to put successively typed keys as far apart as possible favors factor C, thus leading to relatively rapid typing.[45]

The explanation for Norman and Rummelhart's factor C is that during a keystroke, the idle hand prepares for its next keystroke. Thus Sholes's decision to solve a mechanical problem through careful keyboard arrangement may have inadvertently satisfied a fairly important requirement for efficient typing.

The consistent finding in the ergonomic studies is that the results imply no clear advantage for Dvorak. These studies are not explicitly statistical, yet their negative claim seems analogous to the scientific caution that one exercises when measured differences are small relative to unexplained variance. We read these authors as saying that, in light of the imprecision of method, scientific caution precludes rejection of the hypothesis that Dvorak and Qwerty are equivalent. At the very least, the studies indicate that the speed advantage of Dvorak is not anything like the 20–40 percent that is claimed in the Apple advertising copy that David cites. Moreover, the studies suggest that there may be no advantage with the Dvorak keyboard for ordinary typing by skilled typists. It appears that the principles by which Dvorak "rationalized" the keyboard may not have fully captured the actions of experienced typists largely because typing appears to be a fairly complex activity.

A final word on all of this comes from Frank McGurrin, the world's first known touch-typist:

> Let an operator take a new sentence and see how fast he can write it. Then, after practicing the sentence, time himself again, and he will find he can write it much faster; and further practice on the particular sentence will increase the speed on it to nearly or quite double that on the new matter. Now let the operator take another new sentence, and he will find his speed has dropped back to about what it was before he commenced practicing the first sentence. Why is this? The fingers are capable of the same rapidity. It is because the mind is not so familiar with the keys.[46]

Of course, performance in any physical activity can presumably be improved with practice. But the limitations of typing speed, in McGurrin's experiment, appear to have something to do with a mental or, at least, neurological skill and fairly little to do with the limitations on the speeds at which the fingers can complete their required motions.

Typewriter competition

The Sholes typewriter was not invented from whole cloth. Yamada reports that there were fifty-one inventors of prior typewriters, including some earlier commercially produced typewriters. He states: "Examination of these material(s) reveal that almost all ideas incorporated into Sholes' machines, if not all, were at one time or another already used by his predecessors."[47]

Remington's early commercial rivals were numerous, offered substantial variations on the typewriter, and in some cases enjoyed moderate success. There were plenty of competitors after the Sholes machine came to market. The largest and most important of these rivals were the Hall, Caligraph, and Crandall machines. The Yost, another double-keyboard machine, manufactured by an early collaborator of Sholes, used a different inking system and was known particularly for its attractive type. According to production data assembled by Yamada,[48] the machines were close rivals, and they each sold in large numbers. Franz Xavier Wagner, who also worked on the 1873 Remington typewriter, developed a machine that made the type fully visible as it was being typed. This machine was offered to, but rejected by, the Union Typewriter Company, the company formed by the 1893 merger of Remington with six other typewriter manufacturers.[49] In 1895, Wagner joined John T. Underwood to produce his machine. Their company, which later became Underwood, enjoyed rapid growth, producing two hundred typewriters per week by 1898.[50] Wagner's offer to Union also resulted in the spin-off from Union of L. C. Smith, who introduced a visible-type machine in 1904.[51] This firm was the forerunner of the Smith-Corona company.

Two manufacturers offered their own versions of an ideal keyboard: Hammond in 1893 and Blickensderfer in 1889.[52] Each of these machines survived for a time, and each had certain mechanical advantages. Blickensderfer later produced what may have been the first portable and the first electric typewriters. Hammond later produced the Varityper, a standard office type-composing machine that was the antecedent of today's desktop publishing. The alternative keyboard machines produced by these manufacturers came early enough that typewriters and, more important, touch-typing were still not very popular. The Blickensderfer appeared within a year of the famous Cincinnati contest that first publicized touch-typing.

In the 1880s and 1890s typewriters were generally sold to offices not already staffed with typists or into markets in which typists were not readily available. Since the sale of a new machine usually meant training a new typist, a manufacturer that chose to compete using an alternative keyboard had an opportunity. As late as 1923, typewriter manufacturers operated placement services for typists and were an important source of operators. In the earliest days, typewriter salesmen provided much of the limited training available to typists.[53] Since almost every sale required the training of a typist, a typewriter manufacturer that offered a different keyboard was not particularly disadvantaged. Manufacturers internalized training costs in such an environment, so a keyboard that allowed more rapid training might have been particularly attractive.

Offering alternative keyboards was not a terribly expensive tactic. The Blickensderfer used a type-bar configuration similar in principle to the IBM Selectric type ball and, so, could easily offer many different configurations. The others could create alternative keyboard arrangements by simply soldering the type to different bars and attaching the keys to different levers. So apparently the problem of implementing the conversion was not what kept the manufacturers from changing keyboards.

The rival keyboards did ultimately fail, of course.[54] But the Qwerty keyboard cannot have been so well established at the time the rival keyboards were first offered that they were rejected because they were non-standard. Manufacturers of typewriters sought and promoted any technical feature that might give them an advantage in the market. Certainly shorter training and greater speed would have been an attractive selling point for a typewriter with an alternative keyboard. Neither can it be said that the rival keyboards were doomed by inferior mechanical characteristics because these companies went on to produce successful and innovative, though Qwerty-based, typing machines. Thus we cannot attribute our inheritance of the Qwerty keyboard to a lack of alternative keyboards or the chance association of this keyboard arrangement with the only mechanically adequate typewriter.

Typing competitions

Typing competitions provided another test of the Qwerty keyboard. These competitions are somewhat underplayed in the conventional history. David's history mentions only the Cincinnati contest. Wilfred Beeching's history, which has been very influential, also mentions only the Cincinnati contest and attaches great importance to it: "Suddenly, to their horror, it dawned upon both the Remington Company and the Caligraph company officials, torn between pride and despair, that whoever won was likely to put the other out of business!" Beeching refers to the contest as having established the four-bank keyboard of the Remington machine "once and for all."[55]

In fact, typing contests and demonstrations of speed were fairly common during this period. They involved many different machines, with various manufacturers claiming to hold the speed record.

Under the headline "Wonderful Typing," the *New York Times*[56] reported on a typing demonstration given the previous day in Brooklyn by a Mr. Thomas Osborne of Rochester, New York. The *Times* reported that Mr. Osborne "holds the championship for fast typing, having accomplished 126 words a minute at Toronto August 13 last." In the Brooklyn demonstration he typed 142 words per minute in a five-minute test, 179 words per minute in a single minute, and 198 words per minute for 30 seconds. He was accompanied by a Mr. George McBride, who typed 129 words per minute blindfolded. Both men used the non-Qwerty Caligraph machine. The *Times* offered that "the Caligraph people have chosen a very pleasant and effective way of proving not only the superior speed of their machine, but the falsity of reports widely published that writing blindfolded was not feasible on that instrument."[57] Note that this was just months after McGurrin's Cincinnati victory.

There were other contests and a good number of victories for McGurrin and Remington. On August 2, 1888, the *Times*[58] reported a New York contest won by McGurrin with a speed of 95.8 words per minute in a five-minute dictation. In light of the received history, according to which McGurrin is the only person to have memorized the keyboard, it is interesting to note the strong performance of his rivals. Miss May Orr typed 95.2 words per minute, and M. C. Grant typed 93.8 words per minute. Again, on January 9, 1889, the *Times*[59] reported a McGurrin victory under the headline "Remington Still Leads the List."

We should probably avoid the temptation to compare the Caligraph speed with the Remington speeds, given the likely absence of any serious attempts at standardizing the tests. Nevertheless, it appears that the issue of speed was not so readily conceded as is reported in Beeching's history. Typists other than McGurrin could touch-type, and machines other than Remington were competitive. History has largely ignored events that did not build toward the eventual domination by Qwerty. This focus may be reasonable for the history of the Remington Company or the Qwerty keyboard. But if we are interested in whether the Qwerty keyboard's existence can be attributed to more than happenstance or an inventor's whim, these events do matter.

Conclusions

The trap constituted by an obsolete standard may be quite fragile. Because real-world situations present opportunites for agents to profit from changing to a superior standard, we cannot simply rely on an abstract model to conclude that an inferior standard has persisted. Such a claim demands empirical examination.

As an empirical example of market failure, the typewriter keyboard has much appeal. The objective of the keyboard is fairly straightforward: to get words onto the recording medium. There are no conflicting objectives to complicate the interpretation of performance. But the evidence in the standard history of Qwerty versus Dvorak is flawed and incomplete. First, the claims for the superiority of the Dvorak keyboard are suspect. The most dramatic claims are traceable to Dvorak himself, and the best-documented experiments, as well as recent ergonomic studies, suggest little or no advantage for the Dvorak keyboard.[60]

Second, by ignoring the vitality and variety of the rivals to the Remington machine with its Qwerty keyboard, the received history implies that Sholes's and McGurrin's choices, made largely as matters of immediate expediency, established the standard without ever being tested. More careful reading of historical accounts and checks of original sources reveal a different picture: there were touch-typists other than McGurrin; there were competing claims of speed records; and Remington was not so well established that a keyboard offering significant advantages could not have gained a foothold. If the fable is to carry lessons about the workings of markets, we need to know more than just who won. The victory of the tortoise is a different story without the hare.

There is more to this disagreement than a difference in the evidence that was revealed by our search of the historical record. Our reading of this history reflects a more fundamental difference in views of how markets, and social systems more generally, function. David's overriding point is that economic theory must be informed by events in the world. On that we could not agree more strongly. But ironically, or perhaps inevitably, David's interpretation of the historical record is dominated by his own implicit model of markets, a model that seems to underlie much economic thinking. In that model, an exogenous set of goods is offered for sale at a price, take it or leave it. There is little or no role for entrepreneurs. There generally are no guarantees, no rental markets, no mergers, no loss-leader pricing, no advertising, no marketing research. When such complicating institutions are acknowledged, they are incorporated into the model piecemeal. And they are most often introduced to show their potential to create inefficiencies, not to show how an excess of benefit over cost may constitute an opportunity for private gain.

In the world created by such a sterile model of competition, it is not surprising that accidents have considerable permanence. In such a world, embarking on some wrong path provides little chance to jump to an alternative path. The individual benefits of correcting a mistake are too small to make correction worthwhile, and there are no agents who might profit by devising some means of capturing a part of the aggregate benefits of correction.

It is also not surprising that in such a world there are a lot of accidents. Consumers are given very little discretion to avoid starts down wrong paths. A model may assume that consumers have foresight or even that they are perfectly rational, but always in a very limited sense. For example, in the model of Farrell and Saloner, consumers can predict very well the equilibrium among the two candidate standards. But they are attributed no ability to anticipate the existence of some future, better standard. We are not led to ask how the incumbent standard achieved its status; as in David's telling, "It jes' growed."

But at some moment, users must commit resources to a standard or wait. At this moment, they have clear incentives to examine the characteristics of competing standards. They must suffer the consequences of a decision to wait, to discard obsolete equipment or skills, or to continue to function with an inferior standard. Thus, they have a clear incentive to consider what lies down alternative paths. Though their ability to anticipate future events may not be perfect, there is no reason to assume that it is bad relative to any other observers.

Finally, it is consistent that, in a world in which mistakes are frequent and permanent, "scientific approaches" cannot help but make big improvements to market outcomes. In such a world, there is ample room for enlightened reasoning, personified by university professors, to improve on the consequences of myriad independent decisions. What credence can possibly be given to a keyboard that has nothing to accredit it but the trials of a group of mechanics and its adoption by millions of typists? If we use only sterilized models of markets, or ignore the vitality of the rivalry that confronts institutions, we should not be surprised that the historical interpreations that result are not graced with the truth that Cicero asks of historians.

Notes

1 Earlier drafts benefited from seminars at Clemson University and North Carolina State University, and we would like to thank the participants at those seminars. We would also like to thank James Buchanan, Dan Klein, Bill Landes, Nancy Margolis, Craig Newmark, John Palmer, Gregory Rehmke, George Stigler, and Wally Thurman for their suggestions.
2 This trap is treated more seriously in the literature on standards than in other economics literature. This reflects a supposition that foresight, integration, or appropriation are more difficult in the case of standards. The current literature fails to explain why these "externalities" are particularly relevant for standards. We will have more to say about this in forthcoming work.
3 See, for example, Joseph Farrell & Garth Saloner, Standardization, Compatibility, and Innovation, 16 Rand J. Econ. 70 (1985); Michael L. Katz & Carl C. Shapiro, Network Externalities, Competition, and Compatibility, 75 Am. Econ. Rev. 425 (1985); and Jean Tirole, The Theory of Industrial Organization (1988).

4 "Qwerty" stands for the arrangement of letters in the upper lefthand portion of the keyboard below the numbers. This keyboard is also known as the Sholes, or Universal, keyboard.

5 This is also sometimes known as the DSK keyboard, for Dvorak Simplified Keyboard (or the simplified keyboard). As explained below, the letters are arranged in a different order.

6 Paul A. David, Clio and the Economics of QWERTY, 75 Am. Econ. Rev. 332 (1985); and Paul A. David, Understanding the Economics of QWERTY: The Necessity of History, in Economic History and the Modem Economist (William N. Parker ed. 1986).

7 See Ronald H. Coase, The Lighthouse in Economics, 17 J. Law & Econ. 357(1974); and Steven N. Cheung, The Fable of the Bees: An Economic Investigation, 16 J. Law & Econ. 11 (1973). Our debt is obvious.

8 Farrell & Saloner, *supra* note 3.

9 Ronald H. Coase, The Problem of Social Cost, 3 J. Law & Econ. 1 (1960). Of course, inertia is not necessarily inefficient. Some delay in settling on a standard will mean that relatively more is known about the associated technology and the standards themselves by the time most users commit to a technology. Recall the well-known discussion of Harold Demsetz, Information and Efficiency: Another Viewpoint, 12 J. Law & Econ. 1 (1969), on the nature of efficiency. If a God can costlessly cause the adoption of the correct standard, any inertia is excessive (inefficient) in comparison. But it seems ill advised to hold this up as a serious benchmark. Excessive inertia should be defined relative to some achievable result. Further, some reservation in committing to standards will allow their creators to optimize standards rather than rushing them to the market to be first. If the first available standard were always adopted, then standards, like patents, might generate losses from the rush to be first. Creators might rush their standards to market, even where waiting would produce a better and more profitable product.

10 We may ask ourselves why new standards are created if not with the idea of some pecuniary reward. One would hardly expect nonobvious and costly standards to proliferate like manna from heaven.

11 David, Understanding, *supra* note 6. Additionally, see Herkimer County Historical Society, The Story of the Typewriter: 1873–1923 (1923), which notes that in the early 1920s a single typewriter company was placing 100,000 typists a year.

12 Arthur Foulke, Mr. Typewriter: A Biography of Christopher Latham Sholes 106 (1961), which notes: "Present old keyboard machines may be converted to the simplified (Dvorak) keyboard in local typewriter shops. It is now available on any typewriter. And it costs as little as $5 to convert a Standard to a simplified keyboard."

13 David, Clio, *supra* note 6.

14 This history follows David, Clio *supra* note 6, but also see Wilfred A. Beeching, A Century of the Typewriter (1974), as an example of an account with the features and emphasis described here.

15 David, Clio, *supra* note 6, at 332. If true, this would be quite remarkable. A converted Sholes typist will be typing so much faster that whatever the training cost, it is repaid every ten days. Counting only working days, this would imply that the investment in retraining repays itself approximately twenty-three times in a year. Does this seem even remotely possible? Do firms typically ignore investments with returns in the range of 2,200 percent?

16 Farrell & Saloner, *supra* note 3.

17 Tirole, *supra* note 3, at 405, states: "Many observers believe that the Dvorak keyboard is superior to this [Qwerty] standard, even when retraining costs are taken into account. However, it would be foolish for a firm to build this alternative keyboard and for secretaries to switch to it individually." Under some circumstances it might have been foolish for

secretaries and firms to act in this manner. But this type of behavior hardly seems foolish in many real-world situations. For example, large organizations (federal, state, and local governments, Fortune 500 companies, etc.) often have tens of thousands of employees, and these organizations could undertake the training if the costs really are compensated in a short time. See notes 12 and 15 *supra*.

18 For example, see Beeching, *supra* note 14, or Foulke, *supra* note 12.

19 David, Understanding, *supra* note 6, at 34.

20 August Dvorak, Nellie L. Merrick, William L. Dealy, & Gertrude C. Ford, Typewriting Behavior (1936).

21 *Id*. at 226.

22 *Id*. at 210.

23 *Id*. at 217.

24 Foulke, *supra* note 12, at 103.

25 We tried to have the Navy supply us with a copy when our own research librarians could not find it. The Navy research librarian had no more success, even though she checked the Navy records, the Martin Luther King Library, the Library of Congress, the National Archives, the National Technical Communication Service, etc. We were finally able to locate a copy held by an organization, Dvorak International, and would like to thank its director, Virginia Russell, for her assistance. She believes that they obtained their copy from the Underwood Company. We would be more sanguine about the question of the document's history had it been available in a public archive. The copy we received was A Practical Experiment in Simplified Keyboard Retraining—a Report on the Retraining of Fourteen Standard Keyboard Typists on the Simplified Keyboard and a Comparison of Typist Improvement from Training on the Standard Keyboard and Retraining on the Simplified Keyboard, Navy Department, Division of Shore Establishments and Civilian Personnel, Department of Services, Training Section, Washington, D.C. (July and October 1944).

26 It is not an innocuous change. We are told that three Qwerty typists initially scored zero on the typing test but that their scores rose to twenty-nine, thirteen, and sixteen within four days (at 20). We are also told that several other typists had similar improvements in the first four days. These improvements are dismissed as mere testing effects that the researchers wish to eliminate. But the researchers made no effort to eliminate the analogous testing effect for the Dvorak typists. Truncating the measurements to the average of the first four days reduces the reported speed increases for the three typists with zero initial speed by at least thirteen, twelve, and fourteen. Assuming the existence of two other typists with similar size-testing effects, removing this testing effect would reduce the reported speed improvements by 3.6 words per minute, lowering the gain from 46 percent to 28 percent. The effect of the truncation at the end of the measuring period cannot be determined with any accuracy, but there is no testing effect to be removed at this stage of the experiment after many tests have been taken. While the apparent effect of these measurement techniques is significant, the indisputable problem is that they were not applied equally to the Qwerty and Dvorak typists.

27 Navy, *supra* note 25, at 2.

28 *Id*. at 23.

29 *Supra* note 12, at 103.

30 Earle P. Strong, A Comparative Experiment in Simplified Keyboard Retraining and Standard Keyboard Supplementary Training (U.S. General Services Administration 1956). However, Yamada, trying to refute criticisms of Dvorak's keyboard, claims that Dvorak did not conduct these studies, he only provided the typewriters. See Hisao Yamada, A Historical Study of Typewriters and Typing Methods: From the Position of Planning

Japanese Parallels, 2. J. Information Processing 175 (1980). He admits that Dvorak was in the Navy and in Washington when the studies were conducted but denies any linkage. We do not know whom to believe, but we are skeptical that Dvorak would not have had a large influence on these tests, based on the strong circumstantial evidence and given Foulke's identification of Dvorak as the Navy's top expert on such matters. Interestingly, Yamada accuses Strong of being biased against the Dvorak keyboard (at 188). He also impugns Strong's character. He accuses Strong of refusing to provide other (unnamed) researchers with his data. He also implies that Strong stole money from Dvorak because in 1941, when Strong was a supporter of Dvorak's keyboard, he supposedly accepted payment from Dvorak to conduct a study of the DSK keyboard without ever reporting his results to him.

31 Yamada, *supra* note 30.
32 Strong, *supra* note 30.
33 At the time of Strong's experiment, Dvorak had attracted a good deal of attention. At least one trade group had taken the position that, pending confirmation from the Strong study, it would adopt Dvorak as its new standard. See U.S. Plans to Test New Typewriter, New York Times, November 11, 1955; Revolution in the Office, New York Times, November 30, 1955; Key Changes Debated, New York Times, June 18, 1956; U.S. Balks at Teaching Old Typists New Keys, New York Times, July 2, 1956; and Peter White, Pyfgcrl vs. Qwertyuiop, New York Times, January 22, 1956, at 18.
34 In fact, both the Navy and General Service Administration studies found that the best typists took the longest to catch up to their old speed and showed the smallest percentage improvement with retraining.
35 Yamada, *supra* note 30, at 189.
36 Also see note 30 *supra*.
37 Yamada, *supra* note 30, at 185.
38 *Id*. at 188.
39 *Id*.
40 Yamada interprets the Oregon study to support the Dvorak keyboard. To do so, he fits an exponential function to the Oregon data and notes that the limit of the function as hours of training goes to infinity is 17 percent greater than the typist's initial Qwerty speed. This function is extremely flat, however, and even modest gains appear well outside the range of the data. A 10 percent gain, for example, would be projected to occur only after 165 hours of training.
41 A. Miller & J. C. Thomas, Behavioral Issues in the Use of Interactive Systems, 9 Int. J. of Man-Machine Stud. 509 (1977).
42 Cited in Hisao Yamada, Certain Problems Associated with the Design of Input Keyboards for Japanese Writing, in Cognitive Aspects of Skilled Typewriting 336 (William E. Cooper ed. 1983).
43 Cited in *id*. at 365.
44 Donald A. Norman and David E. Rumelhart, Studies of Typing from the LNR Research Group, in Cognitive Aspects of Skilled Typewriting 45, 51 (William E. Cooper ed. 1983).
45 *Id*.
46 George C. Mares, The History of the Typewriter (1909).
47 Yamada, *supra* note 42, at 177.
48 *Id*. at 181.
49 Beeching, *supra* note 14, at 165.
50 *Id*. at 214.
51 *Id*. at 165.

52 David, Understanding, *supra* note 6, at 38. Also see Beeching, *supra* note 14, at 40, 199. Yamada, *supra* note 30, at 184, in discussing the Hammond keyboard arrangement states: "This 'ideal' arrangement was far better than Qwerty, but it did not take root because by then Remington Schools were already turning out a large number of Qwerty typists every year." In 1893, Blickensderfer offered a portable typewriter with the Hammond keyboard.

53 Herkimer County Historical Society, *supra* note 11, at 78.

54 We should also take note of the fact that the Qwerty keyboard, although invented in the United States, has become the dominant keyboard throughout the world. Foreign countries, when introduced to typewriters, need not have adopted this keyboard if superior alternatives existed since there would not yet have been any typists trained on Qwerty. Yet all other keyboard designs fell before the Qwerty juggernaut. In France and some other countries, the keyboard is slightly different than the Qwerty keyboard used in the United States. The major difference is that the top left-hand keys are Azerty (that is also what these keyboard designs are called) and several letters are transposed, but most of the keys are identical.

55 Beeching, *supra* note 14, at 41.

56 New York Times, February 28, 1889, at 8.

57 *Id.*

58 Typewriters, contest for a prize, New York Times, August 2, 1988, at 2.

59 New York Times, January 9, 1889.

60 See text at notes 31–44. There are several versions of the claim that a switch to Dvorak would not be worthwhile. The strongest, which we do not make, is that Qwerty is proven to be the best imaginable keyboard. Neither can we claim that Dvorak is proven to be inferior to Qwerty. Our claim is that there is no scientifically acceptable evidence that Dvorak offers any real advantage over Qwerty. Because of this claim, our assessment of a market failure in this case is rather simple. It might have been more complicated. For example, if Dvorak were found to be superior, it might still be the case that the total social benefits are less than the cost of switching. In that case, we could look for market failure only in the process that started us on the Qwerty keyboard (if the alternative were available at the beginning). Or we might have concluded that Dvorak is better and that all parties could be made better off if we could costlessly command both a switch and any necessary redistribution. Such a finding would constitute a market failure in the sense of mainstream welfare economics. Of course, this circumstance still might not constitute a market failure in the sense of Demsetz, which requires consideration of the costs of feasible institutions that could effect the change.

Bibliography

Beeching, Wilfred. *A Century of the Typewriter*. New York: St. Martin's Press, 1974.

Cheung, Steven N. S. "The Fable of the Bees: An Economic Investigation." *Journal of Law and Economics* 16 (April 1973): 11–33.

Coase, Ronald H. "The Problem of Social Cost." *Journal of Law and Economics* 3 (October 1960): 1–44.

Coase, Ronald H. "The Lighthouse in Economics." *Journal of Law and Economics* 17 (October 1974): 357–76.

David, Paul A. "Clio and the Economics of QWERTY." *American Economic Review* 75 (May 1985): 332–37.

David, Paul A. "Understanding the Economics of QWERTY: The Necessity of History." In *Economic History and the Modern Economis*, edited by W. N. Parker. New York: Basil Blackwell, 1986.

Demsetz, Harold. "Information and Efficiency: Another Viewpoint." *Journal of Law and Economics* 12 (April 1969): 1–22.

Dvorak, August; Merrick, Nellie L.; Dealey, William L.; and Ford, Gertrude C. *Typewriting Behavior*. New York: American Book Co., 1936.

Farrell, Joseph, and Saloner, Garth. "Standardization, Compatibility, and Innovation." *Rand Journal* 16 (Spring 1985): 70–83.

Foulke, Arthur. *Mr. Typewriter: A Biography of Christopher Latham Sholes*. Boston: Christopher Publishing, 1961.

Herkimer County Historical Society. *The Story of the Typewriter: 1873–1923*. New York: Andrew H. Kellogg, 1923.

Katz, Michael L., and Shapiro, Carl. "Network Externalities, Competition, and Compatibility." *American Economic Review* 75 (June 1985): 425–40.

Kinkhead, R. "Typing Speed, Keying Rates, and Optimal Keyboard Layouts." *Proceedings of the Human Factors Society* 19 (1975), pp. 159–61.

Landes, William M., and Posner, Richard A. "Trademark Law: An Economic Perspective." *Journal of Law and Economics* 30 (October 1987): 265–309.

Liebowitz, S. J. "Tie-In Sales and Price Discrimination." *Economic Inquiry* 21 (July 1983): 387–99.

Liebowitz, S. J. "Copying and Indirect Appropriability: Photocopying of Journals." *Journal of Political Economy* 93 (October 1985): 945–57.

Mandeville, Bernard M. *The Fable of the Bees*. New York: Capricorn Books, 1962.

Mares, George C. *The History of the Typewriter*. London: Guilbert Pitman, 1909.

Margolis, Stephen E. "Two Definitions of Efficiency in Law and Economics." *Journal of Legal Studies* 16 (July 1987): 471–82.

Miller, L. A., and Thomas, J. C. "Behavioral Issues in the Use of Interactive Systems." *International Journal of Man-Machine Studies* 9 (1977): 509–36.

Navy Department. *A Practical Experiment in Simplified Keyboard Retraining—a Report on the Retraining of Fourteen Standard Keyboard Typists on the Simplified Keyboard and a Comparison of Typist Improvement from Training on the Standard Keyboard and Retraining on the Simplified Keyboard*. Department of Services, Training Section, Washington, D.C.: Navy Department, Division of Shore Establishments and Civilian Personnel, July 1944 and October 1944.

New York Times. "Typewriters Contest for a Prize." August 2, 1888.

New York Times. "Remington Still Leads the List." January 9, 1889.

New York Times. "Wonderful Typing." February 28, 1889.

New York Times. "U.S. Plans to Test New Typewriter." November 11, 1955.

New York Times. "Revolution in the Office." November 30, 1955.

New York Times. "Pyfgcrl vs. Qwertyuiop." January 22, 1956.

New York Times. "Key Changes Debated." June 18, 1956.

New York Times. "U.S. Balks at Teaching Old Typists New Keys." July 2, 1956.

Norman, Donald A., and Rumelhart, David E. "Studies of Typing from the LNR Research Group." In *Cognitive Aspects of Skilled Typewriting*, edited by William E. Cooper. New York: Springer-Verlag, 1983.

Strong, Earle P. *A Comparative Experiment in Simplified Keyboard Retraining and Standard Keyboard Supplementary Training*. Washington, D.C.: U.S. General Services Administration, 1956.

Tirole, Jean. *The Theory of Industrial Organization*. Cambridge: MIT Press, 1988.

Yamada, Hisao. "A Historical Study of Typewriters and Typing Methods: From the Positon of Planning Japanese Parallels." *Journal of Information Processing* 2 (1980): 175–202.

Yamada, Hisao. "Certain Problems Associated with the Design of Input Keyboards for Japanese Writing." In *Cognitive Aspects of Skilled Typewriting*, edited by William E. Cooper. New York: Springer-Verlag, 1983.

Review and Discussion Questions

1 Was the Qwerty keyboard really designed to be slow?
2 What was the purpose of nineteenth-century typing contests? (Can you believe that people once went to watch typing contests?)
3 Is the Dvorak keyboard sufficiently faster than the Qwerty keyboard that it would pay for a typical individual to switch?
4 Who can profit from leading society to switch to a new, better standard? What are some of the techniques by which this individual can induce society to switch?
5 Liebowitz and Margolis mention another possible coordination problem that the economy faced: why would people buy cars until there were gas stations, but why would anyone build a gas station until people had bought cars? But we manifestly do have gas stations and cars. How do you think the problem was solved?
6 Another alleged coordination problem allegedly stops people from switching from Windows to other, better operating systems. Do you think this coordination problem exists? (For an answer, see the Liebowitz and Margolis book referenced in "Suggestions for Further Reading".)

Suggestions for Further Reading

Cheung, S. N. S. (1973) "The Fable of the Bees," *Journal of Law and Economics*, 16: 11–33.

The classic article discussed in the Munger article about how market transactions internalize the apparent externality of nectar and pollination services.

Fischel, W. A. (2006) "Will I See You in September?" *Journal of Urban Economics*, 59: 236–251.

Why is the school year of American schools from September to June? A well-known answer is that it is inherited from the time when most Americans farmed and most schoolchildren were needed to work during the summers. Fischel shows not only that that explanation is incorrect, he provides both theory and evidence that the current school year is a way of solving a significant coordination problem. The market provides the impetus for the solution.

Liebowitz, S. J. and Margolis, S. E. (2001) *Winners, Losers & Microsoft: Competition and Antitrust in High Technology, Revised Edition* (Oakland: The Independent Institute).

The authors show that Microsoft's products gained and maintained market share, not because of a coordination problem that inhibited customers from switching, but because its products were simply better. The book also argues that the dominance of the VHS format over the beta format for video tapes, and the dominance of the IBM PC over the Apple MacIntosh were not coordination failures.

Pashigian, B. P. and Gould, E. D. (1998) "Internalizing Externalities: The Pricing of Space in Shopping Malls," *Journal of Law and Economics*, 41: 115–142.

Stores located very close to each other in shopping malls would seem to pose a positive externality problem: the big, popular stores induce customers to visit the malls and those customers increase the business of the smaller, lesser-known stores. Won't the smaller stores "free ride" off the larger stores? If so, won't the services of the larger stores be provided less than optimally? Pashigian and Gould demonstrate mall developers can set rents to solve the problem.

Tullock, G. (1999) "Non-Prisoner's Dilemma," *Journal of Economic Organization & Behavior,*" 39: 455–458.

A classic coordination failure occurs in the (one-play) "Prisoner's Dilemma." Tullock criticizes the theory and experimental evidence for the Dilemma. He also describes an experiment that indicates the Dilemma is less common than often supposed.

White, M. W. (2005) "The Economics of Time Zones," http://bpp.wharton.upenn.edu/mawhite/Papers/TimeZones.pdf.

In one day, in 1883, the vast majority of the United States population replaced hundreds of local times zones with a single, national system. And the change was coordinated by private firms, not the government. An example of how profit-seeking entrepreneurs, working through the market, overcame the coordination problem.

PART FIVE

Non-Excludable Goods

Introduction

Some goods are non-excludable. "Non-excludable" means that once a single consumer has purchased the product, the seller finds it very costly, or impossible, to prevent other consumers from using the product, even if they haven't paid for it. The non-payers "free ride" on the payers. It is sometimes thought that government needs to provide non-excludable goods because private providers, unable to exclude free-riders and unable to capture most of the revenue from their products, will refuse.

The three articles in this section discuss instances in which free-riding would seem to be easy, but markets provide the goods anyway. John R. Lott, Jr. notes that in the early days of radio excluding free-riders seemed impossible. Once a radio station beamed a signal, anybody nearby with a radio could listen. Why then would anybody invest in building a radio station? Lott explains why. Daniel B. Klein discusses how roads— another product some observers thought must be provided by government—were privately supplied in early U.S. history. Finally, the article by Richard L. Stroup does two things: it usefully compares the free-rider problem in markets to the free-rider problem in government. Stroup shows that even if the free-rider problem in the market is important, it will almost certainly also be important in government. If the free-rider problem means the market can't provide the good efficiently, it probably also means the government won't provide the good efficiently either. Second, Stroup shows that, contrary to expectation based on the free-rider problem, religious services in the U.S. are provided privately, and they are provided more efficiently than when they were government-supported.

Chapter 17

John R. Lott, Jr.

COMMERCIALIZATION OF RADIO

ANOTHER EXAMPLE OF FREE-RIDING was seen during the early development of radio. Today, virtually everyone takes it for granted that advertising is a sensible way to finance radio broadcasting. Few people realize that free-riding problems initially seemed almost insurmountable in providing radio service. Because no one could figure out how to make listeners pay, radio hosts and entertainers usually had to work for free. For over twenty years, broadcasting primarily involved hobbyists and a few public service transmissions by government stations.

Some people doubted there was any way to make listeners pay. In 1922, Herbert Hoover, then Secretary of Commerce, declared: "Nor do I believe there is any practical method of payment from the listeners."[1] Others assumed that radio transmissions would eventually be funded by paying subscribers, but no one could devise a method for limiting broadcasts to subscribers' receivers. Consequently, some believed the government would have to provide the service. In 1922, *Popular Radio* magazine claimed that radio was "essentially a public utility" and discussed using city telephone wires to sell broadcasts to subscribers—in other words, providing radio service over the phone:[2]

So what happened? Did private businessmen throw up their hands and invite the government to run the industry? Was society denied the benefit of radio because no one could solve the free-riding problem? Of course not. The problem was eventually resolved in 1922 when AT&T discovered it could make money by selling radio advertising airtime. In hindsight, it's hard to believe that private radio almost died in its infancy because people couldn't figure out how it could make money. And it's a good thing that the government decided not to turn radio into a subsidized enterprise, since it is highly unlikely that the state would have distributed payments as efficiently as advertisers do.

Notes

1 Thomas H. White, Financing Radio Broadcasting (1989–1927), in United States Early Radio History (http://earlyradiohistory.us/sec020.htm).
2 Waldemar Kaempffert, "Who will pay for broadcasting? A frank and searching outline of Radio's most pressing problem and the possible ways to solve it," Popular Radio, December, 1922, 236–245.

Review and Discussion Questions

1 Why did it take over twenty years for radio to be commercialized? What, specifically, was the problem?
2 Radio programs were eventually provided by the market because the non-excludable good was tied to another good. Can you think of other cases of non-excludable goods being offered by the market through tie-ins?
3 Software, music, and movies are all widely pirated these days. Firms making these products find it ever more difficult to exclude non-payers. How are the firms able to continue providing these products?

Chapter 18

Daniel B. Klein

PRIVATE HIGHWAYS IN AMERICA, 1792–1916

FIFTEEN YEARS AGO only technology aficionados and laissez-faire idealists entertained the notion of private highways. Today, however, public officials and entrepreneurs are struggling to make the notion a reality. Four private highway projects are underway in California and many other states are following suit.

The notion of private highways, which would seem fantastic to our parents, was commonplace to our great-great-grandparents. Initiated in the 1790s in the growing Republic, these roads stimulated commerce, settlement, and population. During the nineteenth century more than 2,000 private companies financed, built, and operated toll roads. States turned to private initiative for much the same reason they are doing so today: fiscal constraints and insufficient administrative manpower. Knowledge of our toll-road heritage may help encourage today's budding toll-road movement.

The turnpike heyday, 1800–1825

Once the state of Pennsylvania chartered a private company in 1792 to build a road connecting Philadelphia and Lancaster, rival states felt impelled to follow. Private initiative was the only effective means of providing new highways, because state and country finances were almost nonexistent and town resources were meager. Private control and user fees were bold steps, but once taken, states could only continue to move forward. In an age before the canal and railroad, legislators were willing to test community and political custom to get highways built.

The turnpikes were financed by private stock subscription and set up to pay dividends. Built with a surface of gravel and earth, turnpikes were usually 15 to 40 miles in length, and cost $2,000 per mile to build. They were massive undertakings and relied on widespread investment from the community. Stock purchased was more like a contribution to community improvement rather than a business investment.

Some travelers objected to the idea of paying tolls, particularly to a corporate monopoly. Legislators, often suspicious of corporate motives, wrote extensive (and economically, debilitating) restrictions into company characters, specifying conditions for construction maintenance, and toll rates, and toll collection.

The progress of turnpike incorporation is shown in Table 18.1. Only Pennsylvania. Virginia, and Ohio subsidized their turnpike companies; New York chartered the most turnpikes. The opening decade of the nineteenth century saw the most charter activity, though roughly one-third of the companies chartered failed to construct a single-mile of roadway.

The unprofitability of turnpikes soon became obvious. The vast majority of turn pikes paid only very small dividends or none at all. First, toll evasion was rampant, as people would circumvent tollgates—a practice known as "shunpiking." Second, many roads were built in advance of settlement and travel demand was low. Third, legal-restrictions and regulations, limiting both toll rates and countermeasures to shunpiking, hamstrung the turnpikes' abilities to improve their financial situation.

But poor financial returns did not necessarily mean unfruitfulness. Even an unprofitable turnpike stimulated commerce, raised land values, and aided expansion. Therefore, community leaders resorted to a fascinating array of tactics to boost the turnpike cause despite the sad prospects for dividends. Supporters used newspaper appeals, town meetings, door-to-door solicitations, and correspondence to apply social pressure. In this way as in others, American communities relied on voluntarism, as so elegantly described by Alexis de Tocquevile, to meet local needs. The result in terms of turnpike construction in New York is shown in Figure 18.1.

Canals, railroads, and spur turnpikes, 1826–1845

In the late 1820s canals began competing with many of the major turnpikes. Railroads joined in a bit later. Between 1825 and 1845 turnpike mileage dropped considerably.

Table 18.1 Turnpike incorporation, 1792–1845

State	1792–1800	1801–10	1811–20	1821–30	1831–40	1841–45	Total
New Hampshire	4	45	5	1	4	0	59
Vermont	9	19	15	7	4	3	57
Massachusetts	9	80	8	16	1	1	115
Rhode Island	3	13	8	13	3	1	41
Connecticut	23	37	16	24	13	0	113
New York	13	126	133	75	83	27	457
Pennsylvania	5	39	101	59	101	37	342
New Jersey	0	22	22	3	3	0	50
Virginia	0	6	7	8	25	0	46
Maryland	3	9	33	12	14	7	78
Ohio	0	2	14	12	114	62	204
Total	69	398	362	230	365	138	1562

Klein & Fielding, *Transportation* Quarterly (1992).

Figure 18.1 Turnpikes of New York (as of 1830) compiled and drawn by C. T. Baer. 1991.

At the same time, however, the canals and railroads changed the patterns of trade and development, and stimulated new demands for shorter toll roads that would serve as feeders. Table 18.1 shows that turnpike activity by no means ceased with the advent of canals and rails.

Plank road fever, 1847–1853

High hopes for a new kind of short feeder road were placed in the idea of plank roads, organized like turnpikes but surfaced with wooden planks. Plank surfacing promised a smooth, inexpensive alternative to turnpikes, which sometimes resembled a river of mud. Plank road fever struck in the late 1840s and thousands of miles of plank roads were constructed.

Civil engineers and enthusiasts predicted that plank roads would last eight years before needing to be resurfaced. Beginning in 1847, rural Americans financed and constructed plank roads in massive numbers. Table 18.2 shows total incorporation for several states. Figure 18.2 shows the plank road system in New York.

But the planks wore out twice as fast as predicted—usually within four years. The movement ended as suddenly as it had begun. Most plank road companies folded, while others converted their operations to gravel turnpikes.

Table 18.2 Plank road incorporation by state

State	No.	State	No.
New York	350	Georgia	16
Pennsylvania	315	Iowa	14
Ohio	205	Vermont	14
Wisconsin	130	Maryland	13
Michigan	122	Connecticut	7
Illinois	88	Massachusetts	1
North Carolina	54	Rhode Island	0
Missouri	49	Maine	0
New Jersey	25		

Ohio is through 1852; Pennsylvania, New Jersey, and Maryland are through 1857. Few plank roads were chartered after 1857.
Mafewski, Baer & Klein, *Journal of Economic History* (1993).

Figure 18.2 Plank roads of New York, 1845–1860 Compiled and drawn by C. T. Baer 1991.

Toll roads in the far west, 1850–1890

The toll road idea endured to the end of the century. Discoveries of gold, silver, copper, and other minerals in California, Colorado, and Nevada sparked rushes of newcomers. Even before statehood for Colorado and Nevada entrepreneurs organized their own toll road enterprises to serve the mining communities, and some got rich in the process. Well over 360 toll roads were constructed in California, Colorado, and Nevada alone. This experience indicates that private initiative can provide infrastructure for economic development—so long as government respects people's liberty to do so.

The good roads movement and the end of the toll road, 1890–1916

By the end of the nineteenth century, state and county governments had grown in capabilities and new agencies began setting goals for centralized highway management. Independent private toll roads were not thought appropriate in the era of progressive governance, and most of those remaining were bought out or shut down. Observed a county board in New York in 1906;

> The ownership and operation of this road by a private corporation is contrary to
> public sentiment in this county, and the cause of good roads, which has received so
> much attention in this state in recent years, requires that this antiquated system
> should be abolished. . . . That public opinion throughout the state is strongly in favor
> of the abolition of toll roads is indicated by the fact that since the passage of the act
> of 1899, which permits counties to acquire these roads, the boards of supervisors of
> most of the counties where such roads have existed have availed themselves of its
> provisions and have practically abolished the toll road.

Conclusion

In 1991 Congress passed the Intermodal Surface Transportation Efficiency Act (ISTEA), which changed the 75-year policy against toll roads. It permits the use of federal funds on toll roads, including ones designed, constructed, and operated by private groups. It sheds the old requirement that states repay federal funds if the facility is transferred to private control. Although highway financing should be strictly private, ISTEA greatly improves the present system, which relies on unpriced highways built and operated by government. Under ISTEA, America might begin to rediscover the effectiveness of private management and the economic virtue of user charges. With new electronic technologies of toll collection, toll roads make more sense than ever.

As we enter the potentially new era of privately managed highways, the historical experience with toll roads offers some important lessons. First, private operation is more flexible, creative, and motivated to serve than government control. In the nineteenth century, private road companies consistently out-performed their public-sector alternatives. Second, private roads will not be constructed without the prospect of private gain. If governments over-regulate or renege on their promises, private road development will not occur. Finally, infrastructure is an economic good best left to private action.

Private roadways have always made philosophical sense. Now even many public officials understand that they make economic sense as well.

Review and Discussion Questions

1 How do you think the private sector was able to provide highways, when it seems as though excluding non-payers would be costly? See also Klein (1990) and Klein and Yin (1996) in "Suggestions for Further Reading."
2 Are toll roads increasing or decreasing today? Why?

Chapter 19

Richard L. Stroup

FREE RIDERS AND COLLECTIVE ACTION REVISITED[1]

THE FREE-RIDER PROBLEM associated with public goods was recognized by David Hume, even before the time of Adam Smith's writings. Each citizen who can enjoy the benefit of a public good has an incentive to try to lay the whole burden of provision on others, whenever the exclusion of nonpayers is very costly or impossible. Hume recommended in 1739 that government provide the goods in question, such as bridges (Musgrave 1985). Two and a half centuries later, economists typically recommend a similar solution (Arrow 1970; Atkinson and Stightz 1980; Auerbach and Feldstein 1985; Cornes and Sandier 1986; Nicholson 1989; Samuelson 1954).

The public-provision prescription is seldom questioned, although today's economists and policy analysts, having been exposed to public-choice logic and empirical analysis, do recognize that government is an imperfect institution. Government provision of public goods, it is conceded, will not be free of problems (Shleifer 1998). For example, the rational ignorance of voters is widely recognized, and so too is the disproportionate influence of organized special-interest groups. Lobbyists and their campaign contributions are the facets of the problem that receive the most attention.

Even though problems associated with the imperfection of government are commonly recognized, it is seldom noted explicitly that the root of those problems is precisely the same as that of the free-rider problem associated with private production of public goods. The formation and successful control of a government program in the public interest, for any reasonable definition of that nebulous term, are themselves public goods. Who will pay the price in time, effort, and other lobbying costs to originate a program and to control it in the interest of the general public? Does efficiency in serving the public have a constituency? Adam Smith pointed out long ago that no individual can be expected to seek the public interest. Markets work to exhaust the gains from trade and cooperation because each individual has an interest in finding and capturing any and all such gains. Of course, when free riders can enjoy a public good without payment or trade, production and the potential gains from it may never occur. Efforts to originate government programs and to control them in the public interest are no different. As Gordon Tullock (1971) put it, "The public decision-making process is a procedure for generating a public good; and the persons involved in it, whether they are the voters, judges, legislators, or civil servants, all can be expected to treat it as any other public good" (917).

Tullock recognized the point very clearly.[2] He perceived the likelihood of shirking, in the form of spending too little time and effort in researching the issue subject to public decision and in the form of utilizing the decision maker's own preferences rather than the interest of the public in general. For these reasons, public decisions will not necessarily promote the well-being of the general public. Indeed, a program justified in the name of producing a public good may in fact be utilized by special interests to help only themselves, harming the public in the process. Analyses of programs gone awry are common, but the free-rider problem that surely causes many of these problems is seldom mentioned. Tullock's observations, though published in a prominent economics journal, seem not to have made a large impression on policy-relevant discussions by economists since that time. The problem of free riding seems to this day to be discussed almost entirely in the context of *market* failure.

One constructive use of Tullock's basic insight can be in systematic side-by-side comparisons of the incentive problems built into private provision of public goods, on the one hand, and those built into every case of public provision of any good (and of public regulation), on the other. This is the sort of comparison called for by James Buchanan (1987), by Kenneth Shepsle and Barry Weingast (1984), and by Neil Komesar (1994). A careful and realistic evaluation of the incentives facing partici-pants in the public policy process—that is, of the free-rider problem inherent in all politically directed public activity—would be useful in comparing alternative institu-tions whether the *output* of the public policy were a public good or not, and in determining whether a change in policy might provide a superior result.

Public provision of public goods: solving the free-rider problem or expanding it?

Economists who discuss public goods and the free-rider problem use many examples. Among the most common are national defense, public health measures such as mosquito abatement, and roads and bridges (Varian 1984, 253; Atkinson and Stiglitz 1980, 486–87; Nicholson 1989, 727). Each is subject to the most common problem cited: the lack of any producer's ability to exclude beneficiaries in a low-cost fashion, a condition that generates the free-rider problem, resulting in an expectation that the good will be underprovided. The standard solutions offered are government provi-sion of the good, through purchase or production, or government subsidization of its private provision. Each, however, introduces many free-rider problems of its own.

The production of goods and services, whether in the private sector or by the government, is a complex undertaking. In meeting the demand for a good, a starting point is to define specifically the quantity and the qualities of the good to be provided.

Decisions on what to produce and how to produce it

Consider national defense. What is the proper type and level of national defense? What sort of fleet should the navy build and support, and how large should it be? Where should the ships and their support be based in order to provide the best defense for a given expenditure? Similar questions must be answered about the air force and its airplanes and about the army and its forces.

Each of these decisions has intensely important ramifications for military suppliers and for departments within the military bureaucracy. The interest of each of these groups is likely to be well represented in the decision process, both directly and in lobbying. Members of Congress and relevant members of the current administration will be strongly lobbied on behalf of each supplier group and probably by each bureaucratic department.[3]

Who, on the other hand, will persistently lobby for the diffuse interest of the general public by, for example, identifying and then lobbying for the most cost-effective set of resources, or deployment of those resources, to deter potential foreign aggressors? Citizens who are employed by defense contractors or who live in an area where a defense contract is locally important may become active when their specific issue is being debated. For them, economic benefits for themselves and their localities will loom large, whereas the search for cost-effectiveness will surely be secondary. Certainly the firms, the chambers of commerce, and other organized interests will lobby intensively, often with large budgets to do so, as the narrow issues of specific interest to them are being considered.

Most citizens and most groups, however, are not apt to be involved when a specific defense procurement or deployment issue is settled. Each may well recognize that the many decisions on defense procurement and deployment are important; but for each person, the cost of learning about the issue and becoming involved is borne privately by the citizen, whereas the payoff for making better decisions in the service of cost-effectiveness is spread among the general public. The classic free-rider problem presents itself very strongly, even with respect to decisions about *the goals* of public provision of national defense.

The same problem appears in complex decisions on government provision of mosquito abatement. Which wetlands should be treated? Should aerial spraying of mosquitos be utilized? Which chemical pesticides are acceptable to reduce mosquito populations? Which is best in each situation? Again, those with income directly at stake or with strong views on these questions will probably be heard. But by whom will the general public's diffuse interests be strongly and persistently represented? Each ordinary citizen is likely to act as a free rider when the level and description of government provision of a public good is being decided. And such decisions are only the beginning of the government provision process.

Control of the production process

A large literature in economics shows that in the private sector, where minimizing the cost of producing anything (of a chosen quantity and description) is necessary to maximize the profits of a firm, organizing for cost-minimizing production nonetheless remains a complicated process. Thrainn Eggertsson, in his review and extension

244 RICHARD L. STROUP

of this literature, lists the following activities that typically must be undertaken in the production of a good in a modern economy; each is applicable to production or regulation by the government as well:

1. The search for information about the distribution of price and quality of commodities and labor inputs, and the search for potential buyers and sellers and for relevant information about their behavior and circumstances [Who might be the least-cost provider of each good and service needed?]
2. The bargaining that is needed to find the true position of buyers and sellers when prices are endogenous [What prices can actually be negotiated on behalf of the public?]
3. The making of contracts [What specifications and stipulations should be included to reduce future performance problems while controlling costs?]
4. The monitoring of contractual partners to see whether they abide by the terms *of* the contract [Are all parties to the contract complying with its terms?]
5. The enforcement of a contract and the collection of damages when partners fail to observe their contractual obligations [When should contract problems be renegotiated? When should they be taken to court instead? How should these matters be handled, once decisions are made?]
6. The protection of property rights against third-party encroachment [When should the rights of suppliers and those regulated be respected? How should they be protected, and at whose cost?]

(Eggertsson 1990, 15)

The successful performance of each of these activities requires thoughtful and diligent action, good judgment, and intelligent responses to the recognition of mistakes and altered conditions. How will each unit of a bureau be organized to allow each decision maker the latitude to operate intelligently in changing circumstances, while reducing the ability to shirk or to act opportunistically under pressure on behalf of external interests or of the bureaucratic unit's own narrow concerns or even venal interests?[4]

Entrepreneurship is a key to efficiency in a world where technology and relative prices change rapidly. Private firms are constantly adjusting their own organizations to handle changing problems and opportunities. For them the carrot is profit; the stick is failure to survive under competition. Feedback to them from the product market tends to be constant. Each buyer has a personal stake in monitoring the product in order to seek better products and to avoid paying for inferior goods. For managers of publicly traded corporations, there is constant feedback from the stock market as well, concerning both current practices and decisions about the future of the corporation. In the capital market, each investor providing capital to a firm or holding its stock has an incentive to monitor that firm's policies (or to pay a specialized investment advisor to do so) in order to buy a larger stake if the firm's prospects brighten or to bail out by selling ownership rights if adverse events are detected. In the public sector, however, there is no such personal incentive for efficient decision making and typically no such monitoring and feedback. Each voter has a voice, but exit from tax payment is usually difficult or costly, even if the taxpayer studies and disapproves of the government agency's policies or its products.

Who will oversee the efficiency of day-to-day and year-to-year operation of each unit of government in the public interest? Ultimately, voters are in charge. But the individual as a voter, unlike the same individual as a buyer of a product or a share of corporate stock, can seldom benefit *personally* from obtaining better knowledge and applying it more diligently. The individual buyer in a market can easily exercise an option such as selling stock or buying a different product, employing information gathered on the details of how a product will work or how a private corporation is being managed.

The same individual as voter has a more serious problem. Rational voter ignorance is a well-known and well-documented phenomenon. Voters tend to be free riders on the vigilance of others on any issue that is not of unusually concentrated personal interest to them. And there is no capital market that constantly assesses a government program's current performance or the plans for the future. Instead there is constant pressure from special interests, tending to mold each program and its operation to serve their narrow interests.

Some of these problems can be diminished by partially "privatizing" provision, using tax finance and low-bid private sources of supply, or by localizing the provision of goods, so that citizens can more easily choose to "vote with their feet" (Tiebout 1956) in search of better government outcomes. Neither of these tactics eliminates the free-rider problem in the public sector, but together they can reduce it by introducing competition enforced by the possibility that, periodically at least, buyers can exit.

Control of regulators as a public good

We have seen how, when a bureau or a government program is established and given access to the public purse through the budget process, control of the program in the public interest is a public good and subject to the free-rider problem. When the bureau is also given broad regulatory powers, control can be even more difficult. In addition to setting the specific program goals and the general methods of achieving those goals within a budget, regulators are often able to utilize methods that increase costs to others but do not force the spending of the bureau's own funds.

We can expect narrow bureaucratic interests, backed by specific constituencies and afflicted by "tunnel vision,"[5] to attempt to expand their activities well beyond those desired by the broader public. The bureaucrats and their clients see and value the benefits of their program, but do not see, or have no reason to value, the alternative goals given up to gain incremental advantages to their own program. Regulators who can order costly measures to be undertaken, without the check of a budget, will also utilize costly methods, failing to economize except to enhance their own program. No check on cost is present, other than political pressure. Competition of the sort that eliminates waste seldom exists in government. Further, the presence of bureaucratic rule, or "red tape," which is needed because the zeal of an owner or a residual claimant is not present to force cost control, further reduces the ability of bureau leaders to streamline procedures and reduce costs. And as noted previously, because the control and monitoring of government action in the public interest are themselves public goods, the potential controllers and monitors—voters and their elected representatives—tend to free ride rather than to zealously protect the public interest.

As a result, government programs often impose very high costs on society even when the programs imposing the costs produce little in the way of demonstrable, intended benefits.[6] In fact, a bureau can go so far as to cause negative results for the overall goal of its own program. One example is the program to enforce the Endangered Species Act.

The Endangered Species Act

Animal species listed as endangered or threatened are generally protected by the U.S. Fish and Wildlife Service (FWS) under the Endangered Species Act (ESA). The ESA as now written and interpreted gives the FWS the responsibility and authority to preserve each listed species and its habitat without regard to cost. Any habitat, public or private, declared to be important to threatened or endangered species is in effect placed under constraints dictated by FWS project biologists, without regard to cost to the land's private or public owner and without compensation to the owner. FWS habitat decisions may be extremely costly to private resource owners or to other agency missions, but the cost is exempt from the deliberations of the congressional budget process. No compensation is paid. Congress, which took the credit for helping to save species when it approved the ESA many years ago, declines to monitor the program's true costs and benefits. Some members say that they had no idea, when they voted for passage, that the costs for landowners would be so great. But few have even attempted to revise the ESA. Most are, understandably, riding free while taking credit wherever they can.

At least three consequences flow from this arrangement. The first, which was (according to the courts) intended by the Congress, is that there is no limit to the land that may be devoted to the biologist's mission to preserve land from any use other than as habitat for a listed species. The second consequence, presumably unintended, is that land, logically treated by the project biologist as having zero price, is substituted for other, on-budget factors of production, such as professional services, that could be utilized to find less costly conservation plans. The cost of other factors of production would be borne by the FWS, whereas land costs are borne by the landowners. In effect, factor prices for the production of habitat protection are severely distorted. Tunnel vision precludes each program leader from seeing and fully valuing the total social cost of the program's elements. The project managers also ride free. Control of the program in the interest of the general public is, as always, a public good.

The third result, exacerbated by the cost imposed on landowners by the first two, is that prior to being contacted by the FWS, private landowners have an incentive to manage their land in such a way that listed species will not find the land attractive. When no members of the species are present on or near his land, a landowner can avoid bearing the direct costs of the ESA. Landowners can also gain by cooperating with their neighbors to learn and teach techniques for preemptive habitat destruction and even by applying social pressure on those nearby to apply the habitat-modifying techniques. These actions occur even when, as is frequently the case, the species themselves do no harm and would have been welcomed on the land absent the uncompensated financial harm imposed by the ESA.

There is increasing evidence (Stroup 1997; Lueck and Michael 1999) that preemptive habitat destruction is important. Lueck and Michael (1999), for example, find statistically that when a colony of the listed red-cockaded woodpecker is near a forest, costly measures are taken by the landowner to make that forest less attractive to other colonies of red-cockaded woodpeckers. The birds prefer old-growth forests for their nests, so the landowner is more likely to harvest the trees before they reach the normal harvest age.

The unintended negative effect of preemptive habitat destruction by landowners has been noted by close observers of habitat preservation for some time. The effect could be mitigated by putting land-use acquisition on budget for the FWS. That would cause the program biologists and their supervisors to face market prices for land, restoring both the total cost and the true land cost as a factor of production to program decision makers. Less costly and more effective strategies for habitat preservation would be encouraged.

A second unintended negative effect of the ESA program is serious harm to voluntary programs that have been successful over the past several decades. Long before the ESA, wood ducks on the eastern flyway were saved from threatened extinction partly by the voluntary placement of nest boxes by landowners. Eastern bluebirds were saved in a similar way. More recently, the preservation of wetlands habitat in the form of prairie potholes has been effected very economically through the solicitation of landowners' cooperation, again expanding available habitat for important wildlife. These and many other successes would be exceedingly expensive, if not impossible, now in the case of listed species, due to landowners' fear of the uncompensated takings that might easily result under the ESA.

Changing the ESA to avoid uncompensated takings would eliminate both of these unintended negative effects. However, environmental groups oppose such a change, perhaps because the current arrangement is a powerful tool for another purpose: to stop the use of certain tracts of land for timber harvest, development, or even intensive agriculture. The free-rider problem severely reduces the incentive of most voters and elected politicians to carefully monitor the actual results of the ESA program and to demand changes that would make it more effective and minimize its cost.

State forest management

When the benefits of the good produced in the public sector are concentrated on a few beneficiaries and thus have less of the character of a public good, the beneficiaries have a strong incentive to monitor the program. Such close monitoring occurs, for example, in state land programs that are intended to make money for the state's school system.

State land programs that sell timber have been shown to operate much more economically than the U.S. Forest Service program, which is supposed to produce benefits of many kinds for the general public in the national forests. Donald Leal (1996) has shown that the several state programs he examined make money, while the Forest Service timber-sale programs on similar sites nearby operate at a substantial loss. Leal also demonstrated that in Montana, which conducts environmental audits on both state and federal timber lands, the state forest management was environmentally sounder as well.

State programs that are ordered simply to make money for the schools are easier to monitor than their federal counterparts. One need only check: did they make money or not? And watching them are specific interest groups that capture the benefits when the state programs operate more efficiently. The gains they make are concentrated on an organized beneficiary, the government school system. The good the state forest programs produce, in other words, has less of the public-good aspect than the federal program, whose proceeds go into the federal treasury. It may seem ironic that government provision of goods that are less collectively enjoyed and more like private goods should logically be better monitored and thus more efficient, but Leal's evidence is consistent with that logic.

Public goods and public bads: the potential for harms beyond resource waste

The fact that control of a government program in the public interest is a public good implies that groups with far narrower interests may gain control. The actions of such groups not only cause resource waste (from the general public's viewpoint) in the presence of voter shirking because of free riding in the political and bureaucratic processes; but control by those with narrow agendas may indeed cause positive harm. That outcome can easily be produced by regulatory agencies, as illustrated by the case of the FWS and the ESA. Similar outcomes may result from public goods provision.

The classic public good is national defense, as provided by a large standing army. It is intended to protect citizens against threats from hostile foreign nations. But it may be used in ways that increase, rather than reduce, the likelihood of citizens' dying at the hands of hostile foreign nationals. One of the controversial questions surrounding the Vietnam War is whether tens of thousands of Americans would have died at the hands of foreigners if the large standing military force had not been available for quick deployment to serve the aims of the administration sending them. More recently, one wonders whether the likelihood of terrorist attacks in the United States might be increased by certain deployments of the U.S. military abroad. If military forces were smaller, that particular risk would be reduced. Without far more study than we will ever give to the question, most citizen-voters, including this writer, cannot know whether a larger standing army would increase or decrease the risks of harm at the hands of foreigners. In the light of Tullock's basic insight, who would be expected to answer this question on behalf of the general public (if a credible answer is even possible) and then to lobby strongly—perhaps against the interests of military suppliers—for adoption of the policy that best serves the general public?

Production of public goods to reduce natural risks can also result in increased risk, when free riding with regard to control of the program leaves decisions in the hands of narrowly interested parties. Mosquito abatement is a case in point. Is a reduction of mosquito populations worth the risk of extensive aerial spraying of the sort that is so controversial in California? Is it worth disturbing a wetlands ecology? Few citizens have sufficient knowledge to vote intelligently on the issue, even if given a chance in a referendum. Public provision of mosquito abatement, however, unlike private abatement, generally means that the official decision maker is not personally liable if that official's program damages affected citizens. The standard of care is likely to differ as a result of public provision.[7] Again, fighting one danger by establishing pubic provision of a good may worsen other dangers. The free-rider problem among voters, and the poor oversight that results, makes public provision of "protection" from a specific risk potentially dangerous.[8]

Implications of the free-rider problem for public policy and voluntary action

The free-rider problem and its resulting reductions in the efficiency and effectiveness of government actions have important implications. Better understanding of these matters could lead to improvement in institutional choice by society generally as well as by individuals as they choose which institutions to support voluntarily.

Some goods with public-good aspects are provided by a variety of institutions— private individuals, private clubs, and government agencies. For example, wilderness or habitat for endangered species can be provided by individuals, clubs such as the National Audubon Society or the Sierra Club, and government agencies.

In any case, provision requires individuals who are sufficiently well paid or passionate to work hard or make other sacrifices to bring about the production of the public good. Even government provision requires voluntary private sacrifices. For example, establishing public-sector habitat protection in the first place requires strong lobbying by clubs such as the Audubon Society or the Sierra Club. To maintain such programs, lobbying must continue; otherwise the programs will be defeated or distorted by those seeking other goals from the federal budget and federal lands.

The clubs mentioned in fact spend most of their time and money in lobbying for government provision. Might their efforts be more productively spent organizing and campaigning for individual private landowners to help or, instead, on a campaign seeking help from individuals for the private club's efforts to obtain and administer such lands themselves as owners?

The theory of clubs suggests, and observation confirms, that club decisions tend to be made by like-minded individuals who have been drawn together by shared preferences.[9] In clubs, decisions about how the good should be defined and managed are made by like-minded individuals rather than by a median voter in a public election, by politically sensitive (and compromising) politicians, or by bureaucrats under political control. In contrast, government provision must, at least formally in a democracy, be "controlled" by voters, few of whom are likely to be as passionate and motivated and therefore as knowledgeable about the good to be provided as are the self-selected, dues-paying members of a club.

Expanding the responsibility for provision to the level of the general public gains tax support from all taxpayers only by trading off the ability to retain the focus and intensity of like-minded club members. Whether the trade-off is worthwhile can be debated. However, there is some empirical evidence, to be discussed later, that suggests voluntary provision is qualitatively different and can be qualitatively superior.

Each institutional approach requires at least partial solution of the free-rider problem to obtain cooperation among enthusiasts. Each requires work and sacrifice. Government efforts may be the most effective means for some individuals and some groups, who are relatively good at lobbying and other forms of political action.

For them, formation of a club that amounts to a special-interest lobbying group may yield the highest return on their resources.

Yet even when they successfully elicit government action and the provision of the good is assigned to a bureaucratic unit, continuing provision is not guaranteed. Defense of the bureau's budget and control of its actions in the service of specific desired goals are never-ending challenges. Public-sector victories are never bought—only rented. Whether majoritarian interests (and the median voter, who typically is uninformed about provision of the good) prevail or minoritarian special interests (such as those of contracting providers) prevail, the battle is never permanently won, for the courts have consistently held that one legislature cannot bind the next. In the words of one environmental leader, whose specialty is preserving land for wild habitat, "You know what I like? A deed in the courthouse."[10]

The preceding analysis suggests that for an enthusiast seeking to expand the provision of a public good, the same amount of organizational and fund-raising effort might be more successful if applied directly to seeking private provision of that good. The analysis does not indicate that such will necessarily be the case. Depending on the circumstances, the shortfall in payments from some who benefit, and thus the shortfall in provision, caused by the free-rider problem in private provision will be a greater or smaller problem than the reductions in the value (reduced quantity and quality delivered by public provision) that result from the multiple free-rider problems in the public sector. Even with its tax-revenue advantage, however, public provision may still deliver a lesser amount of the good, as the following example illustrates.

When provision of religion became private

As a case study, consider the provision of religious services. At least from Adam Smith's time forward, some have maintained that the church provides positive benefits to the community, beyond those provided to churchgoers. In this view, people who participate in religion become better neighbors, more upstanding citizens, and more honest trading partners (Olds 1994, 280). Such public-good aspects of religious observance, it has been claimed, justify taxpayer subsidies. Even today, many nations have an established (that is, state-supported) church.

Two centuries ago, when Connecticut and Massachusetts were considering disestablishment (ending the subsidy to each state's established church), the argument was made that without taxpayer support, religion would wither. Kelly Olds found, however, that when disestablishment occurred in Massachusetts and Connecticut and all subsidies were abolished, indicators of religious activity rose rather than fell. The statistical evidence indicates that both church membership and the demand for preachers rose rapidly (Olds 1994, 277). Many churches prospered, and their methods of finance varied. The services provided undoubtedly changed. Church leaders, after all, now had to appeal more to individual congregations and less to legislators and state voters as a group. Whatever the reason, the provision of church services increased substantially. Church membership in the United States as a whole rose for nearly all of the nineteenth and twentieth centuries (Iannaccone 1998, 1468). Further, the United States, without an established church, has greater church attendance and a greater percentage of citizens proclaiming themselves to be religious than any of the industrialized nations that provide public funding for their religious establishment (Iannaccone, Finke, and Stark 1997).

Evidently, at least in some cases, private provision allows and encourages appeals to more subgroups than does government provision, which is bound by the need for support by the median voter or by the most powerful interest groups. Indeed, public provision may undercut private support for an activity by replacing it, as it seems to do dollar for dollar in the case of support for university education (Becker and Lindsay 1994). In any event, increased public provision of a good is not an unalloyed benefit to the mission supported, and may on balance harm that mission.

Conclusion

Gordon Tullock first emphasized the importance of the free-rider problem in the public sector. Recognizing this problem should alter our expectation that when the private sector provides a good "imperfectly," citizens have the option to utilize the government in order to achieve an ideal delivery of the good. The public-sector approach is one candidate among several as an institutional means of providing a particular public good. However, the pervasiveness of the free-rider problem in the public sector has several implications:

- Establishing a government program to provide a public good requires voluntary private effort. Keeping the program funded requires continued voluntary private effort.
- Control of a government program in the general public's interest requires voluntary private effort in competition with the many narrow interests that will seek to control the program.
- When taxpayers fund a program, the product will differ from a privately provided product when the preferences of voters as a whole differ from the preferences of those with the greatest zeal and the strongest interest in the activity. The latter group could control a private effort but must compromise with those having less interest when public provision is utilized.
- Private clubs and other private providers have more freedom to choose their methods, and they have full financial responsibility for the cost, so we can expect them to be more efficient providers.
- In light of the preceding points, one expects that private provision may produce more or better-quality public goods. The evidence conforms to that expectation in specific cases such as provision of religious services.

No human institution works perfectly. When a decision about provision of a specific good in a specific case is to be made, each available institutional alternative should be realistically compared.[11] To look at only one option and point out its weaknesses, and hence to conclude that another option must be superior, is exactly the sort of mistake a student makes by supposing that products ought to be manufactured according to absolute advantage rather than comparative advantage. The same factors that make one sector weak may simultaneously weaken an alternative sector. When an externality involves many people, then market provision may be problematic, but so may be government provision. The understanding that "public decisions are public goods," first brought to light by Tullock, and the related considerations discussed in this article should be borne in mind as institutional arrangements are compared.

Notes

1 The research assistance of Charles Steele and Matthew Brown is acknowledged, along with research support from PERC. An earlier version of this article was presented at A Public Choice Conference in Honor of Gordon Tullock and published in *Public Choice Essays in Honor of a Maverick Scholar: Gordon Tullock*, edited by Price V. Fishback, Gary D. Libecap, and Edward Zajac. Boston: Kluwer Academic Press, 1999.

2 Tullock's article spurred my efforts in the present article to push the analysis further and to make it somewhat more concrete.

3 The rent-seeking literature points out the costs to society of competition among special interests to control various aspects of public policy. See Rowley, Tollison, and Tullock 1988.

4 Niskanen (1971) has shown that in certain circumstances the bureaucratic unit may, due to a monopoly of cost information, be able to put the legislature, at budget time, on an all-or-none demand curve so as to maximize the unit's budget. Today that case is generally thought to be an extreme one, even by Niskanen (see Blais and Dion 1991); but the tendency, and some ability to indulge it, may still exist.

5 "Tunnel vision" is the term utilized by U.S. Supreme Court Justice Stephen Breyer (1995) to explain why each regulatory agency tends to go well beyond any social optimum in its activities. It does not experience the opportunity costs of its actions, and it avoids many ordinary constraints in the exercise of regulatory powers granted by the legislative branch. For examples of how tunnel vision affects government programs and program costs in the context of potential risks from toxic chemicals, see Stroup and Meiners 2000.

6 For a concise overview of the high-cost, low-benefit nature of much federal environmental regulation, see Crandall 1992.

7 Precisely this problem helped to generate the Love Canal hazardous-waste problem at Niagara Falls, New York, and led to the creation of the Superfund program. Recognition of potential liability had caused the chemical company to carefully isolate the buried wastes. When the local school board purchased the property, it was explicitly warned of dangers from the waste, but proceeded to utilize "tunnel vision" in managing the land, ignoring the chemicals and, by digging through the containment walls, allowing them to seep out (Zuesse 1981; Stroup 1996, 5–6).

8 *Editor's note:* Nothing better illustrates this truth than the pretense of protection afforded by the regulatory programs of the U.S. Food and Drug Administration. See, for example, Dale H. Gieringer, "The Safety and Efficacy of New Drug Approval," *Cato Journal* 5 (Spring-Summer 1985): 177–201; and Robert Higgs, ed., *Hazardous to Our Health? FDA Regulation of Health Care Products* (Oakland, Calif.: Independent Institute, 1995).

9 The theory of clubs originated with Buchanan 1965; for a discussion, see Mueller 1989.

10 Brent Haglund, executive director of the Sand County Foundation, as quoted by Anderson and Leal (1997, 52).

11 The case for comparative institutional analyses is made in an important book by Neil Komesar (1994). He stresses that analysis should center on comparisons of how concentrated the payoffs are in each case and how many parties are importantly involved.

References

Anderson, Terry L., and Donald R. Leal. 1997. *Enviro-Capitalists.* Lanham, Md.: Rowman and Littlefield.

Arrow, Kenneth J. 1970. The Organization of Economic Activity: Issues Pertinent to the Choice of Market versus Nonmarket Allocation. In *Public Expenditures and Policy Analysis,* edited by Robert Haveman and Julius Margolis. Chicago: Markham.

Atkinson, Anthony B., and Joseph Stiglitz. 1980. Public Goods and Publicly Provided Private Goods. In *Lectures in Public Economics.* New York: McGraw-Hill.

Auerbach, Alan J., and Martin Feldstein, eds. 1985. *Handbook of Public Economics.* Vols. 1 and 2. New York: North-Holland.

Bagnoli, Mark, and Barton L. Lipman. 1992. Private Provision of Public Goods Can Be Efficient. *Public Choice* 74: 59–78.

Becker, Elizabeth, and Cotton M. Lindsay. 1994. Does the Government Free Ride? *Journal of Law and Economics* 37 (April): 277–96.

Blais, Andre, and Stephane Dion, eds. 1991. *The Budget-Maximizing Bureaucrat: Appraisals and Evidence.* Pittsburgh, Pa.: University of Pittsburgh Press.

Breyer, Stephen. 1995. *Breaking the Vicious Circle.* Cambridge, Mass.: Harvard University Press.

Buchanan, James M. 1965. An Economic Theory of Clubs. *Economica* 32 (February): 1–14.

———. 1987. Constitutional Economics. In *The New Palgrave: A Dictionary of Economics,* edited by John Eatwell, Murray Milgate, and Peter Newman, vol. 1, pp. 585–88. London: Macmillan.

Cornes, Richard, and Todd Sandler. 1986. *The Theory of Externalities, Public Goods, and Club Goods.* New York: Cambridge University Press.

Crandall, Robert. 1992. *Why Is the Cost of Environmental Regulation So High?* Policy Study 110, Center for the Study of American Business. St. Louis: Center for the Study of American Business.

Davis, Otto A., and Morton I. Kamien. 1970. Externalities, Information, and Alternative Collective Action. In *Public Expenditures and Policy Analysis,* edited by Robert Haveman and Julius Margolis. Chicago: Markham.

Eggertsson, Thrainn. 1990. *Economic Behavior and Institutions.* Cambridge: Cambridge University Press.

Haveman, Robert H., and Julius Margolis, eds. 1970. *Public Expenditures and Policy Analysis.* Chicago: Markham.

Iannaccone, Laurence R. 1998. Introduction to the Economics of Religion. *Journal of Economic Literature* 86 (September): 1465–96.

Iannaccone, Laurence R., Roger Finke, and Rodney Stark. 1997. Deregulating Religion: The Economics of Church and State. *Economic Inquiry* 35 (April 1997): 350–64.

Komesar, Neil. 1994. *Imperfect Alternatives: Choosing Institutions in Law, Economics, and Public Policy.* Chicago: University of Chicago Press.

Layard, RIG, and A. A. Walters. 1978. *Microeconomic Theory.* New York: McGraw-Hill.

Led, Donald R. 1996. *Turning a Profit on Public Forests.* PERC Policy Series PS-4. Bozeman, Mont.: PERC.

Lueck, Dean, and Jeffrey Michael. 1999. Preemptive Habitat Destruction under the Endangered Species Act. Working paper. Montana State University, Bozeman, Mt.

McMillan, John. 1979. The Free-Rider Problem: A Survey. *Economic Record* 55: 95–107.

Mueller, Dennis. 1989. *Public Choice II.* Cambridge, Eng.: Cambridge University Press.

Musgrave, R. A. 1985. A Brief History of Fiscal Doctrine. In *Handbook of Public Economics,* edited by Alan J. Auerbach and Martin Feldstein, vol. 1, pp. 1–59. New York: North-Holland.

Nicholson, Walter. 1989. *Microeconomic Theory: Basic Principles and Extensions.* 4th ed. Chicago: Dryden Press.

Niskanen, William A., Jr. 1971. *Bureaucracy and Representative Government.* Chicago: Aldine-Atherton.

Oakland, William H. 1985. Theory of Public Goods. In *Handbook of Public Economics,* edited by Alan J. Auerbach and Martin Feldstein, vol. 2, pp. 485–535. New York: North-Holland.

Olds, Kelly. 1994. Privatizing the Church. *Journal of Political Economy* 102: 277–97.

Pornmerehne, Werner W., Lars P. Feld, and Albert Hart. 1994. Voluntary Provision of a Public Good: Results from a Real World Experiment. *Kyklos* 47: 505–18.

Rowley, Charles K., Robert D. Tollison, and Gordon Tullock, eds. 1988. *The Political Economy of Rent-Seeking.* Boston: Kluwer.

Samuelson, Paul A. 1954. The Pure Theory of Public Expenditure. *Review of Economics and Statistics* 36 (November): 387–89.

———. 1955. Diagrammatic Exposition of a Theory of Public Expenditure. *Review of Economics and Statistics* 37 (November): 350–56.

Shepsle, Kenneth A., and Barry R. Weingast. 1984. Political Solutions to Market Problems. *American Political Science Review* 78: 417–34.

Shleifer, Andrei. 1998. State versus Private Ownership. *Journal of Economic Perspectives* 12 (Fall): 133–50.

Steiner, Peter O. 1970. The Public Sector and the Public Interest. In *Public Expenditures and Policy Analysis,* edited by Robert Haveman and Julius Margolis. Chicago: Markham.

Stroup, Richard L. 1995. *The Endangered Species Act: Making Innocent Species the Enemy.* PERC Policy Series PS-3. Bozeman, Mont.: PERC.

———. 1996. *Superfund: The Shortcut that Failed.* PERC Policy Series PS-5. Bozeman, Mont.: PERC.

———. 1997. The Economics of Compensating Property Owners. *Contemporary Economic Policy* 15 (October): 55–65.

Stroup, Richard L. and Roger E. Meiners, eds. 2000. *Cutting Green Tape: Toxic Pollutants, Environmental Regulation and the Law.* New Brunswick, N.J.: Transaction Publishers and The Independent Institute.

Tiebout, Charles M. 1956. A Pure Theory of Local Expenditures. *Journal of Political Economy* 64 (October): 416–24.

Tullock, Gordon. 1971. Public Decisions as Public Goods. *Journal of Political Economy* 79 (July-August): 913–18.

Varian, Hal R. 1984. *Microeconomic Analysis.* 2d ed. New York: W. W. Norton.

Zeckhauser, Richard. 1970. Uncertainty and the Need for Collective Action. In *Public Expenditures and Policy Analysis*, edited by Robert Haveman and Julius Margolis. Chicago: Markham.

Zuesse, Eric. 1981. Love Canal: The Truth Seeps Out. *Reason* 12 (February): 17–33.

Review and Discussion Questions

1 Stroup compares the free-rider problem in private markets to the free-rider problem in government. What does he conclude?

2 What did Stroup find regarding state-supported religions?
3 Research—if necessary—what happened to the Church of Sweden in 2000. Does what happened support Stroup's conclusion?
4 Global warming is widely thought to be caused by the carbon dioxide put into the atmosphere by people. But if everybody but you reduces their carbon dioxide emissions, thus reducing or averting global warming, you will free-ride on the benefit. And, of course, if everybody else recognizes this, there will be little incentive for anybody to reduce production of carbon dioxide. Does this mean that we urgently require government to do something to reduce emissions? What do you think Stroup would say?

Suggestions for Further Reading

Coase, R. (1974) "The Lighthouse in Economics," *Journal of Law and Economics,* 17: 357–376.
Lighthouses were once thought to the quintessential non-excludable good. If a light-house shone its light on one ship, how could it exclude other ships from the light? And didn't that mean lighthouses would not be operated by profit-seeking firms and would have to be government operated? But in this well-known paper, Ronald Coase argues that, for centuries, non-payers *were* effectively excluded, and British light-houses were privately operated. (A couple of recent papers have criticized Coase's research, however, claiming that the British government was also deeply involved in the operation of the lighthouses.)

Demsetz, H. (1964) "The Exchange and Enforcement of Property Rights," *Journal of Law and Economics,* 7: 11–26.
Demsetz argues markets will sometimes provide goods even though free-riding is rampant. Firms provide the goods regardless, if they can tie one good to another. An example is free parking at shopping malls. Why would the merchants provide park-ing without asking customers to pay? The answer is that if the parking increases the merchants' business enough, it is worthwhile to provide. (Does this help explain why malls are often located where land is cheap? Does it help explain why many malls are somewhat isolated, not near other places people would like to visit?)

Klein, D. B. (1990) "The Voluntary Provision of Public Goods? The Turnpike Companies of Early America," *Economic Inquiry,* 28: 788–812.
Circa 1800, roads in America had two potential free-rider problems. Tolls were hard to collect because of legal restrictions. And the benefits of completed roads to the community still accrued to people who didn't help pay for building them. But Klein tells us that communities still managed to build and operate hundreds of turnpike roads.

Klein, D. B. and Yin, C. (1996) "Use, Esteem, and Profit in Voluntary Provision: Toll Roads in California, 1850–1902," *Economic Inquiry,* 34: 678–692.
This article extends Klein's analysis to California toll roads, In California, the profit motive was especially strong and many toll roads operated similar to business enterprises.

Marvel, H. P. (1982) "Exclusive Dealing," *Journal of Law and Economics,* 25: 1–25.
Marvel explains a controversial business practice, exclusive dealing—a contractual requirement by which retailers or distributors promise a manufacturer that they will not handle the goods of competing manufacturers—as a way manufacturers can cope efficiently with a particular type of free-riding.

PART SIX

Asymmetric Information

Introduction

Critics of the market argue that markets will often not work well because consumers have far less information than sellers, that information is "asymmetric." If so, how can buyers ever trust sellers? How can buyers be sure that the products they buy are high quality? How can buyers avoid buying "lemons"?

Here again, the market has ways of reducing or eliminating the problem. The widely cited paper by Benjamin Klein and Keith B. Leffler constructs a model to show how a firm's reputation can induce it to provide high-quality products. The model also offer insights into the pricing and advertising strategies firms adopt to establish good reputations. A paper by Clement G. Krouse and one by Steven N. Wiggins and David G. Raboy apply the model.

A particular version of the asymmetric information problem is the "lemons" problem.[1] A "lemon" is slang for a used car that has one or more defects that the seller knows about but that the buyer doesn't. The lemons problem suggests that buyers will have a lot of trouble trusting sellers of used goods. The problem is thought to be so severe that when a buyer drives a new car off the dealer's lot, its resale price drops significantly almost immediately (because it's then a used car and buyers would wonder whether it was a lemon). But, it turns out, the problem is not serious at all. In an excerpt from John R. Lott, Jr.'s book *Freedomnomics*, Lott contends that almost-new used cars sell for approximately the same price they sell when actually new. Eric W. Bond tests a key implication of the lemons model and finds it mostly unsupported by data on the market for used trucks.

Note

1 The famous paper that originally presented the lemons problem is George Akerlof (1970), "The Market for 'Lemons': Quality Uncertainty and the Market Mechanism," *Quarterly Journal of Economics*, 84: 488–500.

Chapter 20

Benjamin Klein and Keith B. Leffler

THE ROLE OF MARKET FORCES IN ASSURING CONTRACTUAL PERFORMANCE[1]

I Introduction

$\mathbf{A}$N IMPLICIT ASSUMPTION of the economic paradigm of market exchange is the presence of a government to define property rights and enforce contracts. An important element of the legal–philosophical tradition upon which the economic model is built is that without some third-party enforcer to sanction stealing and reneging, market exchange would be impossible.[2] But economists also have long considered "reputations" and brand names to be private devices which provide incentives that assure contract performance in the absence of any third-party enforcer (Hayek 1948, p. 97; Marshall 1949, vol. 4, p. xi). This private-contract enforcement mechanism relies upon the value to the firm of repeat sales to satisfied customers as a means of preventing nonperformance. However, it is possible that economic agents with well-known brand names and reputations for honoring contracts may find it wealth maximizing to break such potentially long-term exchange relationships and obtain a temporary increase in profit. In particular, the determinants of the efficacy of this market method of contract performance and therefore the conditions under which we are likely to observe its use remain unspecified.

This paper examines the nongovernmental repeat-purchase contract-enforcement mechanism. To isolate this force, we assume throughout our analysis that contracts are not enforceable by the government or any other third party. Transactors are assumed to rely solely on the threat of termination of the business relationship for enforcement of contractual promises.[3] This assumption is most realistic for contractual terms concerning difficult-to-measure product characteristics such as the "taste" of a hamburger. However, even when the aspects of a contract are less complicated and subjective and therefore performance more easily measurable by a third party such as a judge, specification, litigation, and other contract-enforcement costs may be substantial. Therefore, explicit guarantees to replace or repair defective goods (warranties) are not costless ways to assure contract performance. Market arrangements such as the value of lost repeat purchases which motivate transactors to honor their promises may be the cheapest method of guaranteeing the guarantee.

While our approach is general in the sense that the value of future exchanges can motivate fulfillment of all types of contractual promises, we focus in this paper on contracts between producers and consumers regarding product quality. In order for a repeat-sale enforcement mechanism to operate, we assume that the identity of firms is known by consumers[4] and that the government enforces property rights to the extent that consumers voluntarily choose whom to deal with and must pay for the goods they receive.[5] In addition, managers of firms are assumed to be wealth maximizing and to place no value on honesty per se.

In Section II, the conditions are outlined under which firms will either honor their commitments to supply a high level of quality or choose to supply a quality lower than promised. In order to emphasize the ability of markets to guarantee quality in the absence of any government enforcement mechanism, a simple model is presented which assumes that consumers costlessly communicate among one another. Therefore, if a firm cheats and supplies to any individual a quality of product less than contracted for, all consumers in the market learn this and all future sales are lost. A major result of our analysis is that even such perfect interconsumer communication conditions are not sufficient to assure high quality supply. Cheating will be prevented and high quality products will be supplied only if firms are earning a continual stream of rental income that will be lost if low quality output is deceptively produced. The present discounted value of this rental stream must be greater than the one-time wealth increase obtained from low quality production.

This condition for the "notorious firm" repeat-purchase mechanism to assure high quality supply is not generally fulfilled by the usual free-entry, perfectly competitive equilibrium conditions of price equal to marginal and average cost. It becomes necessary to distinguish between production costs that are "sunk" firm-specific assets and those production costs that are salvageable (i.e., recoverable) in uses outside the firm. Our analysis implies that firms will not cheat on promises to sell high quality output only if price is sufficiently above salvageable production costs. While the perfectly competitive price may imply such a margin above salvageable costs, this will not necessarily be the case. The fundamental theoretical result of this paper is that market prices above the competitive price and the presence of nonsalvageable capital are means of enforcing quality promises.[6]

In Section III our theoretical model of quality-guaranteeing price premiums above salvageable costs is extended to examine how the capital value of these price-premium payments can be dissipated in a free-entry equilibrium. The quality-guaranteeing nature of nonsalvageable, firm-specific capital investments is developed. Alternative techniques of minimizing the cost to consumers of obtaining an assured high quality are investigated. We also explore market responses to consumer uncertainty about quality-assuring premium levels. Advertising and other production and distribution investments in "conspicuous" assets are examined as competitive responses to simultaneous quality and production-cost uncertainties. Finally, a summary of the analysis and some concluding remarks are presented in Section IV.

II Price premiums and quality assurance

Assume initially that consumers costlessly know all market prices and production technologies but not the qualities of goods offered for sale. For simplicity, the good being considered is assumed to be characterized by a single objective quality measure, q, where quality refers to the level of some desirable characteristic contained in the good. Examples are the quietness of appliance motors, the wrinkle-free or colorfast properties of clothing, or the gasoline mileage of an automobile. We also assume that the economy consists of consumers who consider buying a product x each period, where the length of a period is defined by the life (repurchase period) of product x, and who are assumed to costlessly communicate quality information among one another. Therefore, if a particular firm supplies less-than-contracted-for quality to one consumer, the next period all consumers are assumed to know. In addition, this information is assumed not to depreciate over time.[7]

Identical technology is assumed to be available to all entrepreneurs. Hence, there are many potential firms with identical total cost functions, $C = c(x,q) + F(q)$, where F is fixed (invariant to rate) costs. Higher quality and larger quantities require higher production costs, $F_q > 0, c_q > 0, c_x > 0$, and marginal cost is assumed to increase with quality, $c_{xq} > 0$. Fixed costs are assumed initially to be expenditures made explicitly each period rather than capital costs allocated to the current period. For example, they may include a payment on a short-term (one-period) rental agreement for a machine but not the current forgone interest on a purchased machine or the current period's payment on a long-term rental agreement—both of which imply long-term and hence capital commitments.

We therefore are explicitly distinguishing between "fixed" costs in the sense employed here of constant (invariant to output) current costs and "sunk" (nonsalvageable) capital costs. The usual textbook proposition that a firm will not shut down production as long as price is greater than average variable cost blurs this distinction and implicitly assumes that all fixed costs are also sunk capital costs. Our assumption of the complete absence of any long-term commitments is analytically equivalent to perfect salvageability of all capital assets. If all long-term production-factor commitments were costlessly reversible, that is, all real and financial assets such as the machine or the long-term machine rental contract could be costlessly resold and hence perfectly salvageable, there also would not be any capital costs. Only the non-salvageable part of any long-term commitment should be considered a current sunk capital cost.

If buyers are costlessly informed about quality, the competitive price schedule, P_C, for alternative quality levels is given by the minimum average production costs for each level of quality and is designated by $P_C = P_c(q)$. This is represented in Figure 20.1 for two alternative quality levels, q_h and q_{min}, by the prices P_1 and P_0. Suppose, however, that the quality of product x cannot be determined costlessly before purchase. For simplicity, assume prepurchase inspection reveals only whether quality is below some minimum level, q_{min}, and that the costs are prohibitive of determining whether quality is above q_{min} prior to purchase.[8] Obviously, whenever the market price that consumers will pay for asserted high quality exceeds the cost of producing minimum quality output, the firm can increase its initial period profits by producing the minimum quality output and deceptively selling it as a higher quality product.

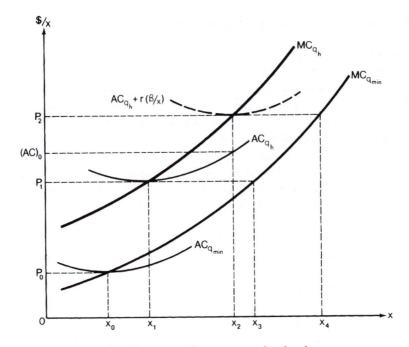

Figure 20.1 Pricing and production of alternative quality levels

If producers are to have an incentive to produce high quality products (in the absence of governmentally enforceable contracts), consumers must somehow reward high quality production and punish low quality production. We assume in this competitive framework that consumers will purchase from particular sellers randomly chosen from the group of homogeneous sellers over which consumer information is transmitted. If a consumer receives a product of a quality at least as high as implicitly contracted for, he will continue to purchase randomly from this group of sellers. On the other hand, if quality is less than contracted for, all consumers cease to purchase from the particular sampled "cheating" firm.

Consider now an initial "competitive" equilibrium in which a single firm contemplates selling a quality below that expected by customers. Given the competitive market price for some high quality, $P_c(q_h) \equiv P_1$, in Figure 20.1, this particular firm could increase its initial period quasi rents by producing minimum quality and selling it at the high quality price. However, since buyers are assumed to communicate fully with one another, all future customers of high quality output, that is, sales at prices greater than $P_c(q_{min}) \equiv P_0$ in Figure 20.1, are lost. That is, a firm that cheats will become known as a "notorious" cheater, and consumers will not purchase from the firm any product the quality of which cannot be determined prepurchase.[9]

Whether sales of high or minimum quality will maximize the firm's wealth depends on whether the capital value of future quasi rents from continued high quality production exceeds the differential initial period quasi rents from quality depreciation. In terms of Figure 20.1, at the perfectly competitive price for high quality output, P_1, price is equal to the average costs of high quality production. Therefore, the quasi rents from continued high quality production are zero. If, alternatively, the firm were to deceptively produce minimum quality output, as a price taker it would expand its production to x_3 (where $P_1 = MC_{q_{min}}$) and receive a one-period quasi rent, the present value of which is equal to:

$$W_1 = \frac{1}{1+r}\left\{(P_1 - P_0)x_3 - \int_{x_0}^{x_3}\left[MC_{q_{min}}(x) - P_0\right]dx\right\} \tag{1}$$

Therefore, at the perfectly competitive price for any quality above q_{min} firms will always cheat consumers and supply q_{min}.

Faced with this possibility, consumers would recognize that regardless of producers' promises they will not obtain the higher quality product. Therefore, consumers would be willing to pay only the costless information price of the minimum quality product whose quality they can verify prepurchase, P_o. Because of such rational consumer anticipations, firms will not be able to cheat, but desired high quality output will not be supplied.

There may, however, be a price higher than the perfectly competitive price of high quality output, P_1, that if it were the equilibrium market price would (a) motivate honest production of the high quality good and (b) not completely dissipate the consumers' surplus from purchase of higher quality. Consider a price such as P_2, in Figure 20.1. A firm supplying high quality output will now expand its production to x_2. The price premium $\tilde{P}$, defined as the increase in the price above minimum average cost of high quality, provides firms supplying high quality with a perpetual stream of quasi rents the present value of which (assuming unchanging cost and demand conditions over time) is equal to:

$$W_2 = \frac{1}{r}\left\{\tilde{P}x_2 - \int_{x_1}^{x_2}\left[MC_h(x) - P_1\right]dx\right\} \tag{2}$$

The price premium also increases the gains to a firm from supplying minimum quality at the high price. A firm that chooses to cheat will now expand its output (in terms of Figure 20.1 to x_4) and earn the extra premium on all units sold.[10] Therefore, the capital value of the quasi rents from supplying quality less than promised is:

$$W_3 = \frac{1}{1+r}\left\{\left[\tilde{P} + (P_1 - P_0)\right]x_4 - \int_{x_0}^{x_4}\left[MC_{q_{min}}(x) - P_0\right]dx\right\} \tag{3}$$

A firm will honor its implicit quality contract as long as the difference between the capital values of the noncheating and cheating strategies, $W_2 - W_3$, is positive. Consider the quasi-rent flow of the cheating and noncheating alternatives, that is, the terms in braces in our expressions (2) and (3). Define QR_2 equal to rW_2 and QR_3 equal to $(1 + r)W_3$. A firm will then elect not to cheat if and only if:

$$\frac{QR_3}{QR_2} \leq \frac{(1+r)}{r} \tag{4}$$

Therefore, there will be a price premium that motivates firms to honestly produce high quality as long as:

$$\lim_{\tilde{P} \to \infty} \left(\frac{QR_3}{QR_2} \right) \leq \frac{(1+r)}{r} \qquad (5)$$

Using L'Hospital's rule, equation (5) will be satisfied as long as

$$\frac{1}{r} > \frac{(x_4 - x_2)}{x_2} \qquad (6)$$

for all $P > P_3$, where P_3 is same finite price. Intuitively, as the price increases it is only the increase in quasi rents on the additional units of minimum quality output that favors the deceptive strategy. Equation (6) insures that price increases beyond some level increase W_2 more than W_3 such that eventually W_2 is greater than W_3.

The condition specified in equation (6) is quite reasonable. It will be satisfied as long as a cheating firm does not accompany cheating with very large output increases. If, for example, the real interest rate were .05 we require only that the output increase by a cheating firm not be more than 20 times the total output that would be produced if the firm were not cheating. Hence, under very general cost conditions a price premium will exist that motivates competitive firms to honor high quality promises because the value of satisfied customers exceeds the cost savings of cheating them.[11]

While we cannot state broad necessary conditions for the form the cost function must take to imply the existence of a quality-assuring price, "reasonable" sufficient conditions can be stated. In particular, all cases of vertically parallel marginal cost curves, as illustrated in Figure 20.1, where quality is produced by a fixed input not subject to decreasing returns to scale (such as the use of a better motor) and where the second derivative of marginal cost is greater than or equal to zero imply the existence of a quality-assuring price. The Appendix contains simulation results under the more unrealistic assumption of isoelastic marginal cost functions.[12] These simulations indicate the exceptional nature of the conditions when equation (6) is not satisfied. When a quality-assuring price does not exist, the cost functions are generally such that at reasonable premiums cheating output would be expanded by very large factors (often factors of many thousands). Since marginal cost functions for most products can be expected to become quite steep if not vertical at output expansions of much less than these factors, a quality-assuring price premium can generally be expected to exist.

Throughout the remainder of the paper we assume the existence of a quality-assuring price. For given cost and demand conditions, the minimum quality-assuring price will depend upon the level of quality considered and is denoted by $P* = P*(q, q_{min}, r)$. Our analysis implies that the quality-assuring price will increase as quality increases, as minimum quality decreases (for all q greater than q_{min}), and as the interest rate increases. These conditions are consistent with the familiar recognition that, given a particular quality level, quality-cheating problems are less severe the higher the level of quality that can be detected prepurchase and the shorter the period of repurchase.[13]

Intuitively, the quality-assuring price treats the potential value of not producing minimum quality as an explicit opportunity cost to the firm of higher quality production.

Hence the quality-assuring price must not only compensate the firm for the increased average production costs incurred when quality above that detectable prior to purchase is produced, but must also yield a normal rate of return on the forgone gains from exploiting consumer ignorance. This price "premium" stream can be thought of as "protection money" paid by consumers to induce contract performance. Although the present discounted value of this stream equals the value of the short-run gain the firm can obtain by cheating, consumers are not indifferent between paying the "premium" over time or permitting the firm to cheat. The price "premium" is a payment for high quality in the face of prepurchase quality-determination costs. The relevant consumer choice is between demanding minimum quality output at a perfectly competitive (costless information) price or paying a competitive price "premium," which is both necessary and sufficient, for higher quality output.[14]

There is a possibility that the required quality-guaranteeing price premium may exceed the increased consumer surplus of purchasing higher quality rather than the minimum quality product. If consumers can easily substitute increased quantity of the low quality product for increased quality, then the value of guaranteed high quality will be relatively low. Therefore, although a quality-guaranteeing price exists, a higher than minimum quality product may not be produced. For those goods where the substitution possibilities between quality and quantity are lower (e.g., drugs), consumer demand for confidence will be relatively high and the high quality guarantee worth the price premium. We assume throughout that we are dealing with products where some demand exists for the high quality good in the range of prices considered.

III Competitive market equilibrium: firm-specific capital investments

Our analysis has focused on the case where costless information (perfectly competitive) prices do not imply sufficient firm-specific rents to motivate high quality production. A price premium was therefore necessary to induce high quality supply. Thus, if price assures quality, the firms producing quality greater than q_{min} appear to earn positive economic profits. However, this cannot describe a full market equilibrium. When the price is high enough to assure a particular high level of quality, additional firms have an incentive to enter the industry. But if additional firms enter, the summation of the individual firms' outputs will exceed the quantity demanded at the quality-assuring price. Yet this output surplus cannot result in price reductions since the quality-assuring price is, in effect, a minimum price constraint "enforced" by rational consumers. All price-taking firms supplying a particular promised quality q above the minimum face a horizontal demand curve at $P* = P*(q)$, which is of an unusual nature in that prices above or below $P*$ result in zero sales. Consumers know that any price below $P*$ for its associated quality results in the supply of q_{min}. They therefore will not purchase from a firm promising that quality at a price lower than $P*$.

A. Brand name capital investments

Competition to dissipate the economic profits being earned by existing firms must therefore occur in nonprice dimensions. However, the zero-profit equilibrium is consistent with only a very particular form of profit-absorbing nonprice competition. The competition involves *firm-specific capital* expenditures. This firm-specific capital competition motivates firms to purchase assets with (nonsalvageable) costs equal to the capital value of the premium rental stream earned when high quality is supplied at the quality-assuring price. That is, if $P^*(q)$ is not to increase, the investment leading to zero profits must be highly firm specific and depreciate to zero if the firm cheats and supplies q_{min}, rather than the anticipated quality. Such firm-specific capital costs could, for example, take the form of sunk investments in the design of a firm logo or an expensive sign promoting the firm's name. Expenditures on these highly firm-specific assets are then said to represent brand name (or selling) capital investments.

The competitive process also forces the firm-specific capital investments to take the form of assets which provide the greatest direct service value to consumers. The consumers' "effective" price of purchasing a quality-assured good, where the effective price is defined as the purchase price of a product, P^*, less the value of the services yielded by the jointly supplied brand name assets, is thereby minimized. Competition among firms in seeking and making the most highly valued firm-specific brand name capital investments will occur until the expected wealth increase and, therefore, the incentive to enter the industry are eliminated.

If the firm decides to cheat it will experience a capital loss equal to its anticipated future profit stream. Since $P^*(q)$ is derived so that the threat of loss of this future profit stream motivates guaranteed quality, the zero-profit equilibrium "brand-name capital," b, which serves as an explicit hostage to prevent cheating, equals, in terms of Figure 20.1, where $P^*(q_h) = P_2$,

$$\beta = \frac{\left[P_2 - \left(AC \right)_0 \right] x_2}{r} \tag{7}$$

That is, the market value of the competitive firm's brand name capital is equal to the value of total specific or "sunk" selling costs made by the firm which, in turn, equals the present value of the anticipated premium stream from high quality output. If we continue to assume that there are no capital (and therefore "sunk") costs of production, the zero-profit equilibrium is shown in Figure 20.1 where average "total" cost (which includes average production costs, AC_{qh}, plus average brand-name capital [i.e., nonsalvageable "selling"] costs, r[b /x]) just equals price, P_2.

What assures high quality supply is the capital loss due to the loss of future business if low quality is produced. Since the imputed value of the firm's brand name capital is determined by the firm's expected quasi rents on future sales, this capital loss from supplying quality lower than promised is represented by the depreciation of this firm-specific asset. The expenditures on brand name capital assets are therefore similar to collateral that the firm loses if it supplies output of less than anticipated quality and in equilibrium the premium stream provides only a normal rate of return on this collateral asset.

Note that the "effective" price paid by consumers, which equals the quality-assuring price less the value of the consumer services yielded by the brand name capital, may be minimized by the investment in specific selling assets with some positive salvage value. Even though this results in an increased quality-guaranteeing price, assets with positive salvage values may yield differentially large direct consumer service flows.

All brand name capital assets must, however, satisfy a necessary condition that the salvage value per unit of output be less than the consumer service value. Firms competing to minimize the effective price will choose specific assets by trading off increased consumer service value with decreased salvage value. This may explain why stores which supply high quality products often have amenities (such as a luxurious carpet cut to fit the particular store) even though only small direct consumer services may be yielded relative to cost.[15]

B. Nonsalvageable productive assets

The market equilibrium we have developed implies an effective price for high quality output that is higher than what would exist in a zero information cost world. While the costless-information solution is meaningless as an achievable standard of "efficiency," alternative marketing arrangements may be usefully compared to this benchmark. Viable, competitive firms will adopt the arrangements which, considering all transacting and contracting costs, minimize the deviations between the costless-information price and the effective price. One potentially efficient alternative or supplement to the pure price-premium method of guaranteeing quality may be the use of nonsalvageable productive assets rather than brand name (selling) assets.

In order to simplify the analysis of price premiums in guaranteeing quality, we have assumed that all production costs, including fixed costs, were noncapital costs and therefore, by definition, salvageable. More realistically, firms can control both the capital intensity of production and the salvage value of any fixed assets employed in the production process. In particular, if the firm uses a production process that has a nonsalvageable capital element, the normal rate of return (quasi-rent stream) on this element of production capital effectively serves as a quality-assuring premium. In terms of our model, the capital value of the quasi-rent stream when a firm cheats (eq. [3]) is now modified so that the net gain from cheating equals W_3 minus this nonsalvageable capital cost. Alternatively, in the zero-profit equilibrium the total level of collateral must still equal the potential gross gains from cheating, but part of the collateral is now provided by the nonsalvageable production assets rather than the brand name capital assets.

For example, if a machine is somewhat illiquid, buying it rather than renting it short term provides some of this collateral and lowers the quality-guaranteeing price. In fact, because of positive selling costs, capital assets generally have a salvage value less than cost. Thus capital inputs, especially those that have a high turnover cost, will have a value in terms of providing quality assurance in addition to their productive value. Even if the asset is not firm specific, if there is any time delay after the firm cheats and is terminated by consumers in selling the asset to another firm, the firm loses the real rate of interest for that time period on the capital. In addition to physical capital, human capital costs, especially entrepreneurial skills, are also often highly nonsalvageable in the face of consumer termination and therefore also provide significant quality assurance.

The general theoretical point is that the presence of positive quality-information costs favors an increase in the capital intensity of production, including the extent of long-term, illiquid contractual arrangements with suppliers of productive inputs. In particular, the minimum-cost production technique is no longer necessarily that which minimizes solely the average cost of production. "Sunk" production capital now accomplishes two functions—the supply of production services and the supply of quality-assuring services. Therefore, increases in average production costs accompanied by larger increases in sunk production assets may minimize the effective consumer product price. Profit maximization requires firms to trade off "inefficient" production technologies and the quality-assurance cost savings implied by the presence of firm-specific (sunk) capital assets in the productive process and hence the reduced necessity for the firm to make sunk selling cost (brand name capital) investments. Although the more capital intensive production technology may increase the perfectly competitive price of high quality output, P_o, it reduces the price premium, P_2-P_1, necessary to assure the supply of that high quality. In fact, even a very slight modification of the minimum production cost technology, such as an alteration in some contractual terms, may imply the existence of large enough nonsalvageable assets so that the need for a quality-guaranteeing price premium is eliminated entirely.[16]

C. Consumer cost uncertainty: a role for advertising

The discussion to this point has assumed complete consumer knowledge of firms' costs of producing alternative quality outputs and knowledge of the extent to which any capital production costs or brand name capital selling costs are salvageable. This knowledge is necessary and sufficient to accurately calculate both the quality-guaranteeing premium and price. However, consumers are generally uncertain about cost conditions and therefore do not know the minimum quality-guaranteeing price with perfect accuracy. In fact, consumers cannot even make perfect anticipated quality rankings across firms on the basis of price. That one firm has a higher price than another may indicate a larger price premium or, alternatively, more inefficient production. In this section, we examine how the more realistic assumption of consumer cost uncertainty influences market responses to prepurchase quality uncertainty.

We have shown that increases in the price premium over average recoverable cost generally increase the relative returns from production of promised (high) quality rather than deceptive minimum (low) quality. The existence of a high price premium also makes expenditures on brand name capital investments economically feasible. The magnitude of brand name capital investments in turn indicates the magnitude of the price premium. When a consumer is uncertain about the cost of producing a particular high quality level of output and therefore the required quality-assuring premium, information about the actual level of the price premium will provide information about the probability of receiving high quality. If consumers are risk averse, this uncertainty about receiving anticipated high or deceptively low quality output will increase the premium that will be paid. The premium will include both a (presumably unbiased) estimate of the quality-assuring premium and an extra payment to reduce the risk of being deceived.

Thus, when consumers do not know the minimum quality-guaranteeing price, the larger is a firm's brand name capital investment relative to sales, the more likely its price premium is sufficient to motivate high quality production. Competitive investment in brand name capital is now no longer constrained to assets which yield direct consumer service flows with a present discounted value greater than the salvage value of the assets. Implicit information about the sufficiency of price as a guarantee can be supplied by "conspicuous" specific asset expenditures. Luxurious storefronts and ornate displays or signs may be supplied by a firm even if yielding no direct consumer service flows. Such firm-specific assets inform consumers of the magnitude of sunk capital costs and thereby supply information about the quasi-rent price-premium stream being earned by the firm and hence the opportunity cost to the firm if it cheats. Both the informational services and the direct utility producing services of assets are now relevant considerations for a firm in deciding upon the most valuable form the brand name capital investment should take.

The value of information about the magnitude of a firm's specific or "sunk" capital cost, and therefore the magnitude of the price premium, is one return from advertising. Indeed, the role of premiums as quality guarantors provides foundation for Nelson's (1974) argument that advertising, by definition, supplies valuable information to consumers—namely, information that the firm is advertising. A sufficient investment in advertising implies that a firm will not engage in short-run quality deception since the advertising indicates a nonsalvageable cost gap between price and production costs, that is, the existence of a price premium. This argument essentially reverses Nelson's logic. It is not that it pays a firm with a "best buy" to advertise more, but rather that advertising implies the supply of "best buys," or more correctly, the supply of promised high quality products. Advertising does not directly "signal" the presence of a "best buy," but "signals" the presence of firm-specific selling costs and therefore the magnitude of the price premium. We would therefore expect, ceteris paribus, a positive correlation not between advertising intensity and "best buys," as Nelson claims, but between advertising intensity and the extent of quality that is costly to determine prepurchase.[17]

Conspicuous sunk costs such as advertising are, like all sunk costs, irrelevant in determining future firm behavior regarding output quality. However, consumers know that such sunk costs can be profitable only if the future quasi rents are large. In particular, if the consumer estimate of the initial sunk expenditure made by the firm is greater than the consumer estimate of the firm's possible short-run cheating gain, then a price premium on future sales sufficient to prevent cheating is estimated to exist. Our analysis therefore implies that independent of excludability or collection costs, advertising that guarantees quality will be sold at a zero price and "tied in" with the marked-up product being advertised.[18]

Our theory also suggests why endorsements by celebrities and other seemingly "noninformative" advertising such as elaborate (obviously costly to produce) commercials, sponsorships of telethons, athletic events, and charities are valuable to consumers. In addition to drawing attention to the product, such advertising indicates the presence of a large sunk "selling" cost and the existence of a price premium. And because the crucial variable is the consumers' estimate of the stock of advertising capital (and not the flow), it also explains why firms advertise that they have advertised in the past (e.g., "as seen on 'The Tonight Show' "). Rather than serving a direct certifying function (e.g., as recommended by *Good Housekeeping* magazine), information about past advertising informs consumers about the magnitude of the total brand name capital investment.[19]

Firms may also provide valuable information by publicizing the large fees paid to celebrities for commercials. Information about large endorsement fees would be closely guarded if the purpose were to simulate an "unsolicited endorsement" of the product's particular quality characteristics rather than to indicate the existence of a price premium. Viewed in this context, it is obviously unnecessary for the celebrity to actually use the particular brand advertised. This is contrary to a recent FTC ruling (see Federal Trade Commission 1980).

This analysis of advertising implies that consumers necessarily receive something when they pay a higher price for an advertised brand. An expensive name brand aspirin, for example, is likely to be better than unadvertised aspirin because it is expensive. The advertising of the name brand product indicates the presence of a current and future price premium. This premium on future sales is the firm's brand name capital which will be lost if the firm supplies lower than anticipated quality. Therefore, firms selling more highly advertised, higher priced products will necessarily take more precautions in production.[20]

We have emphasized the informational value of advertising as a sunk cost. Other marketing activities can serve a similar informational role in indicating the presence of a price premium. For example, free samples, in addition to letting consumers try the product, provide information regarding future premiums and therefore anticipated quality. Such free or low-price samples thus provide information not solely to those consumers that receive the samples but also to anyone aware of the existence and magnitude of the free or low-price sample program. More generally, the supply by a firm of quality greater than anticipated and paid for by consumers is a similar type of brand name capital investment by the firm. By forgoing revenue, the firm provides information to consumers that it has made a nonsalvageable investment of a particular magnitude and that a particular future premium stream is anticipated to cover the initial sunk alternative cost.[21]

Finally, even when consumers systematically underestimate the quality-assuring price because of downward-biased estimates of production or marketing costs or upward-biased estimates of anticipated demand growth, firms in a monopolistically competitive environment may not cheat. Such price-setting firms may possess specific nonsalvageable assets (such as trademarks) upon which they are earning a sufficient quasi-rent premium to induce high quality supply. However, the existence of independent competitive retailers that do not have any ownership stake in this firm-specific asset and yet can significantly influence the quality of the final product supplied to consumers creates a severe quality-cheating problem for the manufacturer. In this context, rational but imperfectly informed consumers will not demand a sufficient premium to prevent retailer cheating. Manufacturers may protect their trademarks by imposing constraints on the retailer competitive process including entry restrictions, exclusive territorial grants, minimum resale price maintenance, and advertising restrictions that will assure quality by creating a sufficiently valuable premium stream for the retailers. If this manufacturer-created premium stream is greater than the potential short-run retailer return from deceptive low quality supply, the magnitude of which is determined in part by the manufacturer by its level of direct policing expenditures, the retailer will not cheat and the consumer will receive anticipated high quality supply.[22]

IV Conclusion

We have shown that even the existence of perfect communication among buyers so that all future sales are lost to a cheating firm is not sufficient to assure noncheating behavior.

We have analyzed the generally unrecognized importance of increased market prices and nonsalvageable capital as possible methods of making quality promises credible. We obviously do not want to claim that consumers "know" this theory in the sense that they can verbalize it but only that they behave in such a way as if they recognize the forces at work. They may, for example, know from past experience that when a particular type of investment is present such as advertising they are much less likely to be deceived. Therefore, survivorship of crude decision rules over time may produce consumer behavior very similar to what would be predicted by this model without the existence of explicit "knowledge" of the forces we have examined.

Our analysis implies that consumers can successfully use price as an indicator of quality. We are not referring to the phenomenon of an ignorant consumer free riding on the information contained in the market price paid by other more informed buyers but rather to the fact that consumer knowledge of a gap between firm price and salvageable costs, that is, the knowledge of the existence of a price premium, supplies quality assurance. The former argument, that a naive buyer in a market dominated by knowledgeable buyers can use price as a quality signal because the relative market price of different products reflects differences in production costs and therefore differences in quality, crucially depends upon a "majority" of the buyers in the market being knowledgeable.

As Scitovsky (1945, p. 101) correctly notes, ". . . the situation becomes paradoxical when price is the index by which the average buyer judges quality. In a market where this happens price ceases to be governed by competition and becomes instead an instrument wherewith the seller can influence his customer's opinions of the quality of his wares." However, even when the "average" buyer uses price as an index of quality, we need not fear, as Scitovsky does, the havoc this supposedly wreaks on the economic theory of choice. All consumers in a market may consistently use price, given their estimates of salvageable production costs, as an indicator of the firm's price-premium stream and therefore as an indicator of the anticipated quality of the output to be supplied by the firm. Scitovsky did not consider that price not only influences buyers' expectations but also influences producers' incentives.

We do not wish to suggest that use of implicit (price premium–specific investment) contracts is always the cheapest way to assure quality supply. When quality characteristics can be specified cheaply and measured by a third party, and hence contract enforcement costs are anticipated to be low, explicit contractual solutions with governmentally enforced penalties (including warranties) may be a less costly solution. When explicit contract costs are high and the extent of short-run profit from deceptively low quality supply and hence the quality-assuring price premium is also high, governmental specification and enforcement of minimum quality standards may be an alternative method of reducing the costs of assuring the supply of high quality products.[23] And, finally, vertical integration, which in this consumer-product context may consist of home production or consumer cooperatives, may be a possible alternative arrangement (see Klein, Crawford, and Alchian 1978).

The three major methods in which to organize transactions can be usefully considered within this framework as (a) explicit contractual or regulatory specification with third-party enforcement, (b) direct (two-party) enforcement of implicit contracts, and (c) one-party organization or vertical integration. This paper has analyzed the brand name repeat-purchase mechanism represented by the second alternative.

More generally, however, all market transactions, including those "within" the firm such as employer–employee agreements, consist of a combination of the two basic forms of contractual arrangements. Some elements of performance will be specified and enforced by third-party sanctions and other elements enforced without invoking the power of some outside party to the transaction but merely by the threat of termination of the transactional relationship.

Our analysis implies that, given a particular level of explicit contract costs, we are more likely to observe an increased reliance on the brand name contract-enforcement mechanism the lower the rate of interest and the lower the level of prepurchase quality-determination costs. The lower the interest rate the greater the capital cost to a firm from the loss of future sales and therefore the lower the equilibrium price premium. Hence we can expect the termination of future exchange method of enforcing contracts to be more effective. More generally, since the interest rate in our model refers to the period of product repurchase, the quality assurance will be less costly for less durable goods that have greater repurchase frequency. Franchising chains, for example, take advantage of this effect by making it possible for consumers to pool information from sales of seemingly disparate sellers, thereby decreasing the period of repurchase and the quality-assuring price.

Similarly, purchase from a diversified firm increases the frequency of repeat purchase and lowers the necessary price premium. As long as consumers react to receiving unexpectedly low quality from a diversified firm by reducing purchases of the firm's entire product line, all the firm's nonsalvageable capital serves to assure the quality of each product it produces. This economy of scale in communicating quality-assurance information to consumers may be one motivation for conglomerate mergers. If a firm sells a set of products, each of which is produced by capital with salvage value less than costs, the quality-guaranteeing price premium on each product will be lower than if production were done by separate firms.

Finally, we can expect greater reliance on the non-third-party method of contract enforcement the lower the direct costs to the consumer of determining quality of the product prepurchase. The higher the costs of producing the minimum quality output that cannot be distinguished prepurchase from a given promised high quality output and the faster these minimum quality production costs rise with increased output, the lower the potential short-run cheating gain and therefore the lower the price premium. When the low quality cost function is such that a cheating firm can expand output a substantial amount with little increase in cost, use of the brand name enforcement mechanism is unlikely.

When the low quality cost function becomes so flat that the premium solution does not exist, the implicit contract-enforcement mechanism we have analyzed will not be used. When this condition is combined with an extremely high cost of quality assurance via explicit contractual guarantees, governmental supply may be the cheapest alternative. An obvious example is the good "money," where the marginal cost of production is essentially zero, the short-run cheating potential extremely large, and where the cost of a commodity money or the necessary bullion reserves to assure performance via convertibility is also extremely high. Governmental supply is the generally adopted but far from costless solution (see Klein 1974). Other products where the "hold-up" potential is very large and where explicit contract costs are high (such as police or fire protection services) are also generally supplied by non-profit-maximizing government agencies rather than by unregulated profit-maximizing firms earning large quasi rents on unsalvageable (firm-specific) capital assets. In general, minimization of the cost of assuring performance will imply an optimal combination of governmental regulation and/or supply, explicit contractual enforcement, vertical integration, and the implicit (brand name) contractual enforcement mechanism we have analyzed.

Notes

1 We thank Armen Alchian, Thomas Borcherding, Harold Demsetz, James Ferguson, Jack Hirshleifer, Matt Lindsay, Roy Kenney, John Long, Ian Macneil, Kevin Murphy, Phillip Nelson, Joseph Ostroy, Peter Pashigian, Sam Peltzman, George Priest, John Riley, Jonathan Skinner, George Stigler, Earl Thompson, and participants at seminars at UCLA and the University of Chicago during 1977–78 for helpful suggestions and comments. Jonathan Skinner also provided valuable research assistance. The Foundation for Research in Economics and Education and the University of Chicago Law School Law and Economics Program provided Klein with research support, and the Center for Research in Government Policy and Business, University of Rochester, provided Leffler with research support.

2 Hobbes ([1651] 1955, pp. 89–90) maintains that "he that performeth first, has no assurance the other will perform after; because the bonds of words are too weak to bridle men's ambition, avarice, anger, and other Passions, without the fear of some coercive Power; which in the condition of here Nature, where all men are equal, and judges of the justness of their own fears cannot possibly be supposed."

3 This assumption is consistent with the pioneering work of Macaulay (1963), where reliance on formal contracts and the threat of explicit legal sanctions was found to be an extremely rare element of interfirm relationships. Macaulay provides some sketchy evidence that business firms prevent nonfulfillment of contracts by the use of effective nonlegal sanctions consisting primarily of the loss of future business. This "relational" nature of contracts has been recently emphasized by Macneil (1974), and also by Goldberg (1976) and Williamson (1979).

4 Nonidentification of firm output leads to quality depreciation via a standard externality argument; i.e., supply by a particular firm of lower than anticipated quality imposes a cost through the loss of future sales not solely on that firm but on all firms in the industry (see Akerlof 1970; Klein 1974).

5 For simplicity, we assume that "theft," as opposed to nonfulfillment of contract, is not possible. While "fraud," in the sense of one party to the transaction intentionally supplying less than contracted for, is analytically similar to "theft," we draw a distinction along this continuum by assuming that the government only permits "voluntary" transactions in the sense that transactors choose whom to trade with. Therefore, while consumers cannot "steal" goods, they can, in principle, pay for the goods they receive with checks that bounce; and while firms cannot rob consumers, they can, in principle, supply goods of lower than promised quality. Although we recognize the great difficulty in practice of separating the underlying government enforcement mechanisms, e.g., property law, from the private promise-enforcing mechanisms we are attempting to analyze, this distinction between theft and fraud is analytically unambiguous.

6 The notion that an increased price can serve as a means of assuring high quality supply by giving the firm a rental stream that will be lost if future sales are not made is not new. Adam Smith ([1776] 1937, p. 105) suggested this force more than 200 years ago when he noted

that "the wages of labour vary according to the small or great trust which must be reposed in the workman. The wages of goldsmiths and jewellers are everywhere superior to those of many other workmen, not only of equal, but of much superior ingenuity; on account of the precious metals with which they are intrusted. We trust our health to the physician; our fortune and sometimes our life and reputation to the lawyer and attorney. Such confidence could not safely be reposed in people of a very mean or low condition." Similar competitive mechanisms recently have been analyzed by Becker and Stigler (1974) and Klein (1974).

7 If we modify the assumptions of our model to make interconsumer communication less than perfect and allow inflows of new ignorant consumers over time and permit individuals to forget, the potential short-run cheating gain by firms would be increased. Therefore, the quality-assuring price premium would be higher than we derive below. In this case increased firm size, by making it more likely that the individuals one is sharing product-quality information with (e.g., family and friends) have purchased from the same firm, lowers the potential short-run cheating gain by essentially reducing the repurchase period.

8 The quality of the good beyond the minimum level is therefore what Nelson (1970) has labeled as an "experience" characteristic. Making the minimum quality level endogenous does not substantially change the following analysis.

9 A terminated firm cannot begin business in this industry under a new name. However, the highest valued alternative use of the entrepreneurial skills is included in salvageable fixed production costs. The firm considered here is assumed to face the same opportunities elsewhere as the firms that are honest in production of x. Therefore, the cheating firm can elect to enter a new industry.

10 Note that although x_2 may be greater or less than x_3 depending on the price premium chosen, given upward-sloping supply functions and the condition that $MC_{qh}(q) > MC_{qmin}(q)$ for all q, it must be the case that $x_4 > x_2 > x_1$.

11 The potential function of price premiums as quality guarantors is also applicable to markets in which firms face downward-sloping demands. In this case, the inability of firms to increase sales without reductions in price limits the gains available from deceptive minimum quality production as price increases. The existence of a price sufficient to guarantee quality now depends on the elasticity of demand in addition to the cost savings from quality reductions at various quantities. In addition, when price-searching firms do not have stable future demands, consumer knowledge of cost and current demand conditions is not sufficient to estimate the quality-assuring price. The anticipated future demand vis-à-vis current demand is also relevant. For example, where consumers expect a growing demand for the output of a firm that continues to produce high quality output, the rate of quasi-rent flow from high quality (or future deceptive minimum quality) production increases over time. As compared to a firm with the same initial but constant demand, the growing firm will receive a larger capital value return at any price from high quality production in the initial period. Firms facing expected demand growth will therefore require smaller quality-assuring price premiums. See Klein, McLaughlin, and Murphy (1980) for an analysis of the less than perfectly elastic firm demand case.

12 The Appendix has been deleted by the editor of this volume.

13 We can complicate our model by dropping the assumption that nondeceiving firms are anticipated to produce forever. If firms have a finite life, and the last period of production is known by both firms and consumers, there will be no premium sufficient to guarantee quality. No matter how high the premium paid by consumers for a high quality good in the last period, firms will supply "deceptive" minimum quality because there are no future sales to lose. Consumers aware of the last period will therefore demand only the minimum quality in that period. But then the next to the last period becomes the last period in the sense

that, independent of the price premium, firm wealth is maximized by supplying minimum quality and going out of business. Consumers will then only pay for minimum quality output in the next to last period, and so on. High quality will never be produced. However, the necessary unraveling of the premium solution to assure high quality requires prior consumer knowledge of a date beyond which the firm will not produce. If consumers merely know that firms have finite lives but cannot with certainty specify a date beyond which a particular firm will not exist, price premiums may assure quality. While consumers are aware that some transactions will be with firms in their last period and hence cheating will occur, the expected gain from purchasing high promised quality can be positive. Our price premium–repeat business quality enforcement mechanism is analytically equivalent in form to the "super-game" solutions to the prisoner's dilemma problem developed in the game-theory literature. A general result of that analysis is that a cooperative solution can exist if one assumes either an infinitely long super game (as we have assumed in our model), or a super game of finite length but with transactors who have sufficient uncertainty regarding the period when the super game will end (see, e.g., Luce and Raiffa [1957], pp. 97–102, or, for a more recent solution to the problem that is similar in emphasis to our approach, Telser [1980]).

14 As opposed to the Darby and Karni (1973) analysis, this particular model implies an equilibrium quantity of "fraud" equal to zero, where fraud is the difference between anticipated and actual quality. Given the symmetrical information assumptions regarding cost functions, parties to a contract know when and by how much a contract will be broken. An unanticipated broken quality contract is therefore not possible. The implicit economic (as opposed to common usage) concept of "contract" refers to anticipated outcomes and not to verbal promises or written agreements; thus there will be no broken quality "contracts."

15 If the "sunk" asset yields absolutely no consumer services, then the firm will not use it. Even though profits would be eliminated by purchase of such an asset, consumers would be indifferent between a firm that invested in the asset and a firm that did not. In a world where consumers do not possess full knowledge of cost conditions, however, use of obviously specific assets may be employed even if yielding no direct consumer service flow because they may efficiently inform consumers regarding the sunk capital cost to the firm. This is discussed in greater detail in Sec. IIIC.

16 For example, franchisers can assure quality by requiring franchisee investment in specific production capital. A general arrangement by which this is accomplished is by not permitting the franchisee to own the land upon which its investments (e.g., capital fixtures) are made. Rather, the franchiser owns or leases the land and leases or subleases it to the franchisee, thereby creating for the franchisee a large nonsalvageable asset if he is terminated by the franchiser. This highly franchiser-specific asset can therefore serve as a form of collateral and potentially eliminate any need for a price premium. See Klein (1980) for a more complete discussion of this franchising solution, including the potential reverse cheating problem that is created by such contractual arrangements.

17 Nelson's argument is based on an assumption similar to the Spence (1973)-type screening assumption regarding the lower cost to more productive individuals of obtaining education. Nelson's argument, however, is circular since consumers react to advertising only because the best buys advertise more and the best buys advertise more only because consumers buy advertised products. Schmalensee (1978) has shown that the Nelson scenario may imply "fly-by-night" producers who advertise the most and also deceptively produce minimum quality. Like Spence's signaling model, the government could, in principle, tax this investment and thereby save real resources without reducing the effectiveness of this information if consumers were aware of the tax rate. However, advertising serves many purposes. In particular, advertising also can supply valuable consumer information about the particular characteristics and availability of products. For optimality the government

would therefore have to determine the appropriate tax rate for each advertising message and consumers would have to be aware of each of these particular tax rates.

18 Mishan (1970) has argued for legislation which would require advertising to be sold separately at a price which covers advertising costs. This would completely destroy the informational value of advertising we are emphasizing here.

19 Note, however, that just as firms may deceive consumers about quality to be supplied, they may also attempt to deceive them about the magnitude of the advertising investments made, e.g., purchasing a local spot on "The Tonight Show" and advertising the advertising as if an expenditure on a national spot was made.

20 The greater is the cost to consumers of obtaining deceptively low quality, the greater will be the demand for quality assurance. The very low market share of "generic" children's aspirin (1 percent) vis-à-vis generic's share of the regular aspirin market (7 percent) is consistent with this implication (see IMS America, Ltd. 1978). Many individuals who claim "all aspirin is alike" apparently pay the extra price for their children where the costs of lower quality are greater and therefore quality assurance is considered more important.

21 Our analysis of advertising also illuminates the monopolistic competition debate. Chamberlin's (1965) distinction between production costs, defined as what is included in the "package" that passes from seller to buyer, and selling costs (e.g., advertising), which are not part of the package transferred, suggests that selling costs usefully may be considered as a privately supplied collective factor. For example, a firm which holds selling costs, such as expenditures on a store sign, constant as his sales increase does not appear to be decreasing the average "quality" of his product. Demsetz (1959, 1968) made the contrary assumption that average quality does fall as sales increase, holding selling costs constant, by merely ignoring Chamberlin's distinction and its possible theoretical significance and identifying quality costs with selling costs (aggregating both into the concept "demand increasing costs"). However, since in a monopolistically competitive environment the price premium that will assure quality depends upon the demand expected in the future, the quality incentive implied by an advertising investment also depends upon consumers' expectations about future demand. In particular, the relevant variable indicating an incentive to produce high quality is the level of advertising capital compared to anticipated future sales. Hence advertising is not a pure public good in a firm's production function as Chamberlin implicitly assumed, and the arbitrary contrary assumption made by Demsetz is possibly justifiable.

22 See Klein et al. (1980) for a complete analysis of this case applied to the FTC Coors litigation. Coors appears to have employed exclusive territories on the wholesale level and resale price maintenance on the retail level to create a sufficient premium to encourage the necessary refrigeration of their nonpasteurized beer. Implications of this analysis in terms of providing a possible rationale for similar constraints on the competitive process enforced by trade associations and government regulatory agencies are also examined.

23 Such governmental regulations, however, do not avoid the contractual problems of ex ante explicitly defining in an enforceable manner all major elements of performance. Nor do they necessarily avoid the implicit contractual conditions of a price-premium stream (created by entry restrictions, an initial forfeitable bond, and/or minimum price restraints) to effectively enforce the governmental regulations (see Klein et al. 1980). In addition, by making it illegal to supply less than the regulated quality, individuals that would voluntarily demand lower quality than the regulated standard incur a loss of consumer surplus. Distribution effects are created, since while the regulation may decrease the cost of supplying high quality output it increases the cost of supplying lower quality output.

References

Akerlof, George A. "The Market for 'Lemons': Quality Uncertainty and the Market Mechanism." *Q. J.E.* 84 (August 1970): 488–500.

Becker, Gary S., and Stigler, George J. "Law Enforcement, Malfeasance, and Compensation of Enforcers."*J. Legal Studies* 3 (January 1974): 1–18.

Chamberlin, Edward H. *The Theory of Monopolistic Competition: A Re-Orientation of the Theory of Value.* 8th ed. Cambridge, Mass.: Harvard Univ. Press, 1965.

Darby, Michael R., and Karni, Edi. "Free Competition and the Optimal Amount of Fraud." *J. Law and Econ.* 16 (April 1973): 67–88.

Demsetz, Harold. "The Nature of Equilibrium in Monopolistic Competition."*J.P.E.* 67, no. 1 (February 1959): 21–30.

———. "Do Competition and Monopolistic Competition Differ?" *J.P.E.* 76, no. 1 (January/February 1968): 146–48.

Federal Trade Commission, Office of the Federal Registrar. *Guides concerning Use of Endorsements and Testimonials in Advertising.* 16 CFR, pt. 255. Washington: Government Printing Office, 1980.

Goldberg, Victor P. "Toward an Expanded Theory of Contract." *J. Econ. Issues* 10 (March 1976): 45–61.

Hayek, Friedrich A. "The Meaning of Competition." In *Individualism and Economic Order.* Chicago: Univ. Chicago Press, 1948.

Hobbes, Thomas. *Leviathan.* Oxford: Blackwell, 1955, first published 1651.

IMS America, Ltd. *U.S. Pharmaceutical Market, Drug Stores and Hospitals, Audit of Purchases.* Bergen, N.J.: IMS America, 1978.

Klein, Benjamin. "The Competitive Supply of Money." *J. Money, Credit and Banking* 6 (November 1974): 423–53.

———. "Borderlines of Law and Economic Theory: Transaction Cost Determinants of 'Unfair' Contractual Arrangements." *A.E.R. Papers and Proc.* 70 (May 1980): 356–62.

Klein, Benjamin; Crawford, Robert G.; and Alchian, Armen A. "Vertical Integration, Appropriable Rents, and the Competitive Contracting Process." *J. Law and Econ.* 21 (October 1978): 297–326.

Klein, Benjamin; McLaughlin, Andrew; and Murphy, Kevin M. "Resale Price Maintenance, Exclusive Territories, and Franchise Termination: The Coors Case." Working Paper, UCLA, 1980.

Leffler, Keith B. "The Role of Price in Guaranteeing Quality." Working Paper no. CPB77-5, Univ. Rochester, June 1977.

Luce, R. Duncan, and Raiffa, Howard. *Games and Decisions: Introduction and Critical Survey.* New York: Wiley, 1957.

Macaulay, Stewart, "Non-Contractual Relations in Business: A Preliminary Study." *American Soc. Rev.* 28 (February 1963): 55–67.

Macneil, Ian. "The Many Futures of Contracts." *Southern California Law Rev.*47 (May 1974): 691–816.

Marshall, Alfred. *Principles of Economics: An Introductory Volume.* 8th ed. New York: Macmillan, 1949.

Mishan, Edward J. *21 Popular Economic Fallacies.* New York: Praeger, 1970.

Nelson, Phillip. "Information and Consumer Behavior." *J.P.E.* 78, no. 2 (March/April 1970): 311–29.

———. "Advertising as Information." *J.P.E.* 82, no. 4 (July/August 1974):729–54.

Schmalensee, Richard. "A Model of Advertising and Product Quality." *J.P.E.* 86, no. 3 (June 1978): 485–503.

Scitovsky, Tibor. "Some Consequences of the Habit of Judging Quality by Price." *Rev. Econ. Studies* 12, no. 2 (1945): 100–105.

Smith, Adam. *An Inquiry into the Nature and Causes of the Wealth of Nations*. New York: Modern Library, 1937, first published 1776.

Spence, A. Michael. "Job Market Signaling." *Q. J.E.* 87 (August 1973): 355–74.

Telser, Lester G. "A Theory of Self-Enforcing Agreements." *J. Bus.* 22, no. 1 (January 1980): 27–44.

Williamson, Oliver E. "Transaction-Cost Economics: The Governance of Contractual Relations." *J. Law and Econ.* 22 (October 1979): 233–61.

Review and Discussion Questions

1 What, in the context of the Klein–Leffler model, does it mean for a firm to "cheat"?
2 Define the "quality-assuring price." Explain why it can deter cheating.
3 What three conditions determine how high the quality-assuring price is?
4 Why doesn't entry of new firms erode the quality-assuring price?
5 What is the role of advertising in maintaining the quality-assuring price?
6 How does the theory explain why endorsements by celebrities are useful to consumers? How does it explain why the amount of money paid to celebrity endorsers is often publicized?

Chapter 21

CLEMENT G. KROUSE

BRAND NAME AS A BARRIER TO ENTRY: THE REALEMON CASE[1]

Introduction

THIS PAPER IS CONCERNED WITH the relationships among consumer demand for and seller supply of product information and market equilibrium: with the effect of brand name on competition, the level of prices, and the extent of product variety on one hand, and with the implications of these results for allocative efficiency and antitrust policy on the other.

Since the pioneering studies of information economics by Scitovsky [13] and Stigler [14] it has been recognized that firms supply only a limited amount of product information and consumers search out only a subset of the available brands of a given commodity. This result of non-negligible, increasing information costs means that consumers have only partial knowledge of market prices and brand characteristics. The residual ignorance in turn implies that prices need not adjust at the margin to equalize actual differences (or nondifferences) in brand quality. The literature has thus come to the understanding that, when product information is costly, some form of monopoly is the proper model of markets and not competition.

While these things have been known for some time, it is not commonly understood that the inelasticity of demand that results in this case, along with the restriction of output and the associated rise in price, does not adversely affect the allocation of resources in any remediable way. When buyers make their consumption decision on the basis of the best available information, the payment of a price in excess of that in a corresponding market with costless information can be regarded as a choice error and a market failure only if it is further presumed either that buyers should have known better or that there is an alternative organization of the industry and exchange to allow information to be provided at lower cost.

These issues are specifically important in understanding the conclusions reached in the matter of *FTC* v. *Borden, Inc. (ReaLemon)*.[2] In the Initial Decision of that case it was found that the Borden Company's ReaLemon Foods Subdivision had unlawfully monopolized the processed lemon juice market. Two key elements of ReaLemon's monopoly were noted: the "premium status" of its brand name, which was said to represent a barrier to entry, and an associated predatory pricing policy.

The Commission's Opinion endorsed the Administrative Law Judge's findings of fact and concurred in his theory of the matter, that the "successful differentiation" of the ReaLemon mark was the underlying source of that brand's monopoly.[3] While stating that a compulsory trademark licensing order was within the range of remedies it had the power to impose, the Commission nonetheless adopted a Final Order prohibiting only the "unreasonably low" pricing employed by Borden. The U.S. Court of Appeals sustained the FTC's finding of monopolization, reaffirmed its conclusions concerning the role played by product differentiation, and upheld the cease and desist order.[4] Whether these conclusions are properly justified upon a reinvestigation of the facts of the case—and particularly when the cost to consumers of determining brand quality are considered—is the present concern.

Some background

The FTC action against the ReaLemon subdivision of Borden, Inc. arose from a complaint originally lodged by ReaLemon's competitor, Golden Crown. Entering the national market for processed lemon juice roughly ten years after Borden, Golden Crown found its sales markedly affected by ReaLemon's "premium brand" status. This was an advantage, Golden Crown maintained, which required it to price its bottled juice some 10 to 15 cents less per quart to equalize. This differential and the pricing policies adopted by ReaLemon were found by the Administrative Law Judge (ALJ) to unfairly exclude Golden Crown from the market. In summary he noted:

> Borden engaged in a number of acts and practices, heretofore described . . . These acts and practices include geographically discriminatory prices, promotional allowances tailored to combat competition in particular areas where competition had arisen, granting to selected key retail stores special allowances designed to eliminate, hinder or restrict sales of competitive processed lemon juices, and taking steps selectively to reduce the retail price of its premium priced product to a level so low as to make it virtually impossible for other producers of processed lemon juice to sell their products at prices above their own cost.
>
> (Initial Decision, p. 770)[5]

Consumers, to be sure, give their trade to those brands they perceive to be best-buys on a quality-adjusted basis, then withdrawing that franchise when the best-buy status is no longer perceived to obtain. In turn, firms compete to be best-buys. When there is a history of experience and advertising exposure for some specific brand, the ALJ (and the Commission in its Final Order) argued in exception to this process of competition: that consumers become "attached" to brands, with disproportionately large price differentials being required to "detach" their custom.[6] Terming this disproportion "successful differentiation" and stressing the role of trademark in differentiating brands provided the plaintiff's theory of the ReaLemon monopoly. Is that a reasonable theory?

Brand name and information cost

With the complete absence of brand-specific information the price of all products in a competitive equilibrium will be the same and equal the marginal value of utility services supplied on average. Such an equilibrium is unstable, however, for if by private research some risk-averse (atomistic) individual surely identifies a particular product which supplies at least the average amount of the otherwise unknown quality, then he is able to better himself by the amount of the difference between the known utility services of this brand and the average taken with risk, less his information cost. If the quality determination costs are not prohibitive, then there are incentives for each consumer to search in this way and gather brand-specific information.

Generally there are economies of scale or specialization in the provision of brand information so that sellers are found to offer information in a public manner, creating the information stock which we call brand name. Given consumers are risk-averse it is in the interest of any firm with a quality level equal to or above the market average to provide evidence of this fact and thereby reduce the risk associated with the purchase of its product relative to a random choice among unknown brands. Consumers in competition then bid up the price of this differentiated brand from that based on the industry (risk discounted) average. Similarly, each firm which supplies a product equal or superior to those remaining undifferentiated has an incentive to provide brand-specific information and distinguish itself by brand name. Such a process continues until the product with the next lowest quality level is then differentiated from that with the lowest quality.

Some details of the above information process can be noted. Of first interest is the fact that brand name is used to identify a product and thereby link information to that product. This link between information and product is perfected by the use of a trademark, for the trademark proprietor has the exclusive right to use the mark for his product. In this way the trademark property rights system enables investments in brand name by assuring that others, being denied any representation by that name, cannot usefully capture returns from those investments. A seller is generally subject to less free-riding on his advertising and sales efforts, and therefore has less difficulty in capturing the gains to whatever investments he makes in increased quality and brand name, when these efforts are made specific to his mark. If, to the contrary, consumers cannot make the link from product to information clearly, then information investments yield less appropriable returns, the amount of information supplied is reduced and, in turn, investment in product quality is restricted, for it would then be more costly for the consumer to identify those brands with greater quality and therefore the individual sellers to capture the gains to such quality through higher price.

The information stock which is brand name leads to perceptions about product quality which can be altered more or less by a single product trial, and altered appreciably with a number of trials. This leads to the second aspect of brand name. If, relative to rivals, some brand name is inconsistent with its quality-adjusted price, then on actual experience consumers will revise the meaning they give to that name. Since such names have limited alternative use and therefore low salvage value, the seller's investments will be substantially forfeited. The result is that firms which cheat on their brand name forego returns to a portion, or all, of these investments.[7] There is thus a second principle: other things equal, those firms having the greatest investment in brand name and thereby the most to lose by cheating on product quality will be less likely to cheat.

Brand-specific information in the ReaLemon case

The view of the processed lemon juice market generally held in *ReaLemon* was that product information could be "costlessly" acquired by consumers, being at most the 50 cents or so required to try a single bottle of Golden Crown. A corollary to this view was that small quality differences across brands could justify only "small" price differences. On the additional assumption that Golden Crown was equivalent in quality with ReaLemon, the implication was that the lower price of Golden Crown should have led, other impediments aside, to rapid shifts in market share much in excess of that which in fact occurred. Presuming this to be a correct characterization of matters, the ALJ and Commission reasoned that Golden Crown's less than dramatic market success owed to an irrational habit of the buying public, the preference for the known ReaLemon brand regardless of its actual qualities relative to Golden Crown.[8] The alternative to this theory of irrationality lies in the value of brand-specific information and how that is provided.

What information is demanded by consumers as they purchase processed lemon juice?

First of all, variations in the quality of processed juice from bottle to bottle are to be expected. Two sources of such variations are likely: from random factors in the production process and from a producer's conscious efforts to cheat by lowering quality relative to that expected by consumers from prior experience and, more generally, brand name. While consumers no doubt value information on both the range and likelihood of such quality variations, it does not seem likely that they would be able to develop this knowledge from a single product trial. Depending on experiences, many trials of a new brand might be required to accurately establish these quality variations.[9] And, as we have noted above, when the brand name is minimal it does not provide a substantial, forfeitable "bond" to guarantee consumers that there will be no future cheating on quality. A lower price, perhaps over a continued period, will be required by consumers in lieu of such a brand name guarantee.

This leads to perhaps the most important consideration: the value consumers place on quality and, derivately, the value of information on quality. The importance of this source of value stems from two considerations. The first is based on the fact that the price to consumers of processed lemon juice is quite small both with respect to the price of the other ingredients with which it is commonly mixed and with respect to the consumer's overall food budget. Secondly, it is of note that a poor quality processed juice mixed with other ingredients results in a low quality combination. Given these conditions it is to be expected that risk-averse users of processed lemon juice would be quite price inelastic in quality demand, meaning that in their purchase they would be willing to pay a high price premium relative to the processed lemon juice price for quality assurance. It is thus reasonable to expect that long-time ReaLemon users, knowing the quality of their brand and uncertain as to the quality of an untried alternative, would demand a substantial price discount to adopt an alternative. Was Golden Crown's 10 to 15 cents per quart sufficient in this regard?

These aspects of information costs and value would seem to be important to explain Golden Crown's less than dramatic success in a more systematic and refutable way than the irrationality explanation. This conclusion is supported by two facts established at the hearing. First, the taste quality of processed lemon juice was shown to be quite sensitive to small variations in the level of the preservative ingredient and thus required strong assurances of quality control. Secondly, the price differential used by Golden Crown, although seemingly large on a percentage basis relative to the ReaLemon price, was small in all respects relative to the price of other ingredients with which the processed juice was typically used on a unit serving basis.[10] In spite of the a priori plausibility of these arguments and these few facts, it is not possible to reach any clear conclusions about the magnitude of information costs and value of information on quality, for these matters were not investigated in any precise way in the proceedings. As a result there is too little in the record on which to base a complete analysis.

Such analysis might be thought as inconsequential, for if Golden Crown and ReaLemon were presumed to be equivalent in quality, then wouldn't compulsory licensing of the ReaLemon mark at royalty rates designed to control quality really be a preferred solution to what monopoly power did exist, whatever its source? And, doesn't knowledge of this quality equivalence and the ability to make that information generally available by a compulsory licensing order mean that ReaLemon's monopoly created remediable inefficiency?

Compulsory trademark licensing: to remedy or not to remedy

ReaLemon's source of monopoly power, however large, lay in the information conveyed by its brand name. If there were no costs of providing information, then each seller of a like product would immediately be recognized as equivalent to ReaLemon, and none could possess a competitive advantage at any instant. The converse case, where there are significant costs of pre- and post-purchase quality determination, is the one of interest not only generally, but in the market specifically for processed lemon juice. While such information costs are capable of producing monopoly power, as long as there is equal access to those investments which provide quality information brand name cannot be a source of long-run monopoly power.[11] With regard to ReaLemon specifically, not only was there no evidence of such assymetrical costs, there were not even qualitative speculations as to the kinds of costs that might be important in this regard. Indeed, the limitations to ReaLemon's monopoly were quite evident: ReaLemon was demonstrably unable to raise its price either to offset rising costs or to bring its product into close substitution with fresh lemon juice, Golden Crown and other *de nova* entrants did continually increase market share by maintaining a price differential, and ReaLemon was forced by this competition to appreciably lower its prices in all geographic markets.

While this market remedy to ReaLemon's monopoly did not occur immediately, this is different from saying it would not occur at all and crucially different from saying that it is a mal-efficient correction mechanism.[12] Still, because of the time involved, wouldn't the compulsory licensing order offer a more immediate, and thus preferred, solution?

Compulsory licensing would have worked by giving the ReaLemon name, label design, and particulars of the Borden production process to all interested firms. With many brands bearing the ReaLemon label, the costs of differentiating one from the other would have been substantally increased and it would have been more difficult for any brand, including Borden's ReaLemon brand, to capture a price premium.

One immediate reaction of the ReaLemon licensees to this state of affairs would have been to use less costly procedures for manufacture and distribution, producing an inferior product coincidentally, and taking in turn the higher margin from selling at the (near) common market price.[13] Such a strategy would have worked since inferior quality (if not too inferior) would have been poorly distinguished pre-purchase from those brands having greater quality. If, in this case, the ReaLemon licensing remedy were taken to mean that any differentiating brand name would be again confiscated, there would have been no subsequent investments in brand information, no significant differentiation, and the above process would have proceeded: product quality would have uniformly deteriorated as each seller attempted to lower its cost and increase its margin relative to average market price (which would be affected only slightly by any individual firm's action).[14]

If, alternatively, there were little fear that the competitive marketing of "successfully differentiated" brands would be found to be monopolizations, then those sellers with superior skills, and motivated by the significant price premium quality appears to command in processed lemon juice, would have chosen "high" quality and invested in brand names to notify consumers of that fact. In this case an industry equilibrium would be reached in which the actual net utility service of each brand (the consumers' value of quality in excess of price) approached zero at the margin, with the extent of any residual monopoly power possessed by any brand being related only to differential production and distribution skills. It is important to note that this second alternative is precisely the market remedy which ReaLemon, Golden Crown, Seneca, Vita-Pakt, Minute Maid, and the other competitive suppliers of processed lemon juice had put in progress prior to the FTC's hearing and decisions.

Conclusions

The extent to which the descriptive features of the neoclassical model of perfect competition do not hold in some industry should not be a general basis for a finding of remediable monopoly power. Rather, antitrust policy in these matters should properly focus on whether or not the degree of rivalry in a market provides for firm demand elasticities at any instant no greater than that which are balanced at the margin with the real costs consumers have in acquiring information and sellers have in producing substitutes and informing consumers of this. The failure to adopt this perspective in antitrust proceedings leads inevitably to the wrong questions being asked and false positions being taken.

The analysis of the productive, or non-productive, purposes of brand names is the case considered here. The tie-in between a seller's product and information specific to it by the use of a trademark is an important device to prevent the critical free-rider problem in information and to make investments in brand name, and therefore investments in brand quality, more fully appropriable. Thus, when some firm creates and sustains a consumer-valued information stock by brand name this allows its product's quality to command the premium in exchange required to assure that that quality level can be supplied.

New entrants to an industry are denied the benefits of brand name created by others as a result of the exclusive rights to use given with a trademark. While such an assignment of rights surely disadvantages would-be producers, it is wrong to think that this creates a remediable imperfection in competition and a loss in market efficiency. While the trademark right generally restricts the output of the marked brand, it just as surely encourages an increase in the number of competing brands and allows a higher level of product quality to be sustained. At the optimum the rights associated with a trademark should equalize the value of additional units of the marked good with the incremental value of variety and sustainable quality. If variety and quality are valued by consumers, then some measure of the new entrant disadvantage necessarily occurs at this optimum. Given this balance has been struck by existing trademark law, then antitrust policy is left only to assure that there is equal access to all the factors necessary to produce and to create brand name. Ex post "corrections" of any brand name disadvantage when there is such equal access can only serve to destroy the efficiency of the balance.

Notes

1 Thanks to William Comanor, Benjamin Klein, Michael Mann, Stanley Ornstein, and Richard Schmalensee for helpful comments. The Research Program in Competition and Business Policy at UCLA provided support for the research and writing.

2 *FTC v. Borden, Inc.*, 92 FTC 669 (1978), hereafter referred to as *ReaLemon*.

3 See Commission Opinion and Final Order pp. 780–81 and 790–91, the Separate Opinion of Chairman Pertschuk pp. 810–11, and the Separate Opinion of Commissioner Pitosky pp. 820–31.

4 *Borden, Inc.* v. *FTC*, No. 79–3028, CA 6 (1982).

5 During the FTC hearing several comparisons of prices with costs were made. Except possibly for a brief period in late 1973 for sales to Acme Markets in Philadelphia, there was no evidence that ReaLemon sold below estimates of its average total cost. While the issue of whether ReaLemon sold below Golden Crown's average total cost was also considered, the ALJ specifically concluded that ReaLemon was not sold below any "relevant" cost, see Initial Decision, pp. 179, 187, and 192. Nonetheless, it was stated by the ALJ that Borden had sold at "unreasonably" and "extraordinarily" low prices which forced its competitors to price near their costs, Initial Decision, pp. 193, 200. The Commission concluded that the "unreasonably" low prices had the effect of injuring competition, see Opinion and Final Order pp. 798–801. Although Borden stated that an "unreasonably low price" criteria for predatory pricing was too vague and unenforceable, the Court of Appeals (at Section VI) upheld the Commission's use of that rule, and decided not to involve the "price less than average variable cost" test offered generally by Areeda–Turner

[3] or the "price less than average total cost" test specifically proposed by Commissioner Pitofsky in his Separate Opinion pp. 820–21.

6 This view of the link between advertising and brand loyalty is a remnant of Kaldor's [8] conjecture. What systematic evidence exists on the subject does not suggest that advertising is an important determinant of brand loyalty. Lambin [10, 117–18], for example, found that buyer "inertia" (his empirical counterpart to brand loyalty) was greatly affected by product qualities, but not necessarily advertising. His conclusion is that advertising influences brand loyalty only to the extent that it supplies product information. Massey and Frank [II] provide strong evidence that price and advertising elasticities are the same for loyal and non-loyal consumers. And, Vernon's [15] investigation of intermarket differences in promotion expenditures on therapeutic drugs specifically found that promotion and the derivative brand name created did not impose barriers to entry, but were a "means of entry." In a more systematic review of the literature. Engel *et al.* [7, Chapter 23] draw similar conclusions.

7 Klein and Leffler [9] show in detail the efficacy of consumer reliance on specific investments by sellers. In addition to specific physical assets which may act to differentiate the brand and form a "bond" which may be forfeited (because of its low value in an alternative use), a future stream of price premiums received for the higher level of quality is also forfeited upon cheating.

8 This irrational behavior was also said to enable Borden to price in a predatory fashion: with its price above average cost, but Golden Crown's below that level.

New entrants to an industry will generally find it necessary to offer compensation to offset the consumer's cost of using a product relatively unknown in quality. Price, being relatively visible (pre-purchase), commonly becomes the basis for the compensating difference. Not only does the lower relative price provide immediate sales, the consumer experience contributes to the entrant's brand name and affects future sales. Because price has this investment character its measurement must be made with care when there is concern with predatory behavior. Any comparison of price with cost would have to be based upon a (volume) weighted average of the present price and the (present value of) future, higher price occuring with the created brand name. A rough estimate at the present value of Golden Crown's brand name investments created in this manner can be found in the terms of its 1974 acquisition. In that merger Seven-Up Inc. paid approximately one-half million dollars in goodwill and committed itself to another $1.75 million in contingent sales performance payments.

9 Demsetz's [6] analysis of relatively rapid market share changes in the frozen orange juice market is not directly applicable here for at least two reasons. First, frozen orange juice does not require a preservative and thus does not involve the major quality problem in bottled lemon juice. Secondly, frozen orange juice is usually consumed by itself (with only added water) and therefore the quality verification problem is easier (i.e., the possibility of having a large number of other ingredients spoiled by a low quality orange juice is much less important).

10 Golden Crown commonly maintained a 10–15 cent differential below ReaLemon's average 50–60 cent per quart price, which represented a 15 to 25 percent range difference. Notice, however, that a 15 cent price difference per quart would represent less than a 0.5 cent difference per one-ounce serving.

11 Schmalensee [12] describes conditions under which uncertainty about product quality make a profitable "pioneering" brand immune from entry. In this model the order-of-entry disadvantage arises not from cost differences, but from the fact that the would-be entrant's demand schedule coincides with that of the pioneer only for prices distinctly

below the pioneer's price. This demand schedule difference owes specifically to the restricted set of pricing strategies Schmalensee considers in an attempt to free his analysis from game-theoretic complications. While important theoretically, the "drastic simplifying assumptions" of his model limits its practical usefulness.

12 It would, of course, be wrong to neglect the increasing cost ReaLemon's rivals faced in accelerating their rate of brand name development. Clarke [4] indirectly provides evidence of these costs, verifying Alchian's [2] general proposition that the cost of any productive activity is directly related to its time rate. During the adjustment period ReaLemon, having first seized the opportunity to develop brand name, enjoyed the associated gains.

13 The fact that ReaLemon was to be a compulsory licensor in the remedy suggests that the simple one-half-of-one-percent royalty fee suggested by the ALJ would have been inadequate to assure quality control. First, the compulsory licensing order means that the due care ReaLemon would normally exercise in the selection of licensees would not have been available, so that ex post quality monitoring costs could not have been appropriately minimized. Second, the ALJ's order gave the direct supervision of licensee product quality control to an independent third party (whose costs ReaLemon was obligated to pay), which surely would have increased ReaLemon's costs of quality assurance. Third, the threat of ultimate termination which might otherwise be exercised to achieve quality standards did not appear to be provided for under the Initial Decision. These factors pose a number of questions not only about ReaLemon's incentives to assure quality, but its actual ability to do so.

14 Such a "lemons equilibrium" was first described by Akerlof [1]. See also Craswell [5].

References

1 Akerlof, G. "The Market for 'Lemons': Qualitative Uncertainty and the Market Mechanism." *Quarterly Journal of Economics*, August 1970, 488–500.

2 Alchian, A. "Costs and Outputs," in *Readings in Microeconomics*, edited by W. Breit and H. Hockman. New York: McGraw-Hill, 1971, 2nd ed.

3 Areeda, P. and D. F. Turner. "Predatory Pricing and Related Practices under Section 2 of the Sherman Act." *Harvard Law Review*, February 1975, 697–733.

4 Clarke, D. "Econometric Measurement of the Duration of the Advertising Effect on Sales." Marketing Science Institute, Cambridge, Mass., Report No. 75–106, April 1975.

5 Craswell, R. "Trademarks, Consumer Information, and Barriers to Competition." FTC Policy Planning Issues Paper, 1979.

6 Demsetz, H. "The Effect of Consumer Experience on Brand Loyalty and the Structure of Market Demand." *Econometrica*, January 1962, 22–33.

7 Engel, J., D. Kollat, and R. Blackwell. *Consumer Behavior*. Hinsdale, Ill.: Dryden Press, 1973.

8 Kaldor, N. "The Economic Aspects of Advertising." *Review of Economic Studies*, 1949–1950, 1–27.

9 Klein, B. and K. Leffler. "The Role of Market Forces in Assuring Contractual Performance." *Journal of Political Economy*, August 1981, 615–41.

10 Lambin, J. *Advertising, Competition, and Market Conduct in Oligopoly Over Time*. Amsterdam: North Holland, 1976.

11 Massey, W. and R. Frank. "Short-term Price and Demand Effects in Selected Market Segments." *Journal of Marketing Research*, May 1965, 171–85.

12 Schmalensee, R. "Product Differentiation Advantages of Pioneering Brands." *American Economic Review*, June 1982, 349–65.

13 Scitovsky, T. "Ignorance as a Source of Oligopoly Power." *American Economic Review*, June 1961, 213–25.

14 Stigler, G. "The Economics of Information." *Journal of Political Economy*, June 1961, 213–25.

15 Vernon, J. "Concentration, Promotion, and Market Share Stability in the Pharmaceutical Industry." *Journal of Industrial Economics*, July 1971, 246–66.

Review and Discussion Questions

1 What is the economic purpose of trademarks?

2 What did the Administrative Law Judge conclude in the ReaLemon case?

3 What, according to the article, is a key characteristic of preserved lemon juice?

4 ReaLemon's 15 to 25 percent price premium equaled how much per quart? How does the Klein–Leffler theory of a quality-assuring price premium apply to ReaLemon's product?

5 Does the article conclude ReaLemon had monopoly power? Why or why not?

Chapter 22

Steven N. Wiggins and David G. Raboy

PRICE PREMIA TO NAME BRANDS: AN EMPIRICAL ANALYSIS[1]

I Introduction

A LONG-STANDING ISSUE in economics concerns the relative importance of objective quality factors, and more subjective influences, in the price-setting process. This issue is particularly controversial in the context of less than perfectly competitive markets where brand-name and generic goods compete side-by-side. Many economists contend that even for goods with highly visible brand-names or trademarks, objective measures of product quality primarily drive prices, while others argue that subjective "product differentiation" factors are more important. The former school contends that brand-names and the associated price premia are efficiency enhancing. The brand-name (or equivalent) serves as a marker for higher quality, and purchasers accordingly pay a price premium as compensation for a quality "guarantee." The latter school contends that brand differentiation is a barrier to entry which impedes consumer choice.[2] Empirical resolution of the issue is elusive due to the difficulty of separating objective quality dimensions from more subjective product differentiation variables for econometric purposes.

This paper empirically examines factors affecting price premia for a specific but interesting market: bananas sold in North America.[3] The banana market is interesting because both objective and subjective dimensions of quality may affect prices, and because there is quantitative data that can isolate dimensions of quality econometrically. Well-known brand-names compete with unbranded production, substantial price variability exists among brands and between branded and unbranded bananas, there is substantial market concentration, and there is evidence of quality-enhancing investment in intangible capital.

There are three well-known companies selling in the North America banana market: Chiquita, Dole, and Del Monte. Although less concentrated in recent years, the market for bananas has been concentrated.[4] As Table 22.1 illustrates, in 1988 Dole

Table 22.1 Banana prices and market shares by company

Company	Weighted average prices by year						Overall average price	1988 market share
	1985	1986	1987	1988	1989	1990		
Chiquita	$6.84	$7.39	$6.62	$8.08	$8.49	$8.63	$7.67	26.94%
Dole	$7.10	$7.49	$6.75	$8.20	$8.63	$8.63	$7.82	29.36%
Del Monte	$6.17	$6.64	$6.13	$7.48	$7.92	$7.90	$7.02	16.78%
Parker-Turbana	$5.45	$6.20	$5.54	$6.94	$7.58	$7.56	$6.57	10.76%
Noboa	$6.19	$6.73	$5.72	$7.47	$7.76	$7.78	$6.98	7.12%

had a 29 percent market share, Chiquita a 27 percent market share, Del Monte a 17 percent market share, and Parker-Turbana (a generic company) an 11 percent market share; the top four sellers held 84 percent of the market.[5] Prices of individual companies vary considerably even within the branded product segment. Table 22.1 also presents weighted average prices by company and year. From 1985 to 1990 average first unrelated-party prices (for 40 pound boxes of bananas) ranged from the high end of $7.82 (Dole) and $7.67 (Chiquita), to an intermediate price of $7.02 (Del Monte) and $6.98 (Noboa), to a low end of $6.57 for Parker-Turbana.

The existence of branding and market concentration would appear initially to support the attribution of price premia to subjective product differentiation. But such a conclusion would be premature. Further observation establishes differences in the rates of investment in quality attributes, sourcing, and other activities, all of which may be related to price differences. Sufficient data exist for the North America banana market to separate some objective from subjective factors and to address several questions: What explains price premia between branded and unbranded bananas? What is the reason for price differences among branded bananas? Are the observed price premia Klein–Leffler quality-related premia tied to specific intangible capital investments, or are they simply associated with product differentiation from advertising in a concentrated market? If they are Klein–Leffler premia, how are price premia related to costs? This paper addresses these issues econometrically.

The remainder of the paper is organized as follows. Section II provides additional background regarding the banana industry, and lays out the empirical model. Section III discusses estimation, presents the econometric analysis, and discusses the findings. Section IV concludes.

II Background: pricing, market structure, and quality

II(i) Characteristics of the market

The five companies previously cited compete in a market where the majority of bananas are sold directly to retail supermarket chains such as Safeway and Giant. Typically, a regional supermarket buyer will purchase bananas at different prices from several suppliers, but will sell all bananas at retail for the same price at a point in time: a weighted-average price plus a markup, regardless of source.[6] That all bananas, regardless of source, sell at the same price at retail is consistent with the concept of a "search" good, where all quality attributes are observable by the consumer.[7] At pre-retail where banana companies sell, however, bananas are "experience" goods with unknown quality characteristics and it is in this market that price variability is evident. Bananas are purchased unseen by supermarkets while they are en route from production sources, and quality attributes can only be observed upon delivery to the retailer.

Bananas consumed in the United States are grown on large plantations in Central and South America, either owned by integrated banana companies or tied to such companies through long-term supply arrangement.[8] In either case, the buying company makes direct investments, or provides low-interest capital to the plantation owners, which lead to long-term buyer–seller relationships facilitating the governance of quality control at the production stage. The same quality standards apply to export-bound production, whether originating from vertically integrated facilities or those governed by long-term contract.

Long distance transportation of bananas from Central and South America to North America presents a major quality-control problem. The transport distances and bananas' delicate ripening process require that bananas be harvested when green. Processes are then needed to delay ripening until it can be induced by supermarkets in special ripening rooms according to rigid stocking schedules. Ripening predictability is a key element of inventory efficiency. To control ripening, bananas need refrigeration within a narrow temperature band, preferably from when they are cleaned and packed in boxes at the plantation until they reach ripening rooms. Quality problems associated with unpredictable ripening are exacerbated by the fruit's susceptibility to bruising, which results from frequent handling of boxes.

There are two primary shipment methods, the choice of which affects product quality. The low-tech method is to stack boxes on large pallets, but this requires frequent handling and leads to bruising as individual pallets are loaded onto trucks, unloaded dockside, reloaded shipboard, and re-handled at each additional transportation stage. This low-tech method also leads to uneven temperature controls as trucks are typically unrefrigerated. On-ship refrigeration is also uneven because in the large open holds of refrigerated "reefer" ships temperature variability is the rule, leading to ripening unpredictability, and therefore spoilage and waste.

High-tech shipment requires that fruit be shipped in specially designed refrigerated semi-truck "containers," in which pallets are stacked and sealed at the plantation. The containers are driven to the dock, and loaded directly onto special ships, minimising handling. The containers also have individual refrigeration and atmosphere control units so that the fruit is refrigerated both in transit and at dockside. These individual units also allow uniform temperature control and monitoring for each individual container during ocean transit, maximizing the predictability of ripening and minimizing spoilage losses. Containerized shipment enhances the quality of fruit for buyers; therefore the choice of shipment method clearly is a measurable quality dimension. Some companies have invested considerable capital in the specialized banana container systems while others have not, and even container-intensive companies still ship substantial quantities via the traditional method, gradually replacing older ships with container ships.

Although not a traditional quality dimension, banana-company sourcing may be important to buyers due to the potential for supply disruption from storms and hurricanes, labor disruptions, political strife, disease and pest infiltration, and transportation problems in production countries. Some banana companies source from multiple countries, while others concentrate their sourcing in a single country. Since country-specific problems can cut off supplies and because banana companies give preferential treatment to existing customers when supplies are tight, diversity of sourcing becomes a valuable service to a buyer. Hence supermarkets may prefer "diverse-sourcing" companies because information costs regarding potential disruptions are greater for the supermarkets than for the banana companies.

Despite these preferences for containerised fruit and diverse sourcing, supermarket buyers have an incentive to diversify across banana companies. Supermarkets will pay a sourcing premium to ensure supplies, and will pay extra for containerized fruit, and then augment their supplies from other sources, saving these premia. For example, a rational purchasing strategy would be to purchase a certain percentage of high quality fruit where ripening can be delayed and controlled; and fill the remainder with low price bananas which may ripen unpredictably and have a greater proportion of damaged fruit. As the unpredictable fruit begins to ripen, it is immediately stocked for retail sale, augmented by the more predictable fruit as needed. Damaged fruit is discarded or sold to the sub-premium trade. The result is that retail buyers may face the same price in a given store at a point in time, but there are quality, potential brand-name, and price differences in the pre-retail market. Similarly, supermarkets will pay a premium to insure some supplies if there is a disruption, but then augment such supplies with cheaper bananas to some extent.

The final dimension of potential price premia is brand recognition: The reader should note that there are competing explanations for the reasons brand-name recognition leads to brand loyalty. One is found in the discussion of trademarks in Landes and Posner [1987]. They stress that "firms with strong trademarks ... will command higher prices for their brands not because of market power but because the search costs associated with their brands are lower." Others, e.g. Scherer [1980], argue that product differentiation is artificial and unrelated to quality. The existence of brands does not necessarily indicate that purely subjective factors are producing observed price premia. A competitive explanation would tie brands to quality-enhancing investment. If the objective factors do not explain price premia while brand existence does, then the suspicion would be that the price premia are caused by purely subjective factors.

A final note on advertising is necessary. With the notable exception of the well-known Chiquita banana ads directed at end consumers through various media, very little promotional activity is directed at brand strengthening. Consumer promotion consists primarily of payments to supermarkets who then advertise weekly specials, often focusing on price, in local outlets such as newspapers. To the extent that traditional brand advertising exists, it is directed at supermarket buyers through trade press advertising, and stresses quality dimensions.

These three factors, shipment method, sourcing, and brand-name, can be analyzed in an econometric pricing model to isolate their respective effects. In such a model shipment method and diversified sourcing represent objective quality factors, while brand recognition in the absence of significant contribution from the other two factors would represent the effect of subjective product differentiation on price premia.

II(ii) The econometric model and the data

Following the arguments above, the basic hedonic pricing model is as follows:

$$P_{icjt} = \alpha + \sum_{i=1}^{2} \beta_i X_i + \sum_{j=1}^{3} \gamma_j Z_j + \sum_{t=1}^{6} \delta_t D_t + \epsilon_{icjt} \tag{1}$$

where P_{icjt}=the price charged to supermarkets for bananas with characteristics I, sold by company c, in region j, in year t, where X_1=container shipment dummy, X_2=individual company fixed effects, Z_2=a set of regional dummy variables where $j=1$ (East), $j=2$ (Central), $j=3$ (West), and D_t=a set of individual year dummy variables and t denotes year. The various components of (1) are measured as follows.

The container variable takes a value of one for premium containerized shipments and is zero otherwise. There is considerable variability among and within companies over the sample period with respect to the use of container shipments. The year fixed effects variables account for any systematic differences in prices across years, correcting for the net effect of supply or demand variation. Region fixed effects in turn account for differences in shipping distances and cost.

To separate diverse-sourcing effects from brand-name influences is somewhat difficult, but company fixed effects variables attempt to provide this separation. Companies that feature diverse sourcing include Dole, Chiquita, and Del Monte; over the sample period each sourced more than 20 percent of supplies from at least three countries, and each has major supplies in both Central and South America. In contrast, the two other companies in the sample, Noboa and Turbana, obtained more than 85 percent of their supplies from a single South American country. Hence we will test for sourcing by determining if the bananas sold by Noboa and Turbana sell at a discount holding other factors constant.

We also use company level fixed effects to glean as much information as possible regarding the impact of brand-names. Market research (Vance [1987]) provides evidence that brand extension does not occur for bananas. As a result, only 7 percent of consumers identifying brand as important identified Del Monte as preferred. Companies that have a more recognizable brand-name include Dole (30 percent brand preferences) and Chiquita (60 percent), who have developed a brand-name tied more directly to bananas. Based on this information it may be plausible to define "brand-name" companies as those having a recognizable brand-name by at least one quarter of those consumers who expressed a brand preference based on market research. Under this definition, the brand-name companies are Dole and Chiquita. Another formulation would include only Chiquita, with more than a 50 percent brand recognition, as a brand-name company. Under either formulation, the significance of the company fixed effects variables, relative to the omitted company, should allow at least tentative conclusions regarding brand-name influence.

The data set includes prices at the point of the first unrelated party sale (to retailers and wholesalers) of 40 pound boxes of bananas for five companies in the three regions for the period 1985–1990. The data report separately total shipments and average prices for both containerized and noncontainerized shipments by company, year, and region.[9] The unbalanced panel has a potential of 180 observations, but there were only 106 observations available because some companies did not sell into some regions in some years.

Summary statistics show a mean of 8,196 thousand boxes per observation and a standard deviation of 4,344, a mean price of $7.31 and a standard deviation of $1.14, and that 25 percent of shipments were containerized. Because of concern about correlation of error terms, even with the year, region, and company fixed effects, we estimated (1) using a Huber correction of OLS standard errors.

III Estimation and results

Table 22.2 presents the regression results. The model explains a large share of the considerable price variation in this market and the relevant coefficients are all of the expected sign and statistically significant. For ease of interpretation the omitted firm fixed effect is Del Monte, a company with diverse sourcing but without brand recognition.

The containerization variable estimate indicates a $.98 per box premium for containerized fruit relative to palletized fruit. The intra- and inter-company variation in the usage of containers, moreover, substantiates that the econometric estimates are directly tied to price differences that individual companies experience when they containerize their fruit. Dole is the leader in containerization, and shipped 62 percent of its bananas in containers in the sample period with the annual percentages varying from 41 percent in 1985 to 81 percent in 1990. Chiquita shipped 41 percent of its shipments in containers and Turbana shipped about 10 percent. Del Monte and Noboa both relied exclusively on palletized shipments. To assess the net impact of the container premium on price differences among companies, these container intensities are employed. Based on the container percentages for Dole and Chiquita, Dole's average company price premium deriving solely from containerization is $.59 per box and Chiquita's is $.39. Comparing these figures with observed intercompany premia shows that the container premium is capable of explaining about two-thirds to three-quarters of the observed differences in the average selling prices of the top two companies compared to the remaining firms.

Identification of a Klein–Leffler type premium requires not just a price premium, but a premium above long run costs. Since containerization is a more capital-intensive transportation method, part of the price premium reflects normal returns to incremental tangible capital and other variable costs. To determine whether containerization involves a net premium over these costs one subtracts them from the price premium. We estimated total per box variable and tangible capital costs for traditionally shipped bananas to be between 85 and 95 percent of those associated with container shipments, depending on capacity utilization. Since containerization costs depend on capacity, we average the incremental costs of containerization across these high and low capacity utilization extremes. Using such a procedure, container shipping requires costs of roughly 33 cents a box above those for traditional methods. Comparing these costs with

Table 22.2 Regressions estimates of determinants of brand-name premia 1985–90

Dependent variable	Price
Constant *	7.820
	(.136)
Container *	.981
	(.097)
Chiquita	.144
	(.120)
Dole	.090
	(.123)
Noboa *	−.246
	(.145)
Turbana *	−.584
	(.126)
1985 *	−1.551
	(.133)
1986 *	−1.077
	(.133)
1987 *	−1.737
	(.128)
1988 *	−.491
	(.126)
1989 *	−.108
	(.125)
East *	.411
	(.091)
West *	−.111
	(.101)
F	(12,93) = 54.48

Standard errors are in parentheses
*Significant at the 5 percent level.

the $.98 estimated premium indicates containerization generates quasi-rents per box of roughly 65 cents. Hence there are substantial returns above the direct costs of containerization, lending substantial support to the notion that there are Klein–Leffler type reputational premia associated with containerized fruit.

One portion of these returns is associated with the sunk investments needed for development of a containerized transportation system. Although containerized shipping would appear to be a standard transportation technique, this is not the case for the specially designed containers and systems unique to the banana trade. A container system involves substantial research and development to create assets unique to banana transportation; creation of an information system to track containerization equipment, including containers, generator sets for refrigeration, and truck chassis in both the producing country and the destination country (where the customer will have possession of this capital for significant periods of time); data systems to monitor, record and control temperature and atmosphere while bananas are in containers;

new maintenance systems; and other firm-specific knowledge. Still, the return to containerization above direct costs is sufficiently large as to suggest that at least a portion of the return represents a quasi-rent to innovation—that is to the early development and adoption of the container system.

These returns suggest that containerization should grow over time, as it has. Dole, Chiquita, and Turbana increased their containerized shipments in the sample, making large, sunk investments in container ships, dockside facilities, containers and other equipment. This process is slowed due to the large investments all companies have in older, long-lived reefer ships. Of the major companies, only Del Monte continues to ship all bananas via the older technology.

Next we turn to diverse sourcing. The two companies without diverse sourcing are Noboa and Turbana. Since the omitted fixed effect is Del Monte, which features diverse sourcing but has little brand recognition in bananas, the best available information in the data for the sourcing effect is the fixed effects of Noboa and Turbana. For both companies the estimated fixed effects are negative as predicted by the analysis of sourcing. Further, an F-test simultaneously restricting both fixed effects to zero is rejected with an F-value of 6.96 (F(2,93)), which is highly significant at the one percent level. The overall point estimate for the discount can be calculated and is also large at $.45 per box.[10] More conservatively, one could estimate the sourcing effect as the fixed effect of Noboa, the smaller of the two fixed effects for the two companies without diverse sourcing, yielding a coefficient of $.25, which is also significant at the 5 percent level. Hence these data offer support for a substantial premium for companies with diverse sourcing, through one should exercise caution in the interpretation since the effects are estimated through company level fixed effects.

The analysis for brand-names is similar in methodology, but the estimated effects of brand-name recognition on price is small and insignificant. In particular both Dole and Chiquita have recognizable brand-names while Del Monte, the omitted fixed effect, does not. Since all three companies have diverse sourcing the difference in fixed effects between Del Monte and Dole and Chiquita provide the best available information regarding brand-name.

One can test for brand-name by testing the hypothesis that the fixed effect for Dole and Chiquita is simultaneously zero. The F-statistic is .47 (F(2,93)), which is not significant. Further, neither of the individual fixed effects of Chiquita or Dole is close to significant, with t-values of 1.2 and .7 respectively, and the point estimates are also small at $.14 and $.09 respectively. Hence these data provide no statistical support for a significant brand premium for either or both of the companies identified as having a well-recognized brand-name by consumers expressing a brand preference.

IV Summary and conclusions

This paper has examined the factors that affect pricing in the banana market. The analysis considered the potential effects on prices of two quality-related factors; the method of shipment and the diversity of sourcing; and a measure of subjective product differentiation relating to brand identity. In this market, econometric evidence supports the hypothesis that quality factors explain the majority of price differences. The price premia associated with containerization are quite robust and explain the bulk of inter-company price differences. Container premia explain two-thirds to three-quarters of observed price differences. Further, while container premia are partially absorbed by returns to tangible investments, there appears to be a residual premium to containerization, likely reflecting a return to intangible investments in the container system—either as a pure opportunity cost of investment or a quasi-rent to innovation.

Diversity of source is a less powerful explanatory factor, and the techniques used in this paper require caution in interpretation, but the evidence suggests that sourcing is important. In contrast, there is no evidence in these data that subjective product differentiation in the form of brand-names has a statistically or economically significant effect on price.

The results must of course be interpreted with caution. The analysis covers only a single market, and bananas may differ significantly from other markets. Nonetheless, quality clearly matters in other fruit and vegetable markets, and name-brand companies sell for significant premia in those markets as well. The analysis presented for bananas may provide a glimpse of a price/quality relationship in other fruit and vegetable markets.

Notes

1 We would like to thank Severin Borenstein, Tom Saving, Curt Taylor, Wes Wilson, two anonymous referees, and Lawrence White for helpful comments. Financial support for Wiggins' research from the Texas Higher Education Coordinating Board Advanced Research Program is gratefully acknowledged.

2 See Klein and Leffler [1981], Shapiro [1982], De Vany and Saving [1983], and Landes and Posner [1987] for examples of work contending that various measures of quality are central determinants of pricing, and Bain [1956], Scherer [1980], and numerous others who contend that simple "product differentiation" is a key determinant of price.

3 The reader should note that the analysis focuses on sales of bananas to grocery stores, which is the same level of the market where there is alleged to be "market power" by sellers of branded products (e.g. Tide detergent and Green Giant vegetables) in standard product differentiation arguments advanced by Bain, Scherer, and others. Still, there are differences between bananas and other products as noted below.

4 It is also arguable that "bananas" are a subset of a broader market for fresh fruit, a market that would be unconcentrated. Some evidence of cross-elasticity exists (see Huang [1993] and Thompson et al. [1990]).

5 The reader should note that these shares are representative for the period; the largest share change in the sample was Chiquita's decline from a 29 percent share in 1985 to a 25 percent share in 1990.

6 Interview with Safeway Corp. executives, Landover, Maryland, April 1991.

7 It is also consistent with the concept of a premium supermarket produce section, where only top-quality produce is displayed. Supermarkets typically place reputational value on the quality of their produce sections. Interview with Safeway Corp. executives, Landover, MD April 1991.

8 The degree of integration varies across countries. In 1992, in Honduras, 57 percent of land associated with export-grade banana plantations was owned by vertically integrated firms. In Costa Rica, the ownership percentage was 58 percent while in Ecuador,

Colombia, Panama, and Guatemala, the percentage of plantation land owned by vertically integrated firms was 8, 51, 72, and 100 percent respectively. Most other supplies were governed by long-term contracts containing strict quality requirements, typically running at least eight years and covering a producer's entire export-grade output.

9 Data for the estimation were gathered from Boca Raton Market Research on behalf of Castle and Cooke, Co., the parent company of Dole during the sample period.

10 Given the use of the fixed effects model where sourcing is measured by the joint effect of Noboa and Turbana, the exercise in the text amounts to calculating the joint fixed effect; the easiest way to mechanically carry out the calculation is to reestimate restricting these companies fixed effects to be the same.

Review and Discussion Questions

1 What are two explanations for the price premia of brand names?
2 Why is the banana market a good market for testing the two explanations?
3 What is the relevance of long-distance transportation and diverse sourcing to the test?
4 What are the results of the test? Which theory seems to better explain the price premia for brand-named bananas?

Chapter 23

John R. Lott, Jr.

A SOUR LEMON STORY

A new car that was bought for $20,000 cannot be resold for more than perhaps $15,000. Why? Because the only person who might logically want to resell a brand-new car is someone who found the car to be a lemon. So even if the car isn't a lemon, a potential buyer assumes that it is. He assumes that the seller has some information about the car that he, the buyer, does not have—and the seller is punished for this assumed information.

And if the car *is* a lemon? The seller would do well to wait a year to sell it. By then, the suspicion of lemonness will have faded; by then, some people will be selling their perfectly good year-old cars, and the lemon can blend in with them, likely selling for more than it is truly worth.[1]

NICE STORY—except that it's wrong. In fact, the widespread perception that a new car loses substantial value as soon as a buyer drives it off the lot is really just a myth, as we shall see.

In a market economy, if anomalies like the well-known lemon problem described by Levitt and Dubner occur, they inevitably create a financial incentive for entrepreneurs to solve them.[2] Suppose you buy a car for $20,000 and decide for whatever reason to resell it quickly. Assuming nothing is wrong with the car, you have a $20,000 car with just a few miles on it, but according to Levitt and Dubner you can only sell it for $15,000 because buyers believe that people only try to sell a new car so quickly when there's something seriously wrong with it. What do you do? Do you really sell the car for a $5,000 loss?

Here is the real question: can you convince someone for, let's say, $4,000 that there is nothing wrong with your car? What about for $500? Could you hire the car's original manufacturer to inspect the car and certify that it's in brand new condition? If you could do this for $500, and inform potential buyers about the certification in your advertisements, you could likely sell the car for the full $20,000, earning for yourself $19,500—not $15,000.

There are, in fact, lots of other possible solutions. For example, car manufacturers also allow warrantees to be transferred to new owners. Whether the warrantee is for three years/36,000 miles or five years/60,000 miles, a person who buys a lemon will not be stuck with it, even if he is the second owner. Furthermore, some places allow you to return a used car for a full refund. For instance, *CarSense,* a certified used car dealer in the Philadelphia area, offers full refunds for cars returned within five days of purchase.[3] And of course, these resale companies want to maintain a reputation for screening out any problematic cars.

Luckily for us, the lemon thesis can easily be tested. I analyzed the prices of fifty-five certified used cars—all 2006 models—in the Philadelphia area, comparing the manufacturers' suggested retail price (MSRP) for brand new cars with the certified used price and the Kelly Bluebook price.[4] The Kelly Bluebook price "reflects a vehicle's actual selling price and is based on tens of thousands of recent real sales transactions from auto dealers across the United States."[5] I looked at forty used cars that were less than a year old, all with about 15,000 miles on them. These were chosen to divine what used cars sell for when they are about a year old. An additional fifteen used cars had been driven less than 5,000 miles on them, averaging 3,340 miles.

One thing immediately became clear: used cars with only a few thousand miles on them sell for almost the same price as when new. (See Table 23.1.) The certified used car price was on average just 3 percent less than the new car MSRP. And it was 3 percent higher than the new car Bluebook prices. The Kelly Bluebook further indicates that the private-transaction used car price was only 4 percent less than the new car Bluebook prices.[6] One explanation for such a small discount on private transactions—in which buyers can't even rely on a brand name dealer's certification—is that manufacturer warrantees still protect buyers.

I called Kelly Bluebook to check if the sample I had was representative and was told that a study of all the cars in their sample would have yielded a similar result; there is surely no 25 percent drop in a car's price as soon as you drive it off the lot. Even more damning, the price of these virtually new cars occasionally rises even above the MSRP. The Kelly Bluebook representatives claim that in order to maintain strong resale price values and prevent customers from feeling as if the dealer is taking advantage of them, manufacturers often ensure that dealers cannot sell their cars— even the most popular models—at more than the MSRP.

If the lemon thesis had been correct and "the seller would do well to wait a year to sell it," as Levitt and Dubner claim, then used cars that are about a year old should not sell for much less than those with only a few thousand miles on them. But, indeed, they do sell for a lot less. Cars that are a year old have substantially lower prices. The certified used car price for these older cars was 14 percent lower than the new car MSRP and 8 percent lower than the new car Bluebook prices.

Notes

1 Levitt and Dubner, *Freakonomics* (2005 ed.), 67.
2 The lemons argument has actually been around for decades, though the person who first brought up the concern realized that there could be strong forces to solve the problem.

Table 23.1 Do car prices plummet as soon as they leave the show room? Looking at used cars being sold with about 3,000 miles (comparing manufacturer suggested retail price with Kelly Bluebook prices and certified used prices for the same 2006 models on September 27, 2006)

Car make and model (All 2006)	Mileage	Transmission	Engine	Drive	Features	MSRP	Kelly Bluebook New Price (actual transaction price of new cars)	Kelly Bluebook Used Price	Certified Used Price (source: Yahoo Auto)	Kelly Bluebook Trade-in Excellent Condition	Kelly Bluebook Private Party Sale Value	Certified Used Price/Kelly Bluebook New	Private Party Sale/Kelly Bluebook New
Ford F150 SXT Supercab 5 1/2	3,841	Automatic	8 cyl	2WD	Standard	$26,300	$23,974	$25,820	$21,595	$17,075	$21,365	90%	89%
Ford Focus 2x4 Sedan 5	4,873	Automatic	4 cyl	2WD	Standard	$14,295	$13,734	$14,215	$14,387	$11,475	$12,495	105%	91%
GMC Canyon 4x4 Crew Cab SLE	1,143	Automatic	4 cyl	4WD	Standard	$24,960	$23,033	$26,470	$22,366	$20,100	$23,210	97%	101%
Toyota Tacoma 4x4 Doublecab	4,483	Automatic	6 cyl	4WD	Standard	$26,460	$24,644	$29,125	$26,855	$25,250	$27,125	109%	110%
Toyota Avalon Sedan XL	3,928	Automatic	6 cyl	2WD	Standard	$27,395	$25,155	$26,350	$24,995	$22,525	$24,435	99%	97%
Volvo S40 2Ai	3,141	Automatic	5 cyl	2WD	Standard	$24,735	$23,561	$26,885	$23,681	$22,800	$24,790	101%	105%
Mercedes-Benz ML 350 SUV	2,673	Automatic	6 cyl	4WD	Standard	$40,525	$38,120	$42,410	$46,995	$36,300	$39,255	123%	103%
Mercedes-Benz R350 Wagon	3,388	Automatic	6 cyl	4WD	Standard	$48,776	$45,869	$47,775	$47,722	$43,275	$45,525	104%	99%
Honda civic EX Sedan	3,998	Automatic	4 cyl	2WD	Standard	$19,055	$18,790	$21,455	$20,995	$18,625	$20,025	112%	107%
KIA Optima LX	3,160	Automatic	4 cyl	2WD	Standard	$18,240	$17,250	$13,655	$16,900	$9,200	$12,385	98%	72%
KIA Am anti	2,653	Automatic	6 cyl	2WD	Standard	$28,675	$26,714	$23,100	$20,659	$16,100	$19,520	77%	73%
Saturn NNE 2.2L	3,974	Automatic	4 cyl	2WD	Standard	$19,345	$18,360	$21,600	$18,995	$16,325	$18,930	103%	103%
Nissan 350Z	4,221	Manual	6 cyl	2WD	Standard	$28,265	$27,004	$27,260	$30,995	$23,675	$25,465	115%	94%
Nissan Pathfinder 4x4	2,030	Automatic	6 cyl	4WD	Standard	$28,050	$26,803	$29,385	$28,665	$22,475	$25,890	107%	97%
Nissan Altima 2.5 S	2,597	Automatic	4 cyl	2WD	Standard	$20,715	$19,900	$20,315	$19,978	$16,750	$18,480	100%	93%
Averages	3,340					$26,386	$24,862	$26,388	$25,719			103%	96%

See George Akerlof, "The Market of Lemons," *Quarterly Journal of Economics*, August, 1970, 488–500. There are other papers that have found evidence that the market solves this lemons problem (Eric W. Bond, "A Direct Test of the 'Lemons' Model: The Market for Used Pickup Trucks," *AER*, 72(4), September 1982, 836–40, and Wimmer and Chezum, "An Empirical Examination of Quality Certification in a 'Lemons Market,'" *Economic Inquiry*, 41(2), April 2003, 279–91).

3 http://www.carsense.com/about.asp.
4 The study was conducted on September 27, 2006.
5 http://www.kbb.corn/kbb/CompanyInfo/FAQ.aspx#nc_1.
6 This assumes that the car is in "excellent" condition.

Review and Discussion Questions

1 What is the "nice story" that Lott argues is wrong?
2 What are the ways that the market can reduce the lemons problem?
3 How does Lott test the nice story? What are the results? What do the results imply for the extent of the lemons problem?

Chapter 24

Eric W. Bond

A DIRECT TEST OF THE "LEMONS" MODEL: THE MARKET FOR USED PICKUP TRUCKS[1]

THIS NOTE PROVIDES an empirical test of one of the implications of models of markets with asymmetric information. In the seminal paper on markets with asymmetric information, George Akerlof (1970) pointed out two possible outcomes that may occur where sellers have better information about the quality of products than do buyers. One possibility is that bad products will drive out good products. If buyers cannot distinguish quality until after the purchase has been made, there will be no incentive for sellers to provide good quality products, and the average quality in the market will decline. In the case of cars, an often-cited example of this phenomenon, owners who discover that they have a "lemon" will attempt to sell it in the used car market to an unsuspecting buyer. The owner of a "creampuff" will not sell his car, since it is indistinguishable from a lemon to buyers and must therefore sell for the price of a car of average quality. The effect of quality uncertainty is to reduce the volume of transactions in the used car market below the socially optimal level.

A second possibility suggested by Akerlof is that institutions may develop to counteract the effects of quality uncertainty. Warranties and brand names can be used to give the buyer some assurance of quality. These institutions may prevent good products from being driven from the market, but they will not necessarily eliminate the inefficiency. These institutions may be costly, and sellers may overinvest in signaling the quality of their product to buyers (for example, see Akerlof, 1976).

The purpose of this note is to test whether bad products drive out good products in the market for used pickup trucks, a market similar to the used car market. The measure of quality chosen here is the amount of maintenance required on a truck, with a lemon being a truck that requires significantly more maintenance than average. Owners will have an idea of the truck's quality from past maintenance experience, but it may be difficult for a potential buyer to predict future maintenance from inspecting the truck. If this informational asymmetry is significant and counteracting institutions do not develop, the lemons model would predict that owners of high maintenance trucks would sell them in the used market. The used truck market would then become a market for lemons, with the abundance of high maintenance trucks driving out sellers of low maintenance trucks as described above. The empirical implication of this model is that a sample of trucks that has been purchased used should have required more maintenance (since it should contain more lemons) than a sample of trucks with similar characteristics that have not been traded. Section I reports the results of such a test using data from the *1977 Truck Inventory and Use (TIU) Survey*.

The results indicate that if the effects of age and lifetime mileage on maintenance are controlled for, there is no difference in maintenance between trucks acquired new and trucks acquired used. This leads to a rejection of the hypothesis that bad products have driven out good, since there is no evidence of an overabundance of lemons among used trucks. One explanation for this finding is that the counteracting institutions of the type discussed by Akerlof may have developed. The provision of warranties on used trucks and the seller's concern about his reputation may prevent sellers from supplying low quality products. A second possible explanation is that buyers are able to obtain enough information from search to eliminate the asymmetry. While the finding that the average quality of original owner and used trucks is the same is consistent with the operation of an efficient market for used trucks, the market could still be inefficient if the informational asymmetry is eliminated through costly counteracting institutions or costly search by buyers.

I Testing the lemons model

As discussed above, the hypothesis that the used truck market contains an overabundance of lemons was tested by comparing the frequency of maintenance between trucks that were acquired used and those that were acquired new in the *TIU Survey*. This section describes the data obtained from the *TIU Survey* and reports the results of the test.

The *TIU Survey* is part of the Census of Transportation. It is based on a stratified probability sample of all trucks registered at motor vehicle departments in the fifty states, and requests information about the characteristics and usage of the trucks. With regard to maintenance, respondents were asked whether their truck had required major maintenance in any of five categories (engine, transmission, brakes, rear axle, and other) in the preceding twelve months.[2] Since the maintenance variable is a dichotomous variable, the frequency of maintenance of a given type in a sample of trucks can be modeled with a binomial distribution if the trucks in the sample are similar. The *TIU Survey* contains information on model year and lifetime mileage, so that it is possible to control for the effects of these observable factors on maintenance. If these factors are controlled, the sample proportion will be an estimate of the probability of maintenance among trucks of that type.

Pickup trucks were selected for study because pickup trucks have the largest noncommercial demand of any trucks in the survey. In the sample, 59 percent of the pickups are used for personal transportation, 21 percent are in agriculture, and the remainder are in various commercial uses (primarily construction, services, and retail trade). It was felt that the large household demand would increase the likelihood of asymmetric information in secondhand markets, since one would expect that household purchasers have less expertise in evaluating used trucks than commercial purchasers.

In addition, several other bits of evidence suggest similarities with the automobile market. Pickup trucks are produced by the major automobile producers (both foreign and domestic), and are sold by many car dealers. The retail markup over dealer cost on a pickup is comparable to that of a full-size car. Finally, the frequency of trading of pickups is comparable to that of autos. Of the trucks purchased during 1976, 60 percent were purchased used. Although data for the same year are not available for automobiles, the 1972 survey of household durable purchases (Department of Commerce, 1973) indicates that 65 percent of automobiles purchased in that year were used.

One question that had to be addressed was the choice of model years to study. Enough time must be allowed for owners to become aware that their trucks are lemons, but if the model year studied is too old, many of the lemons may already have been scrapped.[3] Since the lemons model gives no guidance on this point, trucks that were from one- to five-years old in 1977 (model years 1972–76) were studied to give a fairly wide range of time for the lemons effect to occur.

Table 24.1 shows the number of pickups in the survey, the percentage acquired used, and the proportion of new and used trucks that required major engine maintenance for each model year. The proportion requiring maintenance is slightly higher for used trucks in three of the years. However, this comparison is biased against used trucks since used trucks had significantly higher lifetime mileage in each model year.

If the lemons hypothesis is true, the probability of maintenance should be higher for secondhand trucks than for trucks with similar characteristics that were acquired new. The effects of observable characteristics were controlled for by grouping trucks according to model year and lifetime mileage. Let P_{ijk}^n be the probability of maintenance of type i for trucks of model year j and mileage group k that were acquired new, and let P_{ijk}^u be the corresponding proportion for trucks acquired used. The first test of the lemons model was to test the null hypothesis of no difference in quality between trucks acquired new and trucks acquired used, $P_{ijk}^n = P_{ijk}^u$. If the number of observations is large enough, the difference in group means will be normally distributed. Due to the low frequencies of several types of maintenance and the small number of used trucks in the 1975 and 1976 model years, larger mileage groupings had to be chosen to make the assumption of normality for those years.[4]

Table 24.1 Summary statistics of the sample

Year	Number in sample	Acquired used	Proportion requiring engine maintenance	
			New	Used
1976	2137	.11	.08	.05
1975	1602	.27	.10	.11
1974	2261	.37	.11	.13
1973	2085	.48	.15	.15
1972	1839	.53	.13	.15

The advantage of the test for equality of individual group means is that it allows testing of the hypothesis that only some segments of the market operate inefficiently. For example, suppose that the unreliability of service and large amount of down time associated with operating a lemon precludes its being used very intensively. A buyer of a high mileage truck would then be certain that he was not getting a lemon. If life-time mileage can be used as a signal for unobservable quality, some portions of the market might not contain lemons.

The results of the tests on group means are reported in Table 24.2, with the number of groups in which the used trucks were judged to be inferior at a 10 percent level of significance shown in column 2. The results indicate almost no support for the lemons model in any of the model years. In fact, equally strong support could be found for the hypothesis that trucks in the used market are superior (shown in column 3). There was no evidence that the cases where used trucks were inferior were concentrated in any particular segment of the market.

The data indicated that the probability of maintenance generally increased with the lifetime mileage of the truck, as one would expect.[5] Since maintenance is a dichotomous variable, the relationship between maintenance and mileage can be estimated using a logit model:

$$ln\left[P_i / \left(1 - P_i\right) \right] = \alpha_i + \beta_i x + \varepsilon, \tag{1}$$

where P_i is the probability of maintenance of type i and x is lifetime mileage. A second test of the lemons model was performed by estimating (1) separately for both used and original owner trucks, and then testing whether the slope and constant terms were equal for the two equations. This provides an overall test of whether used trucks and original owner trucks have any difference in quality.

The presence of a market for lemons would be indicated by a constant term in the equation for used trucks that was significantly greater than that for trucks acquired new, or by a combination of differing slope and constant terms that indicate greater maintenance for used trucks over the relevant range. The model was estimated by grouping the data by mileage for both new and used trucks, and then using the group means to estimate (1) with the weighted least squares approximation to the logit discussed by D. R. Cox (1970). Equations were estimated for all five types of maintenance for model years 1973 and 1975. In none of the equations were either the slopes or constant terms significantly different at the 5 percent level between original owner and used trucks. This test provides further support for the hypothesis that there is no dilution of quality in the used market.

Table 24.2 Tests of differences in proportions requiring maintenance

	Number of tests	Used inferior (10 percent level)	Used superior (10 percent level)
1976	19	1	2
1975	27	0	2
1974	44	2	3
1973	57	3	1
1972	67	2	1

II Conclusion

The main finding of this note is that trucks that were purchased used required no more maintenance than trucks of similar age and lifetime mileage that had not been traded. This leads to a rejection of the hypothesis that the used pickup truck market is a market for lemons, which would have required used trucks to show significantly more maintenance. However, it should be noted that the failure to find an overabundance of lemons in the used market is not inconsistent with the commonly expressed notion that cars and trucks are traded when they become "too costly" to maintain. Suppose that there are two types of buyers in the market: one group with high maintenance costs and a second group of handymen with low maintenance costs. As trucks age and require more maintenance, high maintenance cost owners will prefer to sell to low maintenance cost buyers rather than to continue to operate the truck themselves.[6] While it might appear to members of the former group that used trucks are too costly to maintain, this results not from the existence of a market for lemons, but from the reallocation of the stock of assets to those individuals who value them most highly.

Notes

1 I thank Roger McCain, Richard Butler, Arnie Raphaelson and an anonymous referee for helpful comments on this paper. Wayne Morra and John Funk provided computational assistance.

2 It would be preferable to have information on actual maintenance expenditures, since the quality depends not only on the probability of maintenance but also on the costliness of repairs. Unfortunately, expenditure data were not available. However, the costliness of repairs will be partially captured by the fact that the respondents are asked only to indicate major maintenance.

3 The median age of pickup trucks in the *TIU Survey* was 7 years. By the time trucks were five years old, more than 50 percent had been traded at least once.

4 In order for the binomial distribution to be approximately normal, the expected frequency of maintenance should be at least 5 in each group (see R. Hogg and A. Craig, 1978). In order to satisfy this condition, it was necessary to expand the size of the mileage groups for the more recent model years (where relatively few trucks were used) and for transmission and rear axle maintenance (which were more rare events). For the 1972–74 data, the mileage groups were in intervals of 10,000 miles for most maintenance tests. For the 1975–76 data, the groups had to be expanded to 15–20,000 miles intervals for all maintenance tests except the "other" category.

5 An exception to this was maintenance in the "other" category, which was negatively related to lifetime mileage.

6 A complete model of used asset markets with complete information and different types of consumers is presented in my working paper, which also presents evidence that buyers who do their own maintenance are more likely to buy used trucks.

References

Akerlof, George A., "The Market for 'Lemons': Quality Uncertainty and the Market Mechanism," *Quarterly Journal of Economics*, August 1970, *84*, 488–500.

——, "The Economics of Caste and of the Rat Race and Other Woeful Tales," *Quarterly Journal of Economics*, November 1976, *90*, 599–617.

Bond, Eric W., "A Theory of Trade in Used Equipment," working paper 1-81-2, Pennsylvania State University, 1981.

Cox, D. R., *Analysis of Binary Data*, London: Meuthen, 1970.

Hogg, R. and Craig, A., *Introduction to Mathematical Statistics*, New York: Macmillan, 1978.

U.S. Department of Commerce, Bureau of the Census, *Current Population Reports; Consumer Buying Indicators*, P 65, No. 45, Washington: USGPO, 1973.

Review and Discussion Questions

1 If the lemons model were correct, what type of trucks would be sold in the used market?
2 How does Bond test the lemons model? What is the result?
3 Can you think of other situations in which information might be asymmetric and the lemons model might apply? (Hint: what about car or health insurance?)

Suggestions for Further Reading

Gilligan, T. W. (2004) "Lemons and Leases in the Used Business Aircraft Market," *Journal of Political Economy*, 112: 1157–1180.

A study of whether used business aircraft exhibit the lemons effect. Gilligan finds that they do, but he also concludes that the practice of leasing these aircraft tends to reduce the effect.

Karpoff, J.M. and Lott, J.R., Jr. (1993) "The Reputational Penalty Firms Bear from Comm0itting Criminal Fraud," *Journal of Law and Economics*, 36: 757–802.

Can firms commit fraud at will? This is a concern, especially since criminal penalties for fraud seem to many people to be too light. Karpoff and Lott demonstrate that the market has a powerful way of disciplining fraud: firms that commit fraud suffer substantial loss of reputation and market value.

Karpoff, J.M., Lee, D.S., and Martin, G.S. (2008) "The Cost to Firms of Cooking The Books," *Journal of Financial and Quantitative Analysis*, 43: 581–612.

Firms that the SEC cites for financial misrepresentation—"cooking the books"— suffer huge penalties imposed by the market.

Mitchell, M.L. (1989) "The Impact of External Parties on Brand-Name Capital: The 1982 Tylenol Poisonings and Subsequent Cases," *Economic Inquiry*, 27: 601–618.

The infamous Tylenol poisonings had a significant impact on Johnson & Johnson's reputation. The market value of a firm's reputation creates ample incentive for firms to produce safe products.

Mitchell, M. L. and Maloney, M. T. (1989) "Crisis in the Cockpit—The Role of Market Forces in Promoting Air-Travel Safety," *Journal of Law and Economics,* 32: 329–355.

Mitchell and Maloney find that if a plane crashes, and the airline is at fault, the airline loses considerable business. If the airline isn't at fault, there is no evidence that the airline loses business. Together, these imply that an airline's reputation loses value for a crash it is responsible for. The market penalizes bad performance and here again, gives firms ample incentive to operate safely.

Sultan, A. (2008) "Lemons Hypothesis Reconsidered: An Empirical Analysis," *Economics Letters,* 99: 541–544.

A new test, with data on used cars, of the lemons hypothesis. Sultan finds that cars acquired used did not require more maintenance expenditures than those of a similar age that were acquired new. This is inconsistent with used cars being lemons.

PART SEVEN

Monopoly and Collusion

Introduction

The readings in this section make two points. First, the price-raising effects of monopolies and collusive agreements are likely to be short-lived. Market competition tends to weaken monopolies and collusion. David Hemenway discusses a company that controlled virtually the entire market for ice in New York City in 1900. The firm tried to exploit its market position by doubling prices. It even bribed public officials and retaliated violently against would-be competitors—actions most monopolists do not take. But entry occurred anyway, and price fell to the competitive level in about half a year.

The second point is that at least some instances of apparent collusion behavior prove, upon close examination, to have benign explanations. Harold Demsetz's famous paper studies whether the higher profits typically seen in industries with a small number of sellers—also known as high "seller concentration"—is due to collusion. He finds evidence to the contrary, such profits are due to the competitive superiority of the leading firms in those industries.

My first paper in this section examines an antitrust case in which a group of Seattle bakers allegedly attempted to raise bread prices. The government's case seems convincing. Prices in Seattle were 15 percent above the national average for nearly ten years. But the government did not consider that bread prices all along the West Coast were higher than the national average. Wage rates, retail markups, and capital costs were all higher in the West. These factors better explain Seattle's prices than collusion does. My second paper examines why Portland cement prices are higher in cities that have fewer sellers. Collusion is a possible explanation, but I find that cities with fewer sellers have higher costs and that, once again, the collusive explanation does not explain the data as well.

Chapter 25

David Hemenway

THE ICE TRUST

Introduction

THE FIRST GREAT AMERICAN MERGER WAVE had a dramatic effect on the structure of U.S. industry. This early merger movement, culminating in the flurry of consolidations between 1898 and 1902, left an imprint on the American economy that ninety years have not erased. It was during these years that the pattern of concentration characteristic of American business formed and matured.[1] During these four years, 236 important industrial consolidations occurred, with total capital of $6.1 billion.[2] By 1904 the trusts controlled fully 40 percent of the manufacturing capital of the country.[3] It was during this period that U.S. Steel was formed, as were U.S. Rubber, the Tobacco Trust, American Can, U.S. Gypsum, General Electric, International Nickel, International Paper, Allis-Chalmers, United Shoe, United Fruit, Standard Sanitary, National Lead, Pullman Company, National Biscuit Company, The Sugar Trust, International Salt, Western Union, and so forth. Also during this period, a wide variety of less important trusts emerged, including those in bicycles, caramels, grass twine, hominies, chewing gum, buttons, and ice.[4]

This is the story of one of the most fascinating of the lesser trusts, The Ice Trust, which briefly but spectacularly succeeded in gaining monopoly control over the New York City ice supply. It is the story of Charles W. Morse, tycoon and robber baron, founder and president of the American Ice Company, who ruthlessly ordered prices raised and service cut upon securing his monopoly position. And it is the story of the ensuing public outcry, combined with natural competitive forces, which dethroned the ice trust and quickly sent prices tumbling to pretrust levels.

The American Ice Company

At the turn of the century, the residents of New York City received most of their ice from natural sources, principally cuttings from the Hudson and the Penobscot and increasing in both absolute and relative terms, artificial ice still accounted for less than 15 percent of the city's annual four-million-ton consumption.[5] The reliance upon natural ice resulted in pronounced fluctuations in prices and profits depending upon the vagaries of the climate. Warm winters decreased the supply of ice and increased the cost of harvesting.[6] Warm winters also increased the demand, as did hot summers. The warm weather in 1905–1906, for example, raised the winter sales in New York City 50 percent over the previous winter.[7] The effect of the warm weather in 1905–1906 and 1912–13 is shown clearly in the profits of the American Ice Company. In the former period, net profits jumped from $487,000 in 1904–1905 to over $2 million, falling back to $185,000 the next year. And from $369,000 in 1911–12, annual profits climbed the following year to $1,600,000, dropping to $400,000 in 1913–14.[8]

The American Ice Company was the "ice trust," incorporated in 1899 with Charles W. Morse as president. An independent Maine ice operator, Morse, during the warm New York winter of 1890, had been able to acquire control of the ice-starved New York City Ice Company and Consumers' Ice Company. In 1895 these and other small companies were incorporated into the new Consolidated Ice Company, whose stated objectives were to regulate prices, restrict the amount harvested, and hold down competition.[9] The important Knickerbocker Ice Companies of New York and New Jersey soon joined the alliance.[10] Consolidated thus already had substantial control over the New York market at the time of the formation of the American Ice Company.

Incorporated under the friendly laws of New Jersey, the American Ice Company formally merged Consolidated, Knickerbocker of Maine, and a number of smaller manufacturers and distributors. The combination possessed extensive plants for the housing of ice on the Penobscot, Kennebec, Schuylkill, Susquehanna, and Hudson rivers, Rockland Lake, Croton Lake, and many New Jersey lakes. It also controlled a number of plants for manufacturing artificial ice in New York City, Philadelphia, Camden, Atlantic City, Baltimore, and Washington, D.C. and owned dock facilities and real estate in virtually all of these cities. Moody's listed the number of plants acquired as "about 40," and the proportion of the industry controlled locally as 80 percent.[11]

Eliminating competition

Attaining and, especially, maintaining a monopoly position in ice was not an easy proposition. Ice is a largely homogeneous product, and neither a great deal of capital nor technical expertise was required to enter the natural, or even the artificial, ice business.[12] Not only were entry barriers low, but the market was reasonably large and growing. Total U.S. consumption of ice more than tripled between 1880 and 1914.[13] The ice trust engaged in a variety of practices designed to limit competition. One device was the restrictive covenant. Managers of acquired companies were required to sign agreements prohibiting them from engaging in the ice business for a period of ten years.[14] These restrictive covenants seem to have been of some importance. In 1902 *Ice and Refrigeration*, a trade journal, reported that the American Ice Company had obtained a permanent injunction from the Supreme Court restraining certain of the ex-dealers from engaging in the retail ice trade.[15] In late 1909 these covenants were attacked under the New York antitrust statute, but this specific charge was dropped since most of the contracts had expired or were shortly due to expire.[16]

The ice trust had other more ruthless ways of crushing competition. One story reported in the *Times* told of the persecution of independent ice dealer W. A. Wynne. The steamer *Norwich* twice smashed all the ice in front of his place of business. The boat was equipped for this very purpose.[17]

The ice trust's alliance with the Tammany city government seems to have played a key role in eliminating stubborn competitors. One ice dealer, Richard Foster, paid over $2,000 a year to the city for his docking privilege. After he refused to sell to Morse, this privilege was revoked and his ice bridge was cut four times by the Dock Department on the excuse that it obstructed snow dumping. When it was learned that there was to be an official inquiry about such treatment, the harassment stopped.[18] Other ice dealers were told to get out of their berths by the Dock Department, which claimed that the spots were needed for something else. They left, only to watch the ice trust move into the vacated berths.[19]

A further method by which the trust attempted to limit competition was by its strict resale rules to its large (lower price) customers.[20] Restaurants, ice-cream saloons, and liquor dealers were all told that if they sold so much as a pound of ice, even in an emergency, in the case of a contract it would be abrogated, and in the case of a cash customer, she would be left out in the cold.[21]

The price hike

In April 1900, a year after its formation, the ice trust arbitrarily doubled its price. For large customers, prices rose from 15C to 25C per 100 pounds, or $5 per ton. The small consumer was more severely hurt. Here prices rose from 25C to 60C per 100 pounds, with hints of further advances to come. In addition, households were informed that deliveries would be made only three times a week instead of daily. This was a special hardship since few refrigerators in private homes could hold a two-day supply of ice. The trust also eliminated the 5C and 10C chunk, the size most convenient for the poor.[22] (This was at a time when the *Times* cost a penny, the *Sunday Times*, 3C.)

There appears to have been no cost justification for the doubling of prices. While the trust blamed the shortness of supply, *Ice and Refrigeration* refuted the cry of famine. This independent Chicago publication stated: "The much-talked of ice famine apparently exists only in the minds of would-be speculators."[23] The Hudson River crop was only slightly less than normal, and since the previous year's crop had been record breaking (4.3 million tons, or greater than the total New York City ice consumption), there was much left over. Combined with the Maine crop and the manufactured product, there was little shortage in 1900.[24]

Additional evidence attesting to the administered nature of the price rise comes from intercity comparisons. No city had as high a price as New York. In areas where competition existed, prices were little different from previous years. In Buffalo, Boston, Albany, and Bangor, there were no advances. Only in cities like New York and Philadelphia, where the ice trust was strong, did prices increase.[25]

The *Times* claimed that the trust had tried to limit the crop by cutting only four-teen-and twelve-inch ice, whereas ten-inch ice was usually cut, and by leaving much ice unharvested. The trust seems not to have permanently reduced the 1900 supply, however, for when prices returned to their former levels, as they shortly did, no ice shortage occurred in New York City.[26]

Public outcry

The Tammany connection

Public outcry against the price hike was strong and clamorous and had its effect. The quickness of the trust's retreat was probably caused by the immense public resent-ment over the price hike, especially when combined with the subsequent exposure of the trust's shady dealings. The trust did not drop its prices because of a sudden reawak-ening to its social responsibilities. Instead, the quickness of the price reduction is more explicable in terms of crude jawboning, with the bludgeon of state antitrust action clearly visible. But the responsibility lies with an aroused press and citizenry rather than with an alert and concerned government. Indeed, an important portion of the local government had already embraced the trust.

The public first learned of the connection between Tammany and the ice trust in the spring of 1899. On the day that "Boss" Richard Croker's personal representative, John F. Carroll, was to testify before the State Legislative Investigating Committee (the Mazet Committee), a newspaper ran a story charging that Carroll and others were American Ice Company stockholders. When questioned about it, Carroll refused to testify. "It is a personal matter," he said. "I decline to answer it." Boss Croker then took the stand and also initially declined to respond. It was disclosed, however, that Croker had once owned stock but no longer did. "I turned it over to another person." Q: "Who is that?" A: "In my family, my wife." Croker's wife, it was discovered, owned at least 150 shares, then worth some $40 a share. The family further owned substan-tial holdings of the Knickerbocker Ice Company of Philadelphia, which had joined the trust.[27] A year later, less than a month after the famed price hike, the mayor of New York, Robert A. Van Wyck, went on a pleasure trip to Maine, accompanied by John Carroll, both as guests of Charles W. Morse, head of the ice trust.[28] The *Times* edito-rialized, this excursion "cannot escape remark."[29]

Following on the heels of the price advance, a paper's (and people's) crusade began. The *Times* was silent for three weeks but then ran strong editorials against the "hoggish monopoly."[30] The *New York Evening Post* ran articles showing that municipal ice plants could be constructed to produce ice for delivery at 10C per 100 pounds.[31] But the most important action was taken by the *New York Journal*, leading newspaper of the Democratic party. It was the *Journal* that strongly asserted that the Tammany Democratic machine held large blocks of ice trust stock, and it was at the instigation of Randolph Hearst himself that the attorney general of New York began an investiga-tion of the company. None of the criminal or civil cases initially brought against the American Ice Company ever amounted to anything, but the exposed facts had a sen-sational effect.[32]

In June 1900 an official stockholders' list was made public. Mayor Robert Van Wyck was shown to hold 2,660 shares of preferred stock and 3,325 shares of common stock, par value at $100 but selling at $48 in April and falling fast to a record low of $28 on the day after this announcement. It was further disclosed that Morse had let Van Wyck have the stock at "bed-rock price" (half of par) and, in effect, lent him the money with which to buy it![33] (Throughout this trying period there were continual, but false, rumors of the mayor's imminent retirement.)[34]

Another prominent name on the list was the mayor's brother, former judge Augustus Van Wyck, who had unsuccessfully opposed Theodore Roosevelt for governor of New York in 1898 and had been mentioned as a possible vice presidential candidate. It is of interest that Augustus had been touted as the eloquent champion of the movement against the trusts. Wrote the *Independent*: "His utterances against Trust monopolies and exactions are among the most valued campaign documents of his party."[35] The *Independent* felt that the ice scandal might prevent Augustus from being a delegate-at-large at the next convention, though they pointed out that Republican Thurston of Nebraska had recently been elected delegate-at-large upon the platform of denouncing the trusts at the same time that he was defending Standard Oil in court.[36]

Also on the stockholders' list were John Carroll, Boss Crocker's vicegerent, as well as numerous judges and dock commissioners Cram and Murphy. These two officials possessed the principal power to grant or refuse docking facilities to any (ice) firm in New York City. It is estimated that over 50 percent of the property suitable for docking in Manhattan was public or under their control. While Cram had sold his 100 shares of stock, Murphy still possessed his 200, worth close to $10,000 in April 1900.[37]

The scandal had its effect on Tammany. The *Independent* reported that Boss Croker and Carroll turned the Tammany delegation to Bryan and that out-of-city Democrats in New York were preparing to denounce the Ice Company in the coming state convention.[38] At that convention, Tammany did not dare assert itself.[39] In the city the *Times* ran headlines declaring: "Ice Trust's Action Alarms Tammany Men; Rank and File Fear the Effect on Public Sentiment."[40] The Van Wyck brothers were obviously in disfavor. At the subsequent mayoral election, the Tammany candidate was defeated by a "reform mayor," elected by the fusion of all other parties. Interestingly, the major issue was not the ice scandal but the police scandal.[41]

The response of the public to the trust's price hike and the Tammany involvement seems to have been substantial. Continually, the *Times* reported that the trust "is talked of everywhere, from the slums to the clubs, in Wall Street, and on street cars. Plans to thwart the combine are considered by the most lowly as well as by the most intelligent."[42] And, in general, the *Times* concluded, the trust is "now loathed by the community."[43]

The nature of the product

The public outcry against the trust was largely due to the particular nature of the product. Ice was more a necessity than a luxury in 1900. It was virtually essential for the preservation of foods, and doctors had already documented the relationship between infant mortality and drastic heat or ice shortages—times when it was difficult for the poor to preserve milk. The poor spent a noticeable part of their income purchasing ice, a product often bought daily, at a price clearly visible. Further, ice seems to have been thought of not only as a vital necessity but also as something of a gift from nature, or a "free good."[44] Wrote the *Times*: "To corner ice is very much like cornering air and water."[45]

It appears quite important that the product monopolized was ice. Wrote the *Outlook*:

> Had Tammany been prime movers in the organization of the wire and steel trust, their constituents would not have cared, for stock-jobbing operations do not really concern them, and the price of wire fences, or even wire nails, is to them a matter of *supreme* indifference. Had they been *prominent* in the management of the oil trust, they might incur a slight unpopularity, but even the price of oil concerns but little the voters of a great city to whom gas is the cheaper illuminant. But when the leaders of Tammany Hall became connected with the ice trust, and that trust advanced prices 100%, the wrath of the whole East Side was aroused against the hypocrisy as well as the extortion of its professed defenders.[46]

The sensitivity of the public to substantial increases in the price of ice is amply demonstrated by the outrage during the real shortages in 1906 and 1913. Though high prices during these years were prompted principally by demand and supply conditions (these were very warm winters), antitrust action was either brought or seriously considered in New York; Philadelphia; Washington, D.C.; Boston; Baltimore; and Toledo. Little came of these actions, save in Toledo, where a number of businessmen served thirty-seven days in jail.[47] Between 1906 and 1913 there was a great deal of careful attention given to the possibility of government-owned ice plants. In 1910 the mayor of Schenectady was elected partly on his program for "ice-at-cost." The shortage in 1913 prompted the city of New York to finance the Wentworth Report on municipal ice plants. While quite favorable to the construction of municipal plants, the report indicated that there was then only one in existence in the United States, in Weatherford, Oklahoma.[48] With the gradual replacement of manufactured for natural ice, the fluctuations in the supply and price of ice decreased, as did the public clamor for some sort of governmental action.

The hoggish monopoly

The clamor raised against the ice trust in 1900 was due not to the fact that it possessed some degree of monopoly power but that it had used that power so arrogantly and brutally. The *Times*, which went out of its way to explain that it was only averse to "bad" trusts, attacked this "hoggish monopoly" that was "holding up" the community.[49] *Gunton's Magazine* (like the *Times* and most economists of the day) was not against trusts in general but was violently opposed to this "bungling burglar" that would bring discredit to its class. "The people," said *Gunton's*, "can be fooled for a while if the fooling is skillfully done, but not when it is bunglingly performed."[50]

The people obviously were not fooled, and their outcry helped secure the trust's quick defeat. Six weeks after the initial price hike, the trust agreed to sell 5C pieces but "would make no further concessions." The *Times* strongly denounced this "Public be Damned" attitude.[51] Two weeks later, following the official publication of the Tammany Ice Holdings, prices were quietly slashed from 60C to 40C per 100 pounds, which the *Times* editors called "a famous victory."[52] Within the week, prices were 25C for most sectors of the city as the trust met the price of any independent selling below the 40C rate.

In late June the *Times* ran an article under "Ice Plenty and Cheap" (prices still varied from 25C to 50C), which contained this picturesque description of the small ice market:

> Ice was in evidence everywhere on the crowded east side streets. Each block had from one to half a dozen vendors on it, some with huge stores or several tons just from the bridges; others pushed carts which started out with a cake of ice and made journey after journey to the base of supplies as the vendors sold out. Everybody seemed to be buying ice. On stoops and in hallways were women with broods of children and a pitcher of ice-water which was drunk as if it was nectar. Housewives with pans and dishes and cloths left their domestic work to get a chunk of the gelid necessary for 5 or 10C, and each cart or wagon had its following of children who scrambled for small ice refuse and greedily crushed it.[53]

Entry

By November the ice market was glutted.[54] The major cause for the surplus was, as might be expected, the entry of new firms lured by the trust's high prices and profits. Earlier that spring, when prices were high, the *Times* reported the formation of the Empire Ice Company with a manufacturing ice capacity of 600 tons per day and which did "not believe in the exorbitant price which the Trust is asking."[55] The Green Island Ice Company began building a wharf on Sedgwick Street and was expecting to undersell the trust during the summer.[56] The Bronx Consumers Ice Company was incorporated with capital of $100,000, and business purchasers of ice in Brooklyn were seriously considering forming their own "Anti-Trust Ice Company."[57]

The "impetuous rush to form new companies"[58] during "prosperous" times—the perennial fear of the ice industry—seems largely responsible for the oversupply in late 1900. That overentry, or overoptimism of the entrants, was a problem is attested to by company failures large enough to be reported in the *Times*. In the spring of 1901, for example, the Manhattan Ice Company, formed the previous June, employing forty men and serving two thousand customers, toppled.[59] Two years later the People's Co-Op Ice Company, formed in August 1900, with a capital stock of over $1 million, also went under.[60] Fortunately for the industry, while entry was relatively easy, so apparently, was exit.

The rapid entry into the ice industry during the period of high trust prices undoubtedly meant that the public's "famous victory" only speeded the inevitable. For all its ruthlessness, the trust was unable to raise entry barriers to a degree sufficient to allow a large monopoly profit. Its attempt to realize that profit brought a rash of new competitors, decreasing the price and eroding the trust's market position. As the *Times* predicted in the spring of 1900: "It may turn out that the hoggish monopoly has outwitted itself by its hoggishness."[61] "Its recklessness has endangered the health, if it has not insured the death, of the goose relied on to lay the golden eggs."[62]

Was the action of the trust's management in raising prices and inviting entry and condemnation really so irrational? For the longterm health and viability of the American Ice Company, the move was clearly unfortunate. The troubles of the company "really date to the outburst of public condemnation and disfavor in 1900."[63] The stock, selling at $49 in the spring of 1900, fell to $4¾ in 1903 during the general stock market decline.[64] Reported profits dropped from close to a million dollars in 1900, to $650,000 in 1901, to a *deficit* of $162,000 in 1902.[65] The American Ice Company was clearly in dire straits. *Ice and Refrigeration* reported in the spring of 1903: "If a second cool summer with limited demand for ice should come, no holding company scheme could save the big 'ice trust' from dissolution."[66]

Charles W. Morse

While the company and common owners of the stock were severely hurt by the ice trust's attempted "hold-up" of the community, the president of the corporation certainly was not. Though an identity of interests between the owners and controllers of a corporation is sometimes assumed, in this case, what was good for Charles W. Morse was not very good for the American Ice Company. While even Mayor Van Wyck lost money[67] on this weirdly overcapitalized venture (most of the $60 million capitalization was pure "water"), Charlie Morse is reported to have withdrawn from the corporation in 1901 with over $12 million.[68]

Since Morse played such a crucial role in the formation and actions of the ice trust, it is of interest to digress a bit and briefly examine his colorful and checkered career. Morse was far more of a promoter, speculator, and financial manipulator than he was a conservative or conventional businessperson. After his reign as "Ice King" at the turn of the century, he turned more intensively to shipping and banking. By 1907, through a series of brilliant operations, he managed to achieve something close to a monopoly of coastwise shipping from Bangor to Galveston and became known as "the Admiral of the Atlantic." The panic of 1907, however, found the Heinze–Morse banks at the storm center; an investigation resulted in Morse's indictment and conviction for false entries and the misapplication of funds.[69]

While Morse argued that "there is no one in Wall Street who is not daily doing as I have done,"[70] this "fat, squatty little man" with the "masterful inquiring eyes" was sentenced to a fifteen-year term in the Atlanta penitentiary. Every exertion by Morse's friends and relatives to secure a pardon or commutation of sentence from President Taft proved unavailing. Finally, in 1912 Harry Daugherty, later attorney general in the Harding cabinet, contracted with Morse for a retainer of $5,000 and promise of an additional $25,000 in case of success to secure his release. A commission of doctors examined Morse and reported he was suffering from Bright's disease and could not last the year. Taft reluctantly signed a pardon. However, Daugherty's fee remained unpaid, and the attorney general's office received information that before his examination, Morse had drunk a combination of soapsuds and chemicals calculated to produce the desired temporary effects. President Taft later charged he had been deluded in the whole affair, adding that the case "shakes one's faith in expert examination."[71]

In 1916 Morse again made news with a grandiose scheme for organizing an American transoceanic shipping combination. This assumed reality with the formation of a holding company, the United States Shipping Company. The company prospered during the war, but in the subsequent "war frauds" investigation Morse was again indicted. Before that case could be brought, he was further indicted on the charge of using the mails to defraud potential investors. Before this "mail frauds" case was complete, Morse was adjudged too ill to stand trial. He was placed under guardianship, declared too incompetent to handle his own affairs, and died some seven years later in his home town of Bath, Maine at the age of seventy-six.[72]

The American Ice Company after 1903

Morse and his immediate successor seemingly attempted to milk the corporation dry before the crisis of 1903 and the stockholders' revolt. Before that corporate emergency, the common public stockholder had been virtually powerless to take any action. She was unable to discover the actual ownership of the company (it took a court order to get the official listing during the 1900 Tammany-trust investigation), or the actual control (because of the numerous dummy directorates), or even the earnings of the trust. The *Times*, for example, gave this seemingly tongue-in-cheek account of the 1902 stockholders meeting: "It was understood beforehand that the officers of the company would violate the precedent of the past annual meetings and submit a statement of the actual earnings of the company. The corporation regularly pays 6 percent annual dividend on preferred stock, 4 percent on common. ... No precedents were violated however."[73]

The stockholders' meeting in 1903 was a very lively affair. The American Ice Company had just announced a deficit for the preceding year, and stock prices had broken to $4¾. A number of prominent stockholders charged, among other things, that the officers of the trust had declared dividends when there were no earnings, had paid unnecessarily liberal commissions for the sale of bonds, had purchased the Knickerbocker Steam Towage Company at an excessive price benefiting a few insiders in the trust's management, and had used the power of the trust to enhance their own holding in an independent ice company. It was from the pressure of these minority stockholders that an investigating committee, albeit a conservative one, was eventually formed to examine the charges and generally report on the condition of the company.[74]

The report of the stockholders investigating committee helped to document the extent of the trust's overcapitalization and corporate mismanagement. While capitalization had been reduced from $60 to $40 million, the committee reported that the company's real property was worth only $15 million and there was "nothing between this and the preferred stock." The $25 million in common stock, in other words, represented pure "good will."[75] (Note the irony.) The financial difficulties of the company were attributed largely to the payment of unearned dividends. The milking of the corporation was further attested to by the fact that 1903 marked the "first time in several years that the company made liberal expenditures" to improve its real estate.[76] Many of the other charges against the trust were seemingly not examined. Morse undoubtedly made things difficult by generally keeping no books and "destroying all records of deals soon after they were closed."[77]

In 1904, Wesley Oler took over as president of the American Ice Company. Oler was a friend of Morse and a member of the original trust, but he was a sound businessperson and stayed with the company for many years, making it a profitable, if not a growing, concern. Oler died in 1927, two years before the corporation reached its all-time peak sales of $20.8 million and all-time peak profits of $3.4 million. The firm was finally absorbed around 1960, with its sales still in the $15 to $18 million range.[78]

In 1905, Oler again reduced the company's capitalization, but book assets still remained largely "good will account, water rights, and patent rights." These became of less and less value as the natural ice properties were discarded and displaced by manufacturing plants. By the early twenties, virtually all of the business of the American Ice Company was in manufactured ice. Yet, it was well into the Depression before all the natural ice properties were written off.[79]

The American Ice Company made numerous attempts to diversify—into the distribution of coal and wood, the repair of wagons, the distillation of water, and so forth—but the sale of ice continued to provide the vast majority of its revenues into the late twenties and thirties, when electric refrigeration became more common. In 1941 the American Ice Company was still the second largest distributor of manufactured ice in the country, with 50 percent of its $12 million gross sales coming from ice, the rest from fuel oil and laundry services.[80] Of interest in the diversification attempts of the company was the change in its charter made in 1907 to allow it to "acquire, own, equip, operate, and dispose of steamships."[81] This scheme, however, seems to have been quickly dropped when the "Admiral of the Atlantic" was indicted and sent to prison.

Probably the most intriguing episode of the Oler regime occurred in 1906 when a true ice shortage hit New York City, which still relied on the American Ice Company for about half its ice.[82] The general shortage was so acute that for a while, in September, the company was essentially without ice as its fully laden Maine schooners were fogbound in the Atlantic.[83] Prices, of course, were high that year, and the trust made handsome profits, but the company had obviously learned from its 1900 experience. In March, the trust announced its intent "to do everything possible to prevent an increase in public indignation."[84] In June the trust declared that, no matter what, families would not have to pay more than 40C per 100 pounds. If prices were to increase, the burden would be on hotels, stores, and other large customers. Further, the 10C piece (25 lbs.) would remain on sale.[85]

Conclusion

Like many turn-of-the-century trusts, the American Ice Company succeeded in gaining monopoly control over the market. The ice trust, however, had more problems than most in maintaining that position, in some part due to the high visibility and essential nature of the product, but primarily because of the easy entry into the industry. When the trust did abuse its limited economic power, raising prices and decreasing the services associated with the product, these actions proved quite detrimental to its own long-term welfare. (The long-term welfare of the corporation, however, was of no great concern to its early president, whose primary interest was in securing his own short-run profit.) Three years after its formation, the American Ice Company was on the brink of bankruptcy.

While the American Ice Company was only one of the many monopolies formed at the turn of the century, the ice trust was nevertheless a historical phenomenon of some singularity. Among other things, the disclosure of the Tammany-trust connection caused political ripples, and the newspaper crusade demonstrated the effectiveness of public outrage, especially when coupled with strong underlying economic forces. Basically, however, the year of the ice trust provided a unique, if not very pleasant, experience for many residents of New York City—and a lot of money for Charles W. Morse.

Notes

1 J. W. Markham, "Survey of the Evidence and Findings on Mergers," in National Bureau of Economic Research, *Business Concentration and Price Policy* (Princeton, N.J.: NBER, 1955), pp. 141–82.
2 John Moody, *The Truth about Trusts* (New York: Moody Publishing, 1904), pp. 4531–69.
3 Henry Seager and Charles Gulick, Jr., *Trust and Corporation Problems* (New York: Arno, 1929), p. 61.
4 Moody, *The Truth about Trusts*, pp. 205–86.
5 *New York Times*, February 2, 1906.
6 "Some Facts on Present Conditions in the Ice Trade," *Ice and Refrigeration* (July 1906): 16.
7 *New York Times*, March 2, 1906.
8 John Moody, *Railroad and Corporate Securities,* annual, 1905–1915.
9 *New York Times*, May 6, 1900.
10 Richard O. Cummings, *The American Ice Harvests* (Berkeley: University of California Press, 1949), p. 87.
11 Moody, *The Truth about Trusts*, pp. 227–28.
12 As late as 1913, Milwaukee officials estimated the cost of an efficient municipal ice plant at $150,000. Jeanie Wells Wentworth, *A Report on Municipal and Government Ice Plants in the United States and Other Countries* (New York: M. B. Brown, 1913), pp. 60–62.
13 Oscar Edward Anderson, Jr., *Refrigeration in America* (Princeton: Princeton University Press, 1953), p. 114.
14 *New York Times*, May 6, 1900.
15 "Ice Trade Notes," *Ice and Refrigeration* (February 1902): 54.
16 "Ice Trade Notes," *Ice and Refrigeration* (November 1909): 191.
17 *New York Times*, May 9, 1900.
18 Ibid., May 4, 1900.
19 Ibid., May 6, 1900.
20 Ibid.
21 Ibid., March 6, 1900.
22 Ibid., March 26, May 5, June 6, 1900.
23 Ibid., June 6, 1900.
24 *Ice and Refrigeration* (August 1901): 46.
25 Ibid., May 7, 1900.
26 Ibid., May 6, June 2, 1900.
27 Ibid., April 15, 1899.

28 Ibid., May 4, 1900.

29 Ibid., May 5, 1900.

30 Ibid., March 26, May 7, May 8, 1900.

31 "Ice Trust Exactions," *The Outlook*, May 19, 1900, p. 144.

32 "Ice and Politics," *The Independent*, May 31, 1900, p. 1331; Owen Wilson, "Admiral of the Atlantic Coast," *WorldsWork* (April 1907).

33 *New York Times*, June 3, June 10, 1900.

34 Ibid., June 12, 1900.

35 "Ice and Politics," *The Independent,* May 31, 1900, p. 1331.

36 Ibid.

37 *New York Times*, June 10, 1900.

38 "Ice and Politics," *The Independent*, May 31, 1900, p. 1332.

39 "Ice Trust in Politics," *The Outlook*, June 16, 1900.

40 *New York Times*, May 8, 1900.

41 "Robert A. Van Wyck," *Dictionary of American Biography* (New York: Charles Scribner's Sons, 1934).

42 *New York Times*, May 6, 1900.

43 Ibid., April 26, 1900.

44 Ibid., May 29, 1900.

45 Ibid., April 20, 1900.

46 "New York's Ice Trust," *The Outlook*, June 9, 1900, p. 328.

47 *New York Times*, June 26, June 29, July 4, July 7, July 13, 1906; "Ice Trade Notes," *Ice and Refrigeration* (April 1908): 209.

48 Wentworth, *A Report on Municipal and Government Ice Plants*, p. 66. The call for municipal plants in 1900 was cooled by the Tammany-trust connections.

49 *New York Times*, April 26, 1900.

50 "Ice Trust Outrage," *Gunton's Magazine,* June 1900, pp. 515-19.

51 *New York Times*, May 16, May 20, 1900.

52 Ibid., June 8, 1900.

53 Ibid., June 29, 1900.

54 Ibid., November 15, November 18, 1900.

55 Ibid., May 9, 1900.

56 Ibid.

57 *New York Times*, *May* 10, 1900.

58 "Ice Trade Notes," *Ice and Refrigeration* (August 1906): 59.

59 *New York Times*, April 23, 1901.

60 Ibid., October 23, 1903.

61 Ibid., April 26, 1900.

62 Ibid., May 7, 1900.

63 American Ice Company Stockholders Committee Report, 1903, quoted in Moody's *Manual of Industrial and Miscellaneous Securities*, 1904.

64 *Wall Street Journal*, October 24, 1903, quoted in Moody, *The Truth about Trusts*, p. 479.

65 Moody, *The Truth about Trusts*, p. 227.

66 "Ice Trade Notes," *Ice and Refrigeration* (May 1903): 197.

67 The mayor sold all his stock in June 1900 at a slight loss (*New York Times*, November 10, 1900).

68 See Wilson, "Admiral of the Atlantic"; also "Water Still Freezes," *Fortune*, May 1933.

69 "Charles W. Morse," *Dictionary of American Biography* (New York: Charles Scribner's Sons, 1934).

70 "Current Literature," February 1910, p. 153, quoted in *Dictionary of American Biography*.

71 *New York Times*, November 16, 1913, quoted *in Dictionary of American Biography*.

72 "Morse," *Dictionary of American Biography*.

73 *New York Times*, March 12, 1902.

74 Ibid., March 11, April 29, 1903; "Ice Trade Notes," *Ice and Refrigeration* (April 1903): 163.

75 "Ice Trade Notes," *Ice and Refrigeration* (January 1904): 59.

76 Ibid.; *New York Times*, November 21, 1903.

77 John E. MacDonald tried to sue Morse for $200,000 in 1904. The above is from Morse's testimony. See *New York Times*, October 25, 1904; "Ice Trade Notes," *Ice and Refrigeration* (November 1904): 188.

78 Moody's, and then Poor's *Manuals of Corporate Securities* 1900-1960.

79 Moody's *Manual of Railroad and Corporate Securities* 1904, 1905, 1912, 1924; "Water Still Freezes," *Fortune*, May 1933.

80 Moody's (Poor's), 1941.

81 Ibid., 1907.

82 *New York Times*, September 24, 1906.

83 Ibid., September 23, 1906.

84 Ibid., March 14, 1906.

85 Ibid., June 10, 1906.

Review and Discussion Questions

1 What steps did the American Ice Company take to eliminate its competition?
2 After the American Ice Company doubled its price in April 1900, how did the market react?
3 What was more effective in ending the monopolization of ice in New York City, government regulation or market forces? Why?
4 Do you expect monopolization would fail in other industries, or was the turn-of-the-century ice industry in some way unusual? Explain.

Chapter 26

HAROLD DEMSETZ

INDUSTRY STRUCTURE, MARKET RIVALRY, AND PUBLIC POLICY[1]

I Introduction

QUANTITATIVE WORK IN INDUSTRIAL ORGANIZATION has been directed mainly to the task of searching for monopoly even though a vast number of other interesting topics have been available to the student of economic organization. The motives for this preoccupation with monopoly are numerous, but important among them are the desire to be policy-relevant and the ease with which industrial concentration data can be secured. This paper takes a critical view of contemporary doctrine in this area and presents data which suggest that this doctrine offers a dangerous base upon which to build a public policy toward business.

II Concentration through competition

Under the pressure of competitive rivalry, and in the apparent absence of effective barriers to entry, it would seem that the concentration of an industry's output in a few firms could only derive from their superiority in producing and marketing products or in the superiority of a structure of industry in which there are only a few firms. In a world in which information and resource mobility can be secured only at a cost, an industry will become more concentrated under competitive conditions only if a differential advantage in expanding output develops in some firms. Such expansion will increase the degree of concentration at the same time that it increases the rate of return that these firms earn. The cost advantage that gives rise to increased concentration may be reflected in scale economies or in downward shifts in positively sloped marginal cost curves, or it may be reflected in better products which satisfy demand at a lower cost. New efficiencies can, of course, arise in other ways. Some firms might discover ways of lowering cost that require that firms become smaller, so that spinoffs might be in order. In such cases, smaller firms will tend to earn relatively high rates of return. Which type of new efficiency arises most frequently is a question of fact.

Such profits need not be eliminated soon by competition. It may well be that superior competitive performance is unique to the firm, viewed as a team, and unobtainable to others except by purchasing the firm itself. In this case the return to superior performance is in the nature of a gain that is completely captured by the owner of the firm itself, not by its inputs.[2] Here, although the industry structure may change because the superior firm grows, the resulting increase in profit cannot easily serve to guide competitors to similar success. The firm may have established a reputation or goodwill that is difficult to separate from the firm itself and which should be carried at higher value on its books. Or it may be that the members of the employee team derive their higher productivity from the knowledge they possess about each other in the environment of the particular firm in which they work, a source of productivity that may be difficult to transfer piecemeal. It should be remembered that we are discussing complex, large enterprises, many larger (and more productive) than entire nations. One such enterprise happens to "click" for some time while others do not. It may be very difficult for these firms to understand the reasons for this difference in performance or to know to which inputs to attribute the performance of the successful firm. It is not easy to ascertain just why G.M. and I.B.M. perform better than their competitors. The complexity of these organizations defies easy analysis, so that the inputs responsible for success may be undervalued by the market for some time. By the same token, inputs owned by complex, unsuccessful firms may be overvalued for some time. The success of firms will be reflected in higher returns and stock prices, not higher input prices, and lack of success will be recorded in lower returns and stock prices, not lower input prices.

Moreover, inputs are acquired at historic cost, but the use made of these inputs, including the managerial inputs, yields only uncertain outcomes. Because the outcomes of managerial decisions are surrounded by uncertainty and are specific to a particular firm at a particular point in its history, the acquisition cost of inputs may fail to reflect their value to the firm at some subsequent time. By the time their value to the firm is recognized, they are beyond acquisition by other firms at the same historic cost, and, in the interim, shareholders of the successful or lucky firm will have enjoyed higher profit rates. When nature cooperates to make such decisions correct, they can give rise to high accounting returns for several years or to a once and for all capital gain if accountants could value *a priori* decisions that turn out to be correct *ex post*. During the period when such decisions determine the course of events, output will tend to be concentrated in those firms fortunate enough to have made the correct decisions.

None of this is necessarily monopolistic (although monopoly may play some role). Profit does not arise because the firm creates "artificial scarcity" through a reduction in its output. Nor does it arise because of collusion. Superior performance can be attributed to the combination of great uncertainty plus luck or atypical insight by the management of a firm. It is not until the experiments are actually tried that we learn which succeed and which fail. By the time the results are in, it is the shareholder that has captured (some of) the value, positive or negative, of past decisions. Even though the profits that arise from a firm's activities may be eroded by competitive imitation, since information is costly to obtain and techniques are difficult to duplicate, the firm may enjoy growth and a superior rate of return for some time.

Superior ability also may be interpreted as a competitive basis for acquiring a measure of monopoly power. In a world in which information is costly and the future is uncertain, a firm that seizes an opportunity to better serve customers does so because it expects to enjoy some protection from rivals because of their ignorance of this opportunity or because of their inability to imitate quickly. One possible source of some monopoly power is superior entrepreneurship. Our patent, copyright, and trademark laws explicitly provide as a reward for uncovering new methods (and for revealing these methods), legal protection against free imitation, and it may be true in some cases that an astute rival acquires the exclusive rights to some resource that *later* becomes valuable. There is no reason to suppose that competitive behavior never yields monopoly power, although in many cases such power may be exercised not by creating entry barriers, but through the natural frictions and ignorance that characterize any real economy. If rivals seek better ways to satisfy buyers or to produce a product, and if one or a few succeed in such endeavors, then the reward for their entrepreneurial efforts is likely to be some (short term) monopoly power and this may be associated with increased industrial concentration. To destroy such power when it arises may very well remove the incentive for progress. This is to be contrasted with a situation in which a high rate of return is obtained through a successful *collusion* to restrict output; here there is less danger to progress if the collusive agreement is penalized. Evidence presented below suggests that there are definite dangers of decreasing efficiency through the use of deconcentration or anti-merger policies.

III Inefficiency through anti-concentration public policy

The discussion in part II noted that concentration may be brought about because a workable system of incentives implies that firms which better serve buyers will tend to grow relative to other firms. One way in which a firm could better serve buyers is by seizing opportunities to exploit scale economies, although if scale economies are the main cause of concentration, it is difficult to understand why there is no significant trend toward one-firm industries; the lack of such a trend seems to suggest that superiority results in lower but *positively* sloped cost curves in the relevant range of large firm operations. This would set limits to the size of even the successful firms. Successful firms thus would seem to be more closely related to the "superior land" of classical economic rent analysis than to the single firm of natural monopoly theory. Whether or not superiority is reflected in scale economies, deconcentration may have the total effect of promoting inefficiency even though it also may reduce some monopoly-caused inefficiencies.[3]

The classic portrayal of the inefficiency produced by concentration through the exercise of monopoly power is that of a group of firms cooperating somehow to restrict entry and prevent rivalrous price behavior. Successfully pursued, this policy results in a product price and rate of return in excess of that which would have prevailed in the absence of collusion. However, if all firms are able to produce at the same cost, then the rate of return to successfully colluding firms should be independent of the particular sizes adopted by these firms to achieve low cost production. One firm may require a small scale, and hence have a smaller investment, while another may require a large scale, and corresponding large investment. At any given collusive price, the absolute amounts of monopoly profits will be proportional to output, but capital investment also will be proportionate to output, so we can expect the rate of return to be invariant with respect to size of firm.

If one size of firm earns a higher rate of return than another size, given any collusive price, then there must exist differences in the cost of production which favor the firm that earns the higher rate of return. Alternatively, if there is no single price upon which the industry agrees, but, rather a range of prices, then one firm can earn a higher rate of return if it produces a superior product and sells it at a higher price without thereby incurring proportionately higher costs; here, also, the firm that earns the higher rate of return can be judged to be more efficient because it delivers more value per dollar of cost incurred.

A deconcentration or anti-merger policy is more likely to have benign results if small firms in concentrated industries earn the same or higher rates of return than large firms, for, then, deconcentration may reduce collusion,[4] if it is present, while simultaneously allocating larger shares of industry output to smaller firms which are no less efficient than larger firms. But if increased concentration has come about because of the superior efficiency of those firms that have become large, then a deconcentration policy, while it may reduce the ease of colluding, courts the danger of reducing efficiency either by the penalties that it places on innovative success or by the shift in output to smaller, higher cost firms that it brings about. This would seem to be a distinct possibility if large firms in concentrated industries earn higher rates of return than small firms.

The problem posed is how to organize data to shed light on the probability that deconcentration will promote inefficiency. Correlating industry rate of return with concentration will not be enlightening for this problem, for even if concentrated industries exhibit higher rates of return, it is difficult to determine whether it is efficiency or monopoly power that is at work. Similarly, large firms would tend to earn high profit rates in concentrated industries either because they are efficient or because they are colluding. However, partitioning industry data by size of firm does suggest that there exists a real danger from a deconcentration or anti-merger public policy, for the rates of return earned by small firms give no support to the doctrine relating collusion to concentration. A successful collusion is very likely to benefit the smaller firms, and this suggests that there should be a positive correlation between the rate of return earned by small firms and the degree to which the industry is concentrated. By the same token, if efficiency is associated with concentration, there should be a positive correlation between concentration and the difference between the rate of return earned by large firms and that earned by small firms; that is, large firms have become large because they are more efficient than other firms and are able to earn a higher rate of return than other firms.

Tables 26.1 and 26.2 show 1963 rates of return based on internal revenue data partitioned by size of firm and industry concentration for 95 three-digit industries. In these tables, C_{63} designates the four firm concentration ratio measured on industry sales; R_1, R_2, R_3, and R_4, respectively, measure accounting rates of return (profit plus

Table 26.1 Rates of return by size and concentration (unweighted)

C_{63}	Number of industries	R_1	R_2	R_3	R_4	$\bar{R}$
10–20%	14	6.7%	9.0%	10.8%	10.3%	9.2%
20–30	22	4.5	9.1	9.7	10.4	8.4
30–40	24	5.2	8.7	9.9	11.0	8.7
40–50	21	5.8	9.0	9.5	9.0	8.3
50–60	11	6.7	9.8	10.5	13.4	10.1
over 60	3	5.3	10.1	11.5	23.1	12.5

Table 26.2 Rates of return by size and concentration (Weighted by assets)

C_{63}	Number of industries	R_1	R_2	R_3	R_4	$\bar{R}$
10–20%	14	7.3%	9.5%	10.6%	8.0%	8.8%
20–30	22	4.4	8.6	9.9	10.6	8.4
30–40	24	5.1	9.0	9.4	11.7	8.8
40–50	21	4.8	9.5	11.2	9.4	8.7
50–60	11	0.9	9.6	10.8	12.2	8.4
over 60	3	5.0	8.6	10.3	21.6	11.3

interest)/total assets, for firms with asset value less than $500,000, $500,000 to $5,000,000, $5,000,000 to $50,000,000 and over $50,000,000. Table 26.1 is calculated by assigning equal weight to all industries. It is based, therefore, on the assumption that each industry, regardless of size, offers an equally good observational unit for comparing the efficiency and monopolistic aspects of industry structure. Table 26.2 presents the same basic data with accounting rates of return weighted by asset value. Hence, an industry with many assets owned by small firms receives a larger weight in calculating the small firm rate of return for a given interval of concentration ratios.

Both tables fail to reveal the beneficial effects to small firms that we would expect from an association of collusion and industry concentration. The rate of return earned by firms in the smallest asset size does not increase with concentration. This seems to be true for the next two larger asset size classifications also, although in Table 26.1 the 11.5 per cent earned by R_3 firms in industries with concentration ratios higher than 60 per cent offers some indication of a larger rate of return than in less concentrated industries.[5] The data do not seem to support the notion that concentration and collusion are closely related, and, therefore, it is difficult to remain optimistic about the beneficial efficiency effects of a deconcentration or anti-merger public policy. On the contrary, the data suggest that such policies will reduce efficiency by impairing the survival of large firms in concentrated industries, for these firms do seem better able to produce at lower cost than their competitors.[6] Both tables indicate that R_4 size firms in industries with concentration ratios greater than 50 per cent produce at lower average cost.

Since a larger fraction of industry output is produced by larger firms in the more concentrated industries, these industries may exhibit higher rates of return than other industries. That this is so can be seen from the unweighted row averages given by column $\bar{R}$. Industries with $C_{63} > 50$ per cent seem to have earned higher rates of return than less concentrated industries. But this result, which is consistent with some earlier studies, may be attributed to the superior performance of the larger firms and not to collusive practices. Table 26.2 reveals this pattern even more clearly. Because the rates of return of smaller firms receive a larger weight (by total assets) in Table 26.2, industry rates of return are reduced even for concentrated industries in which large firms continue to perform well.

The general pattern of these data can be seen in Table 26.3. The results of regressing differences in profit rates on concentration ratios are shown in this table.

These regressions reveal a significant positive relationship between concentration and differences in rates of return, especially when comparing the largest and smallest firms in an industry.[7] The three regressions taken together indicate a nonlinear, decreasing impact of concentration on relative rates of return as the size of the smaller firms is increased from R_1 to R_3.

The competitive view of industry structure suggests that rapid changes in concentration are brought about by changed cost conditions and not by alterations in the height of entry barriers. Industries experiencing rapid increases in concentration should exhibit greater disparities between large and small rates of return because of the more significant cost differences which are the root cause of rapid alternations in industry structure. The monopoly view of concentration does not imply such a relationship, for if an industry is rapidly achieving workable collusive practices there is no reason to suppose that the difference between large and small firm profit rates should increase. At the time of writing, matching data on concentration were available for both 1963 and 1967. This time span is too short to reveal much variation in concentration ratios, and so we cannot be very confident about evidence gained by regressing differences in profit rates on changes in concentration ratios. However, the persistently positive coefficient of the variable $C_{67} - C_{63}$ in Table 26.4 is consistent with the competitive viewpoint, and must increase our doubts, however slightly, about the beneficial effects of an active deconcentration or anti-merger policy.

Table 26.3

$R_4 - R_1 = -1.4 + .21^*C_{63}$ $\quad\quad\quad (.07)$	$r^2 = .09$
$R_4 - R_2 = -2.6 + .12^{**}C_{63}$ $\quad\quad\quad (.06)$	$r^2 = .04$
$R_4 - R_3 = -3.1 + .10^{**}C_{63}$ $\quad\quad\quad (.05)$	$r^2 = .04$

*, **, significant at the 1% and 5% levels respectively.
Standard errors are shown in parenthesis.

Table 26.4

$R_4 - R_1 = 1.5 + .21*C_{63} + .21(C_{67} - C_{63})$ $r^2 = .09$
          $(.07)$ $(.42)$

$R_4 - R_2 = -2.9 + .12**C_{63} + .37(C_{67} - C_{63})$ $r^2 = .06$
          $(.06)$ $(.28)$

$R_4 - R_3 = -3.4 + .10**C_{63} + .29(C_{67} - C_{63})$ $r^2 = .05$
          $(.05)$ $(.24)$

---

*,**, respectively, 1% and 5% confidence levels.

I have presented an explanation of industry structure and profitability based on competitive superiority. The problem faced by a deconcentration or anti-merger policy was posed on the basis of this explanation. Is there a danger that such a policy will produce more inefficiency than it eliminates? The data presented suggest that this danger should be taken seriously.

Notes

1 The author wishes to thank the Research Program in Competition and Public Policy at U.C.L.A. for assisting in the preparation of this article.

2 A detailed discussion of the implicit notion of team production that underlies these arguments can he found in Armen A. Alchian & Harold Demsetz, Production, Information Costs, and Economic Organization, 62 *Amer. Econ. Rev.* 777 (1972).

3 For a discussion of the social costs that might be incurred by deconcentration, especially in the context of scale economies, see John S. McGee, In Defense of Industrial Concentration 159 (1971).

4 This statement is incorrect if a deconcentration or anti-merger policy causes firms to adopt socially less efficient methods of colluding than would be adopted in the absence of such a policy.

5 Since firms are segregated by absolute size, for some industries the R_3 firms will be relatively large. A better test could be secured by contrasting the rates of return for the 10% largest and 10% smallest firms in each industry. But the data do not allow such a comparison. However, see note 7 for the result of a similar type of adjustment.

6 On the margin of output, however, these large firms need not have an advantage over small firms, just as fertile land has no advantage over poor land for producing marginal units. The failure of the large firms to become more dominant in these industries suggests the absence of such advantage.

7 Three adjustments in procedure and in variables were undertaken to analyze certain problems in the data and the theory.

   (1) It is believed by some that the profits of firms, and especially of small firms, are hidden in administrative wages. To check on the possibility that this phenomenon might have accounted for the data relationships shown above, the data were recalculated after adding back to profits all administrative salaries of firms in the R_1 asset size class. Although this increased very slightly the rates of return for this asset size class, as, of course, must be the case, no correlation between concentration and rate of return was

produced. In fact, rates of return so calculated were virtually perfectly correlated with the rates of return shown above for this asset size.

(2) The asset size categories used to calculate the above data are uniform over all industries. Some industries, however, had no firms in the largest asset size category, and these were dropped from the sample. An alternative method was used to check on the impact of this procedure. For each industry, the largest asset size class was redefined so as to include some firms in every industry. The mechanics of the procedure was to categorize asset sizes more finely and choose the largest three size categories containing some observations for each industry. These were then counted as the larger firms in each industry, and the rate of return for these firms was then compared to those firms contained in the three smaller asset size categories containing some observations. The unweighted average difference between large firm rate of return, R_L, and small firm rate of return, R_s, compared with industry concentration is shown below. This table is consistent with the text tables.

C_{63}	$R_L - R_s$
0–20%	6.4%
20–30	9.4
30–40	7.0
40–50	7.0
50–60	12.8
Over 60	14.0

(3) The efficiency argument suggests that for a given degree of industry concentration, measured by the four firm concentration ratio, the greater the difference between the sizes of the largest firms and the sizes of the smallest firms, the larger will be the disparity between R_4 and R_1. A linear regression of $R_4 - R_1$ on C_{63} and the average size of firms in the R_4 class yields a positive but not highly significant coefficient for the variable "average asset size of firms in the R_4 class." Also, there was a small reduction in the significance of the coefficient of C_{63}.

Review and Discussion Questions

1 What is Demsetz's theory of competitive superiority? What are some possible sources of superiority?

2 How does examining the profits of small-share firms in concentrated industries test the superiority hypothesis?

3 What do the data in Tables 26.1 and 26.2 show?

4 What are the implications of Demsetz's research for antitrust policy?

5 Are there problems with Demsetz's data or approach? (Can you find other academic papers that try to address these problems? What are their results?)

Chapter 27

CRAIG M. NEWMARK

DOES HORIZONTAL PRICE FIXING RAISE PRICE? A LOOK AT THE BAKERS OF WASHINGTON CASE[1]

[T]he enforcement agencies should thus concentrate their efforts in areas (like price fixing) where it can be convincingly argued that successful cases generally create net benefits.[2]

The advocates of strong measures against price fixing and information exchanges should no longer be allowed to treat the welfare case for their position as self-evident. … My analysis provides ample justification for condemning any use of scarce anti-trust enforcement measures to harass small-fry price fixers and low-budget trade associations. Let the local laundries collude in peace.[3]

I Introduction

HOW EFFECTIVE are horizontal price-fixing conspiracies? According to some recent studies, very effective. Producers of asphalt, gymnasium bleachers, rock salt, concrete pipe, and circuit breakers all raised prices through conspiracies.[4] One textbook concludes that the average price-fixing agreement increases price by 10–30 percent.[5] Another text asserts that many conspiracies have increased price by 30–60 percent.[6]

Almost all successful conspiracies shared an important characteristic: government agencies or utilities were major customers of the price fixers. But economists have long predicted that conspiracies against these two types of buyers will be unusually effective.[7] An open question is whether price fixing succeeds against other buyers. We have a small set of empirical studies that suggests that the answer is no: conspiracies against unregulated, for-profit buyers do not raise prices significantly, if at all.[8]

There is, however, an apparent exception to this finding. The staff of the Federal Trade Commission (FTC) presented evidence that the Bakers of Washington conspiracy operated very successfully.[9] The FTC staff concluded that, from 1955 to 1964, this conspiracy increased the retail price of bread in Seattle by at least 15 percent.[10] This conclusion has been widely—and uncritically—cited.[11] Some observers have referred to it when arguing for greater antitrust effort against horizontal price fixing. For example, a diagram illustrating the hypothesized effect of the conspiracy on Seattle's bread price (Figure 27.1) was printed in the *Antitrust Law and Economics Journal* five times in ten years.[12]

This article reexamines the contention that the Bakers of Washington conspiracy raised Seattle's bread price. I present a different explanation of why the Seattle retail price was higher than the U.S. average price during 1955–64 and why the Seattle price fell in 1965. I conclude that the conspiracy did not raise Seattle's price at all.

II The FTC's case against Bakers of Washington

On March 7, 1961, the FTC issued a price-fixing complaint against Bakers of Washington (64 F.T.C. 1089). Formed in 1936, Bakers of Washington was a trade association of bakers located in the western half of Washington State. In September 1961 the association had forty-nine members. Both retail and wholesale bakers belonged to the association, but the great majority of members were wholesale bakers.[13]

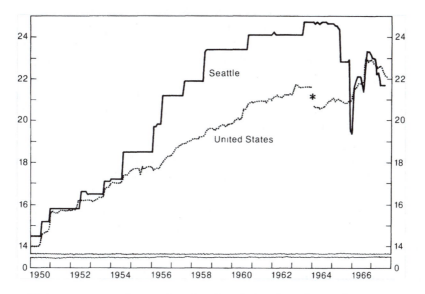

Figure 27.1 Average retail prices for white bread, Seattle and United States, 1950–67. December 1963 and January 1964 prices for the United States are not comparable because of a revision in sampling procedures.

Source. Federal Trade Comm'n, Economic Report on the Baking Industry 67 (1967).

The hearing examiner concluded that "Respondents, using Bakers as a medium, do two things: one, cooperate in the establishment and announcement of price changes; and two, collectively enforce adherence to prices established and announced."[14] In addition to discussing union contracts and labor grievance problems, firm representatives frequently discussed prices at the trade association meetings. The FTC sarcastically dismissed the firms' defense that they made pricing decisions independently:

> Representatives of the larger respondents were something less than persuasive when interrogated about how they happened to have picked a particular date to raise prices and about the reasons for deciding to raise the price by the particular amount chosen. Thus, the 1957 increase had been a 1¢ raise, the 1958 increase had been a 2¢ hike, and the 1960 jump was for only 1¢ again. Why pick 2¢ one year, and 1¢ another? ... Each time a "price leader" raised his prices, it "stuck." The others followed him up quickly. ... The figure he selected—whether 1¢ or 2¢—was always just the amount that his major competitors, also exercising their "independent" business judgement, agreed was neither too large nor too small for the state of the market.[15]

The trade association manager threatened firms that cut prices below the agreed level with the prospect of a retaliatory price war. The commission majority concluded that "[some firms] would not have raised their prices had it not been for the urgings, and sometimes the threats, of the association's manager and certain of their competitors."[16]

In its subsequent report, the FTC staff argued that the price-fixing conspiracy significantly affected the Seattle retail bread price. The report noted that from the mid-1950s through 1964, the Seattle price, as measured by the Bureau of Labor Statistics, averaged 15 percent above the U.S. average price (see Figure 27.1).[17] The conspiracy's effect was also evident, according to the report, in the post-1964 movement of the Seattle retail price.[18] In February 1964 the commission found the trade association and other respondents guilty of price fixing; at the request of a respondent, the commission stayed the effective date of its order and held further hearings. On December 3, 1964, the commission reaffirmed its original judgment and ordered the respondents to cease price fixing. Shortly thereafter, the Seattle retail price began to fall: it fell .3¢ from January to April 1965 and 1.5¢ more in May. While the 1964 Seattle price was 3.9¢ (15.85 percent) above the U.S. average, in 1965 the Seattle price was only .2¢ above the U.S. average; in 1966, .1¢ above; and from 1967 to 1977—when the Bureau of Labor Statistics stopped publishing city food prices—the Seattle price remained below the U.S average. A plausible inference, therefore, is that the commission's action forced Seattle bakers to cut price by approximately 15 percent, a percentage equal to the price-fixing overcharge.

III A Different explanation

In this section, I present evidence that the conspiracy had no effect on Seattle's bread price. The evidence is organized around two contentions. First, after allowing for a higher retail markup on bread, higher wage rates, and a higher normal profit rate in the western United States, the Seattle price during 1955–64 was not unusually high.

Second, the sharp decline of the Seattle price in 1965 was caused by a change in the structure of Seattle's bread market. Bread imported from Canada probably triggered this change.

A The 1955–64 period

I use 1955 as the starting date of the conspiracy, following other authors.[19] My explanation for the difference between Seattle's price and the average U.S. price during 1955–64 builds on the observation that retail bread prices were high all over the West Coast during this period. Prices in San Francisco and Los Angeles were higher than in Seattle, and the Portland price was nearly as high (see Table 27.1).[20] The average price in these other three West Coast cities was 19 percent higher than the average price in sixteen nonwestern cities. Other data show that bread prices were higher all throughout the West.[21]

What was different about bread markets in the West? One difference was that retail markups on bread were larger. When asked why bread prices were higher on the

Table 27.1 1955–63 Average real retail prices of white bread

City	Average price (¢/pound)
San Francisco	18.9
Los Angeles	18.4
New York City	17.7
Seattle	17.7
Portland, Oreg.	17.6
Philadelphia	17.1
Scranton, Pa.	17.0
Pittsburgh	15.8
Cleveland	15.8
Baltimore	15.4
Boston	15.4
Washington, D.C.	15.2
Atlanta	15.1
Kansas City	15.1
St. Louis	14.9
Detroit	14.7
Cincinnati	14.7
Minneapolis	14.3
Chicago	14.3
Houston	13.1
West Coast average price	18.15
Nonwestern average price	15.35

Nominal bread prices from U.S. Dep't of Labor, Bur. of Labor Statistics, Bulletin Numbers 1217, 1254, 1301, and 1446. City Consumer Price Index data from U.S. Dep't of Labor, Bur. of Labor Statistics, Bulletin Number 1256 (Table C-2) and Bulletin Number 1554 (table A).

The nominal price in each city in each year, 1955–63, is deflated by the city Consumer Price Index for that year (1947–49 = 100) before averaging.

West Coast than in Washington, D.C., the president of the Continental Baking Company testified, "I might add that on the west coast the grocers themselves take a larger margin of profit than they do in Washington. In Washington your grocers take approximately 2 cents profit. Out there they take 4 and sometimes as much as 5 cents profit. This makes a difference because you are talking retail prices."[22]

A 1960 Senate report supports the executive's claim. The report lists wholesale prices of major brands of bread in 127 cities. For twenty-one western cities the average wholesale price was less than 9 percent above the nonwestern average price.[23] Thus, approximately half of the difference in retail price between the West and the rest of the country was created by grocery retailers, not by bakers.[24]

Another difference in western markets was that wage rates were higher. Higher labor costs accounted for one quarter of the regional difference in retail prices.[25]

The remaining one quarter of the retail price difference was reflected in larger accounting profits for the western bakers. In 1960 western bakers earned .7 cents/ pound more in pretax profit than bakers in the rest of the country; in 1964, .4 cents/ pound more, according to a survey done for the National Commission on Food Marketing.[26]

Western bakers earned higher profit margins for at least twenty years, 1947–67 (see Table 27.2). Their margins ranged from 6 to 11 percent higher than elsewhere.[27] (Note, though, that until 1967 the margin for Washington State was lower than for the western region as a whole.)

Are these higher margins rates evidence that bakers colluded, either explicitly or implicitly, all throughout the West? Available information provides scant support for a regional collusion hypothesis. Explicit price fixing of bread was detected infrequently in the West.[28] Seller concentration in western markets was not much greater than in other markets. And regression analysis indicates that seller concentration does not explain the western bakers' higher price-cost margin.[29]

This higher margin is better explained by its similarity to the higher margins earned by other manufacturers in the West. Using a list compiled by William Shepherd,

Table 27.2 Regional price–cost margins for bakers, 1947–72

Year	Washington margin	Western region margin	Rest of United States margin (excluding western region)
1947	.1663	.1993	.1817
1954	.1802	.2113	.1946
1958	.2324	.2552	.2300
1963	.2546	.2593	.2452
1967	.2853	.2828	.2618
1972	n.a.	.3002	.2992

U.S. Dep't of Commerce, Bur. of the Census. Census of Manufactures, various years.
The price–cost margins equal value added minus payroll divided by value of shipments for industry SIC nos. 2051–12, "Bread and Related Products—Wholesale Bakeries" (Industry SIC no. 2051 was used for Washington in 1967); n.a. = not available.

I identified sixty-nine four-digit Standard Industrial Classification (SIC) industries as having either local or regional markets.[30] For each of these industries I compared the 1958 price–cost margin in the West to the margin in the nonwestern United States. The western margin was larger for forty-five of the sixty-nine industries. According to the nonparametric sign test,[31] we can reject the null hypothesis that margins were equal in the two regions at the .02 confidence level (two-tailed test). Further, the western margins exceeded the nonwestern margins by an average of 8.4 percent. This average difference is significantly larger than zero, and it explains most of the 11 percent higher margin that western bakers earned in 1958.[32]

Data on regional interest rates also indicate that a higher rate of return on capital prevailed in the West. Interest rates on short-term business loans in the Southwest and West ranged from 4 to 9 percent higher (twenty to thirty-three basis points) than elsewhere in the United States during 1954–64.[33]

B The 1965–66 period

The retail price of bread in Seattle dropped from December 1964 to January 1966, while the U.S. average price rose. Both the unusual size of Seattle's decline, 3.2 cents/pound, and the timing of the decline suggest that a successful price-fixing conspiracy among bakers collapsed in 1965 following the FTC's final judgment in *Bakers of Washington*.[34]

But contrary to what should have occurred had a price-fixing agreement collapsed, the wholesale prices of Seattle's leading brands did *not* fall during 1965–66. By August 1966, the wholesale prices of these leading brands—all produced by alleged conspirators—were 2.3 cents/pound higher than they were in December 1964.[35] This increase was almost identical to the price increases that occurred in other major cities.[36]

Seattle's average bread price fell not because collusion ceased but because several inexpensive, lower-quality brands of bread began selling in Seattle during 1964–66. Principal among these new brands was one manufactured in Canada by Granddad Baking Company. Granddad's bread sold at wholesale for seven cents per pound (nearly 30 percent) less than the leading brands. The other new brands were priced similarly.[37]

I now discuss the reasons why the new brands sold at such a significant discount to the leading brands and why these new brands appeared in Seattle when they did.

The new brands of bread were not identical to the leading brands. The leading brands in Seattle, as in other U.S. cities, were advertised-label brands. Advertised-label bread was sold under the principal trade names of wholesale bakers. Competing against advertised-label bread were private-label brands. Grocery retailers and some wholesale bakers manufactured private-label bread; in either case, grocery retailers sold this type of bread under their own trade names. Private-label bread was generally made from a leaner formula than advertised-label bread, containing less milk, shortening, and sugar.[38] Private-label brands were advertised less intensively than the leading brands.[39]

The two types of bread also were distributed differently.[40] Wholesale bakers employed "driver-salesmen" to distribute their products. Driver-salesmen spent considerable time restocking bread shelves, removing stale loaves, and performing bookkeeping services for retailers. The driver-salesman system was well-suited for deliveries to small, nonchain stores. Large grocery chains employed a less costly method of distribution. The chains' contracts with the Teamsters Union, which represented driver-salesmen as well as chain-store drivers, permitted the chains to pay their drivers a flat hourly wage; in contrast, the union contracts stipulated that driver-salesmen receive a guaranteed hourly wage plus a commission on route sales. The chains also distributed their bread in larger, more efficient lots and relied on cheaper in-store labor for stocking of shelves and removal of stales. Two studies concluded that the large chains could distribute bread for as little as one quarter the cost of wholesale bakers using driver-salesmen.[41]

Because of these differences, grocery retailers priced private-label brands below advertised-label brands. In 1958 the U.S. average retail price for private-label bread was 17 percent below the average price of advertised-label brands.[42] In most areas of the country, retailers occasionally used private-label brands as "loss leaders" by cutting prices to ten cents per pound or less.[43] Retailers increased the discount on private-label brands during the 1960s and 1970s.[44] The discount helped raise private-label brands' share of the national bread market. In 1960 their share was 18 percent; in 1971, 36 percent; and by 1977, approximately 50 percent.[45]

Wholesale bakers recognized early that the chains' less expensive distribution method and lower private-label prices threatened their advertised-label business. The bakers tried to respond by lowering the cost of the driver-salesman system. But the Teamsters Union vigorously resisted any change to this system.[46]

Western Teamsters made a particularly strong effort to maintain the incomes and jobs of driver-salesmen. The union in the West was unusual in its number of members, its leadership, and its activities. The number of Teamsters per capita in the West was nearly twice the national average.[47] This organizational success has been credited to Dave Beck.[48] Beck was president of a Seattle Teamsters local and organizer of the Western Conference of Teamsters. He believed that the key to maintaining the incomes of his members was to insure that Teamsters' employers were profitable. Toward that end, the Western Teamsters tried to restrict entry of firms into many local industries. They refused to serve new firms in "overcrowded" industries. They also, particularly in Seattle, tried to discourage firms from cutting prices.[49] Beck argued, "If [railroad] fares between Seattle and Spokane can be stabilized, why can't we apply the same principle to the prices charged for rye bread and chocolate pies?"[50]

In 1963 a Seattle firm challenged the Teamsters' support of the driver-salesmen. Granddad Baking Company bought bread from a wholesale baker and distributed it to retailers using nonunion drivers.[51] The following year Granddad's supplier stopped selling to Granddad because of "certain pressures" applied by the Teamsters.[52] Because other Seattle wholesale bakers refused to sell to Granddad and because the Canadian dollar had recently fallen against the U.S. dollar, Granddad began importing bread from Canada.[53]

Granddad priced its bread well below the wholesale prices of the advertised-label brands. Retailers typically sold Granddad's bread for more than ten cents per pound (nearly 50 percent) less than the advertised-label brands.[54] This discount was especially attention getting because in Seattle—as all throughout the West—grocers had maintained unusually low discounts on private-label brands.[55]

Although the Teamsters pressured retailers not to sell Granddad's bread, Granddad sold 40,000 loaves a week in 1964 and early 1965.[56] I estimate that this volume equaled a market share of more than 3 percent, probably 5 percent.[57,58] Several Seattle bakers told the FTC Staff that Canadian bread was cutting into their business.[59] And over the period 1966–68, Granddad's volume grew.[60]

The entry of Granddad's Canadian bread apparently prompted Seattle's wholesale bakers and grocery retailers to change their bread-marketing strategies. Both groups spent less effort selling advertised-label brands. In early 1965, Continental Baking Company, the largest wholesale baker in Seattle, introduced a "secondary-label" brand.[61] (Secondary-label brands were similar to private-label brands in that they were advertised little, if at all, and they were made from leaner recipes.) This brand sold at retail for about seven cents per pound less than Continental's advertised-label brand and just three and a half cents per pound more than Granddad's bread.[62] Continental announced that its secondary brand was intended "to meet the competition of Canadian bread."[63] Two other leading wholesale bakers subsequently introduced secondary-label brands.[64] The number of retailers selling private-label brands increased.[65] Retailers also cut prices on private-label bread. In contrast to their practice prior to 1965, Seattle grocers began sharply discounting private-label brands.[66] By 1974 the market share of private-label brands in Seattle had increased so much that in a sample of eighteen large U.S. cities, the city in which private-label brands held the largest market share was Seattle.[67]

That Canadian bread was responsible for the Seattle price decline is also indicated by the movement of bread prices in Detroit. Two Michigan bakers complained during Senate hearings in 1959 that Canadian bread was threatening their business even though Canadian bread held just 2 percent of the Detroit market at that time.[68] The Canadian bread carried a wholesale price of about six cents per pound less than the Detroit bakers' price. From 1959 to 1966, while the U.S. average retail price rose 2.5 cents/pound, the Detroit price rose only .3 cents/pound. (The prices in three other midwestern cities, Chicago, Cleveland, and St. Louis, all rose over two cents/pound.)[69] Among the thirty-two nonwestern cities for which the Bureau of Labor Statistics published 1966 bread prices, Detroit's was third lowest, 3.9 cents/pound (17 percent) below the U.S. average.[70]

IV Conclusion

A comparison of Seattle's retail bread price to the U.S. average retail bread price over the years 1955–66, as shown in Figure 27.1, appears to illustrate dramatically the effect of a successful price-fixing conspiracy. I have argued in this article that neither Seattle's high price during the conspiracy period of 1955–64 nor Seattle's lower price after the conspiracy ended should be interpreted as evidence of an effective price-fixing agreement. Seattle's high price during 1955–64 was matched, even exceeded, in other cities in the western United States. The three reasons why prices were higher in the West were higher retail markups, higher labor costs, and a higher normal rate of return. Given these three regional factors, well beyond the control of Seattle bakers, Seattle's retail price during the conspiracy is seen to be nothing more than the competitive price.

Despite the competitive pricing of Seattle's bakers, new brands of bread entered the market during 1964–66. The first new brand was sold by a firm that imported bread from Canada. This bread carried a much lower price than Seattle's leading brands primarily because of the seller's lower-cost distribution system. After Seattle's wholesale bakers introduced lower-quality brands and grocery retailers slashed the prices on these brands, Seattle's average price fell. Neither group's action could have been, logically, a response to the prosecution of an ineffective conspiracy. And information from several sources indicates that the Seattle bakers' failure to adopt a lower-cost distribution system and their delay in introducing inexpensive brands resulted from extraordinary pressure applied by the Seattle local of the Teamsters Union. The Teamsters' inability, despite considerable effort, to keep out the Canadian bread should be viewed as the probable cause for Seattle's price fall in 1965.

Notes

1 I appreciate the helpful comments of Frank Easterbrook, Robert Fearn, David Flath, Stan Liebowitz, Steve Margolis, Douglas Pearce, and Walter Thurman. I am solely responsible for any errors.
2 Richard Schmalensee, Antitrust and the New Industrial Economics, 72 *Am. Econ. Rev.* 24, 27 (1982).
3 Donald Dewey, Information, Entry, and Welfare: The Case for Collusion, 69 *Am. Econ. Rev.* 587, 594 (1979).
4 See Dale R. Funderbunk, Price-Fixing in the Liquid Asphalt Industry: Economic Analysis versus the "Hot Document," 7 *Antitrust L. & Econ. Rev.* 61 (1974); W. Bruce Erickson, Price Fixing Conspiracies: Their Long-Term Impact, 24 *J. Indus. Econ.* 189 (1976); Alfred L. Parker, Economics in the Courtroom: Proof of Damage in a Price-Fixing Case, 9 *Antitrust L. & Econ. Rev.* 61 (1977); and David F. Lean, Jonathan D. Ogur, & Robert P. Rogers, Does Collusion Pay ... Does Antitrust Work? 51 *S. Econ. J.* 828 (1985).
5 William G. Shepherd, *The Economics of Industrial Organization* 245 (1985).
6 Douglas F. Greer, *Industrial Organization and Public Policy* 264 (1984).
7 See Fred M. Westfield, Regulation and Conspiracy, 55 *Am. Econ. Rev.* 425 (1965); Amen A. Alchian, Electrical Equipment Collusion: Why and How, in *Economic Forces at Work* 259 (Ronald H. Coase ed. 1977); and F. M. Scherer, *Industrial Market Structure and Economic Performance* 224 (1980).
8 For quantitative studies, see George J. Stigler & James K. Kindahl, *The Behavior of Industrial Prices* 92–93 (1971); Erickson, *supra* note 4, at 197–200; James E. Duggan & Gorti V. L. Narasinham, 1981 *Proc. Bus. & Econ. Stat. Sec. Am. Stat. A.* 241 (1981); Michael O. Finkelstein & Hans Levenbach, Regression Estimates of Damages in Price-Fixing Cases, 46 *L. & Contemp. Probs.* 145 (1983); Robert M. Feinberg, The Timing of Antitrust Effects on Pricing, 16 *Applied Econ.* 397 (1984); Robert M. Feinberg, Strategic and Deterrent Pricing Responses to Antitrust Investigations, 2 *Int'l J. Indus. Organ.* 75 (1984); and Franklin M. Fisher, Statisticians, Econometricians, and Adversary Proceedings, 81 *J. Am. Stat. A.* 277 (1986). For a qualitative study of two conspiracies, see Almarin Phillips, Market Structure, Organization and Performance (1962). These studies found that most conspiracies increased price by only a small amount: 2 percent or less.
9 U.S. Federal Trade Comm'n, *Economic Report on the Baking Industry*, 66–71 (1967). (Hereinafter cited as FTC Report.)

10 *Id.* at 52. See also Russell C. Parker, The Baking Industry, 2 *Antitrust L. & Econ. Rev.* Ill (1969).

11 Citations in the professional literature are Louis P. Bucklin, *Competition and Evolution in the Distribution Trades* 250–52 (1972); Leonard W. Weiss, An Analysis of the Allocation of Antitrust Division Resources, in *The Antitrust Dilemma* 39 (James A. Datton & Stanford L. Levin eds. 1974); Andrew James McLaughlin, An Economic Analysis of Resale Price Maintenance 60–74 (unpublished Ph.D. dissertation, Univ. Calif. at Los Angeles 1979); Wesley J. Liebeler, Bureau of Competition: Antitrust Enforcement Activities, in *The Federal Trade Commission since 1970: Economic Regulation and Bureaucratic Behavior* 92 (Kenneth W. Clarkson & Timothy J. Muris eds. 1981); Greer, *supra* note 6; and Bruce W. Marion, *The Organization and Performance of the U.S. Food System* 380–81 (1986). (Weiss qualified his acceptance of the FTC's conclusion, saying that the FTC "seemed" to show that the conspiracy elevated price.) Other citations are William N. Leonard, *Business Size, Market Power, and Public Policy* 215–16 (1969); William Robbins, *The American Food Scandal*, 133–34 (1974); and Jennifer Cross, *The Supermarket Trap* 18 (1976).

12 Willard F. Mueller, Effects of Antitrust Enforcement in the Retail Food Industry: Price Fixing and Merger Policy, 2 *Antitrust L. & Econ. Rev.* 83, 86 (1968–69); Parker, *supra* note 10, at 119; Charles E. Mueller, Lawyer's Guide to the Economic Literature on Competition and Monopoly: An Introduction to the Doctoral Dissertations (I), 5 *Antitrust L. & Econ. Rev.* 83, 92 (1972); Paul D. Scanlon, Measuring the "Performance" of the FTC: The Wrong Kind of Numbers Game Again, 7 *Antitrust L. & Econ. Rev.* 15, 23 (1974); and Mayo J. Thompson, The FTC Strikes Again: Rooting Out "Low" Prices in the Bread Industry, 7 *Antitrust L. & Econ. Rev.* 85, 95 (1974).

13 In the Matter of Bakers of Washington, Inc., *et al.*, 64 F.T.C. 1079 (1964).

14 *Id.* at 1091.

15 *Id.* at 1131.

16 *Id.* at 1134–35. In a vigorous dissent, Commissioner Elman argued that these actions "do not permit an inference of a conspiracy or agreement to fix prices; they form no sinister pattern." *Id.* at 1146.

17 FTC Report, *supra* note 9, at 66.

18 *Id.* at 69–70.

19 W. Mueller, *supra* note 12, at 86–87; and McLaughlin, *supra* note 11, at 67.

20 The twenty cities listed in Table 27.1 are all the cities for which the Bureau of Labor Statistics (BLS) published bread prices. The year 1964 is not included in the averages because BLS published prices for only twelve of these twenty cities for that year.

21 In 1960 in the three West Coast states, the average retail price paid by farmers was 24.0 cents/pound; in the eight Mountain states, 22.0 cents/pound; and in the thirty-seven non-western states, 19.5 cents/pound. Prices were therefore 23 percent higher on the West Coast than in the nonwestern United States and nearly 16 percent higher in the West as a whole. See U.S. Dep't of Agriculture, Statistical Reporting Service, Crop Reporting Board, Agricultural Prices: 1960 Annual Summary, June 1961.

22 U.S. Senate, Committee on the Judiciary, Subcommittee on Antitrust and Monopoly, Hearings on Administered Prices, Part 12, 6125 (1959).

23 U.S. Senate, Committee on the Judiciary, Subcommittee on Antitrust and Monopoly, Administered Prices: Bread (Report No. 1923) 183–86 (1960). I used a median price for cities that had more than one major brand.

24 Why western grocery retailers obtained larger markups on bread is unclear. Company strategies may have played a role in creating the regional difference. Consider A & P, Kroger, and Winn Dixie, the first-, third-, and seventh-largest supermarket chains in 1958. These three chains used their store brands of bread as loss leaders more extensively

than other chains. See Richard G. Walsh & Bert M. Evans, *Economics of Change in Market Structure, Conduct, and Performance: The Baking Industry, 1947–58*, at 106 (1963). But Kroger and Winn Dixie did not operate west of the Rockies, and A & P had only a tiny presence of thirty-seven stores in the West. (See Business Guides, Inc., 1958 *Directory of Supermarket and Grocery Chain Stores*.) Another factor that may have contributed to the difference was that the Teamsters Union tried to restrict the sale of "cheap" bread, and the Teamsters Union was stronger in the West. See Section III*B infra*.

25 Hourly earnings of factory production workers were 14 percent greater on the West Coast than in the rest of the country in 1958. Per capita income in 1957 was 19 percent higher on the West Coast. See M. W. Reder, Trends in Wages, Savings, and Per Capita Income, 82 *Monthly Lab. Rev.* 524, 526–27 (1959). Payroll per employee in wholesale baking firms was 20 percent higher in the West in 1958 and 26 percent higher in 1963 according to Census of Manufactures data. My contention that higher wages accounted for about 25 percent of the retail price difference is based on survey information; see note 26 *infra*.

26 Nat'l Comm'n on Food Marketing, Organization and Competition in the Milling and Baking Industries, Technical Study No. 5, 128–31 (1965). The average wholesale price for bakery products in the nonwestern United States was 18 cents/pound according to this survey. The extra .7 cents/pound in pretax profit earned by western bakers is equal to 4 percent of that price. Since retail bread prices in the West were either 16 percent higher (using state price data, note 21 *supra*) or 18 percent higher (using city price data, Table 27.1 *supra*), this 4 percent is equal to about one quarter of the retail price difference.

27 U.S. Dep't of Commerce, Bur. Census, Census of Manufactures, various years.

28 The Department of Justice filed three price-fixing cases involving western markets during 1955–85. One conspiracy involved firms in Las Vegas and lasted from 1953 to early 1957. Two of the five firms indicted were acquitted. Another conspiracy occurred in Arizona, beginning "sometime before 1963" and lasting until 1974. And a third case was brought against six firms operating in San Diego, but all six firms were acquitted. East of the Rockies, the Justice Department brought six cases from 1955 to 1964 and ten cases from 1965 through 1985. See Block, Nold, & Sidak, The Deterrent Effect of Antitrust Enforcement, 89 *J. Pol. Econ.* 429 (1981); Clabault & Block, *Sherman Act Indictments, 1955–80* (1981); and *Commerce Clearing House, Trade Regulation Reporter*, various issues (1981–85). I could not find any other price-fixing cases filed against bakers by the FTC. One authority notes that FTC price-fixing cases in *any* industry were rare. See Alan Stone, *Economic Regulation and the Public Interest: The Theory and Practice* 90 (1977).

29 Due to its perishability, the relevant geographic market for bread was generally local (FTC Report, *supra* note 9, at 42–44). A special tabulation of Census of Manufactures data lists 1963 seller concentration ratios for eleven metropolitan areas. Los Angeles and San Francisco both had four-firm ratios of .56; the average of the nine nonwestern areas was .51 with a standard derivation of .11. See U.S. Senate Committee on the Judiciary, Concentration Ratios in Manufacturing Industry: 1963, Part II, 338–39 (1963). The FTC staff estimated 1963 concentration in seventeen cities (FTC Report, *supra* note 9, at 44). Four western cities—Denver, Long Beach, Portland, and Phoenix—had four-firm ratios of .46, .59, .58, and .78, respectively. Thirteen nonwestern cities averaged .64. Senate hearings (*supra* note 22, at 6146) contain a bar chart from which lower bounds for four-firm concentration can be estimated for twenty-seven cities for 1957. Five often western cities had ratios equal to at least .50, while nine of seventeen nonwestern cities had ratios at least that large. The available data do not show higher local concentration in the West. The Nat'l Comm'n on Food Marketing (*supra* note 26, at 52–53) reported 1958 four-firm concentration ratios for states. The eleven western states had an average value of .61,

while the thirty-seven other states had an average value of .51 with a standard derivation of .18. These state concentration data can be combined with data from the 1958 Census of Manufactures to crudely test the tacit collusion hypothesis. The dependent variable is the 1958 price–cost margin (in percentages) for each state, for industry SIC no. 2051, "Bread and Related Products." The results (t-statistics are in parentheses):

price–cost margin = 21.9 + .02 concentration ratio + 3.2 western region dummy,

(15.3) (.81)   (3.0)

mean of dependent variable = 23.79.

The higher seller concentration of the western states accounts for little, if any, of western bakers' higher margins.

30 William G. Shepherd, *Market Power and Economic Welfare: An Introduction* 263–67 (1970). Shepherd identified a total of eighty-eight industries, other than bread, as having local or regional markets. For nineteen of these industries I could not compute a western margin because of missing data in the Census of Manufactures, so sixty-nine industries were used for the two tests. I also performed the tests for a set of sixty industries identified by Schwartzman & Bodoff as sold in local or regional markets (David Schwartzman & Joan Bodoff, Concentration in Regional and Local Industries, 37 *S. Econ. J.* 343–48 (1971)). The results were qualitatively the same as those reported in the text.

31 Lothar Sachs, *Applied Statistics: A Handbook of Techniques* 316–18 (2d ed. 1984).

32 The average difference is significantly different from zero using both a nonparametric test and a parametric t-test (t-value = 3.8).

33 U.S. Federal Reserve System, Board of Governors, *Banking and Monetary Statistics, 1941–1970*, at 708 (1976). This publication lists two rates for years before 1967: one rate is the average rate for "7 large northern and eastern cities," and the other rate is an average rate for "11 large southern and western cities." For 1967, the publication breaks out the "southern and western" rate into values for the Southeast, Southwest, and West Coast. The Southeast rate is lower than both the Southwest and West Coast rates, suggesting that 4–9 percent is a lower bound for how much higher western rates were during 1955–64.

34 The coincidental timing of the FTC's final decision on December 3, 1964, and the beginning of Seattle's price fall in May 1965 is less suspicious than it appears because the decision did not end legal action on the case. The major wholesale bakers appealed the decision to the U.S. Circuit Court; on losing in 1966, they appealed for review by the U.S. Supreme Court. That request was denied (386 U.S. 932), but not until February 20, 1967.

35 During 1964 and 1965, the wholesale price of the advertised-label brands was 28¢/loaf, based on a conventional discount of 20 percent from the retail price of 35¢/loaf. See In the Matter of International Telephone and Telegraph Corp., *et al.*, 104 F.T.C. 280, at 327 (1984). (Hereinafter cited as IT&T Case. IT&T owned Continental Baking Co., a large wholesale baker.) *The FTC Report, supra* note 9, at 61–62, based on a survey of Seattle grocers, stated that grocers' markups on advertised-label brands were still exactly 20 per cent in January and August 1966 and that this markup resulted in retail gross margins of 7.4¢/loaf and 7.8¢/loaf. These amounts imply wholesale prices of 29.6¢ and 31.2¢/loaf in these two months. Since the standard loaf weight in Seattle was 22.5 ounces (ITT Case, at 326), the increase of 3.2 cents per loaf from 1964–65 to August 1966 equaled 2.3 cents/pound.

36 Wholesale prices in New York City and Chicago increased 2.4¢/pound over this period. See U.S. Dep't of Labor, Bur. Labor Statistics, Wholesale Prices and Price Indexes, January 1965 and September 1966. The U.S. national average wholesale price increased 1.8¢ pound over the period (FTC Report, *supra* note 9, at 117–19).

37 IT&T Case, *supra* note 35, at 327; and FTC Report, *supra* note 9, at 72–73.

38 See the testimony of R. N. Laughlin, president of Continental Baking Co., and R. A. Jackson, president of Ward Baking Co., in U.S. Senate, *supra* note 22, at 6154 and 6253. And see In the Matter of ITT Continental Baking Co., 84 F.T.C. 1349. at 1370 (1974).

39 FTC Report, *supra* note 9, at 30–31; and U.S. Council of Wage and Price Stability, A Study of Bread Prices 21 (1977). Consumers probably inferred from the heavier advertising of the advertised-label brands that these brands were qualitatively different from private-label brands; see Benjamin Klein & Keith B. Leffler, The Role of Market Process in Assuring Contractual Performance, *89 J. Pol. Econ.* 615 (1981).

40 FTC Report, *supra* note 9, at 29–30; and IT&T Case, *supra* note 35, at 302.

41 Walsh & Evans, *supra* note 24, at 79; and FTC Report, *supra* note 9, at 30.

42 Walsh & Evans, at 127.

43 *Id*. at 106.

44 In the Matter of ITT Continental Baking Co., *supra* note 38, at 1371.

45 IT&T Case, *supra* note 35, at 304.

46 FTC Report, *supra* note 9, at 29–30. See also In the Matter of ITT Continental Baking Co., *supra* note 38, at 1369.

47 Robert D. Leiter, *The Teamsters Union: A Study of Its Economic Impact* 51 (1957).

48 Beck's influence and activities are described in Murray Morgan, *Skid Road: An Informal Portrait of Seattle* 256–63 (1982); Donald Garnel, *The Rise of Teamster Power in the West* 67–77 (1972); Leiter, *supra* note 47, at 49–51; David Bell, Labor's New Men of Power, 47 *Fortune* 148, 156 (1953); Robert Laughlin, The Boss of the Teamsters Rides High, 36 *Life* 122 (1954); and Richard A. Lester, *Labor and Industrial Relations: A General Analysis* 127 (1957).

49 Morgan, *supra* note 48, at 259. See also Garnel, *supra* note 48, at 68–70; and Laughlin, *supra* note 48, at 130.

50 Bell, *supra* note 48, at 156.

51 IT&T Case, *supra* note 35, at 326–27. Granddad may have been encouraged by the example of Ashbrook Bakeries. In 1960 Ashbrook sold bread to a grocer under an arrangement by which the grocer's drivers picked up the bread at Ashbrook's plant. Ashbrook thereby avoided using driver-salesmen. The arrangement was the key issue in collective bargaining between the Seattle Teamsters and the bakers' organization in 1962. The Teamsters won a contract provision forbidding this practice, but the provision permitted bakers already using the arrangement to continue. When Granddad entered the market in 1963, it for a short time purchased bread from Ashbrook. See Granddad Bread v. Continental Baking Co., 612 F.2d 1105 (9th Cir. 1979).

52 See Granddad Bread, note 51 *supra*.

53 *Id*. The Canadian dollar fell 11 percent against the U.S. dollar from 1960 to 1963. International Monetary Fund, Bur. of Statistics, International Financial Statistics Yearbook 222–23 (1985). If the exchange rate movement prompted Granddad's importing, then when the Canadian dollar rose in the 1970s to nearly its 1960 level, Granddad should have stopped importing. And it did: see IT&T Case, *supra* note 35, at 329.

54 IT&T Case, *supra* note 35, at 327. Granddad's low-priced bread was sold in 1964, but Seattle's average retail price, as measured by the BLS, did not decline until 1965. Why? I suspect that the answer lies in BLS's sampling method. At each retail outlet sampled, only the best-selling brand in that outlet was priced. (See Frederick E. Geithman & Bruce W. Marion, A Critique of the Use of BLS Data for Market Structure-Price Analysis, 60 *Am. J. Agric. Econ.* 701, 702 (1978).) It is reasonable, therefore, that a new brand did not affect the BLS-measured price immediately. In this case, not until other Seattle bakers began making cheap bread and Seattle retailers began discounting private-label brands more did the BLS price fall. See text accompanying notes 61–66 *infra*.

55 In 1958 the average retail price difference in the West between advertised-label and private-label brands was just one cent per pound (4 percent). This contrasted with an average 3.3 cents per pound discount (17 percent) nationwide. Walsh & Evans, *supra* note 24, at 127.

56 IT&T Case, *supra* note 35, at 327–30. The initial decision in the IT&T Case concludes discussion of the Seattle market with the finding, "Moreover, it appears that Granddad's principal adversaries in Seattle were Local 227 of the Teamsters Union, Hansen [a whole-sale baker], and the driver-salesmen of all the wholesale bakers." I do not think that the Teamsters were acting simply as a tool of the Bakers of Washington. Just the opposite was probably true. Beck urged businessmen to form trade associations, and in some industries association staffers were former union officials friendly with Beck (Garnel, *supra* note 48, at 70). Beck and the Seattle Teamsters had been working with trade associations to "stabi-lize" prices since 1927, which predates the formation of the bakers' organization (Laughlin, *supra* note 48, at 130).

57 I estimate a lower bound for Granddad's market share as follows. In 1963 $37,226,000 worth of "bread and bread-type rolls" were manufactured in Washington State (source: 1963 Census of Manufactures, at 20E–20). This value is multiplied by the ratio of the wholesale value of "white pan bread" to the wholesale value of "bread and bread-type rolls" sold in the United States, .58812. Dividing by the wholesale price per loaf in Seattle in 1964, $.28 (IT&T Case, *supra* note 35, at 327). I estimate that 78,190,554 loaves of bread were produced in the state. Granddad's sales of 40,000 loaves a week thus consti-tute a market share of 2.66 percent for the *entire state*. But the whole state was larger than the relevant market. Most bread markets consisted of a metropolitan area and an urban-rural fringe (FTC Report, *supra* note 9, at 42). The population of the Seattle area on July 1, 1965, was 1.179 million (U.S. Statistical Abstract). According to the FTC Report, *supra* note 9, at 39, the per capita shipment of white bread in the United States in 1963 equaled 52 pounds. Straightforward computations, given a loaf weight of 22.5 ounces (IT&T Case, *supra* note 35, at 326), yield an estimate of Granddad's share of the Seattle market of 4.77 percent.

58 Three factors restricted Granddad's sales despite its low price. The Teamsters successfully pressured some retailers not to carry Granddad's bread. For example, K-Mart stopped buying 13,000 loaves per week as a result of Teamster pressure (IT&T Case, *supra* note 35, at 329). The efforts of the Teamsters could account for Granddad's use of two nontradi-tional distribution channels: service stations and roadside fruit stands (FTC Report, *supra* note 9, at 71). Second, Granddad did not advertise (FTC Report, at 71). Finally, begin-ning in 1965, Granddad's bread had to compete with other new brands (see text accom-panying notes 61–65 *infra*).

59 FTC Report, *supra* note 9, at 71.

60 IT&T Case, *supra* note 35, at 328.

61 *Id.* at 327.

62 *Id.*

63 *Id.* Continental's reaction to Granddad's entry was similar to Continental's competitive reactions in other cities. For instance, in Denver in August 1964, Continental began sup-plying a private-label brand to a grocery-retailing cooperative to preempt another baker from doing so. The cooperative accounted for only 4 percent of Denver's grocery sales (IT&T Case, *supra* note 35, at 311). In Minneapolis, Los Angeles, San Francisco, and Cleveland, Continental was charged with predatory pricing by several small firms, as well as by the FTC (IT&T Case, *supra* note 35, at 291, 317–25, and 330–65). In most of the instances complained of, Continental chose to fight cheaper bread by producing private and secondary-label brands, *not* by cutting the price of its advertised-label brand.

Other U.S. wholesale bakers made this same choice, even at the cost of a significant loss in market share for their advertised-label brands. See text accompanying note 45 *supra* and In the Matter of ITT Continental Baking Co., *supra* note 38, at 1371. The bakers may have maintained high prices on advertised-label brands because they feared that price cuts would undermine their investment in brand-name capital; see Joseph E. Stiglitz, The Causes and Consequences of the Dependence of Quality on Price, 25 *J. Econ. Literature* 1, 23, 38 (1987).

64 IT&T Case, *supra* note 35, at 327–28.

65 IT&T Case, *supra* note 35, at 328. Private-label brands of large grocery chains held a 21 percent share of the market in 1966, compared to just 4 percent in 1956. See FTC Report, *supra* note 9, at 71.

66 The typical discount in early 1966 was 8.5 cents/pound, compared to 1.0 cent/pound or less during the conspiracy. FTC Report, *supra* note 9, at 72–73. That the retailers' introduction of new brands and their increased discounting was a response to Granddad's and Continental's new brands is suggested by analogy to other cities. For example, the opening of a single store selling inexpensive private-label bread in Minneapolis in 1966 prompted major chains there to cut private label prices by 27.6 percent. IT&T Case, *supra* note 35, at 320. A discount grocery chain's entry into Denver triggered a 25 percent drop in price in 1965. FTC Report, *supra* note 9, at 73–74.

67 U.S. Senate, Select Committee on Nutrition and Human Needs, 1975 Food Price Study, Part 4, 45–145 (1975).

68 U.S. Senate, *supra* note 22, at 6369, 6408. and 6415.

69 U.S. prices are reported in the FTC Report, *supra* note 9, at 103. City prices are reported in U.S. Dep't of Labor, Bur. of Labor Statistics, Estimated Retail Food Prices by City, various annual summary issues.

70 U.S. Dep't of Labor, Bureau of Labor Statistics, City Worker's Family Budget, Autumn 1966 (Bulletin 1570–3). I have no indication that Canadian bread was exported to any of the other thirty-one nonwestern cities in the sample. Bread's perishability would have made it economically infeasible to transport bread far from the Canadian border. The city among the other thirty-one closest to Canada was Buffalo. Interestingly, Buffalo's bread price was also well below the U.S. average (by 13 percent).

Review and Discussion Questions

1 Does Figure 27.1 in the article indicate that the bakers' conspiracy in Seattle raised the price of bread?

2 What is the significance of the data presented in Tables 27.1 and 27.2?

3 Why were bread prices higher than the U.S. average all throughout the West?

4 Doesn't the sharp decline in Seattle's price after 1964 indicate that the government prosecuted successful collusion? Why or why not?

5 Why might collusion be more likely to succeed against government or other non-profit buyers than against for-profit buyers?

Chapter 28

Craig M. Newmark

PRICE AND SELLER CONCENTRATION IN CEMENT: EFFECTIVE OLIGOPOLY OR MISSPECIFIED TRANSPORTATION COST?

1 Introduction

DOZENS OF PAPERS IN THE INDUSTRIAL ORGANIZATION LITERATURE examine a product for which the market is local in extent, such as groceries or gasoline, and ask: are seller concentration and price positively correlated across the markets for the product? Almost all of the papers answer "yes". These results are deemed by survey authors (Schmalensee, 1989, p. 988) and textbook authors (Greer, 1992, pp. 308, 315) to strongly support a key prediction of oligopoly theory: high concentration tends to raise price. A law school dean argues that the findings justify a more active antitrust policy (Thompson, 1986).

Five papers have studied the U.S. Portland cement industry (McBride, 1983; Koller and Weiss, 1989; Allen, 1993; Rosenbaum, 1994; Jans and Rosenbaum, 1997). All five report a positive, statistically significant relation between seller concentration and cement price.[1] Koller and Weiss conclude (p. 36), "Cement offers cleaner evidence of the effects of concentration on price than most industries because of its many geographic markets, its standardized product, and its data on firm market share and price, none of which depend on the census. We feel the evidence gives strong support to the concentration–price hypothesis."

In this paper I argue that the positive correlation between cement prices and seller concentration can be explained in another way. Previous studies have not controlled adequately for an important characteristic of the cement industry—its high transportation cost. The next section of the paper discusses this characteristic. Then I present some new evidence.

2 Transportation costs and economies of scale in the cement industry

The structure of the Portland cement industry has been influenced by two forces: high transportation costs and significant economies of scale in production. Transportation costs were high enough that, in 1964, 90% of U.S. cement shipments traveled less than 160 miles from the point of manufacture to the point of use (U.S. Federal Trade Commission, 1966, p. 18). Scherer et al. (1975) (pp. 429–433) estimated that cement had the second highest transportation cost per dollar of product value—more than double the third-highest industry's cost—in a sample of 101 4-digit manufacturing industries.

Scherer et al. also reported (p. 80) that a plant one-third the size of a minimum optimal scale plant had a unit cost disadvantage of 26%. This degree of disadvantage was more than twice as large as the disadvantage in the industries with the second highest values, steel and glass, of the industries they studied in depth. The F.T.C. (p. 34), cited research that found cement plants with an annual capacity of between 1.2 and 1.9 million barrels per year had an average total cost approximately 50% greater than a plant having a 5.9 million barrel capacity. McBride (1981) concluded (p. 108) that production economies of scale were potentially unlimited because kiln investment costs rose consistently at the rate of capacity raised to the two-thirds power. His regression analysis of data from 1963 to 1965 for a sample of cement plants supported this conclusion.

Confronted by high transportation costs and by significant production economies of scale, cement producers seeking to serve small, geographically isolated markets had two choices. They could build large plants, plants that exploited the production economies, near large markets and they could then ship cement to the more isolated markets. Equilibrium market prices in the distant markets would tend to be higher reflecting the transport cost incurred. This choice was more attractive if the cement could be shipped by water or by rail. Water transport was cheaper than rail transport, and both were far cheaper than transportation by truck.[2]

The other choice for cement producers was to build plants very close to the isolated markets. Equilibrium market prices in the distant markets would then tend to be higher reflecting the higher average cost of producing in small plants. Cement producers sometimes selected this second choice. Allen (1983) (p. 14) observed, "Plants that are inefficiently small may survive if transportation costs are so large that it is rational to trade them off against diseconomies of small-scale production. This is most likely to occur where population and economic activity are sparsely scattered across areas such as the West North Central and Rocky Mountain states."[3]

No matter which choice the cement producers made, market prices in smaller, less densely populated markets tended to be higher. Without adequate control for this condition, tests of the price concentration hypothesis will be biased. The bias will exist because the smaller, isolated markets also had higher seller concentration. Few plants 'fit' economically in those markets; four-firm concentration was necessarily high. But in bigger markets, more plants were economically viable, so the four-firm concentration ratio could be low. A positive correlation between price and seller concentration would thus be caused by exogenous technical and geographic conditions, not necessarily by oligopolistic behavior.

3 Previous studies

Previous studies tried to control for transportation costs and production economies of scale in one of three ways. One study (McBride) included neither a proxy for transport costs nor one for scale economies, but since it used pooled cross-sectional time-series data, it could include market dummy variables to control for omitted factors. Such dummy variables might reduce the statistical problems stemming from omitted transportation costs and scale economies, but they will not eliminate these problems.

One study, Koller and Weiss, included both a proxy for scale economies and a proxy for transportation cost. The scale economies proxy—the reciprocal of the average capacity of all producing plants in the market—was positive and significant for all seven of their sample years. But the transportation cost proxy, defined (p. 19) as the "average distance from the cement plants in a market area to the area's central city weighted by the capacities of the individual plants" had "no consistent effect on price": in four of the seven years they examined, the variable had an unexpected, positive sign (pp. 21 and 22).

The remaining studies (Allen, Rosenbaum, Jans and Rosenbaum) did not include a proxy for transportation cost but included one for scale economies. It was insignificant in Allen's study, but it was significant and had the expected sign in Rosenbaum and in Jans and Rosenbaum. But when Jans and Rosenbaum reestimated their model in first-differenced form, the coefficient on the Herfindahl index changed from positive and significant to negative and insignificant. This result suggests that, despite their inclusion of a scale economies proxy, their specification omits a factor which is correlated with both price and seller concentration and which changes slowly over time. Transportation cost fits that description.

4 Variables and data

4.1 Variables

Previous research has identified a good proxy for transportation cost, and one which has not been used in previous price–concentration studies of the industry. This proxy was discussed by Allen (1983) and Scherer et al. Allen contended that "transport costs should be inversely related to population density" (p. 14). Scherer et al. stated that transportation costs are inversely related to "density of demand per square mile" (p. 90). They continued, "For consumer goods (but less consistently so for producer goods) demand density depends primarily upon the density of the population distribution and the purchasing power of the population." I therefore include population density in my specification. It should be negatively related to price.

To see if transportation cost has any explanatory power independent of plant economies of scale, I follow previous authors and include a proxy for scale economies, the reciprocal of average plant capacity.[4]

The independent variables also include measures of median family income and of the population of the market area. The supply shifter most commonly used by previous studies has been manufacturing wage rates. But direct labor accounts for a relatively small fraction of cement firms' cost; both energy and capital account for larger percentages.[5] I therefore included income to proxy for regional differences in input costs. Research has found income differences to be related to cost-of-living differences.[6] (Income might also proxy for strength of demand as Scherer et al. noted. That income might serve as both a demand shifter and a cost shifter causes no problem for estimating a reduced-form relationship between price and concentration. And, in either case, the expected effect of income on price is positive.) Population is included because, in larger markets, distribution terminals or larger plants should be more economical, lowering cost and thereby price.

4.2 Data

My data on seller concentration are drawn from a special survey conducted by the U.S. Federal Trade Commission (1966) (Appendix C). The F.T.C. computed four-firm concentration ratios based on 1964 shipments for all the U.S. states except Hawaii, California, and Pennsylvania. For each of the latter two states, the F.T.C. computed two concentration ratios: one each for Northern and Southern California and one each for Eastern and Western Pennsylvania.

These F.T.C. concentration ratios have not been used in previous price–concentration investigations. And 1964 is a convenient year. It is exactly in the middle of the period spanned by the seven years Koller and Weiss analyze and close to one of those years, 1965, so my results can be readily contrasted with theirs.

For data on cement prices I use the same source used by all the other price–concentration studies of cement. The U.S. Department of the Interior and Bureau of Mines (1964) published an average mill value per unit for selected geographic districts. It reports (p. 323) these values for 24 districts. Some of these districts are single states and correspond exactly with the state-based concentration ratios. Other districts are multistate regions. For these regions, I attribute the reported price to each of the states in the region.

This reference also reports the number of active plants and the total capacity of those plants at the end of the year for each district. Dividing total capacity by the average number of plants yields an average plant capacity for each district. Values for multistate districts were again attributed to each state in the district.

Data on state population density, population, and median family income are drawn from the U.S. Department of Commerce and Bureau of the Census (1965).[7]

Descriptive statistics for the variables used in the basic analysis are presented in Table 28.1.

5 Results

If price is regressed on concentration alone, a positive, statistically significant coefficient results (Eq. (1), Table 28.2). Both the coefficient, 0.523, and its t-ratio, 3.22, are consistent with values obtained by Koller and Weiss: the median value of the coefficient for the seven years they examined is 0.468 and the median t-ratio is 3.00. (The coefficient using 1965 data is 0.604 and the t-ratio is 3.87.) Adding the reciprocal of average plant capacity and family income also yields expected results. Higher average

Table 28.1 Descriptive statistics

	Price	Concentration	1/(average plant size)	Population density	Income	Population (millions)
Mean	3.25	0.8182	0.000437	90.03	5193	4177.3
Median	3.25	0.8665	0.000395	66.73	5295	3407.0
Standard deviation	0.18	0.1599	0.000159	93.86	972	3598.0
Minimum	2.93	0.4812	0.000198	3.52	2884	343.0
Maximum	3.59	1.0000	0.000837	373.7	6829	17,915.0

plant capacity is associated with lower prices and higher income is associated with higher prices.

The interesting new result is shown in Eq. (3). Population density has the predicted negative effect on price and is statistically significant at the 0.01 level. But with population density in the specification, the effect of seller concentration on price drops very close to zero. The coefficient of 0.025 indicates that were four-firm concentration to increase from the minimum value in the sample, 48.12%, to the maximum, 100%, price would increase only about 1.25 cents per barrel, compared to a sample average price of US$3.25. Population density matters even though a proxy for scale economies is also present in the specification.

In results not shown in Table 28.2, I reestimated Eqs. (3)–(5) with the heteroscedastic-consistent errors of White (1980) and with additional proxies for demand.

Table 28.2 Main regression results

	(1)	(2)	(3)	(4)	(5)
Constant	2.82	2.41	2.63	2.64	2.78
Concentration	0.523	0.351	0.025	0.009	0.031
	(3.22)	(2.41)	(0.14)	(0.05)	(0.15)
1/(average plant capacity)		514.3	428.1	420.5	
		(3.52)	(3.13)	(2.94)	
Income		0.00006	0.00095	0.00097	0.00011
		(2.87)	(4.14)	(3.88)	(4.09)
Population density			−0.0009	−0.0009	−0.0010
			(−2.88)	(−2.62)	(−2.74)
Population				− 0.000002	− 0.000008
				(−0.22)	(−0.87)
Adjusted R^2	0.189	0.452	0.542	0.529	0.429
N	41	41	41	41	41

Dependent variable is price measured in dollars per 376-pound barrel. t-Statistics are in parentheses.

The t-statistics using White's errors were larger in absolute value for all variables except for seller concentration. The demand proxies I tried were the value of construction contracts (from the U.S. Department of Commerce and Bureau of the Census, 1965), the value of total private construction authorized (U.S. Department of Commerce, 1966), and capacity utilization (from U.S. Department of the Interior and Bureau of Mines, 1964). Each of the first two variables entered with the wrong sign, negative, but they were generally insignificant and they changed the values and t-statistics of the other variables very little. Capacity utilization was positive as expected but insignificant and its addition barely affected the results at all.

Another sensitivity test I applied was to aggregate the observations up to the level of the Bureau of Mines districts. My use of prices based on the B.O.M.'s multistate districts attributed to individual states introduced some measurement error. Aggregating the observations to the district level eliminates this error. In regressions not reported here I found that the overall fit of the equations was poorer and the t-statistics were lower, but the results were qualitatively the same: in the modified Eq. (3) the t-statistic for concentration was just 0.39, while the t-statistic for population density was -2.02.

Possible extensions of this analysis include studying other time periods, using delivered prices as the dependent variable, and refining the transportation cost variable beyond the crude proxies of population density and population. The results of a step toward the first of these possibilities are shown in Table 28.3. Jans and Rosenbaum (pp. 407 and 408) published the average (over 1974–1989) cement price and Herfindahl Index for the 25 cities in their study. I combine these data with data on per capita personal income, population density, and natural gas price.[8]

Table 28.3 Results using averaged data and a Herfindahl index

	(1)	(2)	(3)	(4)
Constant	46.3	36.2	44.0	53.3
Herfindahl index	18.3	11.6	6.7	7.2
	(1.96)	(1.23)	(0.71)	(0.80)
Income		0.002	0.002	0.001
		(1.11)	(1.67)	(0.33)
Population density		−0.013		
		(−2.08)		
Log (population density)			−8.07	−11.0
			(−2.65)	(−3.40)
Population				0.0000002
				(0.27)
Natural gas price				4.6
				(2.07)
Adjusted R	0.106	0.196	0.274	0.348
N	25	25	25	25

Dependent variable is price measured in dollars per ton. t-Statistics are in parentheses.

In these data, too, population density is negatively related to price—the log of population density yields a better fit, however—and population density reduces the size and t-statistic of concentration. I conclude that price–concentration studies of the cement industry do not yet yield strong support for a key prediction of oligopoly theory.[9]

Notes

1 McBride does not focus on the price–concentration correlation but on the effect of vertical integration on cement price. He also does not measure seller concentration directly. He includes the variable PLANTS, equal to the total number of cement plants in a market. But he states this variable is a measure of competition in the market and he interprets the negative sign on its coefficient as meaning that "as the number of competitors in the region increases, the average realized price level drops" (p. 1020).
2 Scherer et al. (p. 139) reported that, in the mid-1960s, shipment by truck was about seven times more expensive than shipment by barge. As of the late 1970s the estimated costs were as follows: by barge, 0.3 to 0.5 cent per ton-mile; by rail, 1.5 to 2.0 cents per ton-mile; and by truck, over 6.0 cents per ton mile (U.S. Department of the Interior and Bureau of Mines, 1978, p. 17).
3 See also U.S. Federal Trade Commission (1966) (p. 35), Scherer et al. (p. 24), and McBride (1981) (p. 108).
4 Koller and Weiss (footnote 3, p. 38) chose this measure after also trying average capacity and the natural logarithm of average capacity. They found that the reciprocal provided the best fit.
5 See Federal Trade Commission (p. 34). For discussion of energy costs, see Pitcher (1981), (1990).
6 See, for example, Cebula (1983).
7 County-level data were needed to compute values for the two halves of California and the two halves of Pennsylvania. These data were drawn from U.S. Department of Commerce and Bureau of the Census (1962).
8 The income and population density data are for states, in 1980, and are from U.S. Department of Commerce and Bureau of the Census (1982). State values are attributed to the cities used in the Jans and Rosenbaum data. The gas price is the price of dry natural gas paid by the industrial sector, in 1980, in US$ per million BTU, and is drawn from U.S. Department of Energy (1983). Once again, state values are attributed to cities.
9 The author thanks Steve Margolis for helpful comments.

References

Allen, B.T., 1983. Concentration, scale economies, and the size distribution of plants. *Quarterly Review of Economics and Business* 23, 6–27.
Allen, B.T., 1993. Foreign owners and American cement: old cartel hands, or new kids on the block? *Review of Industrial* Organization 8, 697–715.
Cebula, R.J., 1983. *Geographic Living-cost Differentials*. Lexington Books, Lexington.
Greer, D.F., 1992. *Industrial Organization and Public Policy*. Macmillan, New York.

Jans, I., Rosenbaum, D.I., 1997. Multimarket contact and pricing: evidence from the U.S. cement industry. *International Journal of Industrial Organization* 15, 391–412.

Koller, II, R.H., Weiss, L.W., 1989. Price levels and seller concentration: the case of Portland cement. In: Weiss, L.W. (Ed.), *Concentration and Price*. MIT Press, Cambridge, pp. 17–40.

McBride, M., 1981. The nature and source of economies of scale in cement production. *Southern Economic Journal* 48, 105–115.

McBride, M., 1983. Spatial competition and vertical integration: cement and concrete revisited. *American Economic Review* 73, 1011–1022.

Pitcher, C.B., 1981. Portland cement industry profile: bright prospects but many challenges. *Construction Review* 27, 4–14.

Pitcher, C.B., 1990. The U.S. cement industry: trade and trends. *Construction Review* 36, iii–xiii.

Rosenbaum, D.I., 1994. Efficiency v. collusion: evidence cast in cement. *Review of Industrial Organization* 9, 379–392.

Scherer, F.M. et al., 1975. *The Economics of Multi-plant Operation: An International Comparisons Study*. Harvard University Press, Cambridge.

Schmalensee, R., 1989. Inter-industry studies of structure and performance. In: Schmalensee, R., Willig, R.D. (Eds.), *Handbook of Industrial Organization*, Vol. 2. North-Holland, Amsterdam, pp. 951–1009.

Thompson, Jr., S.C., 1986. A proposal for antitrust merger enforcement reform: repudiating Judge Bork in favor of current economic learning. *The Antitrust Bulletin* 41, 79–136.

White, H., 1980. A heteroscedasticity-consistent covariance matrix estimator and a direct test for heteroscedasticity. *Econometrica* 48, 817–838.

U.S. Department of Commerce, Bureau of the Census, 1962. County and City Data Book.

U.S. Department of Commerce, Bureau of the Census, 1965. U.S. Statistical Abstract.

U.S. Department of Commerce, 1966. *Construction Review*.

U.S. Department of Commerce, Bureau of the Census, 1982. *State and Metropolitan Area Data Book*.

U.S. Department of Energy, Energy Information Admin., 1983. *Energy Price and Expenditure Data Report*, 1970–1980 (State and U.S. Total).

U.S. Department of the Interior, Bureau of Mines, 1964. *Minerals Yearbook*.

U.S. Department of the Interior, Bureau of Mines, 1978. *Mineral Commodity Profiles: Cement*.

U.S. Federal Trade Commission, 1966. *Economic Report on Mergers and Vertical Integration in the Cement Industry*.

Review and Discussion Questions

1 How do previous studies interpret a positive correlation between seller concentration and prices?
2 Why is Portland cement a good industry for a price–concentration test?
3 What two characteristics of the Portland cement industry does the article focus on?
4 Why were population and population density included in the statistical model?
5 What does the statistical analysis show?
6 Are price–concentration studies a good way to examine the effects of seller concentration? What are the possible advantages and disadvantages?

Suggestions for Further Reading

Crandall, R. W. and Winston, C. (2003) "Does Antitrust Policy Improve Consumer Welfare? Assessing the Evidence," *Journal of Economic Perspectives*, 17: 3-26.

> Even if monopolization and collusion were sometimes effective, it's not clear that antitrust actions would yield gains for consumers. Crandall and Winston report that there is little evidence that U.S. antitrust policy is effective against monopolization and explicit collusion.

DeLorme, C. D., Frame, W. S., and Kamerschen, D. R. (1997) "Empirical Evidence on a Special-Interest Group Perspective," *Public Choice*, 92: 317-335.

> Scholars have two theories for why the U.S.'s Sherman (Antitrust) Act was passed. One is that antitrust is in the public interest; the Sherman Act was intended to reduce monopolization and collusion, thereby lowering prices to consumers. The other explanation is that the Sherman Act was a special interest law that actually served to protect smaller, less efficient firms from competition. The empirical results of DeLorme, Frame, and Kamerschen cast doubt on the public interest explanation.

Demsetz, H. (1968) "Why Regulate Utilities?" *Journal of Law and Economics*, 11: 55-65.

> Due to the high fixed costs of plant and equipment, over a large range of output the long-run average cost of a utility firm typically declines. It is often thought, therefore, that in a given market, it is economically efficient for only one firm to serve that market: utilities are "natural monopolies." It seems to follow that utility firms should be regulated, or else they will charge monopoly prices and earn monopoly profits. Demsetz argues that regulation is not logically required: if the firms who wish to be the monopoly provider in a given area are made to *bid for the right to be the monopolist*, competition can cause the price to fall to the breakeven level and excess profits will be competed away.

Newmark, C. M. (1988) "Is Antitrust Enforcement Effective?" *Journal of Political Economy*, 96: 1315-1328.

> Bakers in more cities in the U. S. than just Seattle have been prosecuted for price fixing. But, as for Seattle, there is essentially no evidence that these conspiracies successfully raised price.

Newmark, C. M. (2006) "Price-Concentration Studies: There You Go Again," in Moriati, P. (ed.), *Antitrust Policy Issues* (Hauppauge, NY: Nova Science Publishers, Inc).

> A sizeable recent literature studies products with local markets—bread, gasoline, banking, among others—and investigates whether the markets with higher seller concentration have higher prices. The vast majority of these studies do find that prices are positively correlated with seller concentration. The studies conclude that higher seller concentration facilitates either implicit or explicit collusion. But my review of these studies concludes, to the contrary, that they are seriously flawed. They do not—at least yet—establish that seller concentration harms consumers.

Ravenscraft, D. J. (1983) "Structure–Profit Relationship at the Line of Business and Industry Level," *Review of Economics and Statistics*, 65: 22-31.

> An influential study that confirms Demsetz's result: the competitive superiority of firms with large market shares explains the data better than collusion in highly concentrated industries.

Sproul, M. F. (1993) "Antitrust and Prices," *Journal of Political Economy*, 101:741–754.

> Sproul asks a simple question. If collusive agreements raise prices, then shouldn't prosecution of those agreements results in lower prices? He examines twenty-five collusive conspiracies prosecuted in the United States. He finds that, on average, prices *rose* following prosecution. He concludes that either the government prosecuted benign conspiracies, or the penalties for collusion were too low to discourage further price fixing. But either way, concerning at least those particular collusive agreements, U.S. antitrust policy was apparently ineffective in helping consumers.

PART EIGHT

Abuse of Firm Power

Introduction

Many criticisms of markets ultimately reduce to issues of power. Firms allegedly have the power to make consumers buy items they don't want or which aren't good for them. Firms allegedly have too much power over employees. Firm managers can supposedly exploit shareholders. Firms supposedly can coerce individuals to sign unfair contracts. The articles in this section respond to such concerns by providing evidence that firms' power is frequently much less than it appears. Markets curtail the arbitrary and harmful exercise of firm power.

The first article addresses a question raised in a letter to the editor by a Seattle, Washington resident. If Washington grows some of the finest apples in the world, she wondered, why were a large percentage of the apples in Seattle supermarkets mediocre or worse? Further, why did the Washington-grown apples sold on the East Coast taste so much better? Were local apple growers or supermarkets exerting excessive power against Seattle residents? Similarly, why in France, home of world-class vintners, is some wine sold in cheap *cans*? Eugene Silberberg explains that these outcomes are just an implication of the First Law of Demand (demand curves are negatively sloped).

The second article addresses a question raised by many people. Why do women earn less on average than men? One explanation is that women are discriminated against. Daniel R. Fischel and Edward P. Lazear offer a different explanation: women—at least until recently—often literally *chose* lower-paying occupations because those occupations had significant non-monetary benefits that compensated for the lower pay. Fischel and Lazear do not rule out discrimination, but they provide evidence that the choice hypothesis better explains aspects of the difference in pay than discrimination does.

For decades critics have worried that managers in large publicly held companies can enrich themselves at the expense of shareholders because shareholders don't know much about what the managers are doing. This problem is called "separation of ownership and control": the shareholders own a publicly held firm but they usually do not exercise day-to-day control of it. Harold Demsetz and Kenneth Lehn show that while this separation can be costly it also reduces other costs. They conclude that large publicly held firms tend to efficiently minimize the sum of these costs. Charles R. Knoeber's article shows how golden parachutes—large payments awarded to managers who leave a firm after a change in ownership—promote the interests not just of those managers but also of the shareholders.

The last two articles in this section, by Benjamin Klein and John R. Lott, Jr., show how instances of firms apparently exploiting other parties are not actually abusive. Why would a franchisor insist that its franchisees buy their supplies exclusively from the franchisor? Why do music-publishing companies sign novice songwriters to "unfair" contracts, contracts that grant the publishing companies a very large royalty on future sales? Why is alcohol sold in drinks in restaurants priced much higher than the liquor sold in stores? Why does an airline ticket bought right before the flight leaves costs so much more than one bought well in advance? In each case, the articles explain how the apparent misuse of power is actually economically efficient.

Chapter 29

Eugene Silberberg

SHIPPING THE GOOD APPLES OUT[1]

A N IRATE CONSUMER once wrote to the editor of a Seattle newspaper wondering why it was, in a state known for its apple production, that she had trouble finding high-quality apples in the supermarkets. This complaint, though a casual empiricism at best, is in fact symptomatic of a pervasive phenomenon: higher qualities of goods tend to be shipped farther distances from their point of origin or manufacture than the lower quality items of the same good. Here are some examples.

- The French drink inexpensive, low-quality wine which is often sold in cans. These wines are never exported. Only the higher-quality wines are exported to the U.S. and elsewhere. There are undoubtedly irate French consumers wondering why all the good wine is exported. The average quality of French Fines consumed in North America is higher than that consumed in France.
- Clothing manufacturers wind up with many seconds, clothes that have minor faults due to errors in production. These lower-quality clothes are typically sold in factory outlet stores located close to the factory. Only the high-quality clothes are shipped out to distant locations.
- Most of the high-grade beef (USDA Prime) winds up in restaurants, not in supermarkets for home use. Restaurants sell almost all of this high-grade beef.

The preceding seemingly disparate phenomena are in fact all consequences of the law of demand. Suppose there is some cost, for example, transportation, that increases the price of two varieties of a good by the same amount, irrespective of the quality or other attribute of the good. Transportation costs must be incurred before most goods are consumed; these costs often depend only on attributes of weight and volume that are unrelated to the quality or price of the good itself. Individuals seek ways to mitigate the damages to their incomes because of transportation and like costs. One way to do this is to pack as much of the desirable attributes of a good into the good as practical. For example, people enjoy various aspects of apples—taste, crunchiness, tartness, etc. Good apples have more of these pleasing attributes than poor apples. It costs the same to transport a mediocre apple of a given weight as a good apple. By shipping only good apples, more good attributes are transported for the same cost than would be if only bad apples were shipped. Thus in a real sense the cost of transportation (of attributes of apples) is lowered, if the high-quality apples rather than the low- quality apples are transported. Thus shipping good apples reduces the severity of the constraint on consumption imposed by transportation costs and is thus the behavior which is most commonly observed. The same logic applies to the wine and clothing examples mentioned above. It costs the same amount to ship a poor-grade bottle of wine as a high-grade bottle from France to North America. However, more of what people want in a bottle of wine gets shipped per bottle if the good rather than the poor wine is shipped. Thus only the relatively better grades wind up in the U.S. and elsewhere.

A more formal way of looking at this phenomenon is as follows. Suppose a good apple costs forty cents at locations close to the orchards (e.g., in Washington State, Michigan, New York State, etc.) and a mediocre apple sells for only twenty cents there (see Table 29.1). Then the act of eating a good apple means that two mediocre apples are forgone. The *alternative cost* of a good apple is two mediocre apples; eating two good apples means forgoing *four* mediocre ones. We say the relative price of a good apple is two mediocre apples. Suppose it costs the same amount (and this is a critical assumption), say twenty cents, to ship either type of apple to a distant location, say, New Orleans. In New Orleans these apples would cost sixty and forty cents respectively. Since apples are more expensive in New Orleans than in the producing areas, the law of demand implies that fewer apples will be consumed in New Orleans. More intriguing, however, is the effect on the *mix* of apples consumed. Although both types of apples are more expensive, the good apples are no longer *twice* as expensive as the mediocre apples. They are now only 1.5 times as expensive. Eating two good apples in New Orleans means forgoing only *three*, not four, mediocre apples. In the distant location, the high-quality item has become *relatively cheaper* i.e., cheaper relative to the lower-priced item. With a lower relative price, the law of demand predicts that proportionally more high-quality apples will be consumed, although the total amount of apples consumed will still be lower in distant locations than at locations closer to the orchards.[2]

A really fine steak might cost $4 at home vs. $2 for a so-so steak, but in a restaurant, with perhaps $20 worth of service added (other food, waiters, dishwashers, fine decor, etc.), the prices become $24 vs. $22. At home, with the price ratio of 2:1

Table 29.1

	Close to orchard	Transportation cost	Distant location
Good apple	400	200	600
Mediocre apple	200	200	400
Price ratio	2:1		3:2

($4:$2) most people will eat the less exotic steak, for eating the prime steak costs *two* of the others. At the restaurant price ratio of 12:11 ($24:$22), the law of demand predicts that relatively more prime steak will be consumed. Since steak in restaurants is more expensive than steak at home, more steak will be consumed in the home than in restaurants. However, the *proportion* of excellent to mediocre steak will not be the same in those locations. More of the high-grade steak will be consumed in restaurants because it is relatively cheaper there. For the same reasons, hamburgers never are on the menu in finer restaurants.

Taxes can have a similar effect as transportation costs, depending on how they are levied. In the 1920s, there were two prevalent grades of cigarettes: premium, which cost about ten cents per pack—this was a long time ago—and non-premium, which sold for approximately five cents per pack. With those prices, each premium cigarette smoked meant forgoing two of the lesser quality cigarettes. Many people found that too expensive and smoked the inferior grades. Then, a tax was imposed on cigarettes *by the pack*, raising the prices to twenty and fifteen cents, respectively. At the new prices, smoking three premium cigarettes meant forgoing only four of the others, not six, as would have been the case at the old price ratio. As a result, the lower grades of tobacco virtually disappeared from the market, and the premium grade of tobacco became the standard grade.

In some states, wine is taxed *by the bottle*. This type of taxing scheme will lead to greater relative consumption of higher grades of wine. It is exactly analogous to the transportation cost argument and the above cigarette tax analysis. The impact of the tax on consumption is lessened if one can cram more wine into a bottle. This can be done by increasing the quality of the wine, giving it more desirable attributes per bottle.

It is interesting to note that at the supermarket, produce is sometimes sold by the *piece*, and sometimes by weight. What would account for this? Standard-sized items such as cans of tuna fish, boxes of cereal, cans of coffee, etc., are easily identifiable by weight. There really is no distinction to be made as to whether it is $1.00 for a 7.5-ounce can of tuna or 13.33 cents per ounce. Tuna fish, cereal, coffee, canned fruits and vegetables, etc., are items which are inexpensive to package in standard sizes. This lowers the cost to the consumer of discovering how much of the item is being offered for sale. With produce, however, the story is sometimes different.

Fresh fruits and vegetables never come in standard sizes. Moreover, weighing each individual item is a time-consuming (and therefore costly) activity, and ultimately one the consumer must share. *Counting* heads of lettuce or bunches of carrots is quickly and cheaply done. However, this kind of imprecise measurement can be costly to the supermarket if the variation in the size of the bundles of carrots or heads of lettuce is great, *and* if the produce itself is valuable. We would therefore expect selling produce by the imprecise measure of by the piece to be more prevalent when, other things being equal, the produce is not very expensive. This occurs when the vegetables are in season. During the summer, lettuce will be cheaper than in the winter, because more lettuce is available during the summer than in the winter. We are more apt in the summer to see stores reducing the cost of measurement of lettuce by selling it by the piece rather than weighing each head, than in the winter. The cost of weighing produce stays the same throughout the year. But when the produce is in season, and its price low, the measurement cost is *relatively* high, and so less measuring is done. The produce is sold by the piece. When the gains from precise measurement are less, less measuring will take place, by substituting cruder but cheaper measurements for the goods.

The above principle extends to goods other than produce. Consider that rhinestones and other costume jewelry are measured very crudely. This is because the good itself is not very valuable and precise measurements of weight, angles of cut, etc., would add enormously to the cost. On the other hand, diamonds and other precious gems are extensively measured: their weight is precisely determined, their color is analyzed with a spectrometer, etc. For these gems the costs of measurement are relatively *low*, since the gem is so valuable, and thus much more measurement takes place.

Eric Bertonazzi, Michael Maloney and Robert McCormick investigated the pattern of football tickets purchased for Clemson University's home games. They found that ticket-holders who came to see the games from relatively farther distances from Clemson bought the better, more expensive seats (nearer to the 50 yard line). This case is especially interesting since here, the consumers are being shipped to the goods, rather than the other way around. The reasoning is still valid, if the transportation cost is linked to the good being consumed.

It can be observed that relatively higher-quality houses are built on relatively expensive lots, such as those located with a view. Many people in fact substitute consumption of one fancy house in the city for two lower priced houses, one located in a rural locale.[3] A $100,000 house located on a lot of negligible value costs two $50,000 houses. If the same houses are on view and lots are selling for $50,000, the relative price of the better house falls from 2:1 to 1.5:1. Better houses are relatively cheaper on expensive lots. We expect to see relatively more higher-quality houses located on expensive lots for this reason.[4]

The reasoning extends to the case where the fixed cost (the transportation cost, cost of service in the restaurant, etc.) is not in fact a cost, but a *subsidy*. Here's an example. When professors are recruited and visit the economics department at the University of Washington, the department contributes some fixed amount, say, $10, to offset the cost of going out to dinner. How does this affect the quantity and quality of the meals consumed? Since the subsidy lowers the cost of eating out, the law of demand obviously implies a greater number of restaurant meals. More interestingly, the subsidy lowers the relative price of *cheap* meals. If the price of a good meal is $30 and a lesser meal is $15, eating one good meal out entails the sacrifice of two lesser meals. With the $10 subsidy, however, the prices change to $20 vs. $5; now, eating the good meal costs the consumer *four* cheaper meals! Thus subsidies of fixed amounts lead to greater consumption over all, and relatively greater consumption of the lower-quality items offered in the market.

Notes

1 The argument following was first presented in 1964 by UCLA professors Armen Alchian and William Allen in their "principles" text, *Exchange and Production* (Wadsworth) and in later editions.
2 However, when more than two goods are involved, a fixed cost added to both not only changes the relative prices of these two goods, but also their prices relative to other goods.

Since more than one relative price changes, the law of demand cannot be applied in a straightforward manner. However, Professors Borcherding and Silberberg showed that the result would in general hold unless the goods had highly asymmetric relationships with the remaining goods. See Thomas Borcherding and Eugene Silberberg, "Shipping the Good Apples Out: The Alchian and Allen Theorem Reconsidered," *Journal of Political Economy*, 86, No.1, February, 1978, 131–38.

3 The author, who springs from New York City, finds it mildly surprising that Seattle natives do this, because Seattle was the type of place we went *to* in the summer.

4 It should be mentioned that the effect on income of purchasing an expensive lot is an offsetting influence on this result. Such "income effects," if substantial, can sometimes negate the implications of the law of demand.

Review and Discussion Questions

1 What do Washington state apples, French wines, and the highest-grade beef in the U.S. (USDA Prime) have in common?

2 Explain how fixed transportation costs cause the phenomenon of "shipping the good apples out."

3 Applying the theory, what do you think would happen if the government increased the per-pack tax on cigarettes?

4 The theory applies not only if a good with a fixed transportation cost is shipped to consumers but also if the consumers are "shipped" to the good. What would you predict, therefore, about the kind of vacations in Europe taken by Americans—assuming the Americans have to pay a significant airfare to get to Europe—compared to vacations taken in Europe by resident Europeans? (If your answer depends on income, assume that a statistical analysis has been conducted in which the incomes of the two groups were held constant.)

Chapter 30

Daniel R. Fischel and Edward P. Lazear

COMPARABLE WORTH AND DISCRIMINATION IN LABOR MARKETS[1]

I Introduction

UNDER THE EQUAL PAY ACT OF 1963,[2] employers are prohibited from paying men and women different amounts for identical work if the only justification for the differential is sex. Similarly, Title VII of the Civil Rights Act of 1964[3] prohibits other forms of discrimination against women. For example, employers (with certain narrow exceptions) cannot lawfully refuse to hire women for particular jobs. But an employer in a particular business who treats men and women equally in all respects does not violate either the Equal Pay Act or Title VII. Thus, an employer of nurses who pays female and male nurses the same amount and stands willing to hire both cannot be sued under current anti-discrimination laws. Because such an employer has not discriminated between male and female nurses, he has not acted illegally.

The employer could be liable, however, under the theory of comparable worth. This theory is based on the premise that jobs of equivalent "worth" or value to an employer or to society as a whole should be compensated equally even if the jobs are dissimilar in content. The theory assumes that the proper remedy when two jobs are "comparable," but unequally compensated, is for the employer of the lower-paying job to raise employees' compensation to the level of the higher-paying job. Thus, the employer of nurses who did not discriminate between male and female nurses could nevertheless be liable under a theory of comparable worth if a plaintiff could demonstrate that nurses possessed skills comparable to, say, electricians, but were paid less. The employer would then be required to raise the compensation of nurses to the level of electricians.

Claims brought under Title VII that are explicitly premised on a theory of comparable worth have become much more common in recent years. So far, no court has directly endorsed the theory and several have rejected it outright.[4] The Supreme Court in *Country of Washington v. Gunther*,[5] however, suggested that occupational wage differentials may be actionable under Title VII in certain circumstances. Although the Court expressly refused to address the theory of comparable worth,[6] many commentators have interpreted the decision as a significant expansion of Title VII.[7] Whatever the state of comparable worth in the courts, the issue remains very important. Numerous states and local governments have enacted, or are currently considering, comparable worth legislation for government employees.[8] The same is true of foreign countries.[9]

Comparable worth has been strongly defended as a necessary extension of existing anti-discrimination legislation.[10] Proponents note that women typically earn only sixty cents for every dollar earned by men[11] and this ratio has not changed appreciably over time, notwithstanding the passage of anti-discrimination legislation.[12] Moreover, a high percentage of women in the labor force still tend to be concentrated in a relatively small number of low-paying occupations.[13] Traditional anti-discrimination legislation, proponents claim, is ineffective in remedying this systemic, economy-wide discrimination under which women are segregated into a limited number of low-paying occupations. Only a remedy such as comparable worth which attacks discrimination at the occupational level rather than at the job level, it is argued, can effectively combat this systemic discrimination.

Comparable worth has also attracted its share of critics.[14] The most frequent objection to comparable worth has focused on the premise that the comparability of different jobs can be measured or evaluated apart from values assigned in the marketplace.[15] Critics claim that the "worth" of a job can only be determined by reference to the wage that prevails in the market as a result of the forces of supply and demand. Thus, the critics argue, it is a fundamental contradiction to argue that jobs that are valued differently in the market are nevertheless comparable. The debate about comparable worth, in this view, is simply a modern manifestation of the question that has confounded philosophers for centuries concerning the meaning of a "just" price or wage.

While this standard market critique of comparable worth is powerful, it is not compelling. Many situations exist where market prices are not accepted as final. In antitrust cases, for example, a common inquiry is whether prices charged to consumers are too high as a result of the exercise of market power. Similarly, in cases under the Equal Pay Act, the effect of alleged discrimination on wages paid to men and women is critical. Unless one is willing to argue that the market price should be accepted as dispositive in these other contexts, the standard market critique of comparable worth is not entirely convincing.

We provide a critique of comparable worth that does not depend on acceptance of the market price as dispositive. On the contrary, we freely concede for purposes of argument that observed wage differentials among occupations may, at least in theory, reflect discrimination against women. While we discuss some of the explanations for the wage differentials between men and women—specifically the "crowding" and "choice" hypotheses—we do not attempt to discover the cause of the differentials here. Rather, we argue that comparable worth is never the correct remedy, even if wage differentials and job segregation are the product of discrimination against women.

The essence of our argument is as follows. Assume that women are discriminated against and wrongfully denied entry into a male-dominated occupation, say, electronics.

Women prevented from becoming electricians will flood other occupations such as nursing. The increased supply of women in nursing and other female-dominated occupations may well have the effect of depressing wages. The proper solution, however, is not to raise the wage of nurses while doing nothing about barriers to entry in electronics. Such a remedy would merely combat one inefficiency in the economy (barriers to entry in electronics) by creating a second inefficiency (a minimum wage in nursing). Yet this is precisely the effect of comparable worth.

We then discuss the moral argument that comparable worth is compelled by the need for pay equity for women. We argue that the attempt to justify comparable worth on moral grounds only serves to obscure the effects of comparable worth on various groups. In fact, many women may be hurt by comparable worth. If a consensus exists that women should be compensated for the effects of past discrimination, such compensation should be in the form of a direct public subsidy rather than comparable worth.

Finally, we assess the argument that comparable worth is simply an extension of existing anti-discrimination legislation. Because comparable worth imposes a minimum wage but does nothing about discrimination in the economy, we argue that it is fundamentally inconsistent with, rather than an extension of, existing anti-discrimination legislation. In practice, however, existing anti-discrimination legislation may have the same perverse effects as comparable worth. But even if we assume that Title VII and the Equal Pay Act are beneficial, they still provide no support for comparable worth.

We conclude the article with a discussion of the implications of our analysis for comparable worth cases in the courts and for the *Gunther* case. We argue that *Gunther* provides no support for the theory of comparable worth and is probably wrongly decided on its own facts.

II The significance of earnings differentials

Full-time working women earn approximately sixty percent of what full-time working men earn.[16] Much if not all of this differential is attributable to the disproportionate concentration of women in lower-paying occupations rather than men and women being paid differently for identical work.[17] This much is uncontroversial. The hard question, however, is *why* women are found in lower-paying occupations. We show in this section how wage differentials may or may not reflect discrimination against women. We also demonstrate the deficiencies of job evaluation studies which are frequently performed to analyze whether wage differentials among occupations are a product of discrimination against women.

A Wage differentials and discrimination

Wage differentials among occupations are the norm rather than the exception. Successful athletes and entertainers commonly earn more than Nobel Prize winners; brilliant artists often cannot earn enough to survive while mediocre investment bankers flourish. Within the academic community, law professors generally receive higher salaries (even ignoring consulting opportunities) than professors of political science, even though the skills required for both are quite similar. The examples could be multiplied indefinitely.

Why does anyone choose a lower paid occupation such as political science over a higher paid one such as law? Assuming that individuals are free to choose, the answer must be that they prefer political science (at least at the time the decision is made) even at a lower wage. Perhaps they view the prospect of law school as abhorrent; perhaps they view legal research as dull; perhaps they view lawyers as social parasites or buffoons; perhaps they think law students are more demanding and decide that it would be more enjoyable to teach political science. Whatever the reason, it must be true that individuals who are free to choose law, but voluntarily choose to enter the lower-paying occupation of political science, cannot be worse off. We refer to this scenario as the "choice" explanation for wage differentials.

Now suppose that certain individuals are arbitrarily precluded from entering law. Political science might then be flooded with individuals who would otherwise prefer to teach law, but are crowded out by the entry barrier. Because of the increased supply of individuals going into political science, wages in this area will be artificially low while wages in law will be artificially high. Those willing to work in the lower-paying area of political science may only be willing to do so because they are denied the opportunity to teach law by the entry barrier.[18] We refer to this scenario as the "crowding" explanation for wage differentials.[19]

This simple example of how both the choice and the crowding explanations can explain wage differentials between two occupations when sex is not an issue is illustrative of the ambiguity of statistical disparities in wages when sex is an issue. Women may choose lower-paying occupations because of certain attributes of those occupations; alternatively, they may choose lower-paying occupations because they are denied entry into other higher-paying occupations.

Why might women voluntarily choose lower-paying occupations? One explanation is that many women choose to specialize in child bearing and raising as well as in the production of household services. If women specialize in this manner (while men specialize in the production of income), they may select careers where they are free to enter and leave the workforce with minimum penalty. They may choose to acquire skills that do not depreciate rapidly with temporary absences from the workforce. Conversely, they may avoid occupations (or specialties within occupations) which require long training periods, long and unpredictable hours, willingness to relocate, and other attributes which are inconsistent with specialization in child care and other household responsibilities. Finally, women may expend less effort for any given number of working hours because of their child care and household responsibilities.[20] By choosing to invest less in developing the value of their human capital and to expend less effort, however, women must pay a price in the form of lower wages. But women are not the victims of discrimination under this scenario because they prefer the lower-paying occupations or sub-occupations over higher-paying ones that make production of household services (including child bearing and raising) more difficult.

The alternative explanation for wage differentials is that women do not voluntarily choose lower-paying occupations but, rather, are forced into those occupations by discriminating employers and social prejudices. If employers in certain occupations have a taste for discrimination, they may refuse to hire qualified women.[21] More generally, subtle society-wide prejudices may induce women to avoid certain occupations in favor of others that are perceived as more suitable for women. Indeed, the "choice" of women to specialize in child bearing and raising and the production of household services may itself result from discrimination at the societal level. If this societal discrimination did not exist, women's choices might also be different.[22] Whether the discrimination is by employers in a particular occupation or by society as a whole is irrelevant; the effect will be the same. Women crowded out of certain occupations will flood others and this increase in supply will have a depressing effect on wages in occupations dominated by women. We take up the notion of societal discrimination again in Section C of Part III.

B The empirical evidence

On a theoretical level, it is impossible to decide whether the choice or the crowding explanation better explains wage differentials. The issue is necessarily empirical. Unfortunately, it is extremely difficult to disentangle, even empirically, the sources of the wage differential.

The basic problem is that there is no direct measure for what we would like to test—the causal effect of discrimination on wage differentials. As a result, economists have attempted to measure the effect of discrimination on wages indirectly by measuring how much of the wage differential between men and women can be explained by such factors as education, work experience, seniority, number of hours worked, continuity within the workforce, and so forth. Numerous studies have been performed along these lines.[23] Their general conclusion is that less than half of the wage differential can be explained by taking all these factors into account.[24] Many have interpreted this large unexplained residual as establishing, or at least creating a presumption, that discrimination against women has had a depressing effect on wages in female-dominated occupations.[25]

Others, however, have questioned this interpretation of the data for several reasons.[26] First, the existence of an unexplained residual does not directly establish discrimination. The residual may instead be due to some other factor that is not being tested. Second, when the data is analyzed more carefully, certain basic inconsistencies arise between the data and the crowding hypothesis. The crowding hypothesis would predict, for example, that the wage differential between men and women will not be a function of the marital status of either group. In fact, however, marital status and other family characteristics are crucial.[27]

Women who have never been married appear to have complete wage parity with men who have never been married. Conversely, women who are currently married earn less than half of what men who are currently married earn. Family size is also relevant. The larger the number of children, and the greater the spacing between children, the larger the wage differential. Age matters as well. Earnings differentials are the smallest in the early years, then increase until about age 40, and then decline again.[28]

Each of these statistics is consistent with the choice theory of wage differentials (where women specialize in child bearing and other household services), but inconsistent with the crowding theory. However, the failure of the choice hypothesis to explain much of the wage differential—even when as many factors as possible are held constant—cautions against its easy acceptance. Given the current state of learning, the causes of wage differentials remain something of a mystery.

C Job evaluation studies

The above analysis suggests that wage differentials among occupations are not a subject of concern unless there has been a barrier to entry which makes free choice impossible.

Plaintiffs in comparable worth cases, however, have not established the existence of such barriers. Rather, they have introduced job evaluation studies which purport to demonstrate that certain occupations such as nursing are "comparable" in "worth" to others such as electronics but are paid less.

Such studies of "worth" in labor markets, however, are inherently unreliable. To illustrate this point, it is useful to consider an example drawn from product markets. Consider a hypothetical survey to determine whether water has a value comparable to diamonds. The individual who is conducting the study can resolve this question easily by reference to the market price of water (very low) and diamonds (very high). Of course, this would eliminate the need for the survey in the first place.

But now assume that market prices are discarded because they are somehow biased. What should the author of the study do now? A natural conclusion in the absence of market prices is that since water is necessary for life and diamonds are not, water should rise in price relative to diamonds.

Such a conclusion would, however, overlook the importance of marginal values and thus be a serious error. Water is cheap because of its relative abundance. The first units of water are necessary for life and thus are surely worth more than diamonds. But more water exists than is necessary to support life. Thus, each additional unit of water is worth less than the first and the last marginal units can be used for such nonessential activities as swimming. Raising the price of water to its intrinsic (average) value would preclude its use for swimming even if an ample supply exists for this purpose.

The value of diamonds presents other problems. True, diamonds are scarce, but not as scarce as, say, a painting by one of the authors of this paper. If the author of a "beauty" survey concluded (by some miracle) that our painting was as beautiful as a diamond but more scarce, should our painting sell for more?

Equally intractable problems arise in value studies of labor markets. The criteria for measuring "worth"—e.g., for measuring whether successful athletes are worth more than Nobel Prize winners—are completely subjective and lack any benchmark apart from market price.[29] Moreover, the meaning of "worth" or "value" is not well specified. The value produced by the first worker, the average worker, and the last worker hired by an employer are all different and are likely to differ further across occupations. Which value counts and how is it to be measured apart from employers' willingness to pay? These problems and others doom, for all practical purposes, using job evaluation studies to establish discrimination, particularly where no showing has been made of any barrier to entry into higher-paying occupations.[30]

III The proper remedy

Any persistent wage differential among occupations must either be non-discriminatory (i.e., compensation for attractiveness of work or some other legitimate factor) or must reflect a barrier to entry in higher-paying occupations.[31] In the former situation, the proper course is to do nothing. Eliminating non-discriminatory wage differentials would create misallocations similar to those that would arise if the price differential between water and diamonds were eliminated. For purposes of analysis, we ignore the choice hypothesis in the remainder of this section and assume that occupational wage differentials reflect a barrier to entry. We demonstrate that, even in this situation, comparable worth is the wrong remedy.

A Labor market distortions and the crowding hypothesis

The crowding hypothesis assumes that wages are set by the forces of supply and demand but that women are precluded from entering certain occupations. The spillover of women from the restricted to the unrestricted occupation forces wages up in the former and down in the latter. The restricted occupation becomes male dominated and the unrestricted occupation becomes female dominated. Figure 30.1 illustrates this point.

Panel A shows supply and demand in the unrestricted occupation which ends up being female dominated and Panel B shows supply and demand in the restricted occupation which ends up being male dominated. Without any restrictions on entry into occupation B, the wage would be *WM** and the quantity employed would be *M**. Barriers restricting women from entering occupation B reduce the effective supply of workers from *S** to *S*, driving the wage up to *WM* and the quantity employed down to *M*. The restriction on employment also forces women into occupation A, shifting the supply curve from *S**, where it would be in the absence of mobility restrictions, to *S*. This lowers the wage in the female-dominated occupation from *WF** to *WF* and increases the number employed there from *F** to *F*.

The proper remedy should restore wages and the allocation of labor in the economy to that which would exist were there no restrictions on entry. In the context of Figure 30.1, the goal is to raise wages from *WF* to *WF** in the female-dominated occupation and reduce employment there from *F* to *F**. Similarly, the goal is to lower wages from *WM* to *WM** in the male-dominated occupation and to raise employment there from *M* to *M**. If the barriers to entry were eliminated, the only wage differentials

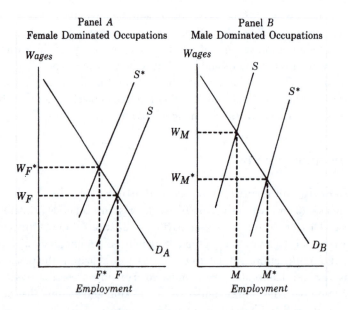

Panel A
Female Dominated Occupations

Panel B
Male Dominated Occupations

Figure 30.1

that would persist are those that resulted from choice and, as discussed above, would thus be compensatory.

Does the remedy of comparable worth, which raises the wage of females to that of males in "comparable" occupations, accomplish this result? Clearly not. The goal should be to raise wages in the female-dominated occupation from WF to WF^* and decrease the level of employment there from F to F^*. Comparable worth, by contrast, raises wages in the female-dominated occupation from WF to WM, not from WF to WF^* as is desired. WM may be above or below WF^* depending on the elasticities of demand in the two occupations. Only in the rarest of circumstances would the "appropriate" wage for females be achieved by this approach. A corollary is that only under the rarest of circumstances will the desired reduction of employment from F to F^* be achieved in the female-dominated occupation.

Significantly, the reduction of employment in the female-dominated occupation under comparable worth is not caused by an exit of women into the male-dominated occupation increasing employment there from M to M^*. This is because comparable worth does nothing to eliminate the barrier to entry in the male-dominated occupation. Thus wages in the male-dominated occupation do not decrease from WM to WM^* and employment does not expand there from M to M^*. The decline in the level of employment in the female-dominated occupation without a corresponding increase in the level of employment in the male-dominated occupation means that previously employed females will now be unemployed. What comparable worth does, in effect, is attack one inefficiency (barriers to entry in the male-dominated occupation) by creating a second inefficiency (a minimum wage in the female-dominated occupation). This is analogous to attacking a cartel of oil producers (which results in an increase in the price of coal as consumers shift to substitute energy sources) by requiring coal producers to lower their prices.

Comparable worth also operates as a penalty against blameless employers. Neither employers in female-dominated occupations nor our analogous coal producers (unlike employers in male-dominated occupations or oil producers) have engaged in any conduct that should be deterred. Both have acted as pure price-takers by setting wages (or prices) at the competitive level, given the market distortion over which they have no control. Indeed, both have mitigated the plight of workers (consumers) caused by others: the employers in the female-dominated occupation by hiring women excluded from other occupations by discriminating employers or unions rather than excluding them as well; the coal producers by expanding production to provide a substitute source of energy. Subjecting them to legal sanction for behaving in a socially desirable way will eliminate their incentive to employ more women or produce more coal. Yet this is precisely the effect of comparable worth; it illustrates why creating a minimum wage is inferior to attacking the source of discrimination directly.

It is also important to recognize that the creation of this minimum wage will only make the underlying problem worse. Wage differentials under the discrimination hypothesis exist because too many women want to enter the female-dominated occupation. The correct solution is to induce some women to exit. Comparable worth has the opposite effect. By raising wages in the female-dominated occupation, comparable worth causes more women (and men) to enter, not less, and at the same time shrinks the number of places available by driving down demand.

B The state as the employer in both the male-dominated and female-dominated occupations

The situation is somewhat more complicated when, as frequently will be the case, the state is the employer in both the male-dominated and female-dominated occupations. An argument could be made that by raising the cost of labor to the state in the female-dominated occupation, the state will be less likely to engage in discrimination in the male-dominated occupation. Attacking the barrier to entry directly, however, is superior to this indirect approach.

The difficulty with the indirect approach is that there is no guarantee that raising the cost of labor to the state in the female-dominated occupation will eliminate the discriminatory entry barrier. The reason is that the incidence of the increased labor costs is indeterminate. The state may simply hire fewer women; alternatively, it may pass on the increased costs to consumers and taxpayers through higher prices or higher taxes. Another alternative is for the state to divest itself of one of the two occupations—i.e., get out of the health care business and thereby not hire nurses.[32] Under any of these alternatives, some groups are worse off (women, consumers, or taxpayers) while barriers to entry in the male-dominated occupation are unaffected. Only by attacking the entry barriers directly can it be guaranteed that discriminating employers will be forced to end their discriminatory practices and that women will be able to enter male-dominated occupations.

C Societal discrimination as the barrier to entry

Some argue that the source of discrimination against women is not employers or unions but society as a whole. This societal discrimination, it is claimed, manifests itself in different ways. Young girls are encouraged to play with dolls while boys play with chemistry sets. Girls are socialized to become full-time wives and mothers and to believe that traits needed for career success are not feminine while boys are socialized to pursue a career and not share the burdens of child rearing and household duties. Because of these and other forms of societal discrimination, the argument runs, women systematically choose low status and low-paying occupations. Implicit in this argument is the assumption that more women would choose to enter male-dominated occupations in the absence of societal discrimination than do at present.

Consistent with our approach throughout, we make no attempt to evaluate the merits of the claim that wage differentials result from societal discrimination. Rather, we assume for purposes of argument that the claim is true and demonstrate that comparable worth is still the wrong remedy.

Suppose that societal discrimination has prevented women from acquiring the skills or the desire to enter the higher-paying male-dominated occupations. Comparable worth is still an inappropriate remedy for a number of reasons. First, it does nothing to correct the initial problem. Women will continue to lack the skills needed for male-dominated occupations, perhaps even more so because the higher wages of the female-dominated occupations make acquiring male skills less attractive. Second, women who are by hypothesis already victims of societal discrimination will be victimized further by comparable worth. Recall that societal discrimination, like other forms of entry barriers, causes too many women to want to enter female-dominated occupations. Comparable worth does not alter the societal discrimination that creates this over-supply of women into certain occupations. It just makes it more difficult for women, given the existence of societal discrimination, to act on their preferences because there will now be greater competition for fewer positions available in female-dominated occupations. Third, since society as a whole is to blame, particular employers should not be subject to legal sanction. It makes no sense to force the particular employers who hire the most women to suffer the greatest costs for actions taken by society as a whole.[33]

In the final analysis, therefore, barriers to entry caused by societal discrimination are no different from barriers to entry caused by the refusal of particular employers or unions to hire qualified women. Whatever the form of barrier to entry, the proper solution is to attack it directly rather than impose comparable worth.

IV The moral argument for comparable worth

Comparable worth is frequently defended on moral grounds. One common claim is that the goal of pay equity for women compels comparable worth. The negative implication of such a claim, of course, is that only those in favor of inequitable treatment of women would oppose comparable worth.

Attempting to seize the moral high ground as a form of argument is a well-known and frequently effective rhetorical device. In the case of comparable worth, however, the moral claim is extremely dubious. The moral claim is obviously weakest if wage differentials are a function of choice rather than crowding. In this event, women (like men) only enter certain occupations if they perceive they are made better off by doing so. Under this scenario, wage differentials between nursing and electronics are no more "inequitable" than differentials among other occupations.

The moral claim for comparable worth is weak even if we assume that wage differentials are the product of discrimination against women. No connection exists in comparable worth cases between the party being penalized and the party who engaged in wrongful discrimination. In addition, the correlation between the victims of discrimination and the beneficiaries of comparable worth is imperfect at best. If a consensus exists that some compensation should be paid to victims of past discrimination, direct financial transfers from general revenues are superior to comparable worth. We expand on these points below and end the section with a brief discussion of an alternative interpretation of comparable worth which attempts to explain its support on non-moral grounds.

A The effects of comparable worth on various groups

1 Women in female-dominated occupations

Comparable worth does nothing about barriers to entry in male-dominated occupations; women who want to enter those occupations are still prevented from doing so. Wages for women remaining in female-dominated occupations will rise to a level that, as we have discussed above, may or may not be higher than what it would be if the barrier to entry were eliminated. This will be of particular benefit to younger women who have long futures in the work force. Older women (who have been in the labor market longer and thus probably have been discriminated against the most) get the higher wage for a lesser number of years.

Comparable worth will also hurt some women. As wages are forced up in the female-dominated occupation, the supply of workers (both men and women) wanting to enter that occupation will increase. At the same time, however, the increased cost of labor will in all probability cause fewer workers to be employed. This greater competition for fewer positions may result in some workers, primarily women (but also men),[34] being fired and fewer being hired in the future. Marginal workers, such as the relatively unskilled, the young, minorities, and middle-aged women who have recently re-entered the workforce will in all probability be the biggest losers. And since comparable worth does nothing about eliminating barriers to entry in male-dominated occupations, there is no place for these women to go. They will be unemployed. Thus, one important (and inequitable) consequence of comparable worth is that it creates intra-occupational inequality among workers where none existed before in an attempt to remedy inter-occupational inequality.

2 Women who are not in the work force

Some women have never entered the work force. One possible reason is that these women value remaining at home more than working and would remain at home even if there were no discrimination against women. A second possibility is that they wanted to enter a male-dominated occupation but were unable to do so. These women are not helped by comparable worth because barriers to entry remain.[35]

Still another possibility is that these women wanted to enter the female-dominated occupation but only at higher wages. Comparable worth will cause some of these women to want to enter the female-dominated occupation. The problem, however, is that comparable worth probably will also result in a reduction of the number of jobs available. Since women who have not entered the work force will in all likelihood not have invested heavily in the development of their human capital, their prospects of entering the female-dominated occupation given the reduction in the number of positions available will not be great. Thus this category of women will not benefit significantly from comparable worth.

3 Employers

Employers in female-dominated occupations are penalized by comparable worth even though they have engaged in no discrimination. Conversely, employers who have created barriers to entry by discriminating against women are unaffected by comparable worth. In fact, comparable worth may well benefit discriminating employers. The reason is that comparable worth raises the labor cost of those who discriminate least relative to the cost of those who discriminate most. The most discriminatory firms do not hire women. By contrast, the least discriminatory firms hire the greatest number of women. Thus these nondiscriminatory firms suffer the largest increase in average wages from comparable worth policies. Discriminating employers who do not hire women in any event are less affected.

As discussed above, the analysis is unaffected if the state is the employer in both the male-dominated and female-dominated occupations. The state has engaged in no wrongful conduct in its capacity as an employer in the female-dominated occupation. It should be punished, if at all, because of its discriminatory practices in male-dominated occupations. Yet comparable worth focuses on the level of wages paid by the state in the female-dominated occupation without regard to whether the state has discriminated in the male-dominated occupation.

B Direct transfers from general revenues as an alternative to comparable worth

In arguing that the moral claim for comparable worth is not compelling, we do not reject the possibility that women, perhaps because of past (and possibly present) societal discrimination, are deserving beneficiaries of wealth transfers. We express no opinion here on the moral entitlement of women to compensation for alleged past or present societal discrimination. Rather, our point is that even if such a moral entitlement exists, comparable worth is the wrong solution. A preferable approach would be a direct transfer to disadvantaged women from general revenues.[36]

Direct transfers avoid the inefficiencies created by comparable worth. They do not distort the relative wages among occupations that give market participants information about the supply and demand for particular skills. Nor do they penalize employers for engaging in socially desirable conduct. Finally, direct transfers do not give employers perverse incentives to create firms which only employ workers in one occupation notwithstanding possible cost increases.

Direct transfers are also more equitable. The costs of remedying discrimination are borne by society as a whole rather than by blameless employers. In addition, victims of discrimination benefit more from direct transfers than from comparable worth in a number of different ways. First, those women who have been prevented by societal discrimination from obtaining certain skills would be compensated under a system of direct transfers. Those women are implicitly penalized by comparable worth since they lack the skills that are "comparable" to those in higher-paying occupations—skills that they would have possessed had they not been victims of societal discrimination. Second, direct transfers could allow those who have been hurt the most—older women—to receive the greatest benefits. Comparable worth, by contrast, provides the greatest benefits to younger workers (those who keep their jobs) even though they have been hurt the least by past discrimination. Finally, direct transfers avoid the unemployment which disproportionately burdens the relatively unskilled and other weaker segments of society.

We do not suggest that implementing a direct transfer system would be easy. Identifying victims and determining how much compensation to pay would be difficult. Moreover, it seems inevitable that the fit between those who have been discriminated against and those who recover would be very imperfect. A transfer to all women, for example, would provide a windfall to some women who would have chosen to specialize in household services in any event. But these problems also exist with comparable worth. Indeed, as we have emphasized, comparable worth either hurts or provides small benefits to those who are most likely to have been victims of discrimination (older women and the relatively unskilled) while providing the greatest benefits to those who have been discriminated against the least if at all (younger skilled women). To the extent that these problems make both a direct transfer system and comparable worth relatively unattractive vehicles, the better course may be to limit recovery to those who can prove, under the Equal Pay Act and Title VII, that they were victims of discrimination by particular employers or entities. We discuss this alternative in Part V below.

C An alternative explanation of comparable worth

While comparable worth is frequently defended on moral grounds, it is possible to analyze the doctrine from an entirely different perspective. Comparable worth can be analyzed as a conventional example of special interest regulation whereby a well organized group (workers represented by unions) attempts to use the courts or the political process to extract wealth from larger, more diffuse groups (i.e., taxpayers).[37]

Interpreting comparable worth as a garden variety form of special interest regulation helps explain comparable worth's strong support among unions.[38] Comparable worth, like minimum wage laws, makes it more costly for employers to substitute relatively unskilled workers for those who are more skilled because the relative prices of the two groups narrows.[39] Because employers are less able to employ lower-priced labor, unions have greater ability to cartelize workers.[40]

The special interest theory also explains why attempts to implement comparable worth have focused on the public sector. Governments are less responsive to competitive pressures than most private firms and can pass the costs of higher wages on to taxpayers. If the full costs of wage increases can be passed on to taxpayers, the pre-comparable worth level of employment can be maintained. In this event, intra-occupational inequality is avoided and comparable worth becomes a pure wealth transfer from taxpayers to workers cloaked in the rhetoric of remedying discrimination.

[Sections V and VI deleted by the editor.]

Notes

1 The authors thank Albert Alschuler, Mary Becker, Richard Epstein, Spencer Kimball, Elisabeth Landes, Bernard Meltzer, Geoffrey Miller, Cass Sunstein, and participants of the Law and Economics Workshop at The University of Chicago for their extremely helpful comments. The authors also thank the John M. Olin Foundation for financial support.

2 29 U.S.C. § 206(d) (1976).

3 42 U.S.C. §§ 2000e-1 to 2000e-17 (1982).

4 See American Nurses Ass'n v. Illinois, 783 F.2d 716 (7th Cir. 1986); American Fed'n of State, County & Mun. Employees (AFSCME) v. Washington, 770 F.2d 1401 (9th Cir. 1985).

5 452 U.S. 161 (1981).

6 Id. at 166, 181.

7 See, e.g., Gasaway, *Comparable Worth: A Post-Gunther Overview*, 69 GEO. LJ. 1123, 1134–36 (1981); Newman & Vonhof, *"Separate But Equal"—Job Segregation and Pay Equity in the Wake of Gunther*, 1981 U. ILL. L. REV. 269, 272–85; Vieira, *Comparable Worth and the Gunther Case: The New Drive for Equal Pay*, 18 U.C.D. L. REV. 449 (1985).

8 See, e.g., *Bureau of National Affairs (BNA), Pay Equity and Comparable Worth* 55–68 (1984) (listing existing and proposed state pay equity legislation); Rothchild, *Overview of Pay Initiatives, 1974–1984*, in 1 *Comparable Worth: Issue for the 80s* 119, 121–23, 128 (US. Comm'n on Civil Rights 1984) (listing state legislation and local initiatives) [hereinafter cited as *Issue for the 80s*].

9 See, e.g., Bellace, *A Foreign Perspective*, in *Comparable Worth: Issues and Alternatives* 137 (E. Livernash ed., 2d ed. 1984) (analyzing the experiences of the European Community, Sweden, Canada, Australia, and New Zealand in trying to achieve "pay equity"); Gasaway, supra note 7, at 1149–55 (discussing comparable worth abroad).

10 See, e.g., Beller, *Occupational Segregation and the Earnings Gap*, in *Issue for the 80s*, supra note 8, at 25–26 (discussing force of Title VII in eliminating occupational segregation); Bergman, *The Economic Case for Comparable Worth*, in *Comparable Worth: New Directions for Research* 71 (H. Hartmann ed. 1985) (offering economic arguments for comparable worth) [hereinafter cited as new directions]; Blumrosen, *Wage Discrimination, Job Segregation, and Title VII of the Civil Rights Act of 1964*, 12 U. MICH. J.L. REF. 397, 490–502 (1979) (arguing that comparable worth is available under Title VII as a remedy for wage discrimination).

11 See *Women in the Work Force: Pay Equity, Hearing before the Joint Economic Committee*, 98th Cong., 2d Sess. 4 (1984) (statement of Heidi Hartmann) ("It is well-known that on average the earnings of women who are employed full-time are approximately 60 percent of those of men who are also employed full-time.") [hereinafter cited as *Hearing*]; *Women, Work, and Wages: Equal Pay for Jobs of Equal Value* 41 (D. Treiman & H. Hartmann eds. 1981) (among full-time, year-round workers, earnings of women average less than 60% of those of men) [hereinafter cited as WOMEN, WORK & WAGES].

12 See, e.g., *Women's Bureau. Office of the Secretary, U.S. Dep't of Labor, the Earnings Gap between Women and Men* 6 (Table 1) (1979) (figures show a persistent earnings gap over a two decade period) [hereinafter cited as *Earnings Gap*]; *Hearing*, supra note 11 at 4 (statement of Heidi Hartmann) ("It is ... well-established that sex segregation in the labor market is extreme and has not changed much since 1900."); Blumrosen, supra note 10, at 411 ("After almost fifteen years of federal legislation prohibiting discrimination in compensation and segregation of jobs, the wage gap is larger now than it was before the legislation."); O'Neill, *The Trend in the Male-Female Wage Gap in the United States*, 3 J. LAB. ECON. S91, S93 (1985) (the female-to-male earnings ratio based on the annual earnings of year-round full time workers was 58% in 1939, 64% in the middle 1950s, 58% again in the mid-1960s, and 62% in 1982). O'Neill predicts that the increasing work experience of women in recent years and other factors will lead to a narrowing of the wage gap in the next 10 years. Id.

13 See *Women, Work & Wages*, supra note 11, at 24–41; Blumrosen, supra note 10, at 415.

14 See, e.g., Killingsworth, *The Economics of Comparable Worth: Analytical, Empirical, and Policy Questions*, in *New Directions*, supra note 10, at 86; Lindsay & Shanor, County of Washington v. Gunther: *Economic and Legal Considerations for Resolving Sex-Based Wage Discrimination Cases*, 1 sup. ct. econ. rev. 185 (1982); O'Neill, *An Argument Against Comparable Worth*, in *Issue for the 80s*, supra note 8, at 177; Rita Ricardo-Campbell, *Women and Comparable Worth* (Hoover Inst. Monograph Series 1985).

15 See, e.g., O'Neill, *supra* note 14, at 178 ("In a free market, wages and prices are not taken as judgments of the inherent value of the worker or the good itself, but reflect a balancing of what people are willing to pay for the services of these goods with how much it costs to supply them. ... There is simply no independent scientific way to determine what pay should be in a particular occupation without recourse to the market.").

16 See sources cited *supra* note 11.

17 See, e.g., *Earnings Gap*, supra note 12, at 2 ("Of prime importance ... in explaining the earnings differential is the concentration of women in relatively low-paying occupations and lower status jobs even within the higher paying occupation groups."); Newman & Vonhof, *supra* note 7, at 270 ("the current disparity is not primarily due to unequal pay for

equal work ... but rather to the concentration of women in low-paying jobs which are different in content from men's jobs") (footnote omitted); Oaxaca, *Male–Female Wage Differentials in Urban Labor Markets,* 14 *Int'l Econ.* Rev. 693, 708 (1973) (same).

18 In all probability, entry barriers would have to be pervasive for there to be a depressing effect on wages for political scientists. For purposes of analysis, we assume that all barriers to entry in one occupation depress wages in other occupations.

19 The crowding explanation for wage differentials in the context of racial discrimination is articulated and formalized in Bergmann, *The Effect on White Incomes of Discrimination in Employment,* 79 *J. Pol. Econ.* 294, 299–301 (1971).

20 G. Becker, *Human Capital, Effort, and the Sexual Division of Labor,* 3 *J. Lab. Econ.* S33 (1985).

21 See generally Gary Becker, *The Economics of Discrimination* 39–50 (2d ed. 1971) (discussing effect of employers' discrimination on labor markets). Alternatively, employers with a taste for discrimination may hire women but pay them less than men. Other groups such as unions or consumers may also have a taste for discrimination. Unions may refuse to admit women to membership; consumers may refuse to patronize firms which do not discriminate against women. Such actions by unions or consumers may create entry barriers to women even if employers do not have a taste for discrimination.

22 See Sunstein, *Legal Interference with Private Preferences,* 54 *U. Chi. I. Rev.* (forthcoming) (discussing adaptive preferences).

23 For a concise summary of these studies, see *Women, Work & Wages, supra* note 11, at 13–42.

24 See, e.g., id. at 42 (attempts to explain differentials on the basis of such factors as education, labor force experience, labor force commitment, or other human capital factors "usually account for less than a quarter and never more than half of the observed earnings differences"); Blinder, *Wage Discrimination: Reduced Form and Structural Estimates,* 8 *J. Human Resources* 436, 449 (1973) (two-thirds of male–female wage differential attributable to outright discrimination in labor markets).

25 See, e.g., *Women, Work & Wages, supra* note 11, at 24 ("[R]esearchers have consistently found that a substantial part of the earnings difference cannot be explained by factors thought to measure productivity differences. Taken at face value, these results create a presumption of additional factors at work, possibly including institutional barriers and discrimination."); Oaxaca, *Theory and Measurement of the Economics of Discrimination,* in *Equal Rights and Industrial Relations* 25 (L. Hausman, O. Ashenfelter, B. Rustin, R. Schubert & D. Slaiman eds. 1977) (discrimination accounts for between 58 and 75% of the gross wage differential).

26 See, e.g., E. Landes, *Sex-Differences in Wages and Employment: A Test of the Specific Capital Hypothesis,* 15 *Econ. Inquiry* 523, 523 (1977) (at least two-thirds of wage differential between men and women within occupations is accounted for by nondiscriminatory employment practices); Lindsay & Shanor, *supra* note 14, at 217–21 (wage differentials could be explained by factors other than discrimination if the data were suitably refined); O'Neill, *supra* note 14, at 183 ("the true effect of sex on occupational differences or wage rates is [an] unresolved issue"); Polachek, *Women in the Economy: Perspectives on Gender Inequality,* in *Issue for the 80s, supra* note 8, at 45 (human capital model explains nearly 100% of the wage differential); Roberts, *Statistical Biases in the Measurement of Employment Discrimination,* in *Comparable Worth: Issues and Alternatives, supra* note 9, at 173–95 (inference of discrimination is largely a function of biases in statistical methodologies).

27 See Polachek, *supra* note 26, at 40–43.

28 Id. at 40.

29 The Ninth Circuit's discussion of the job evaluation study in AFSCME v. Washington, 770
F.2d 1401 (9th Cir. 1985), illustrates the pervasive subjectivity inherent in such studies:

> Comparable worth was calculated by evaluating jobs under four criteria: knowl-
> edge and skills, mental demands, accountability, and working conditions. A max-
> imum number of points was allotted to each category: 280 for knowledge and
> skills, 140 for mental demands, 160 for accountability and 20 for working condi-
> tions. Every job was assigned a numerical value under each of the four criteria.

Id. at 1403. The study found a wage disparity of about 20% between jobs held predominantly by women and jobs held predominantly by men. Id.
The arbitrariness of such a study is obvious. Why are there four as opposed to three or
ten categories that count? Why does each category have the weight that it does? How
are points assigned to different occupations? Who decides all these questions? What
would be the result of application of these four criteria to wage differentials between
law and political science professors?

30 Another problem with using occupational job evaluation studies to establish discrimination is that such studies focus on inter-occupational wage differentials and ignore intra-
occupational differences. As a result, they may conclude that discrimination exists when
none is present. For example, if wages in male-dominated occupations are higher than
wages in "comparable" female-dominated occupations but females in each occupation are
paid more than males, the studies would wrongly predict that women were being subjected to discrimination. Alternatively, occupational job evaluation studies may fail to
recognize discrimination when it exists if it averages out across occupations.

31 If wage differentials were not compensating, and if there were no barriers to entry, all workers would leave the low-paying job for the higher-paying one. This would result in either the
equalization of wages or in the complete extinction of the low-paying occupation.

32 If comparable worth is interpreted to mean that occupations that have the same value to
a particular employer (rather than to society as a whole) must be paid the same, states can
avoid being challenged by providing governmental services only in occupations that are
"non-comparable."

33 See supra Section A of Part III.

34 The case of male employees in female-dominated occupations is slightly different. These
employees are there by choice so they are not directly affected by barriers to entry. While
some men will benefit from the wage increase resulting from comparable worth, some
men will also be hurt. As wages rise and the level of employment in the female-dominated
occupation is reduced, some men previously employed in that field will be unemployed.

35 The harm these women suffer is necessarily less than that suffered by women who work in
female-dominated occupations. A woman who stays out of the labor force reveals implicitly
that she values staying at home more than her potential earnings in the female-dominated
occupation. The harm suffered by these women is the difference between what their wage
would have been in the male-dominated occupation absent discrimination and the value of
staying at home. The loss to women who work in the female-dominated occupation is the
difference between what the wage would have been in the male-dominated occupation
absent discrimination and the current wage in the female-dominated occupation. Since the
wage in the female-dominated occupation is necessarily lower than the value of home time
for those who chose to stay home, the harm suffered by working women is greater.

36 Such transfers could take a variety of forms ranging from direct monetary payments to
subsidies for training or education.

37 For general discussions of the special interest theory of regulation, see Peltzman, *Toward a More General Theory of Regulation*, 19 J.L. & Econ. 211 (1976); Stigler, *The Theory of Economic Regulation*, 2 Bell J. Econ. & Mgt. Sci. 3 (1971), reprinted in George Stigler, *The Citizen and the State: Essays on Regulation* 114 (1975).

38 See, e.g., BNA, *supra* note 8, at 73–78 (discussing union activities in support of comparable worth); *Hearing, supra* note 11, at 136–42 (statement of Brian Turner, Director of Legislation and Economic Policy, Industrial Union Dep't, AFL-CIO).

39 On minimum wage laws, see, for example, Brozen, *The Effect of Statutory Minimum Wage Increases on Teen-Age Employment*, 12 J.L. & Econ. 109 (1969); Linneman, *The Economic Impacts of Minimum Wage Laws: A New Look at an Old Question*, 90 J. Pol. Econ. 443 (1982); Mincer, *Unemployment Effects of Minimum Wage Laws*, 84 J. Pol. Econ. S87 (1976).

40 On the cartelizing effect of unions, and of labor law in general, see Posner, *Some Economics of Labor Law*, 51 U. Chi. L. Rev. 988 (1984).

Review and Discussion Questions

1 What is the discrimination or "crowding" hypothesis?

2 What is the "choice" hypothesis?

3 What evidence seems consistent with the choice hypothesis?

4 Even if discrimination causes male–female wage differences, what would be the disadvantages of a comparable worth law?

5 Polls indicate that college-age women now, more than a generation or two ago, plan to focus on their careers when they graduate. Given this, what should happen to the male–female wage gap if the choice hypothesis is correct?

Chapter 31

Harold Demsetz and Kenneth Lehn

THE STRUCTURE OF CORPORATE OWNERSHIP: CAUSES AND CONSEQUENCES

L ARGE PUBLICLY TRADED CORPORATIONS are frequently characterized as having highly diffuse ownership structures that effectively separate ownership of residual claims from control of corporate decisions. This alleged separation of ownership and control figures prominently both in the economic theory of organization and in the ongoing debate concerning the social significance of the modern corporation, a debate that we join later in this paper.[1] Our primary concern, however, is to explore some of the broad forces that influence the structure of corporate ownership. Our conjectures about the determinants of ownership structure are examined empirically.

Inspection of ownership data reveals that the concentration of equity ownership in U.S. corporations varies widely. For a sample of 511 large U.S. corporations, Table 31.1 lists the distribution of three measures of ownership concentration: the percentage of a firm's outstanding common equity owned by the five largest shareholders (A5), the percentage of shares owned by the 20 largest shareholders (A20), and an approximation of a Herfindahl measure of ownership concentration (AH). This sample and these data will be described more fully later in the paper. We simply note here the variation in ownership concentration. The value of A5 ranges from 1.27 to 87.14 around a mean value of 24.81. Similar variation is found in the values of A20 and AH: A20 ranges from 1.27 to 91.54 and AH ranges from 0.69 to 4,952.38. The corresponding average values of these two variables are 37.66 and 402.75, respectively.

We approach the task of explaining the variation in these data by considering the advantages and disadvantages to the firm's shareholders of greater diffuseness in ownership structure. The most obvious disadvantage is the greater incentive for shirking by *owners* that results. The benefit derived by a shirking owner is his ability to use his time and energies on other tasks and indulgences; this benefit accrues entirely to him.

The cost of his shirking, presumably the poorer performance of the firm, is shared by all owners in proportion to the number of shares of stock they own. The more concentrated is ownership, the greater the degree to which benefits and costs are borne by the same owner. In a firm owned entirely by one individual, all benefits and costs of owner shirking are borne by the sole owner. In this case, no "externalities" confound his decision about attending to the tasks of ownership. In a very diffusely owned firm, the divergence between benefit and costs would be much larger for the typical owner, and he can be expected to respond by neglecting some tasks of ownership.

The inefficiency implied by such externalities, of itself, dictates against diffuse ownership structures, and we would observe no diffuse ownership structures in a "rational" world unless counterbalancing advantages exist. Since these advantages do exist, a decision to alter a firm's ownership structure in favor of greater diffuseness presumably is guided by the goal of value maximization. A theory of ownership structure is based largely on an understanding of what makes these advantages vary in strength from firm to firm.

Determinants of ownership structure

Of the possible general forces affecting ownership structure, three seem important enough to merit investigation. One of these, the *value-maximizing size* of the firm, is not surprising. The second, more subtle and difficult to measure, is the profit potential from exercising more effective control, to which we ascribe the name *control potential*. The third is *systematic regulation*, the general purpose of which is to impose, in one form or another, constraints on the scope and impact of shareholder decisions. In addition to these, we consider the *amenity potential* of firms, about which more will be said below.

Value-maximizing size

The size of firms that compete successfully in product and input markets varies within and among industries. The larger is the competitively viable size, ceteris paribus, the larger are the firm's capital resources and, generally, the greater is the market value of a given fraction of ownership. The higher price of a given fraction of the firm should, in itself, reduce the degree to which ownership is concentrated. Moreover, a given degree of control generally requires a smaller share of the firm the larger is the firm. Both these effects of size imply greater diffuseness of ownership the larger is a firm. This may be termed the risk-neutral effect of size on ownership.

Risk aversion should reinforce the risk-neutral effect. An attempt to preserve effective and concentrated ownership in the face of larger capital needs requires a small group of owners to commit more wealth to a single enterprise. Normal risk aversion implies that they will purchase additional shares only at lower, risk-compensating prices. This increased cost of capital discourages owners of larger firms from attempting to maintain highly concentrated ownership.

As the value-maximizing size of the firm grows, both the risk-neutral and risk-aversion effects of larger size ultimately should weigh more heavily than the shirking cost that may be expected to accompany a more diffuse ownership structure, so that an inverse relationship between firm size and concentration of ownership is to be expected.

Table 31.1 A. Frequency distribution of A5, A20, and AH for 511 firms in sample

Range	A5 Frequency	A5 Cumulative percentage	A20 Frequency	A20 Cumulative percentage	Range	AH Frequency	AH Cumulative percentage
0–4.99	16	3.13	11	2.15	0–19.99	28	5.48
5–9.99	50	12.92	13	4.70	20–39.99	46	14.48
10–14.99	86	29.75	13	7.24	40–59.99	70	22.70
15–19.99	98	48.92	32	13.50	60–79.99	44	31.31
20–24.99	72	63.01	41	21.53	80–99.99	42	39.53
25–29.99	45	71.82	67	34.64	100–119.99	38	46.97
30–34.99	37	79.06	59	46.18	120–139.99	28	52.45
35–39.99	27	84.34	66	59.10	140–159.99	22	56.75
40–44.99	19	88.06	57	70.25	160–179.99	16	59.88
45–49.99	18	91.59	39	77.89	180–199.99	11	62.04
50–54.99	9	93.35	34	84.54	200–219.99	14	64.78
55–59.99	10	95.30	22	88.85	220–239.99	9	66.54
60–64.99	10	97.26	21	92.96	240–289.99	17	69.86
65–69.99	7	98.63	19	96.67	290–369.99	21	73.97
70–74.99	4	99.41	9	98.43	370–479.99	24	78.67
75–79.99	1	99.61	2	98.83	480–539.99	22	82.98
80–84.99	0	99.61	3	99.41	540–779.99	21	87.08
85–89.99	2	100.00	1	99.61	780–1,219.99	25	91.98
90–94.99	0	100.00	2	100.00	1,220–2,279.99	20	95.89
95–100.00	0	100.00	0	100.00	2,280–4,959.99	21	100.00

B. Summary statistics of A5, A20, and AH for 511 Firms in sample

Variable	N	Mean	Standard deviation	Minimum	Maximum
A5	511	24.81	15.77	1.27	87.14
A20	511	37.66	16.73	1.27	91.54
AH	511	402.75	722.99	.69	4,952.38

Larger firms realize a lower *overall* cost with a more diffuse ownership structure than do small firms. The choice by owners of a diffuse ownership structure, therefore, is consistent with stockholder wealth- (or utility-) maximizing behavior.

Control potential

Control potential is the wealth gain achievable through more effective monitoring of managerial performance by a firm's owners. If the market for corporate control and the managerial labor market perfectly aligned the interests of managers and shareholders, then control potential would play no role in explaining corporate ownership structure (although it might then explain the degree to which ownership by professional management is concentrated). We assume, however, that neither of these markets operates costlessly. In addition to the transaction and information costs associated with the acquisition and maintenance of corporate control, Jarrell and Bradley (1980) have shown that there are significant regulatory costs associated with control transactions. These nontrivial costs act effectively as a tax on corporate control transactions. Although we are unaware of similar empirical studies of transaction costs associated with the managerial labor market, we assume that this market also imperfectly disciplines corporate managers who work contrary to the wishes of shareholders. Our view is that these transaction costs impose a specific identity and control potential on firms. Alterations in the structure of corporate ownership, in part, can be understood as a response to these costs.

We seek to uncover elements of a firm's environment that are pervasive and persistent in their effect on control potential. Firm-specific uncertainty is one such factor. Firms that transact in markets characterized by stable prices, stable technology, stable market shares, and so forth are firms in which managerial performance can be monitored at relatively low cost. In less predictable environments, however, managerial behavior simultaneously figures more prominently in a firm's fortunes and becomes more difficult to monitor. Frequent changes in relative prices, technology, and market shares require timely managerial decisions concerning redeployment of corporate assets and personnel. Disentangling the effects of managerial behavior on firm performance from the corresponding effects of these other, largely exogenous factors is costly, however.[2] Accordingly, we believe that a firm's control potential is directly associated with the noisiness of the environment in which it operates. The noisier a firm's environment, the greater the payoff to owners in maintaining tighter control. Hence, noisier environments should give rise to more concentrated ownership structures.[3]

Clearly, we take the view that owners *believe* they can influence the success of their firms and that all outcomes are neither completely random nor completely foreseeable. This belief constitutes an assertion of the existence of risks, opportunities, and managerial shirking that are in some degree controllable by owners for the profit of owners. The profit potential from exercising a given degree of owner control is, we believe, correlated with instability in the firm's environment.

This instability may be measured in many ways, by fluctuations in product and input prices of relevance to a firm, for example, or by variations in a firm's market share. We rely on instability of a firm's profit rate, measured by variation in both stock returns and accounting returns. Profit data are readily available, and profit variability offers a global measure of the impact of the various subcomponents of instability in its environment; profit also is the "bottom line" that so interests stockholders.

The three measures of instability examined here are (1) firm-specific risk (SE), as measured by the standard error of estimate calculated from fitting the "market model," (2) the standard deviation of monthly stock market rates of return (STD_s), and (3) the standard deviation of annual accounting profit rates (STD_a). Our intuition favors firm-specific risk as the factor most strongly associated with the type of instability for which control is most useful. The exercise of control should be particularly important to those operations of a firm that can be influenced and responded to most easily. These would seem to include the inner functioning of the firm and its operations in the markets in which it purchases and sells. These are proximate and specific to the firm. In contrast to these sources of instability, economy-wide events such as the rate of growth of money supply or fluctuations in government tax-expenditure flows are beyond a firm's control and, at best, can be reacted to intelligently. Because of these reactive possibilities, even this more distant and less firm-specific instability is likely to call forth more concentrated ownership, but greater control potential is offered by instability that is more specific to the firm.

We include instability in accounting rates of return among our measures, though we recognize many defects of accounting data. One of these defects is purely statistical: whereas we have collected monthly stock return data, our accounting data are annual data. For any time period, then, there are 12 times as many observations with which to calculate a stock return variance as there are for calculating an accounting return variance. Accounting profits, however, may reflect year-to-year fluctuations in under-lying business conditions better than stock market rates of return, since stock market rates of return reflect expected future developments that may cloak contemporary fluctuations in business conditions. We say "may" because today's accounting rate of return is influenced by past investment expenditures (and other carryover accounting entries), and this also attenuates the impact of "today's" instabilities. It is not clear on a priori grounds which measure is better suited to measure day-to-day or year-to-year variability in the firm's environment.

Regulation

Systematic regulation restricts the options available to owners, thus reducing control potential in ways that may not be reflected fully in profit instability. Regulation also provides some subsidized monitoring and disciplining of the management of regulated firms. A bank whose balance sheet looks too risky to regulators will find itself under considerable pressure to replace its management. These "primary" effects of regulation should reduce ownership concentration to a greater degree than would be predicted simply on the basis of profit instability.

We expect the net impact of regulation to be dominated by these primary effects, which call for greater diffuseness of ownership in regulated industries. There are also well-known problems of amenity consumption by management in a regulated setting. These should be more important than in nonregulated firms because cost-plus price-setting regulation reduces the incentive to hold down cost while it dulls competition. Greater control of management by owners would seem to be called for and, hence, greater concentration of ownership. However, owner incentives to reduce managerial amenity consumption are also dulled by the tendency of commissions to adjust prices toward levels that leave the profit rate unchanged, and this counteracts the desire for greater control of management.

Amenity potential of a firm's output

Those who own large fractions of the outstanding shares of a firm either manage the firm themselves or are positioned to see to it that management serves their interests. Maximizing the value of the firm generally serves these interests well, for this provides the largest possible budget for a shareholder to spend as a "household." The advantage of maximizing profit through the firm and then consuming in the household is based on the implicit assumption that specialization in consumption is productive of maximum utility. However, when owners can obtain their consumption goals better through the firm's business than through household expenditures, they will strive to control that firm more closely to obtain these goals. Just as the potential for higher profit creates a demand for closer monitoring of management by owners, so does the potential for firm-specific amenity consumption.

We refer here to the utility consequences of being able to influence the type of goods produced by the firm, not to the utility derived from providing general leadership to the firm. We believe that there is nonpecuniary income associated with the provision of general leadership and with the ability to deploy resources to suit one's personal preferences, but we are not now prepared to assert how this varies across firms or different ownership structures.[4] However, we do believe that two industries are likely to call forth tight control in order to indulge such personal preferences. These are professional sports clubs and mass media firms. Winning the World Series or believing that one is systematically influencing public opinion plausibly provides utility to some owners even if profit is reduced from levels otherwise achievable. These consumption goals arise from the particular tastes of owners, so their achievement requires owners to be in a position to influence managerial decisions. Hence, ownership should be more concentrated in firms for which this type of amenity potential is greater. Unfortunately, other than a shared perception that the sports and media industries are especially laden with amenity potential for owners, we have no systematic way of tracking amenity potential. On balance, we consider amenity potential a more speculative explanation of ownership concentration in these special industries than are size, control potential, and regulation.

Data and measurements

This study uses ownership data obtained from three directories published by Corporate Data Exchange (CDE): *CDE Stock Ownership Directory: Energy* (1980), *Banking and Finance* (1980), and *Fortune 500* (1981). The sample consists of 511 firms from major sectors of the U.S. economy, including regulated utilities and financial institutions. These firms represent all firms for which we were able to obtain ownership data, accounting data (from the COMPUSTAT tape), and security price data (from the Center for Research on Security Prices [CRSP] tape). We also examine a manufacturing and mining subsample composed of 406 firms.

The ownership data consist of a ranking of all publicly identifiable stockholders who exercised investment power over 0.2 percent or more of the company's common equity. The CDE used the same definition of investment power used by the Securities and Exchange Commission (SEC) in application of 13(f) regulations. Specifically, this definition includes all shares over which the stockholder has the power to buy or sell.

The CDE used various SEC forms to secure data, including forms 3, 4, 13f, 14d-1, and 144, and, in addition, it examined corporate proxy statements, secondary offering and merger prospectuses, public pension plan portfolios, employee stock ownership plan reports, and foundation and educational endowment portfolios. Where institutional investors held shares in a management capacity (e.g., investment advisory agreements or trust agreements), the party for whom they managed the shares is identified as the holder with investment power. Similarly, when nominees held stock, the party for whom they held the stock is identified as the holder with investment power. Holdings by diversified financial holding companies, investment banks, brokerage firms, and investment company managers are listed in the "street name" of the firms when the firms are not holding the shares in a management capacity.

Our statistical work relies heavily on the percentage of shares owned by the most important shareholders, A5 and A20, and the approximation of the Herfindahl index, AH. Different notation is introduced when we discuss institutional and noninstitutional shareholders.

In our regression equations we measure the percentage of shares owned by the top five and top 20 shareholders by applying a logistic transformation to these percentages, using the formula

$$\log \frac{\text{percentage concentration}}{100 - \text{percentage concentration}}$$

The transformation is made to convert an otherwise bounded dependent variable into an unbounded one. A logarithmic transformation is applied to the Herfindahl measure of ownership concentration.[5] We designate the transformed variable by prefixing L, as in LA5, LA20, and LAH.

A glance at a simple correlation matrix for A5, A20, and AH indicates that we can expect similar empirical results from using these alternative measures. The correlation between A20 and AH is weakest, but it is still .71. For purposes of constructing an index of ownership concentration, the 20 largest ownership interests establish a workable outer limit. Beyond 20, it is difficult to interpret the measure as a meaningful index of ownership concentration.

Our measure of firm size (EQUITY) is the average annual market value of the firm's common equity during the period 1976–80, with units in thousands of dollars. We have experimented with other size measures (e.g., book value of assets), but the general nature of the statistical result is unaffected by this choice. Since our ownership data pertain to the ownership of common equity, we prefer to proxy size with a measure of the value of common equity. Our measures of instability of a firm's environment (SE and STD_s) are based on stock market rates of return as determined by 60 monthly stock market returns during the 5-year period 1976–80.[6] Instability measured by the standard deviation in accounting profit rates (STD_a) is based on five annual profit rates over the period 1976–80. Dummy variables take a value of one if the firm is a regulated utility (UTIL), regulated financial institution (FIN), or media firm (MEDIA), and zero otherwise.

Correlation of ownership measures for 511 regulated and nonregulated firms

	A5	A20
A20	.92	...
AH	.86	.71

The second part of our empirical work tests the Berle–Means thesis, which implies that diffuse ownership structures adversely affect corporate performance. We test this by assessing the impact of ownership structure on accounting profit rate (RETURN$_a$). In doing so, it is necessary to control for other factors that may affect accounting profit rate. These other factors include the size of the firm as measured by the book value of assets averaged over 1976–80 (ASSET) and a set of variables that seek to standardize for accounting artifacts. These variables are ratios to sales of capital expenditures (CAP), advertising (ADV), and R & D expenses (RD), all measured as averages from the 1976–80 time period.

Table 31.2 gives summary definitions of all variables used in this paper. Summary statistics for these variables for the 511 firms in our sample are shown in Table 31.3.

Statistical analysis of ownership concentration

Ordinary least squares (OLS) regression estimates of LA5 on three alternative measures of profit instability and four other variables are shown in Table 31.4. All three measures of instability are significantly and positively related to ownership concentration. In addition to linearly estimating ownership concentration as a function of instability, we also estimated this relationship in nonlinear form by including the squared value of the instability measure. The squared values of these variables are negatively related to ownership concentration, indicating that at higher values of these variables the increase in concentration of ownership associated with given increases in instability diminishes. Of the three instability measures, the standard error of estimate from the market model enters most significantly, and the standard deviation in accounting profit rates enters least significantly.[7]

All other variables take the expected signs, and all of the estimated coefficients are statistically significant at the .95 level. Size of firm, as measured by the market value of equity, is negatively related to ownership concentration.[8] The dummy for systematic regulation indicates that the average concentration of ownership for the regulated firms is significantly less than for other firms. The ownership structure of utility firms is affected more by regulation than is that of financial firms. Media firms exhibit significantly more ownership concentration, on average, than other firms, a finding that is consistent with the notion that tighter control is required to achieve the amenity potential offered by the unique output of these firms.

The variation in LA5 explained by these equations is at least 30 percent. When firm-specific risk is the instability measure, 33 percent of the variation is explained. The coefficients of all other variables and their significance are largely unaffected by the measure of instability chosen. Most altered is the coefficient on the market value of equity, which varies from −3.51(E-08) for the nonlinear firm-specific risk equation

Table 31.2 Description of variables

A5	Percentage of shares controlled by top five shareholders: sources: *CDE Stock Ownership Directories: Banking and Finance* (1980), *Energy*, (1980), and *Fortune 500* (1981)
A20	Percentage of shares controlled by top 20 shareholders; sources: same as A5
AH	Herfindahl index of ownership concentration. Calculated by summing the squared percentage of shares controlled by each shareholder; sources: same as A5
F5	Percentage of shares controlled by top five families and individuals; sources: same as A5
I5	Percentage of shares controlled by instituitional investors: sources: same as A5
UTIL	One if firm is electric utility, natural gas pipeline, or natural gas distributor; zero otherwise: source: COMPUSTAT
FIN	One if firm is bank, saving and loan institution, insurance company, or securities firm; zero otherwise; source: COMPUSTAT
MEDIA	One if firm is newspaper publisher, book publisher, magazine publisher, or broadcaster; zero otherwise; source: COMPUSTAT
EQUITY	Market value of common equity in thousands of dollars (annual average, 1976–80); source: CRSP
RETURN$_s$	Stock market rate of return (average monthly return, 1976–80); source: CRSP
RETURN$_a$	Accounting rate of return (annual average of net income to book value of shareholders' equity, 1976–80); source: COMPUSTAT
SE	Standard error of estimate from market model in which firm's average monthly return (1976–80) is regressed on the average monthly return on value-weighted market portfolio (1976–80); source: CRSP
STD$_s$	Standard deviation of monthly stock market rates of return, 1976–80; source: CRSP
STD$_a$	Standard deviation of annual accounting rates of return, 1976–80; source: COMPUSTAT
CAP	Ratio of capital expenditures (annual average, 1976–80) to total sales; source: COMPUSTAT
ADV	Ratio of advertising expenditures (annual average, 1976–80) to total sales; source: COMPUSTAT
RD	Ratio of research and development expenditures (annual average, 1976–80) to total sales; source: COMPUSTAT
ASSET	Value of total assets in millions of dollars (annual average, 1976–80); source: COMPUSTAT

to -5.94(E-08) for the linear equation that includes the standard deviation of accounting profit rate.

Different measures of ownership concentration are regressed on identical sets of explanatory variables for two samples of firms in Table 31.5. The left side of the table continues our investigation of the full sample of regulated and nonregulated firms. The right side of the table uses a smaller sample that systematically excludes regulated firms. Logistically transformed values of the percentage of shares owned by the five and by the 20 largest stockholding interests and the Herfindahl index are used

Table 31.3 Summary statistics of variables for 511 firms in sample

Variable	Mean	Standard deviation	Minimum	Maximum
A5	24.81	15.77	1.27	87.14
A20	37.66	16.73	1.27	91.54
AH	402.75	722.99	.69	4,952.38
F5	9.08	13.03	0	69.39
I5	18.39	11.52	.75	87.14
UTIL	.10	.30	0	1
FIN	.11	.31	0	1
MEDIA	.03	.16	0	1
EQUITY	$1,221,754	$2,698,140	$22,341	$40,587,203
$RETURN_s$	.017	.012	−.013	.074
$RETURN_a$	.238	.105	−.077	.824
SE	.067	.025	.031	.398
STD_s	.084	.029	.034	.412
STD_a	.055	.050	.002	.320
CAP	.089	.103	0	.841
ADV	.011	.023	0	.200
RD	.012	.020	0	.200
ASSET	$3,505	$8,114	$48	$94,162

Table 31.4 OLS estimates of LA5

Intercept	−1.53	−2.10	−1.53	−2.02	−1.20	−1.29
	(13.6)	(11.9)	(12.3)	(10,1)	(20.3)	(15.8)
UTIL	−1.31	−1.20	−1.27	−1.15	−1.36	−1.33
	(11.1)	(10.0)	(10.4)	(9.0)	(11.6)	(11.3)
FIN	−.47	−.47	−.45	−.44	−.45	−.45
	(4.2)	(4.3)	(4.1)	(3.9)	(4.0)	(4.0)
MEDIA	.67	.70	67	.68	.63.	62
	(3.2)	(3.4)	(3.2)	(3.3)	(3.0)	(3.0)
EQUITY*	−4.50	−351	−4.64	−3.99	−5.94	−5.70
	(3.5)	(2.7)	(3.6)	(3.1)	(4.6)	(4.5)
SE	6.86	17.94	...	...	...	...
	(4.8)	(5.9)				
SE^2	...	−39.38	...	...	...	...
		(4.1)				
STD_s	...	...	5.44	13.77	...	
			(4.2)	(4.7)		
STD_s^2	...	...	...	−28.59	...	...
				(3.1)		
STD_a	...	...	...	...	2.84	5.49
					(4.1)	(2.9)
STD_a^2	...	...	...	...	...	−11.78
						(1.5)
N	511	511	511	511	511	511
R^2	.31	.33	.30	.32	.30	.30
F	45.0	41.5	43.6	38.6	43.3	36.5

t-statistics are in parentheses.

* All coefficient estimates on EQUITY should be multiplied by 10^{-8}.

Table 31.5 OLS estimates of ownership concentration

Measurement of ownership concentration	Full sample (N = 511)			Nonregulated sample (N = 406)		
	LA5	LA20	LAH	LA5	LA20	LAH
Intercept	−2.10	−1.01	3.83	−1.92	−.68	4.21
	(11.9)	(6.0)	(13.5)	(9.7)	(4.0)	(13.8)
UTIL	−1.20	−1.44	−2.07	...	....	....
	(10.0)	(12.6)	(10.8)			
FIN	−.47	−.49	−.78	....	....	....
	(4.3)	(4.7)	(4.4)			
MEDIA	.70	.75	.94	.68	.72	.91
	(3.4)	(3.8)	(2.8)	(3.3)	(4.0)	(2.8)
EQUITY*	−3.51	−2.98	−4.25	−3.90	−3.82	−5.09
	(2.7)	(2.4)	(2.0)	(2.9)	(3.3)	(2.5)
SE	17.94	11.14	26.46	14.83	5.60	20.11
	(5.9)	(3.9)	(5.4)	(4.4)	(1.9)	(3.9)
SE^2	−39.38	−25.26	−59.70	−31.98	−12.14	−44.49
	(4.1)	(2.8)	(3.9)	(3.2)	(1.4)	(2.9)
N	511	511	511	406	406	406
R^2	.33	.36	.33	.12	.09	.09
F	41.5	46.5	41.2	13.4	9.3	10.0

t-statistics are in parentheses.

*All coefficient estimates on EQUITY should be multiplied by 10^{-8}.

as alternative measures of ownership concentration. We note the large impact of regulation on R^2.

In Table 31.6 we measure ownership concentration separately for all investors (A5), family and individual investors (F5), and institutional investors (I5). The percentage of shares owned by the five largest shareholding interests (not logistically transformed) of each shareholder class is the dependent variable in these regressions.[9] We examined these classifications of owners to discover whether the significance of the coefficient on the media variable is attributable to the behavior of family and individual owners or to institutional owners. Since the assumption of amenity potential is strongly governed by personal tastes, we do not expect ownership concentration to be significantly higher for institutional owners if the firm is a media firm.

Table 31.6 reveals that the greater ownership concentration in media firms is attributed almost exclusively to greater family and individual holdings. The coefficient estimate on MEDIA is the identical value, 13.30, and it is statistically significant in the equations in which A5 and F5 are the dependent variables. When I5 is the dependent variable, the coefficient estimate on MEDIA drops to 1.40, and it is not statistically significant. These results are consistent with the interpretation we have given to the amenity potential associated with control of media firms.[10]

Table 31.6 Ownership concentration by type of owner

	Dependent variable A5	*Dependent variable F5*	*Dependent variable I5*
Intercept	9.98	1.74	10.66
	(3.0)	(.6)	(4.3)
UTIL	−14.21	−6.86	−9.64
	(6.4)	(3.5)	(5.7)
FIN	−7.32	−3.26	−5.48
	(3.6)	(1.8)	(3.5)
MEDIA	13.30	13.30	1.40
	(3.5)	(3.9)	(.5)
EQUITY*	−5.00	−3.64	−2.88
	(2.1)	(1.7)	(.16)
SE	306.47	154.63	165.85
	(5.4)	(3.1)	(3.9)
SE²	−607.14	−388.16	−315.53
	(3.8)	(2.5)	(2.3)
N	511	511	511
R^2	.23	.10	.16
F	24.7	9.7	15.5

t-statistics are in parentheses.
* All coefficient estimates on EQUITY should be multiplied by 10^{-7}.

Additional evidence that suggests the amenity potential explanation of ownership structure is found by examining ownership data for professional sports clubs. Although we lack systematic ownership, profit, and size data for individual clubs, we show in Table 31.7 aggregate ownership data for 121 clubs in five major sports. These clubs are much more tightly controlled than the 511 firms in our sample. Among the 121 sports clubs, there are 238 owners, an average of 1.97 per club, who either are general partners or control at least 10 percent of the club's stock. Among the 511 firms in our sample, the corresponding numbers are 218 owners and an average of 0.43 owners per firm. Admittedly, sports clubs are smaller than the 511 firms in our sample, which in part explains the increased ownership concentration in the sports industry, and they may operate in less stable environments, although we do not know this to be a fact. Nonetheless, these data are consistent with the amenity explanation of ownership structure.

The impact of regulation on ownership concentration is examined from another perspective in Table 31.8. Salomon Brothers rates the regulatory climates in which electric utility firms operate, assigning letter grades based on such factors as the allowed rate of return, the rate base test period used, the cost items allowed in the rate base, and the time taken by commissions to decide rate appeals. The 1979 rating we use is an average of regulatory jurisdictions, calculated by using revenue weighting for utilities operating in more than one jurisdiction. We divide the electric utilities in our sample into two groups: those that operate in regulatory climates that are less "stringent" than the median (i.e., "more favorable" for investment purposes) and all

Table 31.7 Ownership data on 121 sports firms and 511 nonsports firms

Sample	Number of firms	Number of shareholders owning 10 percent or more of the firm's shares	Number of shareholders owning 10 percent or more of the firm's shares per firm
Sports clubs:			
Major league baseball	26	54	2.1
North American Soccer League	24	54	2.3
National Basketball Association	22	52	2.4
National Football League	28	38	1.4
National Hockey League	21	40	1.9
All sports clubs	121	238	1.97
Demsetz–Lehn sample	511	218	.43

For sports data, North American Soccer League (NASL) v. NFL, no. 78. Civ. 4560-CSH. U.S. District Court. S.D. New York, February 21, 1979.

Table 31.8 OLS Estimates of LA5 for 37 electric utilities

Intercept	−3.94	−8.28	−3.79	10.45	1.18	.29
	(7.4)	(5.4)	(5.3)	(5.2)	(1.9)	(.3)
EQUITY	6.03*	1.10†	6.59*	2.07†	1.72†	2.33†
	(.3)	(.7)	(.3)	(1.0)	(.5)	(.6)
REGULATORY CLIMATE	.44	.13	.68	.27	.92	.81
	(2.1)	(.6)	(2.5)	(1.0)	(2.2)	(1.9)
SE	22.78	.178.21	...	...	....	...
	(2.3)	(3.4)				
SE^2	...	−1,202.00	....	....	...	...
		(3.0)				
STD$_s$	...	...	28.63	244.71	...	...
			(2.3)	(3.9)		
STD$_s^2$	...	....	..	−1,594.26	...	...
				(3.5)		
STD$_a$	...	...	...	...	54.85	156.69
					(2.5)	(2.1)
STD$_a^2$	...	....	..	...	..	−2,374.75
						(1.4)
N	37	37	37	37	37	37
R^2	.27	.43	.30	.49	.28	.32
F	4.0	6.0	4.8	7.8	4.3	3.8

t-statistics are in parentheses.
* Coefficient estimates are multiplied by 10^{-8}.
† Coefficient estimates are multiplied by 10^{-7}.

other electric utilities. The dummy variable, REGULATORY CLIMATE, takes the value of one if the utility is in the former group and zero otherwise.

We expect that this index of regulatory climate is positively related to ownership concentration, less stringent regulation offering owners more control potential through fewer restrictions and less commission monitoring of management. In all three equations where the instability measure enters linearly and in the equation where STD_a enters nonlinearly, REGULATORY CLIMATE enters with a significant and positive estimated coefficient. When SE and STD, enter in nonlinear form, the estimated coefficient on REGULATORY CLIMATE remains positive but is not significant. The firm size variable, contrary to expectations, is not significantly related to ownership concentration. All three of the instability measures are significantly related to ownership concentration in the anticipated direction.

The separation issue

The discussion to this point has focused on the *determinants* of ownership structure. We now empirically examine the alleged *consequence* of diffuse ownership structures for the separation of ownership and control. Berle and Means brought the issue to center stage in 1933 with the publication of *The Modern Corporation and Private Property*. Their interpretation of the issue has remained the focus of debate for more than half a century. Diffuseness in ownership structure, by modifying the link between ownership and control, is seen by them as undermining the role of profit maximization as a guide to resource allocation. Diffuseness of ownership is said to render owners of shares powerless to constrain professional management. Since the interests of management need not, and in general do not, naturally coincide perfectly with those of owners, this would seem to imply that corporate resources are not used entirely in the pursuit of shareholder profit. Although Berle and Means make no great effort to describe how corporate resources are allocated, later discussions of the corporation dwell on management's consumption of amenities at the expense of owner profits.

Berle and Means's work was anticipated by Thorstein Veblen's (1924) volume, *The Engineers and the Price System*. Veblen believed that he was witnessing the transfer of control from capitalistic owners to engineer-managers and that the consequences of this transfer were to become more pronounced as diffusely owned corporations grew in economic importance. In the wake of this transfer of power, Veblen saw the end of the type of profit seeking he associated with capitalists, for he believed that capitalistic owners sought neither efficiency nor increased output so much as monopolistic restrictions to raise prices. The engineers, trained and acculturated to seek technological efficiency, would see to it that the production from the firms they now controlled would rise to higher and socially more desirable levels. The profits of monopoly would be sacrificed on the altar of efficiency.

One of Veblen's famous disciples, John Kenneth Galbraith, shared his teacher's assessment of the change in control but evaluated the outcome differently. In *The New Industrial State* (1967) he argued that the technocrats who had gained control of the diffusely owned modern corporation would sacrifice owner profit to increased output beyond levels that served the real interests of consumers. Enticed to purchase these large output rates by powerful advertising campaigns, consumers would cause the private sector to grow too rapidly and at the expense of the public sector.[11]

Although the three views discussed above concerning the consequences of diffuse ownership structures offer somewhat different evaluations, they unanimously imply a positive correlation between ownership concentration and profit rate. If diffuseness in control allows managers to serve their needs rather than tend to the profits of owners, then more concentrated ownership, by establishing a stronger link between managerial behavior and owner interests, ought to yield higher profit rates.

We expect no such relationship. A decision by shareholders to alter the ownership structure of their firm from concentrated to diffuse should be a decision made in awareness of its consequences for loosening control over professional management. The higher cost and reduced profit that would be associated with this loosening in owner control should be offset by lower capital acquisition cost or other profit-enhancing aspects of diffuse ownership if shareholders choose to broaden ownership. Standardizing on other determinants of profit, Demsetz (1983) has argued that ownership concentration and profit rate should be unrelated.

Table 31.9 reports recursive estimates for coefficients of a profit rate equation in which the key independent variables are alternative predicted measures of ownership concentration: LA5, LA20, and LAH.[12] The dependent variable is the mean value of annual accounting profit after taxes, as a percentage of the book value of equity. The mean is calculated for the 5-year period 1976–80. Stock market rates of return presumably adjust for any divergences between the interests of professional management and owners, so we rely on accounting rates of return to reveal such divergences.

In addition to ownership concentration, we include several other independent variables in this equation. The utilities and financial dummies isolate the impact of systematic regulation. The coefficient on the financial dummy may be explained by accounting procedures, which for these firms include outstanding loans in the asset base. The potential upward bias in asset measurement that results is likely to depress the measured accounting profit rate. Capital, advertising, and R & D expenditures, all as a percentage of sales, standardize for accounting artifacts associated with the decision to expense some of these investments but to depreciate others. The size of the firm is measured by the book value of assets.

The general explanatory power of the profit rate equation is quite low, but regulation does seem to have a negative impact on accounting profit rate. Table 31.9 shows no significant relationship between ownership concentration and accounting profit rate, and especially no significant positive relationship.[13] The data simply lend no support to the Berle–Means thesis.[14]

We have suggested above that certain industries may be characterized as offering greater amenity potential and that this would lead to more concentrated ownership. This does not assert that the more concentrated is ownership, the greater the tendency to cater to amenity potential. If we were to make such an assertion it would imply a negative correlation between profit rate and ownership concentration, and this would tend to hide the opposite correlation suggested by Berle and Means. But, then, this would constitute no evidence more favorable to the Berle–Means hypothesis. Catering to amenity potential is maximizing owner *utility* if not owner profit. Such maximization hardly constitutes evidence of a separation between ownership and control.

Table 31.9 Recursive estimates of mean accounting profit rate

Intercept	.24	.27	.35
	(6.2)	(11.7)	(4.2)
UTIL	−.13	−.10	−.13
	(3.4)	(2.4)	(3.1)
FIN	−.07	−.06	−.07
	(3.6)	(3.3)	(3.5)
CAP	.04	.05	.04
	(.7)	(.8)	(.7)
ADV	.42	.47	.42
	(1.9)	(2.3)	(1.9)
RD	−.11	−.07	−.11
	(.4)	(.3)	(.4)
ASSET*	5.70	8.14	5.97
	(.8)	(1.2)	(.9)
SE	−.29	−.43	−.29
	(1.1)	(2.0)	(1.1)
LA5	−.02	...	...
	(.9)		
LA20	...	−.004	....
		(.2)	
LAH	...	...	−.02
			(.9)
N	511	.511	511
R^2	.10	.10	.10
F	7.2	7.2	7.1

t-statistics are in parentheses.
* Coefficient estimates on ASSET are multiplied by 10^{-7}.

Concluding comments

We have argued, both conceptually and empirically, that the structure of corporate ownership varies systematically in ways that are consistent with value maximization. Understanding some of the forces that determine corporate ownership structure is valuable in its own right, but we also think that our results are germane to a more general theory of property rights. For example, can the land enclosure movement in England be explained in part by the enhanced control potential of landownership during periods of population growth and rising prices of farm and ranch products? Similarly, does greater predictability of an industry's environment make industry regulation politically more tolerable because collectivization of control is likely to be less damaging in such cases? Our analysis suggests a framework for new studies that may shed some light on these broader questions.

Notes

1 Recent literature that has examined the separation of ownership and control includes Jensen and Meckling (1976) and Fama and Jensen (1983*a*, 1983*b*). The debate concerning the social implications of diffuse ownership of corporate equity had its genesis in Berle and Means (1933).

2 The effect of imperfect information on monitoring costs is developed formally in Holmström (1979, 1982).

3 An interesting variant of the hypothesis that corporate ownership structure is, in part, dependent on the stability of a firm's environment is found in Smith (1937, pp. 713–14): "The only trades which it seems possible for a joint stock company to carry on successfully, without an exclusive privilege, are those, of which all the operations are capable of being reduced to what is called a routine, or to such a uniformity of method as admits of little or no variation."

4 Ad hoc examples of the power of dominant owner-managers can be given. The share prices of Disney, Gulf and Western, and Chock Full O'Nuts all rose dramatically on the deaths of their dominant owners. Allegedly the prices of these stocks had been depressed by the policies of Walt Disney to keep a considerable library of Disney films from television, of Charles Bluhdorn to use Gulf and Western to hold a large portfolio of stocks in other companies, and of Charles Black to use Chock Full O'Nuts to maintain large real estate investments. All three policies are associated by the financial community with the personal preferences of the then dominant owner-managers of these companies. Shortly after the deaths of Disney, Bluhdorn, and Black, share prices rose, respectively, 25 percent, 42 percent, and 22 percent. We have no systematic procedure for determining when dominant owners are more likely to exercise their personal preferences in "non-profit-maximizing ways" except for our belief in the amenity potential of mass media and sports industries.

5 Our empirical results remain significant when the equations are estimated using non-transformed ownership variables.

6 We calculated SE by regressing the firm's monthly returns on the returns to a value-weighted market portfolio.

7 Two additional specifications of the ownership equation deserve comment. As an alternative proxy for control potential, we included the intraindustry variability (using four-digit SIC codes) in average accounting profit rates (1976–80) as an independent variable. Plausibly, greater differences in profit rates among firms in the same industry provide an index of the difference in performance that can be wrought by superior control decisions. However, no significant relationship exists between this new index of control potential and ownership concentration. When it is entered as the sole control potential variable, the intraindustry variability of profit rate enters with a positive but statistically insignificant coefficient, and it does not significantly affect the other regression coefficients. When this variable, is added to the regression equations in which SE proxies for control potential, it enters with a positive and statistically insignificant coefficient, and it again leaves all other coefficient estimates essentially unaffected. The simple correlation of the intraindustry variability of profit rate with SE, STD_s and STD_a never exceeds .10. High values of the intraindustry variability of profit rate may correlate with poor census definitions of industries, or they may reflect accounting artifacts that increase the divergence between profit rates within industries, but there is no positive evidence of a linkage to control potential. This absence receives confirmation from a statistical study that regresses ownership concentration on equity, SE, SE^2, and 41 dummy variables, one for each two-digit industry containing our sample firms. The coefficients of only four industries exhibited

statistical significance, and these were either mass media or regulated industries. Industry characteristics other than these bear no relationship to ownership concentration. This absence of significance is puzzling to us, but its implication may be important to industrial organization studies. What the data seem to be saying is that firms are significantly different, even within traditional industry classifications, and that many individual firms may constitute quasi industries in and of themselves in regard to ownership concentration.

8 We also estimated a regression equation in which we entered the logarithm of EQUITY as an independent variable. This variable entered with a negative and statistically significant coefficient, and its inclusion did not significantly affect the other coefficients. Similarly, we included the squared value of EQUITY in addition to EQUITY and the other independent variables. EQUITY continued to enter with a significant, negative coefficient, and its squared value entered with a positive but insignificant coefficient. The other coefficient estimates remained unaffected in this equation.

9 The variables F5 and I5 occasionally take a value of zero, at which point the logistic transformation is undefined. For purposes of estimating these equations, we do not transform the ownership variables.

10 "Softer" evidence reinforces the amenity explanation of ownership concentration in the media industry. In 1984. DOM Jones & Company, 56 percent owned by the Bancroft family, attempted to issue a stock dividend in the form of a new class of stock that would have 10 votes per share compared with the one vote per share of the firm's original common equity. The Dow Jones chairman described the rationale behind this decision: "The purpose … is to try to assure the long term future operation of *The Wall Street Journal* and Dow Jones' other publications and services under the same quasi public trust philosophy that Clarence Barron and his descendants have followed during the company's history. The Bancroft family always has zealously guarded the integrity and independence of the Journal and Dow Jones' other publications. This has been crucial to their growth and financial success. The family … also has encouraged management always to take a long term view, investing heavily for the purpose of building future strength and investment values. The family and the board, acting unanimously and with management's enthusiastic support, are seeking to protect and build Dow Jones' publications in the same manner in the years ahead through continued family control" ("Dow Jones Votes" 1984, p. 5). Similarly, DeAngelo and DeAngelo (1983), in a study of 45 firms that have dual classes of common stock, found that both the *New York Times* and the *Washington Post* have dual classes of common stock that trade with different voting rights.

11 The entire discussion of the separation thesis presumes that diffuseness of ownership is a pervasive phenomenon. Our data cast doubt on this presumption. Our sample is heavily weighted by Fortune 500 firms, precisely the firms that are supposed to suffer from diffuse ownership structures. Yet the mean values of A5 and A20, respectively, are 24.8 percent and 37.7 percent.

12 The predicted measures of LA5, LA20, and LAH were estimated from an OLS equation that included the following independent variables: UTIL, FIN, MEDIA, EQUITY, SE, and SE². The results reported in Table 31.9 do not change significantly when the ownership equations are estimated using alternative specifications that were previously reported.

13 Not reported here is a replication of Table 31.9 in which the profit rate equation is estimated using the actual, not predicted, value of the ownership variable. No changes in conclusions are called for by this replication. We also replicated Table 31.9 on a set of firms for which we were able to obtain the industry four-firm concentration ratio. The concentration ratio enters the profit rate equation with a negative and statistically significant sign, but the coefficient estimates on all three ownership variables remain not significant.

Earlier studies of the profit–concentration relationship show a weakening of the usual positive correlation during periods of rising price levels. The negative relationship revealed in our work may, therefore, reflect the inflationary tenor of the late 1970s. The estimated ownership equation for this subset of firms performs weaker than it does when estimated for the entire sample.

14 Our results are consistent with those of Stigler and Friedland (1983). They reject the separation thesis by demonstrating that management salaries are no higher in "management-controlled" than in "owner-controlled" industries.

References

Berle, Adolf A., and Means, Gardiner C. *The Modern Corporation and Private Property*. New York: Macmillan, 1933.

DeAngelo, Harry, and DeAngelo, Linda. "The Allocation of Voting Rights in Firms with Dual Classes of Common Stock." Mimeographed. Rochester, N.Y.: Univ. Rochester, 1983.

Demsetz, Harold. "The Structure of Ownership and the Theory of the Firm." *J. Law and Econ.* 26 (June 1983): 373–90.

"Dow Jones Votes New Class of Common as Stock Dividend, Raises Payout 20%." *Wall Street J.* (January 19, 1984).

Fama, Eugene F., and Jensen, Michael C. "Agency Problems and Residual Claims." *J. Law and Econ.* 26 (June 1983): 327–49. (*a*)

——. "Separation of Ownership and Control." *J. Law and Econ.* 26 (June 1983): 301–23. (*b*)

Galbraith, John Kenneth. *The New Industrial State*. Boston: Houghton Mifflin, 1967.

Holmström, Bengt. "Moral Hazard and Observability." *Bell J. Econ.* 10 (Spring 1979): 74–91.

——. "Moral Hazard in Teams." *Bell J. Econ.* 13 (Autumn 1982): 324–40.

Jarrell, Gregg A., and Bradley, Michael. "The Economic Effects of Federal and State Regulation of Cash Tender Offers." *J. Law and Econ.* 23 (October 1980): 371–407.

Jensen, Michael C., and Meckling, William H. "Theory and the Firm: Managerial Behavior, Agency Costs and Ownership Structure." *J. Finallcial Econ.* 3 (October 1976): 305–60.

Smith, Adam. *An Inquiry into the Nuture and Causes of the Wealth of Nations*. New York: Modern Library, 1937.

Stigler, George J., and Friedland, Claire. "The Literature of Economics: The Case of Berle and Means." *J. Law and Econ.* 26 (June 1983): 237–68.

Veblen, Thorstein. *The Engineers and the Price System*. New York: Viking, 1924.

Review and Discussion Questions

1 What is diffuse ownership? What is a disadvantage of diffuse ownership? What is an advantage?

2 Why would firms in more stable environments be more likely to have diffuse ownership?

3 Why would regulated firms be more likely to have diffuse ownership?

4 What are the results of the empirical model of ownership concentration?

5 What are the results of the empirical test of whether firms' profit and ownership concentration are related?

Chapter 32

Charles R. Knoeber

GOLDEN PARACHUTES, SHARK REPELLENTS, AND HOSTILE TENDER OFFERS[1]

T HE TENDER OFFER has recently become a popular way to change control over the assets of a firm.[2] Unlike the more traditional merger proposal which must be approved by the target firm's board of directors before it is submitted to a shareholder vote, a tender offer is made directly to the target's shareholders and requires neither approval nor even notification of the target's board of directors. While tender offers and mergers each evoke controversy, a simple argument suggests either is beneficial to both the acquiring firm and the shareholders of the acquired (target) firm. Each is a voluntary exchange and so would be agreed to only if both parties to the exchange expect to benefit. Since mergers require approval of the management of the target firm, however, they add another party to the exchange.[3] Again invoking the argument of mutually beneficial exchange, it must be that, for mergers, not only do the acquiring firm and shareholders of the target benefit but so do the managers of the target. Since target management is not a party to the exchange embodied in a tender offer, though, it need not benefit and indeed may be harmed. This explains why tender offers are sometimes hostile (opposed by management of the target) and sometimes friendly, while mergers are always friendly.

The noninvolvement of target management in a tender offer has further been argued to be a desirable feature of this form of transferring control over corporate assets, since it may provide the additional benefit of displacing poorly performing management. Indeed, the threat of a tender offer is seen as inciting managers to better performance and enriching shareholders (Henry Manne, 1965; Frank Easterbrook and Daniel Fischel, 1981). This argument suggests tender offers are more desirable than mergers, and that recent tender offer experience is an improvement over the previous almost complete reliance on mergers to alter control over corporate assets.

Despite this, much recent activity can be viewed as attempting to discourage hostile tender offers. The Williams Act (1974) provides federal rules regulating tender offers. These rules expand the period during which a tender offer must remain open, dictate substantial disclosure as to the bidders' plans and sources of finance, and contain antifraud provisions that provide target management with the standing to sue for injunctive relief (see Gregg Jarrell and Michael Bradley, 1980). The effect is to better enable target management to obstruct hostile tender offers and so reduce the advantage such offers have over the more traditional merger. Of more interest here are two voluntary measures adopted by a firm's shareholders. The first of these has been labeled "golden parachutes." These are contractual agreements with management that provide substantial (often millions of dollars) payments to managers who elect to (or are forced to) leave the firm when a change of control takes place.[4] A survey of 665 industrial companies in 1982 found 15 percent provided golden parachutes to top management (Ann Morrison, 1982). The obvious effect of this measure is to insulate a target's management from harm even in the case of hostile tender offers. Thus, the advantage of a tender offer over a merger (its policing effect on management) is lost.

The second voluntary measure is the adoption (by shareholder vote) of amendments to corporate charters or bylaws which discourage tender offers. These so-called "shark repellent" amendments provide for super majority voting on mergers and sale of assets, stagger the terms of corporate directors, and impose other impediments to hostile tender offers (for descriptions, see Ronald Gilson, 1982; Harry DeAngelo and Edward Rice, 1983; Scott Linn and John McConnell, 1983). As in the other instances, shark repellents act to dilute the advantage of tender offers over traditional mergers. In all cases, the effect is to make hostile tenders less likely, or to reduce the possibility of an exchange of control of corporate assets not agreed to by current management.

Those who believe in the beneficial effect of hostile tender offers on manager performance typically deplore these recent actions which discourage hostile offers. Most particularly, critics have attacked golden parachutes and shark repellents. The criticisms have led to several proposals to regulate such actions. A legislative rule amending the Williams Act, proposed by Lewis Lowenstein (1983), aims to restrict the actions management can take when confronted with a tender offer. A somewhat similar judicial rule requiring management passivity in the face of tender offers has been proposed by Easterbrook and Fischel. Most recently, an advisory committee to the SEC has recommended rules prohibiting shark repellent amendments to corporate charters and bylaws and restrictions on the use of golden parachutes (*Wall Street Journal*, March 1984).

The fundamental paradox in this attack on obstructions to hostile tender offers is that it is based upon a rejection of the very argument that is used to defend the desirability of any tender offers. This argument is the mutual benefit of voluntary exchange. Tender offers are desirable because they are voluntary and so both the acquiring firm and shareholders of the target benefit. Golden parachutes and shark repellents are viewed as undesirable because they work to the detriment of shareholders. They are, however, voluntarily agreed to by shareholders. How, then, can agreement by these shareholders not be taken as evidence of shareholder benefit (when it is in the case of tender offers)?

The object of this paper is to examine the contractual relation between share-holders and managers, how tender offers (from an outside party) affect this relation, and to suggest that it may well be in shareholders' as well as managers' interest to agree to restrict the possibility for outsiders to disrupt their relation with a hostile tender offer. Quite simply, the same argument used to advocate tender offers can also be made to advocate voluntarily adopted restrictions on hostile tender offers. Doing so casts a considerably different light on recent proposals to regulate such actions as the use of golden parachutes and shark repellent amendments to corporate charters.

The organization of the paper is as follows. Section I characterizes the relation between manager and shareholders and the nature of the contracts which might be expected between the two. Section II considers the effect of hostile tender offers on this contractual relationship and suggests a possible beneficial role for golden para-chutes and shark repellents. Section III focuses empirically on golden parachutes. Here, the earlier sections are used to construct hypotheses about which firms will provide golden parachutes to managers and about the relation between tenure and compensation for managers of firms providing golden parachutes. These hypotheses are then tested on a sample of 331 firms.

I

Shareholders of a firm employ a manager as their agent to make decisions regarding the use of the firm's resources. Shareholders are presumed to be risk neutral and interested only in maximizing the value of their shares (their wealth). The manager is a utility maximizer interested both in his money income and his on-the-job consump-tion. Denote this consumption as a, where a is meant to include activity typically designated as shirking as well as consumption of job perquisites. Consumption a by the manager imposes a cost on shareholders. Consequently, define units of a in terms of their cost to shareholders; each unit entailing a \$1 reduction in the (combined) wealth of shareholders. Some on-the-job consumption is desirable in that the value to the manager exceeds the cost to shareholders. That is, shareholders will want the manager to consume on the job up to the point (call this a^*) where the marginal ben-efit, MB, of a to the manager just equals the marginal cost (\$1) to shareholders. The reason is that compensation in kind, a, is an alternative to compensation in dollars and shareholders minimize their cost of hired management if they choose the cheapest form of compensation.[5] Until $a = a^*$, on-the-job consumption is a cheaper form of compensation than dollar payments.

The manager, however, chooses a and so may select on-the-job consumption greater than that which shareholders desire. If so, some on-the-job consumption costs shareholders more than it is worth and the difference I will call agency cost or the cost of improper incentives provided by the manager.[6]

That is, agency cost, A, is defined a

$$A = \int_{a^*}^{a}(1 - MB(a))\, da. \tag{1}$$

In order to reduce these agency costs or provide correct incentives to the manager, shareholders must somehow tie the manager's dollar compensation to his on-the-job consumption. They must impose a price for on-the-job consumption. (The market for corporate control might also perform this function. The implicit assumption here is that the only discipline imposed on a manager is that of the shareholders. In the empirical section of the paper, this assumption is relaxed.) If a can be measured exactly by shareholders and so is known by both managers and shareholders, then the price can be set equal to \$1 and agency costs are eliminated. For example, the wage contract with the manager might take the following linear form

$$W = \psi_1 - a, \tag{2}$$

where ψ_1 is the fixed salary component and a \$1 penalty is imposed for each unit of a chosen by the manager. If a cannot be measured without error by shareholders, a contract such as (2) may still eliminate agency costs; but only in a special case. Say the shareholders' estimator of a, designated $\hat{a}$, is unbiased,

$$\hat{a} \sim a, \ \sigma_{\hat{a}}^2 \tag{3}$$

If the manager is risk neutral, then a contract like (2) with the shareholder estimator of on-the-job consumption replacing actual on-the-job consumption will again lead the manager to choose $a = a^*$ and eliminate agency costs.

The actual case of managers and shareholders, however, entails both an inability of shareholders to measure exactly on-the-job consumption by the manager and manager risk aversion. Here, the primary problem in principal–agent relationships must be faced. Better incentives provided to the manager entail greater risk bearing by the manager. For example, if a contract like (2) is slightly generalized,

$$W = \psi_1 - \psi_2 \hat{a} \tag{4}$$

As , ψ_2 the price imposed for units of on-the-job consumption, is increased to provide better incentives, the variance of the manager's wage is also increased. Specifically,

$$\sigma_W^2 = \psi_2^2 \sigma_{\hat{a}}^2 \tag{5}$$

So

$$d\sigma_W^2 / d\psi_2 = 2\psi_2 \sigma_{\hat{a}}^2 \tag{6}$$

Now there is a cost of providing better incentives (reducing agency cost) in that additional manager risk bearing is required and the manager must be compensated for such risk bearing to induce him (or her) to accept the contract. Given some $\hat{a}$, the problem faced by the shareholders is to find a contract that maximizes their own wealth, subject to the constraints that the manager chooses a to maximize his expected utility when he faces the contract, and that this manager must receive sufficient compensation that his expected utility is no less than that which he could receive in some other employment. This optimal contract will be such that the marginal risk cost from altering the price (not necessarily a linear price) of measured on-the-job consumption is just offset by the induced change in agency cost.

Define *SW* as shareholder wealth when this optimal contract is selected. Holding constant manager preference for on-the-job consumption and manager attitude toward risk, *SW* is a function of the precision of the shareholder estimator of manager performance (on-the-job consumption), $SW(\sigma_{\hat{a}}^2)$, where

$$dSW / d\sigma_{\hat{a}}^2 < 0 \qquad (7)$$

This is due to the fact that as $\sigma_{\hat{a}}^2$ becomes larger, shareholders must either incur greater agency cost or a greater wage payment or both to compensate the manager for additional risk bearing.

Now assume there are two possible estimators of manager performance. The first, $\hat{a}_1$, employs only current information (say the current performance of the firm) to estimate manager performance. The second, $\hat{a}_2$, employs current information and future information to estimate manager performance. The first estimator cannot be more precise than the second and will likely be (perhaps much) less precise.

$$\sigma_{\hat{a}_1}^2 \geq \sigma_{\hat{a}_2}^2 \qquad (8)$$

Consequently,

$$SW(\hat{a}_1) \leq SW(\hat{a}_2) \qquad (9)$$

Shareholders, then, would generally prefer to use the second estimator of manager performance.

One way to do this would be to initially reward the manager using $\hat{a}_1$, as an estimator of his performance, and then to settle up in the future by making additions or subtractions from this initial payment as better future information becomes available. The difficulty with this method is that the manager must remain in the employ of the shareholders to receive the settling-up increments and decrements. If managers are free to quit at their discretion, as indeed they are, then a manager knowing that shareholders underestimated *a* initially (recall the manager chooses *a* and so knows the extent of mismeasurement) will have an incentive to quit.[7] The manager takes the money and runs. The possibility of such opportunistic behavior by the manager will discourage shareholders from agreeing to such a settling-up contract initially.

Another contract that allows the use of $\hat{a}_2$, but is not susceptible to opportunism by the manager, entails a small payment initially based on the estimator $\hat{a}_1$ and then a non-negative settling-up bonus paid in the future when better information becomes available.[8] This contract that involves deferred compensation removes the incentive for the manager to behave opportunistically, since the deferred compensation acts as a bond (or precommittment) tying the manager to continued employment.[9]

These arguments suggest that in situations where a manager is risk averse and shareholders cannot determine manager performance exactly but can improve their estimator of manager performance as time passes, an optimal contract with the manager will include deferring some expected compensation to be paid in the future.[10] The greater the value of future information or the larger the difference between $\sigma_{\hat{a}1}^2$ and $\sigma_{\hat{a}2}^2$, the greater will be the share of compensation which will be deferred.

Beyond this, the actual amount of deferred compensation is not known, since it depends on information that only becomes available in the future. A contract cannot be written explicitly stating the amount of deferred compensation. Indeed, it is unlikely that a contract can even be written that specifies how this compensation will be determined in the future. This is due to the variety and complexity of information which may become available. Detailing all the future possibilities and contingent payments will at the least be expensive and very likely futile. Consequently, such a long-term deferred compensation contract will be largely implicit.[11]

Obviously, such a contract presents an avenue for shareholders to behave opportunistically. They may fail to pay the deferred compensation and perhaps even discharge the manager. Shareholders may take the money and run. This is not likely, however. The decision to pay the deferred compensation rests with the board of directors. Should they renege on the implicit contract (and should this be known by other managers), the firm would find it difficult to retain or replace managers. The cost of behaving opportunistically would outweigh the gains.[12] The implicit contract would be self-enforcing (see Lester Telser, 1980; Benjamin Klein and Keith Leffler, 1981) and the manager could trust that he will indeed be paid deferred compensation as due.

Optimal contracts between a manager and shareholders (via the board of directors) will often involve deferring compensation until better information about manager performance becomes available. These contracts will necessarily be long term and likely be implicit.[13] However, opportunistic behavior will not be a problem. The manager's deferred compensation acts as a bond, deterring opportunism on his part, and the cost of developing a reputation for unreliability (among other managers) deters opportunism on the part of the board of directors.

II

What effects will tender offers, particularly hostile ones, have in this contracting framework? Importantly, they provide another avenue for shareholder opportunism. A tender offer bypasses the board of directors and appeals directly to shareholders to sell their shares. Once control has changed hands, a manager may be discharged or, if retained, not paid deferred compensation due. The acquiring firm then appropriates this delayed compensation (the prospect of which may be partially responsible for a premium over current stock price paid to tendering shareholders of the acquired firm). Reputation does not prevent shareholders from participating in such opportunism (tendering their shares), as they are essentially anonymous. Nor does reputation deter the bidding firm from such behavior. While this firm would not treat its own managers in such a fashion, developing a reputation for opportunistic behavior in takeovers need not destroy a reputation for reliability in dealing with the firm's own managers ("honor among thieves").

Importantly, the possibility of opportunistic behavior that arises with tender offers is absent with merger proposals. Such proposals must be approved by the board of directors of the acquired firm who have an incentive (to maintain individual reputations and so future employment prospects on other boards for outside directors:[14] obvious financial incentives for inside directors) to assure that any proposal forwarded to shareholders preserves the deferred compensation due management.

This suggests a new explanation for golden parachutes and shark repellents. Both can be viewed as attempts to eliminate the possibility of opportunism toward managers with implicit long-term deferred compensation contracts. A golden parachute is

simply a bond posted by shareholders which accrues to the manager should opportunism accompany a takeover. If the bond is sufficiently large, there is no incentive for
opportunism to occur. The acquiring firm might be able to capture deferred compensation due the manager of the acquired firm but only by forfeiting the bond (golden
parachute payment).[15] Similarly, shark repellent amendments make hostile tender
offers more costly and less likely to succeed. The effect is to make it more advantageous to pursue a friendly tender offer (one approved by management). To gain such
approval, the bidder must assure the current managers of the target that it will not
behave opportunistically. Both golden parachutes and shark repellents, then, deter
opportunistic behavior by bidding (raider) firms.

The advantage to current shareholders of a firm providing golden parachutes or
adopting shark repellents is that by so doing, these shareholders can assure managers
that implicit deferred compensation contracts will not be reneged. Without this assurance, managers would not agree to such contracts. They would require immediate
compensation that would necessitate the use of a less precise measure of manager
performance and so (see equation (9)) less shareholder wealth. These obstructions to
hostile takeovers, then, allow better contracting between manager and shareholders.
Voluntary trade is mutually beneficial.

The prospect of hostile tender offers may indeed impose discipline on a firm's
managers as argued by Manne and so provide a benefit to shareholders. If so, there is
a cost of restricting the possibility of hostile offers with golden parachutes and shark
repellents. The arguments presented here, though, suggest there may also be an offsetting gain. These impediments to hostile tender offers enlarge the contracting possibilities available between managers and shareholders, and, by allowing more effective
contracting, enrich shareholders. This casts golden parachutes and shark repellents in
a new light. They may well be in the interests of shareholders. The case against these
obstructions to hostile tender offers is no longer clear.

Indeed, since these devices are voluntarily adopted by shareholders, it would
seem that, where adopted, the gains from restricting hostile tenders outweigh the
costs. That is, voluntarily adopted restrictions (like any voluntary trade) are mutually
beneficial. Some evidence already seems to confirm this. Linn and McConnell, using
the techniques of empirical finance, found a weak positive effect on stock price (shareholder wealth) due to the adoption of shark repellent amendments to charters or
bylaws.[16] A similar study by Richard Lambert and David Larker (1985) also found
a positive effect on stock price due to the provision of golden parachutes. Further
confirmation is provided in the following section where two sorts of tests are performed. The first examines the incidence across firms of golden parachutes. The
second examines the relation between tenure and compensation, or the importance
of implicit deferred compensation, for managers of firms which do and firms which
do not provide golden parachutes.

III

The above arguments make two important points. First, shareholders have more to
gain from the use of implicit deferred compensation contracts the poorer is current
information about manager performance relative to that which becomes available later.

Second, such contracts become less acceptable to managers the more likely is a hostile tender offer and the attendant possibility of opportunism. These points suggest which firms will be most likely to provide managers with golden parachutes—those firms for which poor current information about manager performance make implicit deferred compensation contracts desirable but that face management resistence due to fear of tender related opportunism. To explain empirically firms' decisions to provide golden parachutes, variables measuring the gain to waiting for future information to evaluate managers and variables measuring the likelihood of a hostile tender offer are required.

I begin with the second task. Empirical researchers have recently examined financial and product market characteristics of firms to discover which affect the likelihood of being acquired by either friendly or hostile means (Robert Harris et al., 1982; Steven Schwartz, 1982). A negative effect of size (as measured by assets) was found. Additionally, measures of the market value of outstanding stock relative to earnings (Harris et al.) or relative to book value of assets (Schwartz) were found to be negatively related to the likelihood of acquisition. Beyond this, no consistent effect of other firm or product market characteristics was found. These findings and the presumption that firms more likely to be acquisition targets are similarly more likely to face a hostile tender offer suggest the following hypotheses. Smaller firms (fewer assets) and firms with lower price-earnings ratios (following Harris et al.) will be more likely to provide golden parachutes to managers.

These hypotheses, though, depend upon the implicit assumption maintained in the first two sections of the paper, that shareholder-manager contracting is the only mechanism which disciplines managers. That is, they consider only the benefit of golden parachutes. Where both such contracting and the market for corporate control work to provide incentives to managers, there is a cost of providing golden parachutes because they impede the incentive effects from the market for control. Where tender offers are more likely, this market will be more effective at motivating managers and so the cost of golden parachutes will be higher. Where tender offers are likely to occur only if manager behavior is egregious, the market for control will be less effective at motivating managers and the cost of golden parachutes will be lower. Increases in firm size and price–earnings ratio reduce the likelihood of a tender offer. Consequently, the cost of golden parachutes should fall with firm size and price–earnings ratio, and they should become more common. This runs counter to the previously predicted negative relation between the existence of golden parachutes and firm size and price earnings ratio. The net effect, then, is unclear and may not be monotonic. For example, if the cost effect dominates for small firms, the incidence of golden parachutes could first rise with increased firm size (as the cost of golden parachutes falls), but then may decline again for very large firms. For these large firms, the cost of golden parachutes is small, but, since tender offers are very unlikely, managers need little assurance of shareholder reliability and so the gains from golden parachutes may be even smaller. The net effect of firm size and price earnings ratio on the likelihood of a golden parachute, then, is of ambiguous sign and may not be monotonic.

An additional variable that may affect the likelihood of a successful hostile tender offer is the fraction of shares held by the manager (or perhaps the board of directors). The larger this fraction, the greater the proportion of other shares that must be tendered for a hostile offer to succeed, and so the less likely such an offer will succeed. As a consequence, golden parachutes are less useful. The resulting hypothesis is that golden parachutes are less likely, the greater the fraction of shares held by the manager (board of directors).

Returning to the first task, variables measuring the gain to waiting for future information must be constructed. Two general characteristics of firms seem to matter. The first is the noise (exogenous influences) encountered when measures of firm performance (outcome realizations) are used to impute manager performance. Waiting for more information allows some of the initial noise to be explained and so allows a more precise estimate of manager performance. The second is the existence of lags between manager performance and outcome realizations for the firm. Where important decisions by managers do not lead to measurable outcomes for several years, current measures of firm performance have little to do with current manager performance. Only by waiting for future information can firm performance be used to impute manager performance. Three instances where such lags may be important are capital expenditure decisions, research and development decisions, and advertising expenditure decisions (particularly where advertising is tied to new product marketing). Accordingly, firms with large capital expenditures (relative to sales), with large R&D expenditures (relative to sales), and with large advertising expenditure (relative to sales) will have more to gain by waiting for future information to evaluate manager performance. The corresponding hypotheses are that firms for which capital expenditures, R&D expenditures, or advertising expenditures are large relative to sales will be more likely to provide managers with golden parachutes.

The noise encountered in using firm performance to impute manager performance increases with the variability of nonmanager (exogenous) influences on firm performance. Taking the rate of return earned by shareholders, r, as the measure of firm performance, the greater the exogenous variation in r the more difficult (less precise) it is to impute manager performance. A measure of the noise encountered when imputing manager performance, then, would be σ_r^2, the variance of the rate of return earned by shareholders. Some variation in r for any firm i, however, can be explained by market (business cycle) factors and so this variation need not introduce noise into the imputation of manager performance. Letting r_m, be the market rate of return, a time-series regression

$$r_i = \beta_0 + \beta_1 r_m + \varepsilon \tag{10}$$

can be used to explain some of the variation in r_i, by market factors. Consequently, an alternative measure of the noise encountered when using r_i to impute manager performance would be the residual variation in (10) or the mean squared error. An hypothesis, then, is that firms for which σ_r^2 or alternatively the mean squared error for (10) is larger will be more likely to provide golden parachutes to managers.

To test the above hypotheses, a random sample of 400 firms in Standard and Poor's COMPUSTAT database was drawn. Firms for which 1982 proxy statements were not available from Q-Data Corporation's Q-File or firms that were not U.S. corporations were deleted from the sample. This left 331 firms. The 1982 proxy statements of these firms were examined for evidence of golden parachutes.[17] Any arrangement awarding managers compensation in the event of a "change in control" of the firm was counted as a golden parachute. Forty-seven firms were found to provide golden parachutes. The qualitative variable *Golden Parachute* was constructed with a value of 1 for firms with golden parachutes and 0 for other firms.

The COMPUSTAT database was then used to construct additional variables for each firm. *Assets* is simply the 1982 value of the firm's assets (in millions of dollars). *Price–Earnings Ratio* is calculated by taking the year-end closing price for the firm's shares and dividing by per share earnings for each year 1980–82 and then averaging these.[18] *Capital Expenditures* is the firm's capital expenditure divided by sales again calculated for 1980–82 and averaged. Because information on *R&D* expenditure and advertising expenditure was not reported for a substantial number of firms, the more inclusive COMPUSTAT data item entitled Selling, General, and Administrative Expenses was used to construct a measure of expenditures (other than capital expenditures) where lags between decisions and outcomes may be important. This data item includes not only advertising expenditures and *R&D* expenditures, but also foreign currency adjustments, marketing expenditures, strike expense, exploration expenditures of extractive firms and other expenditures not directly related to production. The variable *Advertising, Research, and Related Expenditures* is the firm's selling, general, and administrative expenditures divided by sales calculated for 1980–82 and averaged.

The quarterly rate of return to the firm's shareholders was calculated for each quarter 1978–82 (19 quarters) by summing dividends paid and change in share price during the quarter and dividing by share price at the beginning of the quarter. Two variables were constructed from these quarterly rates of return. The first, *Return Variability*, is simply the variance of the firm's quarterly rate of return to shareholders over the period. The second, *Unexplained Return Variability*, is the mean squared error from estimating equation (10) for each firm, using the nineteen quarterly rates of return and letting r_m be the quarterly rate of return on the Standard and Poor 400 index. Finally, information from the 1982 proxy statements was used to construct two measures of manager shareholding. The first, *Fraction Manager Owned*, is the fraction of common stock owned by the manager (defined as the highest paid employee also on the board of directors). The second, *Fraction Manager and Board Owned*, is the fraction of common stock owned by all officers and directors combined.

The empirical model with hypothesized signs of effects is

$$Golden\ Parachute = f(Assets(?),\ Assets^2(?),\ Price–Earnings\ Ratio(?), \qquad (11)$$
Price–Earnings Ratio^2(?), Capital Expenditures(+), Advertising Research and Related Expenditures(+), Return Variability or Unexplained Return Variability(+), Fraction Manager Owned or Fraction Manager and Board Owned(–)),

where the two return variability variables are alternative measures of the noise encountered when using firm performance to impute manager performance and the two ownership variables are alternate measures of manager shareholding. The squared values of *Assets* and the *Price–Earnings Ratio* are included to allow for possible nonlinear effects of these variables. Data were not available for each firm for each variable and so the number of observations in the estimations was 244 or 246. Estimations of the four model specifications are reported in Table 32.1. The signs on each variable are as predicted, but significance levels are not high.[19] Table 32.1 provides modest support for the view of golden parachutes developed here. To determine if this view or the alternative which holds that golden parachutes are a device designed by management to deflect the discipline imposed by the market for corporate control is better supported, note that the alternative implies that golden parachutes are more

Table 32.1 Logit estimates of determinants of incidence of golden parachutes: derivatives of probability of golden parachute evaluated at variable mean[a]

	Variable Means				
Assets	826.220	$.644 \times 10^{-4}$ (1.833)	$.667 \times 10^{-4}$ (1.839)	$.473 \times 10^{-4}$ (1.546)	$.476 \times 10^{-4}$ (1.555)
Assets^2	312.749×10^4	$-.942 \times 10^{-8}$ (1.485)	$-.946 \times 10^{-8}$ (1.488)	$-.724 \times 10^{-8}$ (1.404)	$-.728 \times 10^{-8}$ (1.409)
Price–earnings ratio	13.347	$-.900 \times 10^{-2}$ (1.698)	$-.899 \times 10^{-2}$ (1.696)	$-.807 \times 10^{-2}$ (1.796)	$-.806 \times 10^{-2}$ (1.792)
Price–earnings ratio^2	303.893	$.148 \times 10^{-3}$ (1.999)	1.147×10^{-3} (1.997)	1.146×10^{-3} (2.170)	$.146 \times 10^{-3}$ (2.167)
Capital expenditures	.108	.170 (1.695)	.171 (1.718)	.120 (1.512)	.121 (1.540)
Advertising research, and related expenditure	.174	.182 (.977)	.180 (.970)	.177 (1.116)	.176 (1.109)
Return variability	.102	.071 (.675)		.083 (.972)	
Unexplained return variability	.095		.071 (.662)		.082 (.948)
Fraction manager owned	.060	−.918 (1.836)	−.917 (1.835)		
Fraction manager and board owned				−.676 (2.975)	−.675 (2.973)
Number of observations	244	244	244	246	246
Number of golden parachutes	40	40	40	40	40
ln likelihood		−97.403	−97.412	−92.196	−92.222
χ^2		11.887	11.869	11.917	11.865

[a] Asymptotic t-ratios of logit coefficients are shown in parentheses.

likely where hostile tender offers are more likely. Consequently, the *Assets*, *Price–Earnings Ratio*, and *Fraction Manager Owned* variables would still be predicted to affect the likelihood of a golden parachute. Increases in each should make a golden parachute less likely. Under this alternative view, though, no other variables in (11) would be predicted to affect the likelihood of a golden parachute. To evaluate the merit of the two views, a likelihood ratio test was performed. First, the specifications in Table 32.1 were reestimated restricting all coefficients except those on the *Assets*, *Price–Earnings Ratio*, and *Fraction Manager Owned* variables to be zero. A likelihood ratio statistic, -2 (ln likelihood restricted model—ln likelihood unrestricted model), was then calculated. This statistic is distributed X^2 with degrees of freedom equal to the number of restricted coefficients. It is reported at the bottom of each column in Table 32.1. Each is significant at just under the 5 percent level. The full model performs better than the restricted model. The incidence of golden parachutes is better explained by the view developed in this paper than that which holds they are detrimental to shareholders.

Another implication of the arguments of the previous two sections is that the timing of manager compensation will differ between firms providing and firms not providing golden parachutes. If golden parachutes arise to provide assurance that implicit deferred compensation contracts will not be subject to tender related opportunism, such compensation should be more prevalent for managers of golden parachute firms. An indication of this is a more steeply rising (at least initially) compensation–tenure profile for managers of golden parachute firms. The reason is that where compensation is delayed until better information on manager performance is available, observed compensation will increase with tenure partly because deferred compensation is being paid. This effect will become less important and may disappear as tenure increases.

For example, consider two equally productive managers. Manager *A*'s performance can be observed perfectly this period and he is paid his whole product in the current period. Manager *B*'s performance can be estimated this period but is observed perfectly one period later and so he is paid one-half his estimated product this period and one-half is delayed to be paid next period. If the actual product of both managers is $100,000 in the first period and productivity increases with tenure at a rate of 10 percent each period, then period one compensation will be $100,000 for Manager *A* and $50,000 for Manager *B*. In the second period, Manager *A* will receive $110,000 (a 10 percent increase) while Manager *B* will receive $105,000 (a 110 percent increase). In the third period, Manager *A* will receive $121,000 (again a 10 percent increase) and Manager *B* will receive $115,500 (also a 10 percent increase). So the compensation–tenure profile initially rises more steeply for Manager *B*, but eventually rises at the same rate for both Managers *A* and *B*.

An hypothesis, then, is that compensation will increase more rapidly with tenure for managers of golden parachute firms, but the differential rate of increase will decline as tenure increases. To test this hypothesis, all 1982 compensation of the highest paid manager also on the board of directors was determined from the 1982 proxy statements for each of the 331 firms described previously.[20] This variable is called *Compensation*. The tenure of each manager was also determined from the proxy statements as the number of years of service on the board of directors. Since the hypothesis suggests that the effect of tenure on *Compensation* will differ between golden parachute firms and other firms, a variable *Tenure1* was defined equal to manager tenure for golden parachute firms and zero for other firms. Similarly, *Tenure0* was defined equal to manager tenure for other firms and zero for golden parachute firms. To control for other determinants of manager productivity (and so compensation), two other variables were calculated. These are manager age, *Age*, from the proxy statements and firm size, *Assets*, from COMPUSTAT. Both are expected to be positively related to manager compensation. complete data were available for 316 of the firms.

An empirical model was estimated using the *Tenure*, *Age*, and *Asset* variables and their squared values to explain the logarithm of *Compensation*. The important predictions are that the coefficient on *Tenure1* will be larger than that on *Tenure0* and that the coefficient on *Tenure1²* will be smaller than that on *Tenure0²*. The least squares estimate of the model (*t*-statistics in parentheses) is

$$\text{In } Compensation = 11.495 + -.001 \; Tenure0 + .059 \; Tenure1 + .931 \times 10^{-4} \; Tenure0^2$$
$$(9.849) \quad (-.094) \qquad (2.726) \qquad (.292)$$
$$- .001 \; Tenure1^2 + .028 \; Age \; -.199 \times 10^{-3} Age^2$$
$$(-2.014) \qquad (.625) \quad (-.492)$$
$$+ .600 \times 10^{-4} \; Assets - .500 \times 10^{-9} \; Assets^2$$
$$(5.377) \qquad (-4.577)$$

$$R^2 = .141, \; F\text{-Statistic} = 6.307; \; N = 316.$$

The coefficient on *Tenure1* is indeed larger than that on *Tenure0*, and the coefficient of *Tenure1²* is smaller than that on *Tenure0²*. A test for equality of the coefficients on the two tenure variables has an *F* value of 10.509 with one degree of freedom. Equality can be rejected at a significance level of less than 1 percent. A similar test on the coefficients of the squared tenure variables has an *F* value of 4.843 with one degree of freedom. Here, equality of the coefficients can be rejected at a significance level of 3 percent. As with the previous test on the incidence of golden parachutes, the evidence from this test on the compensation–tenure relationship provides support (albeit mild) for the hypothesis that golden parachutes are beneficial and designed to provide assurance to managers against tender-related opportunism thereby enlarging the contracting possibilities between manager and shareholders.

IV

This paper develops a framework in which golden parachutes and shark repellents may be advantageous. Where contracting between managers and shareholders is an important source of discipline on manager behavior and where the best contract is implicit with much compensation delayed until manager performance can be better evaluated, managers may fear that a hostile tender offer will provide shareholders with an avenue for opportunism. A successful tender will allow the new owners to displace management and capture the delayed compensation due them. Golden parachutes and shark repellents reduce the likelihood that this will happen and so can be viewed as mechanisms adopted by shareholders to assure managers of their reliability and so induce them to accept a contract which makes both better off. It may also be true, though, that golden parachutes and shark repellents impede the disciplinary effect imposed on managers by the market for corporate control. This is the basis for the common view that they are the result of self-serving behavior by managers seeking to avoid discipline of their behavior.

The empirical part of the paper examines the incidence of golden parachutes and the differential compensation–tenure relationship for managers of golden parachute firms in a sample of 331 firms. The evidence provides some support for the view that golden parachutes are advantageous and arise to assure managers against tender related opportunism. While this evidence is not strong, it may give pause to those who would restrict the use of golden parachutes (and by analogy, shark repellents) and so limit the scope for mutually advantageous exchange between manager and shareholders.

Notes

1 Many people have assisted me with useful criticisms. I especially thank Steve Allen, David Ball, Clive Bull, Dwight Grant, Mark Fisher, Jim Hess, Jack Hirshleifer, Steve Margolis, Wally Thurman, and an anonymous referee.

2 In 1960, only 7 tender offers were made for shares in U.S. firms. This represented about four-tenths of 1 percent of all announcements of mergers or acquisitions involving U.S. firms. By 1970, the number of tender offers was 34 or about 2 percent of all acquisition announcements (Patrick Davey, 1977). In 1975, tender offers numbered 71 or 7 percent of acquisition announcements. An apparent high was reached in 1977 with 181 tender offers representing 15 percent of acquisition announcements. The figures for 1980 and 1982 were 123 and 94 tender offers which were 8 and 4 percent of acquisition announcements for the respective years (Douglas Austin, 1980; Austin and Michael Jackson. 1984).

3 It is the board of directors that must approve a merger proposal before it is submitted to shareholders. While managers are represented on the board (inside directors), they need not control board decisions. So merger proposals opposed by management may be submitted to shareholders.

4 Shareholders do not vote explicitly to provide managers with golden parachutes. They are, however, notified of such contracts in proxy statements and so can be viewed as approving them by acquiescence.

5 For a more complete discussion, see Harold Demsetz (1983).

6 Agency cost here includes only a portion of what Michael Jensen and William Meckling (1976) refer to as agency cost.

7 To the extent other employers discover that opportunism occurred (learn the true a), the market for managers may penalize and so discourage such behavior by managers. See Eugene Fama (1980).

8 To ensure that the settling-up bonus is nonnegative, the initial payment may need to be negative. If so, the wealth of the manager becomes a constraint on the use of this sort of contract.

9 Related arguments as to the advantage of deferred compensation and long-term contracts are made by Gary Becker and George Stigler (1974), Jonathan Eaton and Harvey Rosen (1983), and Richard Lambert (1983).

10 The primary reason for deferring compensation here is to allow a more precise determination of manager performance. This reason is not necessary for compensation to be

deferred and has not received primary attention in other studies. For example, Edward Lazear (1979, p. 1272) while acknowledging this monitoring rationale for deferring compensation, develops a model that generates deferred compensation under the assumption that performance is observed perfectly and immediately. This perfect measure of performance allows a worker to contract for an optimal level of performance ($a*$ in my approach), and deferred compensation arises as a mechanism to ensure the worker abides by the contract.

11 Even if the contract can be written, if courts (third-party enforcers) cannot observe the contingencies stated in the contract, as is likely, then an explicit contract will be unenforceable and so equivalent to an implicit contract. See Clive Bull (1983).

12 I presume that firms never find it desirable to renege because of these reputation costs. The present value of the cost of behaving opportunistically, however, is lower when a firm's discount rate is higher. Consequently, firms become more likely to behave opportunistically as this discount rate rises. See Bengt Holmstrom (1983) and H. Lorne Carmichael (1984).

13 As an example, General Motors recently provided bonuses exceeding $1 million to each of its five highest ranking managers. These bonuses are deferred compensation (the previous three years "GM's compensation fell 'way below' other companies": *Wall Street Journal* April 16, 1984, p. 8), paid on long-term, implicit contracts. Their size and timing were not dictated by explicit contracts.

14 See Armen Alchian (1984).

15 If the golden parachute is "too large." exceeding the likely value of deferred compensation due, a manager may voluntarily leave the firm when control changes hands even if no opportunism occurs on the part of the acquiring firm. This suggests a limit to the size of the compensation provided by a golden parachute.

16 A similar study by DeAngelo and Rice, however, found essentially no effect on stock price.

17 Proxy statements must inform shareholders of the existing compensation arrangements with top management. Golden parachutes are a feature of such arrangements and so will be described if they exist.

18 Firms with price–earnings ratios <0 or >100 were deleted.

19 Since golden parachutes and shark repellents are substitutes, stronger results would be expected if firms that had either golden parachutes or shark repellents were treated alike (each given a 1 for purposes of the logit estimations of equation (11)). This was not possible because it could not be determined which firms had adopted shark repellents.

20 All compensation reported in the required Management Remuneration table of the proxy statement was summed to make this calculation. Such compensation includes salary, bonus, cash equivalent benefits, and contingent remuneration. Note that compensation which is *explicitly* deferred, and so represents an explicit legal obligation for the firm, is included in these reported figures even though it is actually paid at a later date. However, implicit deferred compensation which creates no explicit legal obligation for the firm is not included.

References

Alchian, Armen A., " Specificity, Specialization, and Coalitions," *Zeitschrift fur die gesamte Staatswissenschaft*, March 1984, *140*, 34–49.

Austin, Douglas V., "Tender Offer Update 1978–79," *Mergers and Acquisitions*, No. 2, 1980, 15, 13–24.

—— and Jackson, Michael J., "Tender Offer Update: 1984," *Mergers and Acquisitions*, No. 1, 1984, *19*, 60–69.

Becker, Gary S. and Stigler, George J., "Law Enforcement, Malfeasance, and Compensation of Enforcers," *Journal of Legal Studies*, January 1974, *3*, 1–18.

Bull, Clive, "The Existence of Self-Enforcing Implicit Contracts," Research Report No. 83–22, C. V. Starr Center for Applied Economics, New York University, 1983.

Carmichael, H. Lorne, "Reputations in the Labor Market," *American Economic Review*, September 1984, *74*, 713–25.

Davey, Patrick J., *Defenses Against Unnegotiated Cash Tender Offers*, Conference Board Report No. 726, 1977.

DeAngelo, Harry and Rice, Edward M., "Anti-takeover Charter Amendments and Stockholder Wealth," *Journal of Financial Economics*, April 1983, *11*, 329–60.

Demsetz, Harold, "The Structure of Ownership and the Theory of the Firm." *Journal of Law and Economics*, June 1983, *26*, 375–90.

Easterbrook, Frank H. and Fischel, Daniel R., "The Proper Role of a Target's Management in Responding to a Tender Offer," *Harvard Law, Review*, April 1981, *94*, 1161–204.

Eaton, Jonathan and Rosen, Harvey S., "Agency, Delayed Compensation and the Structure of Executive Remuneration," *Journal of Finance*, December 1983, *38*, 1489–505.

Fama, Eugene F., "Agency Problems and the Theory of the Firm," *Journal of Political Economy*, April 1980, *88*, 288-307.

Gilson, Ronald J., "The Case Against Shark Repellent Amendments: Structural Limitations of the Enabling Concept," *Stanford Law Review*, April 1982, *34*, 775–836.

Harris, Robert S. et al., "Characteristics of Acquired Firms: Fixed and Random Coefficient Probit Analyses," *Southern Economic Journal*, July 1982, *49*, 164–84.

Holmstrom, Bengt, "Equilibrium Long-Term Labor Contracts," *Quarterly Journal of Economics*, Suppl., 1983, *98*, 23–54.

Jarrell, Gregg A. and Bradley, Michael, "The Economic Effects of Federal and State Regulations of Cash Tender Offers," *Journal of Law and Economics*, October 1980, *23*, 371–407.

Jensen, Michael C. and Meckling, William H. "Theory of the Firm: Managerial Behavior, Agency Costs and Ownership Structure," *Journal of Financial Economics*, October 1976, *3*, 305–60.

Klein, Benjamin and Letter, Keith B., "The Role of Market Forces in Assuring Contractual Performance," *Journal of Political Economy*, October 1981, *89*, 615–41.

Lambert, Richard A., "Long-Term Contracts and Moral Hazard," *Bell Journal of Economics*, Autumn 1983, *14*, 441–52.

——and Larker, David F., "Golden Parachutes, Executive Decision-Making and Shareholder Wealth," *Journal of Accounting and Economics*, April 1985, 7,179–203.

Lazear, Edward, P., "Why Is There Mandatory Retirement?," *Journal of Political Economy*, December 1979, *87*, 1261–84.

Linn, Scott C. and McConnell, John J., "An Empirical Investigation of the Impact of 'Antitakeover' Amendments on Common Stock Prices," *Journal of Financial Economics*, April 1983, *11*, 361–99.

Lowenstein, Lewis, "Pruning Deadwood in Hostile Takeovers: A Proposal for Legislation," *Columbia Law Review*, March 1983, *83*, 249–334.

Manne, Henry G., "Mergers and the Market for Corporate Control," *Journal of Political Economy*, April 1965, *73*, 110–20.

Morrison, Ann M., "Those Executive Bailout Deals," *Fortune*, December 13, 1982, 82–87.

Schwartz, Steven, "Factors Affecting the Probability of Being Acquired: Evidence for the United States," *Economic Journal*, June 1982, *92*, 391–98.

Telser, Lester G., "A Theory of Self-Enforcing Agreements," *Journal of Business*, January 1980, *53*, 27–44.

Q-Data Corporation, Q-File, 1983.

Standard and Poor's Compustat Services, COMPUSTAT, 1983.

Wall Street Journal "SEC Endorses Major Changes in Merger Fights," March 14, 1984.

——"GM and Ford Bonuses Raise Questions about Import Curbs, Union's Restraint," April 16, 1984, p. 8.

Review and Discussion Questions

1 What is a golden parachute? Who receives them and who awards them?
2 Why would both managers and shareholders favor deferring some of the managers' compensation?
3 Why is it difficult for managers and shareholders to agree to defer the managers' compensation with an *explicit* contract?
4 What do managers have to fear if some of their compensation is deferred? How do golden parachutes address that fear?
5 What is the major prediction of Knoeber's theory? Does the empirical test confirm or disconfirm his theory? Explain.
6 Why does Knoeber's theory also predict that which use golden parachutes will also tend to defer more of their managers' compensation? Does the empirical test confirm or disconfirm this prediction?

Chapter 33

Benjamin Klein

TRANSACTION COST DETERMINANTS OF "UNFAIR" CONTRACTUAL ARRANGEMENTS[1]

T ERMS SUCH AS "UNFAIR" are foreign to the economic model of voluntary exchange which implies anticipated gains to all transactors. However, much recent statutory, regulatory and antitrust activity has run counter to this economic paradigm of the efficiency properties of "freedom of contract." The growth of "dealer day in court" legislation, FTC franchise regulations, favorable judicial consideration of "unequal bargaining power," and unconscionability arguments, are some examples of the recent legal propensity to "protect" transactors. This is done by declaring unenforceable or illegal particular contractual provisions that, although voluntarily agreed upon in the face of significant competition. appear to be one-sided or unfair. Presentation of the standard abstract economic analysis of the mutual gains from voluntary exchange is unlikely to be an effective counterweight to this recent legal movement without an explicit attempt to provide a positive rationale for the presence of the particular unfair contractual term. This paper considers some transaction costs that might explain the voluntary adoption of contractual provisions such as termination at will and long-term exclusive dealing clauses that have been under legal attack.

The "hold-up" problem

In attempting to explain the complicated contractual details of actual market exchange, I start by noting that complete, fully contingent, costlessly enforceable contracts are not possible. This is a proposition obvious to even the most casual observer of economic phenomenon. Rather than the impersonal marketplace of costlessly enforceable contracts represented in standard economic analysis, individuals in most real world transactions are concerned with the possibility of breach and hence the identity and reputation of those with whom they deal. Further, even a cursory examination of actual contracts indicates that the relationship between transacting parties often cannot be fully described by a court-enforceable formal document that the parties have signed (see Stewart Macauley). While the common law of contracts supplies a body of rules and principles which are read into each contract, in many cases explicit terms (which include these general unwritten terms) remain somewhat vague and incomplete.

Contracts are incomplete for two main reasons. First, uncertainty implies the existence of a large number of possible contingencies and it may be very costly to know and specify in advance responses to all of these possibilities. Second, particular contractual performance, such as the level of energy an employee devotes to a complex task, may be very costly to measure. Therefore contractual breach may often be difficult to prove to the satisfaction of a third-party enforcer such as a court.

Given the presence of incomplete contractual arrangements, wealth-maximizing transactors have the ability and often the incentive to renege on the transaction by holding up the other party, in the sense of taking advantage of unspecified or unenforceable elements of the contractual relationship. Such behavior is, by definition, unanticipated and not a long-run equilibrium phenomenon. Oliver Williamson has identified and discussed this phenomenon of "opportunistic behavior," and my recent paper with Robert Crawford and Armen Alchian attempted to make operational some of the conditions under which this hold-up potential is likely to be large. In addition to contract costs, and therefore the incompleteness of the explicit contract, we emphasized the presence of appropriable quasi rents due to highly firm-specific investments. After a firm invests in an asset with a low-salvage value and a quasi-rent stream highly dependent upon some other asset, the owner of the other asset has the potential to hold up by appropriating the quasi-rent stream. For example, one would not build a house on land rented for a short term. After the rental agreement expires, the landowner could raise the rental price to reflect the costs of moving the house to another lot.[2]

The solution we emphasized was vertical integration, that is, one party owning both assets (the house and the land). Because the market for land is competitive, the price paid for the land by the homebuilder does not reflect these potentially appropriable quasi rents. However, this solution will not necessarily be observed. The size of the hold-up potential is a multiplicative function of two factors: the presence of specific capital, that is, appropriable quasi rents, and the cost of contractually specifying and enforcing delivery of the service in question—the incentive for contract violation and the ease of contract violation. Even where there is a large amount of highly specific capital, the performance in question may be cheaply specifiable and measureable and a complete contract legally enforceable at low cost. Therefore, while a short-term rental contract is not feasible, a possible solution may be a long-term lease. In addition, since the cases we will be considering deal with human capital, vertical integration in the sense of outright ownership is not possible.

Contractual solutions

Since the magnitude of the potential holdup may be anticipated, the party to be cheated can merely decrease the initial price he will pay by the amount of the appropriable quasi rents. For example, if an employer knows that an employee will cheat a certain amount each period, it will be reflected in the employee's wage. Contracts can be usefully thought to refer to anticipated rather than stated performance. Therefore the employee's behavior should not even be considered "cheating." A secretary, for example, may miss work one day a week on average. If secretary time is highly substitutable, the employer can cut the secretary's weekly wage 20 percent, hire 20 percent more secretaries and be indifferent. The secretary, on the other hand, presumably values the leisure more than the additional income and therefore is better off. Rather than cheating, we have a voluntarily determined, utility-maximizing contractual relationship.

In many cases, however, letting the party cheat and discounting his wage will not be an economical solution because the gain to the cheater and therefore his acceptable compensating wage discount is less than the cost to the firm from the cheating behavior. For example, it is easy to imagine many cases where a shirking manager will impose costs on the firm much greater than his personal gains. Therefore the stockholders cannot be made indifferent to this behavior, by cutting his salary and hiring more lazy managers. The general point is that there may not be perfect substitutability between quantity and quality of particular services. Hence, even if one knew that an unspecified element of quality would be reduced by a certain amount in attempting the holdup, an *ex ante* compensatory discount in the quoted price of the promised high quality service to the cost of providing the anticipated lower-quality supply would not make the demander of the service indifferent. Individuals would be willing to expend real resources to set up contractual arrangements to prevent such opportunism and assure high-quality supply.

The question then becomes how much of the hold-up problem can be avoided by an explicit government-enforced contract, and how much remains to be handled by an implicit self-enforcing contract. This latter type of contract is one where opportunistic behavior is prevented by the threat of termination of the business relationship rather than by the threat of litigation. A transactor will not cheat if the expected present discounted value of quasi rents he is earning from a relationship is greater than the immediate hold-up wealth gain. The capital loss that can be imposed on the potential cheater by the withdrawal of expected future business is then sufficient to deter cheating.

In our forthcoming article, Keith Leffler and I develop this market-enforcement mechanism in detail. It is demonstrated that one way in which the future-promised rewards necessary to prevent cheating can be arranged is by the payment of a sufficiently high-price "premium." This premium stream can usefully be thought of as "protection money" paid to assure noncheating behavior. The magnitude of this price premium will be related to the potential holdup, that is, to the extent of contractual incompleteness and the degree of specific capital present. In equilibrium, the present discounted value of the price-premium stream will be exactly equal to the appropriable quasi rents, making the potential cheater indifferent between cheating and not. But the individual paying the premium will be in a preferable position as long as the differential consumer's surplus from high-quality (noncheating) supply is greater than the premium.

One method by which this equilibrium quasi-rent stream can be achieved without the existence of positive firm profits is by having the potential cheater put up a forfeit-able-at-will collateral. bond equal to the discounted value of the premium stream. Alternatively, the potential cheater may make a highly firm-specific productive investment which will have only a low-salvage value if he cheats and loses future business. The gap between price and salvageable capital costs is analytically equivalent to a premium stream with the nonsalvageable asset analytically equivalent to a forfeitable collateral bond.

"Unfair" contractual terms

Most actual contractual arrangements consist of a combination of explicit- and implicit-enforcement mechanisms. Some elements of performance will be specified and enforced by third-party sanctions. The residual elements of performance will be enforced without invoking the power of some outside party to the transaction but merely by the threat of termination of the transactional relationship. The details of any particular contract will consist of forms of these general elements chosen to minimize transaction costs (for example, hiring lawyers to discover contingencies and draft explicit terms, paying quality-assurance premiums, and investing in nonsalvageable "brand name" assets) and may imply the existence of what appears to be unfair contract terms.

Consider, for example, the initial capital requirements and termination provisions common in most franchise contractual arrangements. These apparently one-sided terms may be crucial elements of minimum-cost quality-policing arrangements. Given the difficulty of explicitly specifying and enforcing contractually every element of quality to be supplied by a franchisee, there is an incentive for an individual opportunistic franchisee to cheat the franchisor by supplying a lower quality of product than contracted for. Because the franchisee uses a common trademark, this behavior depreciates the reputation and hence the future profit stream of the franchisor.[3]

The franchisor knows, given his direct policing and monitoring expenditures, the expected profit that a franchisee can obtain by cheating. For example, given the number of inspectors hired, he knows the expected time to detect a cheater; given the costs of low-quality inputs he knows the expected extra short-run cheating profit that can be earned. Therefore the franchisor may require an initial lump sum payment from the franchisee equal to this estimated short-run gain from cheating. This is equivalent to a collateral bond forfeitable at the will of the franchisor. The franchisee will earn a normal rate of return on that bond if he does not cheat, but it will be forfeited if he does cheat and is terminated.

In many cases franchisee noncheating rewards may be increased and short-run cheating profits decreased (and therefore franchisor direct policing costs reduced) by the grant of an exclusive territory or the enforcement of minimum resale price restraints (see my paper with Andrew McLaughlin). Franchisors can also assure quality by requiring franchisee investments in specific (nonfully salvageable) production assets that upon termination imply a capital-cost penalty larger than any short-run wealth gain that can be obtained by the franchisee if he cheats. For example, the franchisor may require franchisees to rent from them short term (rather than own) the land upon which their outlet is located. This lease arrangement creates a situation where termination implies that the franchisor can require the franchisee to move and thereby impose a capital loss on him up to the amount of his initial nonsalvageable investment. Hence a form of collateral to deter franchisee cheating is created.[4]

It is important to recognize that franchise termination, if it is to assure quality compliance on the part of franchisees, must be unfair in the sense that the capital cost imposed on the franchisee that will optimally prevent cheating must be larger than the gain to the franchisee from cheating. Given that less than infinite resources are spent by the franchisor to monitor quality, there is some probability that franchisee cheating will go undetected. Therefore termination must become equivalent to a criminal-type sanction. Rather than the usually analyzed case of costlessly detected and policed contract breach, where the remedy of making the breaching party pay the cost of the damages of his specific breach makes economic sense, the sanction here must be large enough to make the expected net gain from cheating equal to zero. The transacting parties contractually agree upon a penalty-type sanction for breach as a means of economizing on direct policing costs. Because contract enforcement costs (including litigation costs which generally are not collectable by the innocent party in the United States) are not zero, this analysis provides a rationale against the common law prohibition of penalty clauses.

The obvious concern with such seemingly unfair contractual arrangements is the possibility that the franchisor may engage in opportunistic behavior by terminating a franchisee without cause, claiming the franchise fee and purchasing the initial franchisee investment at a distress price. Such behavior may be prevented by the depreciation of the franchisor's brand name and therefore decreased future demand by potential franchisees to join the arrangement. However, this protective mechanism is limited by the relative importance of new franchise sales compared to the continuing franchising operation, that is, by the "maturity" of the franchise chain.

More importantly, what limits reverse cheating by franchisors is the possible increased cost of operating the chain through an employee operation compared to a franchise operation when such cheating is communicated among franchisees. As long as the implicit collateral bond put up by the franchisee is less than the present discounted value of this cost difference, franchisor cheating will be deterred. Although explicit bonds and price premium payments cannot simultaneously be made by both the franchisee and the franchisor, the discounted value of the cost difference has the effect of a collateral bond put up by the franchisor to assure his noncheating behavior. This explains why the franchisor does not increase the initial franchise fee to an arbitrarily high level and correspondingly decrease its direct policing expenditures and the probability of detecting franchisee cheating. While such offsetting changes could continue to optimally deter franchisee cheating and save the real resource cost of direct policing, the profit from and hence the incentive for reverse franchisor cheating would become too great for the arrangement to be stable.

Franchisees voluntarily signing these agreements obviously understand the termination-at-will clause separate from the legal consequences of that term to mean nonopportunistic franchisor termination. But this does not imply that the court should judge each termination on these unwritten but understood contract terms and attempt to determine if franchisor cheating has occurred. Franchisees also must recognize that by signing these agreements they are relying on the implicit market-enforcement mechanism outlined above, and not the court to prevent franchisor cheating. It is costly to use the court to regulate these terminations because elements of performance are difficult to contractually specify and to measure. In addition, litigation is costly and time consuming, during which the brand name of the franchisor can be depreciated further. If these costs were not large and the court could cheaply and quickly determine when franchisor cheating had occurred, the competitive process regarding the establishment of contract terms would lead transactors to settle on explicit governmentally enforceable contracts rather than rely on this implicit market-enforcement mechanism.

The potential error here is, after recognizing the importance of transaction costs and the incomplete "relational" nature of most real world contracts, to rely too strongly on the government as a regulator of unspecified terms (see Victor Goldberg). While it is important for economic theory to handle significant contract costs and incomplete explicit contractual arrangements, such complexity does not imply a broad role for government. Rather, all that is implied is a role for brand names and the corresponding implicit market enforcement mechanism I have outlined.

Unequal bargaining power

An argument made against contract provisions such as termination-at-will clauses is that they appear to favor one party at the expense of another. Hence it is alleged that the terms of the agreement must have been reached under conditions of "unequal bargaining power" and therefore should be invalid. However, a further implication of the above analysis is that when both parties can cheat, explicit contractual restraints are often placed on the smaller, less well-established party (the franchisee), while an implicit brand name contract-enforcement mechanism is relied on to prevent cheating by the larger, more well-established party (the franchisor).

If information regarding quality of a product supplied by a large firm is communicated among many small buyers who do not all purchase simultaneously, the potential holdup relative to, say, annual sales is reduced substantially compared to the case where each buyer purchased from a separate independent small firm. There are likely to be economies of scale in the supply of a business brand name, because in effect the large firm's total brand name capital is put on the line with each individual sale. This implies a lower cost of using the implicit contract mechanism, that is, a lower-price premium necessary to assure non-breach, for a large firm compared to a small firm. Therefore one side of the contract will be relatively more incomplete.

For example, in a recent English case using the doctrine of inequality of bargaining power to bar contract enforcement, an individual songwriter signed a long-term (ten-year) exclusive service contract with a music publisher for an agreed royalty percentage.[5] Since it would be extremely costly to write a complete explicit contract for the supply of publishing services (including advertising and other promotion activities whose effects are felt over time and are difficult to measure), after a songwriter becomes established he has an incentive to take advantage of any initial investment made by a publishing firm and shift to another publisher. Rather than rely on the brand name of the songwriter or require him to make a specific investment which can serve as collateral, the exclusive services contract prevents this cheating from occurring.

The major cost of such explicit long-term contractual arrangements is the rigidity that is created by the necessity of setting a price or a price formula *ex ante*. In this song publishing case, the royalty formula may turn out *ex post* to imply too low a price to the songwriter (if, say, his cooperative promotional input is greater than originally anticipated.) If the publisher is concerned about his reputation, these royalty terms will be renegotiated, a common occurrence in continuing business relationships.

If an individual songwriter is a small part of a large publisher's total sales, and if the value of an individual songwriter's ability generally depreciates rapidly or does not persist at peak levels so that signing up new songwriters is an important element of a publisher's continuing business, then cheating an individual songwriter or even all songwriters currently under contract by refusing to renegotiate royalty rates will imply a large capital cost to the publisher. When this behavior is communicated to other actual or potential composers, the publisher's reputation will depreciate and future business will be lost. An individual songwriter, on the other hand, does not generally have large, diversified long-term business concerns and therefore cannot be penalized in that way. It is therefore obvious, independent of any appeal to disparity of bargaining power, why the smaller party would be willing to be bound by an explicit long-term contract while the larger party is bound only implicitly and renegotiates terms that turn out *ex post* to be truly divergent from *ex ante*, but unspecified, anticipations.

However, the possibility of reverse publisher cheating is real. If, for example, the songwriter unexpectedly becomes such a great success that current sales by this one customer represents a large share of the present discounted value of total publisher sales, the implicit contract enforcement mechanism may not work. Individuals knowingly trade off these costs of explicit and implicit enforcement mechanisms in settling upon transaction cost-minimizing contract terms. Although it would be too costly in a stochastic world to attempt to set up an arrangement where no cheating occurs, it is naive to think that courts can cheaply intervene to discover and "fix up" the few cases of opportunistic behavior that will occur. In any event, my analysis makes it clear that one cannot merely look at the agreed upon, seemingly "unfair" terms to determine if opportunism is occurring.

Conclusion

Ronald Coase's fundamental insight defined the problem. With zero transaction costs, the equilibrium form of economic organization is indeterminate. However, rather than distinguishing between the crude alternatives of vertical integration and market exchange, what we really have to explain are different types of market-determined contractual relationships. I have argued that a particular form of transaction cost based upon the existence of incomplete contracts (due to uncertainty and measurement costs)—a transaction cost I have called the hold-up problem—may be an important reason in many cases for termination-at-will and exclusive-dealing contractual arrangements.

The danger is that a discussion of holdup-type transaction costs can lead to *ad hoc* theorizing. The discussion here was meant to be suggestive. If economists are to explain satisfactorily the form of particular complex contracts adopted in the marketplace, they must "get their hands dirty" by closely investigating the facts and state of the law to determine hold-up possibilities and contract enforcement difficulties in particular cases. The most useful legal input to obtain knowledge of the institutional constraints on the trading process, is not likely to come from professors of contract law. Rather, we should consider the knowledge accumulated by practicing attorneys familiar with the likely hold-up problems and the contractual solutions commonly adopted in particular industries. When all firms in a particular industry use similar contractual provisions, it is unlikely to be the result of duress or fraud and should not necessarily be considered (as some courts have) as evidence of collusion. Such uniformity suggests the existence of independent attempts within a competitive environment to solve an important common problem and signals the presence of a prime research prospect.

Notes

1 This paper was written while I was a Law and Economics Fellow at the University of Chicago Law School. Amen Alchian, Roy Kenney, Edmund Kitch, Timothy Muris, Richard Posner, and George Priest provided useful comments on earlier drafts.

2 This problem is different from the standard monopoly or bilateral monopoly problem for two reasons. First, market power is created only after the house investment is made on a particular piece of land. Such postinvestment power can therefore exist in many situations that are purely competitive preinvestment. Second, the problem we are discussing deals with the difficulties of contract enforcement. Even if some preinvestment monopoly power exists (for example, a union supplier of labor services to harvest a crop), if one can write an enforceable contract preinvestment (i.e., before the planting), the present discounted value of the monopoly return may be significantly less than the one-time postinvestment hold-up potential (which may equal the entire value of a crop ready to be harvested).

3 At locations where this incentive is very large, for example, on superhighways where the probability of repeat sales by particular customers is very low, the franchisor may "vertically integrate" and not compensate their employees on any profit-sharing basis. Such fixed wage compensation schemes reduce the incentive to cheat but at the cost of reducing the incentive for workers to supply any effort that is not explicitly specified and measureable by the employer. It is this latter incentive that is harnessed by franchising arrangements.

4 The initial franchise investment also serves as a means of establishing an efficient compensation mechanism. Because the franchise investment is a saleable asset it provides a market measure of future profit and hence a precise incentive on franchisee efforts to build up the business. While an employee contract can contain a profit-sharing arrangement, and retirement and stock option provisions to reward employee efforts that yield a return far in the future and protect the employee's heirs, it would be extremely difficult to write ex ante complete, enforceable (i.e., measureable) contract terms that would as accurately reflect the value of marginal employee efforts.

5 See Macaulay v. Schroeder Publishing Co., Ltd. discussed in M. J. Trebilcock.

REFERENCES

R. J. Coase, "The Nature of the Firm," *Economica*, Nov. 1937, *4*, 386–405.

V. P. Goldberg, "Toward an Expanded Economic Theory of Contract," *J. Econ. Issues*, Mar. 1976, *10*, 45–61.

B. Klein, R. G. Crawford, and A. A. Alchian, "Vertical Integration, Appropriable Rents and the Competitive Contracting Process," *J. Law Econ.*, Oct. 1978, *21*, 297–326.

—— and K. Leffler, "Non-Governmental Enforcement of Contracts: The Role of Market Forces in Guaranteeing Quality," J. *Polit. Econ.*, forthcoming.

—— and A. McLaughlin, "Resale Price Maintenance, Exclusive Territories and Franchise Termination: The Coors Case," unpublished manuscript. Univ. California Los Angeles 1979.

S. Macauley, "Non-Contractual Relations in Business: A Preliminary Study," *Amer. Soc. Rev.*, Feb. 1963, *28*, 55–69.

M. J. Trebilcock, "The Doctrine of Inequality of Bargaining Power: Post-Benthamite Economics in the House of Lords," *Univ. Toronto Law J.*, Fall 1976, *26*, 359–85.

Oliver E. Williamson, *Markets and Hierarchies: Analysis and Antitrust Implications*, New York 1975.

Review and Discussion Questions

1 What is a "termination-at-will" clause?
2 Why are complete contracts difficult to write?
3 What problem is created by the incomplete contracts and specialized assets?
4 Explain how initial capital provisions and termination provisions in frachise contracts and exclusive services contracts can solve the problem in the previous question.
5 What deters franchisors and music publishers from abusing their power?

Chapter 34

John R. Lott, Jr.

TWO EXCERPTS FROM FREEDOMNOMICS

Why are dinners and liquor so expensive in restaurants?

ARE YOU CURIOUS why restaurants charge substantially higher prices for dinner than for lunch? While the size of the dinners are often slightly larger, meal size alone cannot explain the price difference. The knee-jerk answer is that restaurants charge more for dinner simply because they can. In a sense, this is true; restaurants, like any business, will charge the highest price the market allows in order to maximize profits. But if this holds true for dinner, why not for lunch?

This may seem like another case of price discrimination—supposedly, dinner customers are charged more because lunchtime diners typically work near the restaurants they frequent and are more familiar with the local eateries than are dinner customers, who more often travel to other neighborhoods to dine. Thus lunchtime customers could more easily switch to another establishment if a restaurant raised its lunch prices. But this explanation doesn't work, for dinners are more expensive than lunches even in cities such as New York City and Washington, D.C. where dozens of restaurants are crammed into a few square blocks, with prices posted at the front door.[1] It is easy to compare prices in these neighborhoods, and finding the cheaper dinners is not a problem.

So if price discrimination is not at work, and monopolies clearly are not functioning in areas with so many restaurants, how do we explain the price difference? There is a simple answer totally consistent with competitive markets: dinner patrons linger over their meals longer than lunchtime customers, who usually face more severe time constraints.[2] In addition to the cost of the food, the price of a meal has to cover the rental cost of the table. The more leisurely the pace at which people enjoy a meal, the more money a restaurant loses by not selling meals to additional customers at that table. Anyone who regularly frequents restaurants has surely come across waiters who subtly rush patrons with little maneuvers like clearing the table before all the diners have even finished eating. In the restaurant business, time is money.

This time cost of the table also explains why certain kinds of drinks are so much more expensive in restaurants than in stores. Restaurants charge particularly high prices for coffee, tea, and wine because people either linger over these items or linger longer over meals that include them. The mark-up is highest for beverages that people linger over longest. That's why wine typically has a larger absolute mark-up than beer, and why both have larger mark-ups than soda. [3]

Alcohol and coffee also have other costs. Restaurants typically stock all types of liquor, incurring real inventory costs. They also have to throw out many cups of coffee over the day to insure freshness. All these are real costs, just as much as the cost of the alcohol or coffee itself.

The high price of liquor at restaurants has created a popular perception that restaurants break even on food and make huge profits on alcohol. This seems to imply that restaurants have to compete in food service, but can charge whatever they want for drinks. Although restaurants often do break even on meals, their high alcohol prices do not reflect a lack of competition. Restaurants might appear to rake in the money on booze, but drinks also comprise a large part of their costs; that is, the cost of providing a place to linger over a drink.

[...]

Why are last-minute airline tickets so expensive?

Does price discrimination explain why travelers flying on short notice must pay more for a plane ticket than those who book their trips in advance? The Southwest Airlines website clearly shows the relationship between ticket prices and how far in advance a ticket is bought. [4] A one-way flight from Philadelphia to Chicago on December 12, 2006, ranged from $109 for a non-refundable promotional fare purchased twenty-one days in advance to $168 for a ticket bought on the day of the trip. Waiting to buy your ticket until the last day thus raised the ticket price by 54 percent.

It may seem that short-notice travelers are charged more because they are more desperate to fly at a particular time than those who make more leisurely plans. But this would need further explanation: exactly how could airlines charge excessively high monopoly prices when numerous competitors exist and the cost of checking fares is so low? Short-notice travelers can consult Orbitz, Expedia, or other websites that compare ticket prices, or simply call someone who specializes in comparing rates—a travel agent. But the large discrepancy in fares for short-notice and advance-notice travelers exists despite the ease and low cost of shopping around for different fares. This should give us pause before immediately assuming price discrimination. [5]

What airlines are doing, in fact, is charging extra for a particular service—providing a ticket at the last minute. In order to provide this service, airlines must keep "inventories" of seats that are still available at the last minute. As a result, some of these seats can go unsold, and the airlines must be compensated for this loss. This is no different than any other business that stocks inventories—grocery stores, for example, buy more milk than they need in order to ensure that they will not run out. Stores have

Table 34.1 Ticket prices on Southwest Airlines

Type of fare	Price of one way fare from Philadelphia to Chicago's Midway Airport on December 12, 2006, if purchased on November 12, 2006	Required number of days to purchase in advance	Refundable
Promotional	$109	21 days	No
Advance purchase fare	$120.93	14 days	No
Special fare	$158	7 days	No
Refundable anytime	$168	1 hour	Yes

to throw away unsold milk, and this cost is factored into the price. But consumers are willing to pay a little more if it means that milk will always be available.[6]

Airlines can easily sell discounted advanced tickets, to the point that they limit the availability of these offers. For airlines to be willing to hold seats for last-minute travelers, they must earn the same revenue from these seats as they do from seats purchased in advance. Just take a simple numerical example from Table 34-1 for Southwest. Suppose, on average, that just over one-third of the seats set aside for last-minute travelers go unsold; assuming that all these tickets could have been sold at the advanced discount "promotional" price. In that case, the last-minute tickets would have to sell for over 50 percent more than the discount price in order to justify offering the last-minute tickets at all.

Notes

1 After all, New York City had 24,600 restaurants as of September 2006. (David B. Caruso, "NYC weighs ban on artificial trans fats," *Chicago Tribune*, September 27, 2006.)
2 John R. Lott, Jr. and Russell D. Roberts, "A Guide to the Pitfalls of Identifying Price Discrimination," *Economic Inquiry*, vol. 29, no. 1, January 1991, 1819. I would also like to thank my cousin Jim Lyden, who has managed two different Outback Steakhouses, for helpful discussions on these topics.
3 Ibid.
4 http://www.southwest.com.
5 Another puzzle is the requirement that consumers have to spend a Saturday night at their destination in order to receive the discount. This is typically explained as an example of price discrimination against business travelers, but it may only be a form of peak load pricing if those who stay over Saturday night travel on Sunday, the quietest day of the week. The puzzle remains as to why there is not an explicit discount for returning on Sunday, but this is also a problem for the price discrimination explanation.
6 John R. Lott, Jr. and Russell D. Roberts, "A Guide to the Pitfalls of Identifying Price Discrimination," *Economic Inquiry*, vol. 29, no. 1, January 1991.

Review and Discussion Questions

1 Are higher prices for liquor in restaurants evidence that restaurants price discriminate? What about the higher prices that airlines charge for tickets bought shortly before takeoff?

2 Can you think of other instances of apparent price discrimination that might be due instead to different costs? (Hint: what about the high prices of popcorn and snacks in movie theaters?)

Suggestions for Further Reading

Agarwal, A. and Knoeber, C. R. (1996) "Firm Performance and Mechanisms to Control Agency Problems Between Managers and Shareholders," *Journal of Financial and Quantitative Analysis,* 31: 377–397.

Agarwal and Knoeber identify seven ways in which the market addresses the problem of separation of ownership and control, ways in which managers are induced to act in the interest of shareholders. Their empirical results are mostly consistent with the proposition that the seven methods are used in economically sensible ways.

Craig, L. A. and Knoeber, C. R. (1992) "Manager Shareholding, the Market for Managers, and the End-Period Problem: Evidence from the U.S. Whaling Industry," *Journal of Law, Economics, and Organization,* 8: 607–627.

Using data on pre-Civil War U.S. whaling voyages, Craig and Knoeber find evidence that contracting between ship owners and ship masters was economically efficient. Here again, the market is shown to have significant power to reduce the ownership-and-control problem.

Cueller, Steven S. (2005) "Sex, Drugs and the Alchian-Allen Theorem," www.sonoma.edu/users/c/cuellar/research/Sex-Drugs.pdf.

The author states that recent research—outside economics—finds that women who take birth control pills prefer "more masculine" men than women who don't. Why might that be? Cueller argues that the finding can be explained by the same theory that explained why the good apples were shipped out of Seattle.

Kenney, R. W. and Klein, B. (1983) "The Economics of Block Booking," *Journal of Law and Economics,* 26: 497–540.

Block booking was a practice by which movie studios forced theaters to license movies in groups, or blocks. That is, theaters could not license a particular movie to show unless they also agreed to license other movies by the same studio. The U.S. Supreme Court declared the practice illegal because it felt that block booking "extend[ed] monopoly power." But Kenney and Klein note that the monopoly power explanation makes no sense. They summarize an older argument that block booking is economically efficient, and they then present a new argument for its efficiency.

Klein, B. and Saft, L. (1985) "The Law and Economics of Franchise Tying Contracts," *Journal of Law and Economics,* 28: 345–361.

Another business practice alleged to suppress competition is a franchise requirements contract. A franchise requirements contract forces franchisees to buy one or more inputs from the franchisor. Klein and Saft argue that such contracts can be pro-competitive because they can help the franchisor protect its reputation.

Lott, J. R., Jr. (1987) "Should the Wealthy Be Able to 'Buy Justice'?" *Journal of Political Economy,* 95: 1307–1316.

Lott shows that allowing wealthy individuals to hire better, more expensive lawyers—frequently criticized as giving the wealthy too much power—is consistent with the economics of optimal punishment. (It is also, given the higher opportunity costs of wealthy people, consistent with the principle that people committing the same crime should receive equal punishment.)

Index